"Many thanks to John Van Wyk for treating a topic in Edwards studies neglected for too long: his philosophy and practice of education. Edwards served as a teacher from adolescence to his death, from Yale through pastoral ministry to cross-cultural pedagogy at the Stockbridge mission and, finally, at Princeton. This fine book covers it all and offers pedagogical wisdom for thoughtful teachers today."

—DOUGLAS A. SWEENEY, dean of Beeson Divinity School, Samford University

"John Van Wyk here examines both what 'America's greatest theologian' thought about theological education and how he educated aspirants to the ministry as well as everyday disciples, including women and Native Americans. In light of our present crisis in higher theological education, this fascinating study of a past figure proves eminently timely: Jonathan Edwards offers a model of biblical and dialogical pedagogy that strives to foster the knowledge of God to the glory of God."

—KEVIN J. VANHOOZER, research professor of systematic theology, Trinity Evangelical Divinity School

"John Van Wyk has provided us with an outstanding publication on the work of Jonathan Edwards as educator. This brilliantly-researched volume thoughtfully explores the resources, influences, context, and peers who helped to shape the Northampton Puritan's full-orbed, theocentric approach to teaching and learning. Educators, historians, theologians, pastors, and students will all profit from Van Wyk's mature reflection on these important themes, as well as his insights regarding Edwards and his legacy."

—DAVID S. DOCKERY, president, Southwestern Baptist Theological Seminary

"If the expansion of Christ's kingdom was the aim of Jonathan Edwards's life and ministry, education was a vital instrument in achieving this aim. John Van Wyk traces the diverse influences on Edwards's pedagogy and brings to life Edwards's interactions with children, Native Americans, and theological students. A valuable read for anyone who wants a fuller grasp of Edwards's life and times."

—ESMARI POTGIETER, author of *Jonathan Edwards and a Reformational View of the Purpose of Education*

"John Van Wyk has done two things for his readers. In a meticulously researched and well-written volume he has both provided a solid introduction to Edwards the prodigious thinker and contributed a first-ever analysis of Edwards the *educator*."
— GERALD McDERMOTT, author of *Jonathan Edwards Confronts the Gods: Christian Theology, Enlightenment Religion, and Non-Christian Faiths*

"Ideas make a difference in the world. Ideas presented as stories help us to glimpse a life worth living. And for Christians, ideas communicated through sermons, sacraments, schools, and sensations have become leading strategies of spiritual growth in the modern world. Jonathan Edwards exemplifies them all and sets them within his bigger educational agenda, which this book expounds so judiciously, in a thorough, discerning, and edifying way."
— RHYS S. BEZZANT, director, Jonathan Edwards Center, Ridley College, Melbourne, Australia

"In this welcome volume, John Van Wyk explores Jonathan Edwards as an educator. This attention to Edwards contributes valuable insight to the more familiar studies of Edwards as Christian preacher, evangelist, philosopher, and theologian. Present day educators would do well to examine Van Wyk's fine study and Edwards's own writings to deepen their appreciation of Edwards's holistic dialogic methodology, recognition of student agency as responsible image bearers, and encouragement toward lifelong learning."
— DONALD C GUTHRIE, chair in educational leadership, Trinity Evangelical Divinity School

"True to what he describes as Edwards's holistic approach to education, John Van Wyk has produced a study that is both historical and inspirational.... Tracing Edwards's educational theory, practice, sources, and legacy, Van Wyk situates Edwards in the transatlantic theological and philosophical currents of his time, exploring his appropriation and adaptation of those ideas in the lived context of ministry to family, congregation, Native American students, and ministers in training. Edwards the educator emerges as a model for emulation in any age."
— BRADLEY J. GUNDLACH, distinguished professor emeritus of history, Trinity International University

"Van Wyk has put together a commendable survey and fascinating analysis of Edwards's pedagogical philosophy, methodology, and convictions. Thorough, wide-ranging, and insightful . . . Edwards scholars and students alike will enjoy Edwards's emphasis on the dialogical nature of formative education."

—JOSH MOODY, author of *Jonathan Edwards and the Enlightenment: Knowing the Presence of God*

"In this expansive study of 'Edwards the Educator,' John Van Wyk explores the philosophical, theological, and familial influences that shaped Edwards's pedagogy. Of striking importance is Van Wyk's illuminating discussion of Edwards's holistic, dialogical teaching directed at two very different audiences: the Native American children in Stockbridge and the students Edwards mentored in preparation for the ministry."

—DAVID W. KLING, New Divinity scholar and author of *Edwards and the Edwardeans: Jonathan Edwards, the New Divinity, and the Making of a Theological Culture*

To Understand *Things* as Well as *Words*

To Understand *Things* as Well as *Words*

An Examination of Jonathan Edwards as an Educator and His Pedagogical Methodology

JOHN R. VAN WYK

Foreword by Kenneth P. Minkema

☙PICKWICK *Publications* · Eugene, Oregon

TO UNDERSTAND THINGS AS WELL AS WORDS
An Examination of Jonathan Edwards as an Educator and His Pedagogical Methodology

Copyright © 2025 John R. Van Wyk. All rights reserved. Except for brief quotations in critical publications or reviews, no part of this book may be reproduced in any manner without prior written permission from the publisher. Write: Permissions, Wipf and Stock Publishers, 199 W. 8th Ave., Suite 3, Eugene, OR 97401.

Pickwick Publications
An Imprint of Wipf and Stock Publishers
199 W. 8th Ave., Suite 3
Eugene, OR 97401

www.wipfandstock.com

PAPERBACK ISBN: 979-8-3852-1753-3
HARDCOVER ISBN: 979-8-3852-1754-0
EBOOK ISBN: 979-8-3852-1755-7

Cataloguing-in-Publication data:

Names: Van Wyk, John R. [author]. | Minkema, Kenneth P. [foreword writer].

Title: To understand things as well as words : an examination of Jonathan Edwards as an educator and his pedagogical methodology / John R. Van Wky with a foreword by Kenneth P. Minkema.

Description: Eugene, OR: Pickwick Publications, 2025 | Includes bibliographical references.

Identifiers: ISBN 979-8-3852-1753-3 (paperback) | ISBN 979-8-3852-1754-0 (hardcover) | ISBN 979-8-3852-1755-7 (ebook)

Subjects: LCSH: Edwards, Jonathan, 1703–1758. | Education—History. | Christian education—Teaching methods.

Classification: BX7260.E3 V36 2025 (paperback) | BX7260.E3 (ebook)

07/17/25

To my parents, Gerrit and Viola Dockery Van Wyk,
with deepest love and sincerest appreciation

Contents

	Foreword by Kenneth P. Minkema	ix
	Acknowledgments	xi
	Images	xiii
1	Introduction: Jonathan Edwards as an Educator	1
2	Background: Puritanism	21
3	Background: Intellectual Trends Comprising "the Enlightenment(s)"	65
4	Further Influences on Edwards's Pedagogy	117
5	Jonathan Edwards as a Teacher and His Pedagogical Methodology: Background	154
6	Jonathan Edwards's Pedagogical Methodology: Locations	196
7	Edwards as Educator: Review and Educating the "Total Person"	261
8	Conclusion: Edwards as Multidimensional (and Multiple?)	278
	Bibliography	293

Foreword

JONATHAN EDWARDS IS WIDELY known most as a Puritan theologian, as a revivalist of the eighteenth-century "Great Awakening," and as one of the key figures in the development of modern evangelicalism. Scholars consider Edwards the Philosopher, Edwards the Preacher, Edwards the Exegete, and so on. He's not usually thought of as a teacher. Yet, he served as a tutor at Yale College, taught and catechized children and young people, English and Native American, at the churches he served, and ended his career as the president of the College of New Jersey, later known as Princeton University.

Now, in John Van Wyk's book-length study, we have Edwards the Educator. It is the first of its kind, examining Edwards's pedagogical principles and the methods he used to put that approach into practice. Edwards was part of a rich tradition of educational reformers coming out of the Reformation. He also imbibed the New Learning of Locke, Newton, and Berkeley, applying it to the formation of minds and hearts. In the tradition of the parsonage seminary, he prepared a cadre of young candidates for the ministry and for missionary work by taking them into his home and introducing them to the many responsibilities of the pastoral office. And he inherited and adapted a program of educating Native Americans from his predecessor at the mission post of Stockbridge, Massachusetts, which was at once innovative but also controversial for the way it was designed to strip Natives of their language, culture, and beliefs.

In Edwards's world, education reached into all aspects of life. The colony in which he lived mandated public schools in each town. Education was essential for establishing individual historical faith, which in

Foreword

turn was a means of grace and laid a foundation for conversion. It was also formative for godly habits and virtues; although these attributes in and of themselves were not salvific, they were key proofs of holiness. Colonial colleges were established to produce a spiritual and learned clergy who would enlighten and edify their congregations. The nature, purpose and goals of education were debated in Edwards's lifetime, and he himself took part in that debate. Was a Christian spirit a matter of nurture, of a well-formed character, or was it solely a matter of a supernatural, arbitrary invasion of the soul? What was the role of the faculty of reason or understanding, undergirded by the acquisition of knowledge across disciplines, in the cultivation of the self, in the act of choice? What was the role of the beautiful, of delight, in appreciating what the world has to teach? These, and many other issues, occupied Edwards's attention, and his views on God, creation, and the human person still impact us today.

KENNETH P. MINKEMA, PHD
Editor, *The Works of Jonathan Edwards*
Director, The Jonathan Edwards Center
Yale University

Acknowledgments

IT HAS BEEN SAID that writing a dissertation is the closest a male can come to experiencing both the travails and the joys of childbirth and, like childbearing, it is a collaborative effort. Many persons have contributed assistance and encouragement to the work, revised and expanded from my dissertation, which the reader now holds. Although an all-inclusive list would be too lengthy to include here, certain ones should receive special thanks. Foremost are the members of my dissertation committee, Professors Douglas A. Sweeney and John D. Woodbridge of Trinity Evangelical Divinity School and Kenneth P. Minkema of Yale University. Without the wise counsel and invaluable encouragement which they graciously provided, this project would not have come to fruition.

Professors at Wofford College, Erskine Theological Seminary, and Trinity Evangelical Divinity School inspired in me an intellectual curiosity about the history of the Church in general and Jonathan Edwards in particular. Moreover, through equipping me with the requisite academic writing and research skills, they enabled me to pursue this project.

Professor Laurie Matthias's book, *The Cry of a Teacher's Soul*, proved useful in this project. I appreciate her lending a copy of it to me during the preparation of this study. Professor Alice Ott provided helpful advice regarding sources in German and English on Pietism. Comments from fellow members of Dr. Sweeney's dissertation writers' group on an early draft of chapter 1 were useful in writing the final draft. In addition, Rev. Lee Eclov of Village Church of Lincolnshire, Illinois, Dr. James Stamoolis, former Dean of Wheaton College and former Dean of Trinity International University, and Evy Stamoolis read drafts of chapters and offered helpful advice. Importantly, Dr. Stamoolis and Edward Manzo, brothers

Acknowledgments

in Christ and members of Village Church of Lincolnshire, were very supportive of my efforts to get this project published and graciously gave of their time to help me solve formatting issues in the final phase. They and other members of Village Church, and friends at Trinity, offered prayers and encouragement through the various stages of this arduous endeavor. At Trinity's Rolfing Library, Becky Frank was helpful in locating valuable and hard-to-find sources and Rebecca Miller (Donald) proved patient in assisting me in overcoming frustrating formatting issues in the original project. Kris Ford, document assistant at Trinity, went above and beyond the call of duty in finalizing the formatting of the dissertation. Dr. Robin Parry, editor of the present project, Savanah N. Landerholm, typesetter for this project, Stephanie Hough, copy editor, and the others at Wipf & Stock who guided this project to completion, deserve special thanks for the grace, patience, and understanding they showed me as a first-time author of a project of this size, and as someone who did not always get things right the first time.

In the current internet age, I would be remiss in not expressing appreciation to Internet Archive and Google Books, which have greatly simplified accessing rare, antique, or otherwise difficult-to-find sources.

Generations of Edwards scholars of the past and present, on whose work this dissertation builds, and those whose interest keeps (and will continue to keep) the flame of Edwards studies burning brightly to provide both encouragement of heart and spirit in exploring the one whom John Piper has called a "God-entranced man," and illumination of mind in delving into this uniquely brilliant theologian and philosopher, must be acknowledged. Without them, this dissertation would not have happened.

Equally as important are the unstinting and manifold labors of all the many Edwards scholars over the years who assembled the abundant writings of Edwards in one location and who have made the *Works of Jonathan Edwards* available online (*WJEO*). This is the "promised land" of which thousands upon thousands only dreamed. Without the efforts of those who made this a reality, this work, if it came to fruition at all, would have been considerably more difficult.

SOLI DEO GLORIA

Images

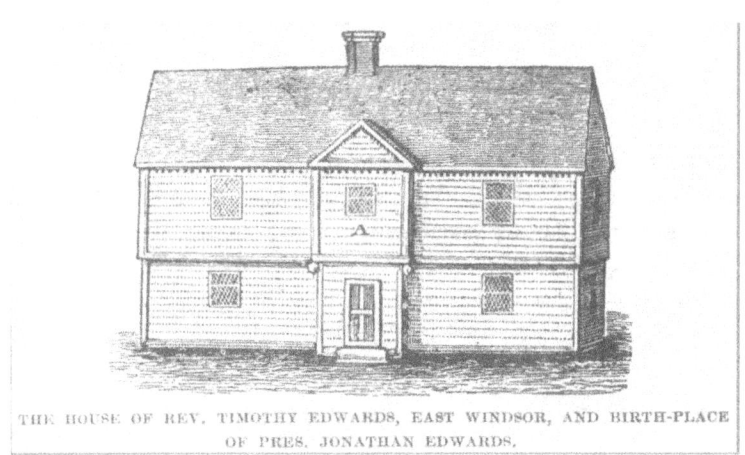

FIGURE 1

The house of Rev. Timothy Edwards (1669–1758) and Esther Stoddard Edwards (1672–1771), and birthplace of Jonathan Edwards (1703–1758) at East Windsor (modern-day South Windsor), Connecticut. Here Edwards received the early education from his parents and older sisters which enabled his admission to the Collegiate School of Connecticut (shortly afterward renamed Yale College) in 1716, and which largely inspired his later commitment to coeducation. (Image in Henry Reed Stiles, *The History and Genealogies of East Windsor, Connecticut* (Hartford, CT: Case, Lockwood and Brainard, 1891–1892), opposite p. 552. Pdf. https://www.loc.gov/item/rc01003324/.

Images

FIGURE 2
Jonathan Edwards instructed his congregants through the sermons he preached in the second First Congregational Meeting House, which stood in Northampton, Massachusetts from 1661 to 1737. Edwards became assistant pastor to his grandfather, Rev. Solomon Stoddard, in 1726/1727; upon Stoddard's death in 1729, Edwards preached in this structure as sole pastor until 1737. (Sketch by C. J. Whitham, 2018, courtesy of www.historicnorthampton.org)

Images

FIGURE 3

The third First Congregational Meeting House, in which Edwards preached from 1737 until his dismissal in 1750. In addition, Edwards instructed young persons in Scripture through use of the *Westminster Shorter Catechism* and his "Questions for Young People" during the period when these two structures stood. (Sketch drawn by William Fenno Pratt, courtesy of www.historicnorthampton.org)

Images

FIGURE 4

The Edwards manse at Northampton. During his pastorate here, the Edwards home thronged with a regular succession of infants, toddlers, young children, older children, parishioners seeking counsel, Bible catechists, and adult ministerial aspirants. Edwards instructed these two last-named groups by dialogues based on sets of theological questions, and mentored them "singly, particularly and closely." (Image courtesy of www.historicnorthampton.org)

Images

FIGURE 5

Known as the "Mission House," this structure, now a National Historic Landmark, is where John Sergeant and Abigail Williams Sergeant lived from around 1742 until his death in 1749. The original missionary to the Stockbridge Indians, Sergeant married Abigail Williams in 1739 and subsequently built this structure for them to live, at her insistence that they live on Prospect Hill, among the English settlers, rather than nearer the Natives. (Image by Daderot at en.wikipedia, Creative Commons Attribution-Share Alike License 4.0)

Images

FIGURE 6

The Edwards house at Stockbridge (left foreground). The Edwards family, in contrast to the Sergeants, lived among the Natives to whom Jonathan ministered. Jonathan Edwards Jr. recalled of his years here that the indigenous persons had been his family's nearest neighbors, with Indian boys as his playmates and schoolmates. (Image in Nathaniel Hillyer Egelston, "A New England Village," *Harper's New Monthly Magazine*, November 1871, 822.

Images

FIGURE 7

The original Nassau Hall at the College of New Jersey (now Princeton University). Completed in 1756 and the largest stone building in the American colonies, this is where Edwards taught senior-class students during his brief time as president. Shown on the right is the President's House, where Edwards lived briefly while Sarah prepared to move most of the household from Stockbridge. (Image courtesy of the John Carter Brown Library, Brown University, Providence, Rhode Island)

1

Introduction
Jonathan Edwards as an Educator

JONATHAN EDWARDS (1703–1758) HAS been routinely showered with reverential superlatives for his achievements as a theologian and philosopher. Among these are, "the most acute early American philosopher and the most brilliant of all American theologians," "the greatest philosophical mind America has produced," "the most influential religious thinker in American history," "the greatest of American thinkers," "America's greatest theologian/philosopher," "America's greatest metaphysical genius," "the greatest philosopher-theologian yet to grace the American scene," "the greatest philosopher of the New World," "the highest speculative genius of the eighteenth century," and the capstone of the monument of praise, "the mightiest mind that has appeared in the modern world."[1] One scholar has concisely summarized the foregoing: "It is not unusual to talk of Edwards in near messianic terms."[2]

1. Marsden, *Jonathan Edwards*, 1; MacCracken, "Sources of Jonathan Edwards' Idealism," 26; Sweeney, "Jonathan Edwards: Legacy"; Gardiner, "Early Idealism of Edwards," 115; Hastings, *Jonathan Edwards and the Life of God*, 1, 1n1; Miller, "General Editor's Note," viii; Miller, "Jonathan Edwards on the Sense of the Heart," 123; Thwing, *History of Higher Education in America*, 119; Fairbairn, "Jonathan Edwards," 151; and Sherman, *Sketches of New England Divines*, 138.

2. Moody, *Jonathan Edwards and the Enlightenment*, 162. See also Moody, *God-Centered Life*, 32: "Accolades cluster around Edwards like bees around a honey pot"; Fairbairn, "Jonathan Edwards," 166; McGiffert, *Jonathan Edwards*, 4, 214; Price, "Jonathan Edwards as a Christian Educator," 1–3; 115–30; Werkmeister, *History of the Philosophical Ideas in America*, 32, 32n19; Morris, "Reappraisal of Edwards," 515–25; Savelle, *Seeds of*

To Understand *Things* as Well as *Words*

His considerable renown extends to multiple areas. He "is regarded by many as the greatest theologian, pastor, preacher, philosopher, and literary artist that America has ever produced."[3] In similar glowing terms, Edwards has earned recognition as "a literary artist, metaphysical theologian, moral prophet, college teacher, nature lover, and civic leader" and is "celebrated as a philosopher, ethicist, moralist, psychologist, [and] preacher."[4] Likewise, this multidimensional figure "is remembered today as a saint, scholar, preacher, pastor, metaphysician, revival leader, theologian, Calvinist—the list goes on."[5] Roland A. Delattre and Jonathan Gibson have been relatively restricted in the scope of their assessments. By way of contrast, in a lengthy, though not exhaustive, enumeration, George Marsden has discerned twenty-six capacities in which Edwards deserves study and notes, "I could add more."[6] One Edwards scholar has noted the consensus from diverse quarters in commenting, "Few students of Edwards's work have failed to take note of the many facets of the man."[7]

Liberty, 47; Morris, "Reappraisal of Edwards," 515–25; and Westra, *Minister's Task and Calling in the Sermons of Jonathan Edwards*, ii–iii, iiin7, iiin8.

3. Ball, *Approaching Jonathan Edwards*, 1.

4. Sweeney, *Edwards the Exegete*, 218; Delattre, "Recent Scholarship on Jonathan Edwards," 369. See also Stout et al., "Introduction," v; Stein, "Introduction," 9.

5. Gibson, "Jonathan Edwards: A Missionary?" 380, and Stout et al., "Introduction," v.

6. Marsden, "Quest for the Historical Edwards," 4. See also Westra, *Minister's Task and Calling*, iii, iii–ivn11; Marsden, "Foreword," vi.

7. Smith, *Jonathan Edwards*, 2. Smith singles out "exegetical preacher," "polemicist," "apologist," "philosopher," and "sacred historian" as facets of Edwards. See also May, "Jonathan Edwards and America," 30: "I think we can agree that Edwards was somehow a great man, whether we admire him most as artist, psychologist, preacher, theologian, or philosopher." Also, Bushman, "Jonathan Edwards as Great Man," 15–46; Weber, "Recovery of Jonathan Edwards," 50–67; Moody, *Jonathan Edwards and the Enlightenment*, 3, 163. ("Notes" to the "Introduction," 10n14–11n18, and 163n4, are especially valuable as being concise but extensive regarding analyses of the multiple interpretations of Edwards.) "Suggestions for Additional Reading," in Moody, *Jonathan Edwards and the Enlightenment*, 111–13, although dealing with Edwards in the context of the Enlightenment, are extensive up to that time regarding analyses of Edwards as a theologian, philosopher, and scientist.

The interpretive variations notwithstanding, the observations regarding Edwards remain true that "he looms as a singular historical figure"; therefore, "[One may] like him or detest him, but in either case [one must] concede his dominant position" in American religious, intellectual, and cultural history; Lucas, "Jonathan Edwards: Between Church and Academy," 236; Minkema and Stout, "Jonathan Edwards Studies: The State of the Field," 246. "Singular historical figure" is an understatement. In the "Postscript" to *After Jonathan Edwards: The Courses of New England Theology*, 254, Crisp and Sweeney conclude, "Edwards has become one of the few Protestant leaders

Introduction

Nor is interest in this fascinating figure confined to a minute or obscure circle or consigned to the distant past. Gone are the days when the assertion that Edwards "is discussed less commonly than his worth merits" can be taken seriously. Both academic and popular fascination with this colonial divine and thinker not only have not declined in recent generations, they are increasing markedly.[8]

---

who have changed the world forever—through his ministry, his writings, and the labors of his followers." McDermott, "Jonathan Edwards and the Future of Global Christianity," 13–19, argues that this result has been achieved partially because "Edwards' theology is a unique bridge-builder in four ways: 1) between Catholics and Protestants, 2) between East and West, 3) between Pentecostals/charismatics and non-charismatics, and 4) between liberals and conservatives," and concludes, "[I]t may be appropriate to cease speaking of Jonathan Edwards as 'America's theologian' and to begin thinking of him as a global theologian for twenty-first century Christianity"; McDermott, "Jonathan Edwards and the Future of Global Christianity," 19. In the global context, for recent discussions among Edwards scholars on the impact this eighteenth-century figure has on the world beyond North America (and on the work remaining to be done in assessing his impact), see the following chapters in *The Oxford Handbook of Jonathan Edwards* (hereafter *OHJE*): Han, "Asia," 514–27; Piggin, "Australia," 528–41; Neele, "Africa," 542–54; and Campos, "Latin America," 555–67.

For analyses reflecting the ways in which emphases in Edwards studies have shifted over time, see Allen, "Place of Edwards in History," 3–31; Riley, "Real Jonathan Edwards," 705–15; Morris, "Reappraisal of Edwards," 515–25; Elwood, *Philosophical Theology of Jonathan Edwards*, 1–11; Holbrook, "Major Patterns," 1–2, 187n1–7; Weber, "Image of Jonathan Edwards in American Culture"; Gerstner, "Jonathan Edwards's Place in the History of Christian Thought," 13–19; Lucas, "Jonathan Edwards: Between Church and Academy," 228–47; Lukasik, "Feeling the Force of Certainty," 223n2; Helm and Crisp, "Introduction," ix–xi; Noll, "Edwards' Theology after Edwards," 292–308; Stein, "Introduction," 1–15; Lesser, "Edwards in 'American Culture,'" 280–99; Lesser, "Introduction," 3–46; Crocco, "Edwards's Intellectual Legacy," 300–24; Chun, *Legacy of Jonathan Edwards in the Theology of Andrew Fuller*, 3–5 (notes 6–17 here are especially useful); and Stievermann, "Studying the History of American Protestantism through Jonathan Edwards," 69–91. See Chun, *Legacy of Jonathan Edwards in the Theology of Andrew Fuller*, 3n9, for a concise but detailed review of recent interpretations of Edwards as a theologian.

8. Quotation is from Suter, "Concept of Morality in the Philosophy of Jonathan Edwards," 265. See, e.g., Lesser, *Jonathan Edwards: A Reference Guide*, xli; Fiering, *Jonathan Edwards's Moral Thought and Its British Context*, 371–79; Hatch and Stout, "Introduction," 3; Oberg and Stout, "Introduction," 3; Lesser, *Jonathan Edwards: An Annotated Bibliography, 1979–1993*; Delattre, "Recent Scholarship on Jonathan Edwards," 369–75; Stout, "Introduction," ix–x; Nichols, *Jonathan Edwards*, 18, 21; Lucas, "Jonathan Edwards," 247; Kling and Sweeney, "Introduction," xi–xii; Taylor, "Introduction," 14; Minkema, "Jonathan Edwards in the Twentieth Century," 659–87; and Hansen, "Young, Restless, and Reformed," 38. The observation that Edwards "was certainly a thinker of the first rank who continues to generate interest today," decidedly understates the case; Helm and Crisp, "Introduction," ix. See Strachan and Sweeney, "Preface," 9: "Three hundred years after his heyday, Jonathan Edwards is more popular than ever . . . . [He] is far more widely read than he was when he lived"; Stout et al.,

To Understand *Things* as Well as *Words*

"Introduction," v: "Even to this day, Edwards's life is studied and his writings consulted on a global basis more than any other American theologian." Nichols, "Jonathan Edwards: His Life and Legacy," 35, 36, observes, "Edwards may be even more well-known and discussed now than he was in his own lifetime," and points out a startling fact: "No other colonial figure, not even Benjamin Franklin or George Washington, has generated the literature . . . [that] Jonathan Edwards has." Byrd, "Introduction," in *Jonathan Edwards for Armchair Theologians*, xiii, comments, "Edwards continues to fascinate scholars in departments that span an entire university campus. For so many—historians, philosophers, ethicists, theologians, literary specialists—Edwards remains interesting because the questions he pondered in his time are dilemmas that remain vital today." As a result of this ongoing fascination, "Study of [Edwards] has become an industry unto itself"; Stout, Minkema, and Neele, "Introduction," x. Moody, *Jonathan Edwards and the Enlightenment*, 3, observes, "The writings [on Edwards] cover so much ground that there are now several works of secondary literature just to keep track of the secondary literature." (See Moody, *Jonathan Edwards and the Enlightenment*, 12n20.)

Yet this may well be a Sisyphean task: "Today, exhaustive reading of secondary sources in the field of Edwards is virtually an impossible endeavor"; Chun, *Legacy of Jonathan Edwards in the Theology of Andrew Fuller*, 2, 2n2: "Minkema has tried to give an overview of what has been done and provides a useful table. See Minkema, 'Jonathan Edwards in the Twentieth Century,' 661–662." Lesser, *Reading Jonathan Edwards: An Annotated Bibliography in Three Parts, 1729-2005*, 31, his most recent bibliographical work on Edwards, notes, "Each of the decades since 1940 has seen almost a doubling of the number of dissertations on Edwards over the previous one." (Sliwoski, "Doctoral Dissertations on Jonathan Edwards," 318–27, provides an extensive listing up to that time.) See also Stievermann, "Studying the History of American Protestantism through Jonathan Edwards," 72: "For decades the number of dissertations, books, and articles on Edwards [has] been steadily increasing, especially in the various areas of theology" (see especially 72n9); Studebaker, *Jonathan Edwards' Social Augustinian Trinitarianism*, 5n3; McDermott, "Introduction: How to Understand the American Theologian," 4–5; Minkema, "Jonathan Edwards's Life and Career: Society and Self," 24–25. Sweeney, *Jonathan Edwards and the Ministry of the Word*, 17, comments, "[Edwards] remains one of the best-studied figures of our past." Even more recently, Edwards scholars observe, "The number of secondary publications on Edwards fast approaches 4,000, making him one of the most studied figures in the history of Christian thought"; Edwards "has been studied and put to use among a wide—indeed, surprising and ironic— array of people, in nearly every part of the world"; Minkema and Stout, "Jonathan Edwards Studies," 251; Crisp and Sweeney, "Postscript," 257. Among his admirers are non-academics. "Especially in evangelical circles, [Edwards] is widely promoted and read as a devotional author, and serves as a cultural and religious hero for many pastors and laypeople"; Stievermann, "Studying the History of American Protestantism through Jonathan Edwards," 72, 72n10.

The mid-twentieth century witnessed the beginning of what has become known as the "Jonathan Edwards Renaissance" which has resulted in "an explosion of first-rate scholarship on Edwards in North America and abroad" produced by "an incredibly rich and growing community of scholars, religious leaders, and others from different backgrounds [and] from different places on the planet"; Sweeney and Stievermann, "Introduction," xv; Minkema, "Foreword," xiv. Regarding the global extent of Edwards's appeal to up-and-coming academicians, "[G]raduate work on Edwards *outside of* the United States now outweighs work on him done *within* the United States"; Minkema, "Foreword," xiv (emphasis added). This phenomenon is manifesting itself

Introduction

In *fine*, in the wide-ranging, decades-long attention he has attracted, Edwards has been appropriated as "America's Theologian," (and is increasingly regarded as a *global*-impacting theologian), has received acclaim as a "revival preacher extraordinaire," has been lauded as "America's pioneer esthetician," and more recently, has been accorded scholarly attention as a "premier exegete of the Holy Writ."[9]

One aspect of Edwards's life and work which has been subjected to comparatively little scholarly examination, however, is that of *educator*. Astonishingly, considering the extensive scrutiny that Edwards's corpus of work has received, relatively little attention has been devoted to his pedagogical philosophy, praxis, or results. This lack of notice is especially puzzling, considering the fact that Edwards invested his entire adult life in instructing various corps of students, both males and females, from pre-teens and early adolescents to adults in their twenties (and possibly older), and ones ranging in socioeconomic status from "savage" and "barbarous" Native Americans to upper-class colonials.[10] Nevertheless, as Kenneth Minkema has noted, "The topic of Edwards as an educator

---

in an immense output of monographs, essays, books, book chapters, dissertations, and journal articles, each addressing "a facet of Edwards's 'greatness,' and his continued 'far-reaching consequence'"; Winslow, *Jonathan Edwards 1703-1758*, 297; Lowe and Gullotta, "Introduction," 13. Nor is the end in sight, as "scholarship on Edwards has only grown in recent years, in nearly every cognate discipline"; Sweeney, "Edwards Studies Today," 570. "The study of Jonathan Edwards continues today, and it will continue in the future . . . . [T]he last word has not yet been written regarding [him], his life and activities, his theology and other ideas, or his reputation and legacy"; Stein, "Introduction," 14. The seemingly boundless fascination with this eighteenth-century historical figure notwithstanding, "much more remains to be done" in terms of fruitful exploration; Sweeney and Stievermann, "Introduction," xv, xix.

9. Cochran, Review of *Edwards the Mentor*; Aldridge, "Edwards and Hutcheson," 35. See Bezzant, *Global Edwards*; Sweeney, *Edwards the Exegete*.

10. Quotations are from Edwards, *Letters and Personal Writings* (hereafter *LPW*), 16:411, 413. See Olsen, "Philosophy of Jonathan Edwards and Its Significance for Educational Thinking," 180: "Edwards began his vocational life in education at Yale, and completed it as president of [present-day] Princeton." The groups of students Edwards taught and his methodology of teaching each will be examined in chapter 6 of this study.

For information about Sir William Pepperrell, Massachusetts' "most famous New Light layman," a military hero, and a supporter of the Stockbridge mission, see Parsons, *Life of Sir William Pepperrell*; Rolde, *Sir William Pepperrell of Colonial New England*; Fairchild, "Pepperrell, Sir William"; Gwyn, "Pepperrell, Sir William"; Marsden, *Jonathan Edwards: A Life*, 210, 402 (source of quotation), 403; Bezzant, "Pepperrell, William (1696-1759)," 436-37.

is something that scholars and devotées often mention but have not discussed in anything like a concerted manner."[11]

Examining this dimension of his work in this study will establish that Edwards regarded education as crucial in achieving the goals to which he devoted his life, those of "glorifying God in the world" by working toward "the advancement and enlargement of Christ's kingdom on earth."[12] As will become evident, Edwards's devotion to these objectives formed a core from which radiated his numerous aspects. Realizing this about Edwards enables a key insight into the periodic discussions of an "essential Edwards" versus "multiple Edwardses," to be examined in the conclusion of this study.

Relatedly, little, if any, effort has been made to determine why Edwards taught the way he did or to examine the instructional methodology(ies) he employed throughout his endeavors as an educator. This study will do so in order to compare techniques Edwards used with the different groups of students he taught. This extensive examination will establish Edwards as a noteworthy education theorist and as an educator by documenting Edwards's systematic use of sets of theological questions and a holistic dialogic model consistently throughout his pedagogy. This in turn will confirm Edwards's view of the significance of the role of educator in both the intellectual and spiritual development of his students.

Regarding Stockbridge specifically, the comparatively scant amount of study devoted to Edwards's teaching there may be at least partially explained by the persistent myth that the Stockbridge mission was a "quiet retreat," allowing him ample time to write while minimally taxing his

---

11. Minkema, "Jonathan Edwards on Education," 31. See also Minkema, "'Informing of the Child's Understanding,'" 159–89.

The present work is the first book-length study specifically focused on Edwards as an educator and his instructional methodology as applied to each group of students he taught. However, Edwards scholar Rhys Bezzant has written notably on Edwards as a mentor, and has observed the necessity, for both Edwards studies and for education studies, of focusing attention on Edwards's pedagogical significance: "Known in some circles as a revivalist and in others as a philosopher-theologian, Edwards must also be understood as an *educator*, who had profound impact on the development and practice of theological education in North America and beyond"; Bezzant, "American Theological Education at the Beginning of the Nineteenth Century," 75, 75n1 (emphasis added). It is the present study's contention that the principles of dialogic instruction applied holistically, with an appropriate emphasis on mentoring students, should characterize education at all levels and in all contexts.

12. *LPW*, 784; *LPW*, 518. See also *LPW*, 797, 800; *LPW*, 518.

Introduction

energies.[13] Twentieth- and twenty-first century Edwards scholars have acted as "mythbusters" regarding this impression, thereby removing this misconception from the field of Edwards studies.[14]

13. Quotation is from McDermott, "Missions and Native Americans," 266. Although this is not McDermott's own view, he notes that others have claimed this. Among these are Levin, *Jonathan Edwards: A Profile*, 74: The Stockbridge years were "a quiet retreat . . . where he had a better opportunity to pursue and finish the work God had for him to do"; Dwight, "Memoirs of Jonathan Edwards, A. M.," cxxvii: The Stockbridge period was a time of "retirement and leisure" enabling Edwards to produce "four of the ablest and most valuable works which the church of Christ has in its possession [*Freedom of the Will, Concerning the End for Which God Created the World, The Nature of True Virtue,* and *Original Sin*];" and Levin, *Jonathan Edwards: A Profile*, xx: The Stockbridge experience was an "isolated assignment [that] freed [Edwards] to write." In addition to noting the sources above, Gibson, "Jonathan Edwards," 380-402, cites Allen, *Life and Writings of Jonathan Edwards*, 2:273-74, and Sedgwick and Marquand, *Stockbridge 1739-1974*, 5, as expressing the same view. Those who do not make this assessment of Edwards's time at Stockbridge nonetheless devote little, if any, attention to Edwards as an educator there, focusing instead on his writings. See, e.g., Holmes, *God of Grace and God of Glory*, 5-6. Holmes characterizes Edwards's time at Stockbridge as "unquestionably hard" but makes no mention of Edwards as an educator. Likewise, Smith, *Jonathan Edwards*, 12: "In Stockbridge [Edwards] preached to the Indians, endured the hardships of being on the edge of the French and Indian wars begun in 1754, published *Freedom of the Will* in the same year, and *Original Sin* in 1758."

14. E.g., Simpson, "Jonathan Edwards—A Historical Review," 4, specifies "teacher" as a task Edwards performed in the "comparative isolation of his pioneer environment" of Stockbridge. Faust and Johnson, *Jonathan Edwards,* xiv, although commenting that Edwards's duties at Stockbridge "gave him leisure to write," note the "local venality and petty caviling" characterizing the mission setting, and observe that a reader of *Freedom of the Will* "should remember that many a chapter must have been temporarily laid aside while [Edwards] paused to catechize the Indian boys or to set them a spelling lesson." Even more recently, Minkema has explored the topic of Edwards as an educator across a broader range by examining Edwards's pedagogical techniques employed with the children at the Stockbridge mission, with young people at his church at Northampton, with ministerial candidates in his home, and with seniors at the College of New Jersey (present-day Princeton University). Nichols, "Last of the Mohican Missionaries: Jonathan Edwards at Stockbridge," writes that is a "mistake to interpret the Stockbridge years merely as an opportunity to devote the necessary time to writing the treatises that earned his reputation as America's greatest philosopher-theologian." Likewise, Claghorn, "Introduction," 17: "Contrary to the received wisdom concerning Edwards' Stockbridge years, he did not view the mission as a retreat where he could hide away and write." Also Minkema, "Jonathan Edwards: A Theological Life," 13: "Stockbridge was no sylvan retreat where [Edwards] could finally sit back and compose the theological treatises he had envisioned for years." In fact, he dealt with "a broad range of complex and divisive issues and individuals" there. Minkema, "Edwardses," 364-65, fleshes out Edwards's "cycle of life at Stockbridge: appealing to the commissioners to meet the Indians' needs, writing to benefactors and interested parties, teaching the children under his charge to read and write, and, in between the many duties to which [he] had to attend, doing his own studying and writing." Perhaps the statement that puts Edwards's work at Stockbridge most in perspective is that of Sweeney, *Jonathan Edwards and the*

To Understand *Things* as Well as *Words*

The present study builds on the work of Minkema and other Edwards scholars by analyzing Edwards as an educator in the following ways: by examining influences on Edwards's pedagogical philosophy and praxis; by focusing on the desired outcomes of his instructional technique at the Stockbridge mission, as expressed in a number of his letters written from there; by making explicit the continuity in his instructional methodology with the "children" at Stockbridge, the "young people" and ministerial candidates at Northampton, and the students at the College of New Jersey (currently Princeton University) through examining Edwards's pedagogical work with each of these groups; and by examining the effects of the dialogic technique used by Edwards, and used and modified by his students Joseph Bellamy and Samuel Hopkins, on the development of the New Divinity movement.[15] Finally, we will examine dialogic instructional technique and the value of mentoring students in the context of a holistic approach to teaching the "total person" in the postmodern world.

We shall now turn to the ways in which Edwards and education intersected throughout his life: Edwards as a student at Yale, his instructing catechists in Scripture and his teaching and mentoring of ministerial candidates during his Northampton pastorate, his instructing Native American and Anglo-colonial children at the Stockbridge mission, and his (albeit brief) instruction at the College of New Jersey, currently Princeton, through sets of theological questions and dialogic interaction. This review will bring into focus the interrelationships between Edwards and education significant for the present work, to be discussed in greater

---

Ministry of the Word, 180, 180n35: "Rather than use his time at Stockbridge as a retreat from worldly affairs, [Edwards] poured his life into Native American ministry."

For an account of English mission efforts in eighteenth-century New England, see Axtell, *Invasion Within*; for an account of the English efforts in education of the Natives, see Axtell, *Invasion Within*, 179–217. See Winslow, *Jonathan Edwards, 1703–1758*, 276–80; Axtell, *Invasion Within*, 197–204; Frazier, *Mohicans of Stockbridge*, 96–123; and Marsden, *Jonathan Edwards: A Life*, 375–94, for accounts of the difficulties at Stockbridge confronting Edwards. Also, Holbrook, "Editor's Introduction," 21–22, and Claghorn, "Introduction," 17–24, give a concise summary of Edwards's struggles at Stockbridge.

15. Minkema, "Jonathan Edwards on Education," 31, 34: "'Children' . . . were for Edwards those younger than fifteen years of age"; "'Young people' Edwards defined as individuals from fifteen to twenty-five years old." See also Minkema, "Jonathan Edwards on Education," 263n2; Minkema, "Old Age and Religion," 674, 675; Edwards's letter to Rev. Thomas Prince, December 12, 1743, 546–47 (also in *LPW*, 116–17); Brekus, "Children of Wrath, Children of Grace: Jonathan Edwards and the Puritan Culture of Child Rearing," 302.

Introduction

detail in chapters 4 and 5: the foundation of Edwards's own education, his assessments of the nature and purposes of education, of the role of educator, his expectations of students, and his pedagogical methodology.

The young Edwards's home environment as relevant to his pedagogical philosophy and praxis will be discussed at some length in chapter 4. Edwards entered Connecticut's Collegiate School (later Yale College) in 1716. There, he encountered the "New Learning" through both his course of studies as an undergraduate and as a Master's degree student, and via the newly-acquired library holdings of the volumes donated by Jeremiah Dummer, the London book agent for the Connecticut and Massachusetts colonies.[16] Included in this intellectually vibrant setting were the works of Isaac Newton and John Locke, the Cambridge Platonists, essayists Joseph Addison and Sir Richard Steele, lexicons, biblical commentaries, Pierre Bayle's *Historical and Critical Dictionary* (1697), "and even an English translation of the Qur'an" via Dummer's donation, as well as the classical formulation of *trivium* (grammar, rhetoric, and logic) and *quadrivium* (algebra, geometry, astronomy, and music) in the curriculum.[17] The program was structured so that students focused on languages at the beginning and mathematics, metaphysics, and logic in the latter stages. "There was also a great deal of reciting: daily from English to Greek, from Hebrew to Greek, from Latin to English; on Fridays from [Swiss Protestant theologian Johannes] Wollebius [(1589–1629)] on Saturdays from William Ames's *Medulla* [*Theologica; Marrow of Sacred*

---

16. Bryant and Patterson, "List of Books Sent by Jeremiah Dummer," 423–92; Opie, "Introduction," vi; Anderson, "Biographical Background," 17–21 (See 19n1); Lukasik, "Feeling the Force of Certainty," 227n9; Brown, "Biblical Exegesis," 371–72. This collection included more than 800 volumes and covered every major branch of learning; Bryant and Patterson, "List of Books Sent by Jeremiah Dummer," 423–92; Thuesen, "Sources of Edwards's Thought," 71; Spencer, "Jonathan Edwards and the Historiography of the American Enlightenment," 23.

17. Maclean, *John Locke and English Literature of the Eighteenth Century*, 7; Townsend, "Introduction," v–vi; Schlaeger, "Jonathan Edwards' Theory of Perception," 2; Thuesen, "Edwards' Intellectual Background," 20; Kimnach et al., "Editors' Introduction," xxiv. See Thuesen, "Edwards' Intellectual Background," 31n10; Opie, "Introduction," vi. For more detailed information regarding Edwards's education at Yale, see Walker, "Jonathan Edwards," 217–63; Davidson, *Jonathan Edwards*, 8–10; Morris, "Genius of Jonathan Edwards," 29–33; Cremin, *American Education*, 315; Fiering, *Jonathan Edwards's Moral Thought and Its British Context*, 25, 30–47; McCracken, *Malebranche and British Philosophy*, 316–17; Marsden, *Jonathan Edwards: A Life*, 59–81; and Sweeney, *Jonathan Edwards and the Ministry of the Word*, 36–40. For a description of the curriculum at Yale in its early years, see Murray, *Jonathan Edwards: A New Biography*, 27, and Schnittjer, "Ingredients of Effective Mentoring," 86–100 (especially 87–88); for a more extensive account, see Warch, *School of the Prophets*, 186–249.

To Understand *Things* as Well as *Words*

Theology] and the *Westminster Assembly's Shorter Catechism*; and on Sundays from Ames again, this time *Cases of Conscience*."[18] Characterized by both discipline and intellectual rigor, Edwards's home environment and his collegiate education provided the foundation on which he built his own instructional philosophy and praxis.[19]

A theme that is central to this study is that Edwards's goal as an educator was two-fold: to assist his students' intellectual *and* spiritual development. In achieving the former, his objective was to enable his students "to understand *things* as well as *words*"; that is, to grasp the concepts of what was being taught through dialogue with the teacher, rather than regurgitating through rote memorization of sounds with no real understanding of their significance.[20] Such interaction, Edwards was convinced, was essential for the students to grasp both words and the ideas the words signify.

In executing this program, Edwards sought, at the introductory level, to expand his students' levels of learning consistent with their aims in studying with him. As we shall see, Edwards's ultimate goal as an educator was to prepare students to receive redemptive grace and the "new spiritual sense" which it brings. This supernatural event is requisite to understanding "spiritual and divine things," his underlying objective as an educator.[21]

As instructor at Stockbridge, Edwards eschewed "the gross defects of the ordinary method of teaching among the English" (i.e., rote memorization), in which "children are habituated to learning without understanding." Instead, he implemented the dialogic (what Edwards termed "familiar") method of pedagogy, in which the teacher engages the students in conversation with questions, eliciting answers and further questions in turn.[22] This procedural schema was foundational to Edwards's teaching praxis throughout his life, with his own children, Bible catechists, ministerial aspirants, Native American and Anglo-colonial elementary students, and college students.

---

18. Minkema, "Informing of the Child's Understanding," 161–62; Morris, *Young Jonathan Edwards*, 64–65. See also Warch, *School of the Prophets*, 193; Anderson, "Editor's Introduction," 11–26.

19. Minkema, "Informing of the Child's Understanding," 162.

20. Quotation is in *LPW*, 408.

21. Quotations are in Edwards, *Religious Affections* (hereafter *RA*), 206, 260. Edwards's pedagogical philosophy, aims, and praxis will be examined in chapters 5 and 6.

22. Quotations are in *LPW*, 408.

Introduction

The second and ultimate purpose for Edwards in thus engaging and developing the mental powers of his students was to help effect spiritual awakening, or salvation, in unregenerate students and to assist in the spiritual development of Christians under his tutelage. In his grand design for the Stockbridge mission that he laid out in his letter to Sir William Pepperrell, dated November 28, 1751, Edwards indicated that, for him, early education inextricably links "informing of the child's understanding, influencing his [or her] heart, and directing its practice . . . [i]n order to promote the salvation of the children, which is the main design of the whole Indian establishment at this place."[23] Thus, no less at the teacher's desk than behind the minister's pulpit, fully as much to his students as to his congregants, Edwards felt "called to be a light to the souls," leading all under his influence to "seek to know the Word of God, that [they] might be instructed by it."[24]

LITERATURE REVIEW

As noted above, the voluminous corpus of Edwards studies contains few analyses of him as an educator. Scholarly examination of his time at Stockbridge, for example, has tended to focus on the major theological works he wrote there and to give little, if any, attention to his teaching the Native Americans and Anglo-colonials at the mission school.

Among the primary sources available, Edwards's writings on the mind (specifically, how the mind forms ideas), on the nature of reality and epistemology, on beauty, and on "true virtue" are critical for the current study. These works illuminate the development of Edwards's theories of epistemology and metaphysics, and, through them, his pedagogy. In addition, Edwards's view of aesthetics affected his choice to include music in the curriculum at Stockbridge.[25]

Edwards's letters from Stockbridge comprise the largest portion of his extant body of correspondence and contain "some of the most elegant prose of his career."[26] This epistolary output reveals him as a mission-

---

23. *LPW*, 408, 409, 411.

24. Edwards, "True Excellency of a Minister of the Gospel," 98; Edwards, "To the Mohawks at the Treaty. August 16, 1751," 107.

25. Edwards, "Of Being," 203–8; Edwards, "Of Atoms," 209–19; Edwards, "Beauty of the World," 306–7; Edwards, "Mind," 333–86; Edwards, "Notes on Knowledge and Existence," 399; Edwards, "Nature of True Virtue" (hereafter *TV*), 539–627.

26. Kimnach in Edwards, *Sermons and Discourses* (hereafter *SD*), *1743–1758*,

ary "deeply involved in the practical affairs" of his setting and confirms "that he considered the [American] Indians and their mission a high priority."[27] These missives are a significant source of material for indicating Edwards's convictions regarding the qualifications and the duties of a teacher, his expectations of students, the nature of the pedagogic program as designed to achieve optimal results, and the ideal outcomes of the teaching/learning enterprise.

Edwards's aforementioned letter to Pepperrell is the "most complete statement of his philosophy of education."[28] It also reveals his "low regard for Indian culture but high trust in Indian potential."[29] In it, Edwards set forth his plan to replace the instructional technique used at the school (where he had recently arrived and where, eventually, he would be placed in charge of the school for Native American and Anglo-colonial children). Rather than relying solely on rote memorization, which had resulted in students "making such and such sounds, on the sight of such and such letters," with no understanding of what they were reading, as noted above, Edwards implemented a dialogic, or "familiar," methodology. That is, "Familiar questions should be put to the child, about the subjects of the lesson; and the child should be encouraged . . . to speak freely, and in his turn also to ask questions."[30] Edwards's other letters from Stockbridge touching on education will be discussed in chapters 5 and 6 in connection with his instructional philosophy and methodology.

Among the secondary sources, six biographies are considered significant treatments of Edwards's life and/or works. Samuel Hopkins penned the first biography of his mentor, *Life and Character of the Late Reverend Mr. Jonathan Edwards* (1765), recording his utmost admiration of Edwards as "one of the greatest—best—and most useful of men" and as someone of great worth to him as a teacher and counselor.

Sereno Edwards Dwight's *Life of President Edwards* (1829), the "first extensive" biography, includes Edwards's notebooks, letters, and manuscripts of "The Mind," "Notes on Natural Science," "Resolutions," "Diary," *Personal Narrative*, and his *Farewell Sermon*. Dwight's rendering of Edwards's dismissal from the Northampton church occupies one-fourth of the volume. This work began creating the myth that the Stockbridge

---

29–30n4.

27. Marsden, *Jonathan Edwards: A Life*, 388; Claghorn, "Introduction," 17.
28. Minkema, "Jonathan Edwards on Education," 32.
29. Marsden, *Jonathan Edwards: A Life*, 389.
30. *LPW*, 407, 408.

Introduction

period was for Edwards primarily a time of "leisure," significant mainly (or solely) because of the major works he wrote there.[31]

Ola Elizabeth Winslow's Pulitzer Prize-winning *Jonathan Edwards, 1703–1758: A Biography* (1940) focuses on the details of Edwards's life and career more than on details of his thought. However, in this work, she maintains that it was a "mistake" for Edwards to have done his life's work in "an outworn dogmatic system." It challenges the idea that his time at Stockbridge was one of idyllic retreat by recounting the hardships Edwards faced in a harsh setting located "beyond the line of the frontier [that was] a mere dot in the wilderness."[32]

Perry Miller's *Jonathan Edwards* (1949) is a biography of Edwards's "life of [the] mind" that aided remarkably in the revival of interest in Puritanism in general and in Edwards studies in particular among American scholars. Miller insisted that Edwards's genius lie in his astuteness in psychology and the natural sciences. One of "America's five or six major artists, who happened to work with ideas," Edwards was "infinitely more than a theologian." Indeed, Miller considered it unfortunate that Edwards was forced by circumstances which were "rigidly circumscribed by narrow doctrinalism" to channel his considerable talents into the area of theology. Miller's biography is significant to the present study mainly for the critical analysis it has attracted and for his interpretation of Locke's influence on Edwards.[33]

Iain Murray's *Jonathan Edwards: A New Biography* (1987), considered by some to be somewhat of a corrective to Miller's "anti-supernatural" bias in his evaluation, is useful for the present project chiefly because of its "Introduction: On Understanding Edwards." In it, Murray notes

---

31. Hopkins, *Life of Edwards*, A2; Dwight, *Life of President Edwards*; Lesser, *Reading Jonathan Edwards*, 73.

32. Winslow, *Jonathan Edwards, 1703–1758: A Biography*, 269. See also Minkema, "Edwardses: A Ministerial Family in Eighteenth-Century New England," 397: "Stockbridge was, even by eighteenth-century standards, a wild and isolated place"; Allen, "Place of Edwards in History," 11.

33. Miller, *Jonathan Edwards*, xi, xii; Lesser, *Reading Jonathan Edwards*, 192; final quotation is in Aldridge, "Edwards and Hutcheson," 35. See Winslow, *Jonathan Edwards, 1703–1758: A Biography*, 327; Miller, "Speculative Genius," 6–7; Miller, *Jonathan Edwards*, xii; Gustafson, "Edwards's Place in Anglo-American Literature," 502–3. Perry Miller's works "remain an important starting point for any serious study of Edwards"; nevertheless, his characterization of Edwards as "modern" has not gone unchallenged; Westra, *Minister's Task and Calling*, 44. See, e.g., Lee, *Philosophical Theology of Jonathan Edwards*, 3n2; and Chun, *Legacy of Jonathan Edwards in the Theology of Andrew Fuller*, 3n8, for samplings of the responses to Miller's assessment.

how Edwards's biographers are divided on how this colonial American should be understood.[34]

George Marsden's *Jonathan Edwards: A Life* (2003) has been hailed as "magisterial" and is considered the definitive comprehensive biography of Edwards to date. Marsden depicts Edwards as a "real person in his own time" and does not seek to elevate any one aspect of Edwards's life to the exclusion of others. This work also gives a detailed account of the difficulties Edwards experienced at Stockbridge and gives valuable information regarding his teaching there, including Edwards's conviction that Bible stories were the best means of engaging the children, his belief that instruction should be co-educational, and his plan to include singing in the school's curriculum.[35]

Erick John Blore has written a thesis and Rebecca Russell Price, D. Campbell Wyckoff, Wesley A. Olsen, and Donald Edd Stelting have written dissertations on intersections between Edwards and education. Of these, each is useful in touching on at least one aspect relevant to the present monograph. However, none examines the influences on Edwards's pedagogical methodology, the use of foundational questions and dialogic technique Edwards employed consistently with his students, the significance of the dialogic methodology Edwards and his first clerical student-mentees, Joseph Bellamy and Samuel Hopkins, utilized, and, which was favored by their students to teach others, for the development of the New Divinity movement, or the value of a holistic dialogic strategy for education today, as the present study seeks to do.[36]

Bernard Bailyn, John Hardin Best, Robert T. Sidwell, James Axtell, Kenneth Lockridge, David Hall, Gerald F. Moran, Maris A. Vinovskis, Jill Lepore, Lisa M. Gordis, David Paul Nord, E. Jennifer Monaghan, and Hugh Amory are among those who have written about the framework of education and the process of learning in colonial New England.[37] Their

---

34. Murray, *Jonathan Edwards: A New Biography*, xix-xxxi; Lesser, *Reading Jonathan Edwards*, 401-2.

35. Marsden, *Jonathan Edwards: A Life*, 390.

36. Blore, "Educational Philosophy of Jonathan Edwards"; Price, "Jonathan Edwards as a Christian Educator"; Wyckoff, "Jonathan Edwards' Contributions to Religious Education"; Olsen, "Philosophy of Jonathan Edwards and its Significance for Educational Thinking"; and Stelting, "Edwards as Educator."

37. Bailyn, *Education in the Forming of American Society*; Best and Sidwell, *American Legacy of Learning*, 5-89; Axtell, *School Upon a Hill*; Lockridge, *Literacy in Colonial New England*; Hall, *Cultures of Print*; Moran and Vinovskis, "Literacy and Education in Eighteenth-Century North America," 186-223; Lepore, "Literacy and Reading in

works discuss the context of education in Edwards's time which put into bold relief his pedagogy.

Chapter 3 will examine written works of four persons whose thoughts exercised a significant influence on Edwards's pedagogical philosophy and praxis. Specifically, John Locke's writings *An Essay Concerning Human Understanding*, *Some Thoughts Concerning Education*, and *The Reasonableness of Christianity* explicate his views on epistemology, pedagogy, and theology.[38] These works will be examined in connection with Edwards's writings and praxis to determine the extent of their influence on Edwards's pedagogical philosophy and methodology. In addition, Isaac Newton's *Philosophiae Naturalis Principia Mathematica* and *Opticks* set forth his views of physics and optics, and will be examined to determine the extent of their influence on Edwards's pedagogy.[39] Lastly, Anthony Ashley Cooper, Third Earl of Shaftesbury's *An Inquiry Concerning Virtue, or Merit* and Francis Hutcheson's *A Short Introduction to Moral Philosophy* and *An Inquiry into the Original of Our Ideas of Beauty and Virtue* will be examined in order to compare them with Edwards's *The Nature of True Virtue* for the purpose of determining Edwards's concept of "true virtue" *contra* the idea of innate morality.[40] Edwards's concept of "true virtue" ("benevolence to Being in general") will then be discussed in connection with its significance for the foundation of his pedagogical philosophy.

Chapter 4 will examine the home environment of Edwards's upbringing as an influence on the foundation, content, scope, and praxis of his pedagogy. In addition, John (Jan) Amos Comenius (1592–1670), a Czech Moravian educator and a major advocate for education and social reform; Nicolas Malebranche (1638–1715), a French priest and philosopher; August Hermann Francke (1663–1727), a German Lutheran minister, biblical scholar, philanthropist, and educator; and Andrew Baxter (1687–1750), a Scottish philosopher, will be discussed as probable

---

Puritan New England," 17–46; Gordis, *Opening Scripture*, 98–99; Nord, *Faith in Reading*, 14, 18; Monaghan, *Learning to Read and Write in Colonial America*; and Amory and Hall, *Colonial Book in the Atlantic World*.

38. Locke, *Essay Concerning Human Understanding*; Locke, *Some Thoughts Concerning Education*; Locke, *Reasonableness of Christianity*.

39. See works by Isaac Newton: *Philosophiae Naturalis Principia Mathematica* and *Opticks, or, A Treatise of the Reflexions, Refractions, Inflexions, and Colours of Light*.

40. Cooper, *Inquiry Concerning Virtue, or Merit*; Hutcheson, *Short Introduction to Moral Philosophy*; Hutcheson, *Inquiry into the Original of Our Ideas of Beauty and Virtue*; *TV*.

influences on Edwards's educational philosophy and praxis by examining the parallels between their ideas and practices regarding education and those of Edwards.

Chapter 5 examines Edwards's pertinent sermons, correspondence, and other writings (e.g., "Miscellanies") and pertinent secondary literature, in order to determine his perspectives on the function of instruction in the office of pastor, on the purpose and on the qualifications of the teacher in the teaching/learning processes, his expectations of students, and his view of the nature of the education experience. Secondary sources regarding the cultural and theological contexts in which Edwards lived will be examined as well.

Chapter 6 documents examples of "Questions for Young People," which Edwards composed in order to initiate a dialogic pedagogy with Bible catechists at his Northampton home. Edwards's first two clerical students, Joseph Bellamy and Samuel Hopkins, manifested in their works and discussed in their correspondence the influence of Edwards on them through his use of sets of theological questions and dialogic technique based on them.[41]

Examples of these "Questions on Theological Subjects" and "Theological Questions of President Edwards Senior" will be discussed in connection with Edwards's pedagogy. Examination of his correspondence from the Stockbridge mission indicates that Edwards used a dialogic method here as well, posing questions to his students based on the *Westminster Shorter Catechism*, as with his own children. Examples of questions from the above-mentioned theological questions posed to seniors at the College of New Jersey in his dialogic pedagogy with them will likewise be documented. Edwards's other writings relevant to education and secondary literature relevant to education in Edwards's milieu will also be examined.

Chapter 7 examines Edwards's "Resolutions," along with his relevant sermons and public writings, in order to confirm his dedication to "glorifying God in the world" by working to achieve "the advancement and enlargement of Christ's kingdom on earth." In addition, his expressed objectives of "informing the [student's] understanding, influencing his [or her] heart, and directing its practice" are discussed in connection with

---

41. Bellamy, *True Religion Delineated*, and Bellamy, *Works of Joseph Bellamy, D. D.*; Hopkins, *System of Doctrines, Contained in Divine Revelation, Explained and Defended*, Hopkins, *Enquiry Concerning the Promises of the Gospel*, Hopkins, *Sketches of the Life of the Late Rev. Samuel Hopkins, D. D.*

Introduction

pertinent works of secondary literature, such as those by Parker Palmer (*Courage to Teach: Exploring the Inner Landscape of a Teacher's Life*, *To Know As We Are Known: Education as a Spiritual Journey*, and *The Heart of Higher Education: A Call to Renewal*). Doing so assesses Edwards's pedagogy by the standard of a holistic approach to education today.

Chapter 8 surveys primary literature (e.g., Edwards's relevant correspondence) and a wide array of secondary literature in order to determine the extent (if any) to which Edwards can be categorized regarding his thought world and whether an "essential Edwards" is identifiable. It also examines Edwards in relation to Laurie Matthias's work, *The Cry of the Teacher's Soul*, in order to determine whether his holistic and dialogic approach to teaching is feasible and desirable today.

RESEARCH QUESTIONS

This work will be constructed to answer: What were the instructional strategies Edwards employed in teaching students throughout his span as an educator? Secondary questions are:

> What philosophy of education undergirded Edwards's pedagogical method(s)?
>
> What does use of these strategies indicate about Edwards's evaluation of the potential for educability of Native Americans compared with that of the Anglo-colonial students he taught?
>
> Who and what influenced Edwards's epistemology and his views on the natural sciences and on the origin and nature of morality, and, through them, his pedagogical methodology?
>
> What does Edwards's letter to Pepperrell setting forth his plan for instruction at the Stockbridge mission indicate about Edwards's view of the proper role of a teacher, of the nature of the education process, and of a teacher's expectations of students?
>
> What was the significance of the dialogic pedagogical technique, begun by Edwards and continued by his students Joseph Bellamy and Samuel Hopkins, for the development of the New Divinity movement?

To Understand *Things* as Well as *Words*

What validity (if any) does a dialogic teaching technique and holistic approach to pedagogy, on which Edwards showed consistent reliance, have in the postmodern era?

METHODOLOGY

This study will examine Edwards's letters from the Stockbridge mission in which he discusses education to see what they reveal about his pedagogical philosophy and his intended educational outcomes. Secondary sources providing information on the educational milieu of Edwards's time will be examined to place Edwards in his context.

Primary and secondary sources dealing with Edwards's early family environment and relevant writings of the four philosophers and educators discussed in chapter 4 will be examined in connection with Edwards's statements on education and with his pedagogical practices to determine if a plausible case can be made for their influence on Edwards's pedagogy.

The sets of theological questions Edwards utilized with Bible catechists, clerical candidates, and college students and the dialogic methodology used in conjunction with them will be examined as well. Edwards's aforementioned letter to Pepperrell and his other correspondence from Stockbridge pertaining to his pedagogy will be examined in order to determine his teaching philosophy, praxis, and objectives with his Stockbridge students, and to assess their uniformity with the foundation, methodology, and expected outcomes of the pedagogy he implemented at the other locations examined. This analysis will demonstrate that his pedagogical technique was consistent across all of these student groups, indicating a thoroughly thought-out philosophy of education and a consistency of expectation of outcomes.

The correspondence of Bellamy and Hopkins that touches on the dialogic instructional technique Edwards used will be examined in order to determine their reactions as students to Edwards as a teacher and to establish their continuation of the dialogic methodology to which he introduced them. In addition, historical records will be examined that establish that the students whom Bellamy and Hopkins taught used the question-based dialogic methodology to teach their students, consisting of the pastor-educators known as the New Divinity.

Introduction

CONTRIBUTIONS

In the mountainous volume of works written about Edwards, comparatively few deal with him as an educator. This lacuna is unfortunate because Edwards considered the role of instructor to be the fundamental function of a minister and he regarded literacy as crucial in salvation and to growth in the Christian life.[42] The present examination will enlarge our understanding and appreciation of Edwards the education theorist and educator by highlighting these largely neglected aspects of his life's work. Doing so will assist in gaining recognition for *educator* as a key dimension of Edwards's Christian evangelization and, thus, will advance Edwards studies.

Specifically, this approach will make three significant secondary contributions to the field of Edwards scholarship: (1) demonstrating that, although to a certain extent Edwards was a "man of his time" as far as his holding certain presuppositions regarding Native American culture common to his era, he nonetheless was convinced that Native Americans were as capable of, and as deserving of, education as their contemporaneous Anglo-colonials, (2) contextualizing the dialogic methodology which Edwards used consistently within the educational milieu of its time, thus highlighting its innovative nature, and (3) noting the significant paradigmatic shift in the role of student, from passive recipient of information to active participant in the learning process, that this methodology enabled. In addition, this examination will contribute to education studies by examining the value of a holistic dialogic methodology in interacting with the "total person" of a student (mind, affections, and behavior), and of mentoring a student "singly, particularly, and closely" in the postmodern era.[43]

Neither deification nor demonization is a useful approach to gaining an accurate understanding of this complex historical figure (although each has been employed).[44] Behind the Jonathan Edwards that has right-

---

42. See Edwards, "True Excellency of a Minister of the Gospel," 85–103; Edwards, "To the Mohawks at the Treaty. August 16, 1751," 105–10.

43. Quotation in *LPW*, 412.

44. "Figures like Edwards deserve neither idolatry nor iconoclasm"; Cochran, "Jonathan Edwards for the Next Generation," 9. A tribute that at least approaches deification is that of Storms, *Tragedy in Eden*, xii: "Edwards justifiably takes his place alongside such Christian 'geniuses' as Augustine, Calvin, and Kuyper, men whose scintillating brilliance and unbridled devotion to the God of sovereign grace cannot be challenged." A prime example of demonization is Marilla Marks Ricker, *Jonathan*

ly been accorded an honored status in history among the heroes of the Christian faith and élite exemplars of intellect, lived a flesh-and-blood human being. This study seeks to shed light on Edwards the person as a *teacher*—an aspect of his life and work which, as noted at the outset, has largely been neglected. In doing so, those who devote their attention to this multifaceted figure, who has fascinated so many in the past and who continues to do so, will gain a greater appreciation of Edwards's commitment to Christ and of his labors for Christ's kingdom that have earned unequaled praise.

This study is undertaken with this stipulation in mind: Any attempt to add luster to the name of Jonathan Edwards is a fool's errand. He has long since ended his life's labors, has passed on to his heavenly reward, and has received the highest accolades humanity can offer. However, to gain a more complete understanding of his life's work by focusing attention on his convictions of what a teacher could and should achieve in the lives of students, and on how he put them into action, is to gain a greater appreciation both of Edwards himself and of what education in its fullest sense can accomplish now and in the future.

Edwards: The Divine Who Filled the Air with Damnation and Proved the Total Depravity of God (American Freethought Tract Society, 1918), quoted in Stout et al., "Introduction," vii: Edwards "believed in the worst God, preached the worst sermons, and had the worst religion of any human being who ever lived on this continent."

2

Background: Puritanism

OBVIOUS THOUGH IT MAY be, it is crucial to realize in assessing Edwards that he did not live in a vacuum. Rather, he was a product of a specific context that was conditioned by particular theological, intellectual, and cultural forces. The eighteenth-century New England environment in which Edwards lived and worked during his adult life was shaped by two primary multidimensional modes of thought: Puritanism (near the end of its dominance in New England) and "the Enlightenment(s)"(toward the beginning of its appearance in colonial America).[1] Each of these was complex and diverse, rather than rigidly unified. Each had specific aspects to which Edwards reacted and which he appropriated that helped shape his pedagogical philosophy and practice. The first of these, that of Puritanism, was brought to colonial America in the seventeenth century by English settlers who, at the most basic level, sought to reform the liturgy, theology, and structure of the Church of England by implementing a bibliocentric focus, and to restructure society to exemplify a Reformed "city on a hill." The second, that of the Enlightenment, made its way to the colonial landscape in the eighteenth century as a result of forces sweeping across Europe that challenged entrenched traditions, sought

---

1. See Best and Sidwell, *American Legacy of Learning*, 85–98, for an overview of the effects of each of these frameworks on American education. The desirability of considering multiple "Enlightenments," rather than a unified phenomenon, will be discussed in the following chapter.

To Understand *Things* as Well as *Words*

to exalt Reason as the primary (if not sole) guide to life, and to promote intellectual inquiry and scientific knowledge as the ways to progress. Defining features of each of these were the nature of mankind and his relationship to God and to the world around him.

A commonplace of Edwards scholarship is that he is somehow connected to both Puritanism and the Enlightenment. If this is taken as a starting point, certain questions remain: "In what way? With what significance for Puritanism? With what significance for the Enlightenment? Around these unanswered questions circles the enigma of Edwards, intriguing because [he is] difficult to tie down. Edwards has captivated an extraordinarily varied expanse of scholarship and commentary."[2] The topics of Edwards as a multifaceted figure who left us a richly diversified legacy will be revisited in the conclusion of this study.

Edwards inhabited each of these worlds as, in significant ways, a "Puritan in the Age of Reason," and as we shall see as we progress, aspects of each impacted his view of teaching.[3] This examination seeks in part to answer the questions Moody raises regarding the relation between Edwards and Puritanism and Edwards and the Enlightenment, specifically by demonstrating how each of these forces influenced Edwards as an educator: his view of the proper role of a teacher, of the true goals of education, and of the pedagogical methodology best suited to achieving them. Doing so will enable us to see Edwards more accurately than was the case previously, by bringing teaching into proper focus among the multiple dimensions that constitute this intriguing figure often considered an "enigma."[4]

This chapter will begin with a brief discussion of Puritanism, then move on to three specific aspects that characterized this movement, and lastly, will demonstrate how these aspects influenced the foundation, content, scope, and focus of Edwards's pedagogical philosophy and praxis. A similar procedure regarding discussion of the Enlightenment will follow in chapter 3. Doing so will enable the reader to see Edwards the educator as partially a product of both Puritanism and the "Enlightenment(s)."

---

2. Moody, *Jonathan Edwards and the Enlightenment*, 3.

3. Quotation is in Opie, "Introduction," vi.

4. See Moody, *Jonathan Edwards and the Enlightenment*, 3, 11n18. Moody, *Jonathan Edwards and the Enlightenment*, 1–9, and Moody, "Notes," 9–16, are valuable sources of information on ways in which Edwards has been evaluated and for a stimulating new analysis of the connection between Edwards and the Enlightenment.

Background: Puritanism

PURITANISM: DIFFICULTIES, DESCRIPTIONS, AND A DEFINITION

At the outset, "Puritanism" must be delimited in such a way as to do justice to the designation and to make the use of it in the present study yield meaningful results. Doing so presents a considerable challenge, since Puritanism was "never monolithic"; a "many-sided and diversified" movement, its components "were in constant flux"; thus, the term "did not mean the same thing to all men at any one time—not even in the sixteenth and seventeenth centuries."[5] One historian has offered a simple, broad overview: "Puritanism concentrates upon the things which are eternal."[6] If this is accepted as a starting point, filling it out has proved problematic. "No scholar would argue that all puritans subscribed to a single coherent orthodoxy that can be labeled 'puritanism.'"[7] Colonial American Puritanism, the variety most relevant to the present study, was "not static"; rather, it "changed its character radically in the space of relatively few years."[8] Hence, the seeker of precise limits pertaining to

---

5. Coffey and Lim, "Introduction," i; Packer, "Foreword," 9; Vaughan and Bremer, "English Background of Puritan New England," 1; Vaughan, *Puritan Tradition in America*, xi–xii. See also Reinitz, "Introduction," 2–3; Hill, "Definition of a Puritan," 24: "[It] is important, in discussing Puritanism, to remember that for contemporaries the word had no narrowly religious connotation"; Morgan, "Problem of Definition," 11–12: "Definitions [of 'Puritan'] were so varied that it is difficult to assimilate them into one coherent understanding of contemporary opinion on the subject; indeed, such a singular comprehension probably did not exist."

6. Henderson, "Puritanism in Eighteenth-Century Scotland," 143.

7. Bremer, *Puritanism*, 35. See Morgan, *Visible Saints*, 61–63; Morgan, *Godly Learning*, 2; Perry, *Intellectual Life in America*, 64. In fact, one writer has characterized the phenomenon of Puritanism as at one point being fraught with "fratricidal cacophony"; Winship, "'Most Glorious Church in the World,'" 71–98.

Weighing the similarities as greater than the differences, Haller, *Rise of Puritanism*, 17, observes, "The disagreements that rendered Puritans into presbyterians, independents, separatists, and baptists were in the long run not [as] significant as the qualities of character, of mind and of imagination, which kept them all alike [as] Puritan." In concurrence with this view is Woodhouse, *Puritanism and Liberty*, 37: "It is unnecessary to posit a *unity* in all Puritan thought; it is sufficient to recognize a *continuity*." Also Lake, "Introduction," 3: Behind the "diverse phenomena" characterizing Puritanism "lay an intense vision of the reality and mutuality of the community of the godly and of the way in which that community could and should be called together through the word [of God], particularly the word preached." See also Tindall, *John Bunyan, Mechanick Preacher*, 5; Murdock, *Literature and Theology in Colonial New England*, 6; Simpson, *Puritanism in Old and New England*, 1–2; Curti, *Growth of American Thought*, 3–4; Hall, "Understanding the Puritans," 343n8, 344n9; Axtell, *School Upon a Hill*, xii-xii.

8. Murdock, "Puritan Legacy," 261. See also Emerson, *Puritanism in America, 1620–1750*, 13.

this topic faces "a peculiar problem of definition": "There is lack of agreement among students of Puritanism concerning even a precise definition of the term 'Puritan,' since "the very essence of Puritanism remains to be determined."[9] Partially out of resignation to this state of affairs, "the words [*Puritan* and *Puritanism*] have been left vague and imprecisely defined" by some writers.[10] Furthermore, "some historians have delighted in the absence of precise definition and [have] made a virtue of vagueness," regarding "[d]efinitional diversity" as a "sign," and possibly even as a "safeguard, of vitality."[11] One leading Puritan authority goes so far as to assert that the term "Puritan" is likely incapable of meaningful definition: "All attempts to distinguish this person, or that idea, or a certain practice or prejudice, as Puritan . . . are liable to fail."[12] Even so, some scholars assure us that the term "Puritanism," though "impossible perhaps to define," is "capable nevertheless of being described."[13]

Among other difficulties one faces in seeking specificity in this area are the fact that Puritanism, as variously conceived, has been both revered and reviled; the shift in cultural sensibilities from the seventeenth and eighteenth centuries to those of recent times, leading to predominantly negative stereotypes; and the reality that the term "Puritan" did

---

9. Vaughan, *Puritan Tradition in America*, xi; Carden, *Puritan Christianity in America*, 11; Oberholzer, "Church in New England Society," 165. See also Greaves, *Puritan Revolution and Educational Thought*, 4; Hall, "Understanding the Puritans," 346n32; Walsham, "Godly and Popular Culture," 277; Bremer, "Introduction," 1:xiii; Gribben, "Eschatology of the Puritan Confessions," 52: "As the debate about the meaning of the term 'puritan' suggests . . . there is little scholarly consensus in understanding what the movement actually was"; Morgan, "Problem of Definition," 9: "Over the last forty years great effort has been expended on the attempt to devise a universally acceptable definition of 'puritan' or 'puritanism'" (See Morgan, "Problem of Definition," 9n1.)

10. Rutman, *American Puritanism*, ix.

11. Rutman, *American Puritanism*, ix; McGiffert, quoted in Rutman, *American Puritanism*, x. Amidst Puritan studies a half-century ago, Vaughan, *Puritan Tradition in America*, xxiv, comments, "Our understanding of that tradition remains far from complete." He quotes McGiffert, after corresponding extensively with forty-six others working in Puritan studies, as concluding, "At present Puritan and New England historiography is remarkable more for vitality than for coherence." In fact, a "recent review" of the field "since Miller's death in 1963 notes the 'dissensus' now prevailing"; Vaughan, *Puritan Tradition in America*, xxii (see also xxivn14; xxiin7).

12. Collinson, *Puritan Character*, 15. See Collinson, *Elizabethans*, 236; Collinson, *Birthpangs of Protestant England*, 143: Puritanism is "not definable in itself but only one half of a stressful relationship," one which depends not only on the context and cultural dynamics of the Puritans' time, but also on the perspective of the one studying them.

13. Rutman, "Mirror of Puritan Authority," 67.

Background: Puritanism

not at its inception occupy Olympian heights and later descend into a state of opprobrium. Rather, it originated as a pejorative.[14]

With this somewhat discouraging beginning, the task still remains to delineate "Puritanism" to an extent that will make this concept useful in understanding the religious, intellectual, and cultural background of Edwards's teaching methodology. Recognizing it as "a reform movement in Tudor and Stuart England and colonial America"; more specifically, one directed at "a national church, the Church of England, which did not fully embrace the Protestant Reformation of the sixteenth century,"

---

14. For discussions of these issues, see, e.g., Murdock, "Puritan Legacy," 260; and Coffey, "Puritan Legacies," 327. See also Waller, "Introduction," v, vii; Vaughan, *Puritan Tradition in America*, xv: "Since the dawn of Puritanism in the sixteenth century, debate has raged over the benevolence or banefulness of its experiment in America"; Vaughan, *Puritan Tradition in America*, xi: "'Everyone who inspects the national consciousness of Englishmen and Americans today,' historian Alan Simpson contends, 'finds Puritanism a part of its makeup.' To some observers that part marks the best in modern America; to others it appears the worst"; Vaughan, *Puritan Tradition in America*, xi. The acceptance of Puritanism's influence in some form(s) and to some extent on subsequent generations in the United States has gone largely unchallenged. See Porterfield, *Protestant Experience*, 11; Miller, "Puritan Way of Life," 4, vii: "Any inventory of the elements that have gone into the making of the 'American mind' would have to commence with Puritanism.... Without some understanding of Puritanism... there is no understanding of America," for the concepts which characterize Puritanism are "fundamental to our culture"; Reinitz, *Tensions in American Puritanism*, 1: "Puritanism... became the single most influential factor in shaping American culture and society."

Cf. Hall, *Religious Background of American Culture*, x, who contends, "Puritanism properly understood has [had] very little to do with marking [American] mentality or giving modes or patterns to our thought." (See 28n21 para. 2, below.)

Regarding negative views of Puritanism, see Mencken, *Mencken Chrestomathy*, 624; Mencken and Nathan, "Clinical Notes," 59; Perry, "Moral Athlete," 98–107 (see 98n1); Bremer, *Puritanism*, 1; Carden, *Puritan Christianity in America*, 11; Gordis, *Opening Scripture*, 1, 223n2; Daniels, *New England Nation*, 2–3, 223–31. Cf. Miller, "Puritan Way of Life," 4–22; Savelle, *Seeds of Liberty*, 25; Stephenson, *Puritan Heritage*, 32, 33; James, "Introduction," 4; Schlatter, "Introductory Essay," 7; Ziff, *Puritanism in America*, 24; Degler, "Were the Puritans 'Puritanical'?" 9–22; Todd, "Puritan Self-Fashioning," 57–58; Middleton, *Colonial America*, 89. Carden, *Puritan Christianity in America*, 11, comments on the demonization by H. L. Mencken and others of the term "Puritan," "Many of the ideas and values today designated as 'Puritanical' were prevalent in the Victorian era of the last century and would have been quite foreign to the Puritans of the seventeenth and early eighteenth centuries"; Murdock, "Puritan Legacy," 261: "Prohibition was glibly called a product of Puritanism, though the Puritans themselves never dreamed of a world without spirits, ale, and wine. Book censorship is decried as a survival of Puritanism by those who forget that the Puritans allowed the importation and circulation of books which in recent years have been banned... in this country or forbidden to enter it"; Hall, "Introduction," xii: Puritans "celebrated the order and beauty of the created world as the handiwork of God and, in everyday life, were far from being prudes or killjoys"; Marini, "Seeing Happiness," 240, 240n3.

begins moving toward a working definition for this study.[15] Adding such details as Puritanism having had Separatist and non-Separatist wings but "no broad institutional organization" fleshes out somewhat a preliminary portrait.[16] Recognition of a coterie encompassing "Protestants, English Protestants, Congregationalists; the heirs of Augustine, Calvin, [Petrus] Ramus, [Thomas] Cartwright, and [William] Perkins; the Christian revolutionists whose slogans were predestination, justification by faith [alone] and the Bible [as] an all-sufficient guide [for faith and practice]" identifies the ecclesiastical and theological orientations characterizing the broadest base of the movement.[17] Assessing those within this scope as embodying "a distinctive style of piety and divinity" consisting of "a synthesis made of strands ... which taken together formed a distinctively Puritan synthesis or style" recognizes that godly lifestyle was as important as correct doctrine (as they understood them).[18]

15. Vaughan and Bremer, "English Background of Puritan New England," 1; Hall, "Introduction," ix. See also Emerson, *John Cotton*, 21–22; Vaughan, *Puritan Tradition in America, 1620–1730*, 1; Hindson, "Introduction to the Puritans," 17 (see Hindson, "Introduction to the Puritans," 17n1); Bremer, xiii–xv.

Taking a broader perspective, Simpson, *Puritanism in Old and New England*, 2, situates Puritanism within the regeneration experience that precedes participation in religious reform: "The essence of Puritanism is an experience of conversion which separates the Puritan from the mass of mankind and endows him with the privileges and duties of the elect. The root of the matter is always a new birth, which brings with it a conviction of salvation and a dedication to warfare against sin." Simpson contends further that the conversion experience was central to a uniquely Puritan sense of purpose: "Puritans were elect spirits, segregated from the mass of mankind by an experience of conversion, fired by the sense that God was using them to revolutionize human history, and committed to the execution of his Will"; Simpson, *Puritanism in Old and New England*, 39. See also Simpson, "Puritan Tradition," 99–114.

See also Rowe, "Introduction," viii: The questions, "[How] are we distinct from other men?" and 'What is our collective relationship to God, history, and the world beyond?" indicate "the complexity of Puritanism as a religious philosophy and historical movement."

16. Vaughan and Bremer, "English Background of Puritan New England," 1. See Savelle, *Seeds of Liberty*, 24; Flower and Murphey, *History of Philosophy in America*, 1:5; Bremer, "Introduction," xiii. Cf. Murdock, "Puritan Legacy," 261, who observes, "[I]n New England the 'movement of dissent' changed to 'an institution with authority.'"

17. Schlatter, "Introductory Essay," 4.

18. Lake, "Defining Puritanism—Again?" 6. Miller, *New England Mind*, 5, defines Puritanism as, "an effort to externalize and systematize" a mood or sensibility he characterizes as "the Augustinian strain of piety," but focuses more of his attention on the New England intellectual system. See Marsden, "Perry Miller's Rehabilitation of the Puritans," 92; Stout, "Word and Order in Colonial New England," 35n3; Carden, *Puritan Christianity in America*, 13: "In attempting to secularize the Puritans, Miller has distorted somewhat our understanding of them"; Simpson, *Puritanism in Old and*

Background: Puritanism

As should have become clear, the fluidity of the terms "Puritan" and "Puritanism" limits the definitive conclusions one may draw concerning those regarded as exemplifying these concepts. Nonetheless, as considered for the purpose of this study, "the Puritan character and Puritanism as a system of belief imply a philosophy of collective values, shared motivations, and a common epistemology," a foundation which shaped the development of a largely "coherent body of ideas and doctrines."[19]

Overall, the Puritans were a cadre of Protestant Christians (concentrated in England and colonial America) who sought to "purify" the Church of England by ridding it of Roman Catholic elements of liturgical, ecclesiastical, and theological faith and practice, and to establish a society in which godliness (by their standards) formed the foundation of all areas of life, including education.[20] To replace the remnants of

---

New England, 21: Miller "has told us too much about the Puritan mind and not enough about the Puritan's feelings . . . . [The Puritans] are people who suffered and yearned and strived with an unbelievable intensity; and no superstructure of logic ought to be allowed to mask that turmoil of feeling."

Cf. Maizlish, "Perry Miller and the Puritans: An Introduction." In his explanations of the Puritans' world, "Historians have complained that Miller focused exclusively on organized thought at the expense of feelings and passion. Nothing could be further from the truth. As he did with ideas and the environment, Miller identified the complex relationship between reason *and* emotion, maintaining that thought could never be completely separated from feeling and favoring an analysis of feeling and emotion . . . . Miller struggled to deconstruct Puritan thought and reveal the complex relationship between reason and passion within it . . . . [Miller] explored the passions and emotions of the Puritans, the 'real being' behind their religious doctrine, and strove to understand their ideas in their own terms" (emphasis added).

19. Rowe, "Introduction," viii; Wright, *Cultural Life of the American Colonies, 1607–1763,* 79, 79n8. See also Bremer, *Puritan Experiment,* viii; Schlatter, "Introductory Essay," 14–17; Rutman, *American Puritanism,* 4–10; Coffey and Lim, "Introduction," 1–15.

20. See Bremer, *Puritanism,* 2; Miller, "Puritan Way of Life," 7–16; Reinitz, *Tensions in American Puritanism,* 1–14; Howard, "Puritans in Old and New England," 92; Carden, *Puritan Christianity in America,* 11–13, 22; Sweeney, *Jonathan Edwards and the Ministry of the Word,* 23n4; Perry, *Puritanism and Democracy,* 65–67: "The Puritans were protestants à outrance . . . . Puritanism in this generic sense [consists of] 'strictness of living and simplicity of worship'—Christianity in its pristine purity, and opposed to fleshly and worldly compromise, as well as to ecclesiasticism, ritualism, the multiplication of sacramental mysteries, and the elaboration of dogma. . . . The puritans in the strictest sense were the left-wing protestants within the Anglican church during the century from the liberal policy of Elizabeth to the repressive policy of Charles II." See also Lei, "'To 'Make a Travailer of Thee,'" 2: "Following [Peter] Lake's approach, I will use the word 'Puritan' in a broad sense to refer to those English Protestants who sought to further reform the liturgy and polity of the church as well as to promote godly living among Christians according to the Scriptures."

Discussions of definitions of "Puritanism" from various perspectives are included in Perry, *Puritanism and Democracy,* 62–81; Simpson, "Puritan Thrust," 1–18; Hall,

"Romanism," these church reformers strove to achieve a simplified worship style and a bibliocentric emphasis, both in matters of Christian faith and in societal life.

All of the mores and institutions of their New England society "bore the Puritan hallmark" in the organizing dynamic.[21] The foundational principles characterizing the society that the Puritans created which will be examined in this study are God-centered worldview, Bible-centered *ethos*, and literacy-centered culture. Let us now consider each of these factors in turn regarding how each influenced Edwards's pedagogy.

"Puritanism," 2:283–96; Hill, "Definition of a Puritan," 13–29; Rutman, "What Is Puritanism? Several Definitions and an Approach," 4–10; Morgan, "Problem of Definition," 9–22 (This chapter and its footnotes provide an especially valuable review of the historiography of this term); Lake, "Defining Puritanism—Again?" 3–29; and Cambers, "Defining Puritanism and Godly Culture," 10–16.

Specifically regarding New England Puritanism, the masterful works of Miller have led to his being considered the premier historian of American Puritanism. Although his conclusions have been challenged in recent years, he has been described recently as "one of the best interpreters of [colonial] New England thought" and his writings remain "the starting point for anyone who would understand the American Puritans"; Kennedy, *First American Evangelical*, 60 (see Reinitz, *Tensions in American Puritanism*, 17). P. Miller's works include *The Puritans: A Sourcebook of Their Writings*, co-written with Thomas H. Johnson; Edwards, *Images or Shadows of Divine Things* (edited by Miller); Miller, "Puritan Way of Life," 4–22; *New England Mind: From Colony to Province*; *New England Mind: The Seventeenth Century*; *Errand into the Wilderness*; *Orthodoxy in Massachusetts, 1630–1650*; and the posthumous *Nature's Nation*. Middlekauff, "Perry Miller," 167–90; McGiffert, "American Puritan Studies in the 1960's," 36–67; Marsden, "Perry Miller's Rehabilitation of the Puritans," 91–105; Reinitz, "Perry Miller and Recent American Historiography," 27–35; Butts, "Perry Miller and the Ordeal of American Freedom"; Butts, "Myth of Perry Miller," 665–94, are among the major assessments of Miller's analyses.

21. Quotation is in Schlatter, "Introductory Essay," 4. See also Oberholzer, "Church in New England Society," 143; Vaughan, *Puritan Tradition in America, 1620–1730*, xii; Hall, "New England Background," 61: "The religious culture of early eighteenth-century New England was recognizably 'Puritan' in important respects despite changes in social and political life" necessitated by the migration from the Old World to the New; Emerson, *Puritanism in America, 1620–1750*, 95: "The creation of New England was doubtless the Puritans' greatest achievement."

A dissenting view is that of Hall, *Religious Background of American Culture*, 97, 109: "The four thousand or more emigrants [who] came over to form the Massachusetts Bay Colony from 1628 on were not in any sense of the word Puritans . . . . In New England the Calvinistic Puritanism was the attitude of too small a class to overcome the resistance of the great body of the colonists and to control their religious life." (See Hall, *Religious Background of American Culture*, 83–109.) Hall situates these colonists, and their influence during their time and on later American society and culture, within "the much older dissenting tradition of England"; i.e., "an older primitive English Protestant type of which [John] Wyclif [ca. 1320–1384] and the Lollards were the main teachers"; Hall, *Religious Background of American Culture*, x, 84.

Background: Puritanism

GOD-CENTERED WORLDVIEW

The God of Reformed orthodoxy was at the center of the Puritans' world, sovereign over each of its aspects: the physical universe, human history and destiny, and individuals' lives.[22] "Puritans had no doubt that God existed, the proof being found in the evidence of creation, in Scripture, and in the apprehension of his presence in their own lives."[23]

The theocentricity of Puritan experience was thoroughgoing: The Puritan faith was "a belief concerning the actual world, to the effect, namely, that a God possessing the attributes of wisdom and goodness is the creative cause and the regulative providence of nature and of history .... [The Puritans'] sense of God ... was continual and pervasive."[24] Pervasive indeed, for everyday life in all particulars was regulated by this principle. "Since God has created the world, the Puritan divines maintained, He governs it in every detail, including the whole of man's existence."[25] In the words of one Puritan minister:

> [God's] hand has made and framed the whole Fabrick of Heaven and Earth. He hath hung out the Globe of this World; hung the Earth upon nothing; drawn over the Canopy of the Heavens; laid the foundation of the earth in its place .... The whole Administration of Providence in the Upholding and Government of all created beings, in a way of highest Wisdom and exact Order, it is *all* His work.[26]

---

22. See Hall, "Understanding the Puritans," 332: "All historians agree that Puritanism belongs within the family of Reformed churches" (see 344n11); therefore, "'Reformed' is a better term than 'Calvinist' [to apply to Puritanism], precisely for the reason that it avoids the unnecessary connotations of direct discipleship. 'Calvinist' is, in any event, an overused and much abused term." Cf. Hall, "Calvin Against the Calvinists," 284–301; Gribben, "Eschatology of the Puritan Confessions," 55, 55n15; Stearns, "Assessing the New England Mind," 249–50; Hall, "Understanding the Puritans," 334–35; Trinterud, "Origins of Puritanism," 37; Bremer, *Puritan Experiment*, 22; Emerson, *Puritanism in America, 1620–1750*, 13.

23. Bremer, *Puritanism*, 35. See also Preston (1587–1628), *Life Eternall*, dedication: "O waking and omnipotent hath ever been the eye and hand of God"; Rutman, *American Puritanism*, 10–13.

24. Perry, *Puritanism and Democracy*, 364.

25. Werkmeister, *History of Philosophical Ideas in America*, 14. See also 11, 16–17; Reinitz, *Tensions in American Puritanism*, 10: "An emphasis on God as power, on human depravity, and on man's dependency on God for everything ... was the essential root of Puritanism and the most profound source of its energies."

26. Adams, *God's Eye on the Contrite*, 6–7. See also Miller, "Puritan Way of Life," 9.

No event is outside the scope of God's sovereignty. Regarding the fate of nations, as Old Testament Israel had been the "chosen people" of God, so those striving for a "pure" Church had received a divine commission to undertake their "errand into the wilderness" to erect "a City upon a Hill" in order to re-create Zion in the New World. This task was intended to form "a modell of Christian charity [love]" displayed to the world as a veritable "model of universal reformation."[27] "It was God who had elected [the Puritans] by his sovereign grace and to his own glory; it was God who had sent them into the howling wilderness; and it was God's glory and Christ's kingship that was being manifested in them."[28] Regarding the composition of society, "God Almightie in his most holy and wise providence hath soe disposed of the Condicion of mankind, as in all times some must be rich some poore, some high and eminent in power and dignitie; others meane and in subjection."[29] Likewise extending to individual circumstances, he "has decreed when and where every [person who] comes into the World shall be Born; and when and where he shall live, in what Country, and in what Town; yea in . . . every [person's] Death, the place and the manner of it . . . . [A]ll is determined in Heaven before it comes to pass on the Earth."[30]

Although this doctrine may seem to some today to be arbitrary and despotic, to the Puritans it provided assurance that a benevolent Divine Being was fully in control of all of their conditions of life. Witness "a piece

---

27. Quotations are from Winthrop, "Modell of Christian Charity," 47, 33; Reinitz, *Tensions in American Puritanism,* 135. See also Wertenbaker, *First Americans, 1607–1690,* 91–92; Schneider, *Puritan Mind,* 26; Cremin, *American Education,* 15; Elliott, *Power and the Pulpit in Puritan New England,* 4 (see also 4n4); Hall, *Puritans in the New World,* 164–70; Heimert and Delbanco, *Puritans in America,* 81–82; Stout, *New England Soul,* 8, 13; Ruland and Bradbury, *From Puritanism to Postmodernism,* 8–11; Porterfield, *Protestant Experience,* 11; Spring, *American School From the Puritans to No Child Left Behind,* 13.

28. Schneider, *Puritan Mind,* 31. See also Higginson, "Attestation to This Church-History of New-England," 11.

29. Winthrop, "Modell of Christian Charity," 33.

30. Unattributed, quoted in Miller, *New England Mind,* 15. See also Walsham, *Providence in Early Modern England*; Stievermann, "History, Providence, and Eschatology," 218: Puritans were disposed to "looking for God's hand in the most minute details of life." See also Chaney, "God's Glorious Work," 18, 18n1: "Everything that happened, significant or insignificant, was in the providence of God. There was nothing, in fact, that was insignificant. Every event was consistent with God's ultimate purpose. The task of the Christian was to 'learne to adore God in all his Providence, and wait to see his ends'"; Eliot, *New Englands First Fruits,* 21. See also 31n33, below

of pious exultation on the part of an ordinary sea captain":[31] "It was God that did draw me by his Providence out of my father's family, and weaned me from it by degrees; it was God that put into my heart to incline to live abroad.... It was God that sent Mr. Maverick, that pious Minister to me, who was unknown to him, to seek me out, that I might come hither. So God ... landed me in health at Nantasket [now Hull, Massachusetts] on the 30th of May—1630.... Blessed be God that brought me here!"[32]

Ideally, the providence of a sovereign God was a source of comfort to the pious Puritan. "A 'cosmic optimism' sustained [the Puritans] and gave them courage to carry on where others might have abandoned hope." Nothing would befall the one living aright that would situate him or her outside the sustenance of God, the "Supreme Governing efficient cause" of life's trials and, ultimately for them, of life's triumphs.[33] As set forth in the best-known work of the eminent Puritan William Ames, *The Marrow of Theology*:

> The providence of God is that efficiency whereby he provides for existing creatures in all things in accordance with the counsel of his will. This providence extends to *all things*, not only general but particular, Ps. 145:15, 16; Prov. 16:9, 33: Exod. 21:13. It ... is both the *universal* and *particular cause* of all things.... Hence our faith [looks] ... to God who alone can relieve all our necessities.[34]

---

31. Schneider, *Puritan Mind*, 33.

32. Clap(p), *Memoirs of Capt. Roger Clapp of Dorchester*, 19. See also Bremer, *Puritan Experiment*, 21.

33. Werkmeister, *History of Philosophical Ideas in America*, 17. See also Walsham, *Providence in Early Modern England*, 282-83; Anderson, *New England's Generation*, 194-95: "Nothing in the Puritans' world happened by accident.... For the doctrine of God's providence taught the settlers to consider the events of their time not as random occurrences, but as a connected chain." Werkmeister, *History of Philosophical Ideas in America*, 17, locates the source of this assurance in divine providence in the Puritans' self-identification: "No matter what the vicissitudes of life, the early Puritans never doubted that ultimately they would triumph, for they were the chosen of God."

34. Ames, *Marrow of Theology* (1629), 107 (emphasis added). Ames's (1576-1633) *Medulla Sacrae Theologiae* (its title in the original Latin; also known in English as *Marrow of Sacred Divinity*) was "the standard text-book of theology in New England"; Miller, "Marrow of Puritan Divinity," 45. See also Hambrick-Stowe, "Practical Divinity and Spirituality," 192-93; Eusden, "Introduction," 1-3. "In England, Holland, and New England nearly all those who aspired to the Puritan way read [*The Marrow of Theology*]. No matter what their aspirations, undergraduates at Emmanuel College [of Cambridge University], Leyden, Harvard, and Yale had to read the *Marrow* in Latin as part of basic instruction in divinity"; Eusden, "Introduction," 1. See also Walton, *Jonathan Edwards*, 77-81.

To Understand *Things* as Well as *Words*

This protection (ideally) meant that the regenerate could live confidently in the security, not only of the providential God, but also of the Master Guide and Supreme Confidante. As expressed by one prominent Puritan:

> I am to resign all my Concerns unto Him, *without whom not a little Bird falls unto the Ground*. And I would so own His Hand, ordering and managing all that betides mee, as that I would rest *contented* therewithal, in a Confidence that is a Dispensation of Him, who is both a *wise Friend* and my *best Friend*; and whose Cravings for mee, are infinitely better than any *Cravings* of my own.[35]

---

35. Mather, *Diary of Cotton Mather, 1681–1724*, 7: 60 (emphasis in original). The subject of accounts "variously describing him as a reactionary and a progressive; as a self-centered neurotic and a sublime mystic; as the last gasp of theocratic Puritanism and the earliest harbinger of the Enlightenment in America," Mather remains today the iconic New England Puritan. "Certainly the most erudite man in the New England of his time," Mather is "still the most salient . . . interesting, controversial, provocative figure [on] the Colonial New England scene." "The chief writer of Boston," Mather authored more than four hundred publications ("making him by far the most prolific author of British North America during the entire colonial period"), among them "theological, scientific, philosophical, and practical writings," including "one of the masterpieces of American literature," the *Magnalia Christi Americana*. These writings "circulated briskly on both sides of the Atlantic, making him perhaps the best-known American of his era among intellectuals in England and on the Continent"; a "scholar with a transatlantic reputation." This influential polymath had scientific works published in the *Transactions of the Royal Society of London*, to which prestigious coterie he was elected in 1713. "The first American evangelical," Mather also edited the massive compilation *Biblia Americana*, the first Bible commentary of colonial America. "The most prominent and controversial minister in Massachusetts" as the pastor of the largest congregation in North America at the Old North Meeting House (Church) in Boston and "the most outstanding religious leader and educator in Puritan New England," Mather was active in a wide variety of endeavors. According to one knowledgeable admirer, "It may justly be said of Cotton Mather, that he was one of the most remarkable men of the age in which he lived; not only remarkable on one, but on many accounts." Mather was admired "by friend and foe alike for his universal learning, exalted piety, extensive charity, and zealous endeavors in the service of Christ"; Lovelace, *American Pietism of Cotton Mather*, 2; Holmes, "Preface," 1:ix; Wendell, *Literary History of America*, 47; Delbanco, "Cotton Mather (1663–1728)," 317; Stievermann, "General Introduction," 2n2; Cremin, *American Education*, 287, 288, 289; Hoselton, "Mather, Cotton (1663–1728)," 366; Winship, "Mather, Cotton (1663–1728)," 1:166; Kennedy, *First American Evangelical*; Elias, *History of Christian Education*, 121; Porterfield, *Protestant Experience*, 136. See also Mather, "Introduction"; Wendell, *Cotton Mather*; Hornberger, "Date, the Source, and the Significance of Cotton Mather's Interest in Science," 413–20; Holmes, *Cotton Mather: A Bibliography of His Works*; Beall and Shryock, *Cotton Mather*; Vartanian, "Cotton Mather and the Puritan Transition into the Enlightenment," 213–24; Bercovitch, "New England Epic: A Literary Study of Cotton Mather's *Magnalia Christi Americana*"; Bercovitch, "New England Epic: Cotton Mather's *Magnalia Christi Americana*," 337–50; Bercovitch, "Cotton Mather,"

Background: Puritanism

Convictions of his supremacy notwithstanding, attempts to comprehend the Divine Being, to fathom the mysteries of his ways, were regarded as merely peering "through a glass darkly" (1 Cor 13:12). "New England Puritanism was dominated by the idea that God is the creator and absolute master of all that exists, [but] remain[s] essentially unknown and unknowable to man."[36] As another who has written on these English and colonial American reformers has stated, "Like other aspects of the supernatural order, [God] was fundamentally incomprehensible."[37] In the words of William Ames, "God, as he is in himself, cannot be understood by any save himself."[38] This is because finite minds cannot lay hold of and comprehend the infinite, which is beyond their experience. As God has declared in Scripture, "For as the heavens are higher than the earth, so are my ways higher than your ways, and my thoughts than your thoughts" (Isa 55:9).

Compounding this situation are the effects of original sin, which corrupted human nature for Adam and his posterity. Man was created in the *imago Dei* as a moral agent capable of exercising free will. Through his choice of disobedience, the Fall resulted in total depravity of humanity, as predisposition to sin became embedded in human nature and thus befouled the human condition. As the Puritan divine Thomas Hooker describes the "hainousness of the hellish nature of sin": "Now by sin we justle the law out of its place, and the Lord out of his Glorious Soveraignty . . . and we say and profess by our practice . . . I will be swayed by mine own will and led by mine own deluded reason and satisfied with my own lusts."[39]

Although the essence of God is hidden from human beings, God has chosen to reveal some of his attributes in his relationship with the

---

93–149; Jeske, "Cotton Mather, Physico-Theologian," 583–94; Smolinski, "How to Go to Heaven, or How Heaven Goes?," 278–329; Middlekauff, *Mathers*, 189–367; Harwood, "Perhaps No One General Answer Will Do"; www.matherproject.org; Bezzant, *Edwards the Mentor*, 29–32. Harwood, "Perhaps No One General Answer Will Do," 9, comments, "Mather remains a controversial figure, particularly because of his role in the [Salem] witchcraft trials, but he died in 1728 having devoted his entire life to serving others and trying, however misguidedly at times, to improve the world around him." See Hoselton, "Introduction," 4n14, for an extensive list of Mather's writings.

36. Werkmeister, *History of Philosophical Ideas in America*, 11.
37. Bremer, *Puritanism*, 35.
38. Ames, *Marrow of Divinity*, 83.
39. Hooker, *Application of Redemption by the Effectual Work*, 53–63. Hooker also authored *A Survey of the Summe of Church-Discipline*, a significant defense of Congregationalism. See Hall, *Puritans in the New World*, 76; Heimert and Delbanco, *The Puritans in America*, 22–23; Foster, "Hooker, Thomas (1586–1647)," 1:130–32.

world. The first significant way in which God has expressed himself is through his covenant with man, expressed as the Covenant of Works (or Adamic Covenant) and then through the Covenant of Grace with the elect.[40] The covenant exercised a mediatorial role in the relationship between holy God and sinful humanity. The construct of the covenant signifies that the God whose ways man could not comprehend through his intellect or whose wrath he could not assuage by his efforts has acted voluntarily toward humanity in his infinite mercy. "[God] is still absolute ruler of the universe, but in the Covenant He has 'given His subjects a bill of inviolable rights.'"[41] In mainstream Puritan theology, God entered into a covenant with Adam based on his obedience to God's commandments. When Adam failed to fulfill it, God made a covenant of grace with mankind, whereby he graciously saves those whom he has predestined to salvation; i.e., those who respond to him in faith. This construct provides a means by which the otherwise unbridgeable chasm between holy God and sinful man can be spanned. As expressed by Thomas Shepard, "What is a Christians comfort, and where doth it chiefly lie, but in this, That the Lord hath made with him an everlasting Covenant, in all things established and sure?"[42]

40. See Stearns, "Assessing the New England Mind," 251 (see also 251n19, 251n20); Minkema, "Edwardses," 17-19, 18, 65n4. See Anderson, "Migrants and Motives," 382: "Religious and social ideals [in New England] became inextricably intertwined as settlers applied the Puritan concept of the covenantal relationship between God and man to their temporal as well as religious affairs . . . . Other British colonists would also strive to create social harmony, but none would do so with the same intensity of religious purpose as New England's founding generation" (see also 382n75.) See Miller, "Marrow of Puritan Divinity," 20-25, for a discussion of the doctrine of the covenant, "the central conception in [Puritan] thought." This essay by Miller (12-42) is also found in its entirety in *Publications of the Colonial Society of Massachusetts* 32 (1937) 247-300, and in *Errand into the Wilderness*, 48-98. Emerson, *Puritanism in America, 1620-1750*, 159n41, considers it "the fullest and most famous discussion of Puritan covenant theology."

However, "Miller's treatment has been frequently challenged"; Emerson, *Puritanism in America, 1620-1750*, 159n41. Carden, *Puritan Christianity in America*, 52, is among those who argue that "Miller has misconceived [the] fundamental Puritan doctrine" of the covenant through a faulty understanding of the imputation of original sin and his attempt to intellectualize what for the Puritans was a matter of faith in the reliability of Scripture.

41. Werkmeister, *History of Philosophical Ideas in America*, 15. See also Oberholzer, "Church in New England Society," 144, 144n4.

42. Shepard, "Salvation by Covenant," vii-viii. This work is "the most important exposition of the concept of the covenant" among Puritan authors; Miller and Johnson, *Puritans*, 1:xlviii. See Werkmeister, *History of Philosophical Ideas in America*, 15n9, and Morgan, *Godly Learning*, 23-40. (N.B.: J. Morgan, *Godly Learning*, 24n4, 26n16, 26n18,

Background: Puritanism

Having examined the theocentricity of the Puritans' worldview, let us now turn our attention to the bibliocentricity of the Puritan societal foundation.

BIBLE-CENTERED ETHOS

As God is at the center of the Puritans' worldview, so is Scripture at the center of their society. Holy Writ is the foundation of the experiment that became the "New Israel" in colonial New England, the "Holy Commonwealth" of the New World.[43] Indeed, "The intensity of the Puritans' beliefs and actions is adequately understood only when one realizes their devotion to the Bible as the Word of God."[44] The Puritans' unshakeable

---

27n21, 29n39, and 30n43 are also valuable sources regarding the doctrine of covenant within Puritan theology.)

43. See Baxter, *Holy Commonwealth*; Wertenbaker, *First Americans, 1607–1690*, 87; Murdock, *Literature and Theology in Colonial New England*, 1; Schneider, *Puritan Mind*, 8–35; Smith, "Jonathan Edwards," 167; Anderson, "Migrants and Motives," 339–83; Staloff, *Making of an American Thinking Class*, 11; Boorstin, *Americans*, 1:5; www.historyproject.ucdavis.edu/lessons/view_lesson.php?id=8: "The main purpose of the [Massachusetts Bay] colony was religious: to establish a society based on the Bible." Cf. Breen and Foster, "Moving to the New World: The Character of Early Massachusetts Immigration," 189–222. In assessing motivation for the Puritans' migration, "The traditional either/or dichotomy—*either* religion *or* economics—makes no sense" (201) Breen and Foster provide a concise historiography of the controversy involving this issue (201n34).

See also Stout, "Word and Order in Colonial New England," 19–38. Noting the general failure of studies of Puritanism adequately to consider the Bible as a factor in the rise of the movement, Stout, "Word and Order in Colonial New England," 19–20, observes that, to the extent that commentators on Puritanism ignore Scripture's influence, "they overlook the basic life work of an entire people whose *sole* reading habit was the vernacular Bible" (emphasis in original). Specifically, two Bible translations, the Genevan version of 1560 and the Authorized ("King James") version of 1611, "dominated at different stages . . . and each of which served different needs and purposes." The latter furnished the primary text on which New England's Puritan society would rest; Stout, "Word and Order in Colonial New England," 20 (see also 35n4). See also Haller, *Rise of Puritanism*, 19; Hall, *Worlds of Wonders, Days of Judgment*, 23; Bremer, "Bible," 2:323–24. Cf. Haller, *Rise of Puritanism*, 8; Alden, "Bible as Printed Word," 11–12; Crockett, "Geneva Bible," 402–4; Hambrick-Stowe, "Practical Divinity and Spirituality," 191: The Geneva Bible (1560) was "the most widely used Bible among Puritans even after the appearance of the Authorized Version in 1611."

44. Carden, *Puritan Christianity in America*, 33. See also Murdock, *Literature and Theology in Colonial New England*, 42; Curti, *Growth of American Thought*, 7; Middleton, *Colonial America*, 77; Hindson, "Introduction to the Puritans," 21: "At the core of Puritan sentiment was an absolutely authoritative Scripture"; Hall, *Worlds of Wonders, Days of Judgment*, 24: "The uniqueness of the Bible was its status as the Word . . . . It

conviction was "the true will of God was revealed, directly or by implication, only and wholly in Scripture," his "holy, absolute, and final" Word.[45] Therefore, "The Word of God governed and disciplined their lives," as Scripture was esteemed as the only source of correct doctrine and right practice.[46] For the Puritans, the Bible impacted all areas of life as "the incarnation of God's will, both as his desire for the world and as his plan for the establishment of a proper order."[47] In summary, the matrix of experience for the seventeenth- and eighteenth-century New England inhabitants was "entirely suffused with the Word of God. It furnished the terms and vocabulary with which they instinctively confronted life's meaning, and interpreted the significance of their collective presence in the New World."[48]

A prominent (if not the primary) motivation for their migration across the Atlantic and the basis of their worldview and lifestyle in colonial New England: Scripture was of prime importance to those we know today as Puritans. This is amply substantiated by their own words in their sermons, their writings, and their creeds. We will now discuss examples in each of these categories in turn.

PURITAN SERMONS

A major result of the liturgical reforms which the Puritans secured in the mother country and transported to the New World was the sermon's

---

was the living speech of God, the 'voice' of Christ, a text that people 'heard.'" Therefore, careful study of Scripture was a "necessary duty" for "all ages, all sexes, all degrees and callings, all high and low, rich and poor, wise and foolish"; Cartwright (ca. 1535–1603), *A Confutation of the Rhemists Translations, Glosses and Annotations on the New Testament*, sig. B3.

45. Wendell, *Cotton Mather*, 6; Curti, *Growth of American Thought*, 7. See also Stout, "Puritanism," 480: The Puritans "acknowledged no authority but Scripture, and resisted any other claimant to absolute truth or authority, be it Crown, church tradition, or private inspiration."

46. Hindson, "Introduction to the Puritans," 21, 23. See also Stearns, "Assessing the New England Mind," 248; Boorstin, *Americans*, 1:18: "If there was any codification of Puritan beliefs, it was the Word of God.... More perhaps than for any other Christians of their age, the Bible was their guide"; Stout, "Puritanism," 480: "For all the diversity of class, region, and dialect, one belief that all Puritans shared was that reading the Bible constituted an essential part of every person's spiritual formation."

47. Morgan, "Problem of Definition," 6.

48. Stout, "Word and Order in New England," 34. See also Bremer, *Puritanism: A Very Short Introduction*, 34; Carden, *Puritan Christianity in America*, 33; Carden, "Word of God in Puritan New England," 1–16.

Background: Puritanism

elevation to preeminence in the public worship experience.[49] The seventeenth- and eighteenth-century New England sermons were thus accorded distinction as a means of communication "whose topical range and social influence were so powerful in shaping cultural values, meanings, and a sense of corporate purpose that even television pales in comparison."[50]

Foundational to the sermon's message was a biblical text to be exposited and a "doctrine" drawn from it and applied to the congregants' circumstances.[51] Puritans regarded with utmost seriousness the biblical

---

49. See Haller, *Rise of Puritanism*, 15; Morgan, *Visible Saints*, 7; Jones and Jones, "Introduction," 3–5; Emerson, *English Puritanism from John Hooper to John Milton*, 44–46; Emerson, *John Cotton*, 31; Vaughan, *Puritan Tradition in America, 1620–1730*, 82: "Puritan [worship] services stressed the reading of the Bible and, especially, sermons by the clergy"; Boorstin, *Americans*, 1:12: "The pulpit, and not the altar, held the place of honor in the New England meeting-house. So, too, the sermon itself . . . was the focus of the best minds in New England." Murdock, *Literature and Theology in Colonial New England*, 217–18n1, provides a valuable review of literature regarding Puritan sermons in England and New England.

In a broader sense, the significance of the Puritan "plain style" of worship was triply emphasized in New England life: The "meetinghouse" (church) where congregations assembled was typically at the center of town; the pulpit ("sacred desk") was at the center of the meetinghouse; the sermon was at the center of community worship. See Boorstin, *Americans*, 1:12–15; Hall, *Faithful Shepherd*, 16; Carden, *Puritan Christianity in America*, 117; Daniels, *New England Nation*, 97; Stout, *New England Soul*, 13–14, 23; Sweeney, *Jonathan Edwards and the Ministry of the Word*, 25.

50. Stout, *New England Soul*, 3. The New England Puritan sermon bore a tremendous *gravitas* in purpose, content, and style. See Boorstin, *Americans*, 1:12; Stout, *New England Soul*, 3; Jones and Jones, "Introduction," 3 (and 167n3); Miller, *New England Mind*, 31. In addition, sermons served the pragmatic function of providing "the knowledge and guidance later generations obtained from public lectures, magazines, and newspaper editorials"; Hart, *Popular Book*, 13. Also Noll, *Protestants in America*, 41: Puritan sermons (delivered at a rate of two and sometimes three a week) were "the center of community life. In both Massachusetts and Connecticut, the sermons functioned as a source of political direction and news from afar, as well as religious instruction." Furthermore, the sermon's duty seems to have been unprecedented in significance: "Seldom, if ever before, did so many people hear the same message of purpose and direction over so long a period of time as did the New England 'Puritans'"; Stout, "Introduction," 3.

51. See Carden, *Puritan Christianity in America*, 119: "The basic structure of Puritan sermons . . . remained essentially constant throughout the seventeenth century and even beyond." (See Carden, *Puritan Christianity in America*, 119–21.) This characteristic configuration was known as "plain style," consisting of a text-doctrine-application format. See Murdock, *Literature and Theology in Colonial New England*, 43–44; Stout, *New England Soul*, 34; Westra, *Minister's Task and Calling in the Sermons of Jonathan Edwards*, 15–16n41.

Greaves, *Puritan Revolution*, 8, comments that the typical Puritan on the pew was not likely to follow "the tedious details of the preacher's arguments, put there more for

admonition of Paul to Timothy, "Preach the Word... [R]eprove, rebuke, exhort with all long-suffering and doctrine" (2 Tim 2:4) and Paul's statement to the church at Rome, "Faith cometh by hearing, and hearing by the Word of God" (Rom 10:17). With Ps 19:7 ("The law of the LORD is perfect, converting the soul; the testimony of the LORD is sure, making wise the simple") and Rom 1:16 ("[T]he gospel of Christ... is the power of God unto salvation") also in their minds and on their hearts, clergy and laity alike considered the sermon to be the principal means of public communication of means of regeneration.[52] Thomas Hooker, esteemed as, "probably the greatest preacher of American Puritanism," proclaimed "The Lord hath ordained and set apart the preaching of the Word, he hath sanctified it... to call the soul.... The Gospel is the means ordained by God to call home the soul unto Him."[53] The Word of God is a healing "physicke" [i.e., medicine] for the soul, by which Christ "doth cast out Devils, and raise men from the death of sinne."[54]

In these expositions, Scripture was regularly proclaimed as the authentic Word of God, having been "breathed by God, and therefore infallible and stamped with Gods own Authority."[55] This conviction was echoed by Puritan ministers through all generations of the Puritan era. As John Eliot, for example, states with simplicity, "The writings of the Bible are the very Words of God."[56] To Increase Mather, the Bible should be "received on [the] sole account of the Authority of the Speaker. Hence often in the Scripture, it is said, Hear the Word of the LORD, and Thus saith the LORD: Intimating that because of the Authority of the Speaker,

---

the benefit of his fellow clergymen than his own congregation." Cf. Stout, *New England Soul*, 34, who notes that ministers' frequent organization of Scripture passages into material for sermon series "facilitated the recall of ordinary listeners who relied on their memories rather than on books to store information and who needed to hear the same truths reiterated week after week." (See 324n5.) Greaves, *Puritan Revolution*, 8, nonetheless concludes there was "a genuine concern on the part of the Puritans to instill in their congregations a sound knowledge of religious principles."

52. See Flynt "Sermon," 59: "[T]he only ordinary way to obtain [saving] faith, is by a diligent attention to the preaching of the Word of God."

53. Emerson, *Puritanism in America, 1620–1750*, 96 (see also 165n2); Hooker, *Soules Vocation or Effectual Calling to Christ*, 33–48.

54. Hoar (1630–1675; President of Harvard College, 1672–1675), *Index Biblicus*, sig. A1 verso.

55. Hall, *Worlds of Wonders, Days of Judgment*, 25; Davenport, *God's Call to His People to Turn Unto Him*, 7.

56. Eliot and Mayhew, *Tears of Repentance*, 39.

men have infinite Reason to Hear and Fear, and to Believe and Obey."[57] Divine inspiration of Scripture was unquestionable, for "there is such a majesty stirring, and such secrets revealed in the Word, that if men will not be willfully blind, they cannot but cry out, 'The voyce of God, and not the voyce of man.'"[58] The sacred volume itself, "the book above all books," bears true witness to its divine source, for it has a "unique aura" and an unequaled power. "There is such a Divine majesty to be seen in it, as is not in any other Book . . . . The Scripture is [God's] Word, for it reaches [the] very thoughts of [the] Heart."[59]

In addition, the Bible was revered as a divine revelation perfect in its completeness and reliability in matters of Christian faith and practice. "Great store-house of truth," "the infallible oracles," and "the RULE" are among the reverential epithets regularly applied to Scripture by Puritans, for it is a "perfect directory, shewing us how we must Serve God, and how we must Serve the Generation wherein we live."[60]

PURITAN WRITINGS

As noted above, *The Marrow of Theology* by eminent minister and scholar William Ames is among the most significant of Puritan literary works. For a century and a half, this writing was regarded as "a clear, persuasive expression of Puritan belief and practice."[61] No less a Puritan personage than Increase Mather believed that the *Marrow* was the only supplement to Scripture itself necessary to make a minister a worthy interpreter

---

57. Mather, *Latter Sign*, 19.

58. Shepard, *Sincere Convert*, 1:10.

59. Eliot, *Harmony of the Gospels*, 32; Hall, *Worlds of Wonder, Days of Judgment*, 25; Mather, "Sermon of March 21," 277.

60. Sermons of March 21 and March 28, in Mather, *Substance of Sermons*, 73, 96; Oakes (President of Harvard College, 1675–1681), *Unconquerable, All-Conquering, and More-Than-Conquering Souldier* [sic], 26; Flynt, "Sermon" 274; Mather, *David Serving His Generation*, 11.

61. Eusden, "Introduction," 1. "From Genesis to Revelation, God's promise and assurance took the form of the covenant of grace, but significant changes did occur [between the Testaments]. Ames sees scriptural unity in the covenant, but also realistic disjunction." Nevertheless, Ames is "one of the very first in the Reformed tradition to seize upon the centrality [to Christianity] of the covenant of grace"; Eusden, "Introduction," 55. Regarding Ames, see Sprunger, *Learned Doctor William Ames*; Fiering, *Jonathan Edwards's Moral Thought and Its British Context*; Fiering, *Moral Philosophy at Seventeenth-Century Harvard*; Hoselton, "Ames, William (1576–1633)," 20–21.

of the Word of God.[62] Ames, although a professor at the University of Franeker (to which he "brought renown as [a] professor, preacher, pastor and theological writer" and where he was rector in 1626) and referred to as "learned doctor," wrote *Marrow* for his students and the laity, not for fellow academics.[63] "More than any other Puritan of [his] time, Ames directs himself to the questions of the Bible's authority and sufficiency."[64] These themes absorbed Ames for much of the *Marrow* and his *Conscience with the Power and Cases Thereof* (1639), and are to what his *Theological Discussion on the Perfection of the Holy Scripture* (1646) is devoted. He discussed these and other theological topics in a manner that has led to his being admired as a "biblical theologian *par excellence* in a biblically minded age."[65]

In his chapter "Holy Scripture" in the *Marrow*, Ames states that God raised up certain "extraordinary ministers" who "received from God the command to write" in order to instruct particular churches and also "for the use and edification of the [universal] Church." To achieve God's purposes, the human writers received the inspiration and guidance of the Holy Spirit in order that their writings be inerrant and be "given to the Church by divine authority and set apart to be its canon or rule."[66] Writes Ames of the Bible:

> It is called Holy Scripture ... partly because of its subject and of its object, which is the true and saving will of God, and partly because of the directive influence which governed its writing, Rom. 1:2; Eph. 3:5; 2 Peter 1:21, 2:22, 3:2; Rev. 18:20 . . . . All things necessary to salvation are contained in the Scriptures and

---

62. Eusden, "Introduction," 1; Horton, "Let Us Not Forget the Mighty William Ames," 434–35.

63. Sprunger, *Learned Doctor William Ames*; Eusden, "Introduction," 2 (see also 2n5); Chisholm, *Encyclopaedia Britannica*, 1:850. See also Carroll, *Puritanism and the Wilderness*, 20; Ames, *Conscience with the Power and Cases Thereof*, Book V, 141; Sprunger, "William Ames and the Settlement of Massachusetts Bay," 66–79. The *Marrow of Sacred Divinity* became influential in colonial America, being both studied by the Massachusetts Puritans generally as "a great favorite [reading] in many seventeenth-century Puritan homes" both in old as well as New England, and academically as "a well-used text at both Harvard and Yale"; Sprunger, "Ames, Ramus, and the Method of Puritan Theology," 133; Sprunger, "William Ames and the Settlement of Massachusetts Bay," 70; Hall, "New England Background," 69; Glanzer et al., *Restoring the Soul of the University*, 48, 48n49.

64. Eusden, "Introduction," 61.

65. Eusden, "Introduction," 61.

66. Ames, *Marrow of Theology*, 185–89.

also those things necessary for the instruction and edification of the Church.... Therefore, Scripture is not a partial but a perfect rule of faith and morals.[67]

Moving now to another of foremost Puritan ministers in the New England of his day, Thomas Shepard (BA, Emmanuel College, Cambridge, 1624; MA, 1627) first earned a reputation for "soul-melting" preaching in his native England, arousing the enmity of Archbishop of Canterbury William Laud. Once in colonial Massachusetts, Shepard became minister of one of the leading churches in the colonies, First Church of Newtown (or New Towne; now Cambridge), Massachusetts, as well as chaplain and a lecturer at Harvard College. Shepard's *First Principles of the Oracles of God* was one of the leading catechisms in use in seventeenth-century New England, helping establish his standing as a "guardian of order and orthodoxy."[68] His other major writings include *The Sincere Convert* and *The Sound Beleever* (volume 1 of the *Works of Thomas Shepard*), *The Parable of the Ten Virgins* (in volume 2 of the *Works*), *Theses Sabbaticae* (volume 3 of the *Works*), *A Short Catechism*, and his autobiography.[69]

Evidence of the divine source of Scripture, Shepard maintained, is provided in "the majesty, glory, holiness" therein; these demonstrate the "truth of [the] God which shines forth in them."[70] Because the Bible is the very Word of God, it is the source of truth and unerring guide for those living the Christian life. It provides "the perfect rule of Faith and Holyness, according to which all doctrines are to be tryed, and all controversies decided."[71] Moreover, in his Word, the Lord "speaks particularly to the very heart of a man" through "the word of the law to humble him, or of gospel to comfort, or of command to guide, as if the Lord meant none but [him]."[72] For these reasons, Shepard, in his work *Theses Sabbaticae*,

---

67. Ames, *Marrow of Theology*, 187.

68. Hambrick-Stowe, "Practical Divinity and Spirituality," 202–3; Emerson, *Puritanism in America, 1620–1750*, 61.

69. Heimert and Delbanco, *The Puritans in America*, 33; Shepard, *Sincere Convert*; Shepard, *The Sound Beleever, or, A Treatise of Evangelicall Conversion, Discovering the Work of Christs Spirit, in Reconciling of a Sinner to God*; Shepard, *Theses Sabbaticae*; Shepard, *The Works of Thomas Shepard*.

70. Shepard, *Short Catechism*, 15.

71. Shepard, *Short Catechism*, 14.

72. Shepard, *Theses Sabbaticae*, 370.

exhorts his readers, "Draw near to God in the word, by looking on it as God speaking to thee."[73]

Having examined Puritan sermons and writings, let us now turn our attention to the statements of faith, the creeds, to which the Puritans subscribed.

PURITAN CREEDS

Historically, the Christian Church has valued creeds and confessions as being codified affirmations of its essential beliefs drawn from Scripture. Although points of doctrine exist concerning which Christians disagree, through the ages, certain biblical teachings have been regarded as essential to the Christian faith and normative for the Christian life. Statements of these beliefs validate the "one, holy, universal, and apostolic" body of Christ in its relationship to God, its members with one another, and its mission in the world. Specifically regarding the seventeenth- and eighteenth century New England Puritans, the creedal statements discussed in this study will be the *Thirty-nine Articles of Religion* (1563), the *Westminster Confession of Faith* (*WCF*, 1646–1648), the *Savoy Declaration* (1658), and the *Confession of Faith* of the "Reforming Synod" of 1679–1680.[74]

As noted at the outset of this chapter, the people group designated as "Puritans" spanned a diverse ideological spectrum. One manifestation of this diversity was in attitudes regarding church polity, with a majority of the ministers who arrived in New England early during the Puritan migration favoring Congregationalism. However, by the 1640s, Anglicanism and Presbyterianism had been established on the New England landscape, as well.[75] Their ecclesiastical differences notwithstanding,

---

73. Shepard, *Theses Sabbaticae*, 381.

74. The best-known of the Puritan Congregationalist creedal statements, the *Cambridge Platform*, is not included in this section because it upholds Congregational ecclesiastical polity, otherwise endorsing the *WCF*. The Massachusetts and Connecticut ministers who composed it fully assented to the *WCF*'s statements concerning the supremacy, sufficiency, and normative nature of Scripture.

75. See Daniels, *New England Nation*, 31; Pope, *Half-Way Covenant*, 3–4: The New England Puritans "discarded the hierarchical structure of Anglicanism and erected in its place independent churches free from the compulsion of bishops or synods. . . . [c]ongregational churches restricted church membership to those who gave reasonable evidence that they were among the 'elect.'" See Emerson, *Puritanism in America, 1620–1750*, 81: "In eighteen years [from Massachusetts Bay's founding in 1630 to the codification of the *Cambridge Platform* in 1646 and 1647 and its publication in 1649] Congregationalism had been solidly established." See Haller, *Rise of Puritanism*, 16–17,

Background: Puritanism

Puritans affirmed the supremacy of scriptural authority for matters of Christian faith and practice. This we shall see as we move to a discussion of the aforementioned creeds.

Irrespective of denominational distinctions, the New England Puritans were in full accord with "Article VI" of the *Thirty-Nine Articles*: "Of the Sufficiency of the Holy Scriptures for Salvation: Holy Scripture containeth all things necessary to salvation: so that whatsoever is not read therein, nor may be proved thereby, is not to be required of any man, believed as an article of the Faith, or be thought requisite or necessary to salvation."[76]

The product of the 121 "learned, godly, and judicious" Puritan clergymen known as the "Westminster Divines," the WCF originated as a major means of actuating the reformation of the Church of England according to Presbyterian polity.[77] Nevertheless, Puritans across ecclesi-

---

for a description of the eleven distinct factions (not including "what not") he identifies (see also 380n11). See also Winship, *Godly Republicanism*, and Noll, "American Christian Politics," for descriptions of various subgroups identified within Puritanism.

76. Originating during a time when the Church of England was defining its doctrinal position with regard to both the Roman Catholic Church and the Protestant reform movements, the *Thirty-Nine Articles* indicate, in the words of one prominent leader of the evangelical branch of the Anglican Church, that if the Church of England "is to be judged by the statements of the *Articles*, [it] must be ranked amongst the Protestant Churches of Europe . . . under that of the Reformed . . . type"; Litton, *Introduction to Dogmatic Theology on the Basis of the Thirty-Nine Articles*, iv. Litton (1813–1897) became Dean of Oriel College, Oxford, in 1843 and wrote his *Dogmatic Theology* while Rector of Naunton Church. He "starts with the fundamental idea that for the Church of England, as for all Protestant churches, the Bible is the sole and absolute rule of faith"; Zenos, Review of E. A. Litton, 406–7. See also Zahl, *Protestant Face of Anglicanism*, 4–5.

77. See *The Points of Difference Between Congregationalism and the Church of England* (1603); Walker, *Creeds and Platforms of Congregationalism*, 77–80.

Regarding the WCF, Gribben, "Eschatology of the Puritan Confessions," 51–78, refers to it as "the most influential of the puritan creedal statements," one that was "deliberately designed as a generally acceptable compromise between parties convinced of various—and often mutually incompatible—systems" (51, 53). Gribben examines the various eschatological approaches taken to the WCF, the *Savoy Confession*, and the *Second Baptist Confession* (1677/1689), and observes that, since none of the creeds cite Revelation 20, it is difficult to classify them as a-, pre-, or post-millennial. Nevertheless, he states that their tone is more conservative theologically than some other writings of the creeds' authors; Gribben, "Eschatology of the Puritan Confessions," 78. Gribben concludes, "The eschatology of the puritan confessions seems as obscure as ever" (78).

Van Dixhoorn, "New Taxonomies of the Westminster Assembly (1643-52)," 82–106, proposes the existence of "theological or hermeneutical reasons for divisions in the assembly," his research having indicated that roughly one-third more of the Assembly's plenary sessions and committees debated theological issues than church government (85). Van Dixhoorn concludes that the designations "Presbyterian" and

astical lines gave hearty assent to its very opening, "Chapter I: Of the holy Scripture." This section of the confession affirms Scripture to be essential in providing "that knowledge of God, and of his will, which is necessary unto salvation."[78] It goes on to uphold Scripture's authority, "for which it ought to be believed and obeyed," as depending "wholly upon God (who is truth itself) the author thereof: and therefore it is to be received, because it is the Word of God."

Furthermore, God's revelation in his Word is sufficient for Christian faith and practice: "The whole counsel of God . . . is either expressly set down in Scripture, or by good and necessary consequence, may be deduced from Scripture." What is set forth in the Sacred Word is redemptively perspicuous; it is "able to make [one] wise unto salvation (II Tim 3:15)": "[T]hose things which are necessary to be known, believed, and observed for salvation" are made sufficiently clear that the learned and unlearned alike, "in a due use of the ordinary means, may attain unto a sufficient understanding of them." Lastly, owing to the reliability and consistency of the internal witness, "The infallible rule of interpretation of Scripture is Scripture itself."[79]

The *Savoy Declaration* is an endorsement of the *WCF* adopted by representatives of Congregationalist churches, with appropriate modification regarding church polity. Likewise, the *Confession of Faith* of the "Reforming Synod" of 1679–1680 is in substance the *WCF* with adjustments made to reflect congregational governance.[80] This indicates that the Puritans, even in the midst of contention regarding ecclesiastical polity, found common ground regarding supremacy and sufficiency of Scripture as a rule and guide for exercise of the Christian faith.[81]

"Independent" are not helpful in analyzing the discussions and voting on the creedal issues. He observes, "At least two alternative non-ecclesiological party-labels for the Assembly may obtain. First, there are those who may be termed creedalists, and then there are excepters or anti-creedalists or Biblicists," but admits, "I have not found a term free of pejorative connotations or anachronisms."

78. www.reformed.org/documents/wcf_with_proofs. All quotations of the *WCF* above are from this source. See Stearns, "Assessing the New England Mind," 248–49: "[M]an's comprehension of the Scriptures and his proper interpretation of them were subject to progressive enlargement and refinement," as the Puritans kept in mind the objective to "grow in grace and in the knowledge of [the] Lord and Savior Jesus Christ (2 Pet 3:18)."

79. www.reformed.org/documents/wcf_with_proofs.

80. See Bremer, "Puritan Experiment in New England, 1630–1660," 139.

81. See Walker, *Creeds and Platforms of Congregationalism*, 441.

Background: Puritanism

In summary, having examined the theocentricity of the Puritans' world and the bibliocentricity of their society, we now turn our attention to the centrality of literacy to their culture.

LITERACY-CENTERED CULTURE

Literacy, considered as "a basic index of cultural attainment," is among the keys to understanding the Puritan period of colonial New England, but evidence of it can be difficult to uncover.[82] "Because the act of reading itself leaves no traces, historians have to look for indirect evidence."[83] Complicating the search is the fact that determination of the extent of literacy among a population depends on measuring two skills, "each with a separate range of competency" and which are not always coequal within an individual.[84]

To work toward an understanding that will be useful for the present study, three spheres of literacy will be considered.[85] The first, the most restricted, is the domestic one and consists of women, children, and domestic servants, including enslaved persons. Those at this level are defined mostly by their relationships with the males with whom they interacted as wives, mothers, mistresses of servants, etc., and are largely "excluded from any kind of direct participation in public life."[86] As one would expect, the level of literacy was generally lowest in this sphere.

Next comes the sphere inhabited by adult white males. At this level, rudimentary skills in reading, writing, or both, facilitating participation in responsibilities of citizenship, can be expected.

82. Quotation is in Bailyn, *Education in the Forming of American Society*, 83.
83. Lynch, "'Every Man Able to Read,'" 1–9.
84. Main, quoted in Lynch, "'Every Man Able to Read,'" 2–3.
85. Monaghan, *Learning to Read and Write in Colonial America*, 11–13. See also Gordon and Gordon, *Literacy in America*, xv: "In the early American colonial era the ability to read at least parts of the Bible was the common definition of literacy." See also Stout, *New England Soul*, 32: "Empirical studies confirm that from highest born to lowest New Englanders were a 'people of the Word' who could and, in most cases, did regularly read their Bibles from cover to cover." This standard is the "lowest common denominator" that was shared by the inhabitants of each of the literacy spheres discussed above. Stevens, "Literacy," 216–18, combines this reading skill test with the writing skill test discussed by Lockridge, *Literacy in Colonial New England*, to produce this standard of literacy in seventeenth-century colonial America: "To be literate often meant the ability to read (recite) from the Bible and to sign one's name"; Stevens, "Literacy," 216.
86. Monaghan, *Learning to Read and Write in Colonial America*, 11.

"The third and most exclusive sphere comprised the founding fathers of New England, who saw themselves as part of an international world of men of letters, committed to shared religious beliefs."[87] The occupants of this rarefied realm, and their counterparts in Europe, had followed a similar path—learning to read at "petty schools," attending "grammar schools," where reading knowledge of Latin, Greek, and a modicum of Hebrew was acquired, graduating from Oxford or Cambridge, which allowed communication in Latin with college graduates from all across Europe.[88]

Within the first two of these spheres is located a spectrum of abilities and interests in reading for acquisition of knowledge and writing as communication. The lower end is inhabited by children and adults for whom reading is generally done aloud in group settings, such as classes. "In this realm reading was valued more than writing because it gave access to the scriptures, and memorizing was key for children to learn to read."[89] At the upper end of this scale, adults read "copiously, intently, and presumably often silently," depending on contexts.[90] Children and adults alike populated an environment in which "oral communication was the norm among the early colonists"; written communication was the exception within social contexts.[91]

In a landmark study designed to discover the extent of literacy in seventeenth-century New England and the degree (if any) to which it expanded during this time period, Kenneth A. Lockridge measured "the level of signatures among a sample of persons leaving wills in colonial New England."[92] Regarding the question, "Do signatures measure literacy?" Lockridge notes, "Scholars agree that the level of signatures runs below but closely parallels reading skills and runs above and roughly

---

87. Monaghan, *Learning to Read and Write in Colonial America*, 12.

88. Monaghan, *Learning to Read and Write in Colonial America*, 11. See also Gordon and Gordon, *Literacy in America*, 4.

89. Monaghan, *Learning to Read and Write in Colonial America*, 12.

90. Monaghan, *Learning to Read and Write in Colonial America*, 12.

91. Monaghan, *Learning to Read and Write in Colonial America*, 13 (see also 394n5). However, Puritans recorded in journals and diaries that were not intended for publication, and some later wrote works for publication.

92. Lockridge, *Literacy in Colonial New England*, 7, 123n2. Cf. Bailyn, *Education in the Forming of American Society*, 84; Morgan, *Godly Learning*, 161n137; Monaghan, "Literacy Instruction and Gender in Colonial New England," 19; Hall, *Worlds of Wonder, Days of Judgment*, 32, 262–63n28; Hall, *Cultures of Print*, 80n2, 90, 90n31, 172–73n9.

parallels writing skills."⁹³ He concludes from his study, "[T]he signatures on wills approximate the literacy [rate] not only of the sample but [also] of the [general] population."⁹⁴ Although admitting that his study used "a biased sample and an ambiguous measure," Lockridge concludes, "[B]etween the middle of the seventeenth century and the end of the eighteenth New England evolved from a society little more than half-literate to a society of nearly universal male literacy."

Furthermore, "[L]iteracy rose faster and to a higher level in New England than in most areas."⁹⁵ Specifically, Lockridge concludes that, among the white male population in New England, literacy stood at roughly 60 percent between 1650 and 1670, rose to 85 percent between 1758 and 1762, and had arrived at a nearly universal level by the end of the eighteenth century.⁹⁶

We can conclude, therefore, that the colonial New England Puritans possessed what may be considered moderate to relatively high levels of reading and writing skills, becoming "one of the most literate peoples in the world" during the 1700s.⁹⁷ Let us briefly examine the factors which produced this result.

93. Lockridge, *Literacy in Colonial New England*, 7, 123n2. See also Mattes, *Handwriting in Early America*.

94. Lockridge, *Literacy in Colonial New England*, 126–28n3, 128n4.

95. Lockridge, *Literacy in Colonial New England*, 3, 132n17.

96. Lockridge, *Literacy in Colonial New England*, 132n19. See also Lynch, "'Every Man Able to Read"; Hart, *Popular Book*, 8; Graff, *Legacies of Literacy*, 163, 164 (434–35n155 provides an extensive review of literature concerning education and literacy in colonial America); Monaghan, "Literacy Instruction and Gender in Colonial New England," 18; Hall, "Readers and Reading in America," 172–73; Urban and Wagoner, *American Education*, 34–35; Beales and Monaghan, "Literacy and Schoolbooks," 1:380–87; Shipton, "Secondary Education in the Puritan Colonies," 650; Gordon and Gordon, *Literacy in America*, xvi: "Male literacy based on signatures on New England wills showed a steady rise throughout the seventeenth and eighteenth centuries" (1650, 60 percent; 1705, 70 percent; 1758, 80 percent; 1795, 90 percent). See Monaghan, *Learning to Read and Write in Colonial America*, 1–8, for a historiography of the studies of literacy in the early colonial American period.

97. Stout, "Word and Order in Colonial New England," 19. See also Stout, *New England Soul*, 32: "No seventeenth-century culture was more uniformly literate than New England"; Stout, "Puritanism," 480: "At a time when less than half of the population in England or Virginia could read, Puritan communities approached universal literacy"; Carden, *Puritan Christianity in America*, 187: "[E]arly New England enjoyed the highest literacy rate in the world at that time." Scotchmer, "Aims of American Education," 104, and Wertenbaker, *Golden Age of Colonial Culture*, 2, 1, place this achievement in perspective by viewing its historical context: "Not all societies have embraced the idea of universal literacy, leastwise societies overwhelmed by the day-to-day struggle simply to survive a cold and harsh environment. But Puritans in New England . . .

To Understand *Things* as Well as *Words*

"Attitudes toward education, values of literacy, and notions about institutions, as well as the larger cultural universe, were brought from one side of the Atlantic to the other with [the Puritans]," necessarily adapted to the unique demands of the New World environment.[98] The founders of New England included a high proportion of men who had been educated at Oxford and Cambridge Universities, among them John Winthrop, Thomas Shepard, John Harvard, Thomas Hooker, and John Cotton. The presence of this number of "scholars of ability" assisted the Puritans considerably in fashioning for their experiment in holiness "a cultural tone unique in the history of colonization."[99]

---

were committed to this cause"; The New England Puritans instituted "a really effective educational system" in an environment in which "most of the people lived in the agricultural villages" and in which life was characterized by "unremitting toil and severe hardships."

98. Graff, *Legacies of Literacy*, 163. See also Carroll, *Puritanism and the Wilderness*, 131: "The seventeenth-century migration to New England embodied both a physical relocation and an intellectual transplantation.... [T]he colonists transported sophisticated ideas about the nature of society into the wilderness. In the early years of the settlement, the Puritans endeavored to incorporate these views into their Wilderness Zion."

Vital among the elements of society that the Puritans sought to recreate from their English environment in the raw New World setting was education. As conceived by the Puritans, education encompassed not only expansion of the intellect and acquisition of knowledge and information, but also character formation. See Wertenbaker, *Golden Age of Colonial Culture*, 5-6; Wright, *Cultural Life of the American Colonies, 1607-1763*, 101; Daniels, *New England Nation*, 78; Tyack, "City upon a Hill," 4: "When the Puritans created schools, they sought to reproduce what they remembered of education in England." See Scotchmer, "Aims of American Education," 99-119; Carden, *Puritan Christianity in America*, 188, for a discussion of three overlapping purposes in the Puritan educational structure: piety (expressed through religious principles), morality (expressed in biblical and civil laws), and utility (expressed through training for vocational calling and intellectual value to society).

99. Wright, *Literary Culture in Early New England, 1620-1730*, 15-17, 17, 16. See Thwing, *History of Higher Education in America*, 1-3; Schneider, *Puritan Mind*, 137n20; Rudolph, *American College and University*, 4: "Approximately a hundred Cambridge men and a third as many Oxford men emigrated to New England before 1646; among them were the founders of Harvard, the fathers of the first generation of Harvard students"; Cremin, *American Education*, 207, 207n13: "Franklin Bowditch Dexter and Samuel Eliot Morison have identified at least 130 university men among those who immigrated [from England to the New World] before 1646; 100 had attended Cambridge, and 32 had attended Oxford (obviously, a few had attended both institutions); 87 held the B.A. degree, and 63 held the M.A."; (Pryde, *Scottish Universities and the Colleges of Colonial America*, 2-3n1: "Of about 100 university men who had come to New England by 1640, some 70 were from Cambridge; the Oxford of William Laud had little affinity with Puritan America"); Dexter, *Influence of the English Universities on the Development of New England*, 3-5. See also Morison, *Founding of Harvard*

Background: Puritanism

The distinctiveness of the New England Puritan worldview derives from the underpinnings of the movement in the mother country which the reformers transported to the colonial American setting. English Puritanism was diversified, but at its core, it "stressed the sovereignty of God, the paramountcy of the Bible in revealing the will of God, and the absolute necessity of men's submitting themselves to God."[100] Salvation could in no way be worked for or earned; it resulted from God's decree of election for those he so favored.

However, "the Puritans were positive that . . . salvation was impossible without" awareness of one's sinful condition and of Christ's offer of redemption revealed in God's Word.[101] The foundational institutions of Puritan society—family, church, school—were devoted to communicating the gospel as conveyed via Reformed orthodoxy as essential to lessons taught at each. In the words of "the patriarch of Stuart Puritans," Richard Baxter, "Education is God's ordinary way for the conveyance of his grace."[102]

College, 40; Wright, *Cultural Life of the American Colonies, 1607–1763*, 101; Morison, *Intellectual Life of Colonial New England*, 17: "A careful combing of lists of emigrants reveals that at least one hundred and thirty [Oxford and Cambridge] university alumni came to New England before 1646"; Gordon and Gordon, *Literacy in America*, 5: "The Puritan migration to Massachusetts included a higher proportion of educated leaders than any other colony, including before 1650 over one hundred Oxford and Cambridge University graduates. Most of these men were pastors of churches. These intellectual leaders, such as John Winthrop, Nathaniel Ward, John Cotton, and John Harvard, gave the community its literacy ideals." (See Gordon and Gordon, 30n12); Carden, *Puritan Christianity in America*, 187: First-generation Puritan immigrants to New England established "a society which boasted a much higher percentage of university trained men than perhaps any other society in the world." Jernegan, "Beginnings of Public Education in New England," 326; Degler, "Were the Puritans 'Puritanical'?" 18, and Daniels, *New England Nation*, 78–79, put this figure in perspective: "The migration [of Puritans] to New England [up] to 1643 is commonly reckoned at about 20,000, or 4,000 families. Thus there would be one person in 40 families, or one for every 200 emigrating, who had received university training. It is estimated that Massachusetts had a population of about 9,000 in 1639"; "At the same date [1640,] not five men in all of Virginia could lay claim to such an educational background"; "Over 150 university graduates immigrated to New England in the founding years— approximately one for every 150 people, compared to one graduate for every 600 people in the home isles." Owing to this relatively high percentage of educated men among the general population, Massachusetts "may well have been the most educated [commonwealth of citizens] in the history of the world to that point"; Cremin, *American Education*, 212.

100. Rutman, *American Puritanism*, 10.

101. Axtell, *School Upon a Hill*, 12.

102. Quotation is from Axtell, *School Upon a Hill*, 12; Baxter, *Autobiography of Richard Baxter*, 10. See also Knight, *Orthodoxies in Massachusetts*, 2–3. Cf. Leader, "In Love with the Image," 174n5. See also Hoeveler, *Creating the American Mind*, 26–29, and the footnotes there.

To Understand *Things* as Well as *Words*

In the Puritan matrix of experience, the God of creation was intensely active in individuals' lives in order to reveal himself and to interact with human beings: "All history, all knowledge, all everyday experience constituted God's education of man."[103] More especially, development of the intellect was necessary in order to participate as fully as possible in the world of God's creation. From the Puritans' perspective, "all of life and learning was worth exploring; true knowledge possessed unity and meaning since it was a creation of God."[104] Life was intended to be lived in accordance with the will of God as declared in the precepts of Scripture, for the truth of God is "the only reasonable answer to man's needs."[105] Genuine knowledge of God's Word would lead to a desire to follow the God who had revealed it. That is, it was the Puritans' conviction that "the ultimate purpose of education was salvation."[106]

---

103. Tyack, "City upon a Hill," 1.

104. Carden, *Puritan Christianity in America*, 185.

105. Hindson, "Introduction to the Puritans," 24. Puritanism was "a philosophy of life that integrated man's whole being with the teaching of Scripture" in a way that brought Scripture to bear on the areas of philosophy and science, and interpreted reality in light of its teachings (23). Cf. Curti, *Growth of American Thought*, 6; Urban and Wagoner, *American Education*, 36: Puritans insisted that "God's word be interpreted in the light of reason and scientific knowledge of the day."

106. Gordon and Gordon, *Literacy in America*, 6. See also Milton, *Of Education*, "The end... of Learning is to repair the ruines of our first Parents by regaining to know God aright, and out of that knowledge to love him, to imitate him, to be like him, ... which being united to the heavenly grace of faith makes up the highest perfection"; The Milton Reading Room, www.dartmouth.edu/~milton/reading_room/of_education/text.shtml; Foxcroft, *Cleansing Our Way in Youth Press'd*, 176; Eavey, *History of Christian Education*, 189; Curti, *Growth of American Thought*, 7; Carden, *Puritan Christianity in America*, 185; Emerson, *Puritanism in America, 1620–1750*, 2; Graff, *Legacies of Literacy*, 163: In the Puritans' view, "Literacy—to gain the holy literature for oneself and to participate in worship fully—should come to all" (see also 434n152); Hall, *Worlds of Wonders, Days of Judgment*, 18: In New England Puritan society, "learning how to read and becoming 'religious' were perceived as one and the same thing." Moreover, "All the institutions of society—school, church, family, civil government—had a common ultimate purpose: the salvation of the individual"; Tyack, *Turning Points in American Educational History*, 2.

Cf. Miller, *Evolution of College English*, 26; Spring, *American School, 1642–2000*, 9; Staloff, *Making of an American Thinking Class*, 13. Reflecting the secular dimension of the Puritans' educational system and bibliocentric society, Spring, *American School, 1642–2000*, 9, states: "In the seventeenth and eighteenth centuries, education in colonial New England was used to maintain the authority of the government and religion. People were taught to read and write so that they could obey the laws of God and the state."

T. Miller has in view both the sacred and the secular in his assessment, "New Englanders looked to public education to perpetuate their values amidst the perceived

Background: Puritanism

In order to re-create as nearly as possible the English Puritan ideal of education in the "howling wilderness" of New England, in 1642 the General Court of Massachusetts Bay enacted the first of the colonial laws regarding education, the 1642 Massachusetts School Law. This legislation upheld and legally enforced the family's (specifically the father's) responsibility for the education of children. This enactment required all children to reach the ability (through being catechized at least weekly) to "read and understand the principles of religion and the capitall laws of this country."

---

barbarism of the frontier, as Bernard Bailyn [*Education in the Forming of American Society: Needs and Opportunities for Study*; repr., New York: Norton, 1972] has discussed" (Miller, *Evolution*, 38). See also Shipton, "Secondary Education in the Puritan Colonies," 646–61. The Puritan education schema was designed to benefit both church and state: "[F]rom the time of founding," the Puritan "regarded education as of value for its own sake and for material as well as for spiritual ends" (648). See also Shipton, Shipton, "Secondary Education in the Puritan Colonies," 646–48, notes 1–9.)

In his discussion, Staloff, *Making of an American Thinking Class*, 13, focuses on ministerial authority: "The foundation of this cultural authority [of ministers] was built on the bedrock of Puritan biblicism . . . . 'Every man was encouraged to read his Bible with his own eyes,' Larzer Ziff informs us, 'but was equally required then to bring his understanding into line with the judgments of the ministry as they were expounded from the pulpit.'" (See Staloff, *Making of an American Thinking Class*, 209n15, 209n16; Ziff, 112; Stout, *New England Soul*, 19.) Stout argues for more of a balance in the clergy-laity dynamic than Staloff and Ziff seem to suggest. Despite the "awesome powers in New England society" ministers enjoyed as the voices of God expounding his Word, "because sermons had to based on *sola Scriptura*, even the ministers' authority was limited . . . . The printed Bible was the bridge linking ministers to congregations, and all who internalized its vocabulary, rhythms, and doctrines could participate in a common community of discourse. In cases where ministers abused that text . . . congregations could dismiss them . . . . Congregations were obliged not only to obey the voice of the sermon but also to read their Bibles and make sure their ministers held true to biblical doctrines"; Stout, *New England Soul*, 19. (See also Stout, *New England Soul*, 320n17.) See also Carden, *Puritan Christianity in America*, 215; Hall, *Worlds of Wonders, Days of Judgment*, 19: "[T]he authority of the [New England Puritan] ministers was held in check by a premise they themselves affirmed, that any version of the 'truth,' whether learned or unlearned, must conform to the Word of God." *Contra* Ziff above, "In practice this idea proved useful to those laymen who disagreed with what the ministers were saying"; Hall, *Worlds of Wonders, Days of Judgment*, 19. Urban and Wagoner, *American Education*, 36, observe that the Reformation doctrine of the "priesthood of all believers," which the Puritans embraced, depended on laypersons who "could read and understand scripture intelligently," and they note the importance of a balanced clergy-laity dynamic to the New Englanders' well-being: "The survival of the Puritan spirit depended on learned ministers *and* on enlightened and literate parishioners"; emphasis added. Curti, *Growth of American Thought*, 6, also recognizes this balance and views it as an impetus of the Puritans' achievements in education: "The conception of a learned clergy capable of expounding the Bible in the light of scholarship and reason implies a sufficiently well-educated laity to follow theological discussions. It is this fact that helps to explain why New England led in supporting secondary education to read their Bibles and make sure their ministers held true to biblical doctrines."

To Understand *Things* as Well as *Words*

Failure to do so resulted in a fine imposed on the families of "twentie shillings for each neglect therein," and could result in the removal of the children from the home and placement with someone competent and willing to perform this duty.[107] A popular catechism for use in homes, churches, and schools was John Cotton's *Spiritual Milk for Boston* [also *American*] *Babes*, the 1656 edition of which is the first known children's book published in colonial America (although it began publication in England before then).[108]

---

107. The 1642 law "is remarkable in that, for the first time in the English-speaking world, a legislative body representing the State ordered that all children should be taught to read"; Cubberley, *Public Education in the United States*, 17. The 1647 law "represents a distinct advance over the Law of 1642" in its results: "The State here, acting again as the servant of the Church, enacted a law for which there were no English precedents. Not only was a school system ordered established ... but, for the first time among English-speaking people, there was the assertion of the right of the State to require communities to establish and maintain schools, under penalty of a fine if they refused to do so." Together, these two laws signify "not only new educational ideas in the English-speaking world ... they also represent the very foundation stones upon which [the] American public school systems have been constructed" (18). See Boone, *Education in the United States*, 44–46; Littlefield, *Early Schools and School-Books of New England*, 75–76; Eavey, *History of Christian Education*, 190–91; Carden, *Puritan Christianity in America*, 213; Spring, *American School, 1642–2000*, 12; Unger, "Massachusetts Laws of 1642 and 1647," 645–46; Eberling, "Massachusetts Education Laws of 1642, 1647, and 1648," 225–26; Scotchmer, "Aims of American Education," 100. See also Jernegan, "Compulsory Education in the American Colonies," 735–36; Littlefield, *Early Schools and School-Books of New England*, 75–76; Eavey, *History of Christian Education*, 190–91; Carden, *Puritan Christianity in America*, 213; Spring, *American School, 1642–2000*, 12; Unger, "Massachusetts Laws of 1642 and 1647," 225–26.

The Puritans are generally regarded today as having established the first public schools in the American colonies as evidence of the esteem with which they viewed education. A fascinating debate in print over whether the appearance of public education in seventeenth-century colonial America is attributable to the Puritans in Massachusetts or to the Dutch in New York is that between Martin, *Evolution of the Massachusetts Public School System* and Draper, "Public School Pioneering"; *Educational Review* 3–5 (1892/1893). See Bailyn, *Education in the Forming of American Society*, 10–12, for a brief discussion of this "paper war" and the issues surrounding it.

108. Cotton, *Spiritual Milk for Boston Babes*; Griswold, "Children's Literature in the USA," 860. *Spiritual Milk for Boston Babes*, "a beginning catechism for children and young Christians, was first published in the 1640s and remained in print continuously for over 200 years .... The oldest surviving copy ... was published in London in 1646. It was reprinted many times on both sides of the Atlantic, and at least eight editions from the seventeenth century are known. Between 1690 and 1701, it was first incorporated into *The New-England Primer*, and it remained an essential component of that work and an integral part of American religious education for the next 150 years"; Royster, Digital Commons@University of Nebraska-Lincoln, www.digitalcommons.unl.edu/etas/18. Cotton (1584–1652) was "the most famous of the early [New England] ministers, eloquent and scholarly" and "by most accounts the preeminent

Background: Puritanism

The 1647 enactment, the "Old Deluder Satan Law" (referring to the enemy of God and mankind, whose "one chief project" is "to keep men from the knowledge of the Scriptures"), "would decisively influence the educational history of New England for the remainder of the colonial period."[109] It required all towns consisting of at least fifty households to hire an instructor "to teach all such children as shall resort to him to write and read." Further, every town of one hundred households was required to establish a grammar school, "the master thereof being able to instruct youth so far as they may be fitted for the university"; that is, at first, Harvard College, founded in 1636.[110]

---

minister and theologian of the Massachusetts Bay Colony"; Thwing, *History of Higher Education in America*, 2; Royster, Digital Commons@University of Nebraska-Lincoln, www.digitalcommons.unl.edu/etas/18. Spring, *American School, 1642-2000*, 13; Stevens, "Literacy," 216, indicates the ideal regarding education which the Puritan community sought to preserve, partially by means of the enactments noted above: Primary instruction "took place in a variety of places, including households, churches, and schools"; "In seventeenth-century colonial America, the task of transmitting literate culture, including literacy skills, was shared by family, church, and school, usually in that order of importance."

Monaghan and Barry, *Writing the Past*, 5, 7, observe that in seventeenth-century New England, the values which the system of instruction at all levels—family, church, and school—was designed to instill were "Christian, Protestant, and Puritan," and the authors outline the standard sequence in which reading was taught as a means of communicating these values; viz., hornbook to primer ("the mainstay of colonial primary education") to psalter to New Testament to entire Bible, "considered the apex of the reading curriculum, at which all the earlier texts aimed." See also Curti, *Growth of American Thought*, 7; Eavey, *History of Christian Education*, 196.

109. Cremin, *American Education*, 181; 180-83. See also Wertenbaker, *First Americans, 1607-1690*, 246-47; and Wright, *Cultural Life of the American Colonies*, 103. The 1647 "Old Deluder Satan" Law is reproduced in "Old Deluder Satan Law of 1647," www.mass.gov/files/documents/2016/08/ob/deludersatan.pdf; *Laws and Liberties of Massachusetts*; Fraser, *School in the United States*, 7-8.

110. Unger, "Massachusetts Laws of 1642 and 1647,"; Littlefield, *Early Schools and School-Books of New England*, 76-77; Eavey, *History of Christian Education*, 190-94; Cremin, *American Education*, 16. See also Wright, *Cultural Life of the American Colonies, 1607-1763*, 102-3; Wertenbaker, *First Americans, 1607-1690*, 244; Morison, *Builders of the Bay Colony*, 187; Degler, "Were the Puritans 'Puritanical'?" 19-20; Bailyn, *Education in the Forming of American Society*, 27. Writing during the Progressive era of the early 1900s, a time in which Puritanism, as then conceived, was not held in high regard, Littlefield, *Early Schools and School-Books of New England*, 101, 328, nonetheless praises a key element of the Puritan legacy: "The magnificent system of public education in the United States to-day is proof of how firmly and broadly our ancestors laid the foundations"; Littlefield is "very strongly of the opinion that the facilities for instruction in the colonial and provincial periods were greater than is generally supposed." See also Shipton, "Secondary Education in the Puritan Colonies," 655, 661. After refuting certain widely-held criticisms of Puritan education, Shipton concludes,

To Understand *Things* as Well as *Words*

At the beginning level, that of the "petty school," in addition to the Bible, the staples of instruction consisted of catechisms, prayer books, and what has been referred to as "the most important book of the eighteenth-century nursery," *The New England Primer*. The first reading tool of its kind designed for colonial America and the most popular and most influential text for primary instruction for a century and a quarter, the *Primer* was regularly reprinted throughout the eighteenth century.[111] It includes instruction in the alphabet, the Lord's (or Model) Prayer, the *Westminster Shorter Catechism*, Cotton's *Spiritual Milk for Boston Babes*, "Advice to His Children" (a versified form of the reputed last words of the first

---

"I believe that the eighteenth century saw, not a decline, but a steady improvement in the [New England] public school system, making education as far as the classics open to the great majority of children in the Puritan colonies, and as far as the colleges to most boys"; "[I]t would seem that there was no permanent collapse of secondary education in Puritan New England such as the earlier studies indicated. The public schools, changed in form to meet the new situation, actually improved in the eighteenth century."

111. Walsh, "New England Primer," 257–58; Eames, Review of *The New England Primer*, 372–73; Monaghan, *Learning to Read and Write in Colonial America*, 98; Eavey, *History of Christian Education*, 195; Smith, *American Reading Instruction*, 18, 19, 25; Mathews, *Teaching to Read Historically Considered*, 17; Hall, *Worlds of Wonder, Days of Judgment*, 37; Spring, *American School From the Puritans to No Child Left Behind*, 16 (also 43n12). The earliest extant edition of the *New England Primer* was printed in Boston by S. Kneeland and T. Green in 1727 and is reproduced in Ford, *New England Primer*; Monaghan and Barry, *Writing the Past*, 7–8. Experiencing remarkable longevity, the *Primer* was produced in 450 editions by 1830; Hall, "Uses of Literacy in New England, 1600–1850," 42–43; Hall, *Cultures of Print*, 74. See Eavey, *History of Christian Education*, 195–96: "*The New England Primer* was found in every home and was sold in all bookstores. It has been estimated that its total sales were at least three million copies," possibly more than five million, and was used in the home, at church, and at school, exerting "a lasting impact on the moral landscape of America" for over one and a half centuries; Lisa, "History of the American Education System"; Smith, "The New-England Primer."

Regarding Puritan use of catechetical instruction, see Eavey, *History of Christian Education*, 191–92; Grant, "Puritan Catechizing," 107–27. "[T]he Puritans subscribed to the now accepted theory that the earlier the training, the more permanent and lasting the results. In all their catechetic writing they were conscious of the need to be simple, clear, and direct. Whenever they felt that a catechism was not simple enough for the littlest children they wrote a more simplified version. Not too infrequently we find pastors publishing such graduated catechisms in one volume, as the Westminster Assembly did . . . . [In] accordance with Mosaic teaching, the Puritans held the family and its extension, the Church, to be the ideal nursery" (108). Before the advent of the medium of Sunday school, catechesis was the primary means of formal instruction, especially of the young, used in churches; Eavey, *History of Christian Education*, 204. "Catechizing was both a church function, conducted by the pastor, and a family affair . . . . Many pastors, following Richard Baxter's example, conducted their catechesis on a family basis"; Grant, "Puritan Catechizing," 108.

Background: Puritanism

of the Protestant Marian martyrs, John Rogers [1500–1555], including, "Keep always God before your Eyes"), and the Ten Commandments.[112] The interconnection in the Puritan mind between secular learning and spiritual growth is illustrated by the *Primer's* use of Scriptural references to teach the alphabet. Both Reformed theology and elementary reading instruction were instilled in students through the inculcation of such couplets as, "In Adam's Fall / We sinned all."

Around the age of seven or eight years, select boys enrolled in grammar schools and prepared for a college curriculum with courses in mathematics, Latin and Greek (and occasionally Hebrew), and classical literature, supplemented by "appropriate training in piety and civility."[113] Girls in this age range typically completed their education at home or at a "dame school," which often was conducted in the teacher's home and gave instruction primarily in reading and writing, and also in useful crafts, such as sewing and cooking.[114]

---

112. See Platner et al., *The Religious History of New England*, 40–41; Price, "Jonathan Edwards as a Christian Educator," 14.

Spring, *American School, 1642–2000*, 13, maintains that the "authoritarian" element of Puritan education is reflected in the fact that the *New England Primer* also contained this verse for children to memorize and to obey: "I will fear God, and honour the KING / I will honour my Father and Mother / I will obey my Superiors / I will Submit to my Elders."

113. Cremin, *American Education*, 186. Cremin, *American Education*, 185–86, gives a detailed description of the grammar school curriculum. See also Mather, "Introduction," xxii–xxiv; Littlefield, *Early Schools and School-Books of New England*, 68–69; Shipton, "Secondary Education in the Puritan Colonies," 655; Hessinger, "Classical Curriculum," 81–82; Middlekauff, *Ancients and Axioms*, 53, 75–88; Eavey, *History of Christian Education*, 196–97; Wertenbaker, *Golden Age of Colonial Culture*, 21; Eberling, "Latin Grammar Schools," 210; and Kennedy, *First American Evangelical*, 12–13. Small, *Early New England Schools*, 30 and Wright, *Literary Culture in Early New England, 1620–1730*, 23n39, give the chronology of the founding of sixteen grammar schools in Massachusetts between 1635/1636 and 1670.

114. Wertenbaker, *First Americans, 1607–1690*, 246; Wright, *Literary Culture in Early New England, 1620–1730*, 23, 102–4; Eavey, *History of Christian Education*, 194; Hewes, "Dame Schools," 106; Carden, *Puritan Christianity in America*, 187; Spring, *American School, 1642–2000*, 13; Gordon and Gordon, *Literacy in America*, 11, 12–14.

Scholars who have focused on literacy "have generally overlooked female readers at the critical moment when their reading assumed significant cultural and economic power"; i.e., before the past two centuries; Hackel and Kelly, "Introduction," 2. "Although the field of women's reading is comparatively undeveloped for the periods before 1800, several contributors to this volume—Mary Ellen Lamb ["Inventing the Early Modern Woman Reader through the World of Goods: Lyly's Gentlewoman Reader and Katherine Stubbes," 15–35], Sasha Roberts ["Engendering the Female Reader: Women's Recreational Reading of Shakespeare in Early Modern England," 36–54], Margaret Ferguson ["'With All Due Reverence and Respect to the Word of God': Aphra Behn as

To Understand *Things* as Well as *Words*

The founding of Harvard College was the capstone of the New England Puritans' monumental efforts to "advance Learning and perpetuate it to Posterity," and, coming as it did a mere six years after the start of the Massachusetts Bay Colony, was an unsurpassed achievement.[115] "[T]he first college in British America," this venerable institution remained the only college in the colonies until the founding of the College of William and Mary in Virginia in 1693 and the only college in New England until the founding of Yale in 1701.[116] Harvard's curriculum was modeled after

---

Skeptical Reader of the Bible and Critical Translator of Fontenelle," 199–216]—have directed scholarly attention to the role of gender in early modern reading and advocated for a more carefully theorized account of the gendering of literacy"; Hackel and Kelly, "Introduction," 3. Among Hackel's and Kelly's contentions ("Introduction," 1–10) are "the emergent 'modern world,'" i.e., the matrix in which printing develops and literacy emerges as at least somewhat quantifiable, "is best viewed in a transnational, transatlantic context," and that "one cannot speak of a singular, unilegible 'Female reader'" (6, 4; see also 9–10n11). See also Monaghan, "Literacy Instruction and Gender in Colonial New England," 18–41. "Several scholars . . . have raised the possibility that some people—particularly women—could read but not write . . . . The thesis of the present study is that this was . . . true of New England"; Monaghan, "Literacy Instruction and Gender in Colonial New England," 19. Wright, *Cultural Life of the American Colonies, 1607–1763*, 103, observes without quantification, "A large proportion of New England women were literate, and they learned to read somewhere," largely through the dame schools.

115. Quotation is from *New England's First Fruits*, 242. Jannenga, "Making College Colonial," 1, offers an astute observation contextualizing this achievement: "To prioritize a privilege such as higher education, at a time when the simple act of surviving from one year to the next was uncertain, means that the education of their young men was of utmost importance to the English migrants." See Rudolph, *American College and University*, 5–6: "[T]he really important fact about Harvard College is that it was absolutely necessary. Puritan Massachusetts could not have done without it . . . . [because] In the future the state would need competent rulers, the church would require a learned clergy, and society itself would need the adornment of cultured men." See Tewksbury, *Founding of American Colleges and Universities Before the Civil War*, 32n82: "Although the Act of 1636 [establishing Harvard] did not explicitly grant the institution the right to confer degrees, this right was implied in the establishment of the institution, and degrees were actually conferred, beginning in August 1642. A full charter was not granted to Harvard until 1650." Under the 1636 charter, four tutors and six professors began teaching in 1638, the year Miller, *Brief Retrospect of the Eighteenth Century*, gives as the date of its founding. See also Quincy, *History of Harvard University*, 2: Appendix; Hornberger, "Date, the Source, and the Significance of Cotton Mather's Interest in Science," 7.

116. Quotation is from Wertenbaker, *First Americans, 1607–1690*, 247. Jannega, "Making College Colonial," 27, gives an intriguing historical perspective on the establishment of institutions of higher learning in colonial America vis-a-vis those in England: "[I]t took the English in the motherland over 600 years after they established Cambridge [in 1209] to establish the University of Durham [in1832], yet the colonists founded nine colleges in the colonies in less than 140 years."

Background: Puritanism

that of Emmanuel College at Cambridge, a bastion of English Puritanism.[117] Its course of studies was based on "the best learning of the day" and included biblical languages ("Chaldee," i.e., Aramaic, and Syriac, in addition to Hebrew and Greek), Latin, rhetoric, logic, physics, geometry, astronomy, botany, and ethics.[118] The focus of academic preparation for ministerial students was mastery of Scripture through study of its original languages and proficiency in orthodox Reformed interpretation and exposition.[119]

---

117. See Degler, "Were the Puritans 'Puritanical'?" 19; Rudolph, *American College and University*, 24; Pryde, *Scottish Universities and the Colleges of Colonial America*, 2; Carden, *Puritan Christianity in America*, 187; Sloan, *Scottish Enlightenment and the American College Ideal*, 20–21n39: Morison's "well-documented conclusion [in *The Founding of Harvard College*, 40, 92–107 (see also 92n1); Morison, *Builders of the Bay Colony*, 205–6] is that the most influential model for Harvard was Emmanuel College at Cambridge, which many of the Massachusetts founders had attended"; Hoeveler, *Creating the American Mind*, 7, 7n14, 8, 9, 9n17.

See also Thwing, *History of Higher Education in America*, 56, 65, who detects two strains of British influence on the colonial colleges, one English, represented by Harvard, and the other Scottish, represented by William and Mary. See also Sloan, *Scottish Enlightenment and the American College Ideal*, 249. Sloan's bibliography (249–80) is extensive regarding Scottish influence on the origins and development of American education. Two significant works dealing with the development of college curricula generally are those of Snow, *College Curriculum in the United States*, and Hangartner, "Movements to Change American College Teaching, 1700–1830."

118. Snow, *College Curriculum in the United States*, 31–33, 46–48; Wertenbaker, *First Americans, 1607–1690*, 248; Degler, "Were the Puritans 'Puritanical'?" 19; Norton, "Harvard Text-Books and Reference Books of the Seventeenth Century," 364; Rand, "Liberal Education in Seventeenth-Century Harvard," 525–51; Wertenbaker, *Golden Age of Colonial Culture*, 22–23, 28; Carden, *Puritan Christianity in America*, 187; Cremin, *American Education*, 102–4, 211, 216; Wright, *Literary Culture in Early New England, 1620–1730*, 19–20. See Wright, *Cultural Life of the American Colonies, 1607–1763*, 220, 220n6. Hans, *New Trends in Education in the Eighteenth Century*, provides a basis for comparison of the English and colonial educational systems during this time period. Cremin, *American Education*, 211–23, provides an extensive account of Harvard's early years. For even fuller examinations, see Morison's works, *Founding of Harvard College*; *Harvard College in the Seventeenth Century*, *Three Centuries of Harvard, 1636–1936*, 3–50 ("The Puritan Age," 1636–1707), 53–163 ("Aaron's Rod," 1708–1806).

119. Although *New England's First Fruits*, 1:242 (also found in Morison, *Founding of Harvard College*, Appendix D, 304–5) focuses on the desire to avoid an "illiterate ministry" as the motivation behind the establishing of Harvard, it is a myth that that institution existed to educate solely or primarily those preparing to enter the ranks of the clergy. From its beginning, Harvard prepared students for other learned professions, as well. See Morison, *Harvard College in the Seventeenth Century*, 562; Morison, *Intellectual Life of Colonial New England*, 42; Wertenbaker, *Golden Age of Colonial Culture*, 152–53; Fink, "Purposes of the American Colonial Colleges"; Ranz, "History of the Printed Book Catalogue in the United States," 50; Carden, *Puritan Christianity in America*, 187: "While theology permeated the curriculum, so did the liberal arts, and

To Understand *Things* as Well as *Words*

As we have seen, New England Puritans, across all socioeconomic strata, were a people of the Word. In each household was at least one Bible, which was read and studied regularly in family devotions, in individual study, and in the education of children.[120] Furthermore, as "religious literature came increasingly to be within the access of the common folk," typically, Puritans also owned such materials as catechisms, prayer books (such as *The Christians Daily Walke in Holy Securitie and Peace* (1627) by Henry Scudder (d. 1659?), and *The Whole Book of Psalms*, popularly known as the *Bay Psalm Book* ("America's first best seller," printed in 1640 at the Cambridge press and which "achieved iconic status") or other hymnals (such as *Hymns and Spiritual Songs* [1707] by Isaac Watts [1674–1748], sometimes in combination). In addition, volumes on theology, medicine, and law; works elucidating such topics as farming, stock-raising, and shipping; and "the most popular of all mundane books," almanacs, such as the *New England Almanac* (first printed in 1639 at the Cambridge press), were all valuable "to assist an agricultural and maritime people" to survive, to adapt, and (in the Puritan vision), to conquer their untamed environment, and were common in family libraries.[121]

---

in the seventeenth century less than half of Harvard's graduates entered the ministry"; Eavey, *History of Christian Education*, 197: Harvard was founded "to supply the church with ministers and the colony with teachers and civil officers"; Hoeveler, *Creating the American Mind*, 32: Harvard existed "to educate leaders of church and state and to equip all others who entered its doors with the intellectual foundations of Puritanism." Spring, *American School, 1642–1990*, 12, itemizes the occupations which Harvard graduates entered between 1642 and 1689. Roughly half (180 of 368) entered the ministry.

120. See Price, "Jonathan Edwards as a Christian Educator," 14; Curti, *Growth of American Thought*, 7; Carden, *Puritan Christianity in America*, 215; Cambers, *Godly Reading*, 80; Anderson, *New England's Generation*, 173–74.

Among the works dealing with the presence of Scripture in the colonial New England environment are those of Hill, *English Bible and the Seventeenth-Century Revolution*, 7; Stout, "Word and Order in Colonial New England,"; Cressy, "Books as Totems in Seventeenth-Century England and New England," 92–106; Alden, "Bible as Printed Word," 9–28. Amory, "'Bible and Other Books,'" 58–79, provides a specialized study of Bibles in various formats for 765 estates in Essex County, Massachusetts from 1635 to 1681 (see also 78n35).

121. Graff, *Legacies of Literacy*, 159 (see also 433n142); Hart, *Popular Book*, 9, 13, 14; Wright, *Cultural Life of the American Colonies, 1607–1763*, 126–53; Smith, *American Reading Instruction*, 17–18; Hall, *Cultures of Print*, 57; Amory, "Printing and Bookselling in New England, 1638–1713," 103; also in Hall, *Bibliography and the Book Trades*, 127; Carden, *Puritan Christianity in America*, 189; Sleeper, "Puritan Prayer Books," 2:509–10; Amory, *Bibliography and the Book Trades*, 12, 130–31; Ruland and Bradbury, *From Puritanism to Postmodernism*, 8.

Stout's characterization in *New England Soul*, 32, that "besides their Bibles [the Puritans] read practically nothing else," and thus inhabited a "literate but nearly bookless

Background: Puritanism

A number of Massachusetts' settlers brought libraries with them from England, and the more affluent New Englanders enjoyed access to printed materials from booksellers. These included classical works by authors such as Homer, Aristotle, Virgil, Livy, Pliny, and Plutarch; histories such as *Actes and Monuments* (first edition, 1583; commonly

---

society," is somewhat of an exaggeration. See Carden, *Puritan Christianity in America*, 189–90; Wright, *Literary Culture in Early New England, 1620–1730*. 54, 61: Fragmentary evidence suggests that "the early settlers did not suffer for books, either old or new, since the good libraries they brought with them were constantly increased by importations. Also, the colonists could increase their range of reading materials by "borrowing, or to assist their friends by lending"; Puritans "were not without the means of culture and had access to a moderate amount of real literature." Wright, *Cultural Life of the American Colonies, 1607–1763*, 127, 144, confidently states, "No one who has assessed the evidence properly will say that seventeenth-century America was without literary culture"; "Proof is ample of the presence of books among the possessions of the colonists in the first century of settlement. The ruling classes and even many humbler folk possessed works which they prized as important to their lives and prosperity"; "The traditional literary heritage of England was transmitted to the New World. . . . Writers of the early Renaissance, of Elizabethan and early seventeenth-century England, continued to influence Englishmen in America. [These works] provided nourishment for a developing intellectual life that came to maturity in the later eighteenth and nineteenth centuries." Bremer, *Puritan Experiment*, 19, puts the matter in a theological context: "The Puritans read all Christian authors, but they used their works as aids to understanding the Scriptures." "Although the average New Englander bought books expounding the intricacies of theology and the subtleties of ecclesiastical polity" to supplement the Bible, "he probably turned more often to practical guides to godliness." The most popular of these was *The Practice of Piety* by Lewis Bayly (1580–1631), a devotional guide that achieved bestseller status in seventeenth-century England. It "included dialogues between characters that illustrated morality and the tenets of religion, selections from the Psalms, and examples of morning prayers," thus combining bibliocentric theology and practical application of Scripture. Highly valued in New England as well, it was "one of the few books [other than the Bible] thought to warrant the pains of translation and publication in the tongue of the Massachusetts Indians"; Keeble, "Puritanism and Literature," 311; Melton, "Pietism, Politics, and the Public Sphere in Germany," 296–97 (see 327n8); Sleeper, "Puritan Best-Sellers," 502; Hart, *Popular Book*, 12; Cremin, *American Education*, 44.

It is important to keep the Puritans' literary preferences in perspective. "The Puritans read religious books, but then so did any cultivated man of the day. . . . The actual number as well as the proportion of religious works was higher in New England's book collections" than in those of the other colonies, yet it is not true that "the Puritans of New England confined their literary interest to theology"; Hart, *Popular Book,* 10, 11; Wright, *Cultural Life of the American Colonies, 1607–1763*, 144. See also Carden, *Puritan Christianity in America*, 211; Herrick, "Early New Englanders," 1–17; Seigel, "Puritan Light Reading," 185–99. In summary, Puritans were among the most well-read of all early Americans, and typically owned or could access reading materials other than the Bible, including those by classical "pagan" authors and other learned works that they believed helpful. Nevertheless, the materials in large measure explicated and reinforced biblical teachings.

To Understand *Things* as Well as *Words*

known as Foxe's *Book of Martyrs*) by John Foxe (1517–1587), *A History of New England* (1654; better known as *Wonder-Working Providence of Sion's Savior in New England*) by Edward Johnson (1598–1672), *Historie of the World* (1614; "favored by the Puritans because it demonstrated the divine purpose in human events") by Sir Walter Raleigh (1552–1618), and the "majestic" *Magnalia Christi Americana* (1702) by Cotton Mather, essays such as *The Advancement of Learning* (1605; "read and quoted as an authority by preachers, schoolmasters, and politicians") by Sir Francis Bacon (1561–1626; "throughout the seventeenth century a name to conjure with in America"); and works of practical piety, such as *The Plaine Man's Pathway to Heaven* (1601) by Arthur Dent (d. 1607) and the iconic *Pilgrim's Progress* (1681) by John Bunyan (1628–1688).[122] Overall, the New England Puritans who were able to do so regularly gained entry into the literary world through purchases and by "borrowing freely from their neighbors near and remote."[123]

---

122. Wertenbaker, *Golden Age of Colonial Culture*, 26–27, 153; Wright, *Literary Culture in Early New England, 1620–1730*, 25–61; Murdock, *Literature and Theology in Colonial New England*, 68–69; Wright, *Cultural Life of the American Colonies, 1607–1763*, 131, 133, 135, 159; Clement, "Colonial Book Production, 1638–1783," 7; Knight, *Orthodoxies in Massachusetts*, 1; Hall, *Cultures of Print*, 86; Hall, *Bibliography and the Book Trades*, 127–28; also in Amory and Hall, *Colonial Book in the Atlantic World*, 103; Ruland and Bradbury, *From Puritanism to Postmodernism*, 14–16. See also Werkmeister, *History of Philosophical Ideas in America*, 32–33: "Through almanacs and popularized commentaries the essence of Newtonian mechanics became known throughout the colonies . . . . Newton's *Principia Mathematica* was well-known in America, as was Locke's *An Essay Concerning Human Understanding*"; Carden, *Puritan Christianity in America*, 189. Hall, *Cultures of Print*, 79–96, and in Amory and Hall, *Colonial Book in the Atlantic World*, details the means of Puritans' acquisition of books (Amory, "Printing and Bookselling in New England, 1638–1713," 83–116, is expanded and reprinted in Hall, *Bibliography and the Book Trades*, 105–45). Wroth, "Printing in the Colonial Period, 1638–1783," 7–59, provides a detailed history of the origins, development, and output of colonial American printing of books, newspapers, and periodicals. Hall, "Readers and Writers in Early New England," 51–59, describes selling books through subscription method, book "pedlars," and auctions. See also Farren, "Subscription."

123. Wright, *Literary Culture in Early New England, 1620–1730*, 61 (see also 135–36). See Anderson, *New England's Generation*, 173–75; Hart, *Popular Book*, 15–16. See also Wright, *Literary Culture in Early New England, 1620–1730*, 219–24. In addition, "Libraries were present in colonial America in a variety of forms, if not in large numbers"; Ranz, "History of the Printed Book Catalogue in the United States," 49, 50; "By the early years of the eighteenth century, increasing prosperity and urbanity led to the multiplication of private libraries in all the colonies, the beginnings of libraries designed to serve a wider public, and a well-developed book trade in such towns as Boston, New York, Philadelphia, and Charleston"; Wright, *Cultural Life of the American Colonies*, 144. Among these were the libraries founded by each of the nine colonial colleges, town libraries, such as those of Boston and New Haven, commercial libraries

CONCLUSION

We have seen the interrelationship of the three characteristics of Puritanism discussed above: The sovereign God has disclosed his commandments and his covenant of grace in Scripture as his authoritative Word. Standing in the Reformation lineage, the Puritans affirmed the centrality of Scripture to their faith as the written Word that has revealed the living Word, Christ, as "the way, the truth, and the life (John 14:6)."[124] Literacy was regarded as a "universal prerequisite to spiritual preparedness, the central duty of the covenant."[125] "The ability to read the Scriptures therefore was a way to salvation, and men and women had a religious obligation to teach their children this essential art."[126] Let us now examine how each of these dimensions influenced Edwards's pedagogy.

("enterprises organized to lend books to the public for a fee"), and personal holdings .

Once having acquired literacy skills, Puritans became "notoriously prolific" in writing, as well as reading, literature; Degler, "Were the Puritans 'Puritanical?'" 552; Wertenbaker, *First Americans, 1607-1690*, 242-44. Sermons and religious treatises, historical works (e.g., Edward Johnson's *Wonder-Working Providence of Sion's Savior in New England*, 1654, and Cotton Mather's *Magnalia Christi Americana*, 1702), biographies (e.g., John Norton's biography of John Cotton, *Abel being Dead Yet Speaketh*, 1658), diaries, autobiographies (e.g., Thomas Shepard's *Autobiography* and *Journal*, 1630s?), and poetry (e.g., Bradstreet's *The Tenth Muse, Lately Sprung Up in America*, 1650, and Wigglesworth's *Day of Doom*, 1662), are among their notable works; Carden, *Puritan Christianity in America*, 189-90; Cappello, "Authority of Self-Definition in Thomas Shepard's *Autobiography* and *Journal*," 35-51; Wright, *Literary Culture in Early New England, 1620-1730*, 82-95; Murdock, *Literature and Theology in Colonial New England*, 99-172; Hall, *Worlds of Wonder, Days of Judgment*, 126. Wright, *Literary Culture in Early New England, 1620-1730*, 82-95, 159-68, 205-15, discusses Puritan writings during the periods 1620-1670, 1670-1700, and 1700-1727, respectively.

See also selections by John Winthrop, Samuel Danforth, John Cotton, Cotton Mather, and Anne Bradstreet in Delbanco, *Writing New England*. Selections by Bradstreet are also in Hall, *Puritans in the New World*, 135-39, 188-92.

124. The Reformation concept of "the priesthood of all believers" fundamentally altered the relationship between the individual Christian and the Church. Although situating the regenerate person within a community of saints, it "made each man's relationship to God his own terrifying responsibility"; Degler, "Were the Puritans 'Puritanical?'" 16. Those in the Reformation tradition considered the individual Christian as having a direct relationship with God, necessitating literacy in order to know God's covenant requirements and man's responsibilities revealed in Scripture. See Urban and Wagoner, *American Education*, 36 (N.B. the caution expressed in 36n35); Gordon and Gordon, *Literacy in America*, 4; Wright, *Cultural Life of the American Colonies, 1607-1763*, 98; Hall, *Worlds of Wonder, Days of Judgment*, 18.

125. Axtell, *School Upon a Hill*, 13.

126. Wright, *Cultural Life of the American Colonies, 1607-1763*, 98. See also Monaghan, *Learning to Read and Write in Colonial America*, 11; Murdock, *Literature and Theology in Colonial New England*, 2; Smith, *American Reading Instruction*, 12; Graff, *Legacies of Literacy*, 164 (see also 435n160); Spring, *American School, 1642-2000*, 13.

To Understand *Things* as Well as *Words*

As a "scion of the Puritans," the world in which Edwards the child and young adult lived was predominantly one which they had shaped and permeated, one in which the inhabitants were "God-centered in their thoughts and God-fearing in their hearts."[127] On the primary level, from his Puritan family, peers, and college instructors, Edwards learned to read and to study, and to appreciate the role which learning played in his environment. Far from restricting the activity of the mind to narrow academic confines, "from [the Puritans] he inherited the supreme challenge of reconciling all of life and learning to the dictates of God's law as contained in Scripture and in nature."[128] Education was a crucial means of accomplishing this feat.

For Edwards, as well as for his Puritan forebears and contemporaries, God, Scripture, and literacy were intertwined. As previously discussed, in Reformed orthodoxy, God has sovereignly elected some members of fallen humanity to receive his redemptive grace and has appointed evangelization as the means of reaching them with the gospel message. Edwards strove indefatigably, no less as an educator than as a pastor, to spread this "good news." "There is such a thing as conversion," he declared, and "'tis the most important thing in the world; and they are happy [who] have been the subjects of it and they are most miserable [who] have not."[129] Those who have received this saving grace have received the gift of the Holy Spirit to reorient their lives and to impart to their minds new spiritual understanding. They have "acquired a *taste* for God, a new and profound sense of joy and confidence in divine things."[130] As Edwards expressed it, those who have received this new spiritual sense have "a true sense of the divine excellency of the things revealed in the Word of God, and a conviction of the truth and reality of them."[131]

As we have seen and as further examination in chapter 5 will make even clearer, expansion of his students' intellects was an important goal of Edwards as an educator. Foremost, however, was instruction as a vehicle for the grace of conversion for the unregenerate and for the spiritual development of Christians. In Edwards's words, "[T]he most excellent knowledge [is] to understand the Word of God." Therefore, "The

---

127. Quotations are in Sweeney, *Edwards the Exegete*, 20; Packer, "Introductory Essay," 1.
128. Quotation is in Smith et al., "Editors' Introduction," vii.
129. Edwards, "Reality of Conversion," 83, 92.
130. Sweeney, *Jonathan Edwards and the Ministry of the Word*, 118.
131. Edwards, "Divine and Supernatural Light," 126.

Christian enjoys the pleasure of the most excellent knowledge. 'Tis natural to the reasonable creature to love knowledge . . . and to delight in the attainment of knowledge. [T]he believer has the most excellent kind of knowledge: he has the pleasure of knowing the most glorious truths, the most excellent verities."[132]

Scripture, for Edwards, is the supreme source of true wisdom and the most unerring guide to life. He praises its pages as being "full of wondrous things," even "the most excellent things in the world." Scriptural precepts provide "not only a perfect Rule of Truth but of Life." The Bible as God's Word is the very "word of life . . . the light of life; a sweet, excellent, life-giving word." Edwards further extols, "[W]hat a precious treasure God has committed into our hands in that he has given us the Bible . . . . What an excellent book is this, and how far exceeding all human writings," expressing "the most excellent things that man can exercise his thoughts about."[133]

Furthermore, the "book of Scripture" is necessary to make knowledge gained from the "book of nature" intelligible: "All that is visible to the eye is unintelligible and vain, without the Word of God to instruct and guide the mind." Human beings doubtless should "make it [their] chief business to improve" the faculty of understanding through gaining knowledge of the natural world. Doing so, however, should lead to the realization that "God gave man the faculty of understanding, chiefly, that he might understand divine things."[134] Edwards the educator, as much as Edwards the minister, sought to instruct those in his charge in the principles of Scripture, that they may be made "wise unto salvation" (2 Tim 3:15) and may "grow in grace and in the knowledge of [the] Lord and Savior Jesus Christ" (2 Pet 3:18).

Without meaning to belabor the obvious, literacy opens to Edwards's students access to both the natural world and divine things in the supernatural sphere. Literacy is necessary to be able to read sacred Scripture, and thereby to place oneself in the way to receive saving grace and to appropriate scriptural lessons for spiritual development.[135] Edwards

---

132. Edwards, "Profitable Hearers of the Word," 252; Edwards, "Pleasantness of Religion," 21.

133. Edwards, *History of the Work of Redemption* (hereafter *HWR*), 290–91; Edwards, "Personal Narrative," 801; Edwards, "Heeding the Word, and Losing It," 46; Edwards, "Divine Love Alone Lasts Eternally," 363.

134. Edwards, *HWR*, 290; Edwards, "Heeding the Word, and Losing It," 46; Edwards, "Importance and Advantage," 34, 35.

135. See Monoghan, *Learning to Read and Write in Colonial America*, 11; Sleeper,

made this connection clear in his sermon to a group of Native Americans on August 16, 1751. He chastised, "[F]ew of your children have been taught to read. And therefore you know but little of the Word of God, for you [are not] able to read it." This is most unfortunate, because all "should seek to know the Word of God, that [they] might be instructed by it." Scripture is regenerative: "When the light of God's Word shines into the heart, it gives new life to the soul."[136]

Let us now move on to examine the influence on Edwards the educator of the other predominant intellectual and cultural force of his lifetime, the "Enlightenment(s)."

"Puritan Prayer Books," 510: "The very act of reading the Bible, prayer books, and other devotional manuals was central to puritan religion because it opened the heart to receive grace." See Edwards, "Sermon 307." This sermon illustrates Edwards's evangelistic practice of "calling men and women to seek salvation through the means of grace because of the divine initiative provided by the awakening stream of God's Spirit"; Stratton, "Jonathan Edwards' (1703–1758) Theology of Spiritual Awakening and Spiritual Formation Leadership in Higher Education," 101 (see 101–13, for elaboration on means of grace).

136. Edwards, "To the Mohawks at the Treaty, August 16, 1751," 107, 110. See Baines, "Thy Kingdom Come," 117: "To envision a thriving redeemed community apart from the fundamental ability to read and apply the Word of God was outside of Edwards's frame of reference. It was not just unlikely; it was simply not possible."

3

Background: Intellectual Trends Comprising "the Enlightenment(s)"

"Neither Puritanism nor the Enlightenment can be neatly defined, and yet we have no difficulty in recognizing both as distinctive and enduring strands in American thought and culture."[1] This observation by a noted American philosopher summarizes two salient features that characterize each of the "two main clusters of ideas influential in early America": ambiguous regarding exact delimitations, yet discernible in its effects.[2]

The difficulties in defining "Puritanism" were discussed briefly in chapter 2. Yet, despite the elusiveness of a definition that will prove completely satisfactory regarding this topic, we have seen that specific aspects which comprise Puritanism influenced Edwards's conception of the purposes of education and the function of a teacher in the education process.

Similarly, this chapter acknowledges the complexity of "the Enlightenment(s)" but nevertheless identifies certain Enlightenment components to which Edwards responded that assisted in shaping his pedagogical philosophy and practice.

---

1. Smith, "Puritanism and Enlightenment," 195.
2. Quotation is in May, *Enlightenment in America*, xiii.

To Understand *Things* as Well as *Words*

ENLIGHTENMENT: DIFFICULTIES, DESCRIPTION, AND A DEFINITION

It is acknowledged at the outset that "the Enlightenment" (also known as the "Age of Reason") is a term originating in the late nineteenth century and is of imprecise consented-to chronological and geographical referents.[3] In recent years, accounts of this set of historical phenomena "have become increasingly layered and contextualized." A notable result of these more comprehensive analyses is that the assertion by one recognized authority, "There was only *one* Enlightenment," has given way, first, to the recognition of nationally contextualized movements of individual character and, more recently, to the acknowledgement that the term "Enlightenment," rather than applying to "a set of propositions commonly espoused in a set time period," is an anachronistic construct imposed on ideas, vantage points, and discussions, which "may be characteristic of other times and people" than eighteenth-century thinkers.[4] Although an

---

3. "Enlightenment," *Oxford English Dictionary*, 1897; Hill, *Faith in the Age of Reason*, 6; Beck, "Introduction," 1; Anchor, *Enlightenment Tradition*, 1–12; Lough, "Reflections on Enlightenment and Lumières," 1–15; Barnett, *Enlightenment and Religion*, 1; Himmelfarb, *Roads to Modernity*, 7; Moody, *Jonathan Edwards and the Enlightenment*, 5; Woodbridge and James, *From Pre-Reformation to the Present Day*, 358; Thomas, "Great Fight Over the Enlightenment," 68–72.

Similarly to "Puritan" and "Puritanism," "Enlightenment(s)" is "at once obvious and elusive"; "one of those useful but difficult terms . . . which paradoxically are about as indefinable as they are indispensable"; Kesler, "Different Enlightenments," 102; Eliot and Stern, "Introduction," 1:1. Approximate starting points for the "Enlightenment(s)" that have been proposed include Rene Descartes's (1596–1650) proclamation of the radical departure in epistemology from external authority to internal certainty, "*Cogito ergo sum*," in 1637; the conclusion of Great Britain's Thirty Years' War in 1648; mid-seventeenth century; the publication of Isaac Newton's *Philosophiae Naturalis Principia Mathematica* in 1687; Great Britain's Glorious Revolution of 1688; and the dawn of the eighteenth century. The publication in 1781 of Immanuel Kant's (1724–1804) *Critique of Pure Reason* or the publication in 1790 of his *Critique of Judgment* (the third and final *Critique*) ; the beginning of the French Revolution in 1789; the Reign of Terror in France in 1793; and the Napoleonic Wars (1804–1815) have been suggested as approximate ending points; Heidegger, "Age of World Picture," 115–54; Ingraffia, *Postmodern Theory and Biblical Theology*, 126; Swazo, *Crisis Theory and World Order*, 97–99; "Age of Enlightenment," *New World Encyclopedia*, www.newworldencyclopedia.org/entry/Age_of_Enlightenment; Hourly History, *Age of Enlightenment*.

4. Spencer, "JE and the Historiography of the American Enlightenment," 36; Gay, *Enlightenment*, 1:3 (emphasis added; see also Gay, *Enlightenment*, 1:x); Moody, *Jonathan Edwards and the Enlightenment*, 4, 12n27. See also White, "Editor's Introduction," ix–xix; Behrens, Book Review of *The Enlightenment: An Interpretation*, 190–95; May, *Enlightenment in America*; Pocock, "Post-Puritan England and the Problem of the Enlightenment," 91–112; Noll, "Rise and Long Life of the Protestant Enlightenment

Background: Intellectual Trends Comprising "the Enlightenment(s)"

all-encompassing definition remains elusive, a serviceable perspective on the "Enlightenment(s)" for the purposes of this work is, multiple efforts to emancipate humanity from the restrictions of previously accepted authorities and entrenched traditions and "superstitions," in order to achieve progress through development and use of Reason in the scientific, philosophical, theological, ethical, social, and political areas of life.[5]

---

in America," 88–124; Pocock, *Barbarism and Religion*, 9; Pocock, "Re-Description of Enlightenment," 101–17; Dupré, "Definition and a Provisional Justification," 1–7; Woodbridge and James, *From Pre-Reformation to the Present Day*, 356–488; Outram, "What Is Enlightenment?" 1–9; and Himmelfarb, *Roads to Modernity*, 239n10.

Issues surrounding the nature and extent of "the Enlightenment(s)" continue to provoke scholarly debate. See *Eighteenth-Century Studies* 49 (2015) for the following articles on the topic, "Was There a Counter-Enlightenment?": Caradonna, "There Was No Counter-Enlightenment," 51–69; Piirrimäe, "Berlin, Herder, and the Counter-Enlightenment," 71–76; Garrard, "Tilting at Counter-Enlightenment Windmills," 77–81; Schmidt, "Counter-Enlightenment," 83–86; and Caradonna, "Roundtable Discussion Conclusion," 87–88. My thanks go to Dr. John Woodbridge for bringing this discussion to my attention.

5. "A European intellectual movement of the late 17th and 18th centuries emphasizing reason and individualism rather than tradition," an era and a *zeitgeist* in which reason was "eulogized, apostrophized, invoked and venerated . . . . Reason was a strong, unified force; it could with the aid of sense and evidence lead men to the way of both truth and light," "the notion that the world had existed in varying stages of darkness beforehand, and that it was only at this point that everyone awoke from a kind of intellectual stupor," and the "guiding thought was that human reason was adequate to [meet] human needs," have been proposed as conveying the essence of the movement(s); www.google.com/?gws_rd=ssl#safe=strict&q=enlighten; Redwood, *Reason, Ridicule and Religion*, 198; Hill, *Faith in the Age of Reason*, 6; Beck, "Introduction," 3. When the dawning "light of Reason" shone in all its splendor, it would "dispel the oppressive darkness of superstition, ignorance, metaphysical speculation, fanaticism, and intolerance allegedly engendered by the Christian faith"; Woodbridge and James, *From Pre-Reformation to the Present Day*, 357. See also Kennedy, *First American Evangelical*, 106–7. The movement(s)' keynote was "knowledge was to be gained by observation rather than received on the authority of past, nonempirical centuries"; Cassara, *Enlightenment in America*, 16.

The term "Enlightenment(s)" continues to resist precise definition, as no one attempt at categorization is adequately inclusive. Even a statement that may seem incontestable regarding the "Age of Reason," "'Reason' becomes the unifying and central point of the [eighteenth] century, expressing all that it longs and strives for, and all that it achieves"; Cassirer, *Philosophy of the Enlightenment*, 5, is challenged: There was not "unity within the Enlightenment on perhaps the central plank of Enlightenment doctrine, the role of reason in the future of civilization"; Barnett, *Enlightenment and Religion*, 1. "The fact that the expression *Enlightened* bore different connotations in various European countries . . . reveals that not all contemporaries experienced or defined the "Enlightenment" in the same way . . . . Various "Enlightenments" . . . existed in eighteenth-century Europe with different intellectual shadings"; Woodbridge and James, *From Pre-Reformation to the Present Day*, 358. May, *Enlightenment in America*, xiii, laments, "No definition of the Enlightenment fits all the men usually assumed to belong to it,"

To Understand *Things* as Well as *Words*

Yet as this study proceeds, it is with the realization that an examination of Edwards's responses to specific intellectual trends of his time will be more productive than an attempt to classify these currents of thought under what has proved to be as imprecise a category as the "Enlightenment(s)."

The geographical remoteness of colonial New England from the mother country and from the continent of Europe did not mean, for Edwards, intellectual isolation from the outpourings of "the most important cultural and intellectual movement of his time."[6] The late seventeenth and early eighteenth centuries were a period "of great fertility and interchange of ideas" among the leading thinkers of the day.[7] In this intellectually lively and fruitful milieu, through his active participation in the "Republic of Letters," Edwards interacted with a wide array of the *illuminaires* of his era, becoming deeply enmeshed in the theological, philosophical, and scientific thought worlds of the "Age of Reason."[8]

---

observing, "Any definition that includes optimism about human nature excludes Voltaire, Hume, and many French materialists. Any that centers on rationalism excludes Hume and Rousseau. A definition that emphasizes empiricism raises serious questions about Rousseau, Paine, and Condorcet." May distinguishes four categorizations: "The Moderate Enlightenment (1688–1787)"; "The Skeptical Enlightenment (1750–1789)"; "The Revolutionary Enlightenment (1776–1800)"; and "The Didactic Enlightenment (1800–1815)." In his analysis, May has demonstrated the effects of "a series of interrelated movements with diverse emphases and perspectives"; McDermott, *Jonathan Edwards Confronts the Gods*, 217. Kennedy, *First American Evangelical*, 106, sees a unity in the diversity: "The various branches of enlightenment share a similarity that gives them their common label: their participants believed they were turning on the lights" in order to dispel darkness as variously conceived. See also Noll, "Rise and Long Life of the Protestant Enlightenment in America," 93; Woodbridge and James, *From Pre-Reformation to the Present Day*, 359–60.

6. Moody, *Jonathan Edwards and the Enlightenment*, 3.

7. Fiering, *Jonathan Edwards's Moral Thought and Its British Context*, 15, 38; Chamberlain, "Edwards and Social Issues," 329.

8. Opie, "Introduction," v. See also Moody, *Jonathan Edwards and the Enlightenment*, 4, 13n32; Fiering, "Transatlantic Republic of Letters," 642–60. Edwards gained information about "new books published, new ideas advanced, and the state of the argument on any given issue" through his participation in this network; Fiering, "Transatlantic Republic of Letters," 643; Bezzant, "Introduction," 7. Even though Edwards should be understood within the Anglo-colonial context in which he interacted, "it is his trans-Atlantic context, both during and after the eighteenth century, that is of critical importance in understanding his world as his world understood itself . . . . The trans-Atlantic Republic of Letters, consisting of a multidirectional coterie of thinkers, set Edwards and his New World colleagues within the bigger frame of reference of European thinkers," allowing Edwards to engage with their "Enlightenment(s)" participants.

Background: Intellectual Trends Comprising "the Enlightenment(s)"

"The Enlightenment was a period of profound intellectual upheaval that placed unique demands on Christian thinkers."[9] Edwards recognized and accepted the direct challenge posed to orthodox Christianity by the *ethos* of the times deriving from the philosophical inquiries and scientific discoveries during that era regarding the physical and metaphysical worlds. These seemed to many to depose the God of orthodoxy from his throne and to coronate man as master of his own domain.[10] The three major intellectual and cultural trends prevalent during what Edwards ironically called "this age of light and inquiry," which will be examined in turn in this work are Lockean epistemology, Newtonian physics and optics, and innate morality.[11]

LOCKEAN EPISTEMOLOGY: LOCKE AND EDWARDS REGARDING IDEAS

Much discussed among Edwards scholars have been the questions of whether, and to what extent, the philosophy of British empiricist John Locke (1632–1704) influenced Edwards. As the details are well-known, a brief introductory review will suffice here. Samuel Hopkins, Edwards's first biographer, records:

> In [Edwards's] second Year at College, and the thirteenth of his Age, he read Locke on the human Understanding, with great delight and profit.... Taking that Book into his Hand... not long before his Death, he said to some of his select Friends... That he was beyond Expression entertain'd and Pleas'd with it, when he read it in his Youth at College; that he was as much engaged, and had more satisfaction and Pleasure in studying it,

---

9. Studebaker, *Jonathan Edwards' Social Augustinian Trinitarianism*, 207. See also Zakai, "Age of Enlightenment," 81, 89: "The 'enlightened age' witnessed the replacement of religion by reason as the main agent for providing 'objective truths' about the world in which human life is set. The supremacy and primacy of divine revelation were attacked," as Reason's role was magnified and revelation's role was minimized or discounted completely; "The 'enlightened age' posed grave implications for traditional Christian thought"; Marsden, "Biography," 23: "Edwards was ... countering some of the most prevalent trends in the progressive thought of the ['Enlightenment(s)'] era." Cf. Woodbridge and James, *Pre-Reformation to the Present Day*, 358.

10. See Opie, "Introduction," v–vi; McDermott, *Jonathan Edwards Confronts the Gods*, 227; Marsden, "Challenging the Presumptions of the Age," 99–113; Moody, *Jonathan Edwards and the Enlightenment*, 7; Zakai, "Age of Enlightenment," 81; Zakai, *Jonathan Edwards's Philosophy of Nature*, 210, 232.

11. Quotation is from Edwards, "Conclusion," 437.

than the most greedy Miser in gathering up handfuls of Silver and Gold from some new discover'd Treasure.[12]

In the decades since this biography's publication, controversy has existed among Edwards scholars regarding whether an influence of Locke is discernible in Edwards's thought and, if so, its significance.[13] In support of a Lockean influence, claims have been advanced such as, "There is no doubt that Locke's *Essay [Concerning Human Understanding]* was a major factor in the philosophical development of Jonathan Edwards," demonstrating an "obvious and lasting impact" on the course of Edwards's epistemology.[14] Although not hesitating to disagree with Locke "on specific points," Edwards "quickly accepted most of the Lockean philosophy."[15] In fact, this landmark work by Locke exerted such an "enormous influence on Edwards' thought" that it formed "the general framework within which he worked."[16] At one point in this historiography, the acceptance of the "long unquestioned assumption" of the influence of Locke's epistemology on Edwards had become such a commonplace that it "scarcely needs asserting."[17]

---

12. Hopkins, *Life and Character of the Late Reverend Mr. Jonathan Edwards* (hereafter *Life of Edwards*), 3. "The extent of Locke's influence on Edwards has been a subject of some debate among contemporary students of Edwards, especially since Perry Miller's suggestion in 1949 that Edwards thoroughly embraced Locke's empiricism"; Cherry, *Theology of Jonathan Edwards*, 15. The extent to which Miller's analysis is considered correct by contemporary Edwards scholars is discussed briefly in this chapter and in the notes below. See also Spencer, "Jonathan Edwards and the Historiography of the American Enlightenment," 22–23.

13. See Schweitzer, *God Is a Communicative Being*, 20n36. Although acknowledging that "the genealogy of Edwards' philosophy has been debated," Schweitzer argues Edwards "formulated a Christian version of idealism that incorporated certain aspects of Locke as well as Malebranche" (20). See also Hastings, *Jonathan Edwards and the Life of God*, 9. Influences on Edwards "included continental scholastic Reformed theologians Francis Turretin (1623–1687) and Petrus van Mastricht (1630–1706) as well as Enlightenment thinkers such as John Locke and Nicolas Malebranche"; Spencer, "Jonathan Edwards and the Historiography of the American Enlightenment," 23–24, 23n8, 23n9, 24n10, 24n11.

14. Helm, "John Locke and Jonathan Edwards," 51–61; Helm, "Epistemology," 104; Laurence, "Jonathan Edwards, John Locke, and the Canon of Experience," 107–23.

15. Flower and Murphey, *History of Philosophy in America*, 1:140.

16. White, *Science and Sentiment in America*, 35; Thuesen, "Edwards' Intellectual Background," 16–33.

17. Smith, "Jonathan Edwards and 'The Way of Ideas,'" 153–73. See Ramsey, "Edwards and John Locke," 1:47–65.

Background: Intellectual Trends Comprising "the Enlightenment(s)"

The foremost proponent of this thesis is Perry Miller, who is "normally imputed with having started the modern analysis of Edwards in relation to Locke."[18] In his biography of Edwards, Miller writes that Edwards's exposure to the *Essay Concerning Human Understanding* by Locke, "the master-spirit of the age," constituted "the central and decisive event in his intellectual life."[19] Reading this momentous essay at the age of thirteen (if Hopkins's account is correct), Edwards "grasped in a flash" that the "'new way of thinking by ideas' would determine the intellectual career of the eighteenth century."[20] Edwards's study of Locke made the young college student realize, in a "permanent and abiding" way, "how meet and suitable it was that God should govern the world, and order all things according to his own pleasure."[21]

The main opponent of the thesis that Locke exerted a major influence on Edwards's epistemology is Norman Fiering. After extensive examination of the intellectual context of the eighteenth century, Fiering concludes, "That Edwards studied Locke's *Essay* closely, was stimulated by it, and learned from it is not at issue. But the notion that the *Essay* played a key functional role in the development of Edwards's metaphysics is not sustainable."[22] Paul Copan, along with Fiering, argues for a more direct and discernible connection between the thought of the French philosopher Nicolas Malebranche (1638–1715) and Edwards than that

---

18. Moody, *Jonathan Edwards and the Enlightenment*, 11n16. Perry Miller lauded Edwards as one of "those pure artists through whom the deepest urgencies of their age and country become articulate," and considered it tragic that Edwards was confined to the theology of his time to express his genius; Miller, *Jonathan Edwards*, xi. Moody, *Jonathan Edwards and the Enlightenment*, 11n16, provides a concise but detailed review of recent analyses of the issue of Edwards as "Lockean" or "non-Lockean." See also Chun, *Legacy of Jonathan Edwards in the Theology of Andrew Fuller*, 3n8.

19. Miller, *Jonathan Edwards*, 52. See also Miller, "Jonathan Edwards on the Sense of the Heart," 121–45. In this article, Miller includes what has since been published as Edwards, "Miscellany 782," 18:452–66.

20. Miller, *Jonathan Edwards*, 52.

21. Miller *Jonathan Edwards*, 54; Edwards, "Personal Narrative," 804. Edwards locates the observation quoted here as having occurred on a Saturday in January 1738/1739, but Miller argues that Edwards's study of Locke while in college opened the way to this insight.

22. Fiering, "Rationalist Foundations of Jonathan Edwards's Metaphysics," 92. See also Fiering, *Jonathan Edwards's Moral Thought*, 23–45; Spencer, "Jonathan Edwards and the Historiography of the American Enlightenment," 23, 23n9. See Walton, *Jonathan Edwards, Religious Affections, and the Puritan Analysis of True Piety, Spiritual Sensation and Heart Religion*, 25–30, for a detailed review of analyses denying an influence of Locke on Edwards.

of Locke. Likewise, Charles J. McCracken presents a case for the influence of Malebranche's works *Concerning the Search after Truth* (*De la Recherche de la Vérité*) and *Elucidations* as being more predominant than Locke's *Essay* in Edwards's thought.[23]

At this point, caveats are in order. Undeniably, Edwards was an original thinker "who called no man, Father [or Master]," but, rather, "thought and judged for himself."[24] "[L]ike all geniuses, he did not merely accept unquestioningly truths," or concepts accepted as truths, "from the past."[25] By no means an unimaginative or uncritical devotee of Locke (or anyone else), Edwards accepted even the designation "Calvinist" with some reluctance: "I utterly disclaim a dependence on Calvin, or believing the doctrines which I hold, because he believed and taught them; and cannot justly be charged with believing in everything just as he taught."[26]

---

23. Copan, "Jonathan Edwards' Philosophical Influences," 107–24; McCracken, *Malebranche and British Philosophy*, 316–40. See also Spencer, "Jonathan Edwards and the Historiography of the American Enlightenment," 21–39; Cuthbert, "'More Swiftly Propagating the Gospel,'" 153n2; Kim, "Jonathan Edwards's Reshaping of Lockean Terminology," 105n5. Brown, "Edwards, Locke, and the Bible," 361–84 (at 361n1), Lukasik, "Feeling the Force of Certainty," 222–45 (at 224n3), and Kim, "Jonathan Edwards's Reshaping of Lockean Terminology," 103–22 (at 103–4n2), provide extensive lists of other notable responses to Miller's argument regarding the Lockean influence on Edwards. See Spencer, "Jonathan Edwards and the Historiography of the American Enlightenment," 26–30, for a critical analysis of Miller's understanding of Edwards; see especially 27–28, 27n26, for other scholars who have built on Miller's work. The plausible influence of Malebranche on Edwards will be examined in the following chapter.

24. Hopkins, *Life and Character of Edwards*, 41. See also Erdt, *Jonathan Edwards: Art and the Sense of the Heart*, 26: Edwards was "the master and not the slave of his sources"; Elwood, *Philosophical Theology of Jonathan Edwards*, 169–70n51. After a detailed listing of studies of possible influences on Edwards's early thoughts on idealism, Elwood concludes, "Every study of [Edwards's] sources . . . has led to the conclusion that Edwards was not dependent on any one author or school of thought, and that his originality stands out in every comparison. Perhaps the soundest judgment on this matter is expressed by H. W. Schneider when he concludes that further discussion of the sources of Edwards' thought now seems superfluous (*History of American Philosophy* [New York: Columbia University Press, 1963], p. 31.)"

25. Smith et al., "Editors' Introduction," vii. See also viii: "Like all creative geniuses, Edwards borrowed from much of the best of his time and place without being beholden to any."

26. Edwards, "Freedom of the Will" (hereafter *FW*), 131. See also *EW*, 167. For differences between Calvin's theology and that of Edwards, see Cooey, *Jonathan Edwards on Nature and Destiny*, 2: "Concern with divine destiny [as Creator and Redeemer] as exemplified or communicated through nature ['minimally defined as sensible and sentient reality'] and history . . . distinguishes Edwards'. . . Christology and his Trinitarian thought from Calvin's"; 138: "In the *Freedom of the Will*, Edwards, in a radical departure from Calvin, argues that God *permits*, rather than directly *wills*, evil as a means to a greater

Background: Intellectual Trends Comprising "the Enlightenment(s)"

Nevertheless, Locke's *Essay Concerning Human Understanding* (hereafter *Essay*) likely provides Edwards with both a point of connection and a point of departure in developing his own epistemological schema.[27]

---

good" (emphasis added. see 249n35); Erdt, *Jonathan Edwards: Art and the Sense of the Heart*, 22, 42: "Edwards reaffirmed a traditional Calvinist teaching on the sense [of the heart] in describing it as a unique feeling of sweetness. But whereas Calvin and Puritan divines generally spoke of the feeling as one of gratefulness for God's mercy, Edwards, finding that moral perfection is an aesthetic quality, portrayed it as a response to divine beauty." The concept of beauty as a means of communication of God to man will be discussed later in this chapter.

27. It seems safe to conclude that Miller overstated the connection between Locke's thought and that of Edwards. See Leader, "In Love with the Image," 178n24, 178n26, for discussions of scholarly critiques of Miller's analysis of Locke's influence on Edwards. See especially 178n26. Spencer, "Jonathan Edwards and the Historiography of the American Enlightenment," 21–39, provides an incisive assessment of how the relationship between Edwards and the "Enlightenment(s)" has been analyzed since the early twentieth century. For overall assessments of Miller's presentation of Edwards, see Leader, "In Love with the Image," 174n4, 177–78n24, 178n26; Strobel, *Jonathan Edwards's Theology*, 1; Spencer, "Jonathan Edwards and the Historiography of the American Enlightenment," 27, 27n26; McClymond, "Spiritual Perception in Jonathan Edwards," 199, 199n13; Holmes, *God of Grace and God of Glory*, 20; and Schweitzer, *God Is a Communicative Being*, 1. Marsden considers Miller's biography of Edwards "influential, brilliant, and often misleading," and laments that "the most influential historian of New England" allowed "his creativity to get the best of him" in producing it. Marsden concludes, "Miller's [biographical] portrait is to [the actual] Edwards what Hamlet is to the actual Danish prince, a triumph of the imagination"; Marsden, *Jonathan Edwards*, 60, 61. Perhaps the most pungent critique of Miller's analysis is that offered in Fiering, *Jonathan Edwards's Moral Thought*, 373: "Rhetorically brilliant but utterly misleading in content, Miller's *Edwards* can only be judged an unaccountable lapse in scholarship in one of the greatest of American historians. Miller appears to have relied primarily on intuition in writing about Edwards, rather than on dogged research." Cf. Butts, "Perry Miller and the Ordeal of American Freedom," and Butts, "Myth of Perry Miller," 665–94.

Simonson, Leon Howard, Helm, and Morris have presented arguments advocating Edwards's more discriminating use of Locke: The importance of a Locke-Edwards connection is "what [Edwards] was able to assimilate from [Locke], and what stimulus he found in him for his own unusual powers"; Morris, *Young Jonathan Edwards*, 130. "That Locke was a major force behind [Edwards's intellectual] growth does not . . . lessen the claim that Edwards . . . was an independent thinker . . . . Although seized by Locke's ideas," Edwards strove "to push beyond Locke." "The peculiar nature of Locke's influence seems to have been in the questions he raised" and what his ideas "challenged [Edwards] to work out for himself," rather than in the answers he provided; Simonson, 24, 95. Edwards "was more disposed to peck at Locke than to swallow him"; if Edwards gathered up "handfuls of silver and gold" from Locke, it was done "not to hoard but to appraise"; Howard, *"The Mind" of Jonathan Edwards*, 125, 121. Edwards "draws on arguments from 'the new way of ideas' only when these serve his wider aims"; Helm, "John Locke and Jonathan Edwards," 51. Helm observes here that Edwards also utilized Locke's thoughts on human action in *FW* and on personal identity in Edwards, *Great Christian Doctrine of Original Sin Defended* (hereafter *OS*). See Ramsey, "Edwards and John Locke," 47–65,

To Understand *Things* as Well as *Words*

Locke's renown as the one in whom "the new currents of thought [in his day] all seemed to flow together," indeed as "the Father of the Enlightenment," rests largely on his landmark work, *Essay* (1690).[28] In it, he argues that a human being is born with a mind as a blank slate (*tabula rasa*), thus rejecting innate ideas. Simply stated, all human knowledge is derived from sensory experience. Ideas are formed as impressions received through the senses are unified in the mind into "one continuum of experience."[29]

Setting as his goal, "to inquire into the Original, Certainty, and Extent of humane [*sic*] Knowledge," Locke queries, "How comes [the mind] to be furnished? Whence comes it by that vast store, which the busy and boundless Fancy of Man has painted on it with an almost endless variety? Whence has it all the materials of Reason and Knowledge? To this I answer in one word, From *Experience*: In that all our Knowledge is

---

for a detailed discussion of the similarities and differences between Edwards and Locke regarding human will and understanding. See also Cherry, *Theology of Jonathan Edwards*, 15: "Above all, Locke's treatment of the human faculties and his theory of the 'simple idea' became useful for Edwards in a description of the internal dynamics of the act of faith"; Helm, "Human Self and the Divine Trinity," 93: "[Edwards's] blueprint for an understanding of the Trinity is the account of the human mind offered by John Locke" in the *Essay*. "Edwards' Lockeanism in [*Discourse on the Trinity*] is much more pervasive than has so far been appreciated." In fact, "Locke's views provide the conceptual structure for Edwards' understanding of the Trinity," with Edwards's modifications. Likewise, S. Lee: "Edwards articulates the doctrine of the Trinity using both the logic of dispositional ontology and also John Locke's psychology of the self–namely, the self, the self's reflexive idea of the self, and the self's love of the reflexive idea. The three distinctions in God, says Edwards, are "God, the idea of God, and delight in God"; Lee, "Does History Matter to God?," 3.

To argue for a Lockean influence on Edwards is not to deny that Edwards was an original thinker or that he drew upon sources other than Locke when to do so suited his purposes. See Smith, "Jonathan Edwards as Philosophical Theologian," 311n8: "The dependence on Locke must not be exaggerated as Perry Miller was inclined to do. The Cambridge Platonists were equally important, and their influence has been insufficiently emphasized." See Cherry, *Theology of Jonathan Edwards*, 19: "Though Locke proved helpful to Edwards for spelling out the type of knowledge involved in the act of faith, Edwards was by no means solely dependent in this enterprise upon Lockean insights and categories." Perhaps Edwards's stance toward Lockean epistemology is more accurately characterized as one of adoption and modification than as a "dependence." See also Phillips, "Last Edwardsean," 10–11, 11n13; Reklis, "Imagination and Hermeneutics," 311–12.

28. Locke, *Essay Concerning Human Understanding*. See Hampson, *Enlightenment*, 38; Hill, *Faith in the Age of Reason*, 34; Cassara, *Enlightenment in America*, 16; Capaldi, *Enlightenment*, 42.

29. Quotation is in Lyttle, "Sixth Sense of Jonathan Edwards," 51.

Background: Intellectual Trends Comprising "the Enlightenment(s)"

founded, and from that it ultimately derives it self."[30] Locke recognizes a two-fold division in "the Fountains of Knowledge" whence come "all the *Ideas* we have, or can naturally have."

One division is "depending wholly upon our Senses, and derived by them to the Understanding," which he calls *sensation*; the other is "the *Perception of the Operations of our own Minds* within us, as it is employed about the *Ideas* it has got," which he calls internal sense or *reflection*."[31] In summary, Locke's *Essay* begins with an extensive rejection of innate ideas, then moves to a demonstration of how knowledge is derived from ideas conveyed through the sense organs to internal sensation or reflection.[32]

Locke goes on to distinguish two categories of ideas, *simple* and *complex*. Simple ideas, "the materials of all our knowledge," are sensations such as hardness, coldness, loudness, and blueness that arrive in the mind via the senses, or reflections on these sensations. "When the understanding is once stored with these *simple ideas*, it has the power

---

30. Locke, *Essay*, 43, 104 (I.1.2; II.1.2). A major factor in his being "considered by his contemporaries one of the more dangerous and important writers of [his] day" was this *tour de force*. "Among the most widely-read philosophical texts of the eighteenth century," it appeared singly in nine English editions, and in four editions of Locke's collected works, between 1727 and 1760; Ayer, "Editorial Foreword," 11–22; MacLean, *John Locke and English Literature of the Eighteenth Century*, 3. See Taylor, *Sources of the Self*, 169: From Locke's perspective, "the whole *Essay* is directed against those who would control others by specious principles supposedly beyond question, like the ones that are allegedly 'innate.'" Through this work, Locke is credited with having founded empirical psychology; Yolton, "Preface," ix. Moreover, Locke offers here a new concept of experience and makes sweeping claims regarding its significance. This landmark essay "ultimately seeks to transform our whole sense of philosophy itself"; Chai, *Jonathan Edwards and the Limits of the Enlightenment*, 3. See McClymond, "Spiritual Perception in Jonathan Edwards," 203n27. Among the citations there are Cragg, *Reason and Authority in the Eighteenth Century*, 5–6: "Locke, beyond any other writer, was to be the moving spirit of the eighteenth century.... In every branch of intellectual endeavor his influence was supreme." Hazard, *European Thought in the Eighteenth Century*, 41, comments that in his day, "[Locke's] supremacy seemed unchallenged, and unchallengeable," and that there may be "no thinker who exerted a profounder influence on the minds of his contemporaries than did he." Indeed, "'Locke is universal,' said [William] Warburton"; MacLean, *John Locke and English Literature of the Eighteenth Century*, 2, 2n13: "*Letters from a Late Eminent Prelate* [Warburton] *to One of His Friends* [Hurd], London, [1808], p. 207. Letter of March 3, 1759." See also Fiering, *Jonathan Edwards's Moral Thought*, 40, 41n69; McCracken, *Malebranche and British Philosophy*, 18, 18n79; Henry, "Locke, John (1632–1704)," 353–54. See Ayer, "Editorial Foreword," 11–22; Yolton, "Introduction," 9: "Locke is a good place to look for anyone interested in the basic problems of philosophy."

31. Locke, *Essay*, II.1.2, II.1.3, 4.

32. Locke, *Essay*, I.1.2–3.2. See also White, *Science and Sentiment*, 11–12; Lee, *Philosophical Theology of Jonathan Edwards*, 118.

to repeat, compare, and unite them . . . and so can make at pleasure new *complex ideas.*"[33]

Up to this point, Edwards is in agreement with Locke's framework.[34] In preparation Edwards made for a work he had conceived on "The Natural History of the Mental World," he penned thoughts he classified as "Subjects to be Handled in the Treatise on the Mind." In number 29 of these, "Sensation," regarding, "How far all acts of the mind are from sensation," Edwards writes, "[A]ll ideas begin from [sensations], and there never can be any idea, thought or act of the mind unless the mind first received some ideas from sensation, or some other way equivalent, wherein the mind is wholly passive in receiving them."[35]

Furthermore, in "The Mind [42]," Edwards argues for the existence of an "infallible agreement between simple ideas" of "sounds, smells, tastes and other sensations" that allows the mind to categorize the sensations properly.[36] He explicates, "The mind perceives that some of its ideas agree, in a manner very different from all its other ideas."[37] This phenomenon activates the predisposed "habit of the mind" to order and to classify ideas: "The mind therefore is determined to rank those ideas together in its thoughts; and all new ideas it receives with the like agreement it naturally and habitually and at once places to the same rank and order and calls them by the same name; and by the nature, determination, and habit of the mind the idea of one excites the idea of others."[38] For example, because all sensations classified as sounds share a common

33. Locke, *Essay*, III.2.1–2 (emphasis added). See also Lyttle, "Supernatural Light," 2–10.

34. "In his Yale notebook [Edwards] writes that he planned to show 'how the mind would be without ideas, except as suggested by the senses.' Thus, like Locke, he held that we have no knowledge of nature until our minds are activated by the natural world"; Lyttle, "Sixth Sense of Jonathan Edwards," 50. See also Schlaeger, "Jonathan Edwards' Theory of Perception," 40.

35. Edwards, "Subjects to be Handled in the Treatise on the Mind," 390. For Edwards's further exposition of the categories of ideas, see Edwards, "Miscellany 782," 452–66. See also Anderson, "Editor's Introduction," 1–136; Chai, *Jonathan Edwards and the Limits of Enlightenment Philosophy*, 39–55; Studebaker, *Jonathan Edwards' Social Augustinian Trinitarianism*, 176–88 (N.B.: 176n129 and Studebaker's discussion of Edwards's theory of ideas in connection with Wallace Anderson's and Chai's work).

Regarding Edwards on ideas, see, e.g., Morris, "Genius of Jonathan Edwards," 35; Erdt, *Jonathan Edwards*, 26.

36. Edwards, "Mind [42]," 360. See also Edwards, "Mind [71]," 329.

37. Edwards, "Mind [42]," 361.

38. Edwards, "Mind [42]," 361. See also Lee, *Philosophical Theology of Jonathan Edwards*, 129–34.

Background: Intellectual Trends Comprising "the Enlightenment(s)"

agreement that sets them apart from other sensations, "if we had never had any such sensation as the head-ache, and should have it, I do not think we [would] call that a new sound; for there would be so manifest a disagreement between those simple ideas, of another kind from what simple ideas have one with another."[39] To summarize this point, knowledge of the natural world is gained through simple ideas as sensations from direct contact with the world.[40]

Far from maintaining solely an academic interest in epistemological questions, Edwards relished the delights of "a beautiful and lovely world" even as he analyzed how the human senses convey sensations to the mind to provide our ideas of this world.[41] In his sermon, "The Pleasantness of Religion," Edwards praises God for having "given us of his redundant bounty many things for the delight of our senses, for our pleasure and gratification . . . . There are none of the senses but God allows of the gratification of; yea, he has made much provision for their gratification."[42] Edwards's work, "Beauty of the World," is both a rhapsody to and a reflection on the sense experiences possible of the created order.[43] In it, with "the wonderful suit-

---

39. Edwards, "Mind [42]" 361.

40. See Lee, *Philosophical Theology of Jonathan Edwards*, 124. Up to this point, "Edwards accepted the fundamental concerns of Locke's empiricism." See also Smith, "Jonathan Edwards and 'The Way of Ideas,'" 153; Laurence, "Jonathan Edwards, John Locke, and the Canon of Experience," 107–23; and Kim, "Jonathan Edwards's Reshaping of Lockean Terminology," 108–9.

41. Quotation is in Edwards, "Beauty of the World," 306. This selection is also included in Edwards, *Images or Shadows of Divine Things*, 135–37, and in Smith et al., *Jonathan Edwards Reader* (hereafter *JER*) 14–15.

42. Edwards, "Pleasantness of Religion," 102; Kimnach et al., *Sermons of Jonathan Edwards: A Reader* (hereafter *SJER*), 15.

43. Foremost for Edwards, his "depiction of nature itself as a vehicle through which God speaks to the believer without nature becoming deified or merging with the identity of the viewer never strays from the orthodox Calvinism he so staunchly defended; there was a broad precedent in Protestant thought for interpreting just how 'the heavens declare the glory of God; and the firmament sheweth his handywork (Ps 19),'" with which Edwards was familiar. In setting forth his view of creation/nature as a medium of divine communication, Edwards "locates in the natural world a typological rather than pantheistic or romantic sense of the divine; the boundaries between natural type and supernatural antitype are held in a tension that ensures both their separateness and their continued 'desire' for each other, a connection that evokes an 'iconic' rather than an idolatrous response from Edwards"; Leader, "'In Love with the Image,'" 174n5, 172. Overall, to Edwards, the natural world is "a shadow of divinity," an "image or shadow of divine things" that demonstrates the wisdom and creativity of the "divine designing consciousness"; Lyttle, "Supernatural Light," 1; Edwards, *Images or Shadows of Divine Things*; Jenson, *America's Theologian*, 15–18; Schlaeger, "Jonathan Edwards' Theory of Perception," 1. "[T]he whole outward creation, which is but the shadows of beings, is

ableness of green for the grass and plants, the blue of the sky, the white of the clouds, the colors of flowers . . . the gentle motions of trees, of lily, etc." on his mind, Edwards contemplates what properties allow the ideas which the sense experiences present to the mind to appear with such magnificence: viz., "a complicated proportion . . . one with another, either in the magnitude of the rays, the number of vibrations that are caused in the optic nerve, or some other way."[44] He then distinguishes between "beauties that are more palpable and explicable," that "[please] us and we can tell why," and "hidden and secret beauties" which "delight us and we can't tell why."[45] Those in the latter category principally constitute the world, muses Edwards: "These hidden beauties are commonly by far the greatest, because the more complex a beauty is, the more hidden is it."[46]

This realization provides Edwards with his point of departure from Locke's epistemological structure.[47] Natural, unregenerate human beings can experience sensations from the world only through the natural senses. As Locke observes, all the ideas a person can "*naturally* have" derive from the natural senses and from reflection on these ideas, because these senses and this capacity of reflection are the only cognitive faculties that natural man possesses.[48] For Edwards the theologian, this is a result of

---

so made as to represent spiritual things"; Lane, "Jonathan Edwards on Beauty, Desire, and the Sensory World," 44–72; Marini, "Seeing Happiness," 251: "In [Edwards's] encounters with nature, language, and fellow humans, there [were] no mute elements. *Everything* in Edwards's cosmology had some internal truth to communicate" (emphasis in original); For Edwards, the natural world is a "school of desire" in which regenerate persons "learn to apprehend God's glory"; Lane, "Jonathan Edwards on Beauty, Desire, and the Sensory World," 44. The "inferior and shadowy parts of [God's] works . . . represent those things that are more real and excellent, spiritual and divine" so as "to shadow them forth"; Edwards, "Miscellany 362," 434. See also Edwards, "Personal Narrative," 793; Bush, "Jesus Christ in the Theology of Jonathan Edwards," 249–50; Cooey, *Jonathan Edwards on Nature and Destiny*, 12, 15, 160, 161; Schweitzer, *God Is a Communicative Being*, 27; Stievermann, "History, Providence, and Eschatology," 217–18. The theme of creation as reflecting the beauty and harmony of the Godhead will be examined later in this chapter.

44. Edwards, "Beauty of the World," 305; Edwards, *Images or Shadows of Divine Things*, 135; *JER*, 14.

45. Edwards, "Beauty of the World," 305; Edwards, *Images or Shadows of Divine Things*, 136; *JER*, 15.

46. Edwards, "Beauty of the World," 306; Edwards, *Images or Shadows of Divine Things*, 136; *JER*, 15.

47. See Edwards, *Religious Affections* (hereafter *RA*), 205–39; Miller's introduction in Edwards, *Images or Shadows of Divine Things*, 19; Elwood, *Philosophical Theology of Jonathan Edwards*, 123–25; Schlaeger, "Jonathan Edwards' Theory of Perception," 70–73.

48. Quotation is from Locke, *Essay*, II.1.2 (emphasis added.) See also Locke, III.1.

the Fall and its consequent curse on Adam's posterity. As created, there existed a two-fold image of God in man: "his moral or spiritual image," which is "the image of God's moral excellency," and "God's natural image," manifested in human beings' "Reason, understanding, [and] natural ability."[49] The original sin of disobedience resulted in God's withdrawing from humanity's primordial parents the "superior principles ... wherein consisted the spiritual image of God, and man's righteousness and true holiness; which are called in Scripture the *divine nature*."[50] This resulted in the loss of the "moral excellency" aspect of the *imago Dei* in man.[51]

These divinely-implanted attributes were "summarily comprehended in divine love [and] may, in some sense, be called supernatural."[52] These "superior principles" empowered "man's union and communion with God, or divine communications and influences of God's Spirit," and, thus, enabled Adam and Eve to maintain a right relationship with God through rightly ordered affectional orientations.[53] Their withdrawal and the loss of the moral image of God in man left human beings only with the "inferior principles of self-love and natural appetite," or "mere human nature."[54] Consequently, "communion with God ... entirely ceased," as a result of the disordering of the primordial parents' affections and the loss of their *will* (but not natural *ability*) to communicate with God.[55]

1–6, IV. xviii. 4: A person "has no greater assurance than that of his sense"; Schlaeger, "Jonathan Edwards' Theory of Perception," 72–74.

49. *RA*, 256; Edwards, "Chapter IV: Literary Theory and Practice," 195: "Reason ... is the natural image of God in man"; Strobel, "Being Seen and Being Known," 160. See also Faust, "Jonathan Edwards' View of Human Nature"; Barnett, "Doctrine of Man in the Theology of Jonathan Edwards"; Crabtree, *Jonathan Edwards' View of Man*, 21–22; Oliphint, "Jonathan Edwards on Apologetics," 135–43 (complete selection is 131–46). See McDermott, *Jonathan Edwards Confronts the Gods*, 56; Edwards, "Miscellany 210. Spirit of God"; Edwards, "Sermon 110. On Job 31:3, 1729," 195; Edwards, "Sermon 373. Rom. 2:10. Decem[ber] 17, 1735"; Edwards, Sermon "Wicked Men's Slavery to Sin," 347; Edwards, *OS*, 168; Edwards, "Value of Salvation," 309; McDermott, *Jonathan Edwards Confronts the Gods*, 56n3.

50. Edwards, *OS*, 381. See also Strobel, "Being Seen and Being Known," 161–63; Slater, *Children in the New England Mind in Death and in Life*, 60–61; Brekus, "Children of Wrath, Children of Grace," 310.

51. *RA*, 256; Edwards, "Pure in Heart Blessed," 67. See also Crabtree, *Jonathan Edwards' View of Man*, 24–26; Oliphint, "Jonathan Edwards on Apologetics," 136; Studebaker, *Jonathan Edwards' Social Augustinian Trinitarianism*, 140n13–42n23.

52. Edwards, *OS*, 381.

53. Edwards, *OS*, 382.

54. Edwards, *OS*, 381. See also Edwards, "Sermon 795," 1086.

55. Edwards, *OS*, 382.

This corrupted human nature has been inherited by Adam's posterity, as all of humanity sinned in him.[56] "And therefore, as God withdrew spiritual communion and his vital gracious influence from the common head [i.e., Adam], so he withholds the same from all the members, as they come into existence."[57] As a result, unregenerate persons are equipped only with the "natural and inferior principles; and so become wholly corrupt, as Adam did."[58]

A solution, however, is possible; one which removes the curse of the Fall. Conversion, or regeneration, "through the saving influences of the Spirit of God," brings about "a new inward perception or sensation" in the mind of a person who experiences it that is "entirely of a new sort," "entirely different in its nature and kind" from any sensation he or she could have experienced previously.[59] Edwards the philosopher, adopting Locke's terminology, refers to this as "a new simple idea."[60] Being "an entirely new

---

56. Edwards, OS, 382, 398–99. See also Crabtree, *Jonathan Edwards' View of Man*, 23, 35; Lyttle, "Jonathan Edwards on Personal Identity," 21–32; Keating, "Personal Identity in Jonathan Edwards"; Chaney, "God's Glorious Work," 28–29; Storms, *Tragedy in Eden*; Helm, "Jonathan Edwards on Original Sin," 152–76; Holifield, "Edwards as Theologian," 150; Everhard, "Original Sin [Doctrine]," 424–27; Biehl, "*Original Sin* (1758)," 427–30.

This section of OS contains a significant instance of Edwards using a Lockean concept as a point of departure for his own purpose. In his argument contending for the constitution of humanity in Adam, Edwards uses Locke's definition of personal identity to argue that it is necessary but not sufficient: "[I]f we come even to the *personal identity* of created intelligent beings, though this be not allowed to consist wholly in that which Mr. Locke places it in, i.e., *same consciousness*; yet I think it can't be denied, that this is one thing essential to it." Edwards goes on to maintain that "identity of consciousness depends wholly on a law of nature, and so, on the sovereign will and agency of God; and therefore, that personal identity, and so the derivation of the pollution and guilt of past sins in the same person, depends on an arbitrary divine constitution"; Locke, *Essay*, II.27.19; Edwards, OS, 398, 399 (emphasis in original). See Cooley, "New England Theology and the Atonement," 56–57 and 57–58n67.

57. Edwards, OS, 383. See Minkema, "Edwardses," 275–81; see Van Vlastuin, "Federalism and Reformed Scholasticism," 183–98, for an examination of Edwards's stance on the covenant of works and the covenant of grace applied to Adam and his posterity in the context of the Reformed tradition.

58. Edwards, OS. 383. See also Edwards, "Part III: First Sign," 208–39.

59. RA, 205.

60. RA, 205. Edwards acknowledges that this term has originated with "some metaphysicians," but it seems clear that Locke is one source in mind. See Locke, *Essay*, II.2. 1, II.7. 1–10, II.8.1; Morris, "Genius of Jonathan Edwards," 34; Smith, "Jonathan Edwards as Philosophical Theologian," 311; Cherry, *Theology of Jonathan Edwards*, 15; Helm, "Forensic Dilemma," 45; Helm, "Epistemology," 112; Chamberlain, "Editor's Introduction," 39.

kind of principle," it produces "in the soul a new sort of exercises which it is conscious of, which the soul knew nothing of before."[61] This "new spiritual sense" is "a new foundation laid in the nature of the soul" that allows regenerate persons ("saints") to delight in "spiritual and divine things," that is, "a real sense of the excellency of God, and Jesus Christ, and of the work of redemption, and of the ways and works of God revealed in the gospel."[62]

In his sermon, "A Divine and Supernatural Light," Edwards gives a detailed analysis of the "twofold understanding or knowledge of good, that God has made the mind of man capable of": "The first [is] that which is merely *speculative* or *notional*: as when a person only speculatively judges, which by the agreement of mankind, is called good or excellent."[63] Here, Edwards is making use of Locke's analysis: "*The Mind often exercises an active Power in making these* several *Combinations*" of simple ideas. Once furnished with simple ideas, the mind can combine them into complex ideas; "and hence, I think, it is, that these *Ideas* are called *Notions*."[64] In addition, in what Edwards calls "a 'speculative' approach," a person "considers the problem abstractly but is not engaged."[65] Either a regenerate or an unregenerate person can judge in this way regarding whether a complex idea would "by the agreement of mankind" be "called good or excellent" by reflection on "that which is most to general advantage . . . and the like."[66]

---

61. *RA*, 205.

62. *RA*, 206; Edwards, "Divine and Supernatural Light," 413 (the complete selection is 408–26). This selection is also included in Edwards, *Jonathan Edwards: Representative Selections* (hereafter *JERS*), 102–11 (passage cited here is on 106), and included with the year of its delivery as 1734 in *JER*, 105–24 (passage cited here is on 111), and in *SJER*, 121–40 (passage cited here is on 127.) See also Holifield, "Edwards as Theologian," 147; Edwards, "Personal Narrative," 790–804, 794, 793. Hambrick-Stowe, "'Inward, Sweet Sense' of Christ in Jonathan Edwards," 79–95, provides an extensive examination of the "Personal Narrative" in the context of Edwards's struggles with his conversion experience and his post-conversion spiritual condition.

63. Edwards, "Divine and Supernatural Light," 413; *JERS*, 106; *JER*, 111; *SJER*, 127.

64. Locke, *Essay*, II.22.2.

65. Smith, "Editor's Introduction," 47. See also Edwards, "Mind," 374: Humans "are capable of reflecting upon what passes in their own minds . . . [persons] are capable of viewing what is in themselves contemplatively . . . . [T]he minds of [human beings] are not only passive but [also] abundantly active"; Tan, "Anthropology, Affections, and Free Will," 251: "The intellect includes [both] the passive and active powers for perception and speculation."

66. Edwards, "Divine and Supernatural Light," 413; *JERS*, 106–7; *JER*, 111; *SJER*, 127.

The second, more profound understanding of which Edwards speaks is "super-empirical" or "supraphysical"; that is, it transcends knowledge provided by the natural senses.[67] This new understanding to which Edwards refers consists in "a new spiritual sense that the mind has" which enables "an entirely new kind of perception or spiritual sensation" of "spiritual and divine things."[68] To use a favorite example of Edwards's, the supernatural things perceived by the exercise of this spiritual sense are as qualitatively different from perceptions via the natural senses "as the sweet taste of honey is diverse from the ideas men get of honey by only looking on it, and feeling of it."[69]

LOCKE AND EDWARDS REGARDING EDUCATION

A study of Locke's and Edwards's views on education reveals significant differences regarding both the foundation of and the purposes of education. These differences result from these two men's fundamentally dissimilar conceptions of human nature, the essence of Christianity, and the definition of "virtue."

At the outset, a striking contrast is evident in each one's presuppositions concerning human nature. As noted above, Locke argues that persons are born with no innate ideas, with minds as "blank slates" upon which experiences of sense data (and reflections on them) inscribe all knowledge. He also rejects the orthodox Reformed view of innate depravity through imputation of original sin.[70] On the subject of "a state of necessary sinning and provoking God in every action that men do" as a consequence of the curse of the Fall, Locke writes disbelievingly,

---

67. White, *Science and Sentiment in America*, 34; Elwood, *Philosophical Theology of Jonathan Edwards*, 123.

68. RA, 205. However, "God deals with man as with a rational creature" in the conversion process through impression on the senses and on the faculty of understanding; Edwards, "Importance and Advantage," 88, 31.

69. RA, 206. Edwards's use of the descriptions "new spiritual sense that the *mind* has" and "this new sense of the *mind*" emphasizes the mind's *consciousness* of this sense and of its effects. His use of the description "the sense of the *heart*" emphasizes the *effects* themselves on a person's *will* or *inclination* on the basis of this sense. See Edwards, "Divine and Supernatural Light," 413; JERS, 107; JER, 111; SJER, 127–28; White, *Science and Sentiment in America*, 33. RA, 96, goes into a fuller discussion of this distinction.

70. Yolton, *Locke: An Introduction*, 35; Aaron, *John Locke*, 296: "Justification by Faith does not . . . in Locke's opinion, involve Original Sin, and so it does not involve Atonement in the usual sense." See also Schweitzer, *God Is a Communicative Being*, 21n41; Hill, *Faith in the Age of Reason*, 155–56.

Background: Intellectual Trends Comprising "the Enlightenment(s)"

"Could a *worthy man* be supposed to put such terms upon the obedience of his subjects? Much less can the *righteous God* be supposed, as the punishment of one sin [of Adam] wherein he is displeased, to put man under the necessity of sinning continually, and so multiplying the provocation."[71] He continues, "If by death, threatened to Adam, were meant the corruption of human nature in his posterity, it is strange that the New Testament should not anywhere take notice of it and tell us that corruption seized upon all because of Adam's transgression."[72] Most significantly, Locke maintains that Reason should be the judge of revelation as the "explainer, developer, and utilizer" of ideas. Owing to "man's innate capacity to reason," there exist "self-declared and self-evidenced criteria of truth, of things within the reach of his natural faculties."[73]

Regarding a pedagogical program, instruction in character and inculcation primarily in virtue (as Locke conceived it) and also in manners and industriousness, matter more to Locke than education in specific subjects. Locke's concept of educational goals is contextualized by "the seventeenth-century notion of a young gentleman," in which "virtue is the health of the soul [and] the aim of education is to produce a healthy, virtuous person."[74] Central to achieving this objective is a method that has as its primary purpose making "the Principles and Practices of Vertue, and good Breeding" part of a child's nature.[75] In doing so, emphasized is the "efficacy of right habits formed early in life" while taking into account differences in children's "temperaments and rhythms of development," so as to accommodate "the educational program to the child, not the child to the program."[76] Specifically, Locke urges instruction in Scripture to children. However, this seems to be set in a context of the necessity of a

---

71. Locke, *Reasonableness of Christianity as Delivered in the Scriptures*, 9, emphasis added. Woodbridge and James, *From Pre-Reformation to the Present Day*, 371, observe that this very title "underscore[s] the central role reason played in [Locke's] formulation of Christianity."

72. Locke, *Reasonableness of Christianity*, 9–10. In fact, the New Testament states this doctrine of imputation in Rom 5:12.

73. Ewing, *Reasonableness of Christianity*, xvii–xviii. See Locke, *Essay*, IV. 28. 2–11; Brown, "Edwards, Locke, and the Bible," 367–69.

74. See Locke, *Some Thoughts Concerning Education*, 128–33 (§ 70–§ 71, 94); Yolton, *Locke: An Introduction*, 35; Yolton, *John Locke and Education*, 69; Yolton and Yolton, "Introduction," 18.

75. Locke, *Some Thoughts Concerning Education*, § 70, 94. See also Locke, *Of the Conduct of the Understanding*, 87, 63; Cremin, *American Education: The Colonial Experience, 1607–1783*, 364, 364n7.

76. Axtell, "'Education' in Context," 52.

To Understand *Things* as Well as *Words*

"Knowledge of Vertue" through being "informed in [its] Principles and Precepts" and "Moral Rules" for the "Conduct of his Life" being essential in the make-up of a "Vertuous and well-behaved young man."[77]

Locke self-identified as a Christian.[78] Nevertheless, he and Edwards conceived of Christianity in decidedly distinct ways. Locke's approach is one in which what is scripturally normative is subject to discovery by (and apparently capable of obedience by) the right use of Reason, for "Reason is the voice of God in man."[79] Human beings, as a gift from their Maker, "have light enough to lead them to the knowledge of their Maker, and [to] the sight of their own duties" of worship and obedience owed to him. Thus, for Locke, moral rules are either laws of nature or derivations from such laws. "Discovery of the laws of nature can be made by reading the Scriptures . . . But laws of nature (and hence moral rules as well) are also laws of reason."[80] Therefore, no divine revelation in Scripture will contradict what can be discovered by reason, for "Christianity is reasonable."[81]

---

77. Locke, *Some Thoughts Concerning Education*, 160, § 185; 135, § 159; 160–61, § 186.

78. "Second Vindication of the Reasonableness of Christianity (1697)," in Locke, *Works of John Locke*, 7:359: "A Christian I am sure I am." See also Locke, "Letter to the Right Reverend Edward," 4:96; Locke, "Letter to the Reverend Mr. Richard King," 10:306; Cremin, *American Education*, 278; Woodbridge and James, *From Pre-Reformation to the Present Day*, 370, 371. Cf. McLachlan, *Religious Opinions of Milton, Locke, and Newton*, 107; Schweitzer, *God Is a Communicative Being*, 21n41; Hill, *Faith in the Age of Reason*, 155–56; Stephen, *History of English Thought in the Eighteenth Century*, 1:83–84; Yolton, *Locke Reader*, 3–4, 4n6; Redwood, *Reason, Ridicule and Religion*, 101, 162; Lucci, *Scripture and Deism*, 44–52. N.B.: "[I]t was, above all, Locke's 'way of ideas' that influenced deistic hermeneutical methodologies, especially [John] Toland's and [Anthony] Collins's biblical criticism" (44); "The deists were strongly influenced by Locke's theories on religion" (51).

79. Yolton, *Locke: An Introduction*, 35.

80. Ewing, "Introduction," xviii. See Locke, *Essay*, I.II.3, I.IV.31: "The Candle [of natural Reason], which is set up in us, shines bright[ly] enough for *all* our Purposes (emphasis added); God "hath furnished Man with those Faculties which will serve for the sufficient discovery of all things requisite for the discovery of such a Being." See also Morris, *Young Jonathan Edwards*, 140, commenting on Locke's position: "We [humans] are given light sufficient for our purposes."

81. Aaron, *John Locke*, 296. See also Aaron, *John Locke*, 25–27; Yolton and Yolton, "Introduction," 26: "Locke's answer to the question, 'How am I to recognize the obligation to obey God?', is that reason tells us we are God's creatures and hence should obey his laws. Revelation supports reason (being indeed described as 'natural reason'), and the prospect of eternal punishment or reward gives an incentive towards virtue." See Locke, *Essay*, IV.18.1–6; Cremin, *American Education*, 274–75; Laurence, "Jonathan Edwards, John Locke, and the Canon of Experience," 110; Helm, "Epistemology," 112; Nichols, *Absolute Sort of Certainty*, 40: "In short, Locke's work posits the autonomy of

Background: Intellectual Trends Comprising "the Enlightenment(s)"

In Locke's interpretation, "What we are now required to believe ['under the revelation of the gospel'] to obtain eternal life" is "believing on the Son"; i.e., that Jesus Christ is the Son of God.[82] He continues, "[I]t is plain [in John 4] that believing on the Son is the believing that Jesus was the Messiah, giving credit to the miracles he did and the profession he made of himself."[83] Notably absent from this exegesis is awareness of a necessity of individual supernatural conversion in order to meet this standard.[84]

---

reason [and] dismisses the Reformation principles of the authority and necessity of Scripture.... Edwards could not disagree more with these conclusions."

Cf. Edwards: "Christian divinity ... is not evident by the light of nature; it depends on [divine] revelation. Such are our circumstances now in our fallen state, that nothing which is needful for us to know concerning God, is manifest by the light of nature in the manner in which it is necessary for us to know it"; Edwards, "Importance and Advantage," 86, 29; Oliphint, "Jonathan Edwards on Apologetics," 137: "Though people may have a kind of knowledge that is useful and helpful in a limited way, that knowledge, when according to the natural image [of reason after the Fall] will not and cannot produce spiritual light"; Crabtree, *Jonathan Edwards' View of Man*, 37: To Edwards, "apart from God's revelation in Christ we can know nothing of his grace and forgiveness"(cf. Crabtree, 38–39). In man's natural state, *awareness* of a moral obligation does not *enable* one to meet it; *inclination* toward reward and away from punishment does not *enable* one to achieve the one and avoid the other.

82. Locke, *Reasonableness of Christianity*, 26.

83. Locke, *Reasonableness of Christianity*, 26–27. See Lyttle, "Sixth Sense of Jonathan Edwards," 52–53.

84. Herein lies a fundamental contrast between Locke and Edwards. See Walton, *Jonathan Edwards, Religious Affections, and the Puritan Analysis*, 25, 25n102: "Whereas Locke denied that personal illumination was a necessary and indispensable qualification for a true Christian, Edwards defined the true Christian according to this very criterion. Locke considered 'submission to Scripture' and 'assent to the religious truths set forth in scripture' sufficient to make a true Christian. For Edwards, mere assent of this kind was not enough to constitute genuine piety."

Cf. Turner, "John Locke, Christian Mission, and Colonial America," 267–97. Citing both previously neglected and new documentary evidence, Turner argues that "Locke both supported organized efforts to spread Christianity among New World slaves and Indians and used his influence within King William's Board of Trade [as secretary] to advance these efforts." Turner locates Locke's support for evangelization within his commitment to religious toleration (270). "Locke exemplifies the early Enlightenment tradition of evangelical tolerationism" (284). In his *Second Letter Concerning Toleration* (1690), Locke argues against use of force in evangelization, writing, "We pray every day for their conversion," regarding pagans, Muslims, and Jews; Turner, "John Locke, Christian Mission, and Colonial America," 291. Additionally, Turner argues, "Locke nicely conjoins the issues of Christian mission and toleration when he voices contempt for 'those men' who, however much they pray for Pagans, are so unconcerned for their conversion that they 'will neither go to them to instruct them, nor suffer them to come to us for the means of conversion'"; *Third Letter for Toleration* (1692), in Locke, *Works of John Locke*, 234; Turner, "John Locke, Christian Mission, and Colonial America," 293, 293n126. However, nowhere does this article cite Locke's definition of "conversion." It

Formed by substantially different convictions, Edwards's educational ideal stands in contrast to that of Locke. "The Bible formed the core of Edwards's understanding of reality," and sanctified Reason was necessary to comprehend correctly both it and the world.[85] Additionally, coming as he did from a Puritan background, for Edwards, character formation was an essential objective of a proper education. This aim was shaped, however, by what was believed to be possible given the human condition. As has been made clear, Edwards, in contradistinction to Locke, considered human nature to be corrupted by original sin. In an extensive polemic that constitutes one of his major works, Edwards examined "whether we have any evidence that the heart of man is naturally of a corrupt and evil disposition," and, if so, the cause(s).[86] In *The Great Christian Doctrine of Original Sin Defended* (known as *Original Sin*, 1758), he explicates the depravity of the human heart as fact from observable experience and the imputation of Adam's sin to his posterity on scriptural grounds.

The "corrupt and depraved" natural state of mankind is demonstrated by the "universal effectual tendency to sin," manifesting itself in "mankind in general, through all countries, nations, and ages, and in all conditions."[87] This proclivity results from a "pernicious tendency belonging to [human] nature," which is "corrupt as [a person] comes into the world."[88] This tendency begins appearing early in individual lives because of a fixed internal cause, that is, "the established union between Adam and his posterity" (similar to the union of the roots and branches of a tree as constituting one organism), and leads to individual commission of sins.[89]

---

seems established that Locke did not hold to the Christian orthodox view of imputation of guilt of original sin. If this is true, it would follow that he and Edwards would not have had the same concept of Christian conversion. Therefore, for the purposes of this study, Locke's influence on Edwards's pedagogical methodology through partial agreement regarding the nature of ideas seems conclusive, but not on Edwards's view of the fallen condition of human nature and of the ultimate goal of education.

85. Quotation is in Brown, "Biblical Exegesis," 370.
86. Quotation is in *OS*, 107.
87. *OS*, 113, 126, 125.
88. *OS*, 126, 137.
89. *OS*, 193, 408. See also Holifield, "Edwards as Theologian," 150; Brekus, "Children of Wrath, Children of Grace," 309: In *OS*, Edwards "moved beyond the traditional view of 'imputation' to offer a *new interpretation* of original sin," insisting that "all humans had been metaphysically present with Adam in the Garden of Eden. Just as a tree had many branches but was still one discrete organism, all of humanity was a single entity" (emphasis added); Allen, "Holy Children are Happy Children," 24. Cf. Everhard, 329–30: In *OS*, "Edwards labors hard to defend the *traditional view* of original sin.... Like Adam, all of humanity share in the consequences of our foreparents' rebellious

Background: Intellectual Trends Comprising "the Enlightenment(s)"

Moreover, how Locke and Edwards each viewed "virtue" also differs markedly. "True virtue," to Edwards, consists in "a 'relish' and 'taste' for divine things, that loving consent to Being as such."[90] As he expresses it, "True virtue most essentially consists in benevolence to being in general," or, more simply stated, love of God, which is "exercised in a general good will."[91] Edwards expounds elsewhere, "holiness comprehends all the true moral excellency of intelligent beings: there is no other true virtue, but real holiness."[92] Furthermore, "Holiness comprehends all the true virtue of a good [person], his love to God, his gracious love to [persons], his justice, his charity, and bowels of mercies, his gracious meekness and gentleness, and all other true Christian virtues that he has, belong to his holiness."[93]

While instilling in students standards of ethical behavior is an essential component of education, "true virtue" can result only from regeneration and the "new spiritual sense" to experience and to comprehend the things of God that it brings. Virtue in its fullest sense is not simply moral behavior according to prescribed rules. *Contra* Locke, it cannot be

---

action in the Garden of Eden . . . . Edwards argues for the *traditional view* of sin . . . [but] uses creative arguments never before utilized in the long history of this discussion" (emphasis added). See also Slater, *Children in the New England Mind in Death and in Life,* 20: In the "Augustinian-federal" (or "covenant") conception of original sin, Adam "had covenanted with God to serve as the representative of the human race for all time to come. His crime [of disobedience] was therefore humanity's crime, the resultant guilt charged ('imputed') to each and every one of Adam's descendents down through the ages." This view "meant that all future [human beings] inherited depraved natures" that are "the cause[s] of the many sins that each individual personally committed during his life ('actual sin')"; see Slater, *Children in the New England Mind in Death and in Life,* 168–69n24; see Crabtree, *Jonathan Edwards' View of Man,* 31–36, for a discussion of Edwards's "Idealistic Identity" view of personal identity. Van Vlastuin, "Federalism and Reformed Scholasticism," 183–98, concludes, "In the broader Reformed and Puritan tradition Edwards has his own place," and contends, "[His] approach differs from the understanding of the covenant in the Reformation and in the *Westminster Confession*," 195. See also Holifield, "Edwards as Theologian," 157–58. See Crisp, "On the Theological Pedigree of Jonathan Edwards' Doctrine of Imputation," 308–27; Crisp, *Jonathan Edwards and the Metaphysics of Sin;* Helm, "Different Kind of Calvinism?," 91–103; Campos, "Re-formed Understanding of Imputation in Jonathan Edwards's Original Sin," 223–43; Barshinger, "Sin and Evil," 235–49, especially 241–46; Hussey and McClymond, "Creation and Predestination," 199–214, especially 209–11.

90. Holbrook, "Editor's Introduction," 36.
91. *TV,* 540. See also Crabtree, *Jonathan Edwards' View of Man,* 29–30.
92. *RA,* 255.
93. *RA,* 255.

taught; it can only be pointed toward and encouraged as students are put on the way to receive regenerating grace.[94]

As an educator, Edwards was particularly concerned with developing in his students both of the senses of understanding discussed above. In a detailed declaration of his pedagogical philosophy and his view of the aims of education, Edwards laments the inadequacies of the method of education then used at the Stockbridge mission school, whereby the children there were "habituated to learning without understanding."[95] Instruction by rote memorization had produced results no more extensive than the "habit of making such and such sounds, on the sight of such and such marks, with a perfect inattentiveness to any meaning."[96] This means that the students were not developing the capacities to associate words with their referents, to reflect on the connections between ideas and the words which served as their signs, or to reflect on the associations of ideas and of words with one another.

In his discussion of children's acquisition of knowledge through ideas, Locke observes of the process by which language is learned thus: "The Senses at first let in particular *Ideas*, and furnish the yet empty Cabinet."[97] Through the repetition of these occurrences, the mind becomes familiar with them and they "are lodged in the Memory, and Names [affixed] to them. Afterwards the Mind, proceeding farther, abstracts them, and by Degrees learns the use of general Names. In this manner the Mind comes to be furnished with *Ideas* and Language, the Materials about which to exercise its discursive Faculty."[98] Since Locke rejected the concept of innate ideas, a person's learning to develop these capacities required guidance through instruction.

An egregious inadequacy of the instructional system at Stockbridge before Edwards assumed its control was the fact that this progression was not happening. In Lockean terminology, the students were failing (through neglect in their instruction) to reflect on the connections between ideas (simple and complex) and words as *signs* of the ideas, and on connections of ideas and words with one another.[99] Moreover, this

---

94. See Lovejoy, "Samuel Hopkins," 232; Price, "Jonathan Edwards as a Christian Educator," 56.

95. *LPW*, 407.

96. *LPW*, 407.

97. Locke, *Essay*, I.2.15; II.25.1–33.19.

98. Locke, *Essay*, I.2.15; II.25.1–33.19.

99. Locke, *Essay*, III.2.1–8.

Background: Intellectual Trends Comprising "the Enlightenment(s)"

defective program of education was not limited to the youngest students. Edwards notes that, regrettably, it persisted "even a long time after [the children] are capable of understanding."[100]

As a remedy, Edwards proposed a radical departure from this system. Memorization would be kept to the minimum necessary for the introductory material. The teacher and the students would ask questions of each other in a dialogic approach to lessons in which the students would be encouraged to participate freely. In this procedure, the instructor would be responsible "that the [students] be made to attend to, and understand, the meaning[s] of the words and sentences which [they read]."[101]

This would require development of the capacities of understanding that were being neglected in the system that Edwards deplored. Edwards was convinced that, by age-appropriate means, an educator should stimulate and assist in advancing students' capabilities of comprehension through dialogic interaction. In Edwards's analysis, this methodology would benefit the student as "his [or her] mind will gradually open and expand with knowledge, and his capacity for reasoning [be] improved," as he or she would come to make the proper associations between ideas and words and draw conclusions from doing so.[102]

Of equal significance, as the student would come to see the connections among the words learned, the ideas they signify, and the world which the student, the ideas, and the words and their referents inhabit, "learning will be rendered pleasant, entertaining and profitable."[103] Beyond the specific subject matter taught in this way, this procedure would set the student on the path to becoming a lifelong learner: If begun early, it would "accustom the child . . . to think and reflect, and to beget in it an early taste for knowledge, and a regularly increasing appetite for it."[104]

As vital as development of students' natural understanding and intellectual capacities was to Edwards, it was preparatory to his ultimate pedagogical goal. Crucial to Edwards as an educator was placing students in the way to receive the "new simple idea" of regeneration in order for them to experience the "new spiritual sense." In his credo on education that he shared in the aforementioned letter to Pepperrell, Edwards stated that the Bible, Psalter, and catechism, through being

100. *LPW*, 407.
101. *LPW*, 408.
102. *LPW*, 407.
103. *LPW*, 407.
104. *LPW*, 408.

communicated in a "familiar [i.e., dialogic] manner," should be "opened to the child's understanding."[105] The teacher, envisioned Edwards, encouraging the students to "speak freely, and [each] in his turn also to ask questions," should teach lessons based on "a short general scheme of the scriptural history," based on stories drawn from both the Old and New Testaments.[106]

This methodology would achieve a threefold goal: developing in students "the habit of conversation on divine things," encouraging the students to read Scripture on their own as they become able to do so, and placing them, through openness to Scripture and the gospel, on the way to conversion, "the main design of the whole Indian establishment at this place."[107] Thus, for Edwards, ultimately successful pedagogical technique is holistic, engaging the entire capacities of intellect, will, and affections to achieve a tripartite objective: "informing [a student's] under-standing, influencing his heart, and directing its practice."[108]

Although Locke and Edwards differed fundamentally regarding the nature of the Christian faith and the purpose of education, Locke does seem to have influenced Edwards's pedagogy with respect to the connection between words and ideas. Witness Edwards's work *Misrepresentations Corrected, and Truth Vindicated* (1752), which arises out of the "communion controversy" that was the primary factor in his dismissal from his Northampton pastorate. A response in print to an attack by Solomon Williams on Edwards's position on qualifications for communion, the treatise is divided into three parts, the first treating concisely the "general misrepresentations" that Williams makes of the *Humble Inquiry*, the second providing a cogent examination of Williams's own design, and the third offering a commentary on Willams's line of reasoning.[109]

Regarding Williams's position on communion, to Edwards's astonishment, "it must be agreeable to Mr. Williams' scheme, that a man has a right to make a profession of godliness, without having godliness, and without any dictate of his conscience that he has the thing he professes, yea, though he knows he has it not!"[110] This leads Edwards to comment, "This notion of a solemn profession of godliness, in words of a double

---

105. *LPW*, 408.
106. *LPW*, 409.
107. *LPW*, 411.
108. *LPW*, 409.
109. See Hall, "Misrepresentations Corrected," 74–77.
110. *EW*, 388–89.

meaning, without any marks of difference in their signification, is the great peculiarity of Mr. Williams' scheme; and in all his controversy with me, this appears to be the main hinge, the crisis of the whole affair."[111] Edwards then goes on to state that if someone uses words "which have no distinguishing signification, or without any signs or discriminating marks by which men may be enabled to distinguish what he means," the words convey no meaning: They are "vain to the pretended purpose . . . which is to convey the thing meant to others' understanding."[112] Here, Edwards notes, "Mr. Locke says, *Human Understanding*, ed. 7, vol. 2. p.103. 'He that uses words of any language without distinct ideas in his mind, to which he applies them does so far as he uses [them], in discourse, only make[s] a noise without any sense or significations.'"[113]

A significant criticism Edwards made of the method of instruction at Stockbridge in place upon his arrival was that a similar confusion there prevented genuine learning from occurring. Instruction by rote memorization had produced only the children's "habit of making such and such sounds, on the sight of such and such letters," with no comprehension of the meanings of the sounds.[114] Edwards determined as a teacher to enable the students to come to associate the words with the ideas they signified. Having examined Locke in connection with Edwards's pedagogy, let us now move on to the influence of Newtonian physics and optics on Edwards the educator.

NEWTONIAN SCIENCE

Although the claim that Edwards "learned his philosophy from Locke and his science from Newton" may be an exaggeration, no less so than

---

111. *EW*, 389.

112. *EW*, 389.

113. *EW*, 389n4: "John Locke, *An Essay concerning Human Understanding. In Four Books. The Seventh Edition, with large Additions* (London, 1716)." See also Edwards, "Controversies" Notebook, "One method used to explode everything that is in the least difficult to the understanding not of religion, is to ridicule all distinctions in religion. The unreasonableness of this may appear from what Mr. Locke observes concerning discerning and judgment. *Human Understanding*, Bk. II, ch. II; note 80, Locke, *Essay* (7th ed.), vol. I, Bk. II, ch. II, sec. 2. p. 117." See, e.g., Morris, *Young Jonathan Edwards*, 134. See Anderson, "Editor's Introduction," 28; Edwards, *Catalogues of Books*, 27, for other references to Locke by Edwards.

114. *LPW*, 407. See also Minkema, "Jonathan Edwards on Education," 32, 265n32.

Locke, the work of Sir Isaac Newton was a major influence on his thinking.[115] One close examiner of Edwards's reading patterns has observed, "The two authors whom Edwards most venerated were Isaac Newton and John Locke, and nothing they published escaped his notice."[116] As with Locke, certain features of Newton's thought provided both points of contact and points of departure for Edwards in the development of his philosophical and theological worldview. The influence of Newton's discoveries in physics and optics is evident in Edwards's scientific and philosophical writings. However, it is perhaps in Edwards's development of his theological vision of a God communicating to humanity the beauty and harmony of the Trinity through creation that Newton's insights are given their fullest expression in the Edwardian system of thought.

Edwards's admission as a student into Yale provided him access to the second edition of Newton's *Philosophiae Naturalis Principia Mathematica* and the first Latin edition of his *Optics*.[117] During his college

---

115. Quotation is in Townsend, "Introduction," v. "Edwards's debt to Newton is no less great than his to Locke"; Hall, "Enlightenment," 199; "Edwards's early thought was shaped by the great English figures of the previous generation, Isaac Newton and John Locke." Marsden, "Biography," 19. See also Schlaeger, "Jonathan Edwards' Theory of Perception," 2; Jenson, *America's Theologian*, 17, 23; Meyer, *Democratic Enlightenment*, 9; Marsden, "Biography," 22; Everhard, "Jonathan Edwards," 323; Minkema, "Foreword," 11; Opie, "Introduction," vi; Moody, *Jonathan Edwards and the Enlightenment*, 6; Helm, "Epistemology," 111. See also Moody, *Jonathan Edwards and the Enlightenment*, 13–14n39; Howard, *"Mind" of Jonathan Edwards*, 121, 125; Anderson, "Editor's Introduction," 41; Hall, "Enlightenment," 198–200.

Nevertheless, as with Locke, so Edwards was more an adopter and modifier of Newton's thoughts than an uncritical admirer. See Henry, "Locke, John (1632–1704)," 353–54: Jonathan Edwards used Locke's works "extensively though selectively, and not uncritically . . . . Scholars continue to debate whether and how extensively Edwards adapted Locke's thoughts . . . . One should always remember that Edwards adapted Locke; he did not slavishly follow him."

116. Johnson, "Jonathan Edwards' Background of Reading," 210. See also Hornberger, "Effect of the New Science upon the Thought of Jonathan Edwards," 200. Gardiner, "Early Idealism of Jonathan Edwards," 590, considers the influences on Edwards's philosophical thought as being "mainly from three sources: from Locke with his doctrine of ideas, from Newton with his doctrine of colors, and from [leading Cambridge Platonist figure Ralph] Cudworth with his diffused Platonism."

Cf. Zakai, "The Medieval and Scholastic Dimensions of Edwards' Philosophy of Nature," 17; Zakai, *Jonathan Edwards's Philosophy of Nature*, 11–50. Objecting to what he sees as the tendency to "perpetuate the myth of the modernity of Edwards's scientific thought" by Perry Miller and Wallace Anderson, Zakai situates Edwards instead within medieval, Scholastic, and Renaissance contexts.

117. Johnson, *Samuel Johnson, President of King's College*, 1:8–9; Townsend, "Introduction," vii; Anderson, "Editor's Introduction," 15, 18, 18n5; Lukasik, "Feeling the Force of Certainty," 230: "Edwards's involvement with Newton's theories at New Haven

Background: Intellectual Trends Comprising "the Enlightenment(s)"

days, Edwards began work on the essay, "Of Being," part of a larger work, "Notes on Natural Science." One scholar regards this as a "curiously interesting document," and believes there is good reason to consider it as "the first of the series [of notes in "The Mind"] setting forth [Edwards's] idealistic view."[118]

A complete exposition of Edwards's philosophical viewpoint would be both a laborious undertaking and outside the necessary scope of this study. In brief, Edwards adopted an idealist (or "immaterialist") position that "nothing has any existence anywhere else but in consciousness."[119] This should not be taken to mean that he denied the existence of a world outside the mind. Indeed, it is "impossible . . . that all the world is contained in the narrow compass of a few inches of space, in little ideas in the place of the brain; for that would be a contradiction."[120] Rather, "the principles we lay down . . . [do not] make void natural philosophy, or the science of the causes or reasons of corporeal changes; for to find out the

---

is a critical commonplace"; see also 227n13. Edwards's exposure to Newton's works at Yale was through Jeremiah Dummer's donation of some 800 volumes in 1718. Cf. Schafer, "Concept of Being in the Thought of Jonathan Edwards," 5n4: Edwards "had read Newton's *Opticks*, probably from the family library, before he went to college."

118. Gardiner, "Early Idealism of Jonathan Edwards," 579. See also Rupp, "'Idealism' of Jonathan Edwards," 209. See Gardiner, "Early Idealism of Jonathan Edwards," 579n3.

See Anderson, "Note on 'Natural Philosophy,'" 173–91, for a detailed historiography of the chronology and dating of these writings. Anderson regards Edwards's idealistic stance in "Of Being" as subordinate to "the much more general metaphysical principle that nothing whatever can be without being known"; Anderson, "Editor's Introduction," 77. See also Edwards, "Miscellany pp. God," 188.

119. Edwards, "Of Being," 204. See also Edwards, "Notes on Knowledge and Existence," 398: [T]here is no such thing as material substance truly and properly distinct from all those that are called sensible qualities." See also Leader, "'In Love with the Image,'" 176n17: "In brief, Edwards's idealism differs from Kant's in that reality is based in God's mind rather than man's. It differs from Bishop Berkeley's subjective idealism in the sense that Edwards stressed that in the world humanity experiences God's ideas directly rather than weakened reflections of God's ideas. Substantive treatments of Edwards's idealism may be found in Claude A. Smith, "Jonathan Edwards and 'the Way of Ideas,'"; Bruce Kuklick, *Churchmen and Philosophers: From Jonathan Edwards to John Dewey*; Anderson's introductions to *Works [of Jonathan Edwards,]* [vols.] 6 and 11; Richard A. S. Hall, "Did Berkeley Influence Edwards? Their Common Critique of the Moral Sense Theory"; and McClymond, *Encounters with God.*"

See Guelzo, "Edwards, Jonathan," 1:390–92. Spencer, "Jonathan Edwards and the Historiography of the American Enlightenment," 36, notes that "Edwards was one of the few Americans given an individual entry" in this work, the *Encyclopedia of the Enlightenment*.

120. Edwards, "Mind [34]," 353.

reasons of things in natural philosophy is only to find out the proportion of God's acting." This is the case "whether we suppose the world to be only mental in our sense, or no."[121]

Although his intended work, "The Natural History of the Mental World," did not come to fruition, Edwards set forth conclusions he had reached while laboring on it in his other writings. His critical examination had led him to what he considered a "fundamental metaphysical principle, one to which our understanding of all things must conform."[122] Essentially, Edwards formulated an ontological structure in which all reality exists in the mind of, and hence is known by, God: "God is the sum of all being and there is no being without His being. All things are in Him, and He [is] in all."[123] A corollary of this is that subjective perception is necessary for existence: "the universe can exist only as it is perceived by finite and created minds, or as it is known by God."[124] Among his subordinate conclusions are the necessity of existence, the understanding of space as "necessary, eternal, infinite, and omnipresent," the composition of all bodies in the universe of indivisible, solid particles that interact

---

121. Edwards, "Mind [34]," 353.

122. Anderson, "Editor's Introduction," 76.

123. Edwards, "Miscellany 880," 121–39; Edwards, "Miscellany 976," 280–86. See also Edwards, "Notes on Knowledge and Existence"; Edwards, "Mind," 344; Rehnman, "Idealism and Aetiology," 337–50, especially 338–42; Holifield, "Edwards as Theologian," 148; Suter, "Philosophy of Jonathan Edwards"; Schafer, "Concept of Being in the Thought of Jonathan Edwards"; Noll, "Rise and Long Life of the Protestant Enlightenment in America," 98: "Edwards held that Newtonian physics required an idealistic metaphysics everywhere dependent on God."

Regarding the progression of Edwards's metaphysics and ontology, see, e.g., Gardiner, "Early Idealism of Jonathan Edwards," 595–96; Elwood, *Philosophical Theology of Jonathan Edwards*, 44, 173n34; Anderson, "Mind and Nature in the Early Philosophical Writings of Jonathan Edwards"; Anderson, "Development of Edwards' Philosophical Thought," 52–136; Anderson, "Editor's Introduction," 26; Colacurcio, "Example of Edwards," 55–106 (98–106, contains extensive and valuable notes); 97–98: "Edwards can give essentially Christian ideas . . . a perfectly respectable standing within an idealist metaphysic. Or, alternatively, he can offer, within that same metaphysic, a perfectly 'Christian' understanding of secular ideas . . . . 'Philosophically,' we can argue, it all flows from an insight into 'substance' considered as that which enjoys the privilege of self-existence. And 'theologically,' we can easily sense, such an insight readily supports, or is supported by, Scripture's treasured revelation of the Divine Name. But about which came first it seems 'safe' not to decide."

124. Anderson, "Editor's Introduction," 76. See also Holifield, "Edwards as Theologian," 148; Edwards, "Mind [10]," 342: "[I]t is evident that all things are self-evident to God"; Edwards, "Miscellany pp. God," 188.

with one another according to universal laws, and a universal gravitational attraction.[125]

A Newtonian influence upon Edwards's formulation of the scientific basis of his idealist philosophy is evident in a number of his writings. In "Of Being," for example, Newton's conception of space as a three-dimensional sensorium of God and his law of universal gravitation undergird Edwards's conclusion, "space is God."[126] The concept of a force of universal gravitation became a major component in Edwards's philosophical and theological thought. In fact, "upon reading Newton, especially the Queries at the end of the *Optics*, Edwards took up the idea of universal gravitational attraction with enthusiasm, applying it wherever he could in cosmology, physics, and optics."[127]

---

125. Edwards, "That there should absolutely be nothing at all is utterly impossible"; "Of Being," 202; see also Edwards, "Of Atoms," 208; Edwards, "Things to be Considered an(d) Written Fully About, [*Long Series*]" (hereafter *LS*), 231, Numbers 14, 15, 18, 20, 22, 23[a], 23, 24.

126. Isaac Newton, *Philosophiae Naturalis Principia Mathematica*, Bk I, prop. 69, *Scholium*; Edwards, "Of Being," 203; Heim, *Christian Faith and Natural Science*, 170–72, 108; Elwood, *Philosophical Theology of Jonathan Edwards*, 42. See also Schlaeger, "Jonathan Edwards' Theory of Perception," 4; Lukasik, "Feeling the Force of Certainty," 228n14. This is another example of Edwards's use of an idea adopted from another source for his own purpose. Whereas Newton viewed gravity as not being an essential property of bodies and he declined to specify a cause, Edwards stated, "Solidity is gravity; so that, in some sense, the essence of bodies is gravity" and it proceeds from "the immediate operation of God" and "divine influence"; Isaac Newton, "Rules of Reasoning in Philosophy," Rule III in *Principia*, Bk. III, 357–58; Edwards, *LS*, 234. Also, in "Miscellany 931," Edwards makes use of Newton's work with sunlight to support his argument for the horrors of hellfire, and in "Miscellany 984," he refers to Newton's work in his argument for the age of the human race; Isaac Newton, *Opticks, or, A Treatise of the Reflexions, Refractions, Inflexions, and Colours of Light*; Isaac Newton, *Chronology of the Ancient Kingdoms Amended*, 174–90; Edwards, "Miscellany 931," 185; Edwards, "Miscellany 984," 309.

127. Anderson, "Editor's Introduction," 45. The significance of Newton's Universal Law of Gravitation can scarcely be overstated. In formulating it, Newton is "establishing and clearly expressing a—rather *the*—cosmic law." In his doing so, "thus was the victory of human knowledge decided and an elemental power of knowledge had been discovered which seemed equal to the elemental power of nature"; Cassirer, *Philosophy of the Enlightenment*, 43. Edwards used this scientific advancement as a major basis of his idealistic philosophy; see, e.g., *LS*, 14, 20, 22, 231, 232, 234; Edwards, "[7] Gravity," 265–66.

For Newton's own religious viewpoint, see his "Letter I" to Richard Bentley, Decemb[er] 10, 1692, in Newton, *Four Letters*, 1–12. See also Redwood, *Reason, Ridicule and Religion*, 93–114; Woodbridge and James, *From Pre-Reformation to the Present Day*, 364: "Voltaire knew that Newton was a Christian, albeit with Arian [anti-Trinitarian] proclivities." Cf. Plato, "Newton, Isaac (1642–1727)," 407: "Though devout

This is because Edwards sees a vital connection between the force of gravity as a natural law and the divine presence of the lawgiver and law enforcer:

> Because it is universally allowed that gravity depends immediately on the divine influence; and because it may be proved that solidity and gravity are in a good sense the same, and resolvable into each other; and because solidity has been proved to be the very being of a body: therefore we may infallibly conclude that the very being, and the manner of being, and the whole of bodies depends immediately on the divine power.[128]

Likewise, in "Of Atoms," Edwards begins with the observation, "All bodies whatsoever, except atoms themselves, must of absolute necessity be composed of atoms, or of bodies . . . that cannot be made less."[129] By relentless logic, he continues that "solidity results from the immediate exercise of God's power, causing there to be indefinite resistance [to divisibility] . . . where it is"; "all body [or solidity] is nothing but what immediately results from the exercise of divine power"; and "motion, also . . . is from the immediate exercise of divine power so communicating that resistance, according to certain conditions which we call the laws of motion."[130] Edwards concludes, "So that, speaking most strictly, there is no proper substance but God himself (we speak at present with respect to bodies only). How truly, then, he is said to be *ens entium* [i.e, Being of beings]."[131]

---

in his own way, Newton could not be described as an orthodox Christian, as he rejected the doctrine of the Trinity. See Zakai, "Age of Enlightenment," 97n43; Woodbridge and James, *From Pre-Reformation to the Present Day,* 382–84, for a discussion of how Newton's work was appropriated by both orthodox Christians and by Deists in support of each.

128. *LS*, 22, 23. See also Anderson, "'Natural Philosophy' and Related Papers," 234n3. See Marsden, "Jonathan Edwards in the Twenty-First Century," 155: "Edwards's universe was, like Newton's, a universe of relationships. A change in one part changed the relationships of the whole. Yet Edwards's universe, while having room for scientific laws of *physical* relationships, was ultimately a universe of *persons* and *personal* relationships" (emphasis added).

129. Edwards, "Of Atoms," 208. See also *LS*, 14–17, 231. "Many theologians stressed divine sovereignty; Edwards's concrete application of the idea [as in the selections cited here] was extraordinary"; Fiering, "Rationalist Foundations of Edwards's Metaphysics," 79.

130. Edwards, "Of Atoms," 215, 216.

131. Edwards, "Of Atoms," 215. See also 44; Edwards, "Notes on Knowledge and Existence," 398; Daniel, "Edwards as Philosopher," 163, 166–70; Morris, "Genius of Jonathan Edwards," 35; Colacurcio, "Example of Edwards," 104n53.

Edwards applied Newton's law of cause-and-effect to the realm of human actions as well as to the physical universe. In his analysis of what determines the will to act, Edwards discusses the possibility of "the most minute effects of the Creator's power" achieving "very great and important consequences" in a "whole series of events."[132] He takes as his starting point, "If the laws of motion and gravitation, laid down by Sir Isaac Newton, hold universally, there is not one atom, nor the least assignable part of an atom, but what has influence every moment throughout the whole material universe, to cause every part to be otherwise than it would be if it were not for that particular corporeal existence."[133]

Likewise, in his examination of the bearing of "the laws of nature" on the imputation of original sin, Edwards again invokes Newton as a witness. Proceeding from the proposition, "A steady effect argues [for] a steady cause," Edwards contends, "It is the will of the mind that is the first cause, that gives a subsistence and efficacy to all those laws, who is the efficient cause that produces the phenomena, which appear in analogy, harmony, and agreement, according to these laws."[134] This holds true for the actions of human beings as well as for the motions of atoms, for "The same principles must take place in things pertaining to moral, as well as natural philosophy."[135]

---

132. *FW*, 392.

133. *FW*, 392–93. See also Edwards, "Miscellany 1263," 201–12; Stievermann, "History, Providence, and Eschatology," 218: Although God's normal *modus operandi* is through "certain, fixed, invariable laws" which "we call LAWS OF NATURE," God is not bound by these. By his "sovereign pleasure," he is free to redirect or to suspend these to accomplish his purposes.

134. *OS*, 121; Newton, quoted in Turnbull, *The Principles of Moral Philosophy*, vol. 1 of *The Principles of Moral and Christian Philosophy*, 7; cited in *OS*, 399.

135. Newton, quoted in Turnbull, *The Principles of Moral Philosophy*, 9; cited in *OS*, 399. The passage from which Edwards's selection quoted above is taken has been commended thus: "In all colonial literature there is perhaps no more acute analysis of the scientific method"; Hornberger, "Effect of the New Science upon the Thought of Jonathan Edwards," 203.

Cf. Cherry, *Theology of Jonathan Edwards*, 98–99, for a critique of Perry Miller's proposal that Edwards "drew upon his study of Newton in [Edwards's] theory of the relation between faith and salvation." Cherry considers the argument that Newton assisted Edwards in regarding the faith-salvation connection as one of antecedent-subsequent "highly suggestive" but "somewhat strained." Cherry argues that in Edwards's rejection of the belief that faith merits salvation, Edwards is "more evidently reclaiming a view central to earliest Calvinism than he is calling upon Newtonian insights." See also Colacurcio, "Example of Edwards," 61; Erdt, *Jonathan Edwards*, 21–42.

Lastly, Edwards was intrigued by Newton's study of optics.[136] In "Of Insects," he investigates why spider webs appear notably larger from a distance than when seen close up. After considering and rejecting a competing theory, Edwards concludes that "the chief reason must be referred to that incurvation of the [light] rays passing by the edge of any body, which Sir Isaac Newton has proved."[137] Furthermore, light rays' effects on the appearances of cosmic phenomena aroused Edwards's curiosity. He determined "[t]o shew, from Isaac Newton's principles of light and colors, why the sky is blue; the sun not perfectly white, as it would be if there were no atmosphere . . . why the sun is yellow rising and setting, and sometimes, in smoky weather, of a blood red."[138] Finally, contemplation of the origin and nature of the reflection of light that produces rainbows motivated Edwards's "endeavor to give a full account of the rainbow; and such [a] one as we think, if well understood, will be satisfactory to anybody, if they are fully satisfied of Sir Isaac Newton's study of different reflexibility and refrangibility of the rays of light."[139]

Edwards's absorption by such subjects of inquiry went well beyond the merely scientific. The motions of atoms, the blue sky, rainbows, and the other wonders of nature are components of his theory of a unified reality in which God communicates to human beings the beauty and harmony of the Trinity through the beauty and harmony of creation. In Edwards's ontological vision, the physical world, consisting "wholly of sweet mutual consents, either within itself, or with the Supreme Being," is but a "shadow" or "image" of the world of "things divine and spiritual."[140]

136. "Although Edwards addresses himself to a very wide range of topics in his scientific writings, various problems in optics were of particular interest to him throughout"; Anderson, "Editor's Introduction," 41.

137. Edwards, "Of Insects," 159. See Anderson, "'Spider Papers,'" 6:159n4, 159n5. Evidence such as comparisons of Edwards's handwriting and spelling in his essay "Of Insects" with other such samples establishes a probable time of its composition as his senior year at Yale or his first year of graduate study there (1719–20). During this time, he may not have studied Newton's *Optics* itself, but had become acquainted with Newton's work through interpreters such as William Derham's *Astro-Theology* (1714) or William Whiston's *Astronomical Lectures* (1715), or Whiston's *Sir Isaac Newton's Mathematick Philosophy more easily Demonstrated* (1716). When Edwards turned to Newton's works shortly afterward, "optics became a central area of his scientific interests"; Anderson, "'Spider Papers,'" 6:150; Anderson, "Editor's Introduction," 22, 42.

138. *LS*, 221.

139. Edwards, "Of the Rainbow," 298, *SPW*, 298n1, indicates that Edwards's reference here is "[Newton's] *Optics*, Bk. I, prop. 2, theor. 2; prop. 3, theor. 3."

140. See Edwards, *Images or Shadows of Divine Things*, Cochran, "Jonathan Edwards and His World of Harmony," 25, 25n7: "Edwards observed that the presence of harmony

Foundational to this vision is Edwards's conception of beauty. In a detailed discussion of the nature of "excellency," Edwards sets forth his ideas on what constitutes beauty. Beginning with a discussion of the preliminary concepts of proportion and equality, he continues, "simple equality, without proportion, is the lowest kind of regularity, and may be called simple beauty; all other beauties and excellencies may be resolved into it."[141] Further, "Proportion is complex beauty." Edwards theorizes, "all beauty consists in similarities, or identity of relation."[142] Proceeding from this, two bodies of similar shapes, for example, exhibit agreement of "being with being," and thus, "agreement to being in general" and to a "perceiving being."[143] This kind of agreement, or "correspondency, symmetry, regularity, and the like, may be resolved into equalities," which perceiving beings find pleasant.[144] "Of these [equalities]," maintained Edwards, "consist the beautiful shape of flowers, the beauty of the body of man and of the bodies of other animals."[145] Beauty of this sort is known as "natural" and it displays "a very complicated harmony" of proportions in its "mutual consent and agreement," known as order, symmetry, harmony, and so on.[146]

For Edwards, *primary beauty*, "variously referred to as true, highest, moral, spiritual, divine, or original beauty," is superior to *secondary* (or *natural*) *beauty* and consists in "that consent, agreement, or union of being to being" that characterizes "spiritual and moral beings."[147] This

---

in the natural world foreshadowed the presence of harmony in the spiritual world"; Edwards, "Beauty of the World," 305; Edwards, "Miscellany 119," 284. See also Helm, "Epistemology," 116–17. Schlaeger, "Jonathan Edwards' Theory of Perception," 203, notes the all-encompassing scope of Edwards's vision of reality, which in the "divine design" is interconnected, involving "all natural law, all phenomena of nature, all human activity, and all human thought."

141. Edwards, "The Mind. [1] Excellency," 332, 333.

142. Edwards, "The Mind. [1] Excellency," 333, 334. See also Suter, "Concept of Morality in the Philosophy of Jonathan Edwards," 271; Mitchell, *Jonathan Edwards on the Experience of Beauty*, 1–4; Holifield, "Edwards as Theologian," 145.

143. Edwards, "The Mind. [1] Excellency," 335; *TV*, in Edwards, Ecclesiastical Writings (hereafter *EW*), 561–62; also *TV*, 28.

144. Edwards, "The Mind. [1] Excellency," 335; *TV*, in *EW*, 561–62; Edwards, *TV*, 28. See also Edwards, "The Mind." [1] Excellency," 338.

145. Edwards, "The Mind. [1] Excellency," 335; *TV*, in *EW*, 564; also *TV*, 28.

146. Edwards, "The Mind. [1] Excellency," 335; *TV*, in *EW*, 561–62; also *TV*, 28.

147. Edwards, "Chapter III," 561; *TV*, 27; Delattre, *Beauty and Sensibility in the Thought of Jonathan Edwards*, 17; Erdt, *Jonathan Edwards*, 21–42; Mitchell, *Jonathan Edwards on the Experience of Beauty*, 4; Suter, "Concept of Morality in the Philosophy of Jonathan Edwards," 272; Dyrness and Wells, "Aesthetics," 296–308, especially 299–301.

is exemplified in its ultimate form in the communication of love among the Persons of the Trinity.[148] God manifests his infinite excellence as he "exerts himself towards himself . . . in infinitely loving and delighting in himself, in the mutual love of the Father and the Son" (the Father's perfect idea of himself), with the Holy Spirit the bond of love between them as "God's love to and delight in himself," which is expressed *ad intra* as God's "infinite consent to being in general."[149]

Having a "good disposition in his nature to communicate of his own fullness in general," and directing his goodness in particular to receptive beings in his creation, indicate that "God is a communicative being." Specifically, God is glorifying himself as he communicates *ad extra* in two ways: "(1) by appearing to [human beings], being manifested to their *understandings*; (2) in communicating himself to their *hearts*, and in their rejoicing and delighting in, and enjoying the manifestations which he makes of himself."[150] Edwards elaborates on God's purposes in doing so: "This

---

148. See Edwards, "Miscellany 104," 272–75; Edwards, "Discourse on the Trinity," 109–44; Erdt, *Jonathan Edwards, Art and the Sense of the Heart*, 42: "The ultimate beauty of existence is that love or harmony between the Father and the Son which is the Holy Spirit."

149. Edwards, "The Mind [45]," 364; Edwards, "Miscellany 405," 468; Edwards, "Miscellany 94," 264. See also Edwards, "Discourse on the Trinity," 131. See also Studebaker, *Jonathan Edwards' Social Augustinian Trinitarianism*, 167–99; Bush, "Jesus Christ in the Theology of Jonathan Edwards," 178; Holbrook, *Ethics of Jonathan Edwards*, 101: "God is the proper entity in which greatness and consent to being cohere."

150. Schweitzer, *God Is a Communicative Being*, 12 (see also 17, 23); Edwards, "Dissertation I: Concerning the End For Which God Created the World," 433–35, 439; Edwards, "Miscellany 96," 263–64, Edwards, "Miscellany 104," 272; Edwards, "Miscellany 271," 374, Edwards, "Miscellany 332," 410, Edwards, "Miscellany 448," 495 (emphasis added); Edwards, "Miscellany 553," 97; Edwards, "Miscellany 769." Studebaker, *Jonathan Edwards' Social Augustinian Trinitarianism*, 136, observes, "The disposition of the divine nature for self-communication is perhaps Edwards' most fundamental theological conviction." See Marini, "Seeing Happiness," 248: The idea that "God is a communicative being" is "at once simple and seismic," and she notes that it "would form the basis of the second of [his] two dissertations, *The Ends for Which God Created in the Earth* [sic]," in which he "formalizes this most important insight about the nature of God." (Actually, *The End for Which God Created the World* is the first of the two works; *The Nature of True Virtue* is the second. She correctly identifies this work on 244–45, but refers to it as *The Ends for Which God Created the Earth* on 256.)

Sang Hyun Lee has argued persistently for Edwards having maintained a dispositional ontology. See Lee, "Concept of Habit in the Thought of Jonathan Edwards"; Lee, *Philosophical Theology of Jonathan Edwards*; Lee, "Edwards on God and Nature: Resources for Contemporary Theology," in *Edwards in Our Time: Jonathan Edwards and the Shaping of American Religion*, 20, 22: "The creation of the world, for Edwards . . . is for the purpose of the external exercises of God's dispositional essence."

Cf. Strobel, *Jonathan Edwards's Theology*, 18–19, 18n34; Strobel, "Nature of God and

communication is really only to intelligent beings: the communication of himself to their understandings is [for] *his glory*, and the communication of himself with respect to their wills, their enjoying faculty, is [for] *their happiness*."[151] That is, God is glorified in the communication of himself to man's understanding, and his glory is magnified when his communication is "rejoiced in, when those [who] see it delight in it."[152] Thus, this divine communication calls for a response with both "noetic and beatific [or cognitive and affective] elements."[153]

The "one grand medium" through which God implements the "grand design" of his communication project is Jesus Christ, the God-man (*theanthropos*), who both communicates God the Father to his creation and glorifies the Father in doing so.[154] The means by which Christ communicates are Scripture ("revealed religion"), nature ("creation"), and history ("providence").[155] Edwards elaborates on these major themes in a number of his writings and sermons. Scripture is the Word of God containing the record of God's revelation to man and "the rule which

---

the Trinity," 118–34; Holmes, "Does Jonathan Edwards Use a Dispositional Ontology?," 99–114; Crisp, "Jonathan Edwards's Ontology," 1–20; See Dyrness and Wells, "Aesthetics," 298n2; Hussey and McClymond, "Creation and Predestination," 200–201, for a discussion of Lee's and Crisp's positions on this issue.

151. Edwards, "Miscellany 332," 410 (emphasis added). See also Edwards, "Dissertation I," 434, 435; Schlaeger, "Jonathan Edwards' Theory of Perception," 155, 156.

152. Edwards, "Miscellany 448," 495. See also Holifield, "Edwards as Theologian," 145–54; Wainwright, "Ontology," 97; Cooey, *Jonathan Edwards on Nature and Destiny*, 117; Lane, "Jonathan Edwards on Beauty, Desire, and the Sensory World," 72.

153. Schweitzer, *God Is a Communicative Being*, 27. See *RA*, 201; Edwards, "Dissertation I," 531; Ward, "Love," 357; S. Edwards, "Affections," 11–12. See also Dupré, "Definition and a Provisional Justification," 328; Erdt, *Jonathan Edwards*, 42.

154. Edwards, "Approaching the End of God's Grand Design," 116, 117. See also *RA*, 246; Edwards, "Excellency of Christ," 563–95; McDermott, *Jonathan Edwards Confronts the Gods*, 66; Williamson, "Excellency of Christ"; Bush, "Jesus Christ in the Theology of Jonathan Edwards," 184–96; Holifield, "Edwards as Theologian," 149.

The ultimate purpose of Christ's communicating God the Father to human beings is that described by Bezzant, *Edwards the Mentor*, 90: "Drawing on 2 Peter 1:4, our participation in the life of God (sometimes known as theosis, or divinization) is achieved through our union with Christ by faith, who as the ultimate image of God restores that image in us"; Edwards, "God Glorified in Man's Dependence," 208.

155. Edwards, "Miscellany 706," 324; Edwards, "Duty of Hearkening to God's Voice," 440–41. See Boss, "Wheels of a Watch," 278: "Jonathan Edwards, situated in the midst of [the] new Enlightenment constructs of history, did not accept the new de-divinizational trends . . . . Edwards's view of history was theocentric; God was the author of history. The major events of history were . . . divine acts." See Hussey and McClymond, "Creation and Predestination," 199–214.

To Understand *Things* as Well as *Words*

God hath given to the world to be their guide" in the quest for "things divine and supernatural."[156] The natural world of creation, consisting of "sweet mutual consents" of being to being, is "an extension of the divine will" as it "shadows forth" the world of spiritual things while displaying the wisdom of the Creator in its "contrivance."[157] History is theo-centric; it is the medium through which is being directed "the greatest of all the works of God," the redemption of fallen humanity, from eternity past to its completion in the eschaton.[158]

---

156. Edwards, "The Importance and Advantage of a Thorough Knowledge of Divine Truth," 86; *SJER*, 29; Edwards, "Miscellany 119," 284.

157. Edwards, "Beauty of the World," 305; Edwards, "Miscellany 362," 434, 435; Cooey, *Jonathan Edwards on Nature and Destiny*, 33; Edwards, "Beauty of the World," 14; Edwards, "Images of Divine Things 7," 44; Edwards, "Images of Divine Things 7," 16; Edwards, "Wisdom in the Contrivance of the World," 307–10. See also Bush, "Jesus Christ in the Theology of Jonathan Edwards," 250; Zakai, "Medieval and Scholastic Dimensions of Edwards' Philosophy of Nature," 15–31; Zakai, *Jonathan Edwards's Philosophy of Nature*, 233; Lee, "Edwards on Education," 79: "The knowledge God enjoyed in the Trinity is revealed to mankind throughout history," 140: Edwards "sees a unified universe in which every blade of grass, every historical event, every pattern of nature, and ultimately, every atom all exist to communicate who God is to his creation. This communication centers around God's redemptive work of history in Christ." Edwards "developed a singular philosophy of nature" as an essential component in his formulation of "a unique view regarding the essential nature of reality"; Zakai, *Jonathan Edwards's Philosophy of Nature*, 232.

158. Edwards, *HWR*, 512, 513. See also Strobel, "Being Seen and Being Known," 175; Holifield, "Edwards as Theologian," 154; Wheeler, "History," 291–92; Stievermann, "History, Providence, and Eschatology," 215–33; Holifield, "Edwards as Theologian," 154. Zakai, *Jonathan Edwards's Philosophy of History*, xv. Zhu, "Jonathan Edwards and Chinese Millennial Movements," 51, 51n43, describes Edwards's grand concept as "a cosmic redemptive-historical scheme" which "transcends both time and space, covering pre-historical, historical, and post-historical dimensions"; see also *LPW*, 728.

Cooey, *Jonathan Edwards on Nature and Destiny*, 33, notes the unity of the three divinely-used media: "The book of nature, read in light of scripture, communicates the destiny of divine being" through redemption history. She observes, "Edwards' 'philosophy of history' is redemption history extended to include the redemption of the cosmos." Nature and history were, for Edwards, "the unified playing out of divine being communicating its destiny [as both Creator and Redeemer] as it reached fulfillment"; Cooey, *Jonathan Edwards on Nature and Destiny*, 117: Nature as a "book of types" is a medium, through the "secondary beauty " of which, the "primary beauty" of the "excellency of divine things" is communicated.

See also *LPW*, 727–28; Stout, "Preface to the Period," 9, 14–23; Zhu, "Jonathan Edwards and Chinese Millennial Movements," 51; Bush, "Jesus Christ in the Theology of Jonathan Edwards," 17–23; Stout, "Jonathan Edwards' Tri-World Vision," 28–32; Stout, "Edwards as Revivalist," 125–43, especially 130–36. See Stievermann, "History, Providence, and Eschatology," 222: The thirty-sermon series to which Edwards referred as his "Redemption Discourse" is based on one biblical text (Isa 51:8) and "affirms the unity of history as salvation history on all three levels of traditional Christian cosmology (heaven, earth, and hell)"; Wilson, "Editor's Introduction," 1.

Background: Intellectual Trends Comprising "the Enlightenment(s)"

As will be discussed more fully in chapter 5, Edwards regarded his calling as a teacher to be twofold. In the pedagogical process, assisting students through "improv[ing their] under-standing by acquiring knowledge" was necessary to enable them to participate as fully as possible in the natural world by expanding their God-given intellects.[159]

Nonetheless, with the deep conviction that "God gave man the faculty of understanding, chiefly, that he might understand *divine things*," for Edwards, this step was introductory to engaging with his students in such a manner as to put them on the way to receiving "the divine and supernatural light" and the "new spiritual sense" that it enables.[160] Thus regenerated, they would become as originally intended, "created for life with God who is the fountain of beauty and love," each one a very "partaker of God's beauty and Christ's joy." Their faculties properly reoriented, Edwards's charges would experience true fellowship with each person of the Godhead; the students could therefore savor being in communion with the God who yearns to communicate his love to them. In such a condition, theirs would be the reward of "a view of those things that are immensely the most exquisitely beautiful, and capable of delighting the eye of the understanding."[161] Nothing less than faithfully delivering this message to students would have been service worthy of the God who had engineered so grand an interconnection of Scripture, nature, and history to communicate his love to fallen humanity.

INNATE MORALITY

As noted in some detail at the outset of this work, Edwards has been analyzed from a number of varying perspectives and has been assigned, with equal ardor and certainty, within a variety of (sometimes mutually exclusive) camps. Nevertheless, bearing in mind his imperviousness to simple categorization, the description of him as a "Puritan in the Age of Reason" is somewhat useful in understanding the two major influences on his life

---

159. Edwards, "Importance and Advantage," 90; *SJER*, 34.

160. Edwards, "Importance and Advantage," 90, 91; *SJER*, 35 (emphasis added).

161. Strobel, "Being Seen and Being Known," 160; Edwards, *RA*, 201; Edwards, "Divine and Supernatural Light," 424; *SJER*, 139; *JER*, 123. See also Edwards, "Honey from the Rock," 136; Strobel, "Being Seen and Being Known," 163–68. In Edwards's exquisitely unique idiom, "It is a thing truly happifying to the soul of men to see God"; Edwards, "Pure in Heart Blessed," 61.

and work that have been examined thus far.[162] As a "scion of the Puritans" and a critical appraiser and appropriator of the "Enlightenment(s)," the *ethos* of each world shaped his responses to the intellectual trends of the eighteenth century.[163]

Edwards inhabited (and confronted) a reality in which "the new worlds of matter and spirit proposed by Descartes, Newton, and Locke" and the developing notion of man as "a fundamentally rational, benevolently inclined individual" were emerging as the accepted premises of "the expansionist mood of Western culture," which, to a large extent, "had already conquered the western mind."[164] As Reason's hegemony increased its domain, the "spirit of inquiry, which was opening new areas of knowledge in the physical world, was applied also to the realm" of the metaphysical.[165] The efforts to liberate humanity from "antiquated restraints" on mind, soul, and spirit had created an "enlightened" religion, in which everyone was free to peruse the "marketplace of ideas" for what was most agreeable to one's reason and conscience.[166]

This "religion of humanity" claimed for its sacred text the Book of Nature and held to the tenet, "If man's Reason was capable of evaluating the empirical evidence gained in scientific pursuit, it certainly had the ability to evaluate the claims of contending religious groups and weigh them against experience."[167] Worship of the god of Reason necessitated the rejection of religious claims based on supernatural revelation or

---

162. Quotation is in Opie, vi. See also Thuesen, "Editor's Introduction," 3.

163. Quotation is in Sweeney, "Edwards, Jonathan (1703–1758)," 397; see Marini, "Seeing Happiness," 243; Todd, "Populist Puritan," 140; Everhard, "Jonathan Edwards," 317; McDermott, *Jonathan Edwards Confronts the Gods*, 3–4; Brekus, "Children of Wrath, Children of Grace," 309; Ahlstrom, *Theology in America*, 149; Hastings, *Jonathan Edwards and the Life of God*, 9; Smith et al., "Editors' Introduction." That is, Edwards both adopted and modified certain components of the intellectual trends of his time in order to pursue his goal of Christian evangelism. See also McDermott, *Jonathan Edwards Confronts the Gods*; Fiering, *Jonathan Edwards's Moral Thought*, 150.

164. Opie, "Introduction," vi; Holbrook, "Editor's Introduction," 1. See also Cragg, *Church and the Age of Reason*, 157–73; Savelle, *Colonial Origins of American Thought*, 52–53. Cf. Woodbridge and James, *From Pre-Reformation to the Present Day*, 389–90.

165. Cragg, *Reason and Authority in the Eighteenth Century*, 62; Cassara, *Enlightenment in America*, 117; Zakai, "Age of Enlightenment," 80.

166. See Savelle, *Colonial Origins of American Thought*, 41, 45–46, 54–65; Cassara, *Enlightenment in America*, 116–44; Dupré, "Definition and a Provisional Justification," 230.

167. Cassara, *Enlightenment in America*, 116, 117.

Background: Intellectual Trends Comprising "the Enlightenment(s)"

supported solely by traditional authority.[168] Luminaries such as Locke, Lord Shaftesbury, and Francis Hutcheson (to be discussed below) "began

168. See Cassara, *Enlightenment in America*, 117. "Deism was the religion of the Enlightenment"; "Deism was the most crystallized version of the Enlightenment religion in the eighteenth century"; McDermott, *Jonathan Edwards Confronts the Gods* 34, 217; Zakai, "Age of Enlightenment," 81–85; Gundlach, "Foundations of Christian Higher Education: *Learning from Church History*," 133: "[T]he Enlightenment . . . produced deism, a deep and deliberate challenge to revealed religion. Universal reason, modeled on Newton's . . . physical laws, offered a very attractive alternative to the seemingly endless dogmatic controversies and 'wars of religion.' By the end of the eighteenth century, deism's assault on Christianity enjoyed wide popularity." Although acknowledging that "the 'deists' did not all think alike," and, consequently, "minimal intellectual coherence" existed among those he (and others) have designated as "Deists," a "lowest-common-denominator" functioning identification useful for this study regarding adherents is, persons dedicated to promoting a system of "rational," benevolent, utilitarian morality loosely united around certain basic ideals; quotations are in McDermott, *Jonathan Edwards Confronts the Gods*, 19, 20. See McDermott, *Jonathan Edwards Confronts the Gods*, 17–85; McDermott, "Franklin, Jefferson, and Edwards on Religion and Religions," 65–85; Zakai, "Age of Enlightenment," 81–85; Marsden, "Biography," 23; Marko, "Deism," 136–38. Cf. Lucci, *Scripture and Deism*, 17–63.

N.B.: Lucci, *Scripture and Deism*, 20–23; McDermott, *Jonathan Edwards Confronts the Gods*, 19–21; Chun, *Legacy of Jonathan Edwards in the Theology of Andrew Fuller*, 136n116. For delineations of minimal commonly-held Deistic beliefs, see Lord Edward Herbert of Cherbury, *De Veritate*, 289–307, summarized in McDermott, *Jonathan Edwards Confronts the Gods*, 28; Paine, *The Writings of Thomas Paine*, Chapter 1; Franklin, "Letter to Ezra Stiles," 10:84. See also Morais, *Deism in Eighteenth Century America*. For "what came to be considered the most complete statement of deistic belief," also known as the "Deist's Bible," see Tindal, *Christianity as Old as the Creation*, http://www.preteristarchive.com/Books/1730_tindal_christianity-creation.html; Gambrell, "Ministerial Training in Eighteenth-Century New England," 39. For a more detailed analysis, see Woodbridge and James, *From Pre-Reformation to the Present Day*, 418: "In his *Demonstration of the Being and Attributes of God* [London: Will. Botham, (1704–6)], Samuel Clarke identified four types of deists: 1. Those who pretend to believe [in] the existence of an eternal, infinite, independent, intelligent Being; and teach also that this Supreme Being made the world, though at the same time, they fancy God does not at all concern himself in the government of the world, nor has any regard to, or care of, what is done therein; 2. Those who also believe in divine [general] providence [but not in particular providence]; 3. Those who also believe in the divine perfections of God; 4. Those who believe we have duties to God who rewards or punishes us in a world to come." In each of these last three cases, persons thus categorized believed in God's governance and sustenance of the physical universe, but not in his superintendence of and intervention in the lives of individual persons.

Regarding the "scandal of particularity," which to many Deists was "the greatest theoretical problem of orthodox Christianity," i.e., the fact that "the Jewish and Christian God [had] revealed himself to only one-sixth of the world seemed manifestly unjust," see McDermott, *Jonathan Edwards Confronts the Gods*, 130–45; quotations are on 131. Moreover, as McDermott observes, "Deism was more than just a set of religious claims. Its interests and influence extended further—to epistemology, ethics, ontology, and even politics" (217).

to forge a new understanding of human nature that undermined [or at least challenged] older Christian interpretations," in the process fashioning "a more liberal understanding of both humanity and God."[169] Altogether, *l'esprit de l'epoque* was amenable to acceptance of this "kinder, gentler" God and a more meritorious humanity than had dominated thinking in years past.

Foremost among the doctrines of Christian orthodoxy that had been critically examined and rejected by the proponents of Reason was that of imputation of guilt through original sin.[170] The moral philosophy that was developed in this environment, the "school of the 'moral sense,'" constituted a substantial "part of the modern project that made nature normative for understanding the self and self-understanding normative for morality."[171] Conscience (or a "moral sense") was considered innate in human nature and the light of Reason, after all, would lead to all knowledge and truth. Two major prophets of the gospel of the innate goodness of man and of benevolence of human beings toward one another, with attendant optimism for the present and the future, were Anthony Ashley Cooper, third Earl of Shaftesbury (1671–1713) and Francis Hutcheson (1694–1746).[172]

---

169. Brekus, "Children of Wrath, Children of Grace," 308, 309. See also Brekus, "Children of Wrath, Children of Grace," 309n23.

170. In 1738 or 1740 (see Holbrook, "Editor's Introduction," 2n5), John Taylor (1694–1761), a British dissenting minister and theologian, wrote *The Scripture-Doctrine of Original Sin, Proposed to Free and Candid Examination*. Creating quite a storm, "Taylor seemed to have succeeded in undermining not only the Calvinist system, but the entire drama of salvation for which human depravity provided the first act"; Holbrook, "Editor's Introduction," 17; Allen, "Children as 'White Paper,'" 174–75. "Edwards considered the doctrine of original sin so important because it was intertwined with doctrines of saving faith and divine sovereignty. Attacks on this doctrine amounted to attacks on the Gospel itself"; Barshinger, "Sin and Evil," 241. In response, Edwards penned *The Great Christian Doctrine of Original Sin Defended* (*Original Sin*) in 1758.

171. Marsden, "Challenging the Presumptions of the Age," 105.

172. See Fiering, *Jonathan Edwards's Moral Thought*, 148, 8. See Marsden, "Challenging the Presumptions of the Age," 105–6, for a concise account of the intellectual background of this time period. See also Zakai, "Age of Enlightenment," 91–95; Cassara, *Enlightenment in America*, 124, 132–33; Cragg, *Reason and Authority in the Eighteenth Century*, 62–92; Hill, *Faith in the Age of Reason*, 153–71; Studebaker, *Jonathan Edwards' Social Augustinian Trinitarianism*, 210–27; Minkema, "Cooper, Anthony A., Third Earl of Shaftesbury (1671–1713)," 114. See Morris, *The Young Jonathan Edwards*, 170: "If, for Edwards, to read Locke was like for a miser to gather handfuls of gold, then to read Shaftesbury must have been like panning the gold he had found so richly. For in Shaftesbury he came full force into contact with the eighteenth century, and the philosophical aspects of the Enlightenment mind."

Background: Intellectual Trends Comprising "the Enlightenment(s)"

In 1711, Lord Shaftesbury collected his mature works into a single volume and added to them extensive notes and commentary, entitling the collection, *Characteristics of Men, Manners, Opinions, Times*.[173] His *An Inquiry Concerning Virtue, or Merit* (1714) is divided into two books, the first of which discusses virtue and its relation to religion; the second discusses obligation and its relation to happiness. In the latter, Lord Shaftesbury states as his first goal "to see if we can clearly determine what Quality is to which we can give the Name of *Goodness*, or VIRTUE."[174] Regarding natural morality, he posits a moral sense innate in humans that functions reliably to lead humanity to the moral principles which a benevolent creator had built into the universe.[175]

Proceeding teleologically, Lord Shaftesbury maintains that all things are part of a harmonious cosmic order, arrayed in ever-expanding communities, and argues that something is good if it contributes to the "existence or well-being" of the system of which it is a part.[176] "This view of a system and its parts explains Shaftesbury's view of the content of goodness ... Virtue or merit ... involves not merely acting for the good of the system but performing such actions in a self-aware or reflective manner."[177]

In his discussion of self-love or self-interest as a motive for actions, Lord Shaftesbury contends, "If the affection towards private or Self-Good, however selfish it may be esteem'd, is in reality not only consistent with publick Good, but in some measure contributing to it ... 'tis so far from being ill, or blameable in any other sense, that it must be acknowledg'd absolutely necessary to constitute a Creature Good."[178] For example, enlightened self-interest may motivate the formation of standards and norms for a larger community in which a person lives. Each member of the community may reason, "I do not want someone to kill me, steal from me, etc. Therefore, the larger community should have standards by

---

173. Gill, "Lord Shaftesbury."

174. Cooper, *Inquiry Concerning Virtue, or Merit*, Book I, Part II, § 22, 8.

175. Marsden, "Challenging the Presumptions of the Age," 106, 106n14; Dupré, "Definition and a Provisional Justification," 120–24; Conforti, *Samuel Hopkins and the New Divinity Movement*, 13.

176. Cooper, *Inquiry Concerning Virtue, or Merit*, Book I, Part II, § 24–29, 9–11; Lord Shaftesbury, *Characteristics of Men, Manners, Opinions, Times*, 1:II.I.245.

177. Gill, www.plato.stanford.edu/entries/shaftesbury. See Cooper, *Inquiry Concerning Virtue, or Merit*, Part I, Book II, § 54, 18.

178. Cooper, *Inquiry Concerning Virtue, or Merit*, Part I, Book II, § 38, 13.

which murder, robbery, etc., are treated as being wrong and punishable." Lord Shaftesbury concludes, "in this case alone it is we call any Creature Worthy or Virtuous, when it can have the Notion of a publick Interest, and can attain the Speculation or Science of what is morally good or ill, admirable or blameable, right or wrong."[179] We shall now examine the second of Edwards's conversation partners regarding innate morality, Francis Hutcheson.

Scots-Irish "ex-Calvinist" minister and philosopher Francis Hutcheson was the most influential moral philosopher of his era in both political theory and ethics.[180] An academic as well as a cleric, he was appointed professor and chair of Moral Philosophy at the University of Glasgow in 1729. For philosophers and psychologists, Hutcheson's significance arises from his theories of human nature, which include an account of an innate benevolence toward others and of the internal senses (including the moral sense). The latter were central to the Scottish Enlightenment's theory of aesthetics, and all of Hutcheson's theories helped shape the British moralism known as the "moral sense" perspective.[181] Hutcheson's most influential writings were *An Inquiry into the Original of Our Ideas of Beauty and Virtue* (1725) and *An Essay on the Nature and Conduct of the Passions and Affections, with Illustrations of the Moral Sense* (1728).

"Hutcheson's thorough treatment of the internal senses, especially of beauty, grandeur, harmony, novelty, order and design in the Inquiry, is what specifically moved the focus of study from rational explanations to the sensations."[182] As did Locke, Hutcheson argues that all knowledge derives from sense perceptions. Hutcheson accordingly defines different senses as the powers "of receiving . . . different Perceptions" and maintains that humans also acquire the material for our aesthetic and ethical knowledge by some sort of perception.[183]

---

179. Cooper, *Inquiry Concerning Virtue, or Merit*, Part I, Book II, § 53, 18. See Meyer, 32.

180. Marsden, "Challenging the Presumptions of the Age," 106. See also Dupré, "Definition and a Provisional Justification," 127–30; Minkema, "Hutcheson, Francis (1694–1746)," 312–13.

181. Vandenberg and DeHart, "Francis Hutcheson (1694—1745)," www.iep.utm.edu/hutcheso/; Minkema, "Hutcheson, Francis (1694—1745)," 312–13.

182. Vandenberg and DeHart, "Francis Hutcheson (1694—1745)."

183. Hutcheson, *Inquiry into the Original of Our Ideas of Beauty and Virtue*, www.oll.libertyfund.org/titles/2462, I. I. §§ I, II.

Background: Intellectual Trends Comprising "the Enlightenment(s)"

Moreover, Hutcheson, like Lord Shaftesbury, claims moral judgments are made in the human faculty that Shaftesbury calls a moral sense. Writes Hutcheson, "What is approved by this sense we count as *right* and *beautiful*, and call it *virtue*; what is condemned, we count as *base* and *deformed* and [*vicious*.]"[184] A concern for others exhibited through the moral sense is innate in humankind, Hutcheson contends: Nature has constituted human beings to be "endued . . . with various reflex senses"; by these senses, "that application of our natural powers is immediately approved . . . which is most beneficial either to the individual or to mankind."[185]

EDWARDS REGARDING "TRUE VIRTUE"

In opposition to the theories prevalent in his time of innate morality and natural benevolence of human beings, Edwards set forth his conception of "true virtue."[186] As noted above, Edwards distinguished two types of beauty. The inferior, or secondary, type can be perceived by the natural senses as displaying pleasing harmony, proportion, symmetry,

---

184. Hutcheson, *Short Introduction to Moral Philosophy*, 1:17 (emphasis in original); Marsden, "Challenging the Presumptions of the Age," 106. See also Hutcheson, *Inquiry into the Original of Our Ideas of Beauty and Virtue*, 2, 7, 14; Dyrness and Wells, "Aesthetics," 298, 298n3.

185. Hutcheson, *Short Introduction to Moral Philosophy*, I:14–15; Hutcheson, *Inquiry into the Original of Our Ideas of Beauty and Virtue*, www.oll.libertyfund.org/titles/2462, I.I.I.VIII. 83; I.411; Vandenberg and DeHart, "Francis Hutcheson (1694–1745)". See *TV*, 562, 562n1, 562n 2, 566, 566n9; Fiering, *Jonathan Edwards's Moral Thought*, 8–9; Aldridge, "Edwards and Hutcheson," 35–53; Faust, "Introduction," lxxviii; Dyrness and Wells, "Aesthetics," 298; Marsden, "Challenging the Presumptions of the Age," 106–07; Faust, "Introduction," lxxx; Opie, "Introduction," 70. Cf. Dupré, "Definition and a Provisional Justification," 128. See also Danaher, "Beauty, Benevolence, and Virtue in Jonathan Edwards's *The Nature of True Virtue*," 386–410, and his argument that Edwards's *End for Which God Created the World* and *TV* should be understood as "apologetical engagements of the moral sense philosophy" of Hutcheson (388).

186. See Hall, "Abolitionism of Samuel Hopkins," 296–313, especially 303–6; Brekus, "Children of Wrath, Children of Grace," 309; Noll, "Rise and Long Life of the Protestant Enlightenment in America," 97–98: "Edwards's books on free will and original sin, and especially his work, *The Nature of True Virtue*, called into question the natural moral capacities that had become so important to the ethics of the Enlightenment and especially of Scottish moral philosophy," of which Hutcheson was a major exponent. Cf. Cochran, "Ethics," 281–95: "Edwards understands virtue as fundamentally a divine quality, and a commitment to viewing Jesus Christ as a paradigmatic moral exemplar is central to his ethic." A combination of "reflecting on God's self-revelation [in Scripture]" and of "discerning God's presence in the world provides a necessary . . . starting point for the pursuit of moral actions" (293, 294).

etc. The superior, or primary, type "is relished by a spiritual or divine sense."[187] Virtue is a beauty in the latter category, involving "acts of the mind that are of a *moral* nature, i.e., such as are attended with desert or worthiness of *praise* or *blame*."[188] Such acts are not merely speculative in nature; rather, they entail deliberate choices put into action: They are in the sphere of "the disposition and will, or (to use a general word I suppose commonly well understood) to the heart."[189] The ultimate beauty of virtue which humans can attain is "benevolence to being in general" or "consent, propensity and union of heart to being in general"; that is, "true virtue must chiefly consist in love to God."[190]

As Edwards demonstrated in *Original Sin*, this is not an inherent inclination of human nature because of God's withdrawal of the "superior principles" from humanity that made benevolence toward God and toward other human beings possible. The human nature that mankind has inherited since the Fall contains only the "inferior principles of self-love and natural appetite." In the absence of the "governour and guide" of the regulating "superior principles," self-love tends to run unchecked and chaos reigns in the soul: Self-love "breaks out into all manner of exorbitancies, and becomes in innumerable cases a vile and odious disposition, and causes thousands of unlovely and hateful actions." The tragic result is "a *fatal catastrophe*, a turning of all things upside down, and the succession of a state of the most odious and dreadful confusion."[191]

---

187. Frankena, "Foreword," ix. See also Dyrness and Wells, "Aesthetics," 299–300; Edwards, "Mind," 333–36, 362; Holifield, "Edwards as Theologian," 145.

188. *TV*, 539 (emphasis in original); *TV*, 1–2. Edwards also discusses a secondary type of virtue; i.e, a common morality that can be practiced by the unregenerate. See Ramsey, "Editor's Introduction," 33–53.

189. *TV*, 539 (emphasis in original); *TV*, 2. See also Faust, "Introduction," lxxvi–lxxvii.

190. *TV*, 540; 3. "The dynamic of God's sovereignty is that God's love is at the heart of the universe and that the universe was created in order to share that love with other intelligent beings capable of returning that love." *Ergo*, "Because of its intra-Trinitarian origins, beauty for Edwards is essentially personal. It is the beauty of love." One who encounters this love "is transformed to love what God loves." Such a one comes to realize that the "dynamic beauty of love . . . is at the center of reality," and ultimately, "seeing the beauty of the redemptive love of Christ as the true center of reality," will "love God and all that he has created"; Marsden, "Foreword," vii; Marsden, "Jonathan Edwards in the Twenty-First Century," 163; Marsden, *Infinite Fountain of Light*, 50; Marsden, *Jonathan Edwards: A Life*, 505.

191. *OS*, 382 (emphasis in original); *EW*, 252, 43. See also Tan, "Anthropology, Affections, and Free Will," 251; Tan, "Learning from Jonathan Edwards," 179–202. See also Tan, *Fullness Received and Returned*; Edwards, "Miscellany 1253," 186–88; Edwards,

Background: Intellectual Trends Comprising "the Enlightenment(s)"

In his discussion of conscience, Edwards observed that in human beings following the principle, "Do unto others as you would have them do unto you," a measure of self-love is involved: "To do that to another, which we should be angry with him for doing to us ... is to disagree with ourselves, and contradict ourselves." On the other hand, in pure love to others, "i.e., love not arising from self-love, there is [a] union of the heart with others; a kind of enlargement of the mind, whereby it so extends itself as to take others into [one]self."[192] The former case is private and involves a "natural principle." The latter case, however, is public and is motivated by "a sense of the primary beauty of true virtue" and requires being "united with Being in general, and supreme love to God."[193]

Actions in the latter category display "an agreement or union of heart to the great system, and to God the head of it, who is all and all in it—[it] is a divine principle."[194] The unregenerate conscience of natural man is motivated by the "natural principle" of recognizing "the uniformity and natural agreement ... between loving others, and being accepted and favoured by others" and "between hating and doing ill to others, and being hated by them, and suffering ill from them."[195] Although a "moral sense which is natural to mankind," "arising from a sense of the general beauty and harmony of things," exists, it does not rise to a level beyond self-love or above a "sense of desert and approbation of that natural agreement there is, in manner and measure, in justice."[196] In summary, a "dis-

---

"Discourse on the Trinity," 116, 141, 143; Edwards, "Miscellany 370," 442; Edwards, "Miscellany 1084," 467; Edwards, "Miscellany 1094," 483.

192. *TV*, 43, 589, 61, 590, 62–63. See also Schlaeger, "Jonathan Edwards' Theory of Perception," 180.

193. *TV*, 590, 594, 67.

194. *TV*, 590, 596–97, 70; Edwards, "Mind. [39]," 356. See also Faust, "Introduction," lxxxviii–xci; Holifield, "Edwards as Theologian," 152.

195. *TV*, 594, 596–97, *TV*, 70; Edwards, "Mind. [39]," 356.

196. *EW*, 596; *SPW*, 356; *EW*, 596. See also Noll, "Rise and Long Life of the Protestant Enlightenment in America," 98. Spohn, "Sovereign Beauty," 395–96, observes that *TV* and Edwards's *Concerning the End for which God Created the World*, "Dissertation I," in *EW*, 405–536, published together as *Two Dissertations* (Boston: S. Kneeland, 1765), are "parts of a single argument which holds that the love of God is the necessary context for all truly moral acts and that morality finds its proper ground and fulfillment in authentic religion." In the latter stages of Edwards's thought, "Morality and love of God" were unified in that "virtuous acts must be *dependent upon* the love of God and *subordinate to* the good of Being in general"; Quinn, "Master Argument of the Nature of True Virtue," 79–97. See also Jenson, *America's Theologian*, 169–76; Gaustad, "Nature of True—and Useful—Virtue," 42–57; and Danaher, "Beauty, Benevolence, and Virtue in Jonathan Edwards's *The Nature of True Virtue*," 386–410, and his review of the historiography of interpretations of Edwards's *TV*.

interested moral sense" is not "universal in the world of mankind"; it is activated only by the "new spiritual sense" that enables "consent to being in general."[197]

A significant example of Edwards demonstrating "true virtue" is his conduct toward the Native Americans at the Stockbridge mission, despite his condescending attitude toward their culture at the beginning of his service there. His advocacy on their behalf in the face of hostility, mistreatment, and exploitation toward them on the part of some of the English settlers and English and French missionaries (at tremendous cost to Edwards himself) included a massive flurry of letter-writing to those in authority, both local and distant. These efforts acquainted those in power with abuses to the native peoples and assisted in securing a partial end to the ill treatment. In addition to preaching regularly to the Native Americans and teaching weekly at the mission school, Edwards's actions ranged from "rooting out a corrupt official who exploited the boys as slaves and embezzled funds, to inviting students into his own house for private instruction and opening it up for the tribal councils of the Mohawks."[198] Demonstrating amelioration of his initial attitude toward the native peoples, Edwards came to accept them as human beings made in the image of God who deserved education and the proclamation of the gospel. Edwards's Stockbridge experience will be discussed more fully in chapters 5 and 6.

As an educator, Edwards believed that only someone of "true virtue," someone who was committed, ultimately, to placing students in "the way of grace" to receive the "new spiritual sense," could teach in the truest sense. Only someone who practices "true virtue" can desire and

---

197. *EW*, 596; *RA*, 26, 32, 206, 207, 209, 220, 271; *SPW*, 336, 337, 363, 364.

198. Quotation is in Blore, "Educational Philosophy of Jonathan Edwards," 37. See Wheeler, "Edwards as Missionary," 201; Wheeler, "'Friends to Your Souls,'" 749–50. Of the approximately 1,200 compositions in the Edwards sermon corpus, 187 were written specifically for the Stockbridge Indians. Adding to this total the number of sermons Edwards repreached at the mission that had been delivered earlier brings the figure to approximately 233. "Even a conservative estimate of 250 sermons preached over the full seven years from January 1751 to January 1758 results in an average of three times a month in the pulpit." In addition, see Wheeler, "'Friends to Your Souls,'" 748, 748n42: At Stockbridge, "Edwards proved to be a diligent advocate for Indian rights, as his dozens of letters to mission backers and Massachusetts officials attest"; Blore, "Educational Philosophy of Jonathan Edwards," 37: In his service at Stockbridge, Edwards exercised a "dedication to his community and the interests of the minority population that could rival any in American history."

Background: Intellectual Trends Comprising "the Enlightenment(s)"

seek for someone else to receive it. This, as we shall see later, he earnestly strove to do.

CONCLUSION

Noted at the outset of this chapter was the diversity of the "Enlightenment(s)" projects to the point of resistance to precise definition.[199] Nevertheless, taken together, the philosophical inquiries and scientific discoveries characterizing the "Age of Enlightenment(s)" occasioned a seismic shift in how humans viewed the world around them and their place in it.[200] Some of those directing the movement(s) considered their goal as nothing less than the conquest of the entire cosmos under the banner of humanity's "Empire of Reason."[201] Yet God had not surrendered his sovereignty, nor had humanity become nobler, with the dawn of the eighteenth century.

Acutely aware of these realities, Edwards interacted with the intellectual forces of his day, intent on seizing the advancements in learning to further the cause of Christ. Locke aided Edwards in describing the "new spiritual sense," Newton assisted in the refining of Edwards's ideas about the order and beauty of the cosmos being a reflection of the Godhead, and the British moralists served as interlocutors in the formulation of Edwards's definition of true virtue.[202]

---

199. See Woodbridge and James, *From Pre-Reformation to the Present Day*, 358–59. Not only did the "Enlightenment(s)" movements differ in character and impact from one country to another, not all areas in a given country were impacted equally: "Several streams of Enlightenment thought might course through one city or province and leave another region relatively untouched." For example, "The Roman Catholic 'Enlightenment' in Bavaria had different traits from the *Aufklärung* in towns of northern Protestant Germany such as Halle or Berlin."

200. See Zakai, *Jonathan Edwards's Philosophy of Nature*, 208; Holmes, *God of Grace and God of Glory*, 1: The Enlightenment is "perhaps still the greatest change in Western intellectual self-understanding since the Renaissance of the fifteenth century."

201. See Henry Steele Commager's description of the "Enlightenment(s)" movement(s) in Europe and the American colonies: The eighteenth-century "Age of Enlightenment" was a time in which those driving the movement(s) "had emancipated themselves from . . . the past of ignorance, credulity, and superstition—and now . . . they hurled themselves upon a new world and a new universe. They were not interested in the next world; they were interested in the world about them"; Commager, *Empire of Reason*, 1. See also Cragg, *Church and the Age of Reason*, 234–55; N.B.: 237: The "natural consequence of [the *philosophes*'] glorification of the Newtonian revolution [was] having 'deified nature,' they 'denatured God.'"

202. See Ramsey, "Edwards and His Antagonists," 65–118; Cuthbert, "More Swiftly

To Understand *Things* as Well as *Words*

Even as Edwards was a discerning appropriator of their thoughts, he understood that underlying much of the "Enlightenment(s)'" manifestations was a naïve optimism concerning the extent and the capabilities of unassisted human Reason.[203] To a great extent, "the light of nature and Reason" is well-suited for comprehending and coping with the natural world around us, and "it must be a great part of man's principal business, to improve his understanding by acquiring knowledge."[204] Yet this endeavor is not an end in itself. As Edwards expounded, properly used, "learning is the handmaid of the Lord" in understanding the things of this world and of the supernatural realm.[205] For Edwards, knowledge of

---

Propagating the Gospel," 153–54: Both Edwards and those with whose thinking he engaged drew on ideas of luminaries such as Locke, Malebranche, and Newton to promote their respective agendas. "What both narratives hold in common is their understanding of the goal of Enlightenment; as the name suggests, it is the process of bringing light into darkness, begging questions of Edwards's understanding of light and darkness. For many in this period, the light of reason was brought to bear on the darkness of tradition, superstition, and ignorance. Edwards drew on this imagery and discourse to explain his theological commitments."

203. See Todd, "Populist Puritan," 137: In the age of ideas in which Edwards lived and with which he engaged, "From Newtonian physics to Lockean epistemology to the new moral philosophy, the Enlightenment injected new ideas into virtually every arena of medieval thought." As examined in this chapter, in precisely each of these spheres did Edwards interact with interlocutors and engage with their thoughts in order to fashion new defenses of orthodox Christianity. See also Capaldi, "Introduction," 7, 8. To the extent that participants in the "Enlightenment(s)" shared a common goal, Capaldi considers it to have been social reform, out of which grew the social sciences. He therefore offers this as a matter-of-fact statement of purpose, rather than as one theory among others: "How the Enlightenment came to signify the knowledge of man's nature and how that knowledge might be used to improve the human condition."

204. Edwards, "Importance and Advantage," 90; *SJER*, 34.

205. See Zakai, *Jonathan Edwards's Philosophy of Nature*, 233; Guelzo, "Learning Is the Handmaid of the Lord," 1–18.

See Edwards, "Sermon 998," 741; Edwards, "Miscellany 986," 310. In this respect, Edwards's view of the relationship between Scripture and reason is similar to that of August Hermann Francke, a German Pietist whose influence on Edwards's pedagogy will be discussed in the following chapter. See Sattler, *Nobler Than the Angels*, 67: "The great stress placed on education by Pietist pedagogues indicates quite a high regard for the intellect . . . . Francke even calls *Wissenschaft* a gift of God, whereas ignorance works to Satan's advantage"; see Sattler, *Nobler Than the Angels*, 67n107; Francke, *Lectiones Paraeneticae*, 7:376. See also Sattler, *Nobler Than the Angels*, 68n108: "See E. Peschke, 'August Hermann Francke und die Bibel,' in *Pietismus und Bibel*, hrsg. Von Kurt Aland, (Witten, 1970), pp. 579ff." In this chapter, "the Pietist view of the proper role and limitations of human reason is made clear. We must remember, too, that Francke had Christian Wolff expelled from the faculty at Halle for teaching that unaided human reason could attain to moral truth. In [doing] this, Wolff had claimed for reason territory which, in Pietist thought, belonged solely to the divinely illumined mind. See also F.

Background: Intellectual Trends Comprising "the Enlightenment(s)"

the physical world points to the world of divine and supernatural things, of which the former, notwithstanding its splendor, is but a pale reflection.

"In [the Lord's] light shall we see light" to see the world aright (Ps 36:9). The light of human Reason, even though the crowning legacy of the *imago Dei* remaining in post-Fall humanity, has its limits. All the optimism which both impelled and was engendered by the "Age of Enlightenment" and the progress in human knowledge that it produced neither eliminated nor alleviated the problem which lay at the root of ills plaguing humanity: humanity's fallen condition.

Therefore, armed with Scripture, Edwards marched with resolute steps into the pseudo-Paradise named *Civitatem Hominis*, which unalloyed *hubris* and undimmed hope were constructing as a monument to unfettered human Reason and unlimited human potential, strode its streets paved with fool's gold and stood in its midst, in effect proclaiming, "In the name of the Lord, hear ye! The 'light of reason' has its uses. But only 'the divine and supernatural light' can penetrate and illuminate the darkness of the human soul. Only with the 'new spiritual sense' can one understand the ultimate things of life. Only in heartfelt 'consent to being in general' can life be lived as the Creator, the Giver and Sustainer of life, intends." With unwavering devotion and eloquent voice, Edwards communicated this message as a minister, as a philosopher, as a theologian, and as a teacher.

In summary, Edwards maintained "an ambivalent relationship with the age in which he lived," one which was characterized by his appropriation and resistance alike. As we have seen, this figure who bridged the period which witnessed the waning of Puritanism in New England and the dawning of the colonial American "Enlighten-ment(s)" made use of key elements of eighteenth-century thought. Simultaneously, he rejected the anthropocentric direction of certain protagonists of the "Age of Reason" and their attempted "all-encompassing programmatic estrangement" of humanity from God which resulted.[206] In these labors, Edwards made

---

DeBoor, 'Erfahrung gegen Vernunft," in *Der Pietismus in Gestalt und Wirkungen*, hrsg. Von H. Bornkamm, u. a., (Bielefeld, 1975), pp. 120–138"; Sattler, *Nobler Than the Angels,* 68n108. See also Cherry, "Imagery and Analysis," 21: "[G]enuine religion includes both light and heat, head and heart, understanding and affection, and . . . the one yields the other'; *RA*, 120: In "true religion," there must be "light in the understanding, as well as an affected fervent heart." Neither "heat without light" nor "light without heat" in a person's life indicates the activity of scripturally normative Christianity.

206. Minkema, "Foreword," 11; Ball, *Approaching Jonathan Edwards,* 36; Zakai, "Jonathan Edwards, the Enlightenment, and the Formation of Protestant Tradition in

"substantial withdrawals from the Enlightenment bank, particularly the proto-Enlightenment [or "Moderate Enlightenment" or "early Christian Enlightenment"] of Locke and Newton, but only to invest in his own, essentially Biblical, view of reality."[207] Let us now examine five further influences on Edwards's pedagogical philosophy and praxis that he likewise regarded as providing support for his own ideas.

America," 183, 190.

207. Moody, *Jonathan Edwards and the Enlightenment*, 7; May, *Enlightenment in America*, 3–104; Crisp, "Foreword," iii-v. See also Holifield, "Edwards as Theologian," 144; Zakai, "Natural Sciences and Philosophy of Nature," 335; Hall, "Enlightenment," 198–200: "All in all, Edwards was an enlightened Calvinist, or, as historian Sydney Ahlstrom dubbed him, 'a Dordtian *philosophe*'.... Edwards used philosophical ideas of the Enlightenment in defense and support of Reformed theology and evangelical Calvinism; in so doing, he engaged in the perennial task of reconciling faith with reason"; Minkema, "'Dordtian Philosophe.'"

4

Further Influences on Edwards's Pedagogy

As discussed in the previous chapter, in engaging with "the Enlightenment(s)," Edwards straightforwardly responded to challenges to Christian orthodoxy, resulting in his modification of some of the ideas forming his source material. This chapter continues the discussion of Edwards as educator by focusing on five further influences on the foundation, content, scope, and methodology of his pedagogy.

Edwards scholar Peter Thuesen has observed, "A favourite pastime of intellectual historians is to trace the antecedents of a great mind." In the case of Edwards, this activity has proved particularly tantalizing. This is partially because of the fact that Edwards at times used the thoughts of others as springboards to reach new vistas from his own perspective. In doing so, some debts (e.g., to Newton) are explicitly acknowledged. In other cases (e.g., that of Locke), adoption and adaptation of a specific idea seems evident, but the reader is without the benefit of the confirmation of a name in print.[1] Therefore, to a great extent, this chapter engages in speculation and posits plausibilities. With this in mind, let us proceed.

1. Thuesen, "Sources of Edwards's Thought," 69. Copan, "Jonathan Edwards' Philosophical Influences," 117; McCracken, *Malebranche and British Philosophy*, 329: "It seems clear that [Edwards] owed much to Locke and Newton." However, "it cannot always be established whether, or to what extent, he owed his doctrines to others [and] to what extent they were of his own devising." This difficulty may be partially

To Understand *Things* as Well as *Words*

HOME ENVIRONMENT

At the risk of stating the obvious for some readers, the two earliest and most profound influences on Edwards were Scripture and his father, the minister Timothy Edwards, through both his preaching and his teaching. Together, these sources inform "the idiom and rhetorical conventions for much of his later writing."[2]

The only son among eleven children, Jonathan Edwards was especially blessed regarding his early education, receiving both the benefits of the "refined female society" of his scholarly mother and sisters and the "rich treasures of [his father's] well-stored mind."[3] The young Edwards

---

attributable to Edwards's idiosyncrasies regarding use of and citation of sources. Holbrook, "Editor's Introduction," 23–25, 67–68, details discrepancies between authors Edwards mentions in preparation for his works and citations that appear in editions of the works themselves. For example, Holbrook, "Editor's Introduction," 67: "[R]emarkably few of the authors [Edwards] had explored ['in the 'Book of Controversies,' 'Miscellanies,' and other preparatory writings'] are cited in the first edition [of *OS*]." Specifically, Holbrook notes that extensive citations of six authors appear in Edwards's "Miscellanies" in preparation for *OS*, "yet the majority of these citations are found nowhere in the [completed] *OS*, although other citations from the same authors do occur"; Holbrook, "Editor's Introduction," 25. Another example is that of Solomon Stoddard. In Edwards, "Miscellany 301," 387, Edwards writes, "The best philosophy that I have met with of original sin and all sinful inclinations, habits and principles, is undoubtedly that of Mr. Stoddard's, of this town of Northampton"; see also Holbrook, "Jonathan Edwards and His Detractors," 387n4. "However, Stoddard is nowhere given credit in the final work"; Holbrook, "Editor's Introduction," 25. Nevertheless, "the most original of thinkers has his sources, even if what he derives from them is transformed in his hands and made into a new thing"; McCracken, *Malebranche and British Philosophy*, 20. See Rehnman, "Idealism and Aetiology," 338: Various Edwards scholars have argued that Edwards "worked with a wide variety of sources in the context of the early modern Atlantic intellectual community," known as the "Republic of Letters." Rehnman cites here Anderson, "Editor's Introduction," 1–143; Fiering, "Rationalist Foundation of Jonathan Edwards's Metaphysics," 73–101; Thuesen, "Editor's Introduction," 1–116; Rehnman, *Edwards on God*, 338. Thuesen, "Edwards' Intellectual Background," 16–33, and Thuesen, "Sources of Edwards's Thought," 69–88, are two valuable analyses of sources that Edwards used in fashioning his own thought systems.

2. Thuesen, "Editor's Introduction," 4; Kimnach, "Early Experiences and Formal Education," 4.

3. Hollister, *History of Connecticut*, 2:587; Stoughton, *"Windsor Farmes,"* 76, 77. Minkema, "Hannah and Her Sisters," 35–56, is an invaluable source of information and insight regarding Jonathan Edwards's mother and siblings as persons of keen intelligence and determination who displayed nonconformity in certain respects to social conventions of their time. Women of "deep religious involvement," they likewise exemplified "highly cultivated intelligence," were "characteristically headstrong and assertive," and thus, not surprisingly, "espoused views on gender and marriage roles well in advance of when historians have identified such views"; Minkema, "Hannah and Her

Further Influences on Edwards's Pedagogy

early on came under the tutelage of his father, an exacting taskmaster who taught a Latin grammar school set up in his home.[4] Living in an era when the village parson typically was well-educated and represented the voice of authority in most community matters, the senior Edwards was both "the most learned and most important man [Jonathan] knew."[5]

In addition, Jonathan's mother, Esther Stoddard Edwards, a person "of strong intellect and much cultivation," was known as one who had received a superior education (for its time) in Boston, who was well-acquainted with literature, and who possessed more "native vigor of understanding" than her husband, "whose knowledge was more esoteric."[6]

Sisters," 36. See Minkema, "Hannah and Her Sisters," 35n1, for an outline of the names and brief biographical information on Edwards and his sisters, taken from Smith, "Descendants of William Edwards," (1940) 217-24, 323-32 and (1941) 124-25; Marsden, *Jonathan Edwards: A Life*, 510; taken from Minkema, "Hannah and Her Sisters," 35n1.

4. For information on Timothy Edwards, including biographical details, analysis of his preaching technique, and examination of his interaction with the culture of his time, see Minkema, "Edwardses," 15-152; see 640-44; 645-65. See Plunkett, "Ten Co-educated Girls Two Hundred Years Ago," 451-52; Kimnach, "Editor's Introduction," 4; Minkema, "'Informing of the Child's Understanding, Influencing His Heart, and Directing Its Practice," 160; Minkema, "Hannah and Her Sisters," 41; Thuesen, "Edwards' Intellectual Background," 17; Thuesen, "Editor's Introduction," 4-5; Minkema, "Edwards, Timothy (father) (1669-1758)," 185-86.

5. Kimnach, "Editor's Introduction," 4. See also Plunkett, "Ten Co-educated Girls Two Hundred Years Ago," 453: In early-eighteenth-century colonial New England, "the minister was the dominant figure in every community"; Stelting, "Edwards as Educator," 4: This was "an age and setting which held that clergymen were the intellectual and moral leaders of their society." Specifically, Rev. Timothy Edwards pastored his East Windsor (now South Windsor), Connecticut church for over sixty years and was esteemed in area parishes as "a very influential man in all religious matters—in fact was *the* man to whom other parishes looked for counsel when in difficulties (which was not seldom)"; Plunkett, "Ten Co-educated Girls Two Hundred Years Ago," 452. See also Chamberlain, "Family Life," 4: The elder Edwards was a regular source of comfort and advice throughout his son's life. Timothy and Jonathan, over time, "developed a relationship more of companionable friendship than [the early] filial deference." Cf. Minkema, "Edwards, Timothy (father) (1669-1758)," 185-86: Timothy Edwards was possessed "[o]f an obsessive, controlling temperament," which may have persisted to an extent into son Jonathan's adulthood.

6. "Timothy Edwards," in Wilson and Fiske, *Appleton's Cyclopaedia of American Biography*, 2:309; Dwight, *Life of President Edwards*, 1:16; Wetmore, *Wetmore Family of America and Its Collateral Branches*, 299; Minkema, "Edwardses," 152, 198n12; Minkema, "'Informing of the Child's Understanding," 161; Minkema, "Hannah and Her Sisters," 40; MacLeod, "Jonathan Edwards (1703-58)"; Esther Stoddard Edwards was a multitalented, erudite, and godly mother; Powers, "Women in Colonial America Were More Powerful Than We Give Them Credit For." Dwight, *Life of President Edwards*, 1:16, writes that "a considerable number" of neighbors who had been "well-acquainted with Mrs. Edwards" described her as a person of "remarkable judgment and

To Understand *Things* as Well as *Words*

In addition to providing the usual maternal nurture and admonitions, Esther assisted her husband in their only son's academic preparation for college.[7]

Lastly, figuring prominently in Jonathan's early learning environment were his ten sisters. When Timothy's duties called him away from home, as was often the case as a prominent minister and an army chaplain, he entrusted Jonathan's instruction (and that of other college-bound students who were instructed in their home) to his accomplished daughters.[8] Persons of wide-ranging abilities and extensive interests for their day, they "consulted Bible commentaries in Latin, read [Joseph] Addison and [Sir Richard] Steele [editors of the British periodical *The Guardian*], and, in contrast to their brother, wielded rapier-like wits."[9] Edwards's sisters were set apart "even from the majority of young women of the colonial gentry" as beneficiaries of highly-regarded education in Boston.[10] They lived, both within a household that "took very seriously

---

prudence" who possessed "an exact sense of propriety," and who also was characterized by "singular conscientiousness, piety and excellence of character."

7. Minkema, "Edwardses," 152; Minkema, "'Informing of the Child's Understanding,'" 161; Minkema, "Edwards, Esther Stoddard (1672–1771)." In addition, after the passing of her husband, Esther taught theology to neighborhood women; Minkema, "Edwardses," 152, 198n13; Minkema, "'Informing of the Child's Understanding,'" 161; Minkema, "Hannah and Her Sisters," 40, 40n18. See also Dwight, *Life of President Edwards*, 1:16; Schafer, "Concept of Being in the Thought of Jonathan Edwards," 5.

8. Plunkett, "Ten Co-educated Girls Two Hundred Years Ago," 452; Marsden, "Historical and Ecclesiastical Contexts," 38–39.

9. Plunkett, "Ten Co-educated Girls Two Hundred Years Ago," 452; Minkema, "Informing of the Child's Understanding," 161. Timothy Edwards demonstrated equal concern for the education of Jonathan and of Jonathan's sisters. When he was away from home (e.g., as an army chaplain in 1711), he wrote to Esther to ensure that Jonathan and their daughters not slacken in their studies by having them teach him in areas where they had advanced beyond him, and vice versa. See letter, "C5. Timothy Edwards to Esther Stoddard Edwards. C005, TE-ESE 8-3-11 [August 3, 1711]" and letter, "C6. Timothy Edwards to Esther Stoddard Edwards. C006, August 7, 1711 TE-ESE 8-7-11." See also Thuesen, "Editor's Introduction," 1, 1n1.

The Edwards household of Jonathan's early years was one in which evangelical values and fervent piety were conjoined with a genteel ambience fitting for a family of upper social station. Of his sisters, "Theirs was rather a life of the parlor than of the field"; Minkema, "Private Writings of Hannah Edwards (Hannah Edwards Wetmore)."

10. Minkema, "Hannah and Her Sisters," 41. See Minkema, "Hannah and Her Sisters," 41n20: The only Edwards sister not to have been educated in Boston, "Mary Edwards attended a finishing school in Hadley, Massachusetts so as to be near her grandparents in Northampton, for whom she was caring." See also Minkema, "Edwards, Mary (1701–1776)," 181: Mary Edwards was the only one of Jonathan's sisters who lived to maturity not to marry, and she cared for her parents in their advanced years.

Further Influences on Edwards's Pedagogy

the intellectual and spiritual capacities of women" and in their larger community, as exemplars of "distinguished intellectual achievement and high moral worth."[11] In summary, from Jonathan's earliest days, the Edwards household was characterized by piety and devotion, permeated by erudition, and recognized as a location at which sound instruction was standard. Such was the reputation of the Edwards parsonage school for excellence that students who had survived its rigors were rarely given college entrance examinations, it being expected that its graduates would meet or exceed college proficiency standards.[12]

Timothy Edwards received his Bachelor's and Master's degrees from Harvard College in 1694 on the same day (July 4)—"an unprecedented act" on the part of the school as a mark of respect for the "extraordinary"

---

11. Minkema, "Hannah and Her Sisters," 45; Plunkett, "Ten Co-educated Girls Two Hundred Years Ago," 456. See also Minkema, "Hannah and Her Sisters," 41, 46, for specific recognitions the Edwards daughters Esther, Mary, Hannah, and Martha received for their achievements. See also Minkema, "Edwardses," 155–56; Gierer, "Hannah Edwards Wetmore and Her Joyful Death," 197; Edwards's sister Jerusha "exemplified the spirituality of the Edwards children in her strict virtue, solitariness, and devotional zeal"; in effect, serving as the "moral regulator" among the siblings, in such ways as reading the Bible and praying long after the rest of the household was asleep. Hannah, the ninth child of Timothy and Esther Stoddard Edwards, along with her sisters, was "[e]xceptionally well educated for an eighteenth-century woman" and is owed her due with her sister Esther Edwards Burr as a diarist. Possessing an "exceptionally analytical mind," she "periodically recorded her philosophical, theological, and personal reflections in writing . . . with a grace and clarity of thought that makes her work distinct among the scant examples of women's writing from the pre-Revolutionary era." In fact, though her writings are "sporadic, their early date–from 1736 to her death in 1773–make them of great value, since it is difficult to find compositions by colonial New England females from before the [American] Revolution." Overall, her literary output is distinguished by "the fluency of the style, the poignancy of the subject matter, and the deftness of the intellect" that the compositions reveal; Gierer, "Hannah Edwards Wetmore and Her Joyful Death," 202, 189, 189n2; Minkema, "Private Writings of Hannah Edwards (Hannah Edwards Wetmore)." See Burr, *Journal of Esther Edwards Burr, 1754–1757* (hereafter *Burr's Journal*). Plunkett, "Ten Co-educated Girls Two Hundred Years Ago," 456, continues: All of Edwards's sisters "stand at the head of one line of what [Oliver Wendell] Holmes [Sr.] calls 'the Brahmin caste of New England.' [in *Elsie Venner: A Romance of Destiny* (Boston and New York: Houghton, Mifflin, 1862), 4]. In describing those whom he thus classifies, he says: 'Their names are always on some college catalogue or other, they break out every generation or two in some learned labor which calls them up after they seem to have died out. A newer name seems to take their place—but you enquire a little, and you find it is the blood of the Edwardses [. . .] disguised under the altered name of a female descendent.'"

12. Claghorn, "Introduction," 6. See also Stoughton, *"Windsor Farmes,"* 76, 77; Plunkett, "Ten Co-educated Girls Two Hundred Years Ago," 451; Stelting, "Edwards as Educator," 42, 61n17; Minkema,"'Informing of the Child's Understanding," 161.

To Understand *Things* as Well as *Words*

and "unsurpassed scholarship" he had demonstrated.[13] In his instructional technique, "Timothy Edwards was extremely conscientious, careful of the slightest detail, systematic and plodding in all his processes."[14] He was especially knowledgeable regarding Hebrew, Greek, and Latin languages and literature, and also was "skilled in the intricacies of Puritan divinity."[15] Overall, the elder Edwards acquired a reputation as a person of wide-ranging reading interests who was "familiar with the latest learning" of the time, and he honed his students (including his daughters as well as Jonathan) in the catechism, English composition, grammar, logic, classical languages, natural philosophy, and Church history.[16]

The Edwards home environment was a venue at which learning was venerated in another way, as well: Its library was replete with grammar aids in Greek, Latin, and English; classical texts by such notables as Cicero, Ovid, and Virgil; lexicons; and a number of textbooks for educating children, such as *The English Academy* (London, 1677) by John Newton and *Sententiae Pueriles* (*Sentences for Children, English and Latin*; London, 1612; repr. Boston, 1702) by Leonhard Culmann.[17]

The instruction young Jonathan received at home produced the desired result. So proficient a student was this scion of cerebral parentage that he arrived at the Collegiate School of Connecticut (soon to be

---

13. Quotations are in Plunkett, "Ten Co-educated Girls Two Hundred Years Ago," 451; Minkema, "Edwardses," 30, 67n31. See also Stelting, "Edwards as Educator," 42, 61n16; Minkema, "Edwards, Timothy (father) (1669–1758)," 185–86. Cf. Fiering, *Jonathan Edwards's Moral Thought*, 23, 23n27. Plunkett, "Ten Co-educated Girls Two Hundred Years Ago," 450, adds that the elder Edwards's mind "was always kept bright, and never allowed to lapse into desuetude, during a long life." Among the ways in which this gift was exercised were the theological notebooks he kept throughout his life, consisting of his thoughts on his readings and other observations, and his poetry; Minkema, "Edwardses," 65n5: There are four of Timothy Edwards's notebooks extant, demonstrating that he "paraphrased and quoted [sources] on a roughly equal basis," 150–51, 198n6, 198n7, 198n8. See also Minkema, "Edwardses,"660–65, for "a list of books that [Timothy] Edwards cited or quoted from in his notebooks."

14. Schafer, "Concept of Being in the Thought of Jonathan Edwards," 4–5.

15. Schafer, "Concept of Being in the Thought of Jonathan Edwards," 4; Dwight, *Life of President Edwards*, 16; Minkema, "Edwardses," 149–50; Minkema, "'Informing of the Child's Understanding,'" 160.

16. Simonson, *Jonathan Edwards*, 23–24; Thuesen, "Edwards' Intellectual Background," 20; Minkema, "Edwardses," 150–52; Minkema, "'Informing of the Child's Understanding,'" 160; Anderson, "Editor's Introduction," 4–5; Kimnach et al., "Editors' Introduction," xxiv.

17. Minkema, "'Informing of the Child's Understanding,'" 160, 160n1; Thuesen, "Edwards' Intellectual Background," 17; Thuesen, "Editor's Introduction," 5, 367, 397; Thuesen, "Sources of Edwards's Thought," 70.

Further Influences on Edwards's Pedagogy

renamed Yale) with a reading knowledge of Latin, Greek, and Hebrew, and also with a substantial interest in the natural sciences, which his father had cultivated with painstaking effort.[18] Edwards emerged from Yale's combination of classical and "new learning" to graduate in 1720 as class valedictorian.[19]

Characterized by a healthy appreciation of learning manifested in enforced discipline and intellectual rigor, Edwards's home environment provided the earliest "foundation on which Jonathan Edwards built his own instructional theories and method."[20] The young Edwards's familial experiences as a child impressed on him the reality that females as well as males could cultivate an active and developed intellect. In his formative years, Edwards witnessed in his sisters models of "[mental] acuity, argumentativeness, and capacity for single-minded resolve."[21] Everyone in the young Edwards's household was known from without as someone to be reckoned with and respected; from within, each member fully participated in an intellectually lively family atmosphere.[22]

As noted at the outset of this chapter, another foundation stone of Edwards's pedagogy that was laid in his early home environment, a "laboratory in Christian living," was the centrality of Scripture in instruction.[23] From the fount of sacred Scripture come both practical lessons for everyday living and divine guidance in the deeper things of life regarding regeneration and preparation for the life hereafter. In keeping with the Puritan norm, the upbringing of Jonathan and his siblings focused on nurture of the soul through a daily regimen of Scripture reading, prayer, and meditation on Scripture, both individually and as a family. To the Edwardses, as with all those in the Puritan lineage, "education was central because it provided the requisite knowledge of Christian

---

18. McGiffert, *Jonathan Edwards*, 3; Warch, *School of the Prophets*, 189; Schafer, "Concept of Being in the Thought of Jonathan Edwards," 5, 5n4.

19. Oviatt, *Beginnings of Yale (1701–1726)*, 239; Morris, "Genius of Jonathan Edwards," 29–30; Stelting, "Edwards as Educator," 154.

20. Minkema, "Informing of the Child's Understanding," 162. See also Minkema, "Jonathan Edwards on Education," 33.

21. Minkema, "Hannah and Her Sisters," 36.

22. Minkema, "Hannah and Her Sisters," 38. As patriarch and *paterfamilias*, Timothy Edwards strove to "duplicate in his own home the loving, pious, and intellectual atmosphere that his father [Richard Edwards (1647–1718)] had done his best to foster"; Minkema, "Edwardses," 26. For ways in which Timothy's and Esther's parenting strengths complemented each other, see Minkema, "Edwardses," 152–53.

23. Quotation is in Price, "Jonathan Edwards as a Christian Educator," 91.

truths and ability to read the Scriptures and 'other good books,' which were the seedbeds for salvation."[24] That is, in the Edwards family, the ultimate purpose of education was as preparation of the mind and heart for regeneration by placing the student in the way of receiving the Lord's redeeming grace.[25]

The lessons Edwards absorbed while coming of age were robustly expressed in his pedagogical philosophy and praxis. As discussed previously, Edwards's conviction was "the things of divinity are the things to know [for] which we had the faculty of reason given us," for "[D]ivine subjects ... are the things which appertain to the end of our being, and to the great business for which we are made."[26] The emphasis accorded Scripture as, above all, making one "wise unto salvation" (2 Tim 3:15) that Edwards imbibed with his mother's milk provided the primary basis for his convictions of the purpose of education and the proper role of a teacher: ultimately, to facilitate students' conversions and their receiving

---

24. Minkema, "Hannah and Her Sisters," 40; Minkema, "Private Writings of Hannah Edwards (Hannah Edwards Wetmore)." See also Minkema, "Hannah and Her Sisters," 40n17: "[Edmund S.] Morgan, *The Puritan Family* [*:Religion and Domestic Relations in Seventeenth-Century New England* (New York: Harper, 1944; rev. and enlarged ed., 1966),] pp. 87–108."

25. In this respect, the Edwardses demonstrate their commitment to "the formal goal of [the] Calvinist domestic-education theory," subscribed to by their Puritan contemporaries: "the child's reception of purifying grace: 'The most important object of education is unattained, so long as the heart remains unsubdued by the saving power of evangelical truth'"; Slater, *Children in the New England Mind in Death and in Life* 130; Antipas, "Comparative Importance of Moral and Intellectual Culture," 575; Senex, "On Christian Education," 563. See Edwards, "Importance and Advantage," 22:91; *SJER*, 35; Edwards, "Sermon 770, on Psalms 78:5–7"; "Appendix: Dated Sermons, January 1743–February 1758, Undated Sermons, and Sermon Fragments": "The religious education of children is one of the principle [sic] means of grace that God has appointed in his church"; February 1745. Quarterly lecture. Repreached June 1755; Edwards, "A Farewell Sermon Preached At The First Precinct," 484: "[F]amily education and order are some of the chief of the means of grace. If these fail, all other means are like to prove ineffectual. If these are duly maintained, all the means of grace will be like[ly] to prosper and be successful." See also Minkema, "Informing of the Child's Understanding," 162; Slater, *Children in the New England Mind in Death and in Life,* 134: "For [persons] beyond infancy, evangelical training constituted an essential step in the process of conversion"; Morgan, *Puritan Family,* 88: "The Puritans insisted upon education [both within the home and in the schools established by the law discussed in chapter 2, 53–55 above] in order to insure the religious welfare of their children .... Children were taught to read in order that they might gain a first-hand knowledge of the Bible"; "The Puritans sought knowledge ... [ultimately] because salvation was impossible without it."

26. Edwards, "Importance and Advantage," 89; *SJER*, 33; Edwards, "Sermon 525."

Further Influences on Edwards's Pedagogy

the "new spiritual sense." Edwards's pedagogical philosophy and praxis will be discussed in the following chapters.

In addition, having had examples of educated and polished women set before him from his earliest years, Edwards was well-acquainted with what education could produce in persons of the female gender. As we shall see in chapter 6, instruction of male and female students together early in life (as had been the case in his home) was an innovation Edwards sought and achieved at the Stockbridge mission. Furthermore, coeducation was not the prevalent practice at that time in that milieu, limiting the range of possible influences on his decision to implement this system. In summary, one may reasonably conclude that Edwards's home environment influenced his vision of the goal of education and its scope as encompassing instruction of females.

JOHN AMOS COMENIUS (1592-1670)

John (also *Jan* or *Johann*) Amos Comenius (Latinized form of *Komensky*), a Czech Moravian educator and the last bishop of the first Moravian group known as the Unity of the Brethren (*Unitas Fratrum*), experienced somewhat of a diminution of fame during a time of eclipse since his passing. Nonetheless, as one who combined zeal for his church with a dedication to teaching, this educational revolutionary "brought together a mystical piety with an emphasis on practical application, scientific progress, and innovative pedagogy, to become one of the most visionary reformers of his time."[27] Accorded recognition he was once denied, today he is considered "the most significant reform educator of the early

---

27. Minkema, "'Universal Education' in Early New Haven," 2-3. See also Minkema, "Reforming Harvard," 319-40. So highly was Comenius regarded during his lifetime that "the Massachusetts Puritans offered him the presidency of Harvard," which he declined so as to devote himself to the leadership of the Moravian Church; Comenius, *Orbis Pictus of John Amos Comenius*, ii, quoting Cotton Mather, *Magnalia Christi Americana*, 2:14, 4:128; Anonymous, "Harvard College, 1636-1654," 135; Cremin, *American Education*, 213; Roucek, "Czechoslovakia's Higher Education and Its Changing Fortunes," 22; Murphy, *Comenius*, 28; Armstrong, *Patron Saints for Postmoderns*, 103. See also Matthews, "Comenius and Harvard College," 146-90; Turnbull, *Hartlib, Dury and Comenius*, 368, 368n6. Matthews "considers it probable that Comenius was known personally to John Winthrop, junior, and that the latter discussed with Comenius some time in 1641-2, when he [Winthrop] was on a visit to Europe, the question of an offer of the Presidency of Harvard to Comenius when a vacancy should occur"; Matthews, "Comenius and Harvard College," 368n6.

To Understand *Things* as Well as *Words*

modern period"; indeed, "the father of modern education."[28] Moreover, this figure who was "captivated by the possibilities of human learning" can now be regarded as a "patron saint for postmoderns" through his legacy of his innovations in the theoretical foundations, methodology, and scope of education.[29] Despite the eclipse of his fame during most of the eighteenth and a portion of the nineteenth centuries, few since his time have exerted as great an influence on educational theory and practice.[30] The twentieth century witnessed recognition given once again to the place of "commanding importance" he holds in the history of education.[31] In effulgent prose, this encomium summarizes his standing in the world of pedagogy: "What Petrarch was to the revival of learning, what Wycliffe was to religious thought, what Copernicus was to modern science, and what Bacon and Descartes were to modern philosophy, Comenius was to educational practice and thinking."[32] Today, primary schools in several cities in Germany, a teachers' college at the University of Miskolc in Hungary, Comenius University in Bratislava, Slovakia (the largest university in that country), and the Comenius Medal, "a UNESCO award honoring outstanding achievements in education research and innovation," all stand as memorials to the legacy of the one lauded as "that incomparable Moravian."[33]

A prolific and imaginative writer, Comenius authored more than 150 works. These include *Janua Linguarum Reserata* (*The Gate of*

---

28. Lindberg, "Introduction," 7; "John Amos Comenius"; "Comenius Biography," www.comeniusfoundation.org/pages/why-comenius/comenius-biography.php; Duchan, "John Amos Comenius (1592–1670)," http://www.acsu.buffalo.edu/~duchan/new_history/early_modern/comenius.html; Spinka, *John Amos Comenius*, 153. See also Comenius, *Patterne of Universall Knowledge*; Sadler, *J. A. Comenius and the Concept of Universal Education*; Sadler, *Comenius*; Keatinge, *Great Didactic of John Amos Comenius*; Monroe, *Comenius and the Beginnings of Educational Reform*; Cubberley, *History of Education*, 408–21; Reed, *History of Christian Education*, 229.

29. Armstrong, *Patron Saints for Postmoderns*, 92–111.

30. See Gilman et al., "Comenius, Johann Amos"; Spinka, *John Amos Comenius*, 152.

31. Quotation by Butler (President of the National Education Association, 1895, President of Columbia University, 1901–1945, President of the Carnegie Endowment for International Peace, 1925–1945) is in Cubberley, *Readings in the History of Education*, 356.

32. Cubberley, *History of Education*, 415.

33. See www.uni-miskolc,hu/en; www.uniba.sk/en; www.unesdoc.unesco.org; www.newworldencyclopedia.org. In addition, Comenius is the eponym of the Comenius Foundation, "dedicated to using film and television to promote faith, learning, and love," and of the asteroid "1861 Komensky," and is commemorated on the Calendar of Saints of the Evangelical Church of Germany on November 16; www.comeniusfoundation.org; Schmadel, "1861 Komensky"; *Liturgische Konferenz*, "Das Kirchenjahr."

Further Influences on Edwards's Pedagogy

Languages Unlocked, 1632), which, through statements about the world in both Latin and Czech, "revolutionized Latin teaching and was translated into sixteen languages," and *Orbis [Sensualium] Pictus (The Visible World in Pictures*, 1658). The latter is "probably the most renowned and most widely circulated of school textbooks" because of its innovative use of illustrations as teaching aids and, thus, is "the forerunner of the illustrated schoolbook of later times."[34]

The influence Comenius exerted on education extends to schools' systematic structure, pedagogical practice, and educational content. In his most comprehensive work, *Didactica Magna (The Great Didactic*, 1649), Comenius outlined his vision of reform of education.[35] Beginning in infancy and continuing through adulthood, "The ideal of universal education, as conceived by Comenius, was concerned with the cultivation of an integrated concept of wisdom that comprehended three main elements: learning, morality, and faith."[36] In this "Pansophic ideal" (i.e., the aim of teaching the entire range of human knowledge under Comenius's rubric of "pansophy" or "pansophism") was "emphasized the unity and interconnectedness of all knowledge," in a way in which, ultimately, the "[a]rts and sciences alike pointed the way to God."[37]

To achieve this mightily ambitious goal, Comenius advocated a four-fold division of instruction based on age and advancement: (1) infancy-home; (2) childhood (ages six to twelve years)-vernacular school; (3) older childhood (ages twelve to eighteen years)-Latin School or

---

34. Sadler, "John Amos Comenius: Czech Educator"; Gilman et al., "Comenius, Johann Amos"; *Janua Linguarum Reserata* "became the standard Latin textbook in Europe and America throughout the seventeenth and much of the eighteenth centuries." Also, *Orbis [Sensualium] Pictus* was "enormously popular in Europe and America [and] was printed in the United States until 1887"; Johann Comenius (1592–1670), http://education.stateuniversity.com/pages/1868/Comenius-Johann-1592-1670.html#ixzz3tL49Ac4d; Armstrong, *Patron Saints for Postmoderns*, 103. Drucker, *New Realities*, 262, identifies Comenius as "the first person to advocate universal literacy" and the one who "invented the textbook and the primer"; Cubberley, *History of Education*, 441: *Orbis Pictus* was "the first illustrated schoolbook ever written." See also Turnbull, *Dury and Comenius*, 440–49, for a compilation of Comenius's writings.

35. See Monroe, *Comenius and the Beginnings of Educational Reform*, 83–85. This *magnum opus* was planned in 1628, written in Czech, translated into Latin and published in Amsterdam in 1657. Its first complete translation into English was done by M. W. Keatinge of Edinburgh in 1896.

36. D. Murphy, *Comenius*, 79.

37. Hill, "Wordsworth, Comenius, and the Meaning of Education," 303. See also Comenius, *Pampaedia, or Universal Education*.

To Understand *Things* as Well as *Words*

Gymnasium; (4) youth (ages eighteen to twenty-four years)-university.[38] This product of his vision and labors is realized today as "the exact counterpart of the existing American system of kindergarten, elementary school, secondary school, college, and university."[39]

All areas of the arts and sciences were to be taught in accordance with the students' individual capacities and progress (i.e., learner-centered), based on a "dialectic" (i.e., question-and-answer) methodology carried on between teachers and students.[40] This churchman and pedagogic innovator anticipated a wide dispersion of schools to facilitate the learning he proposed: "A [Home]-School should exist in every house; a Vernacular School in every hamlet and village; a Gymnasium in every city; and a University in every kingdom or province."[41]

A monumental innovation that Comenius advocated was universal education of both sexes (at least through the Latin school stage), irrespective of social or economic class: All children alike, "boys and girls, both noble and ignoble, rich and poor, in all cities and towns, villages and hamlets, should be sent to school."[42] He goes on to observe that female students "also are formed in the image of God, and share in His grace and in the kingdom of the world to come."[43] Moreover, females "are endowed with equal sharpness of mind and capacity for knowledge (often with more than the opposite sex), and they are able to attain the highest positions, since they have often been called by God Himself to rule over nations . . . and [to do] other things which benefit the human race."[44]

---

38. Comenius, *Great Didactic*, 255, 256. See also Sadler, *J. A. Comenius and the Concept of Universal Education*, 215–39. Why Comenius considered persons eighteen years of age and older "youths" is unclear.

39. Gilman et al., "Comenius, Johann Amos." See also Murphy, *Comenius*, 90–91: "What [Comenius] envisaged—both in terms of its uniform character, its ethos, its organizational structures, its curriculum, and range of activities—strongly resembles the modern comprehensive school, though he saw both elementary and secondary schooling as merely phases in the process of lifelong education, for . . . which he envisaged . . . alternative institutions."

40. Comenius, *Great Didactic*, 58–59, 137, 156, 261. See also Minkema, "'Universal Education' in Early New Haven," 3–4; Minkema, "Reforming Harvard," 337.

41. Comenius, *Great Didactic*, 256.

42. Comenius, *Great Didactic*, 66. See also Comenius, *Great Didactic*, 55: "Education is indeed necessary for all;" 70: "[E]veryone ought to receive a universal education, and this at school."

43. Comenius, *Great Didactic*, 68.

44. Comenius, *Great Didactic*, 68. See also Armstrong, *Patron Saints for Postmoderns*, 103.

Further Influences on Edwards's Pedagogy

Similarly to Edwards, Comenius held the conviction that the ultimate purpose of education is comprehension of spiritual things in preparation for eternity. Human beings, writes Comenius, are "destined to a higher end than all other creatures, that of being united with God, the culmination of all perfection, glory and happiness, and of enjoying with Him absolute glory and happiness for ever."[45] This destiny is not to be taken for granted as occurring without preparation. Human beings "must be taught eternal things, because being destined for eternity they cannot be ignorant of their end without risk of eternal loss."[46] To accomplish this goal, students "should be enlightened through their intellects [and] sanctified through their consciences."[47] The ideal end of the educational process is the formation of Christian character and practice through instilling piety in a threefold procedure: instruction in and meditation on Scripture, reflection on God's handiwork in creation, and in the practice of the Christian virtues of faith, hope, and love.[48]

COMENIUS TO MATHER TO EDWARDS

A major channel of Comenius's influence on Edwards is through that "icon of Puritan New England," Cotton Mather.[49] Three of Comenius's works, including *De Bono Unitatis* (London, 1710), appear in Mather's

---

45. Comenius, *Great Didactic*, 27. See also Laurie, *John Amos Comenius*, 75–76: Comenius's "whole purpose was to lead youth to God through *things*—to God as the source of all, and as the crown of knowledge and the end of life"; Cubberley, *History of Education*, 410: "[T]o know God aright [Comenius] held to be the highest aim" of education.

46. Comenius, *Via Lucis*, 115.

47. Comenius, *Great Didactic*, 74.

48. Comenius, *Great Didactic*, 218–30. N.B.: "In Christian schools . . . God's Book should rank before all other books; that, like Timothy, all the Christian youth, may, from [childhood], know the sacred writings which are able to make them wise unto salvation (II Tim. iii. 15)"; Comenius, *Great Didactic*, 223.

49. Quotation is in Minkema, "Reforming Harvard," 319. Cotton Mather has been described as "perhaps the single most influential Puritan in colonial New England"; Stout, "Preface," ix. For "a direct line" from Cotton Mather to Edwards, see Hoselton, "Mather, Cotton (1663–1728)," 366; Park, "Stoddard, Solomon (1643–1729)," 553; Everhard, "Jonathan Edwards," 319, 319n4. See also Stievermann and Hoselton, "Spiritual Meaning and Experimental Piety in the Exegesis of Cotton Mather and Jonathan Edwards," 144–62; Minkema, "Cotton Mather, Jonathan Edwards, and the Relationship Between Historical and Spiritual Exegesis in Early Evangelicalism," 182–99, as examples of works examining similarities in the "blended providential-prophetic-typological hermeneutic that both of these exegetes employed"; Minkema, "Cotton Mather," 196.

library, and Comenius is among the most frequently cited of Pietist authors in Mather's writings.[50] The gravitas of Comenius permeated the Puritan *ethos* in which Mather lived. In addition to having been influential enough among the Massachusetts Puritans to have been offered the presidency of Harvard, Comenius's works were well-regarded at Harvard and at the Boston Public Latin School, his textbooks having been assigned at both since the 1650s.[51]

A significant way in which Comenius influenced Mather was through the use of the dialogic, or conversational, technique in learning, through the means of what Mather refers to as "Sodalities." In his diary and in his work *Manuductio ad Ministerium,* Mather urges ministerial students to form "sodalities," or societies, which would "meet every Week, for the Communications of their Acquisitions [of knowledge] to one another" through "profitable conversations"[52] In these, one student acting as director would moderate the exchange of questions and answers on such subjects as philology, philosophy, mathematics, and history.[53] To summarize, overall, the evidence leads one to conclude that Comenius's "pedagogical principles ... doubtless presented themselves to Mather as a model."[54]

In turn, Mather influenced Edwards. Mather was close to Edwards's family while Jonathan was growing up, and a number of Mather's works appeared in Timothy Edwards's library, along with those of his father, Increase, amounting to 20 percent of the total.[55] Late in Mather's life, Edwards was a prominent member of the rising generation of ministers whom Mather praised as, "*Excellent Young Men* who Study and Resolve their Duty, and are the *Rain-bows* of our Churches."[56] Edwards was impressed enough by Mather's *Manuductio* to have obtained a copy of it soon after its publication. Evidence indicates he regarded this work

---

50. Lovelace, *American Pietism of Cotton Mather*, 58, 311n99.

51. Minkema, "Reforming Harvard," 337.

52. Mather, *Diary of Cotton Mather, 1709–1724,* 8:724; Mather, *Manuductio ad Ministerium,* 72–74. See also Minkema, "Reforming Harvard," 338.

53. Mather, *Manuductio ad Ministerium,* 73.

54. Minkema, "Reforming Harvard," 337.

55. Kennedy, *First American Evangelical,* 141; Thuesen, "Editor's Introduction," 3; Minkema, "Appendix A," 363; Gierer, "Hannah Edwards Wetmore and Her Joyful Death," 196.

56. Mather, *Minister,* 45. See Bezzant, *Edwards the Mentor,* 31, 31n106: "In the estimation of Lovelace [*American Pietism of Cotton Mather,* 199], Cotton Mather was to Jonathan Edwards as John the Baptist was to the coming one [i.e., Christ]."

Further Influences on Edwards's Pedagogy

highly, citing its book recommendations ten times in his *Catalogue of Books*. Furthermore, considering the nexus between their two families, Edwards likely relied on Mather's counsel in other instances not indicated in the *Catalogue*.[57]

Significantly, as a Puritan, Mather shared Edwards's conviction that "the chief purpose of education is to prepare [students] for conversion, and the way to accomplish this is through an understanding of the Bible."[58] For Mather, piety (expressed through regeneration's effects) is "the chief end of education and the decisive element in determining its content and character."[59] Displaying a keen awareness of the significance of proper instruction in a person's development and of the various responsibilities parents, ministers, and teachers each discharge in providing it, Mather dealt in detail with these themes in *A Family Well-Ordered* (1699), *Cares About the Nurseries* (1702), *Corderius Americanus* (1708), and *Bonifacius (An Essay Upon the Good,* 1710).[60] In scriptural terms, education should lead to the realization, regarding the physical world, that "all things were created by [Christ], and for him: and by him all things consist (Col 1:16–17)." Further, this awareness should lead to regeneration through the Scriptures, which make one "wise unto salvation through faith which is in Christ Jesus (2 Tim 3:15)."

In his magisterial work on colonial American education, Lawrence Cremin sees Mather, through his "supernatural rationalism," as having begun a theme running through American Puritanism that dominated the eighteenth-century scene. He terms it, "the brilliantly rationalized orthodoxy of Jonathan Edwards," which demonstrates an "insistence upon an education concerning itself not merely with an understanding and conduct but also with the affections."[61] This focus centers on "such

---

57. Silverman, *Life and Times of Cotton Mather,* 401; Thuesen, "Editor's Introduction," 26, 26n3. See also Minkema, "Appendix A," in *Catalogues of Books,* 381: "The Mathers' significant influence on Edwards is reflected in this catalogue." See also Stievermann and Hoselton, "Spiritual Meaning and Experimental Piety in the Exegesis of Cotton Mather and Jonathan Edwards," 86–105.

58. Cremin, *American Education,* 290.

59. Cremin, *American Education,* 289. A la Edwards, Mather also was convinced that "Children must be made familiar with the historical portion of the Bible, so that they may draw appropriate religious lessons from the narratives." In addition, "They must acquire doctrinal knowledge . . . with the aid of a proper catechism"; Cremin, *American Education,* 290.

60. See Cremin, *American Education,* 288.

61. Cremin, *American Education,* 293. See also Middlekauff, *Mathers*; Kennedy, *First American Evangelical,* 13.

books" as the Bible and devotional literature, and learning that inclines one's study and meditation toward scriptural truths, "as [having] a tendency deeply to affect the hearts of those who attend these means."[62]

No references to Comenius are included in Edwards's *Catalogues of Books*. However, in addition to a plausible influence on Mather, the Moravian bishop and educator directly influenced the pedagogical philosophy and practice of the German Pietist August Hermann Francke, and Francke likely influenced Edwards's educational outlook, as will be discussed later in this chapter.[63] As we shall see in the following chapters, Edwards put into practice education of students of both sexes and various economic backgrounds through use of a dialogic methodology, paralleling Comenius's vision and praxis. In Edwards's time, neither of these concepts was much, if at all, in evidence in colonial America, Therefore, an influence of Comenius on the scope and methodology of Edwards's pedagogy is probable.

NICOLAS MALEBRANCHE (1638-1715)

A French philosopher and priest in the Oratory, Malebranche, "the philosopher of French classicism," is known principally for synthesizing the views of St. Augustine and René Descartes into an ontology of Occasionalism (i.e., the position that God is the only true cause of events).[64] He set

---

62. *RA*, 96, 121.

63. In addition to a plausible direct influence on Edwards's pedagogical philosophy, Comenius also directly influenced August Hermann Francke, and thus, influenced Edwards through Francke. See Sadler, J. A. *Comenius and the Concept of Universal Education*, 183: "In Germany the ideas of Comenius found their clearest expression in the educational and philanthropic institutions of Francke." See also Bunge, "Education and the Child in Eighteenth-Century German Pietism," 248–49n5: "Francke was highly informed by Comenius; he mentions Comenius in his writings, and many texts by Comenius can be found in the library of Francke's institutes. For a discussion of Francke's relation to Comenius, see Erhard Peschke, 'Die Reformideen des Comenius und ihr Verhältnis zu A. H. Franckes Plan einer realen Verbesserung in der ganzen Welt,' in *Der Pietismus in Gestalten und Wirkungen*, 368–82; and Hofmann, 'A. H. Franckes Idee der 'Universal-Verbesserung' und die Weltreformpläne des Comenius,' in *Hallesche Universitätsreden*." See also Sparn, "Der Philosophiebegriff in Halle," 233–40; Loch, "Historische Zusammenhänge und phänomenologische Unterschiede," 264–68; Loch, "Die Konzeption der Kindheit als Prinzip der Pädagogik," 272; Loch, "Weltverbesserung durch Erziehungseinrichtungen," 279; Müller-Bahlke, "Naturwissenschaft und Technik im Gedankenhorizont des Halleschen Pietismus," 363–64.

64. Quotation is in Lennon and Olscamp, "Introduction," vii. A full-orbed Occasionialist may be described as one subscribing to the following two tenets: "(1) the positive

Further Influences on Edwards's Pedagogy

out to demonstrate that "there is only one true cause because there is only one true God; . . . the nature or power of each thing is nothing but the will of God; . . . all natural causes are not *true* causes but only *occasional* causes [i.e., occasions on which God acts to produce causes]."⁶⁵

At the outset, perhaps a recognition issue should be dealt with for the modern reader. To claim that this cleric-philosopher influenced the development of Edwards's thought may seem strange today, "since everybody assumes that Locke and Newton were the master-spirits of [the 'Enlightenment(s)'], and Malebranche seems exceedingly esoteric by comparison."⁶⁶ Regrettably, "time and circumstance have played tricks" over the years with the reputation of one who has continuously received accolades from his countrymen.⁶⁷ Malebranche's contemporary Pierre Bayle (himself one whose "erudition was second to none in his, or perhaps any, period") lauded him as "the premier philosopher of our age," and he is now considered "the most famous occasionalist of the Western philosophical tradition."⁶⁸ The way in which he explored how the mind

---

thesis that God is the only genuine cause; (2) the negative thesis that no creaturely cause is a genuine cause but at most an occasional cause . . . . The occasionalist resists a blanket, univocal understanding of . . . apparent causal interactions, and argues that we distinguish two types of relations in the world, that of genuine causation and that of occasional causation, wherein the latter relations are ultimately and fundamentally grounded in the former"; Sukjae Lee, "Occasionalism," www.plato.stanford.edu/entries/occasionalism.

65. Malebranche, *Oeuvres completes de Malebranche*, 2:312; Malebranche, *Search After Truth and Elucidations*, 448. See also Stewart, *Collected Works of Dugald Stewart*, 157; Minkema, "Malebranche, Nicolas (1638–1715)," 360: "A Cartesian, Malebranche distinguished himself for his theocentric idealism, or his conception of 'seeing all things in God,' and his occasionalism, or the notion that there are no efficient causes other than God."

66. Fiering, *Jonathan Edwards's Moral Thought*, 40.

67. Fiering, *Jonathan Edwards's Moral Thought*, 40.

68. Fiering, *Jonathan Edwards's Moral Thought*, 40; Lennon and Hickson, "Pierre Bayle," www.plato.stanford.edu/entries/bayle; Schmaltz, "Nicolas Malebranche," www.plato.stanford.edu/entries/malebranche; Sukjae Lee, "Occasionalism," www.plato.stanford.edu/entries/occasionalism. See also Stewart, *Collected Works of Dugald Stewart*, 151: Malebranche was "a writer formerly so universally admired" as the "author of some of the most refined speculations claimed by the theorists of the eighteenth century"; Hazard, *European Mind*, 134: The fame that Malebranche was once accorded "penetrated far beyond the frontiers of [France], and it lasted longer than his life. He had his army of readers, his devoted disciples, his fanatic admirers"; Mastin, "Nicolas Malebranche," www.philosophybasics.com/philosophers_malebranche.html: "Although his reputation outside France diminished during the [eighteenth century], many have begun to argue in recent years that the originality and unity of his philosophical system merits him a place alongside such Rationalist figures as Descartes,

functions has earned him recognition as being in the company of notables such as Descartes, Pascal, Antoine Arnauld, Locke, and Leibniz.[69]

The decline of Cartesian metaphysics after having been "overturned by the Newtonian" system and the eccentricity to some critics of his "curious doctrine about causality," that is, his vision of "all things consisting in God," partially account for why Malebranche's "huge reputation at the end of the seventeenth century" later "[sank] into obscurity."[70] The realization that "in London, Oxford, and Dublin, *Malebranche* was a name to conjure with as the eighteenth century dawned" and the observation that "Malebranche exerted much greater influence [than Spinoza] on the course of late seventeenth- and early eighteenth-century philosophy" occasion reflections on the vagaries of fame.[71] Late in the twentieth century, this once-prominent figure again began to attract scholarly attention, befitting one who, at the time of his death, "was considered one of the three or four most important living European philosophers."[72]

Devotées of this French priest and thinker included royalty: "[King] James II was reputed to have been an admirer of [Malebranche's] books, and it is known that shortly after James was deposed and took refuge in France, he paid a visit to Malebranche at the Oratory."[73] Moreover,

---

Spinoza, and Leibniz." See also Lewin, *Die Lehre von den Ideen bei Malebranche*; Gueroult, *Malebranche*; Rodis-Lewis, *Nicolas Malebranche*; Robinet, *Système et existence dans l'oeuvre de Malebranche*; Radner, *Malebranche*; Nadler, *Malebranche and Ideas*; Schmaltz, *Malebranche's Theory of the Soul*; Bardout, *Malebranche et la métaphysique*; Bardout, *La vertu de la philosophie*; Nadler, *Cambridge Companion to Malebranche*; Schmaltz, "Cartesian Causation," 362–73; Downing, "Occasionalism and Strict Mechanism," 206–30; LoLordo, "Descartes and Malebranche on Thought, Sensation, and the Nature of Mind," 387–402; Schmaltz, "Occasionalism and Mechanism," 293–313; Stencil, "Malebranche and the General Will of God," 1107–29.

69. Woodbridge and James, *From Pre-Reformation to the Present Day*, 292.

70. Warburton, "Letter CXXVII" 283; McCracken, *Malebranche and British Philosophy*, 1; Fiering, *Jonathan Edwards's Moral Thought*, 40; Warburton, "Letter CXXVII," 282. See McCracken, *Malebranche and British Philosophy*, 1–20, 316–40; Fiering, *Jonathan Edwards's Moral Thought*, 40–45; Fiering, "Rationalist Foundations of Jonathan Edwards's Metaphysics," 84–88, for discussions of the vicissitudes of Malebranche's stature and his influence during and since his lifetime.

71. McCracken, *Malebranche and British Philosophy*, 10; Loeb, *From Descartes to Hume*, 193. The inclusion of Malebranche among the "minor Cartesians" was not a judgment on his merit and influence of his day; "it was Spinoza, not Malebranche, who was largely ignored or dismissed until late in the eighteenth century" (191); "For a brief account, see [Stuart] Hampshire, [*Spinoza*, Baltimore: Pelican Books,] 1951, pp. 26–28" (191n2).

72. Riley, "Biographical Note," xii.

73. McCracken, *Malebranche and British Philosophy*, 2, 2n7.

Further Influences on Edwards's Pedagogy

many of the luminaries in the literary and philosophical spheres during and after his time were impressed with Malebranche's thought. Ephraim Chambers's *Cyclopaedia* (1728) used *The Search After Truth* as "a principal authority on many philosophical and psychological subjects; Alexander Pope placed Malebranche in the company of Locke and Bolingbroke, both of whom he exceedingly admired."[74]

In addition, in the early eighteenth century, Bishop George Berkeley, founder of immaterialism, was "rightly regarded as a disciple of Malebranche."[75] "Hume's debt to Malebranche is, if anything, greater than that of his illustrious predecessor in British empiricism [i.e., Berkeley]. Rarely do authors cite other authors in this period, but the name of Malebranche appears four times in [*Enquiries concerning the Human Understanding and concerning the Principles of Morals* (1777)], and only seven other names are cited in the *Treatise* [*of Human Nature* (1738)]."[76] As further evidence of Malebranche as a name of renown:

> Leibniz discussed [Malebranche] at great length in the *Theodicée*; Montesquieu called him one of the 'four great poets' (with Plato, Montaigne, and [Lord] Shaftesbury); Rousseau was soon to rank him with Plato and Locke—his favourite ancient and modern thinkers. Even Kant would soon say that the 'fathers' of modern philosophy were Descartes, Leibniz, and Malebranche.[77]

---

74. Fiering, *Jonathan Edwards's Moral Thought*, 42. "Pope to Jonathan Swift, Sept. 15, 1734, in George Sherburn, ed., *The Correspondence of Alexander Pope*, III (Oxford [: Clarendon], 1956), 433" (42n76). Chambers's *Cyclopaedia, or An Universal Dictionary of Arts and Sciences*, was one of the first general encyclopedias published in English and was "the primary inspiration for Diderot and d'Alembert's *Encyclopdie*"; Chambers' Cyclopaedia, www.artfl-project.uchicago.edu/content/chambers-cyclopaedia.

75. Fiering, *Jonathan Edwards's Moral Thought*, 41.

76. Lennon and Olscamp, "Introduction," xxii.

77. Riley, "Biographical Note," xii–xiii. See also McCracken, *Malebranche and British Philosophy*, 315: "[T]hat thinkers as diverse as Norris, Locke, Berkeley, Hume, and Reid found in Malebranche ideas of the first importance is a good indication of his philosophical stature."

Admittedly, Malebranche was not without his critics. See Lennon and Olscamp, "Introduction," xiv–xx; Bossuet, *Politics Drawn from the Very Words of Holy Scripture*. Among the most prominent of these was Bishop Jacques-Bénigne Bossuet (1627–1704), author of *Discourse on Universal History* (1681) and *Politics drawn from the Very Words of Holy Scripture*, published in ten books in 1709; Bossuet had completed this work, which "remains the most extraordinary defense of divine-right absolute monarchy in the whole of French political thought," by the time of his death; Riley, "Introduction," xv.

To Understand *Things* as Well as *Words*

The time seems to have passed when "the prominent place accorded Malebranche in the history of thought by his own countrymen stands in remarkable contrast to his obscurity in the English-speaking world."[78] This imbalance has begun being redressed, for, within the recent past, this onetime eminence in theology and philosophy has once again begun receiving due acclaim. The twentieth century witnessed the first publication of English translations of this "frail, gentle, and modest" Gallic Oratorian's writings since 1700, in keeping with the reality that "the latter half of the twentieth century has returned to the view of Malebranche as [a] philosopher of the first rank."[79] In fact, the renewed awareness of this once-neglected churchman-philosopher makes it possible now to see him as "a heroic figure" who "establishes an extraordinary synthesis of science, philosophy, and hard-headed faith."[80]

Recherche de la Vérité (*The Search After Truth*) is the foundation of Malebranche's fame, as it is his "first, longest, and most important work."[81] Appearing in six editions from 1674–75 to 1712 and divided into six books, each edition underwent fairly extensive modifications that reflected the development of Malebranche's thinking during the project's production. "The work is therefore an account of his initial interests, mature thought, and abiding philosophical concerns."[82]

Malebranche's encounter with Descartes's *Traité de L'homme* (*Treatise of Man*) at age twenty-five in 1664 reputedly produced much the same reaction that Edwards's introduction to Locke, in Edwards lore, activated for the Yale student.[83] The first fruit of the French philosopher-priest's

---

78. McCracken, *Malebranche and British Philosophy*, 2.

79. Rome, *Philosophy of Malebranche*, 3; Lennon and Olscamp, "Introduction," xxii. See Malebranche, *Dialogues on Metaphysics and on Religion*; Malebranche, *Search and Elucidations*.

80. Rome, 6.

81. Lennon and Olscamp, "Introduction," xv.

82. Lennon and Olscamp, "Introduction," xv.

83. "[I]n [Yves Marie] André's celebrated account (*Vie du R. P. Malebranche*[Paris: Librarie Poussielgue Fréres, 1886]), he was so 'ecstatic' that he experienced 'such violent palpitations of the heart that he was obliged to leave his book at frequent intervals, and to interrupt his reading of it in order to breathe more easily.'"; Riley, "Biographical Note," xi. This account of the effect of Descartes upon Malebranche also appears in Stewart's *Collected Works*, 1:149–50, as having been related by Bernard Le Bovier de Fontenelle (1657–1757). See also Rome, *Philosophy of Malebranche*, 3–4, 353n1, 353–54n2.

efforts to synthesize Augustianism and Cartesianism was *The Search After Truth* (hereafter *Search*; volume I, 1674; volume II, 1675), which was widely admired.[84] In 1694–95, two translations were produced of this, Malebranche's principal philosophical work; one by Thomas Taylor at Oxford, the other by Richard Sault in London.

A luminary widely read and well-regarded in some leading circles, Malebranche produced in *Search* a work that has been praised in these effulgent terms: "Few [other] books can be mentioned, combining, in so great a degree, the utmost depth and abstraction of thought, with the most pleasing sallies of imagination and eloquence; and none, where they who delight in the observation of intellectual character may find more ample illustrations, both of the strength and weakness of the human understanding."[85] Moreover, this landmark work has been esteemed as one of "the three great monuments to the advancement of learning," in the company of Descartes's *Meditations on First Philosophy* and Locke's *Essay Concerning Human Understanding*.[86]

Malebranche begins *Search* by stating the proposition, "Error is the cause of men's misery; it is the sinister principle that has produced the evil in the world; it generates and maintains in our soul[s] all the evil that afflicts us."[87] He then attributes the origin and continuation of this tragic human condition to the Fall: "Sacred Scripture teaches us that [human beings] are miserable only because they are sinners and criminals, and they would be neither if they had not enslaved themselves to sin by consenting to error."[88] Not for this Oratorian, then, was the blithely benevolent view of mankind as innately good espoused by many during Edwards's time.

Malebranche proceeds to describe the mind as "a simple, indivisible substance without composition of parts" consisting of two faculties, "the

---

84. Riley, "Biographical Note," xi; Ginsberg, "Translator's Preface," 16.

See Lennon and Olscamp, "Introduction," xi: Malebranche's epistemology, "Malebranche's signature doctrine of the vision of all things in God, finds support in Augustine, at least in broad outline, and certainly comports with Augustine's insistence on man's dependence on God in all things, including even cognition." Regarding Descartes's influence, Malebranche's admiration of him was not uncritical; see Lennon and Olscamp, "Introduction," x-xiv.

85. Stewart, *Collected Works*, 1:150.

86. McCracken, *Malebranche and British Philosophy*, 9; Wotton, *Reflections upon Ancient and Modern Learning*, 156–58.

87. Malebranche, *Search and Elucidations*, Book 1, Chapter 1, 1 (1.1.1).

88. Malebranche, *Search and Elucidations*, 1.1.1.

understanding and the *will*."⁸⁹ The understanding is the faculty "of receiving various *ideas*, that is, of perceiving various things; the will is "that of receiving inclinations, or of willing different things."⁹⁰ He explicates further, "I understand by this word understanding that passive faculty of the soul by means of which it receives all the modifications [i.e., 'sensations' or 'modes of the mind'] of which it is capable."⁹¹

Malebranche then delineates his view of the basis of human action: "I propose to designate by the word WILL as "the capacity the soul has of loving different goods" as exercised through "the impression or natural impulse that carries us toward general and indeterminate good."⁹² Freedom of the will is "the power that the mind has of turning this impression toward objects that please us so that our natural inclinations are made to settle upon some particular object."⁹³ In Malebranche's ontology, God "alone is the general good" toward which actions are directed "because He alone contains in Himself all goods."⁹⁴

The essence of Malebranche's philosophical and theological vision is outlined in Book III, chapter six of *Search*. After considering and rejecting four possible ways in which a person may perceive external objects (i.e., the ideas we have of objects originate from the objects themselves; humans have the power to produce the ideas themselves; God has produced the ideas in humans when creating their souls or at every instance in which humans think of the objects; souls themselves contain all the "perfections" perceived in objects), Malebranche expounds the view which has earned his standing among scholars of the mind and of the Church: "We see *all things* in God."⁹⁵ This is the case since "God must have within Himself the ideas of all the beings He has created (since otherwise He could not have created them), and thus He sees all these beings by considering the perfections He contains to which they are related."⁹⁶ Continuing in this vein, "Only God," Malebranche contends,

---

89. Malebranche, *Search and Elucidations*, 1:1:2.
90. Malebranche, *Search and Elucidations*, 1:1:1.
91. Malebranche, *Search and Elucidations*, 1:1:3, 2.
92. Malebranche, *Search and Elucidations*, 1:1:5.
93. Malebranche, *Search and Elucidations*, 1:1:5.
94. Malebranche, *Search and Elucidations*, 1:1:5.
95. Malebranche, *Search and Elucidations*, 1:1:5, 3:1:219, 3:6:230 (emphasis added). See also Rome, *Philosophy of Malebranche*, 74–119; Fiering, "Rationalist Foundations," 86.
96. Malebranche, *Search and Elucidations*, 1:1:5, 3:6:230.

Further Influences on Edwards's Pedagogy

do we know through Himself, for . . . only He can act on our mind[s] and reveal Himself to [them]. Only God do we perceive by a direct and immediate perception. Only He can enlighten our mind[s] with His own substance. Finally, only through the union we have with Him are we capable in this life of knowing what we know . . . for He is the only master, according to St. Augustine, ruling our mind[s] without the mediation of any creature.[97]

Malebranche further underscores human dependence on divine sovereignty thus:

> God created the world because He willed it. "Dixit, & facta sunt" Ps. 32:9]; and He moves all things, and thus produces all the effects that we see happening, because He also willed certain laws according to which motion is communicated upon the collision of bodies . . . , whereas [per se] bodies cannot act . . . . But not only are bodies incapable of being the true causes of whatever exists: the most noble minds are in a similar state of impotence. They can know nothing unless God enlightens them. They can sense nothing unless God modifies them [i.e., acts upon the senses]. They are incapable of willing anything unless God moves them toward good in general, i.e., toward Himself . . . . Men can only love because God incessantly pushes them toward the good in general, i.e., toward Himself; for God having created them only for Himself, He never preserves them without turning and pushing them toward Himself.[98]

---

97. Malebranche, *Search and Elucidations*, 1:1:5, 3:7:236–37; 1:1:5, 237a: "Humanis mentibus nulla interposita natura praesidet,' Aug. *De vera relig[ione]* ch. 55."
On the dispute between Pierre-Sylvain Régis and Malebranche on the nature of ideas, "from it emerged the clear statement of Malebranche's doctrine on the efficacy of ideas. Régis had been prepared to concede that God creates and preserves the soul, and causes all its ideas and sensations, but he insisted that this dependence is the only union that the soul has with God. In reply, Malebranche underlined the soul's dependence on God, not only as the efficient cause of its perceptions, but also on God's ideas as the formal cause of those perceptions"; Lennon and Olscamp, "Introduction," xviii. See also Schmaltz, "Nicolas Malebranche," www.plato.stanford.edu/entries/malebranche: "In the 1693 *Réponse à Régis (Response to Régis)*, Malebranche emphasized his Augustinian position that we can be instructed as to the nature of bodies only through a union with God. However, he put a new spin on this position when he noted that the union with God involves an 'affecting' or 'touching' of our mind by God's idea of extension."

98. Malebranche, *Search and Elucidations*, 6:3:449. In his discussion on "The mind's limitations is the source of many errors," Malebranche refers to "the means God has for reconciling His decrees with our freedom"; 3:2:205. See also Schmaltz, "Nicolas Malebranche," www.plato.stanford.edu/entries/malebranche.

To Understand *Things* as Well as *Words*

The parallel in this regard of Edwards the colonial minister-philosopher with the French priest and thinker is obvious. The absolute sovereignty of God in every dimension of the universe is unquestionably the foundation of Edwards's theological and philosophical reflections. He expounds that "God is as it were the only substance" and "the sum of all being"; "there is no being without His being. All things are in Him, and He [is] in all."[99] As "the sum of all being," God is the only true, ultimate cause of events, for "all other positive existence is but a communication from him."[100] That is, the existence and continuation of "the properties of bodies" in the universe is upheld by "the immediate exercise of divine power" by "[him] by whom all things consist."[101]

It should be noted, however, that Malebranche was subjected to severe criticism for his apparent lack of belief in God's particular providence over individual lives. Perhaps the most prominent such critic was Bishop Jacques-Bénigne Bossuet (1607–1724). Malebranche's argument, "God acts by general wills [*volontés générales*] when he acts as a consequence of general laws which he has established," in order to "construct or preserve his work by the simplest means, by an action [that is] always uniform, constant, perfectly worthy of an infinite wisdom and of a universal cause," encountered a "violently hostile reaction" from the French cleric, theologian, and philosopher, who is regarded as a "great controversialist and defender of Catholic orthodoxy" on a variety of fronts.[102]

Edwards makes clear his conviction that "God's moral government over mankind, his treating them as moral agents, making them the objects of his commands, counsels, calls, warnings, expostulations, promises, threatenings, rewards and punishments, is not inconsistent with a determining disposal of all events, of every kind, throughout the universe, in his providence."[103] Malebranche's vision of all reality consisting in God seems to have been an idea which Edwards appropriated (similarly to Locke's concept of simple ideas) and made use of in his own

---

99. Edwards, "Notes on Knowledge and Existence," 398; Edwards, "Miscellany 880," 122. See also *LS*, 44.

100. Edwards, "Miscellany 1077," 460.

101. Edwards, "The Mind [61]," 380; Edwards, "Of Atoms," 216.

102. Malebranche, *Treatise on Nature and Grace*, 5:147–48; Riley, "Introduction," xiv. For a detailed account of the debate between Malebranche and Bossuet on this issue, see Riley, "Introduction," xxi–xxviii.

103. *FW*, 431.

Further Influences on Edwards's Pedagogy

way by ensuring that his vision included a positive stance toward particular providence.

In sum, a strong, if speculative, case can be made for Malebranche's influence on Edwards.[104] The second London edition of *Search* was included in the Jeremiah Dummer Collection gifted to Yale, and at some point, Edwards became aware of and seems to have read it, as well as works by two of Malebranche's British followers, John Norris and Arthur Collier.[105] Furthermore, Malebranche's views on certain metaphysical and epistemological issues have caused him to be situated within the category of "theocentric metaphysicians," "a sub-branch of the so-called Continental school" of philosophy.[106] The three criteria for this categorization are "the denial that certain kinds of causal relations obtain (between matter and spirit, spirit and matter, or matter and matter); the attribution of considerable metaphysical importance to the problem of such relations; and the belief that the standard of knowledge is strict demonstration based upon intuition and deduction."[107] By these metrics, both Malebranche and Edwards qualify for such inclusion.

Overall, Edwards's metaphysical orientation can be summarized in five general principles or tenets: (1) the affirmation of total divine sovereignty regarding events, to the exclusion of contingency with respect to causality (i.e., God is the only true cause); (2) the belief in the divine concurrence in events and in the continuous conservation and re-creation of the existing universe (i.e., God re-creates the world at every moment); (3) the conviction that all reality exists for an ultimate divine purpose; (4) the acceptance of a Neoplatonic typology of Forms or Ideas (i.e., one of divine archetypes and their ectypal representations on earth); and (5)

---

104. It is not definite that Edwards read *Search*, but I believe the evidence for Malebranche's influence on Edwards is compelling. In addition, what Malebranche writes in *Treatise on Nature and Grace* aside, the passages from *Search* quoted above seem to allow an interpretation of particular providence of God not inconsistent with Edwards's view.

105. Morris, *Young Jonthan Edwards*, 137, 137n27; Thuesen, "Editor's Introduction," 7, 75; Fiering, *Jonathan Edwards's Moral Thought*, 43–44, 44n82. Thuesen, "Editor's Introduction," 75, indicates that Edwards's entry number for *Search* is 303; for Norris, 26; for Collier, 664. Fiering, *Jonathan Edwards's Moral Thought*, 44, believes it is "almost certain" that entry number 303 and number 130, in *Catalogues*, 115, for "some of Malebranches writings," were made before 1726.

106. Fiering, "Rationalist Foundations," 77; Loeb, *From Descartes to Hume*, 29–30. See also Daniel, "Edwards as Philosopher," 162, 162n1.

107. Fiering, "Rationalist Foundations," 77; Loeb, 320, 37–56.

the rejection of the Cartesian idea that extension is the essence of matter.[108] "With some minor variations, these five tenets fit quite nicely within the philosophical framework of Malebranche and of others like Norris, who were influenced by him and who, in turn, exerted an influence on Edwards."[109]

Taken together, the evidence shows "some striking similarities between Malebranche's views and Edwards's" on major points: Proceeding from a Christocentric theology, "Both held that God is *being in general*, a view . . . that is developed in remarkably similar ways by [these] two thinkers. Both believed that the perceived world is really an 'ideal world' in God, made known to us by the direct action of God on our minds. And both taught a thoroughgoing doctrine of Occasionalism."[110] This has led a number of writers to posit Malebranche as an influence on Edwards.[111] Among their conclusions are, "The great thoughts of . . . Malebranche . . . became familiar to [Edwards], probably through the personal reading of [his work]"; "The impact of Malebranche on Edwards, even if indirect, seems clear enough," and, more specifically, "Edwards's point of view [in metaphysics] was consolidated, there is reason to believe, by his reading of Malebranche in the early 1720s."[112]

It is, therefore, plausible to conclude that Malebranche influenced the content of Edwards's teaching through the vision of all reality existing in God—God's sovereignty as "Being in general" extending to causation of all events in a world that he re-creates at every moment. Commentators on Edwards have referred to this as his "God-centered vision of

---

108. Fiering, "Rationalist Foundations," 78; Copan, 113. Edwards arrives at these positions through a combination of engagement with Scripture, interaction with literary sources, and philosophical speculation. See, e.g., Holbrook, "Editor's Introduction," 17–97.

109. Copan, "Jonathan Edwards' Philosophical Influences," 113.

110. Wainwright, "Ontology," 95; McCracken, *Malebranche and British Philosophy*, 331.

111. McCracken, *Malebranche and British Philosophy*, 329, 329n36; Lyon, *L'Idéalisme en Angleterre au XVIIIe siècle*, 430–33; Allen, *Jonathan Edwards*, 12; Elwood, *Philosophical Theology of Jonathan Edwards*, 26; Danaher, *Trinitarian Ethics of Jonathan Edwards*, 21; Hastings, *Jonathan Edwards and the Life of God*, 9, 125, 167; Daniel, "Edwards as Philosopher," 177, 177n57; Helm, "Epistemology," 105–6; Minkema, "Malebranche, Nicolas (1638–1715)," 360: "Norman Fiering has convincingly made a case for the influence of Malebranche [on Edwards], whom Edwards also read as a young man." Danaher, *Trinitarian Ethics of Jonathan Edwards*, 130, invokes "Malebranche as the source of Edwards's idealism."

112. Foster, *Genetic History of the New England Theology*, 48; Copan, "Jonathan Edwards' Philosophical Influences," 117; Fiering, "Rationalist Foundations," 78.

all things," his affirmation of the biblical truth that all things are "from [God] and through him and to him (Rom 11:36)."[113] In Edwards's words, "The whole [of reality] is *of* God, and *in* God, and *to* God, and God is the beginning, middle and end in this affair."[114] Underlying Edwards's worldview, this is the vision he articulated throughout his adult life.

Regarding his pedagogy, the God who is sovereign over all events and directs all persons' lives is the God who seeks to communicate his love through creation, through his Word, and through the revelation of his Son, Jesus Christ. Since education is one of "the chief of the means of grace" which God has appointed, as we shall see in chapter 5, communicating this message to students was Edwards's ultimate goal as a teacher.[115]

AUGUST HERMANN FRANCKE (1663–1727)

August Hermann Francke, "Pietist *par excellence*," was a German Lutheran minister, biblical scholar, philanthropist, and educator who taught Greek and Oriental languages at the University of Halle.[116] A person of diverse aptitudes and interests, "Francke was both a theologian with a pedagogical inclination and a rational entrepreneur with commercial acumen."[117] "Francke is acknowledged not only for his institutions and

113. Quotation is in Taylor, "Introduction," 14.
114. Edwards, "Dissertation I," 531 (emphasis added).
115. Edwards, "Farewell Sermon Preached," 484.
116. Quotation is in Sattler, *God's Glory, Neighbor's Good*, ix.
Regarding the Pietists, of whom Francke was a luminary: "The myriad ways they read, preached, interpreted, translated, and practiced the Bible are inextricable from how they pursued religious and social reform [in which Francke participated prominently], fashioned new forms of devotion, founded new institutions [foremost among them the *Franckesche Stiftungen*, discussed later in this section], engaged the early Enlightenment, and made sense of their world . . . . They applied the Word to liberate souls from the bondage of sin, unshackle true religion from the manmade traditions and hierarchies of Christendom, and unyoke civil rights and freedom of conscience from political tyranny" [in all of which Francke engaged consistently]; Hoselton, "Introduction," 1, 10.
See also Shantz, "Bible Editions, Translations, and Commentaries in German Pietism," 20: "Jurgen Quack identifies Francke's 'Einfaltiger Unterreich wie man die H. Shrifft zu seiner wahren Erbauung lesen solle' [Halle, 1694] as the most popular and most-published of all German prefaces [to the Bible] along with Luther's. Francke's 'Einfaltiger Unterreich' was included in most of the Bibles published by the Canstein Bible Society in Halle."
117. Matthias, "August Hermann Francke (1663–1727)," 100. See also Olson, "Pietism," 8–9. See Russell, *German Higher Schools*, 64, quoted in Cubberley, *History of Education*, 419–20: "Francke had the rare ability to see clearly what needed doing, and then do it regardless of obstacles or consequences. The magnitude of his work in Halle

remarkable organizational skills but also for his innovative approach to education. He incorporated the ideas of several religious thinkers who were also concerned about education . . . especially Johannes Amos Comenius (1592–1670), and he is recognized for putting these ideas into practice in a highly visible way."[118]

This multidimensional figure was hailed as one of the most productive leaders of the German Pietist movement. Two major streams characterized Francke's activities: conceiving and activating a potent combination of both scholarly and practical interest in Scripture, and concern for living out Scripture's precepts regarding love of neighbor and attention to the needs of children.[119] Among Francke's notable accomplishments, those in the area of education have been singled out for special praise. Indeed, Francke "cannot be understood apart from his very impressive contribution to the field of education, and his achievements in this area must be seen in the light of his vision of the future, which shaped his educational philosophy."[120] His involvement in education and social welfare ushered in a new era in how learning and Christian-based reforms should be conceived and practiced, resulting in an astonishing

---

is simply marvelous, and yet what he actually accomplished is insignificant in comparison with what he inspired others to do. He showed how practical Christianity could be incorporated in the work of the common schools; his plan was immediately adopted by Frederick William I [1688–1740; King of Prussia, 1713–1740] and made well-nigh universal in Prussia. He showed how the *Realien* could be profitably employed in a Latin school, and even made a constituent part of a university preparatory course; as a result of his methods, and especially of his suggestion that schools should be founded for the exclusive purpose of fitting the youth of the citizen class for practical life, there has since grown up in Germany a class of *Real*-schools."

118. Bunge, "Education and the Child in Eighteenth-Century German Pietism," 248–49. See also *SJER*, 210n1; Goen, "[All Christians Should Honor God in Every Way]," 528n4: "[August Hermann Francke (1663–1727) may be credited with institutionalizing the Pietistic movement in German Lutheranism begun by Philipp Jakob Spener (1635–1707). Appointed to a professorship at the University of Halle (in Saxony) in 1691, Francke by the time of his death had made the school a center of Pietism. His influence was multiplied many times over through educational foundations, philanthropic institutions, and evangelistic missions throughout the world]"; Shantz, *Introduction to German Pietism*, 122–23. N.B.: "From the beginning, Francke was inspired . . . by a pedagogical philosophy that he described as 'guiding the children to true godliness and Christian intelligence,'" (401n26).

119. Bunge, "Education and the Child in Eighteenth-Century German Pietism," 247–8.

120. Stoeffler, *German Pietism During the Eighteenth Century*, 23–24, 24n1. See also Stoeffler, *Continental Pietism and Early American Christianity*; Hoselton, "Introduction," 1n3, 2n5.

Further Influences on Edwards's Pedagogy

number of institutions, to be discussed below.[121] Rejecting the typical approaches to education of his day, Francke advocated coeducation and education of children of all socioeconomic strata. In championing the general causes of grand reforms, Francke did not lose sight of the particular; he "paid attention to the individual needs and abilities of students." In all of his labors, this preeminent Pietist "emphasized not only the acquisition of knowledge but also the development of character."[122]

In 1686 in Leipzig, Francke co-founded the *Collegium Philobiblicum*, which originally focused on study of the Bible in the original languages among academics, and later was reoriented toward devotional exercises in spiritual growth.[123] This pastor and educator sets forth his vision for institutional reform in his *magnum opus*, now known as *Der Grosse Aufsatz (The Great Essay*, 1704).[124] Becoming convinced of the need of a complete, worldwide revision of all levels of the school system, Francke determined to establish "a model educational community on all levels of the educational enterprise."[125]

---

121. See Sattler, *God's Glory, Neighbor's Good*, 47.

122. Bunge, "Education and the Child in Eighteenth-Century German Pietism," 249.

123. Ripley and Dana, "Francke, August Hermann"; Falbusch, "Francke, August Hermann," 2:345; Saebø et al., "Francke, August Hermann," 2:909; Matthias, "August Hermann Francke (1663–1727)," 101. See also Yoder, *Pietism and the Sacraments*. See Shantz, Introduction to *German Pietism*, 104, for the names and brief biographical information on the seven co-founders with Francke of the *Collegium Philobiblicum*.

124. See Stoeffler, *German Pietism During the Eighteenth Century*, 24n1: "Francke's educational vision is embodied most fully in a tract to which Gustav Krämer gave the title *Der grosse Aufsatz* in 1882, and which since that time goes under that name. Francke himself gave it the title *Offenherzige und gründliche Nachricht von der innerem Beschaffenheit und Wichtigkeit des Werks des Herrn zu Halle—sowohl— als was unter dem ferneren Segen Gottes davon zu hoffen*. It was written in 1704 and most painstakingly edited by Otto Podczeck in *Abhand lungen der sächsischen Akademie der Wissenschaft zu Leipzig* in 1962. We refer to it as his *Great Essay*." See also Shantz, Introduction to *German Pietism*, 129–30: "In 1704 Francke composed a 125-page report that he sent to supporters and friends. Entitled *A Sincere and Thorough Report concerning the Inward State and Importance of the Work of the Lord in Halle, in the Duchy of Magdeburg*, it became known simply as *The Great Project (Der Grosse Aufsatz)*. It has long been considered the most important literary reflection of the goals and vision of Halle Pietism"; Shantz, Introduction to *German Pietism*, 129. In this work, Francke sets forth his plan for worldwide social reform "through reform of Christian education" (129).

125. Stoeffler, *German Pietism During the Eighteenth Century*, 25. See Shantz, Introduction to *German Pietism*, 123: Regarding all of the schools established in the Halle project, "The schools' reputation and progressive program attracted children from all over Europe."

To Understand *Things* as Well as *Words*

The results were astounding and were much of Francke's adult life in the making. Coming under Francke's direction between 1695 and his death in 1727 were what were known as "Francke's Institutes" (*Franckesche Stiftungen*): a school for the poor, a Latin school for preparing sons of ordinary citizens for the university and for careers in medicine, law, and theology; a *Pedagogium* for instructing the sons of the upper class and nobility in positions in the military and government; a school and seminary for training teachers for these establishments (the Seminarium Praeceptorium, established in 1697, was "the first teachers' training school in German lands, and the teachers he trained served to scatter his educational ideas over the German States"), as well as pastors and missionaries; a large-scale print shop (that "dispatched pious books as far off as Siberia and in a few years issued more editions of the Bible" ("about two million complete Bibles and one million New Testaments in the eighteenth century") in various languages "'than in the whole Period of the Time, from the *Reformation* until *Now*"); a bookstore ("one of the largest in Germany at that time"); a pharmacy; a library; a small home for widows; a pediatric hospital (perhaps the first one in Germany), and an orphanage ("the hallmark of this [network], the largest after the Reformation social reform movement of the early modern period").[126]

What this enterprise encompassed was nothing short of astonishing in its scope. This interconnection of projects was "unheard of" at the time, covering nearly thirty-seven acres and engaging almost three thousand students, teachers, and staff.[127] This network of reform programs "distinguished itself from similar contemporary 'modish' ideas of utopia"

---

126. See Mather, *Nuncia Bona*; Schmid, *Die Geschichte des Pietismus*, 286-320; Francke, *Faith's Work Perfected*, 84-89; Schmidt, *Wiedergeburt und Neuer Menschs*, 195-237; Stoeffler, *German Pietism During the Eighteenth Century*, 25-27; Tappert, "Influence of Pietism in Colonial American Lutheranism," 31, 32; Sattler, *God's Glory, Neighbor's Good*, 47-67; Bunge, "Education and the Child in Eighteenth-Century German Pietism," 248, 254-55; Matthias, "August Hermann Francke (1663-1727)," 101; Herzog, *European Pietism Reviewed*, 20-21; Sweeney, *American Evangelical Story*, 36; Olson, "Pietism: Myths and Realities," 8; Loch, "Historische Zusammenhänge und phänomenologische Unterschiede," 264-308; Silverman, *Life and Times of Cotton Mather*, 231-32; Woodbridge and James, *From Pre-Reformation to the Present Day*, 262; Hoselton, "Bible in Early Pietist and Evangelical Missions," 117-18, 118n31; Shantz, *Introduction to German Pietism*, 117-19; Minkema, "Reforming Harvard," 339; Obst, *August Hermann Francke und Sein Werk*, 73-99; Cubberley, *History of Education*, 418-19.

127. Bunge, "Education and the Child in Eighteenth-Century German Pietism," 248, 254-55, 255n29; Ward, *Protestant Evangelical Awakening*, 62. See also Stoeffler, *German Pietism During the Eighteenth Century*, 1-38; Herzog, *European Pietism Reviewed*, 20-21, 46n80.

Further Influences on Edwards's Pedagogy

by actual functional and practical results.[128] Largely through the activities of Francke, Halle became a hub from which Pietism as orthodoxy and as orthopraxy was widely diffused all over Germany, beyond Europe, and even into the New World, producing "Christian leaders for all spheres of society who could advance spiritual and social renewal."[129]

Finding the breadth and the success of the enterprise at Halle "dazzling," Cotton Mather trumpeted Francke's Institutes in his publication *Nuncia Bona* (1715) and initiated a correspondence with their founder, beginning in 1710 and continuing through 1724.[130] In depicting Francke

128. See Bunge, "Education and the Child in Eighteenth-Century German Pietism," 248n3, 248n4, 254n26, 255n29, 255n30; Shantz, *Introduction to German Pietism*, 123, 402n28, Minkema, "Reforming Harvard," 339, for statistics regarding the capacities and outputs of the various components of the *Franckesche Stiftungen*.

129. "Francke, August Hermann"; Chisholm, *Encyclopaedia Britannica*, 2:4–5; Shantz, *Introduction to German Pietism*, 129; Minkema, "Reforming Harvard," 339. See also Matthias, "August Hermann Francke (1663–1727)," 102; Bunge, "Education and the Child in Eighteenth-Century German Pietism," 248; Woodbridge and James, *From Pre-Reformation to the Present Day*, 262: For nearly four decades, Francke's "energetic endeavors established Halle as the center of German Pietism and its diffusion" throughout the world. A specific example of Francke's influence extending into colonial America is that of the orphanage he founded serving as the model for a similar institution "established in 1738 by the Salzburg Lutherans in Georgia"; Tappert, "Influence of Pietism in Colonial American Lutheranism," 32. See also Bunge, "Education and the Child in Eighteenth-Century German Pietism," 248n4, in part: "See Klaus Deppermann, "August Hermann Francke," in *Orthodoxie und Pietismus*, ed. Martin Greschat (Stuttgart: Kohlhammer, 1982), 257; and Udo Sträter, "Pietismus und Socialtätigkeit: Zur Frage nach der Wirkungsgeschichte des 'Waisenhauses' in Halle und des Frankfurter Armen-, Waisen-, und Arbeithauses," *Pietismus und Neuzeit* 8 (1982): 201–30. For the influence of Francke's institutes in other countries, see, e.g., Wolf Oschlies, *Die Arbeits- und Berufspädagogik August Hermann Franckes (1663–1727): Schule und Leben im Menschenbild des Hauptvertreters des halleschen Pietismus* (Wittenberg: Luther-Verlag, 1969), 41–46; for their influence in the United States, see, e.g., Hermann Winde, "Die Frühgeschichte der Lutherischen Kirche in Georgia" (unpublished dissertation, Martin- Luther-Universität Halle-Wittenberg, 1960), 135–48; and Thomas J. Müller, *Kirche zwischen zwei Welten: die Obrigkeitsproblematik bei Heinrich Melchior Muehlenberg und die Kirchengründung der deutschen Lutheraner in Pennsylvania* (Stuttgart: Steiner, 1994)."

130. Silverman, *Life and Times of Cotton Mather*, 232. "I have followed the text of *Nuncia Bona* in Kuno Francke, 'Further Documents Concerning Cotton Mather and August Hermann Francke,' *Americana Germanica*, I (New York, 1897), 54–66" (448); Minkema, "Reforming Harvard," 338; Thuesen, "Editor's Introduction," 67. Regarding the correspondence between Mather and Francke, see Benz, "Pietist and Puritan Sources of Early Protestant World Missions," 28–55; Splitter, "Fact and Fiction of Cotton Mather's Correspondence," 102–22; Scheiding, "World as Parish," 131–66. Benz, "Pietist and Puritan Sources," argues that a personal correspondence between Mather and Francke and their "intimate exchange of thought about the meaning and task of Protestant missions" contributed significantly to the early development of

To Understand *Things* as Well as *Words*

in *Nuncia Bona* as "a seminal force in modern Christianity," Mather effuses, "More than all Europe will soon feel, yea, has already felt the precious Effects of the *Franckian* education."[131] This approbation indicates that Francke influenced Cotton Mather's perspective on learning through his having instituted coeducation and the ideal of universal education at the *Franckesche Stiftungen* at Halle.

The English translation of Francke's first report of Pietist activities throughout Europe was called *Pietas Hallensis*. This work began giving Boston Puritans an outstanding impression of the projects themselves and of the attitude of the Pietists as allies of the Puritans in completing the Reformation of the Church and of society.[132] In a letter written in 1717

---

eighteenth-century missions (29).
Cf. Splitter, "Fact and Fiction of Cotton Mather's Correspondence," who discovers minimal evidence of direct correspondence between the two and argues that the letters they exchanged "contain little of substance or import" (103). Furthermore, "According to the current state of research, no more than six letters, written in Latin in 1711, 1712, 1714, 1715, 1719, and 1724, are known to have been sent or received by Mather or Francke over a period of thirteen years" (106, see also 106n14, 106n15, 106n16). Splitter concludes that it is a "decided exaggeration to refer to the intermittent, limited contact between Mather and Francke as a "correspondence"" (122). Commenting on Francke's apparent lack of reciprocity in the epistolary exchange with Mather, Scheiding observes, "no one has considered that Francke's response to the books, letters, and money that Mather mailed to Halle may not have been transacted as continuous exchange of personal letters, but instead took the form of what Böhme called a 'Historical Narrative' (in Francke's *Pietas Hallensis* v), that is, of quasi-official reports (or circulars) about activities in Halle"; "Fact and Fiction of Cotton Mather's Correspondence," 137. Scheiding (citing Silverman, *Life and Times of Cotton Mather*, 199) notes that Mather produced "the largest extant correspondence of an American Puritan," at approximately 600 letters. Francke "had about 5,000 correspondents and was in constant contact with at least three to four hundred of them'"; Scheiding, "World as Parish," 133. Although Mather was not among Francke's main correspondents, their "Boston-Halle connection is of real significance that is easily overlooked" by focusing only on their exchange of letters. The interaction between Mather and Francke offers insights into "the genuine affinities and, most importantly, mutual exchange of ideas that existed between Franckean Pietism and third-generation American Puritanism." In fact, their transatlantic conversation "enjoyed much greater reciprocity in terms of mutual interest and influence than is commonly understood or acknowledged"; Scheiding, "World as Parish," 133, 133n4.

131. Silverman, *Life and Times of Cotton Mather*, 232. See also Beall and Shryock, *Cotton Mather*, 93: The connection between Francke and Mather is "an especially significant instance" of continuous intellectual contact between early modern Germany and the New World.

132. *Pietas Hallensis: or a publick demonstration of the foot-steps of a divine being yet in the world* (London: J. Downing, 1705). See Benz, "Pietist and Puritan Sources of Early Protestant World Missions," 28–55; Benz, "Ecumenical Relations," 163; Silverman, *Life and Times of Cotton Mather*, 231. The English translation *Pietas Hallensis*

Further Influences on Edwards's Pedagogy

in which he responds to Francke's report, Mather refers to the "blessing light of the gospel" that was shining on the Continent and, newly, in the colonies: "The sun of righteousness of blessedness arose. This is the work of God, and is a miracle to our eyes as well as to all believers."[133] In addition, in the preface to his *Manuductio*, Mather lavishly praises (in Latin) the Frederician Academy "wherewith Halle blooms and shines, and with which all the academic world, as the copy of this criterion, ought to be shining"[134] In summary, in recognition of his deep spirituality, entrepreneurial acumen, and organizational skills, to Mather, as someone he "loved and deeply respected," the founder of the vast network at Halle was truly "the incomparable Dr. Franckius."[135]

Francke also earned the respect of Edwards. In a letter dated June 1, 1740 to Josiah Willard, "a widely connected evangelical and secretary of the Massachusetts Province," Edwards inquired concerning "the latest accounts of the progress of that affair at Halle in Saxony. I have seen nothing since the account we had of Dr. Francke's life, published by Mr. Samuel Mather [Cotton Mather's son] in Boston."[136] In addition, Edwards spoke and wrote publicly of his admiration for the practical manifestations of Francke's godliness and talents. In two sermons, one included in *A History of the Work of Redemption* (1739) and also his "Much in Deeds of Charity" (1741), as well as in his musings, "Some Thoughts Concerning the Revival" (1743), Edwards spoke glowingly of the labor Francke expended in doing "the great work that God wrought by him," which "has now been carried on for above thirty years." The result was "a wonderful

---

was done by Anton Wilhelm Böhme (1673–1722), the German chaplain at the Court of St. James in London, of Francke's work *Segensvolle Fusstapfen des noch lebenden und waltenden liebreichen und getreuen Gottes* (1701), "an institutional history of the charity school at Halle," which "documented the accomplishments of the educational and social reforms" there; Scheiding, "World as Parish," 134 (see also 134n6, 135n7); Benz, "Pietist and Puritan Sources of Early Protestant World Missions," 32, 39–40; Wallmann, *Der Pietismus*, 131–32; Yeide, *Studies in Classical Pietism*, 39–61. For the importance of Böhme's work as a translator and as someone involved in ecumenical relations, see Benz, "Ecumenical Relations," 160–62.

133. Benz, "Ecumenical Relations," 166.

134. Mather, *Manuductio ad Ministerium*, xiv.

135. Lovelace, *American Pietism of Cotton Mather*, 4; Mather, *Man Eating the Food of Angels*, 63; Mather, "Preface," ; Silverman, *Life and Times of Cotton Mather*, 231; Thuesen, "Editor's Introduction," 67; Splitter, Fact and Fiction of Cotton Mather's Correspondence," 111n37, 114n54. See also Scheiding, "World as Parish," 131–66; Harwood, "Perhaps No One General Answer Will Do," 24–25.

136. Stout, "Revivals as Millennial Harbingers," 24; *LPW*, 83.

reformation and revival of religion, and a spirit of piety in the city and university of Halle." Francke's undertakings not only "had great influence in many other places in Germany," but had "spread its happy influences into many parts of the world," seeming "remarkably to stir up multitudes to their imitation."[137] Edwards's tribute makes it clear that he esteemed Francke as an example of "religious affections," of true Christianity in action, both by teaching "doctrine and precept" and by practicing "instance and example," in the same manner as he did David Brainerd.[138]

Edwards's view of the role of a teacher and his pedagogical methodology will be examined in the following chapters. Given (1) the high regard in which Edwards held Francke, (2) the parallel between each one's convictions that education should be for the ultimate purpose of preparing students for the regenerated life and the work of Christ, and that education should be available to all, regardless of gender or economic status, and (3) the fact that educating male and female students in the same environment beyond the home was not widely practiced in Edwards's milieu, and, thus, immediate positive examples of this practice were not readily at hand, an influence of Francke on Edwards's pedagogical philosophy and practice is highly probable.

ANDREW BAXTER (1686/7–1750)

Andrew Baxter was a Scottish metaphysician who "maintained the distinction between matter and spirit," and thus "resisted the more advanced British epistemology" of his time. Baxter's view of human freedom in his work *An Enquiry Into the Nature of the Human Soul* (1733) Edwards quoted approvingly in *Freedom of the Will*.[139] A measure of Baxter's standing with his contemporaries is the fact that a second edition of his *Enquiry* was considered necessary in only four years, and critical notice was taken

---

137. Edwards, "Sermon Twenty-Four," 436; Edwards, "Much in Deeds of Charity," 210; Edwards, "Some Thoughts Concerning the Revival: Part IV," 528. See also Hoselton, "Bible in Early Pietist and Evangelical Missions," 109–28, 118n35; Hoselton, "Jonathan Edwards, Halle Pietism, and Benevolent Activism in Early Awakened Protestantism," 51–68; Stievermann, "German Pietism," 248, 249.

138. Quotations are in Edwards, "Author's Preface," 89.

139. "Andrew Baxter: Scottish Philosopher," www.britannica.com/topic/rationalism; Baxter, *Enquiry Into the Nature of the Human Soul*. See Edwards, *Freedom of the Will*, 379n, 386n2, and 392n5. N.B.: "Edwards later quoted the third edition of Baxter in footnotes to *Freedom of the Will*"; Thuesen, "Editor's Introduction," 76. See also Chisolm, *Encyclopaedia Britannica*, 3:551; Stephen, "Baxter, Andrew (1686–1750)," 3:425.

Further Influences on Edwards's Pedagogy

of this work within two years of its first printing.[140] Additionally, Baxter authored *Matho: or, Cosmotheoria Puerilis* (1738), in which he constructs a dialog between a six-year-old boy and a teacher regarding philosophy and science. This work appears in Edwards's *Catalogue of Books* as one which he regards favorably and recommends for its educative value.[141]

Matho consists of two volumes containing ten dialogues in six "conferences" between Matho, "a boy of genius" who is "very desirous of knowing" certain things, and his friend, Philon, who agrees to assist him.[142] They begin with questions about the rotation of the earth and gravity, move on to such subjects as motion of objects in the air moving contrary to the rotation of the earth, and conclude with a discussion of the divine power and creativity displayed in creation.

Matho's exchanges with Philon lead the earnest student to conclude, "[I]t is the most grievous absurdity, and a contradiction to nature, to suppose the *non-existence* of the Deity. If the Deity did not exist, nothing at all could ever have existed . . . Hence I see that being and perfection must be infinite and necessary." To this, Philon asks, "Does this necessity hold as well to eternity as from eternity?" Matho responds, "To suppose that this necessity could ever cease, is to suppose the necessity of being and perfection a *possibility* only of being and perfection!"[143] Thus, the dialogic interaction has led to the conclusion, "Eternal truths discover [i.e., reveal] to us, immediately and by themselves, an eternal intellect."[144]

Yet again, plausibility based on parallels between a pedagogical practice of Edwards's and an example of such a practice from someone

---

140. Bracken, "Andrew Baxter, Critic of Berkeley," 183–4, 184n5. "[A] few pages of [Baxter's] reasonings have not only more sense and substance than all the elegant discourses of Dr. [George] Berkeley, but infinitely better entitle him to the character of a great genius"; Fraser, *Works of George Berkeley*, 3:400; Bracken, "Andrew Baxter, Critic of Berkeley," 184n7. Baxter's *Enquiry* seems to have influenced Scottish Common-Sense philosophers Thomas Reid and James Beattie; Bracken, "Andrew Baxter, Critic of Berkeley," 184, 184n8. See also Reid, *Inquiry into the Human Mind on the Principles of Common Sense*; Beattie, *Essay on the Nature and Immutability of Truth in Opposition to Sophistry and Scepticism*.

141. Baxter, *Matho: or, Cosmotheoria Puerilis*; Edwards, *Catalogues of Books*, 37, 76, 179. See Edwards, *Catalogues of Books*, 700: Baxter's *Matho* is included on a list Edwards compiled in 1751 of books which he recommended to Sir William Pepperrell for use in teaching Native Americans in his "Letter 135," 406–14; Minkema, "Informing of the Child's Understanding," 168; Potgieter, "Education," 412.

142. A. Baxter, *Matho*, 1:1–3.

143. Baxter, *Matho*, 1:320–21.

144. Baxter, *Matho*, "Table of Contents.

of whom he was aware comes to the fore here. At Stockbridge, Edwards lamented "the gross defects of the ordinary method of teaching among the English" and "the common methods of instruction in New England," which were founded on rote memorization, and he implemented instead a dialogic methodology.[145] Judging by Edwards's characterization, at least to his knowledge, simple memorization was the common pedagogical methodology in the colonial New England of that time. This makes an example of someone other than Baxter, of someone actually practicing dialogic instruction, unlikely. Therefore, given Edwards's awareness of and approval of Baxter's *Matho* and his own affirmation of the dialogic approach to instruction, an influence by Baxter on Edwards's pedagogical praxis is virtually conclusive.

CONCLUSION

Even the most innovative of thinkers draws upon sources of inspiration, reworks them, builds on others' ideas, and takes them in new directions. As discussed in the previous two chapters, this Edwards did as a product of a Puritan background responding to the challenges posed to Christian orthodoxy by certain key currents of "the Enlightenment(s)." The historian's task in tracing the development of a person's ideas is aided if the person being studied has left records in which he or she acknowledges debts to those whose ideas have proved useful to him or her. This Edwards has done in the cases of Locke (to some extent) and Newton.

On the other hand, evidence is frustratingly scant regarding the origins and development of his pedagogy. Thus, the historian is presented with three options: abandonment of the search, continuation of the search, or reliance on plausibility of influence in the cases of similarity of ideas and parallelism of praxis. We have certain facts at hand: (1) Edwards was brought up in an environment in which he was surrounded by educated women who participated in educating him. (2) Instruction from the Bible in preparation for salvation was foundational in his home. (3) Through the fame Comenius experienced in Edwards's time for his advocacy of universal education and Edwards's participation in the Republic of Letters, Edwards was likely aware of Comenius's views on education. (4) Evidence demonstrates that Edwards was aware of and admired Francke's work, including his pedagogical philosophy.

---

145. *LPW*, 407, 409.

Further Influences on Edwards's Pedagogy

(5) Parallels exist between Edwards's early family environment (erudite females having predominated), Comenius's and Francke's convictions regarding educating females, and Edwards's vision of and practice of instructing female as well as male students. (6) Edwards was aware of and approved of Baxter's *Matho*, which details a dialogue between a student and a teacher, and Edwards advocated and used a dialogic methodology with his students throughout his teaching experience. (7) Coeducational praxis and dialogic pedagogical methodology were not much (if at all) in evidence in Edwards's environment during his time, limiting the scope of possible influences on his views to persons of whom he was aware. (8) Lastly, there is no known evidence of Edwards having disclaimed any influence of his home, Comenius, Francke, or Baxter on the formation of his pedagogy.

Taken together, this evidence makes it probable (1) that Edwards's early domestic environment influenced his view of the centrality of instruction in Scripture to the purpose of education and educational content, and the scope of education as properly including females; (2) that Malebranche influenced the content of what Edwards taught via reinforcing his underlying worldview; (3) that Comenius (perhaps indirectly) and Francke also influenced Edwards's commitment to theocentric content and coeducational praxis; and (4) that Baxter bolstered Edwards's use of dialogic methodology. It is unlikely that Comenius, Malebranche, Franke, or Baxter persuaded Edwards to abandon a view he held in favor of another. Rather, Edwards likely found in each of these a kindred spirit who reinforced a way of thinking to which Edwards had already (at least largely) committed.

Thus far, this study has examined ways in which Edwards was influenced by elements of Puritanism and intellectual trends of "the Enlightenment(s)," prevalent in his day. A case has been presented for the plausible influence of Edwards's parents and sisters and of four persons active in educational theory and/or practice on Edwards's pedagogy. In the following chapter, we move beyond speculation and plausibility in order to examine the philosophical background of Edwards's pedagogical philosophy and praxis.

5

Jonathan Edwards as a Teacher and His Pedagogical Methodology

Background

THIS CHAPTER WILL MOVE beyond the influences on Edwards's pedagogy and will examine the background of what Edwards sought to achieve as an educator and what he in fact achieved (to the extent evidence permits this outcome). His written words in records of his private thoughts and in his correspondence, his spoken words from the pulpit, and his actions as a pastor and as an educator, indicate that Edwards employed a consistent, fully developed pedagogical philosophy which was holistic in application, and a praxis which was dialogic in foundation. Gleaned from the *ethos* of his Puritan background, the spiritual and intellectual environment of his upbringing, ideas adopted and modified from the influences examined in chapters 3 and 4 of this study, and his own thoughts, Edwards applied an approach to teaching that was bibliocentric in content, learner-centered in character, and God-focused in direction. As we shall see in the following chapter, this he did in his own familial environment, with Bible students and with ministerial aspirants at Northampton, with Native American and Anglo-colonial students at Stockbridge, and with senior-class students at the College of New Jersey.

Furthermore, throughout his adult life, teaching (both as a pastor in the pulpit and as an educator in the classroom) occupied a substantial amount of Edwards's time and claimed much of the effort he expended.

Jonathan Edwards as a Teacher and His Pedagogical Methodology

Therefore, his view of the nature and purposes of education and the function of a teacher in terms of expected outcomes regarding students will be examined. Since children and Native Americans are two cohorts of students whom Edwards taught, his view of each of these categories of persons will be discussed in turn.

In addition, his instructional methodology will be examined in relation to the pedagogical praxis common at that time. The revolutionary paradigmatic shift in the role of the student that Edwards's methodology entailed will also be discussed. These examinations set the stage for the following chapter, in which the pedagogical philosophy and praxis which characterized Edwards's teaching will be analyzed as employed by his students Francis Bellamy and Samuel Hopkins. This evaluation will highlight the role of dialogic holistic education on what became known as the New Divinity movement. In doing so, some of the key ministers who comprised the New Divinity and major ways in which the New Divinity movement impacted eighteenth and nineteenth-century America will be examined.

EDWARDS'S VIEW OF THE ROLE OF TEACHING IN PASTORAL MINISTRY

Teaching (considered as imparting knowledge or conveying information to someone, and encouraging and enabling the development of skills, habits, values, and goals) was integral to all of the public functions Edwards performed in his adult life.[1] Christian evangelism in the form of

---

1. A formal definition of education does not appear in Edwards's works. However, see Stelting, "Edwards as Educator," 214, who summarizes education as Edwards would have conceived it as, "those deliberate experiences which, engaging the senses of the student, produces [sic] understanding and inclination; these are demonstrated in the intentional actions of the student." See also Jannenga, "Making College Colonial," 21, for perhaps the most basic definition of teaching (or "pedagogy"), as referring to "the methods and practices utilized by educators to impart knowledge to their students"; Knight, *Philosophy of Education*, 9: "Learning," as distinguished from formal education occurring in a school setting, may be defined as "'the process that produces the capability of exhibiting new or changed human behavior . . . provided that the new behavior or behavior change cannot be explained on the basis of some other process or experience'—such as aging or fatigue"; Laska, *Schooling and Education*, 6. See also Frankena, "Model for Analyzing a Philosophy of Education," 9: "Education is primarily a process in which educators and [persons being] educated interact," which is intended to produce "certain desired or desirable abilities, habits, dispositions, skills, character traits, beliefs, or bodies of knowledge"; Coley et al., *Transformational Teaching*, 48: "The aim of education is to promote the development of each human being as he/she

communicating the gospel in order to achieve "the advancement and enlargement of Christ's kingdom on earth," and thus to "glorify God in the world," motivated Edwards's actions as a minister, as a theologian, as a philosopher, and as an educator.[2] This is evident from what Edwards wrote throughout his life in his corpus of correspondence, as well as in his published works and his public sermons. Each of these capacities requires instruction in order to inform someone's understanding and to bring about a desired result in the formation or transformation of a person's intellect, character, and/or nature. Comparing Edwards's written statements concerning the significance of education with his actions as a minister and as an educator reveals the consistency of his words with his deeds regarding education's function in preparation for this life and for the next.

"Edwards stands firmly in the evangelical tradition of [the Apostle] Paul, Augustine, and Calvin, in holding that preaching as a means of conversion and grace is a collaboration of the 'word of God' [i.e., the minister as the voice of God and the message preached] and the Word of God."[3] Always paramount in Edwards's mind was awareness of instruction in Scripture being the primary function of a minister: God, having set in place those he has appointed to be proclaimers and expositers of the sacred text in churches "to be *teachers*, . . . he [has] made it their business *to impart knowledge . . . of divinity*." Therefore, teaching is essential to the proper performance of preaching in imparting the divine message as revealing the will of God. A minister stands as Christ's ambassador and proxy to exposit Scripture to his listeners in order that they might "know the Word of God, [so] that [they] might be instructed by it" concerning

---

was intended to be as an image-bearer of God, [as] one who reflects his character"; Matthias, "Faith and Learning," 179: "Learning" can be defined either as "a body of knowledge related to particular academic disciplines or as an intellectual process . . . . The latter includes any intellectual activity or use of one's mind to acquire, assimilate, interpret, and evaluate [the] body of knowledge." Palmer, *To Know As We Are Known*, 88, emphasized the outworking of the teaching/learning process is his definition, "To teach is to create a space in which obedience to truth is practiced." Edwards strove to bring about learning in school settings in the form of changed behavior from students resulting from both acquisition and assimilation of knowledge, informed understanding, and "the new spiritual sense" given in regeneration. As importantly, his teaching and his mentoring of students encouraged and enabled his students to discover scriptural truth and to practice (to put into action) obedience to it.

2. Quotations are in *LPW*, 518; Edwards, "Diary, February 25, 1723/24," 784, Edwards, "Personal Narrative," 800.

3. Westra, *Minister's Task and Calling in the Sermons of Jonathan Edwards*, 56.

its meaning and application, in order to "Let the word of Christ dwell in [them] richly in all wisdom" (Col 3:16), so that, ultimately, they would be "conformed to the image of [Christ] (Rom 8:29).[4]

"As a student of divinity and searcher of the Word of God, the gospel minister becomes expert in 'that science of doctrine which comprehends all those truths and rules which concern the great business of religion.'"[5] The edification of a minister's flock in the Sacred Word, with the great ends in view of converting the unregenerate and of guiding and strengthening the people of God, is a task of divine appointment. "Speaking 'as the oracles of God' in their commission to preach the full gospel, ministers are painstakingly to search the Scriptures they are especially chosen to safeguard and transmit to God's people."[6] Firmly rooted in his Puritan heritage, Edwards regarded the Bible as "a book of divine instructions," from which issues "the light of life; a sweet, excellent, life-giving word."

With this in mind, Edwards strove "to unpack the text [of Scripture] in a pedagogical way, with the formation of disciples at the forefront of his mind. He interpreted its language for the edification of everyday sinners *cum* saints . . . teaching lessons from the Bible in a systematic manner and applying them to the daily lives of everyone who listened."[7] As a minister of the Word, Edwards was divinely commissioned to explicate and to apply to his congregants the "most noble, and worthy, and most entertaining objects of man's most noble faculty, viz. his understanding, the most excellent things that man can exercise his thoughts about."[8] For Edwards, as Christ's ambassadors, ministers of the gospel are to follow

---

4. Edwards, "Sermon 525," Edwards, "To the Mohawks at the Treaty. August 16, 1751," 107. See Snoddy, "Preaching," 457–59. "Preaching, for Jonathan Edwards, was an exalted task, the heroic work of one chosen and called to serve as Christ's 'ambassador' or earthly representative" (457).

5. Westra, *Minister's Task and Calling*, 25; Edwards, "Importance and Advantage," 85.

6. Westra, *Minister's Task and Calling*, 24; Edwards, "Warning to Professors," 4:531. See also Holloway, "Homiletical Theology of Jonathan Edwards, Gilbert Tennent, and Samuel Davies," 77–78.

7. SD, 1739–1742, 93; Edwards, "Personal Narrative," 801; Sweeney, *Edwards the Exegete*, 188. See also Stelting, "Edwards as Educator," 168: "Edwards viewed the ministry as would an educator"; Stelting, "Edwards as Educator," 170: "When Edwards mounted the pulpit, he came to instruct his congregation," his goal being the explication and application of God's Word to his hearers.

8. Edwards, "Heeding the Word, and Losing It," 46. See also Edwards, "525. *Heb. 5:12*": "The truths of divinity are of superlative excellency"; in divine things are "the most excellent truths, and the most beautiful and amiable objects held forth to view."

their Lord's example by being "wont to take opportunities to deliver heavenly instructions to teach [persons] those things that [pertain] to their salvation."[9] Indeed, a minister acting on Christ's behalf, under his "infallible guidance," is "sent forth to *teach the world* the will of Christ."[10]

As Edwards further expounds, ministers are divinely commissioned to spread the seed of the Word widely and indiscriminately; to "teach Christ's laws," that is, "to teach [persons] what Christ would have them to do and to teach them who doth these things and who doth them not."[11] In a striking example, in what "might well be both his most mystical and his most sensual ministerial sermon," one abounding in conjugal imagery, Edwards takes care to note that ministers are "the instructors . . . of God's people" in order that the Church as Christ's bride may be "properly educated."[12] Likewise, in his "Farewell Sermon," in which he delivered what he believed would be his closing message to his Northampton congregation, he reminded his listeners, "Ministers are set [in place] as . . . teachers" of a congregation who "meet their people from time to time in order to instruct and enlighten them."[13] Fulfilling this mission signifies the expositors of Scripture as having been "set [in place] to be lights to the souls of men . . . as they are to be the means of imparting divine truth to them."[14]

The teaching function was crucial to Edwards in preaching because God has appointed the senses and rational understanding as the means of receiving knowledge of his redeeming grace and all things of divinity. Whatever takes hold of the heart and is manifested in one's actions must first pass through the door of one's understanding. "God, in letting this [supernatural] light into the soul, deals with man according to his nature, or as a rational creature; and makes use of his human faculties."[15] There-

9. Edwards, "Sermon 086. Luke 14:16"; Edwards, "Sermon 525. *Heb. 5:12.*"
10. Edwards, "Miscellany 40," 222 (emphasis added).
11. Edwards, "Miscellany qq," 188; Edwards, "Miscellany 40," 222.
12. Westra, *Minister's Task and Calling,* 169; Edwards, "Church's Marriage to Her Sons, and to Her God," 169, 187.
13. Edwards, "Farewell Sermon Preached At The First Precinct In Northampton," 466. In fact, Edwards preached to the Northampton congregation after this date, because of the church's difficulty in securing another minister. See Winslow, *Jonathan Edwards, 1703–1758,* 260–67; Sweeney, "River Gods and Related Minor Deities," 2:449; Marsden, *Jonathan Edwards: A Life,* 364.
14. Edwards, "True Excellency of a Minister of the Gospel," 90.
15. Edwards, "Divine and Supernatural Light," 416; Edwards, "Divine and Supernatural Light," 114. See also Snoddy, "Preaching," 457: "It was in the context of

fore, "He that doth not understand, can receive no faith, nor any other grace."[16] As Edwards explicated, "No speech can be any means of grace, but by conveying knowledge."[17] This reality places a high demand on one who proclaims and seeks to explain the Divine Word, as, "All teaching is in vain, without learning."[18]

EDWARDS'S VIEW OF THE ROLE OF TEACHER IN EDUCATION

Educating students in a classroom was equally as vital an evangelistic ministry to Edwards as was instructing congregants via his sermons. In each of these capacities, Edwards personified "the teacher who affects eternity." Through instructing parishioners and students alike in the holy verities of Scripture, he opened the way for them to receive the "divine and supernatural light" of regenerative grace and to have imparted to them the "new spiritual sense." By God's grace blessing these efforts, Edwards's listeners were given priceless lessons in how best to live the present life and how to prepare for the world to come.

It was Edwards's conviction that "the art of teaching," particularly of children (for Edwards, persons younger than fifteen years of age) as the formation of their mental capacities is beginning, required someone of "superior abilities and education" and "superior talents," including "great prudence, faithfulness, and constant application" to the task.[19] Equal to

---

preaching, Edwards held, that God ordinarily imparted a *simple idea* by a supernatural light" (emphasis added). This means of expression emphasizes Edwards's appropriation of Locke's concept of "simple ideas" in the service of God's bringing his congregants the "supernatural light" through Edwards's preaching.

16. Edwards, "Importance and Advantage," 88.
17. Edwards, "Importance and Advantage," 88.
18. Edwards, "Importance and Advantage," 87; Edwards, "525. Heb. 5:12."

Westra, *Minister's Task and Calling*, 26, records a way in which Edwards indicates his awareness of this responsibility, other than through his public utterances in the sermons themselves: "Along the margin of his Bible, Edwards . . . observes that the most important 'business and labours of a minister of the gospel' is 'to explain and apply the word of God to his hearers'"; see Westra, *Minister's Task and Calling*, 26n80: "P. 814 of the interleaved Bible in the Beinecke Edwards MSS Collection."

19. Adams, *Education of Henry Adams*, Chapter 20: "A teacher affects eternity; he [or she] can never tell where his [or her] influence stops." Although intended negatively by Adams, who criticizes his Harvard education in his autobiography, this quotation is usually taken in a positive sense regarding the effects a teacher has on his or her students' lives. It is meant in this sense here; *LPW*, 433. Edwards discusses "the divine and supernatural light" and "the new spiritual sense" in his sermon, "Divine and

other qualifications are "uncommon prudence and steadiness of mind" and having one's "heart much in the affair [of teaching]," as evidenced by one's willingness to devote "all the care and strength and skill and constant attendance" possible to the work of leading students on the path to knowledge.[20] Edwards's description of the ideal teacher sets a high standard for pedagogic aspirants and practitioners by requiring someone of a unique combination of gifts, skills, and temperament. A divine calling rather than an occupation, Edwards esteemed the mission of education as being second only to the exposition of Scripture in its significance for preparation for this life and the next.[21]

With this in mind, Edwards sought to open the understanding of the students he taught in classroom settings to the material presented, with an ultimate view to putting the unregenerate on the way to receiving the "new spiritual sense." Edwards stood in the Puritan tradition in his conviction, as expressed by "the patriarch of Stuart Puritans," Richard

---

Supernatural Light" and extensively in *RA*, e.g., 206, 207, 209, and 271. For Edwards's definition of children, see Minkema, "Jonathan Edwards on Education," 31, 263n2: "'Children' . . . were for Edwards those younger than fifteen years of age"; Minkema, "Old Age and Religion," 674, 675; Edwards's letter to Rev. Thomas Prince, December 12, 1743, in Edwards, *Great Awakening* (hereafter GA), 546–47 (*LPW*, 116–17); Brekus, "Children of Wrath, Children of Grace," 302. Quotations are in *LPW*, 433; *LPW*, 447.

20. *LPW*, 433; *LPW*, 447. Teaching effectively is a formidable task, requiring someone of not only of serious purpose, but also of pure heart and astute mind, since "An educator is responsible to steward the *process* of learning as well as the *content*"; Colwill, "Dialogical Learning and a Renewed Epistemology," 155 (emphasis added).

21. "Piety," "prudence," an even temperament, ability to inspire trust in one's good will, and sound character, weigh as heavily on Edwards's scales as do one's learning and communicative ability in his criteria for teaching effectively; see *LPW*, 422–30; *LPW*, 434–47; *LPW*, 493–509; and *LPW*, 629–43. These qualifications make clear that only a regenerated person would meet Edwards's standards for a teaching position. In addition to the letters noted in note 20 above, in *LPW*, 422–30; *LPW*, 434–47; *LPW*, 493–509; and *LPW*, 629–43, Edwards indicates the esteem in which he holds the calling of teacher through the qualifications he lists as being necessary.

In this regard, Edwards's concepts both of a teacher and of the teaching enterprise parallel those of "that incomparable Moravian": See Comenius, *Outline of a Pansophic School (Delineatio)*, 3:35–60; Comenius, *Pampaedia*, 80–81. "Comenius believed that the teacher was God's servant on earth . . . . Education, stated Comenius . . . meant the cultivation of wisdom, virtue, and piety"; Mayer, *Road to Modern Education*, 164. See also Murphy, *Comenius*, 112.

Note also the similarity in this regard to Francke: See Francke, *Pädagogische Schriften*, 93: Education is of no avail if the teacher is not "thoroughly turned to God. The work of education is beyond all powers of the natural man." "Education is not only a demanding and eminently significant task, it is also a divinely appointed labor which requires the power of God and a born-again instructor"; Sattler, *God's Glory, Neighbor's Good*, 53.

Jonathan Edwards as a Teacher and His Pedagogical Methodology

Baxter, that "education is God's ordinary way for the conveyance of his grace."²² Edwards himself affirmed education as being one of "the chief of the means of grace" which God has appointed to effect conversion, through evangelization and instruction in Scripture.²³ He attested, "God gave man the faculty of understanding, chiefly, that he might understand divine things."²⁴ Therefore, in the conversion process, "God deals with man as a rational creature," through presentation of Scripture to the understanding.²⁵ As Edwards emphasized, "There is no other way by which any means of grace whatsoever can be of any benefit, but by knowledge . . . . Such is the nature of man, that nothing can come at the heart but through the door of the understanding."²⁶ Ultimately, which students received the grace conveyed by his teaching was determined by God, but Edwards fulfills the ideal that he holds of an educator by preparing the way for them to receive it.

Edwards considered the understanding "as including the whole faculty of perception or apprehension, and not merely reason or judgment."²⁷ It is the means by which a person "is capable of perception and speculation, or by which it discerns and views and judges things."²⁸ That being the case, education is a primary factor that, once "introduced

---

22. Axtell, *School Upon a Hill*, 12; Baxter, *Autobiography of Richard Baxter*, 10.

23. Edwards, "Farewell Sermon," 484. See also Edwards, "Writings on the Trinity, Grace, and Faith," 21:58–59: "God makes use of means; but it is not as mediate causes to produce this effect . . . . The Word of God is only made use to convey to the mind the subject matter of this saving instruction: and this indeed it doth convey to us by natural force of influence"; Edwards "taught his [Northampton] congregation that conversion was in general a process achieved by the use of means. 'The way to obtain grace is daily to wait upon God for it in the use of the means of His appointment'"; Minkema, "Edwardses," 216–17; Edwards, "Prov. 8:34," *Sermons, Series II, 1731–1732*; "Edwardses," 217n34. "Though the means in themselves had 'no influence to produce grace either as causes or instruments,' yet they were necessary for the 'production of grace'; Minkema, "Edwardses," 219; Edwards, "Miscellany 539," 84, 88; Minkema, "Edwardses," 219n44.

24. Edwards, "Importance and Advantage of Divine Truth (1739)," 35; Edwards, "525. Heb. 5:12."

25. Edwards, "Importance and Advantage of Divine Truth (1739)," 31. See also Edwards, "Divine and Supernatural Light," 130: "God, in letting in this ['divine and supernatural'] light into the soul, deals with man according to his nature, or as a rational creature; and makes use of his human faculties."

26. Edwards, "Importance and Advantage of Divine Truth (1739)," 31–32; Edwards, "525. Heb. 5:12."

27. *RA*, 96.

28. *FW*, 147. See also Minkema, "Jonathan Edwards on Education," 33: "Knowledge is acquired, and thereby choices informed, through understanding."

and established" in the mind, informs a person's choices and determines one's will.²⁹

This astute pedagogic theorist envisioned education as being a holistic undertaking. The proper function of an educator is that of engaging the entire faculties of the person being taught (the intellect, will, and affections) by "informing [a student's] understanding, influencing his [or her] heart, and directing its practice."³⁰ To Edwards, in a truly complete educational process, a student has his or her knowledge of the subject(s) taught augmented in a way that leads to the realizations that "the fear of the LORD is the beginning of knowledge" (Prov 1:7a) and "everything is related because everything is related to God"; the understanding informs the will of the need for regeneration; and "religious affections" become the student's choices and actions.³¹ Learning should be *formative* and

---

29. *LPW*, 409. See also Blore, "Educational Philosophy of Jonathan Edwards," 37: "[T]he gospel was for Edwards at the center of all endeavors to educate"; *The Development of a Curriculum of Religious Education* (1928), 38, quoted in Wyckoff, *Theory and Design of Christian Education Curriculum*, 35: "The objective of religious education from the viewpoint of the evangelical denominations is complete Christian living[,] which includes personal acceptance of Jesus Christ as Savior and his way of life . . . [and] the Christian motive in the making of life choices." See also Price, "Jonathan Edwards as a Christian Educator"; Wyckoff, "Jonathan Edwards' Contributions to Religious Education"; Wyckoff, *Task of Christian Education*, 25–39, 127–49; Wyckoff, *Gospel and Christian Education*; Wyckoff, *Theory and Design of Christian Education Curriculum*, 17: "The task of Christian education is the [formation and] the nurture of the Christian life. . . . The curriculum task is that of designing a plan for the communicative transaction . . . centering upon a learner or a learning group"; Byrne, *Christian Approach to Education*; Clark, *Christian Philosophy of Education*; Noddings, *Philosophy of Education*; Lee, "Edwards on Education."

See also Colwill, "Dialogical Learning and a New Epistemology," 116–17. In effective learning, considered as a process of transformation involving teacher and student, "The *whole person* imbibes knowledge. Learning is no longer considered an exclusively rational enterprise. [Jane] Vella states, 'All learning involves cognitive, affective, and psychomotor elements.' Knowing, being, [and] doing are inseparable in the learner"; Vella, "Spirited Epistemology," 15; emphasis added. Although Colwill focuses on adult learning in the postmodern era, her conclusion that effective learning engages and affects the combined faculties of a student applies also to Edwards's pedagogical approach to all groups of students he taught.

30. *LPW*, 409.

31. Quotation is in Marsden, *Jonathan Edwards: A Life*, 460. Once "sinners experience God's love" when regeneration occurs, "they begin to love what he loves," and this experience enables "a God-centered vision of all things"; Marsden, *Jonathan Edwards: A Life*, 460; Taylor, "Introduction," 14. See also Marsden, *Infinite Fountain of Light: Jonathan Edwards for the Twenty-First Century*, 129. Regarding the quotation from Marsden, *Jonathan Edwards: A Life*, 460, "everything is related because everything is related to God," another expression of the relatedness of all of reality to God is the aphorism, "All truth is God's truth"; see also Gundlach, "Foundations of Christian Higher Education," 136: "[A]ll truth finds its origin and end in God."

transformative, as well as *informative*. That is, a truly complete educational process not merely *informs what a person knows*; it *transforms how a person lives*.³² In Edwards's ideal, only someone who has had his or her understanding, will, and affections thus awakened and enlivened is

---

"Though the minister cannot change or convert a single soul, he prepares the way for the moving of the affections [by the Holy Spirit]. When the Holy Spirit acts to convert . . . it acts upon the matter that the preaching of the word has furnished to the understanding of the hearer"; Westra, *Minister's Task and Calling in the Sermons of Jonathan Edwards*, 117. Edwards considered this true of teaching, as well. See also Minkema, "Edwardses," 219: "Edwards stated that the more an individual was supplied with 'notions or speculative ideas of the things of religion,' the more objects there were [in the soul] for grace to act upon. The stronger and more lively the ideas of divine things were in the soul, the greater the opportunity for [saving] grace" to act on the soul. As a minister through his preaching and as an educator through his teaching, Edwards sought to maximize the opportunities for those in his charge to receive God's grace.

32. See Colwill, "Dialogical Learning and a New Epistemology," 129–30: "Dialogical education is concerned with transformation at its core. Transformation is not merely cognitive; *the whole person* in the relational context is in view. [Paulo] Freire believed, 'for education to be liberating, one's consciousness must be transformed.' [Jane] Vella asserts, 'transformation is not grasping an external set of information, knowledge, or skills, but rather a change into one's new self, informed by the new knowledge and skills'"; Merriam et al., *Learning in Adulthood*, 325; Vella, "Spirited Epistemology," 7 (emphasis added).

Transformation is a process in which not only the student, but the teacher, as well, is involved. See also Fant, "Teaching and Learning in the Humanities," 217: "Transformational education is the result of incarnational teaching. By this I mean that the educator embodies what it means to be human, including the godly humility that precedes learning, the spiritual disciplines that allow for the Christ follower to flourish, and the personal presence that has a direct impact on students' lives."

A full exposition of the concepts grouped in the category of "Transformative Learning Theory," pioneered by Jack Mezirow and developed by others, is not feasible here. However, "transformative learning," defined as, "the process of effecting change in a frame of reference," often precipitated by a "disorienting dilemma" for the student, holds potential as a significant means by which the type of holistic dialogic instruction Edwards employed could be positively applied in the postmodern world. Edwards realized that each student he taught (and, indeed, every human being) is oriented in a particular context, in which he or she perceives and relates to the world in a particular way, based on an "embodied understanding." This is informed by input from, e.g., one's sensory organs and one's psychological presuppositions. Learning reorients a student by providing opportunities "to embrace [inevitable] disorienting dilemmas or tensions" so as to "engage in deeper learning," i.e., "transformative learning." For Edwards, the ultimate re-orientation was the regeneration effectuated by the "new spiritual sense." Regeneration placed the learner in the proper orientation to God, who is the source of wisdom and strength for continuing "disorientations" the learner would encounter; Mezirow, "Perspective Transformation," 100–110; Mezirow, "Transformative Learning," 5; Lakoff and Johnson, *Philosophy of the Flesh*, 102; Backfish, "Transformative Learning Theory as a Hermeneutic," 281–95.

prepared to teach others, continuing the line of raising up qualified teachers and producing godly students.

In order to achieve these objectives, Edwards considered it necessary to move beyond teaching exclusively by rote memorization ("the common method of teaching among the English") by initiating an interactive dynamic with the student.[33] By the time Edwards delineated his pedagogical philosophy in his aforementioned letter to Pepperrell, he had formed his conception of what a teacher should do and had experience in putting it into practice, as we shall see when we examine Edwards's teaching methodology in the following chapter.[34]

Edwards's recognition of the fact that "all teaching is in vain, without learning" led him to adopt an educational model consisting of a collaboration between teacher and student.[35] In his conception, each party

---

33. Quotation is in *LPW*, 407.

34. Edwards was a tutor at Yale from June 1724 to September 1726, while he was a graduate student there. Although there is some evidence of what he taught and accounts that he taught well there, no record exists that he used the dialogic technique that he used in his later teaching. See Sergeant, *Valedictorian Oration*, 22–24; Warch, *School of the Prophets*, 126; Anderson, "Editor's Introduction," 32; Claghorn, "Introduction," 7.

As noted previously, Edwards's letter to Pepperrell (number 135 in *LPW*) is his most complete statement of his educational philosophy. Edwards's letters from Stockbridge constitute the largest portion of his extant body of correspondence (which comprises over four hundred pages in the Yale *WJE* edition) and they "confirm that he considered the Indians and their mission a high priority"; Marsden, *Jonathan Edwards: A Life*, 388; Claghorn, "Introduction," 17. A substantial portion of this corpus is the result of a large-scale campaign Edwards conducted to alert Rev. Isaac Hollis (the chief financial sponsor of the mission, living near London) and area officials to the difficulties both he himself and the mission were experiencing. As part of this, in order to outline his ideas and plans concerning education in general and instruction at Stockbridge specifically (e.g., *LPW*, 387–90), Edwards bemoaned (as in his letter to Pepperrell) the inadequacies of the rote memorization method of instruction then in use and urged that greater effort be made to teach the Native Americans there English.

Edwards's view of proper teaching qualifications parallels that of Jan Comenius. See Murphy, *Comenius*, 112; Comenius, *Outline of a Pansophic School (Delineatio)*, 3:35–60; Comenius, *Pampaedia*, 80–81. Note also the similarity to August Francke: "Education is not only a demanding and eminently significant task, it is also a divinely appointed labor which requires the power of God and a born-again instructor." Education is of no avail if the teacher is not "thoroughly turned to God. The work of education is beyond all powers of the natural man"; Sattler, *God's Glory, Neighbor's Good*, 53; Francke, *Pädagogische Schriften*, 93.

35. Quotation is in Edwards, "Importance and Advantage," 87; *SJER*, 31. *LPW*, 407–14, is the source of his statements on his pedagogical philosophy and goals for this section, unless otherwise noted. See *LPW*, 408–9, for Edwards's conception of the "familiar," or dialogic, technique of teaching.

assumes a responsibility in a reciprocal relationship. The teacher sets as goals both conveying portions of "the knowledge of human arts and sciences, and skill in temporal affairs" and directing the learning process toward engendering the student's interest in gaining "a true sense of the divine excellency of the things revealed in the Word of God, and a conviction of the truth and reality of them, thence arising."[36]

Edwards realized that the achievement of this ultimate outcome (especially in the case of children) necessitated a process that could be many years in the making. He therefore envisioned as a function of an instructor, not only teaching the subject at hand, but also encouraging and enabling the student to become a life-long learner. Once properly set on the path of learning, the student would develop the capacities "to think and reflect" on what is learned and would acquire "a regularly increasing appetite" for knowledge.[37] Consequently, a teacher, as conceptualized by Edwards, exerts an enduring influence, extending well beyond the amount of time a student spends in a classroom. As significant for the development of the "total person" as stimulating the intellect is, it is inadequate alone. For Edwards, integral to a fully complete educational program is a spiritual component: Accompanying the instruction in the classroom is mentoring of the student "singly, particularly and closely, about the state and concerns of his soul," with an emphasis on the significance of prayer.[38]

---

36. Edwards, "Divine and Supernatural Light," 409, 414; *JER*, 106, 111; *SJER*, 122, 126. See Blore, "Educational Philosophy of Jonathan Edwards," 37n112: "[T]he gospel was for Edwards at the center of all endeavors to educate." Edwards's conviction was that the spiritual component of education should not only begin early in life but also continue as a vital part of the entire schooling process. He considered it necessary for "the governors and instructors of the colleges particularly, singly and frequently to converse with the students about the state of their souls"; *GA*, 512.

37. *LPW*, 408. See also Potgieter, "Education," 410.

38. *LPW*, 412. See also Bezzant, "'Singly, Particularly, Closely,'" 205–25, and Bezzant, *Edwards the Mentor*. "Mentoring" Bezzant defines as "that intentional activity between two people which seeks to empower for spiritual development, often with the result of enhancing skills and attitudes for leadership"; Bezzant, "Singly, Particularly, Closely," 207. As we shall see in the following chapter, Edwards considered this an essential component of education.

Schnittjer, "Ingredients of Effective Mentoring," 86–100, discusses another mentoring model from eighteenth-century colonial America. See also Bezzant, *Edwards the Mentor*, 157n159.

To Understand *Things* as Well as *Words*

Edwards's educational philosophy and praxis brought about a shift in the way in which students were viewed that was groundbreaking for its time and place. He rejected viewing a student as a passive recipient of information who was expected to store it and reproduce it on demand. Instead, Edwards treated the student as an active participant in the learning process through interactive engagement with the instructor. When actuated, this conception had an empowering and dignifying effect on the student by recognizing him or her as a human being made in the image of God with the capacities of understanding and reasoning.

EDWARDS'S VIEW OF CHILDREN: "CHILDREN OF WRATH"

A gruesome image of Edwards has long captured the popular imagination—that of a "curious, rather mad eighteenth-century preacher, preoccupied with hell-fire [and with] a God of wrath" who unleashed on humanity "the hatred of 'all of Adam's children with a hatred bordering on the pathological.'"[39] However embedded in the collective psyche and deeply ingrained in American culture it has become, this picture is distorted. Underlying Edwards's complex view of humanity is his grasp of the paradox of the human condition: corrupted and sinful, yet rational and redeemable.[40] We shall now examine this reality as it applies to chil-

---

39. Angoff, *Literary History of the American People*, 1:302; Cherry, *Theology of Jonathan Edwards*, 1. See Storms, *Tragedy in Eden*, 1: "Mental portraits often have a way of embedding themselves in the American consciousness and are expunged, if at all, only by the most diligent effort. Contemporary perception of Jonathan Edwards, the mere mention of whom evokes the image of a deranged fanatic infatuated with eternal torment and a God of vengeance, is a case in point"; Cherry, *Theology of Jonathan Edwards*, 1: "Images have a way of fixing themselves in the American consciousness, and this image of Edwards is not easily shattered . . . . [However,] Clyde Holbrook has directed us to the fact that the caricatures are as much a commentary on the interpreters of Edwards as on Edwards himself"; Cherry, *Theology of Jonathan Edwards*, 1–2; Holbrook, "Jonathan Edwards and His Detractors," 388.

40. "Nobler than the angels, lower than a worm," is the Pietist expression of this paradoxical condition; see Sattler, *Nobler Than the Angels, Lower Than a Worm*. "Nobler than the angels" because of what a person *is* as the supreme work of the Creator and *becomes* through regeneration; "lower than a worm" in the fallen condition, apart from God. Both the Pietists and the Puritans are in the Augustinian/Reformed lineage with regard to the *imago Dei* being present in humanity, but being damaged and diminished by the Fall, and thus accounting for the duality of human nature. "[T]he credit, glory, and initiative for the individual's conversion are ascribed to God, but there needs to be some remnant of the *imago Dei* which is yet capable of renewal and of responding to the promptings of the Holy Spirit." By having been created in the *imago Dei*, human nature is capable of being united in Christ with the nature of God. This view is "seen

dren; as it applies to Native Americans will be discussed in the following section.

The two sides of the coin regarding Edwards's outlook toward the youngest human beings are as "children of wrath" and "children of grace"; that is, persons "indelibly tainted with original sin, and yet also capable of genuine faith."[41] Regarding the former proposition, the extent to which Edwards was "hardly sentimental in his attitudes toward children" may well be repulsive to modern sensibilities.[42] "The proofs of natural goodness [of humanity] adduced in Edwards's time were sometimes quite sophisticated and not easily dismissed"—even more so, it would seem, in the case of children, whose immoral actions would not have persisted for as long, nor have reached the level of culpability, of their adult contemporaries.[43]

Yet Edwards forthrightly rejected the "common inclinations" among many in his day to rationalize away eternal punishment as excessive and unjust, especially of children.[44] He staunchly defended (albeit perhaps in a novel way) the Calvinistic doctrine of all humanity's being born with the taint of guilt of original sin imputed to Adam's posterity.[45] Edwards

---

in Francke's pedagogical thinking wherein he encourages teachers to 'paint with living colors' the 'soul's true nobility as it exists in its renewal in the image of God'" (xi, 33, 32, 32n10, 32n11). See also Clifton-Soderstrom, *Angels, Worms, and Bogeys*, 7, 7n8.

41. See Brekus, "Children of Wrath, Children of Grace," 300–328; 301. See also Brekus, "Remembering Jonathan Edwards's Ministry to Children," 40–60; Slater, *Children in the New England Mind in Death and in Life*, 22: "The Puritans viewed the child as a paradox: an innocent façade behind which lurked all sorts of wicked desires." For example, Samuel Willard describes infants as, "innocent vipers": *Mourners Cordial Against Excessive Sorrow*, 77. See also Fleming, *Children and Puritanism*. Cf. Ryken, *Worldly Saints*, 84: "Despite their harsh comments about the depraved nature of children, the Puritans actually had an optimistic view of the possibility of children becoming youthful Christians."

During his Northampton pastorate, Edwards preached thirty messages specifically to children and young persons; Kistler, "Preface," v. These messages blended warnings of their fates if remaining "children of wrath" with appeals to their becoming "children of grace" and consequent rewards.

42. Quotation is in Brekus, "Children of Wrath, Children of Grace," 301. See also Chamberlain, "Edwards and Social Issues," 331.

43. Quotation is in Fiering, *Jonathan Edwards's Moral Thought and Its British Context*, 175.

44. Quotation is in Edwards, "Miscellany 1226," 158. See also Holbrook, "Editor's Introduction," 1–67, for the "clearest explanation of Edwards's complicated understanding of original sin"; Brekus, "Children of Wrath, Children of Grace," 311n27.

45. Regarding the relationship between Edwards and "orthodox Calvinism," see Muller, "Jonathan Edwards and the Absence of Free Choice," 3–22; McClymond,

wrote that it is "exceeding just, that God should take the soul of a newborn infant and cast it into eternal torments," explaining that no one who is saved is "saved by the death of Christ from damnation that have not deserved damnation."[46]

In further explication, Edwards observed that God's perspective on all of the unregenerate is the same: All human beings "are by nature the children of wrath and heirs of hell; and that every one that has not been born again, whether he be young or old, is exposed every moment to eternal destruction, under the wrath of Almighty God."[47] Furthermore, in the case of unregenerate children, the divine perspective differs from that of

---

"Hearing the Symphony," 67-92; Helm, "Different Kind of Calvinism?," 91-103; Pederson, "Orthodoxy," 430: "Edwards's Trinitarianism was articulated within the context of a 'classical' Christian orthodoxy that upheld the triunity of God, the distinction between persons of the Trinity, and the incarnation of God's Son. Thus, overall, Edwards can be seen as standing within the line of orthodox Calvinism," although his "relation to his tradition" in certain respects "has been contested; that debate will no doubt continue"; Barshinger, "Sin and Evil," 248: "Edwards did not merely repeat theological tropes but creatively defended old doctrines"; Smith et al., "Editors' Introduction," viii: By appropriating and modifying traditional Calvinist tenets and the ideas of such luminaries as Newton, Locke, and Malebranche, Edwards "fashioned . . . an 'Edwardsean' worldview whose conceptual and metaphorical pillars upheld traditional doctrines in compelling new ways"; Everhard, "Jonathan Edwards," 234: "Jonathan Edwards both defended a Calvinism that was at least as conservative as that which his ancestors bequeathed to him; yet . . . doing so from an empirical and rational methodology that was in some ways wildly creative; Marsden, *Jonathan Edwards: A Life,* 458: "Edwards' defense of [the Reformed doctrine of] original sin demonstrates "that he was simultaneously a strict conservative and an innovator . . . . Edwards's genius was to show how his core theological views were intellectually viable in the Enlightenment era."

46. Edwards, "Miscellany n. Damnation of Infants," 169. Cf. Allen, "Children as 'White Paper,'" 169-85, especially 175-79; Allen, "Holy Children are Happy Children," 17. Edwards's view of original sin affecting children must be nuanced with respect to his historical context. As a "Puritan in the Age of Reason" who was an adapter of "Enlightenment(s)" ideas in defense of Christian doctrines, Edwards was "a transitional figure during the rapidly changing eighteenth century . . . . In many ways, Edwards became not only the eighteenth century's greatest articulator" of the paradox of the human condition, highlighted through "Calvinist interactions with Enlightenment principles"; he "also offered the finest attempts to reconcile it." "As with many other topics, Edwards saw in Enlightened childhood philosophy new ways to make sense of his traditional beliefs . . . . His comments about childhood were not written as a grand topical discourse but were rather necessitated by local circumstances and common attitudes. As a result, Edwards's view of childhood cannot be explained without understanding its immediate context"; Allen, "Children as 'White Paper,'" 173, 174. Significantly, Allen, "Holy Children are Happy Children," 30, observes that Edwards "never explicitly states that all unborn infants *are* sent to Hell, only that *if* they are, it would be fair" (emphasis in original). (Cf. Brekus, "Remembering Jonathan Edwards's Ministry to Children," 51-52.) See also Allen, "Holy Children are Happy Children," 34-38.

47. Edwards, "Some Thoughts Concerning the Revival: Part III," 394.

humans: "As innocent as children seem to be to us, yet if they are out of Christ, they are not so in God's sight, but are young vipers, and are infinitely more hateful than vipers, and are in a most miserable condition."[48]

It is doubtless difficult for modern readers, far removed from Puritan culture and its underlying presuppositions, to sympathize with Edwards's view in this matter. A contention of this analysis is that Edwards was a complex combination of a person at once defined by his eighteenth-century colonial milieu and a person not limited by such constraints. Regarding his viewpoint toward the unregenerate, including children, Edwards was definitely a product of his Puritan heritage and environment, in which punishment for God's wrath continually loomed as a genuine prospect.[49] Those in Edwards's religious tradition found scriptural support for the guilt of original sin resting on children as well

---

48. Edwards, "Some Thoughts Concerning the Revival: Part III," 394. In some interpretations, Edwards's view of imputation of guilt and the taint of original sin is not as harsh as it may seem here. See, e.g., Slater, *Children in the New England Mind in Death and in Life*, 60, 61: "Edwards rejected the old idea that there was some sort of taint, pollution, fountain of evil or the like in the soul at birth, deserving of punishment in itself. Native depravity could instead be explained by God's withdrawal of the divine principles that had been present in human nature before the race's joint apostasy.... Evil was not intrinsic to human nature, but was the invariable result of it: 'These inferior principles [that remained in human nature after the fall] are like fire in [a] house; which, we say, is a good servant, but a bad master'"; "The correct explanation [of human depravity] was that human nature's constituent principles of self-love, passion, and appetite, although not evil as such, always coerced the will by improper motives, except when combined with the divine elements that the regenerate obtained through grace"; Edwards, *OS*, 382–83; Brekus, "Children of Wrath, Children of Grace," 310: "[I]nfluenced by Thomas Aquinas, [Edwards] described sin as privative: it was the inevitable result of human frailty after Adam's fall." Adam's loss of holiness as a result of the divine, or "superior principles," had resulted in an inability to control his passions. This "mere human nature" was passed on to all of his posterity. As a result, infants "were morally *neutral* at birth, not corrupt, but without God's indwelling spirit, they began to sin as soon as they were 'capable' of it"; see Brekus, "Children of Wrath, Children of Grace," 310n26; Brekus, "Remembering Jonathan Edwards's Ministry to Children," 45; Edwards, *OS*, 50–51, 134, 135–6n2. In any case, it is "no wonder that Edwards regarded children as anything but little victims, for they came into the world with the human's 'infallible disposition to be wicked as soon as possible'"; Slater, *Children in the New England Mind in Death and in Life*, 61; *OS*, 283.

Edwards's statement, "Little children are innocent and harmless," should be understood in the context of his propensity for typological interpretation; it helps explain a "spirit of love, meekness, quietness, forgiveness and mercy, as appeared in Christ," and the reason that Christ "represents all his disciples, all the heirs of heaven, as little children"; *RA*, 349, 345; McClymond and McDermott, *Theology of Jonathan Edwards*, 118; Allen, "Children as 'White Paper,'" 177, 177n44.

49. See Brekus, "Children of Wrath, Children of Grace," 306–10, for a concise discussion of factors affecting the cultural and intellectual context of Edwards's time.

as adults in Ps 51:5, "I was shapen in iniquity; and in sin did my mother conceive me" and Romans 5:12: "[A]s by one man sin entered into the world, and death by sin; and so death passed upon all men, for that all have sinned."

In addition, "the Puritans fed their children a steady diet of catechisms and books" which warned them of a wrathful God provoked by sin, *all* sins, including those of children.[50] For example, in the words of the *Westminster Confession of Faith*, because of the disobedience of mankind's primordial parents, "They being the root of *all mankind*, the guilt of this sin was imputed; and the same death in sin, and corrupted nature, conveyed to *all their posterity* descending from them by ordinary generation."[51]

Therefore, "From this original corruption, whereby *we* [all humans, including children] are utterly indisposed, disabled, and made opposite to all good, and wholly inclined to all evil, do proceed all actual transgressions."[52] Corruption of the original human nature produced a result characterized by total depravity; therefore, when "God looks to the heart," he sees a heart full of "heart whoredom, heart sodomy, heart blasphemy, heart drunkenness, heart buggery, heart oppression, heart idolatry; and these are the sins that terribly provoke the wrath of Almighty God."[53]

The outlook was no less bleak for children than for adults. In a bestselling book of 1662, Rev. Michael Wigglesworth depicts an angry God condemning sinners—even children—to "endless pains and scalding flames."[54] Among those portrayed in this work are ones whose lives

---

50. Quotation is in Brekus, "Children of Wrath, Children of Grace," 304. See also Brekus, "Remembering Jonathan Edwards's Ministry to Children," 41. (See note 57; below.)

51. *Westminster Confession of Faith*, 19 (emphasis added).

52. *Westminster Confession of Faith*, 19 (emphasis added).

53. Shepard, *Works of Thomas Shepard*, I:29.

54. Wigglesworth, *Day of Doom* (quotation is in Stanza 37, 10); see also Cotton, *Spiritual Milk for Boston Babes*; Brekus, "Children of Wrath, Children of Grace," 304, 304n10.

The Day of Doom is considered "the most popular poem that New England has ever known" and "America's first best-seller," selling out its 1,800 copies on the day it was published. This equaled approximately one for every twenty persons in New England at the time. It remained a staple of Puritan households, its status as a popular classic persisting into the following century. In fact, many persons reputedly were able to repeat it from memory as late as 1828. At 224 stanzas, it is the longest poem of the colonial period; Cremin, *American Education*, 131; 16; Trent and Wells, *Colonial Prose and Poetry*, 49–60; Murdoch, *Day of Doom*, x; Daniels, *Puritans at Play*, 38; Allen, "Holy Children are Happy Children," 72n45.

Jonathan Edwards as a Teacher and His Pedagogical Methodology

ended in youth and who plead, "Short was our time, for in its prime / our youthful pow'r was cropt; / We dy'd in youth before full growth, / so was our purpose stopt." This leads to their appeal, "Let our good will to turn from ill, / and sin to have forsaken, / Accepted be, O Lord, by thee, / and in good part be taken."[55] Rather than mercy, this earns a rebuke from the "Judge" for their not having repented during the time that "Free Grace" had given them. In a stern tone comes the unwelcome reprimand, "You had a season; what was your reason / such precious hours to waste? / What could you find, what could you mind / that was of greater haste?"[56]

It is in this context of assurance of eternal punishment for the unregenerate, young and old alike, that Edwards sounded his warnings to "flee from the wrath to come (Luke 3:7)."[57] In a private meeting with chil-

---

55. Wigglesworth, *Day of Doom*, Stanza 108, 28.

56. Wigglesworth, *Day of Doom*, Stanza 110, 28.

57. Brekus's statement, "The Puritans, as many historians have lamented, raised their children in a climate of fear" ("Children of Wrath, Children of Grace," 304; Brekus, "Remembering Jonathan Edwards's Ministry to Children," 42) is misleading, as it lacks a sufficient explanation or contextualizing nuancing. "[I]t would be a mistake to misrepresent the Puritans as unusually harsh or controlling parents, who lacked an awareness of children's special nature"; Mintz, *Huck's Raft*, 10. The "earliest and most often reprinted statements" of the Puritans' child rearing advice, such as Robert Cleaver's *A Godly Form of Household Government* and William Gouge's *Of Domesticall Duties*, "give a rather different impression than the popular stereotype" of Puritans as repressive and tyrannical parents; Sommerville, *Rise and Fall of Childhood*, 127.

Moreover, Puritan parents considered it their sacred duty to do as much as possible to place their children on the way to receiving redemptive grace through "dedicating them to God and praying for them, but also instructing, counseling and warning them and so endeavor to bring 'em into the strait gate, and carry 'em along in the narrow way that leads to life"; Edwards, "Miscellany 849," 76. "According to Puritan doctrine, infants who died unconverted were doomed to eternal torment in hell," since "From a Puritan perspective, childhood was fundamentally tied to the concept of original sin. Beginning at conception, all people possessed a sinful nature and flawed disposition, eternally separating them from God" if remaining unregenerate; Mintz, *Huck's Raft*, 15; Allen, "Children as 'White Paper,'" 170; 170n8; see also Allen, "Holy Children are Happy Children," 17. Given their theological convictions, what some from outside their community may consider a "climate of fear," from the Puritans' viewpoint, was not pointless or cruel. "A true love for [children, Edwards] argued, would wish them born anew and delivered from the curse of sin as soon as possible"; Goen, "Editor's Introduction," 73. In this light, the parents' actions were intended to bring about their children's conversion, partially through warnings of the fate awaiting the unregenerate (see Mintz, *Huck's Raft*, 19).

"Death came easy in the eighteenth century" to young and old alike; "Death was . . . a prominent presence in eighteenth-century lives" ; "maternal deaths were common and children themselves often faced fatal diseases"; therefore, "As early as possible, children were taught to prepare for death." An important point to consider is the infant mortality rate during this period: In an environment in which "as many as three out

To Understand *Things* as Well as *Words*

dren, he warned them not to live in sin in their younger years, because

of every ten infants in New England [in Edwards's time] did not survive to their first birthday (a death rate ten times higher than in the modern United States)," (see also Mintz, *Huck's Raft*, 14–15, 15n15) there existed in Puritan culture a heightened awareness of the necessity of preparing children for salvation as early as possible; Lowe and Gulotta, "Introduction," 16; Marsden, *Jonathan Edwards: A Life*, 413; Bezzant, *Edwards the Mentor*, 101; Mintz, *Huck's Raft*, 20; Brekus, "Children of Wrath, Children of Grace," 316, 316n45; Allen, "Holy Children are Happy Children," 27n35. See Piper, "Sarah Edwards," 73: "How easily might a woman die in childbirth. How easily might a child die of fever. How easily might one be struck by a shot or an arrow of war. How easily might a fireplace ignite a house fire, with all asleep and lost"; See also Slater, *Children in the New England Mind in Death and in Life*, 130: "[S]ince, as parents knew only too well, death could strike anyone at any time ... the sooner conversion with its guarantee of heaven occurred the better." Slater puts the infant mortality rate figure in perspective, noting that "the death rates for children in New England towns" during the "Puritan era (defined as New England's first century, the 1620s to the 1720s)," "although high in comparison with modern levels, were often lower than contemporary European ones" (19, 168n20).

Regarding Edwards, his sermons to parents and to children alike warning of the fate of unregenerate souls were delivered in an era in which "Puritan sermons and moral tracts portrayed children as riddled by corruption," containing such pronouncements as, "'Your *Children* are born with deadly *wounds* of Sin upon their souls'; There is a *Corrupt Nature* in Every Child, in its Infancy: Yea from the *very Birth, they Go Astray Speaking Lyes*'"; Mintz, *Huck's Raft* 11; (see also 11n9); Mather, *Family Well-Ordered*, 11; Lawson, *Duty and Property of a Religious Householder*, 42; Moodey, *Vain Youth Summoned to Appear at Christs Bar* [preached in 1701], 8–9; Paine, *Doctrine of Original Sin Proved and Applyed*, 13; see Slater, *Children in the New England Mind in Death and in Life*, 169n25. In reality, "Privately, [Edwards] seemed to share Cotton Mather's assumption that 'the infants of the godly [who] die in infancy are saved'"; Brekus, "Children of Wrath, Children of Grace," 306; Brekus, "Remembering Jonathan Edwards's Ministry to Children," 42; Edwards, "Miscellany 849," 75: "infants stand fair for being really God's people, and of his church, in God's ordinary way of dealing with mankind." Moreover, although undergirding the Puritan religious ethos was the conception of hell as a reality that spared not the young unregenerate, "Explicit suggestions [from the pulpit] that a particular child might be bound for hell were put forth only in exceptional circumstances"; Slater, *Children in the New England Mind in Death and in Life*, 40. See also Holbrook, "Editor's Introduction," 27n8; Edwards, *"Controversies" Notebook*, 4–6, 10b, 11a, 15, 33, 51, 56, 59–60, 63, 65–6, 69, 73, 87.

In the Puritans' covenant theology, children of church members were considered members of the covenant who were placed "in the way of grace," but were expected to "own the covenant" through participation in the sacraments and church life after conversion. See the *Westminster Confession of Faith*, "Chapter XXV: Of the Church, Section II," 75: "The visible Church ... consists of all those throughout the world that profess the true religion; *and of their children*" (emphasis added). See also Morgan, *Puritan Family*, 7: "[T]hough the covenant of grace was made with an individual believer, the promises he made [to God] were undertaken not just for himself but [on] behalf of his whole household." See also Morgan, *Puritan Family*, 65–86, for a discussion of the relationships between parents and their children, and Morgan, *Puritan Family*, 87–108, regarding parents' responsibility to educate their children; Demos, *Little Commonwealth*, 59–190, for examinations of the composition of the household structure and methods

Jonathan Edwards as a Teacher and His Pedagogical Methodology

"many times persons, by giving way to sin when young, get those customs of sinning that they never leave as long as they live." Thus, regrettably, "many Persons Never Get Rid of the Guilt of the sins of their Youth but it attends them to their Graves & Goes with them into Eternity" if they remain unconverted.

Probably Edwards's bluntest warning to children came in a February 1741 sermon on 2 Kgs 2:23–24 (dealing with the unfortunate fate of "little children" who had mocked the prophet Elisha). Bearing his duty as pastor, as the one to whom "Christ has committed the care of [their] souls," Edwards the quintessential shepherd proceeded to "earnestly seek [their] salvation" by severely warning his young listeners, "God is very angry at the sins of children." Edwards spared no feelings as he made it clear that the outcome of uncorrected, unregenerate behavior is to be "cast . . . into hell [for] all eternity" and to "burn in hell forever."[58] That

---

of dealing with life transitions in a typical Plymouth Colony family. Regarding the fate of unconverted infants, "Over time the Puritans softened the Calvinist emphasis on infant depravity. By the end of the seventeenth century, a growing number accepted the possibility that baptism washed away a child's sins and protected it from damnation"; Mintz, *Huck's Raft*, 15.

Despite the caricature of New England Puritans as "emotionally cold and humorless" as parents who delighted in terrorizing their children with threatening images of "damnation and hellfire," the reality is they "were among the first groups to reflect seriously and systematically on children's nature and the process of childhood development"; Mintz, *Huck's Raft*, 11–12; Huffman, "Train Up a Child in the Way He Should Go," 14: "Interestingly, Puritans were progressive in their understanding of childhood development. They were the first to stress the importance of early learning (even in infancy) as well as the importance of leading by example as well as word"; "The Puritan theory of child development stressed that children were, like their parents, fallen creatures whose sinful bent needed to be redirected toward God and moral goodness. The threefold foundation of Puritan childbearing [likely "childrearing" is intended] was the importance of early training, the influence of example as well as precept, and a balance between restraint and positive support"; Ryken, *Worldly Saints*, 87; Huffman, "Train Up a Child in the Way He Should Go," 14. N.B. Morgan, *Puritan Family*, 108: "Granted its purposes and assumptions, Puritan education was intelligently planned, and the relationship between parent and child which it envisaged was not one of harshness and severity but of tenderness and sympathy."

58. Edwards, "Sins of Youth Go with Them to Eternity," 35; this sermon is also found as Edwards, "Sermon 274"; Edwards, "God is Very Angry at the Sins of Children," 57; this sermon is also found as Edwards, "Sermon 592," 544. See also Holmes, *God of Grace and God of Glory*, 211–40.

See Chun, *Legacy of Jonathan Edwards in the Theology of Andrew Fuller*, 3n7: For recent interpretations of Edwards's view of damnation, "see Jonathan Kvanvig, 'Jonathan Edwards on Hell,' 1–11, and William Wainwright, 'Jonathan Edwards and the Doctrine of Hell,' 13–26, in *Jonathan Edwards Philosophical Theologian*[, ed. Paul Helm and Oliver D. Crisp] (Aldershot: Ashgate, 2003); see also Holmes, *God of Grace*, 199–272. Cf. John

is, "They would spend eternity in a dark pit; they would be tormented by monsters; and no matter how much they wept for mercy, they would be utterly alone, forsaken by their parents."[59] Although this message may be considered today as a harsh exploitation of childhood fears inflicting damage on fragile psyches, in the context of its time it constituted a potent weapon in the arsenal against Satan by warning of the fate of those who succumb to his wiles.

EDWARDS'S VIEW OF CHILDREN: "CHILDREN OF GRACE"

The other side of the coin, the other half of the paradox that is humanity's condition, is that human beings can become "children of grace." Although "Jonathan Edwards knew his hell," and was uncompromising in his efforts to get his listeners to shun it, "he knew his heaven better," and labored equally unstintingly to win souls to it.[60] Acutely aware that "children, like adults, were fully human," Edwards understood that this entailed "they had the potential to be full of sin [if remaining unconverted], but also full of grace."[61]

Gerstner, *Jonathan Edwards on Heaven and Hell* ([Grand Rapids: Baker Book House, 1980; repr.,] Morgan, [PA]: Soli Deo Gloria Ministries, 1999); Chris Morgan, *Jonathan Edwards and Hell* (Glasgow: Mentor, 2004)." See Woznicki, "To Hell with the Enlightenment," 304: "Edwards believed that those in hell exist forever in that state; he denied annihilationism"; see 304n23; Edwards, "Sermon 152." See also Colwell, "Glory of God's Justice and the Glory of God's Grace," 291–308; Trueman, "Heaven and Hell," 75–85; and Holmes, *God of Grace*, 201–11, for discussions of this doctrine in eighteenth-century Puritan theology. (See, e.g., the *"poena sensus-poena damni* distinction," borrowed from Scholastic thinkers; Trueman, "Heaven and Hell," 77; Holmes, "Does Jonathan Edwards Use a Dispositional Ontology?," 202, 202n12; Woznicki, "To Hell with the Enlightenment," 308–9.)

59. Brekus, "Children of Wrath, Children of Grace," 317; Brekus, "Remembering Jonathan Edwards's Ministry to Children," 46. See also Edwards, "End of the Wicked Contemplated by the Righteous," 223. Brekus, "Children of Wrath, Children of Grace," 317, comments, "This sermon echoed Wigglesworth's *Day of Doom.*"

60. Quotation is in Gerstner, "Jonathan Edwards's Place in the History of Christian Thought," 9.

61. Brekus, "Children of Wrath, Children of Grace," 312. See Allen, "Holy Children are Happy Children," 60: "While still viewing children as sinful as 'vipers,' Edwards recognized their malleability and potential for goodness" (See also Mintz, *Huck's Raft*, 11, 11n8). Adapting "Enlightenment(s)" ideas in the defense of Puritan ideals and goals, "Edwards believed in the depravity of children, but treated them as rational persons with misplaced desires"; Slater, *Children in the New England Mind in Death and in Life,* 129–30: "Infants might be a special case" to some in the orthodox Christian tradition

Jonathan Edwards as a Teacher and His Pedagogical Methodology

In point of fact, Edwards's perspective on children brings into focus both his grasp of the paradox of the human condition and his efforts to modify the Lockean construct of persons entering the world as *tabulae rasae*. Edwards's thoughts on persons in childhood resist precise categorization, being "complicated and seemingly contradictory." While viewing children as in a sense "little vipers," he also considered them as "white paper" who enter the world free from "any prepossessions or prejudices of any Judgm[en]t formed or habit Contracted." Because of "the mutual Relation & Circumstances of Parents and Chil[dren]," parents should constantly bear in mind the fact that children "naturally Learn [from] their Parents and are Influenced by them especially when little." It was therefore incumbent upon parents to exercise utmost caution regarding how they influenced their children and what impressions they made on them.

As a means of influencing children himself, the Northampton pastor took care to instruct them directly that Christ died for them as much as for other persons; that "He is reconciled to them & [has] become their Friend." Furthermore, he "Highly prizes them," "Delights in them" and "will surely seek their Good," if they are "willing to give thems[elves] wholly to Him and to "follow & serve him as long as they live."[62] Rather than imposing unbearable restrictions on their enjoyments, following

---

regarding deserving damnation, but "once past three or four years of age the moral situation of a child was essentially the same as an adult's. Without the receipt of saving grace, the depraved individual was certain to be subjected to the unending miseries of hell; with grace he was assured of the eternal bliss of heaven."

I remember an apt comment from one of my seminary professors, Dr. Loyd Melton: "The only people who believe in the innocence of children are those who don't have any." In any case, see Allen, "Children as 'White Paper,'" 169–85. "It was in children that the complexities of human depravity, innocence, and faith could best be understood. They were the future of society, and as a pastor, Edwards held a special responsibility for their eternal state"; Allen, "Children as 'White Paper,'" 174; Allen, "Holy Children are Happy Children," 5: "In children, Edwards saw all the possibilities of the future. As a pastor, he felt that he would be held responsible for their eternity."

62. Edwards, "Sermon, 251." This sermon is also included in Edwards, "Don't Lead Others into Sin," 111–32 (quotation is on 128). Allen, "Children as 'White Paper,'" 170; Edwards, "Sermon 1171," to English children while catechizing, August 1756. See also Edwards, "Most Direct Way to Happiness," 54; Allen, "Children as 'White Paper,'" 182, 182n70. Regarding the importance of the parent-child relationship in its connection to salvation, see Allen, "Holy Children are Happy Children," 58: "Edwards believed [Christian] nurture [by parents] to be essentially tied to a child's salvation. Since children were most malleable and naturally prepared to receive the gospel [as 'white paper'], it would be a great sin [for parents] to fail in Christian nurture." I am thankful to Russell Allen for acquainting me with the sermons cited in this note.

such a course early in life would ensure "obtain[ing] vastly more Excellent Pleas[ures] than [obtainable] by spending yout[h] in sin & vanity"; pleasures that are not "vile & brutish," but rather, "delights of a more sublime nature" and "vastly sweeter & more Exquisitely delighting."

An integral element of Edwards's evangelistic strategy was preaching to both parents and children as a means of putting children in the way of grace. On one occasion, Edwards delivered an American Puritan jeremiad, in which he bewailed the numerous sins and vices which had afflicted his Northampton townspeople, denouncing them as wicked. Lamenting licentiousness among the young people, he indicts, "[P]arents are very much to blame" for laxity and indifference toward their children, resulting in a "vast declension in family education and government"; "How little care do parents take in instructing [and] governing [their children]." Let "heads of families" be "exhorted to take heed," therefore, for "When a people are corrupted, they are not soon purged from it."[63]

In a September 1733 sermon, Edwards reissued his admonitions to parents in a less severe tone. "Persons should be much concerned to know whether they do not live in some way of sin." Here, Edwards reminded parents of their responsibility to teach their children, both by precept and example, through family Bible study and prayer, instruction in the catechism, and by modeling Christian virtue. Parents should be, admonished Edwards, "as Carefull [sic] about the welfare of [their children's] souls as you are about their bodies."[64]

Seizing yet another opportunity to rouse his listeners out of complacency, Edwards took his warnings to parents to their logical conclusion. He called upon his congregation's parents to imagine their feelings if their offspring died young (a realistic possibility). What reaction would watching their "Children [on] their death bed[s] in the sensible [i.e., visible] approaches of death ... Gasping and dying," produce?[65] Could they at least take comfort in the fact that they had fulfilled their parental responsibilities by having exposed their children as much as possible to the means of redeeming grace and having brought them up "in the nurture

---

63. Edwards, "Sermon 323"; Edwards, "Sin and Wickedness Bring Calamity and Misery on a People," 505; Minkema in Edwards, "Sin and Wickedness Bring Calamity and Misery on a People," 484.

64. Edwards, "Sermon 297," 457. See also Edwards, "Sermon 136," 549: "'Tis the [duty] of wise and pious parents, to maintain a true concern of mind towards their children, lest they should fall into sin."

65. Edwards, "Sermon 891."

and admonition of the Lord" (Eph 6:4)? Alternatively, would they regret their negligence as their young ones were "Cast, Gone down into Hell"?[66] In an ultimate worst-case scenario, lax parents of unregenerate children would face the prospect of their condemned offspring "Accusing [them] and Crying out against [them]" before God as judge as having been a "Great occasion of [their] Ruin" through their carelessness regarding instruction and their negative parental example. Parents, therefore, should constantly make "the necessary means of obtaining [salvation]" available to their children, as well as set a Christ-like example, always keeping in mind "That these things be done with the Love[,] compassion[,] & Gentleness of X [i.e., Christ]."[67]

In a December 1740 message, Edwards adopted a revivalistic stance. In "the epitome of the 'awakening sermon,'" he noted the number of conversions among children and young persons during a period of "great and general awakening," and posed a challenge to older congregants who may have grown hardened in their sins: "As we see now, God chiefly moves on the hearts of those that are very young . . . . Shall children, babies and sucklings go into the kingdom of God before you?"[68]

Even though Edwards rejected sentimentalization of childhood with its saccharine images of childlike innocence, he was convinced that "it was possible for God to choose even the tiniest infants for salvation" to make them "children of grace."[69] He mused that God in his sovereignty chooses the time of election: "As to the Time of bestowm[en]t of Conv[ersion], when G[od] hath a design of mercy, he sometimes bestows it on Persons when young or even in Childhood."[70]

Drawing on this thought, in his sermons specifically directed to children, Edwards explained that two paths were open to them (following or rejecting Jesus Christ as Lord) and what lay at the end of each. "When people don't give their youth to God, but spend it all in sin and [in] the service of the devil, what a sin do such people commit." At the

66. Edwards, "Sermon 891."

67. Edwards, "Sermon 251"; Edwards, "Sermon 891."

68. *SD, 1739–1742*, 262; Edwards, "Sinners in Zion," 283, 284; Edwards, "Sermon 585,"; Minkema, "Old Age and Religion," 693, 693n54.

69. Brekus, "Children of Wrath, Children of Grace," 311; Brekus, "Remembering Jonathan Edwards's Ministry to Children," 46.

70. Edwards, "Sermon 345." The idea that conversion could occur at any age is also expressed by some other ministers in Edwards's Puritan tradition. See Hooker, *Unbeleevers Preparing for Christ*, 195; Hooker, *Application of Redemption, and Spirit of Christ*, 266; Beales, "Search for the Historical Child," 385–86.

end of this road lay grievous consequences: "How much willful sin, how many dreadful provocations, what great guilt do such [persons] contract, what uncleanness, and the like?" Clearly indicating that he believed they were capable of receiving redeeming grace, Edwards exhorted them to "[s]eek [the] divine grace in your heart whereby your soul may be beautiful, adorned, and rendered lovely in the eyes of God." "We are all born in sin," Edwards explained; "We come into the world estranged from God, but "an infinitely wise God" has so ordered childhood to be "the freest opportunity to spend their time in seeking God and their salvation," through having provided "Christ for [their] recovery." The appeal to heed the call of the Lord early in life was based partially on the pragmatic recognition that continuation in sin over a period of years hardens one's heart to this call: "If you live in sin in youth, 'tis much less probable that you will be converted afterwards, because the heart grows harder and harder the older you are and the older your sin is."[71]

These messages blend explanations of Scripture appropriate for their level with simple imagery they would find appealing. For example, in "Children Ought to Love the Lord Jesus Christ Above All," Edwards exposited Matt 10:37 as the text.[72] Edwards explained that the first half of this verse applies especially to children toward their parents, while the second half applies particularly to parents toward children. He then praised Christ as being "greater and higher than all the kings of the earth," while being "good and full of mercy and love." Proceeding thence to employ simple imagery, Edwards depicts the love and grace of Christ as so far exceeding anything in this world as the light of the sun, "the brightest of all things," exceeds that of a candle.[73] Christ also exceeds the brightest

---

71. Edwards, "Most Direct Way to Happiness," 53, 55; Edwards, "Sermon 525": "[T]he time of youth is especially the time for learning; it is peculiarly proper for gaining and storing up knowledge"; Edwards, "Early Piety Is Especially Acceptable to God," 5 (also Edwards, "Sermon 341," 801). Likewise, Edwards, "Time of Youth Is the Best Time to Be Improved for Religious Purposes," 12–25, is also in *Sermons, Series II 1731–1732, WJEO*, vol. 46; Edwards, "Ps 119:60a [Summer 1724]": "We ought to make religion our present and immediate business." This sermon is published in McMullen, *Blessing of God*, 89–105. See also Slater, *Children in the New England Mind in Death and in Life*, 130: "[T]he clergy emphasized that [regeneration] was more likely to happen in the early portions [of one's life] than in the middle and late ones when he had become hardened and set in sin"; Cf. Beales, "Search for the Historical Child," 386; Hooker, *Unbeleevers Preparing for Christ*, 198; Hooker, *Application of Redemption*, 268.

72. Edwards, "Children Ought to Love," 167–80.

73. Edwards, "Children Ought to Love," 171.

star, the loveliest flower, and (in an instance of a favorite Edwardian image), the sweetest honey.

Moreover, Edwards reminded his listeners of Christ's love for and attention to children during his earthly life and assured them that his atoning death was "not only for grown persons but for children" as well.[74] Christ's love is irrespective of wealth or social standing; rather, "he stands as it were with the arms of his love open to receive *all children* . . . that he may bless them" and receive them "into communion with him."[75] Regenerate youths' rewards for living in this communion with Christ are "a very sweet life" on earth and will include, in heaven, "a glorious crown . . . which will be a thousand times more excellent than the best crown that is worn by any king or queen."[76]

In this sermon, Edwards stated explicitly his view of paradoxical human nature: "All children are by nature *children of wrath* and are in danger of eternal damnation in hell. But children that live under the gospel have an opportunity to . . . become the *children of God*," and be blessed by Christ, who "stands as it were with the arms of his love open to receive all children" and "to give them sweet manifestations of his love."[77] In doing so, he presents both the precarious situation in which the unregenerate live and the offer Christ extends to them "to seek earnestly that they may be converted [so] that God would fill their hearts with love to Christ now while they are young."[78]

EDWARDS AS A FATHER AND AS AN OBSERVER REGARDING CONVERSIONS OF CHILDREN

In addition to his pulpit pronouncements, Edwards's private musings, his private actions as a father, and his observations of his own children and of other children and young adults, attest to his conviction that even those in the tenderest years of life could be "savingly wrought upon." In a note in which he meditated on the possibility that the standard Puritan morphology of conversion may not apply to all persons who become regenerated, Edwards concluded that persons truly exist who are "regenerated in

---

74. Edwards, "Children Ought to Love," 171.
75. Edwards, "Children Ought to Love," 174 (emphasis added).
76. Edwards, "Children Ought to Love," 175.
77. Edwards, "Children Ought to Love," 174, 175 (emphasis added.)
78. Edwards, "Children Ought to Love," 177.

their infancy [who] live till they are adult[s]," and "without doubt [they] exercise grace gradually as they exercise their reason."[79]

As a father, Edwards's "chief and constant desire for his own children was their salvation," toward which he directed considerable effort.[80] Striving to place his young ones "in the way of grace," he "took much pains to instruct them in the principles of religion."[81] Executing this goal, he regularly interacted with his children "in his study, singly and particularly, about their own soul's concerns; and to . . . give them warning, exhortation, and direction, as he saw occasion."[82] At least three of the Edwards children (Sarah, Jerusha, and Esther), having been put "in the way of grace," to Edwards's understanding were "savingly wrought upon" during the First Great Awakening in March 1740/41. Under their parents' guidance, "the strong spiritual commitment characteristic of conscientious Puritans" flowered during this expression of religious fervency, of which Jonathan was such a vital force.[83]

On the other hand, Edwards's daughter Mary and son Timothy seem to have caused him particular concern regarding conversion. In a July 1749 letter to then-fifteen-year-old Mary, who was away on an extended visit and who "was not yet considered to be in a state of grace," Edwards assured her, "my greatest concern is for your soul's good."[84] In an effusive expression of both parental and pastoral concern, Edwards wrote, "My desire and daily prayer is that you may . . . meet with God where you be, and have much of his divine influences on your heart wherever you may be, and that in God's due time you may be returned to us again in all

---

79. Edwards, "Miscellany 302," 389.

80. Hopkins, *Life of Edwards*, quoted in Dwight, *Life of President Edwards*, 1:587; Price, "Jonathan Edwards as a Christian Educator," 84.

81. Hopkins, *Life of Edwards*, 43. See also Levin, 43; Minkema, "Edwardses," 155; Minkema, "'Informing of the Child's Understanding,'" 162; Goen, "Editor's Introduction," 73n7.

82. Hopkins, *Life of Edwards*, 43. See also Chamberlain, "Family Life," 13; Brekus, "Children of Wrath, Children of Grace," 327: "According to the Reverend Samuel Hopkins, Edwards was a remarkably patient father who taught his children to obey him through love, not fear"; Blore, "Educational Philosophy of Jonathan Edwards," 82.

83. *LPW*, 88. The phrase, "savingly wrought upon" also appears in *RA*, 136; *LPW*, 49, 56; Minkema, "Edwardses," 246; Karlsen and Crumpacker, *Journal of Esther Edwards Burr*, 8.

84. Marsden, *Jonathan Edwards: A Life*, 355; *LPW*, 289; Price, "Jonathan Edwards as a Christian Educator," 84.

respects under the smiles of heaven."[85] He entreated her to "seek effectually for that divine grace and comfort."[86]

The prevalence of serious illness and death during childhood in Edwards's environment provided him opportunities for encouragement of his children's conversions. In letters to his children, "he often reminded them—not morbidly, but almost as a matter of fact [which it was]—how close death might be."[87] For example, in an April 1753 letter (written during a smallpox epidemic) to Timothy, then age fourteen, Edwards pleaded, "whether you are sick or well, like[ly] to die or like[ly] to live, I hope you are earnestly seeking your salvation."[88] Recounting the "warnings you have had in word and in providence," Edwards concludes, "I earnestly desire that God would make you wise [un]to salvation."[89] Similarly, after his expression of tenderness, "I am full of concern for you, often think of you, and often pray for you," Edwards uses the death of a playmate of ten-year-old Jonathan Jr. to exhort his namesake, "This is a loud call of God to you to prepare for death . . . . Never give yourself any rest unless you have good evidence that you are converted and [have] become a new creature."[90]

Lastly, Edwards recorded his personal observations of conversions of children and young persons. The best-known of these accounts is that of Phebe Bartlet, a four-year-old girl with whom Edwards became acquainted in the spring of 1735.[91] After apparently having been witnessed to by her older brother (who had been "hopefully converted a little before" this), Bartlet's parents began observing her retiring to their closet "several times in a day, they concluded, for secret prayer."[92] On July 31, 1735, Bartlet's mother heard her saying from within the closet, in the voice of someone "exceeding[ly] importune and engaged," "Pray, blessed Lord, give me salvation! I pray, beg, pardon all my sins!"[93] Her mother's

85. *LPW*, 289.

86. *LPW*, 290.

87. Piper and Taylor, *God-Entranced Vision of All Things*, 73.

88. *LPW*, 580. Timothy Edwards was in Newark, New Jersey, then the site of the College of New Jersey, as a student.

89. *LPW*, 580.

90. *LPW*, 666–67; also in Ferm, *Jonathan Edwards the Younger, 1745–1801*, 15–16; Marsden, *Jonathan Edwards: A Life*, 412; Piper and Taylor, *God-Entranced Vision of All Things*, 73–74.

91. Edwards, *Faithful Narrative of the Surprising Work of God* (hereafter *FN*), 199–205.

92. [*Two Notable Converts*], *FN*, 199.

93. *FN*, 200.

subsequent attempts to relieve her anguish proved unsuccessful, "till at length [Bartlet] suddenly ceased crying, and began to smile, and presently said with a smiling countenance, 'Mother, the kingdom of heaven is come to me!'"[94]

Edwards indicated by including this account in his *Faithful Narrative* his assurance that she was "savingly wrought upon, and remarkably changed in [her] childhood."[95] In fact, Edwards regarded this account of spiritual rebirth, now considered "the most famous conversion in the eighteenth century," as significant enough to set Phebe Bartlet apart as being the younger of the "two notable converts" during the first wave of what has become known as the "First Great Awakening."[96] In summary,

---

94. *FN*, 200.

95. *FN*, 191, 158. See Karlsen and Crumpacker, *Journal of Esther Edwards Burr*, 21: "It is not surprising that Edwards chose Phebe Bartlet, Abigail Hutchinson, and his wife Sarah as his three exemplars of heartfelt religion, and undoubtedly encouraged evangelical women in particular to keep written accounts of their souls' concerns."

96. Beales, "Search for the Historical Child," 387. See also Allen, "Children as 'White Paper,'" 183. Goen in *GA*, 74, notes that "If any doubted the propriety or efficacy" of Edwards's efforts to evangelize those of tender age, "he could always point to Phebe Bartlet, who was soundly converted at the age of four and was still living a convincing Christian life" some years later (e.g., she had manifested "an uncommon degree of a spirit of charity"); *FN*, 204. See Newcomb, *Memoir of Phebe Bartlett, of Northampton, Mass.*; Parker, "Bartlett, Phebe," 59–60. At age 24, Bartlet(t) married Northampton native Noah Parsons (1731–1814), an American Revolution veteran who fought in battles at Boston, Lexington, Ticonderoga, and East Hoosac, and together, they had six children; www.myheritage.com/names/phebe_parsons www.worcesterfamily.com/Parsons%20Family.htm. "Those who knew her, say that she was a very prayerful, sincere, and devout Christian"; *Memoir*, 34. The headstone at her grave in Northampton reads, "In Memory of Mrs. Phebe Parsons, Wife of Mr. Noah Parsons; Who Died, January 5,1805, In the 74th Year of Her Age"; *Memoir*, 35. See also Gustafson, "Edwards's Place in Anglo-American Literature," 501. In *FN*, Edwards's account of "the young Phebe Bartlett demonstrates the emerging possibilities for infant conversion." The other "notable convert" referenced is Abigail Hutchison, a teenager who, despite being frail, experienced a joyful conversion whose "ecstatic spiritual visions and resignation under extreme physical suffering framed an influential type of female holiness"; see *FN*, 191–99. Stein, "Introduction," 4. Edwards's "Account of Abigail Hutchison," excerpted from *FN*, was reprinted by the American Tract Society in "thousands upon thousands of copies" in the early 1800s; Gura, "Edwards and American Literature," 276.

In Edwards's record, "near[ly] thirty" persons between the ages of ten and fourteen experienced conversion in the revival detailed in *FN*, two between the ages of nine and ten, and one (Phebe Bartlet) about the age of four; *FN*, 158. See also Minkema, "Old Age and Religion," 689: "At Northampton, the 1734–1735 awakening dramatically, though only temporarily, reversed the trend in the church's aging membership. Edwards's success in drawing in the younger generations during revivals is amply demonstrated." See Chamberlain, "Edwards and Social Issues," 331–32, 332n21; Brekus, "Children of Wrath, Children of Grace," 301; Minkema, "Old Age and Religion," 687–704, for

Jonathan Edwards as a Teacher and His Pedagogical Methodology

Edwards held the conviction that children, as is the case of all humanity, though by nature heirs of hell, could, by redeeming grace, become heirs of heaven. The following section will examine the paradox of the human condition as it applies to Native Americans.

EDWARDS'S VIEW OF NATIVE AMERICANS

"Edwards had low regard for [colonial American] Indian culture but high trust in [colonial American] Indian potential."[97] This statement encapsulates Edwards's perspective on Native Americans as their being encompassed within the paradoxical condition of humanity. It also indicates that he was in some ways captive to the limitations of his environment and in other ways a person not restricted by his historical context.

On the one hand, Edwards had absorbed an expectation of deference to social rank from his childhood onward and he held typical political and economic views for an eighteenth-century Anglo-colonial Protestant. He also expressed the contempt for Native American culture that was common among those of his time, place, and social standing. In unsparing terms, Edwards denounced the customs and mores of those tribes who had not received "the divine and supernatural light" of regeneration as being "savage" and "barbarous," characterized by "coarseness, and filth and degradation."[98] Specifically, their languages were totally un-

---

information on the fluctuation of the composition of the Northampton church by gender and age groups as affected by reactions to the revivals of the 1730s and 1740s. Cf. Beales, "Search for the Historical Child," 387, for data on ages of new communicants in churches in Massachusetts and Connecticut from approximately mid-seventeenth century to mid-eighteenth century.

97. Marsden, *Jonathan Edwards: A Life*, 389.

98. *LPW*, 411, 413. See Valeri, "Politics and Economics," 446-60; Marsden, "Historical and Ecclesiastical Contexts," 39; Winslow, *Jonathan Edwards (1703-1758)*, 274; Marsden, *Jonathan Edwards: A Life*, 394: Edwards "shared many of the English prejudices of [his] time, assuming the inferiority of almost everything in [American] Indian culture"; McDermott, "Missions and Native Americans," 267: "Edwards shared the overwhelming white consensus that [American] Indian culture was inferior and despicable"; Wheeler, "Edwards as Missionary," 202: "Edwards differed little from his contemporaries in his views of Indian culture"; Wheeler, *To Live Upon Hope*, 212-13; Smith, "God Has Made Us to Differ," 48: "Edwards also shared with his fellow white colonists a number of presumptions about Indian culture rooted in white Anglo-Protestant racial and cultural superiority in opposition to pagan Indian barbarism that began with the very first contacts between Europeans and Native peoples."

Cf. Claghorn in *LPW*, 22: "Although [Edwards] did make prejudicial comments about the 'barbarous' quality of the Indian languages, he also spoke of the genius of the

suitable for conveying the thoughts of a virtuous or an intellectual people, being "very ill-fitted for communicating things moral and divine, or even things speculative and abstract."[99] It was unthinkable that a people possessed of a culture of "civilization, knowledge and refinement" would attempt to communicate in so primitive a manner.[100] In order to remedy this intolerable situation, it was "necessary that the [Native American students] should be taught the English tongue" and be exposed to English customs, values, and modes of behavior, in order to "bring [about] that civility which is to be found among the English." "Civilization" (read, "Anglicization") was essential to lift all "heathen" peoples out of the "barbarism and brutality" to which they are naturally inclined.[101]

---

native people, and he did not view Indian education as a one-way street"; Minkema, "Jonathan Edwards's Life and Career," 21: "For much of his life, [Edwards] adhered to the accepted wisdom of the [eighteenth century] that Africans, [American] Indians, and Jews were culturally inferior to white Christian Europeans. However, his daily exposure to Indians at Stockbridge caused him to reevaluate his views of human nature to some degree; he came to see that Europeans and Indians differ, in the end, not innately but only in circumstance and providence. He came to respect many of the natives he served and considered them better Christians than some of the English inhabitants" (27n10); McDermott, "Missions and Native Americans," 268: While at Stockbridge, "Edwards referred to [the Native Americans] as 'my people'"; *LPW*, 610. See also Marsden, *Jonathan Edwards: A Life*, 385. Edwards respected Christians regardless of ethnicity. He wrote of Abraham Conaughstansey, the elder brother of Chief Hendrick of the Mohawk tribe, "I can't but look upon [him] as a remarkable man"; *LPW*, 398. Hendrick and Conaughstansey were both Christians and supporters of the mission and the school there; Marsden, *Jonathan Edwards: A Life*, 385, 386.

99. *LPW*, 413. Compare Jennings, *Invasion of America*, 50: "When Cotton [Mather] got no response to his effort to exorcize a demon from a young [American Indian] woman by using Indian words for his incantation, he petulantly concluded that the Indian language was so hard and stupid that not even demons understood it."

100. *LPW*, 413.

101. *LPW*, 413, 411. See Bowden, *American Indians and Christian Missions*, 136: In 1710, "Cotton Mather expressed the popular attitude [of 'White disdain for Indian cultures in Massachusetts'] in the following words:

The best thing we can do for our Indians is to Anglicize them in all agreeable instances; and in that of Language as well as others. They can scarce retain their language, without a Tincture of other Salvage [sic] Inclinations, which do but ill suit, either with the Honor, or with the design of Christianity"; "Mather, as cited in *MHS Collections*, ser. 6, 1 (1886) 401–2." This quotation appears in Bowden, *American Indians and Christian Missions*, 228n3. By 1721, Mather had concluded (as he expressed it to the commissioners of a missionary society, the New England Company): "to Humanize these Miserable *Animals* [i.e., the Native Americans], and in any measure to *Cicurate* [i.e., tame] them & *Civilize* them, were a work of no little Difficulty; and a Performance little short of what One of our most famous *Physicians* esteemed the *Greatest Cure* that ever himself had wrought in all his Practice; *To bring an Idiot into the Use of Reason*"; Mather, *India Christiana*, 28–29. This quotation appears in Axtell, *Invasion Within*,

Jonathan Edwards as a Teacher and His Pedagogical Methodology

133, 350n14. See also remainder of Axtell, *Invasion Within*, 350n14: "[Robert] Gray, *A Good Speed to Virginia* [(London, 1609)], sig. Blv, C2v, C4r-v, and [Samuel] Purchas, [*Virginia's Verger*, in *Hakluytus Posthumus; or, Purchas His Pilgrimes* [(London, 1625; Glasgow, 1903–5)], 19: 231." The colonists in eighteenth-century Massachusetts "who gave any thought to saving Indian souls made it plain that religious benefits accrued only to those who adopted English beliefs and habits"; Bowden, *American Indians and Christian Missions*, 136.

"Civilization" (i.e., "Anglicization") and Christianity went hand-in-hand in missionary efforts, either as the former being the precursor to the latter, or the two being virtually identical. See Wheeler, "Edwards as Missionary," 203; Beaver, *Pioneers in Mission*, 17: The objective of Christian evangelism toward the Natives was to effect their being "conformed to the model of the Puritan churchman, the Puritan church, and English civilization, all of these being identified with fundamental Christian faith." The missionary mindset was largely to bring about the converts "relating to the English community and [coming] to dress, eat, live, think, and behave like Englishmen"; Axtell, *European and the Indian*, 169, who notes the early link between these two goals: "The English, like their French rivals, began their colonizing ventures in North America with a sincere interest in converting the Indians to Christianity and civilization." "The problem with the Indians, as the English saw it, was their unpredictability and their 'savagery,' both of which stemmed from glaring cultural deficiencies: their lives were ungoverned by civil and social order; they, especially the men, were strangers to work; their dress and manners lacked all modesty and taste; and their religion knew [not] God Almighty, Jesus Christ, nor John Calvin" (266). A degree of contention between the Natives and the colonials came to the fore at the creation of the Stockbridge mission, resulting from resistance on the part of some Natives to the plan by John Sergeant and Governor Jonathan Belcher, "to *civilize* [the Indians] will be the readiest way to *Christianize* them"; Miles, "Red Man Dispossessed," 48n6 (emphasis in original). See also Axtell, *Invasion Within*, 133: To English missionaries, "While the Indians were potentially salvable, their savage condition was not felt to be fertile ground for the holy seeds of Christianity.... Until the 1760s it was the opinion of 'the most sensible Writers on this Subject' that it was necessary to 'civilize savages before they can be converted to Christianity, & that in order to make them Christians, they must first be made Men'"; Axtell, *Invasion Within*, 350n12: "Letter from Charles Inglis to William Johnson, March 28, 1770, in *The Papers of Sir William Johnson* (hereafter *Johnson Papers*), ed. James Sullivan, et. al. (Albany, NY: University of the State of New York, 1931), 7: 506." Axtell continues that the implication the Native Americans were not yet men signified one of three things: (1) The Indians "were the children of the human race, their passions still largely unrestrained by reason"; (2): They "were little better than animals, incapable of reason and enslaved by the most brutal passions"; (3): "The third and by far most prevalent meaning... was simply that the Indians had not mastered the 'Arts of civil Life & Humanity,' which is to say, the classical liberal arts.'" These refinements must "go before, or at least in the rising Generation accompany, the Teaching of Christianity to them" (133, 135); "Letter from William Smith to William Johnson," 511.

Furthermore, Axtell observes, throughout the colonial period, as English missionaries tried to convert native adults, "their emphasis shifted perceptibly toward the young, just the opposite direction taken by the Jesuits" (for more on Jesuit missions, see Bowden, 75–95). Education was the favored means to reach Indian children and adults at the same time. For the young, instruction meant evangelization: "To the English, learning to read was synonymous with learning the elements of Protestant Christianity from primers, psalters, and catechisms such as John Cotton's *Milk for Babes* and the Westminster Assembly's *Shorter Catechism*"; Axtell, *Invasion Within*, 79, 188; 351n26.

To Understand *Things* as Well as *Words*

And yet, as we shall see in the following chapter, Edwards was convinced that the Native Americans were as capable of being taught by dialogic interaction as were the Anglo-colonial students who came under his tutelage.[102] The *imago Dei* has been inherited by all human

---

At least some of the indigenous people who interacted with missionaries seem to have employed a strategy which allowed their survival without total capitulation to "white man's ways": See Winiarski, "Native American Popular Religion in New England's Old Colony, 1670–1770," 147–86. "[C]urrent studies of Native religion in the decades preceding the American Revolution suggest that Indians preserved traditional culture by grafting Christianity onto a preexisting grid of beliefs and practices.... Most Wampanoag families in New England's 'Old Colony' lived between cultures–neither fully integrated into English society nor fully traditional in their identities or worldview.... [F]or the majority of Native Christians who lived and worked side-by-side with their English neighbors, religion remained an eclectic affair as they deployed a variety of spiritual resources to combat the vicissitudes and uncertainties of everyday life" (147).

For the history of the often contentious relationship between the Natives in the Stockbridge area and the Anglo-colonials, particularly members of the Williams family, two important sources are Miles, "Red Man Dispossessed," 46–76, and Sweeney, "River Gods and Related Minor Deities." See also Smith, "God Has Made Us to Differ," 56–57: "The choice of Edwards over Ezra Stiles to succeed John Sergeant as missionary to Stockbridge 'reflects [Timothy] Woodbridge's New Light [i.e., pro-revival] inclinations and the Indian preference for evangelicalism, while the Old Light-leaning Williamses fretted that Stockbridge would become a radical New Light enclave," (57, 57n24); Marsden, *Jonathan Edwards: A Life*, 378–82. Timothy Woodbridge was a teacher who was popular with the Natives who sought an English education; Marsden, *Jonathan Edwards: A Life*, 380; Smith, "God Has Made Us to Differ," 56. "By the time Edwards arrived at Stockbridge in the 1750s, the forces of economic self-interest [represented by the Williamses] were, as he was especially alert to see, in control"; Marsden, *Jonathan Edwards: A Life*, 382. Certain members of the Williams family positioned themselves as particular nemeses of Edwards both at Northampton and at Stockbridge, and emerged as formidable enemies by having intermarried with most of the prominent families in the Connecticut Valley area, giving them powerful connections to the major local leaders in business, politics, and the clergy. Claghorn in *LPW*, 20, 23, provides a succinct account of the Williamses' antagonism toward Edwards, set in the overall contentious environment of the forces at work at the mission: Ephraim Williams and some other members of his family opposed Edwards's installation as missionary at Stockbridge at the outset; Wright, *Colonel Ephraim Williams*, 61–62. Claghorn in *LPW*, 23: "Edwards's struggle [at Stockbridge] was no easy task, as the Williams clan did all it could to thwart him. In addition to the ploys of the immediate Ephraim Williams family, other Williamses [all of whom enjoyed high status and favorable connections in the community] became active opponents of Edwards as well. Ephraim's cousins, Col. Israel Williams ... Rev. Solomon Williams ... and Col. Elisha Williams ... each actively opposed Edwards in both Northampton and Stockbridge."

102. See *LPW*, 411: "All children are capable of being informed, and having an idea of these things" to be taught; Wheeler, *To Live Upon Hope*, 213–14: "Although Edwards believed [American] Indian culture to be lacking in many respects, he believed that [American] Indian children had an equal capacity to learn [as others].... [Edwards's] educational philosophy reflects his conviction that humans are fundamentally equal, differing only in circumstance and environment."

Jonathan Edwards as a Teacher and His Pedagogical Methodology

beings (who are diminished and damaged, but not destroyed, by the Fall) of all races and nations. As Edwards explained in a sermon to his indigenous congregants, "God has given [all human beings] reason and understanding," an inheritance of "man being made in God's image."[103] As a result, notwithstanding Satan's schemes and the colonials' amalgam of intermittent evangelistic indifference and outright hostility, the native peoples were capable of receiving and acting upon the gospel as revealed in Scripture if it were shared with them.

The manner in which Edwards communicated with the Native Americans, albeit adapted to an "uncivilized" audience via story-telling, did not sacrifice "the aesthetic dimension of his theological vision."[104] One of his first sermons to his Stockbridge Indian congregation majored on the point, "Men are naturally blind, so that they don't [see] the main things in the Word of God." Expounding Ps 119:18 as the text ("Open thou mine eyes, [O LORD], that I may behold wondrous things out of thy Law"), Edwards explained that the "chief things" that Christ must open one's eyes to see are his "Glory and Excellency."[105]

In a message he delivered for a celebration of communion (the standard for admission to which, as his pastoral career indicates, he considered of vital importance), Edwards sounded a theme dear to him: a true

---

103. Edwards, "Sermon 998," 739.

104. McDermott, *Jonathan Edwards Confronts the Gods*, 201. See Wheeler, "'Friends to your Souls,'" 750; Wheeler, "Edwards as Missionary," 204; Gibson, "Jonathan Edwards: A Missionary?" 389; Harder, "True Excellency," 68; Franklin, "Missions and Missiology," 385; Snoddy, "Preaching," 458: "Among the Indians at Stockbridge [Edwards] employed simpler, often narrative-driven, forms [of sermons]." The majority of the sermons Edwards preached to the Natives at Stockbridge were new, written specifically for that congregation, and largely made use of the New Testament, such as parables from the Gospels of Matthew and Luke. "From these two gospels, [Edwards] could draw on stories of farmers, fisherman, drought, and difficult travel. All these images were part of everyday life for his Indian audience"; Grigg, "Missions," 421, 422; Harder, "True Excellency," 71. Minkema, "Writing and Preaching Sermons," 400–401, observes that, at Stockbridge, Edwards simplified his sermon structure from his previous tripartite outline, resulting in his preaching becoming "more narrative in style." In addition, "His sermons became more practical, even more pietistic.... Most notably, he became a story-teller, choosing biblical characters such as Mary or Cornelius and then, in a 'Once-upon-a-time' manner, telling the story of Christianity down to the present, with the Natives before him as the next chapter in the unfolding saga." This narrative mode drew his congregants into the "divine drama" of redemption history in which God seeks to draw human beings to participate, as discussed below.

105. Edwards, "Sermon 1007," 742; McDermott, *Jonathan Edwards Confronts the Gods*, 201.

Christian "Loves G[od] above all else for his own Beauty."[106] Edwards's messages at Stockbridge indicate his assurance that, if communicated in appropriate imagery, his audience could grasp their "rarified themes" so that he might share the same magnificent vision of a glorious God that he had communicated at Northampton.[107]

Of further theological import, Edwards's sermons at Stockbridge indicate that, in his view of human nature in general and of American Indians in particular, he "reawakened the latent egalitarian undercurrent of Calvinism" by contending that the Fall "had rendered all humanity equally helpless and in need of God's regenerating grace."[108] In a note on Job 31:15 (Job's words regarding his manservant, "Did not he who made me in the womb make him? And did not one fashion us in the womb?") Edwards wrote in the early 1730s in his extensive interleaved biblical commentary to which he referred as his "Blank Bible": "We are made of the same human race, and [God] has given us the same human nature." Pertaining to the human race *qua* all of its individual members, "We are all ... by nature, *companions* in a miserable helpless condition," whereby all "mankind are corrupt by nature."[109] These observations, coupled with his interactions with the Natives at the mission, his previous experiences at his Northampton pastorate, and his ongoing contentions with the Williamses and with their allies, served as background for his sermon emphases. Edwards fully and forthrightly covered the topics of the Indians' inherent sinfulness, of their need of divine light, and of the punishment awaiting the unconverted. Importantly, these admonitions were balanced by his assurances that "we [i.e., Caucasians, including the English] are no better than you," that Christ died for "some [persons] of all nations," and that Christ "shall save his people from their sins."[110]

106. Edwards, "Sermon 1031," 743.

107. Quotation is in McDermott, *Jonathan Edwards Confronts the Gods*, 201.

108. Wheeler, "'Friends to Your Souls,'" 737; Kling, "Edwards in the Context of International Revivals and Missions," 63. See also Wheeler, "Lessons from Stockbridge," 131–40; Mailer, "Freedom From Spiritual Slavery, But From Civil Too," 69n27; Holbrook, *Ethics of Jonathan Edwards*, 14, 140–45; *OS*, 124.

109. Edwards, "Blank Bible," 458; Edwards, *OS*, 424 (emphasis in original).

110. See Wheeler, "'Friends to Your Souls,'" 737n5; 738, 765; Wheeler, *To Live Upon Hope*, 213–19; Edwards, "To the Mohawks at the Treaty, August 16, 1751," 108; Edwards, "Sermon 1152," 753; Marsden, *Jonathan Edwards: A Life*, 393–94; Wheeler, "Edwards as Missionary," 207; Wheeler, "Lessons from Stockbridge," 134: "Had it not been for his mission experience, I believe Edwards might not have emphasized in *Original Sin* the equality in human depravity to the extent that he did"; Grigg, "Missions," 422, 423: Edwards's "exposure to the unjust practices of the English at Stockbridge [regarding

Jonathan Edwards as a Teacher and His Pedagogical Methodology

Sounding these themes, Edwards observed in a message in August 1751 to his Mohawk audience, *all* mankind is equally under the curse of the Fall, originating "when man sinned against God, [and consequently] he lost his [principle of] holiness, and then the light that was in his mind was put out."[111] However, God the Father in his mercy sent his Son into the world "to die for sinners and more fully to instruct the world" regarding repentance and the ways of God. In fulfilling this mission, "Christ commanded that his word contained in the Bible should be ope[ne]d to all nations, and that all should be instructed out of it."[112] In doing so, God has revealed that he would have persons "be saved and come to

---

mistreatment and exploitation of the Natives], following on from his own expulsion from Northampton, convinced him that humans were all equal in their sinfulness." A Native who was exposed to the gospel via English culture was as likely to receive salvation as was an English settler. The positive response of some Stockbridge Natives to Edwards's ministry "and the concomitant depravity of the English" may have been a major influence on *OS*, written while at the mission; Grigg, "Missions," 423; Wheeler, "'Friends to Your Souls,'" 736–65; Wheeler, *To Live Upon Hope*; *SD, 1743–1758*, "The Stockbridge Mission," 30n5.

See Hoselton, "Bible in Early Pietist and Evangelical Missions," 122, 122n46: In his sermon, "To the Mohawks at the Treaty," Edwards explained to his Native congregants there existed "'two sorts' of people 'that have the Bible.' The first sort of 'white people [who] came over the seas and settled in these parts' had disregarded the Bible's light and consequently had failed in their duty to share and apply the Word rightly among the Native Americans." The French, English, and Dutch had chosen to keep the Natives illiterate and ignorant of Scripture. "But another sort [of people] cherished the Word and acknowledged that they 'are no better than you,' for sin had ruined all mankind equally." The ones of the latter sort desired to share the Scriptures with the Natives to share the message that, "'When the light of God's Word shines into the heart ... it gives new life to the soul' that 'is sweeter than honey.' Edwards wished to share that honey freely."

Edwards preached from approximately 190 to over 200 original sermons to his Native congregation at Stockbridge; Wheeler, "Edwards as Missionary," 204n44; Wheeler, "Lessons from Stockbridge," 132; Franklin, "Missions and Missiology," 385. See Wheeler, "Edwards as Missionary," 204n44, for source of calculation of number of original sermons. In contrast, twenty-nine of the 165 sermons to the English-speaking congregation were new messages; Harder, "True Excellency," 65. As shown in this chapter, in these messages, Edwards preached in a simpler, more narrative-based format than he did to his Anglo-colonial congregation. See also Marsden, *Jonathan Edwards: A Life*, 385. Edwards respected Christians regardless of ethnicity. He wrote of Abraham Conaughstansey, the elder brother of Chief Hendrick of the Mohawk tribe, "I can't but look upon [him] as a remarkable man"; *LPW*, 398. Hendrick and Conaughstansey were both Christians and supporters of the mission and the school there; Marsden, *Jonathan Edwards: A Life*, 385, 386.

111. Edwards, "To the Mohawks at the Treaty, August 16, 1751," 105; Edwards, *OS*, 124.

112. Edwards, "To the Mohawks at the Treaty, August 16, 1751," 106. See also Edwards, "1225. No text. Fragment," 760.

the knowledge of the truth," irrespective of social status, ethnicity, or national identity.[113] In a sermon on Luke 24:47 later that year to this Native American congregation, Edwards emphasized that "forgiveness is offered" through Christ "to *all nations* if they will repent."[114] In yet another message, preached to all of the Stockbridge Indians and, on another occasion, to the Mohawks specifically, Edwards left no doubt as to the breadth of the gospel's application: "Christ calls *all*, men and women, young and old, and little children. *All* are invited to look to him [so] that they may be saved." In a 1751 address specifically to the Mohawks, yet again he sounded the theme that Christ does not discriminate with regard to ethnicity, with specific application to his congregation: "He makes no diff[erence] between English & Indians[;] white or black, all are alike wellcome [sic]."[115]

Significantly, regenerated members of all socioeconomic, ethnic, and national classifications will savor the reward of the Christian life lived on earth; that is, being in the eternal presence of God, in the millennial kingdom: "[God's] kingdom shall fill the earth; that all people, nations and languages should serve and obey him; and so, that all nations should go up to the mountain of the house of the Lord, that he might teach them his ways, and that they might walk in his paths."[116] In this idyll of universal peace and equality, "all nations, in all parts, on every side of the globe, shall then be knit together in sweet harmony."[117] In summary, in

113. Edwards, "To the Mohawks at the Treaty, August 16, 1751," in *SJER*, 107.

114. Edwards, "Sermon 1008. Oct. 1751. Stockbridge Indians and Mohawks," in *SD, 1743–1758*: "Appendix: Dated Sermons, January 1743–February 1758, Undated Sermons, And Sermon Fragments," 742 (emphasis added); Valeri, "Politics and Economics," 457–58.

115. Edwards, "Sermon 975," 111–20 and Edwards, *Blessing of God*, 237–46 (emphasis added); Edwards, "1003."

116. *FW*, 246. See also Mailer, "Freedom from Spiritual Slavery," 66, 66n17.

117. *HWR*, 483. See also *HWR*, 472, 473: "[T]he kingdom of Christ shall in the most strict and literal sense extend to all nations and the whole earth." In this respect, Edwards was more optimistic than some others in eighteenth-century New England Protestantism. "In 1772 Samuel Kirkland, arguably the most effective Protestant missionary to the Iroquois, confessed that . . . he had concluded against his fondest hopes that the Indians were 'in a peculiar sense & manner under the curse of Heaven' and 'as a people or Nation' would never be called to God in the millennium. A visit to [the] Oneida [tribe] some years later persuaded the Reverend Jeremy Belknap that conversion of Indians was indeed 'a hopeless business'"; Axtell, *Invasion Within*, 272; Letter from Samuel Kirkland to Rev. Mr. John Rodgers, June 20, 1772 (draft), in *Samuel Kirkland Papers*, Hamilton College Collection https://www.hamilton.edu/documents/IndexSamKirklandPapers.pdf; McDermott, *Jonathan Edwards Confronts the Gods*,

Jonathan Edwards as a Teacher and His Pedagogical Methodology

his Stockbridge sermons, Edwards was fully committed to affirming the Reformed doctrines of original sin and total depravity, but he emphasized the gospel's uplifting aspects to the Native Americans. Capitalizing on his observations and experiences both at the Northampton church and at the Stockbridge mission, the manner in which Edwards preached to the Indians and to the Anglo-colonials held out hope to the lowly and humbled the mighty.[118]

200, 200n30; Axtell, *Invasion Within*, 370n7; Axtell, *Invasion Within*, 370n8: "Gideon Hawley to Jonathan Walter Edwards, Feb. 18, 1801, Yale University Library; [Jeremy Belknap] . 'Has the Discovery of America Been Useful or Hurtful to Mankind?' *Boston Magazine* (May 1784), 281–85, at 283."

118. See Wheeler, "'Friends to Your Souls,'" 737, 765; Wheeler, "Edwards as Missionary," 205; Wheeler, "Lessons from Stockbridge," 133; Wheeler, "Jonathan Edwards: Missionary"; Marsden, *Jonathan Edwards: A Life*, 393–94; McDermott, "Jonathan Edwards and American Indians," 549–50; Valeri, "Politics and Economics," 457–58: "[Edwards] frequently preached to his Native parishioners in Stockbridge about a God who offered belonging and forgiveness to all people and therefore regarded no nation or race above another"; Grigg, "Missions," 421–22; Saillant, "Ministry to the Bound and Enslaved," 432; Kimnach, "Stockbridge Mission," 27: In his sermons at the Stockbridge mission, Edwards assured the Natives "that despite their inherent sins as human beings, and their peculiar sins as Indians, they are in a very hopeful situation at the mission" through hearing the gospel preached. In his sermons to his indigenous congregation, Edwards "deftly balance[d] the fear of punishment and the hope of reward."

Wheeler, "'Friends to Your Souls,'" 736, makes an intriguing observation about the sermonic distinction Edwards drew between his two congregations at the mission. In the summer of 1756, in a "simple yet extraordinary" message to the Native Americans, he "counseled his listeners that God 'advises us to be friends to our own souls' by seeking after holiness. Edwards encouraged his Indian congregants to take tender care of their souls, to 'forsake wickedness and seek after Holiness'" and not to be "Enemies to your soul." In sharp contrast, in a sermon preached only a month earlier to his English listeners, Edwards "railed at them that he would 'rather go into Sodom and preach to the men of Sodom than preach to you and should have a great deal more hopes of success.'" The only redeeming aspect of this circumstance is the assurance that "'God is almighty and he can make the [W]ord pierce your hearts tho' [they] be harder than a rock'" Edwards, "Sermon 1166," 754.

In a similar vein, Harder, "True Excellency," 74–75, points out two sermons, each drawn from the Book of Job and preached the same week (in January 1753), which illustrate the contrasts in Edwards's perspectives on his two Stockbridge congregations. "God is Infinitely Strong," *SD, 1743–1758*, 641–46, "a model of what had become his method of preaching to the Indians," emphasizes God's omniscience, omnipresence, and omnipotence in a simple narrative style, leading to the exhortation, "Fear him; trust in him; be humble.... [God] sees all you do, sees in the night, [and] remembers all. Here is encouragement to pray to God.... He can save you from the devil." "God's Use of Affliction," *SD, 1743–1758*, 646–53, utilizes a "relatively elaborate scheme of three doctrinal propositions" to stress that, in a world in which "all [persons] deserve God's displeasure" and "God is the orderer of affliction," it behooves his listeners to heed that "Afflictions that are brought on [persons] in this world are from the hand of God" for sin, but the object of God's correction "is said to be happy" and turn "from that which is evil to that

To Understand *Things* as Well as *Words*

Given that the eternal destinies of souls were at stake, Edwards excoriated the English for their "shameful neglect" of the Native Americans regarding their minimal efforts to evangelize them and to teach them Scripture.[119] By having been blessed with the light of the gospel for far longer than the nations where it had only recently begun to shine, the English should have made more progress toward enlarging Christ's kingdom. Instead, "they have not done their duty" to the indigenous peoples; rather, "they have greatly neglected" them.[120] Edwards observed that "the great God has undoubtedly been made very angry" by the laxity of the

---

which is truly good." Turning to God will yield the realization that God can "cause [it; i.e., affliction] to work for good, but [God] is able to destroy [us], if [we] despise [his chastisements]" and fail to turn to him"; Kimnach, "Stockbridge Mission," 641, 646.

119. Edwards, "To the Mohawks at the Treaty, August 16, 1751," 107.

120. Edwards, "To the Mohawks at the Treaty, August 16, 1751," 107. See McDermott, *Jonathan Edwards Confronts the Gods*, 201: Edwards considered Native Americans "to be less morally culpable than their white, nominally Christian counterparts." See Edwards, *OS*, 183: "The poor savage Americans are mere babes and fools (if I may so speak) as to proficiency in wickedness, in comparison of multitudes that the Christian world throngs with." The colonists' response to the charge that they had accomplished little in the way of evangelization of the native peoples by mid-eighteenth century divided the responsibility among God, the Natives, and the colonials themselves. "[In] his infinite but mysterious wisdom, God had not see fit 'till of late' to give the Indians the grace to recognize their pitiful condition and seek salvation." Moreover, the settlers had initially attempted to woo the natives by their "exemplary civility," but had encountered a mixture of indifference and hostility to both the gospel and the English as messengers. For example, the "Apostle to the Indians," John Eliot (1604-1690), lamented that the Indians were "never willing to hear" the gospel "until he began to preach to them in 1646." In addition, Edward Johnson, "one of New England's earliest historians," claimed that "'at their first coming' the English did make an effort to introduce the local natives to Christianity, 'but yet,' he admitted, 'very little was done that way, till in process of time [the Native Americans,] by continuall coming to the English, became better able to understand them.'" A major hindrance to the evangelization efforts of the settlers was the "brutish and sottish spirit" of the natives that prevented them from recognizing the example they had attempted to set for "the Heathen." Eliot's translation and publication of the Bible into the Massachusett language in 1663 and his establishment of the towns of "praying Indians" were highlights in the efforts at evangelization. Finally, Edwards was among those who admitted that not enough had been done to reach the Native Americans with the gospel. This was especially frustrating to him, since he viewed the evangelization of Indians as a necessary step in the history of redemption, leading to the millennium; *HWR*, 434; Axtell, *Invasion within*, 218, 219; Eliot and Mayhew, *Tears of Repentance*, 197-260; Johnson, *History of New England*, 263-64; Shepard, *Clear Sun-Shine of the Gospel Breaking Forth upon the Indians in New-England*, 55; Stoddard, *Question*, 8; *LPW*, 436-47.

The "Popish" French fare no better than the English in Edwards's evaluation. See Edwards, "To the Mohawks at the Treaty, August 16, 1751," 107; Edwards, "Things That Belong to True Religion"; *LPW*, 436-47. See also Marsden, *Jonathan Edwards: A Life*, 385-86; Baines, "Thy Kingdom Come," 116n284.

English in evangelizing Native Americans.[121] In this respect, he echoed his grandfather and pastoral supervisor at Northampton, Solomon Stoddard, who posed a similar challenge a quarter-century earlier to his countrymen's evangelistic lethargy.[122]

Edwards's attitude toward Native Americans tempered contempt for their culture with sympathy for their situation. Satan, he believed, had deliberately isolated them away from the gospel in order to render them his captives. In Edwards's analysis, the dispersion of the nations over the earth after God halted the construction of the Tower of Babel led to the "inhabited world [being] chiefly in the Roman empire in the times immediately after Christ."[123] Subsequently, "The devil . . . led many nations unto remote parts of the world to that end to get 'em out of the way of the gospel, [and so] led 'em unto America."[124]

Once on the "American continent . . . the devil had the nations that inhabited this part of the world, as it were, secure to himself, out of the reach of the light of the gospel and so . . . [held] in his dominion over

---

121. Edwards, "To the Mohawks at the Treaty, August 16, 1751," 107. See also *LPW*, 436, 440; Wheeler, *To Live Upon Hope*, 212, 302n102. "The [English settlers] had the [gospel] light all around them, they had been catechized since their earliest days, they had the Scriptures in their own tongue and they had been taught to read and write." Having these advantages, compared with the Natives, the whites were more culpable for their sins and were blameworthy for not having done more to evangelize the Indians; Baines, "Thy Kingdom Come," 130.

122. Stoddard, *Question*. Stoddard emerged as "a controversial figure because of his public criticism of the treatment of the Indians" by the New England colonials; Kidd, *Protestant Interest*, 160. The zeal for evangelism Stoddard displayed in *Question*, a combination of a "blistering attack on New Englanders for their failure to heed God's command to evangelize the Indians" and a defense of the colonials' initial inactivity resulting from the natives' "brutish and sottish spirit," signals a transformation from his attitude toward Native Americans expressed two decades earlier; McDermott, *Jonathan Edwards Confronts the Gods*, 197; Axtell, *Invasion Within*, 219. See Stoddard', "Letter to [Massachusetts Bay] Gov. [Joseph] Dudley, Oct. 22, 1703," 235–37, in which, because the town of Deerfield, Massachusetts "has suffered much formerly from the Indians," he proposes that the townspeople "may be put into a way to Hunt the Indians with dogs . . . trained up to hunt Indians as they doe Bears." Stoddard reflects, "If the Indians were as other people are, & did manage their warr fairly after the manner of other nations, it might be looked upon as inhumane to pursue them in such, a manner." He argues, however, "they are to be looked upon as theives [sic] and murderers, they doe acts of hostility, without proclaiming war. they don't appear openly in the field to bid us battle, they use those cruelly that fall into their hands. they act like wolves & are to be dealt withall as wolves." See also Davies, "'Prepare Ye the Way of the Lord,'" 71–72; McDermott, "Jonathan Edwards and American Indians," 544, 544n21.

123. Edwards, "Sermon Three," 155.

124. Edwards, "Sermon Three," 155. See also Edwards, "Sermon 1082," 27.

them."[125] As a horrendous consequence of this historical reality and the lackadaisical attitude toward missions that kept the gospel "confined to the opposite side of the globe . . . the many nations of Indians from age to age worshiped [the Devil] as God."[126] Consequently, they continued in bondage to the Prince of Darkness, who had made the American Indians his unwitting victims. In Edwards's graphic description, "The devil sucks their blood and eats their bowels and vitals" as he kept them locked into a lifestyle that would lead only to the misery of hell.[127]

In the end, his ministrations in the frontier wilderness molded a maturing experience for Edwards regarding his attitude toward the native peoples of colonial America. During the imbroglio of Stockbridge, he won the confidence of the Boston Commissioners of Indian Affairs as someone who had "acquired the general affections of the Indians, and influence over them, which he constantly employs for the best purposes."[128]

For his own part, serving those whom he taught and to whom he preached enabled Edwards to come to consider as friends and to esteem as "my people" who "steadfastly adhere to me," those whom he had once scorned as "barbarous" and "savage."[129] As a work in progress during his

125. Edwards, "Sermon Twenty-Four," 433-34.

126. Edwards, "Sermon Twenty-Four," 434. See McDermott, *Jonathan Edwards Confronts the Gods*, 194n1, 194n2: The belief that the Native Americans had been led by Satan to North America to isolate them from the gospel "was something of a consensus among colonial religious leaders such as Cotton Mather. [*The Life of David Brainerd* (hereafter *LDB*), ed. Norman Pettit, *WJE*, vol. 7 (New Haven: Yale University Press, 1984)], 11-12; [William R.] Hutchison, [*Errand to the World: American Protestant Thought and Foreign Missions* (Chicago: University of Chicago Press, 1987)], 39; [Alden T.] Vaughan, *New England Frontier*[: *Puritans and Indians, 1620-1675* (Boston: Little, Brown, 1965)], 20." See also McDermott, *Jonathan Edwards Confronts the Gods*, 194n3: "[Edwards,] Sermon on 1 John 3:10, March 1756; *HWR*, 472. On the assertion that the Native Americans worshiped the devil, also *LDB*, 261."

127. Edwards, "Sermon 105." See also Edwards, "Sermon 973"; McMullen, *Blessing of God*, 225-30; McDermott, *Jonathan Edwards Confronts the Gods*, 195n6.

128. Letter from Josiah Willard to Sir William Pepperrell, February 1753, quoted in Marsden, *Jonathan Edwards: A Life*, 403.

129. *LPW*, 420; *LPW*, 562; *LPW*, 610. See Grigg, "Missions," 424: "There is no question . . . that his time at Stockbridge had deeply transformed Edwards . . . . His daily interactions with Native Americans, conflict with the Williams clan, Moravian [missionary] influence, the example of [missionary David] Brainerd, and probably his own maturing were surely all part of the mix. Together they meant that while Edwards the missionary saw success at Stockbridge, Edwards the man was changed by his time at the mission"; Franklin, "Missions and Missiology," 385: Edwards's service at Stockbridge was characterized by "his consistent defense of the Indian residents"; Smith, "God Has Made Us to Differ," 59: "Edwards's seven years at Stockbridge fundamentally changed his mind about Indians. Although he clearly favored Christianized Indians

time there, Edwards came to look more favorably upon colonial American Indians. Comprehending *abstractly* at the outset of his missionary venture the fallen nature of all human beings at birth, Edwards's work "in the trenches" at Stockbridge convinced him *experientially* that the Mahicans and the Mohawks to whom he ministered were no worse, no more fallen, than any other unregenerate persons. Sin favors no ethnicity; it speaks equally well every language. Wickedness respects no nation's borders and bows in deference and submission before no socioeconomic class. Fallenness knows no division into "us" and "them." "Total depravity" was as likely to have an Anglo-colonial face as a Native one. Edwards the missionary came to realize that, ultimately, though lost and ignorant of the Word by nature, his Indian neighbors were nonetheless capable of salvation and instruction.[130]

In summary, we have discussed Edwards's assessment of the role of a teacher both in the meeting house and at the schoolhouse, and his views of children and Native Americans, two of the cohorts he taught. In the following chapter, we shall examine Edwards's teaching methodology and his application of it in each location at which he taught.

---

over their 'pagan' counterparts, he grew in his conviction that all Indian souls deserved God's grace as much as any white person. He became their champion and defender against Anglo-American exploitation, making no distinction between Mahicans who had accepted Christ and those who refused to do so."

Ironically, the Native Americans toward whom Edwards felt this affection were more "his people" than those members of the Williamses who opposed him at Northampton and at Stockbridge, who were relatives of his. See Marsden, *Jonathan Edwards: A Life*, 508-9; McDermott, *Jonathan Edwards Confronts the Gods*, 203.

130. See McDermott, "Jonathan Edwards and American Indians," 557. Cf. Frazier, *Mohicans of Stockbridge*, 14: Edwards, "who was acquainted with the Housatonics, once remarked in a mixture of paternalism and condescension reflective of the times that 'the Indians, wild as they are, have some sense of the shamefulness of vice and of the value of virtue, good order and civilization, and they have some sense of the worth of knowledge. If any one among them is able to read and write, it is looked upon as a great attainment. And they esteem it as a thing much to be valued to be able to read and understand the Bible'"; *LPW*, 441. If paternalism was, in fact, present at this point in Edwards's attitude toward the Native Americans with whom he had begun interacting, it seems to have been replaced with affection and at least a modicum of respect by the end of his service at Stockbridge.

6

Jonathan Edwards's Pedagogical Methodology

Locations

EDWARDS'S PEDAGOGICAL METHODOLOGY

"The child should be taught to understand *things*, as well as *words*."[1] This conviction expresses Edwards's philosophy of education with his students at Stockbridge and, *mutatis mutandis*, with the young persons (those from fifteen to twenty-five years of age) and adults whom he taught throughout his instructional experience.[2] To teach students to understand *words* meant enabling them to associate words with the ideas which they signify and to reflect on the connections between the words and the ideas, and between those connections and the world which they inhabit. "To understand *words*" serves as a metaphor for his introductory goal with the other groups of students whom he taught: to grasp the subject matter in a way that would enlarge the students' understandings and would inform their choices appropriately.

---

1. *LPW*, 408.
2. For Edwards's definition of "young person," see Minkema, "Jonathan Edwards on Education," 34, 263n2: "'Young people' Edwards defined as individuals from fifteen to twenty-five years old"; Minkema, "Old Age and Religion," 675; *LPW*, 116–17; Brekus, "Children of Wrath, Children of Grace," 302.

Jonathan Edwards's Pedagogical Methodology

To Edwards, "The end . . . of Learning is to repair the ruines of our first Parents by regaining to know God aright and out of that knowledge to love him, to imitate him, to be like him."[3] In Edwards's words, "Man's happiness consists in his union with his Creator."[4] Because of the corruption of human nature consequent upon original sin, human beings are "born into the world [as] universally of an unholy nature," which prevents the communion with the Creator that "our first Parents" enjoyed.[5] Only receiving the "new spiritual sense" can restore the "holiness of nature" that constitutes "conformity of nature to God."[6] Learning is among "the chief of the means of grace" to effectuate the regeneration that enables restoration of communion of humans with God.[7]

For all students, "to understand *things*" to Edwards meant to understand "*spiritual and divine things*;" to have one's understanding informed in such a way that one's will is affected by the "new spiritual sense" so that one displays "holy affections" (evidence of regeneration, i.e., "fruit of the Spirit" Gal 5:22–23).[8] This is possible only through "being united to the heavenly grace of faith" in the God who communicates through his creation, and through his Word and his appointed means of instruction therein.[9]

We shall now examine the pedagogical methodology Edwards used to achieve the educational objectives that formed a vital part of his overall evangelistic mission. Doing so reveals him to be an intricate figure who erected ideas adapted from "Enlightenment(s)" thinkers onto a Puritan theological foundation to bring innovation to education in the service of his Lord Jesus Christ.

Edwards's experience with dialogic instruction began in his home, as it were, "a little Church, and a little commonwealth." Lessons in Scripture and personal piety formed an essential part of the upbringing of each of the Edwardses' eleven children, taking as a model young Jonathan's family environment. Edwards's paternal approach to teaching emphasized interaction: "He made use of the [*Westminster*] *Assembly's*

---

3. Milton, "Milton Reading Room."
4. Edwards, "Reality of Conversion," 84.
5. Edwards, "Reality of Conversion," 85.
6. Edwards, "Reality of Conversion," 85.
7. Edwards, "Farewell Sermon," 484.
8. Quotations are in *RA*, 95, 117, 182, 205, 206, 254, 256; Edwards, "Treatise Concerning Religious Affections," 141, 160, 161.
9. Quotation is in Milton, "Milton Reading Room."

To Understand *Things* as Well as *Words*

[*Shorter*] *Catechism*: not merely by taking care that [his children] learned it by heart, but by leading them into an understanding of the doctrines therein taught, by asking them questions on each answer, and explaining it to them." Thereupon a dialogue ensued, as "he also posed questions back to his children, and expounded on them."[10] Thus, the pedagogy of Edwards the *paterfamilias* prefigured the philosophy and praxis of Edwards the educator in the world outside his home.

The Saturday evening instruction was buttressed by morning devotions in which his questions were appropriate for each participant (children as well as servants). Edwards was acutely aware that both the Puritan tenets and the norms of Anglo-colonial society at that time dictated that he was the religious leader of his home, which was the locus of learning and character development. Edwards took this responsibility with utmost seriousness, acting out in private his public proclamations that the family is a microcosm of the Church. As such, in the Edwards home, instructions in Christian living came in both "doctrine and precept" through Scripture and in "instance and example" through modeling Christian faith and practice.[11]

From early in life, each of the Edwards children was started on the path of discipline, instruction, and counseling intended (per the Puritan paradigm) to lead him or her to be well-grounded in sound decision making and, ultimately, to receive redemptive grace. Edwards's effectiveness as a counselor to his children extended past their formative years. At age twenty-four, Esther Edwards Burr, for example, attests to "some free discourse with [her] Father on the great things that concern [her] best interest." An uninhibited discussion they carried on removed "some distressing doubts that discouraged [her] much in [her] Christian warfare." "Excellent directions" from her original family head prompted her to exclaim, "What a mercy that I have such a Father! Such a guide!"[12]

---

10. Gouge, *Of Domesticall Duties: Eight Treatises*, 18; Hopkins, *Life of Edwards*, 43. See also Chamberlain, "Family Life," 13, 14.

11. Quotations in Edwards, "Author's Preface," 89. See Chamberlain, "Family Life," 13–15; Mintz, *Huck's Raft*, ix, 17–21.
Prominent among "instance and example" of Christianity in the Edwards household was the "uncommon union" between Jonathan and Sarah, which included minimal domestic conflict, despite a regular succession over a number of years of infants, toddlers, young children, older children, parishioners seeking counsel, and adult ministerial aspirants; *Burr's Journal*, 7, 7n11.

12. Hopkins, *Life of Edwards*, 44; Marsden, *Jonathan Edwards: A Life*, 321; Minkema, "Edwardses," 365–70; Karlsen and Crumpacker, *Journal of Esther Edwards Burr*, 7–8; Potgieter, "Education," 407; Burr, Karlsen and Crumpacker, *Journal of Esther Edwards Burr*, 224.

Jonathan Edwards's Pedagogical Methodology

The result of this upbringing was each of the Edwards offsprings was planted firmly on Scripture as the spiritual foundation of life. Again, daughter Esther provides an example in her letter of November 2, 1757, to her father following the death of her husband (Reverend Aaron Burr Sr.), in which she attests, "['T]is my comfort in this disappointment as well as under all my afflictions that God knows what is best for me and for his own glory . . . . God has carried me throu[gh] new tryals [sic] and given [me] new supports . . . . O how good is God!"[13] Let us now examine how Edwards applied a holistic dialogic instructional methodology at the Stockbridge mission.

EDWARDS'S PEDAGOGY AT STOCKBRIDGE

We begin at the Stockbridge mission because it is here that Edwards clearly articulates his philosophy of education, his perspectives on the necessary qualifications and on the responsibilities of educators, and his expectations of learning outcomes for students which underlie his pedagogy in each of the settings analyzed in this study. Also, examining Edwards at Stockbridge situates him in an environment in which he applied the dialogic methodology he had begun at his Northampton home to persons in the same age range as seven of his own children during this time period, within a wider interaction matrix, consisting of participants both inside and outside of his own social and ethnic classes (i.e., a cross-cultural mission).[14] Analyzing the evidence available from his mission

---

13. Letter of Esther Edwards Burr to Jonathan Edwards, Nov[embe]r 2, 1757, 295–96. Esther Burr's letters to Sarah Prince of Boston (1728–1771) published in her journal "provide one of the earliest glimpses into eighteenth-century colonial life from the perspective of a woman, and tell us much about Esther's attitudes regarding female spiritual and intellectual life, relations between men and women, and provincial affairs"; Weaver, "Burr, Esther Edwards (1732–1758)," 79. See also Hedberg, "Child Rearing," 87; Ledwith, "Family," 221–24.

14. See Marsden, *Jonathan Edwards: A Life*, 511–12, for the birth dates of each of the Edwardses' children. On the history of the Stockbridge mission and Edwards's service there, see Sweeney, "River Gods and Related Minor Deities," 2:459n84. See also Bezzant, *Edwards the Mentor*, 69: "Edwards was an accomplished preacher, but his enjoyment of dialogue and his commitment to the Socratic method were no less pedagogically significant features of his ministry." Bezzant, *Edwards the Mentor*, 69n175, observes the similarity between Edwards's pedagogical commitments and the priorities of Comenius regarding the philosophy and praxis of education.

Regarding Edwards's service at Stockbridge, corrections to certain recent inaccuracies are in order. Davies, "'Prepare Ye the Way of the Lord,'" locates Edwards's missiological motivation and activities within an historical and contemporaneous Reformed

To Understand *Things* as Well as *Words*

context. Davies presents an extensive historiological and theological background for Edwards at Stockbridge and details some of the difficulties Edwards faced there. However, his assertion on p. 193, "As we shall see, [Edwards's] gifts seemed to be more along the lines of missionary strategy and administration, rather than direct personal involvement in the task" of missionary ignores the "direct personal involvement" Edwards poured into teaching and mentoring students at the mission. Although Davies goes into detail regarding the letters Edwards wrote from Stockbridge concerning his plans for the school, the topic of Edwards as a teacher is given scant attention in one sentence on p. 206. In the one paragraph "regarding the methods of education" that Edwards planned and executed, no mention is made of the innovation which the dialogic methodology Edwards employed there represented as a departure from reliance on rote memorization (210). Davies gives a good description of Edwards's activities as a missionary on p. 65 of Davies, "Jonathan Edwards," 60–68, and concludes, "Among the many-sided activity of [Edwards's] comparatively short life, his missionary interest, involvement, and influence deserve recognition." Yet he still fails to credit Edwards as *educator* among his mission duties.

In its conception, "Stockbridge was the best planned, best organized, and best financed of any eighteenth-century Indian mission"; Hankins, "Bringing the Good News," 124. (Cf. Sweeney, "River Gods and Related Minor Deities," 2:458: "The missionary experiment at Stockbridge . . . had been flawed from its inception. From the beginning, the project lacked unified administration and suffered from intermittent direction from too many white chiefs, who were far removed from the mission itself.") In reality, however, the mission experiment conducted there "failed to become a model Indian-English town," partially because the English settlers generally (led by certain members of the Williams family) did not share the zeal of Edwards and others, such as Isaac Hollis, to evangelize the Natives. Instead, the Stockbridge area was viewed as an opportunity for settlers to exploit the Natives and encroach on their land; see, e.g., Miles, "Red Man Dispossessed," 46–76, Sweeney, "River Gods and Related Minor Deities," Hankins, "Bringing the Good News," 126–29; Kimnach, "Stockbridge Mission," 28. Hankins states "one of the most important" reasons for this failure was "the New England Company's inability to supply the new town with missionaries who had enough ability or influence to protect the Indians from the encroachment of English settlers"; 124. Hankins comments that Edwards's departure from Stockbridge "deprived the Indians of one of their strongest champions (p. 130)," and commends him as one of only three of a total of at least seven missionary-ministers in Stockbridge's forty-year history who "demonstrate[d] a personal commitment to the ideal of a Christian Indian community"; 133. Additionally, she notes, "Edwards spent six or seven years trying to reconcile the factions in Stockbridge who were wrangling over control of funds supplied by [Reverend Isaac] Hollis, the New England Company, and the province of Massachusetts for Indian work"; 128. In doing so, she points out one difficulty Edwards faced at the mission: diffusion of power among individual patrons, the missionary society, and boards of commissioners, resulting in an unclear line of authority for much of his time there. Hankins goes into no detail about Edwards's missionary activities there, which include a massive letter-writing campaign to secure support for the mission and to alert authorities to circumstances created by "a broad range of complex and divisive issues and individuals," regularly preaching to Native and English congregations two and three times weekly, teaching weekly at the mission school, writing what Hankins considers "theological works as unintelligible to most colonists as they were to the Indians (p. 130)," but which have been considered "four of the ablest and most valuable works which the church of Christ has in its possession"; all the while, fending off attempts to drive him away by persons who opposed his presence

experience reveals a pedagogical methodology rooted both in Puritan values and ideals and in the new thinking of the "Enlightenment(s)," as well as Edwards as a theorist and as a teacher who is ambitious concerning expected outcomes.[15]

---

at the mission; Minkema, "Jonathan Edwards: A Theological Life," 13; Dwight, *Life of President Edwards*, cxxvii. It is unfortunate, as Hankins points out, that the Stockbridge mission did not achieve its promise, but Edwards should have received more credit for his efforts than she gives. She compounds this omission by resurrecting a myth that has long since been put to rest. On p. 130, Hankins's description of Edwards as one of the greatest of the Indians' defenders is prefaced by, "Even though Edwards may have spent most of his time at Stockbridge" writing. It is unfortunate that Hankins's work, an overall valuable resource regarding eighteenth-century missions activity, did not treat Edwards's missions efforts more fully and accurately.

A lapse of scholarship by a respected Edwards authority that is even more egregious, occurring as it does by someone who knows that research has proven this to be untrue, is the same assertion by Stout, "Parish Ministry," 30, that while at Stockbridge, "mostly Edwards dedicated his time and energy to completing his philosophical and theological treatises, which would come to define his fame, both then and to posterity." Admittedly, Edwards's written works, including *HWR* and *LDB*, as well as the ones composed at Stockbridge, were considered "indispensable" by "virtually every well-known Protestant missionary and mission society of the nineteenth century." However, so, too, did they consider his example as a deeply invested evangelizer as "paramount"; Franklin, "Missions and Missiology," 385. Edwards's written compositions at Stockbridge should be appreciated within the context of his overall ordeal there, and the sum total of his Stockbridge service should be evaluated as a key component of a life devoted to Christ in which instruction was a crucial element of his evangelism. It is my earnest desire that the present study will assist in securing for Edwards the recognition as a pedagogical theorist and as an educator which his extraordinary and self-sacrificial labors and far-reaching results merit.

15. See Claghorn in *LPW*, 22: "Edwards' letters–particularly those written to [Rev. Isaac] Hollis (July 2, 1751), Sir William Pepperrell (Nov. 28, 1751), and Joseph Paice (Feb. 24, 1752)—provide the reader with an unparalleled view of his philosophy of Indian education." Significantly, the epistolary evidence from Stockbridge, the largest single division of his extant correspondence, indicates that Edwards devoted a substantial amount of attention to education-related matters, in addition to teaching itself, e.g., designing the curriculum, improving the school facilities, and securing support for education at the mission from those best situated to provide it; see *LPW*, 388–90; *LPW*, 406–14; *LPW*, 435–47. See Claghorn, "Introduction," 17; Potgieter, "Education," 407: "Edwards's practical side as an educator is seen at its clearest in his correspondence from Stockbridge. He reminds sponsors and political leaders of the importance of instructing the Indian children. He stresses the need for able trustees and educators. He mentions the weekly instruction he himself gives to the children and he details plans for a female school."

"[Edwards's] hope was to turn the mission into a regional center for the Indians' religious instruction, and he garnered support for this educational vision from both [Sir William] Johnson [who, in the late 1740s, became sole Commissary for Indian Affairs in New York and in 1755 became Britain's first Superintendent of Indian Affairs] and the Stockbridge tribal leaders"; Claghorn in *LPW*, 22, 21. Edwards seemed to have planned for Stockbridge during his service there to have been modeled to a degree on

To Understand *Things* as Well as *Words*

Edwards had long been invested in missions as a means of evangelism, and in the Stockbridge mission specifically from its outset. He was a member of the committee that established Stockbridge in 1734, and served as a receiver and disburser of funds for the school there. Given his high expectations, the review of the mission Edwards conducted prior to actively assuming his duties there left him sorely disappointed. "The previous fifteen years of instruction at the [mission] school had been wasted."[16] Edwards was dismayed that the ineffective instruction was preventing the seeds of learning from being planted in the fertile soil of receptive minds.

The effects of this failure were being realized on two levels. As noted previously, opportunities for the students actually to gain an understanding of English (and anything else supposedly "taught") were being missed because the Native children had merely made sounds for signs, achieving no comprehension of what they were reading.[17] This meant that the students were not learning at the introductory level: They were not able to associate the sounds of the words they were memorizing with their referents, not reflecting on those associations, and not contextualizing the words and the ideas within the physical world which the words, ideas, and the students inhabited.[18]

This in turn led to the failure to achieve what, to Edwards, was learning's ultimate goal: The students were not coming to understand the physical world as the creation of the God who seeks to use his creation as a means of communication to human beings, whom he desires to draw to himself. This failure hindered winning souls to Christ through conversion, which Edwards observed is "the main design of the whole Indian establishment at this place."[19]

Francke's establishment at Halle (although not as ambitious in scope), including a mission, at least one school, and a distribution center for religious literature; See Minkema, "Francke, August Hermann (1663–1727)," 233.

16. Chaney, 89, 89n3; Claghorn, "Editor's Introduction," 18n9; Franklin, "Missions and Missiology," 384; Gibson, "Jonathan Edwards: A Missionary," 3.8n38; Winslow, *Jonathan Edwards (1703–1758)*, 277. See also Marsden, *Jonathan Edwards: A Life*, 389; Wheeler, *To Live Upon Hope*, 213.

17. See Winslow, *Jonathan Edwards (1703–1758)*, 277; LPW, 407.

18. See Stelting, "Edwards as Educator," 176.

19. *LPW*, 411; Smith, "God has Made Us to Differ," 54–55. See Baines, "Thy Kingdom Come," 117n286. Parsons, *Life of Sir William Pepperrell*, 245–54, recounts interactions between Edwards and Pepperrell during the time of Edwards's missionary service. I appreciate Ronald Baines's dissertation acquainting me with this biography of Pepperrell.

Jonathan Edwards's Pedagogical Methodology

Edwards considered "the ordinary method of teaching among the English" to be marred by "gross defects" and, in particular, "the common methods of instruction in New England," regrettably, were "grossly defective."[20] Consequently, he set about remedying this situation by teaching via an emphasis on dialogic interaction with the students, a technique he had used, and was still using, effectively with his own children.[21] He recognized that responding to questions and formulating other questions in turn require connecting words with ideas and reflecting on the connections, which are more advanced skills than rote memorization requires. This procedure should begin early in the student's life to accrue maximum benefit, not only in the acquisition of knowledge in particular subjects, but also in the early formation of a positive attitude toward learning: This methodology would "accustom the child, from its infancy, to think and reflect, and to beget in it an early taste for knowledge, and a regularly increasing appetite for it."[22]

As argued previously, Edwards was a composite of someone whose mindset was contextualized by eighteenth-century colonial American norms and values, and thus bore his environment's limitations, and also of someone forward-thinking who escaped its limitations in ways which would surprise us today.[23] As we shall now discover, Edwards the educator reveals himself in each of these identities.

---

20. *LPW*, 407, 409.

21. Although Wheeler, *To Live Upon Hope*, 213, correctly notes, "Edwards proposed novel educational techniques for teaching his Indian charges," her assertion, "Edwards saw stories as a means to engage the minds of children in a way that teaching by rote simply could not," while true, fails to account for the value of the *teacher-student dialogue* based on *questions* about the stories.

See Bezzant, *Edwards the Mentor*, 69n175, who observes that Edwards's commitment to dialogical pedagogy was also reflected in the priorities of Jan Comenius, "whose pedagogical theory in the seventeenth century encouraged exchange, fun, and models of learning from the natural world, which may have been mediated to New England through John Winthrop. See Howard Louthan and Andrea Sterk, "Introduction," in *John Comenius: The Labyrinth of the World and the Paradise of the Heart* (The Classics of Western Spirituality 90; New York: Paulist Press, 1998), 13, 14." As discussed in chapter 4 of this study, I believe Comenius plausibly influenced Edwards's commitment to dialogic interaction with students and his belief in the value of story-telling as a pedagogic technique.

22. *LPW*, 408.

23. See Marsden, "Jonathan Edwards in the Twenty-First Century," 154: Edwards was someone "who was deeply loyal to the Puritan and wider Reformed or Calvinistic traditions of the seventeenth century and who was also informed by the Newtonian revolution and profoundly challenged by the British Enlightenment of his own era."

To Understand *Things* as Well as *Words*

Edwards expressed disdain for Native American languages, convinced they were "extremely barbarous and barren," altogether unfit for proper communication of intellectual or spiritual thoughts.[24] The Native American students would therefore need to be taught English to permit their receiving instruction. Rather than stress constant rote memorization

---

24. *LPW*, 413. Claghorn, in *LPW*, 22, observes, "The most urgent need [at the mission], Edwards believed, was to teach the Indians how to speak and read English," because of the "unfitness" of the Native languages to communicate sophisticated ideas effectively. For Edwards, "even a rudimentary education required the reading of European works in a wide range of liberal arts and sciences; to translate them all from English into the relevant Indian languages would, in Edwards' view, simply take too long"; Claghorn in *LPW*, 22. Edwards did not learn the Mohawk and Mahican (also known as Housatonic or Housatunnock, Brotherton, or generally as "Stockbridge Indians"; see Winslow, *Jonathan Edwards (1703–1758)*, 270–92; Axtell, *European and the Indian*, 49; Marsden, *Jonathan Edwards: A Life*, 375, 578n1) languages during his service at Stockbridge. He indicates that his view of the Indian languages is based on information from others; i.e., "on almost every account," Native American means of communication are deficient; *LPW*, 413. Likely this is at least a partial reflection of his colonial American's overall condescension toward "inferior" cultures.

Interestingly, Jonathan Jr. learned Native American dialects while his family was living at Stockbridge, in preparation for a potential career as a missionary envisioned by his father. During his time there, he "seldom heard English outside [his] home. 'I knew the names of some things in Indian,' he later recalled, 'which I did not know in English; even all my thoughts ran in Indian'"; Marsden, *Jonathan Edwards: A Life*, 391, 580n33, Ferm, 15–16. "Clearly, [Edwards] thought learning Indian languages a better investment for the young [than for him], eventually sending young Jonathan Jr. along on a mission to live among the Indians"; Marsden, *Jonathan Edwards: A Life*, 580n33. Marsden here refers to Edwards Jr. leaving home at age fifteen to live at the Iroquois village of Onohoquaga, New York, under the instruction of Gideon Hawley; Bezzant, *Edwards the Mentor*, 114, 114n2. The senior Edwards viewed this venture of his son as part of a broader project with wider implications: "As indicated by his decision to send his young son Jonathan Jr., to New York with missionary colleague Gideon Hawley to develop his facility with Indian languages and gain firsthand experience of tribal customs [which proved successful], Edwards knew that the English had something to learn from Indian languages and cultures[,] and believed that a genuine understanding of the curriculum would entail a bilingual appropriation of Western knowledge (see also the letter to Joseph Bellamy, June 1756 [217, *LPW*, 688–89]); Claghorn in *LPW*, 22. Edwards Jr. apparently was well-received by the Indians as a result of his efforts; see Gideon Hawley MS, Congregational Library, Boston, 4, November 20, 1755, quoted in Sibley, *Sibley's Harvard Graduates*, 12:396; Marsden, *Jonathan Edwards: A Life*, 412, 412n55.

Cf. Stelting, "Edwards as Educator," 175–76: "[Edwards's] concern [that the Indians did not know English] was a practical one. The native Indian languages did not have words for concepts inherent to the matters being taught. This was especially true of the Christian doctrines which were of extreme importance to the purpose of the mission." Whether this information is the result of Stelting's own research or whether he has simply taken Edwards's statements about the American Indian languages at face value is unclear. See also Baines, "Thy Kingdom Come," 120.

Jonathan Edwards's Pedagogical Methodology

or teach via a traditional monologic mode, Edwards designed a "familiar," or conversational, interaction between teacher and students. In this procedure, "Familiar [i.e., dialogic, sometimes known as Socratic] questions should be put to the child, about the subjects of the lesson; and the child should be drawn on, to speak freely, and in his [or her] turn also to ask questions, for the resolution of his [or her] own doubts."[25] That is, the teacher would present a lesson and initiate a dialogue, encouraging the students to ask questions and asking questions of them in turn. Being taught the English words for objects and actions in the dialogic manner (in Edwards's assessment) would enable the students to connect the words with the ideas they represent; thus, "the things which the lesson treats of" would be "opened to the child's understanding."[26]

Edwards made a noteworthy observation regarding an effective pedagogic method of ensuring students' understanding lessons: A teacher should "not only [explain] the words and sentences, but also from time to time [vary] the phraseology, putting the question in different words of the same sense, and also intermixing with the questions and answers . . . some improvement or application . . . founded on the answers that have been given"[27] This technique would assist the students in expanding their vocabularies and in developing the ability to associate different words expressing the same idea with the idea itself and to reflect speculatively on these connections.

Although planning for students to be taught a full range of subjects such as spelling and arithmetic along with reading, Edwards particularly concentrated on history as a medium in the learning process. Using Scripture, a psalter, and the *Westminster Shorter Catechism* as materials (well-known to him both as a pastor and as a father), he envisioned "The teacher, in familiar [i.e, dialogic] discourses . . . [giving] the children a short general scheme of the scriptural history," beginning with the creation account in Genesis and progressing through the "larger divisions" of the Old and New Testaments, "giving them some idea of their connection one with another."[28]

In Edwards's outlook, teaching by means of stories centered around major scriptural events, such as the Flood and the Exodus in the Old Testament and (not surprisingly), "the birth of Christ, some of the chief

25. *LPW*, 408.
26. *LPW*, 408.
27. *LPW*, 409.
28. *LPW*, 409.

acts of his life, his death, his resurrection, [and] his ascension," and Pentecost in the New Testament, would awaken in the students the desire to "obtain the knowledge of [the events] themselves" through reading on their own.[29] Pursuing this activity would yield benefits on both levels of education. Reading would increase their information about their world and thus assist in developing their intellects, and reading sacred and devotional literature would also be a key means of the students' placing themselves on the way to receiving redemptive grace.[30]

Moreover, Edwards formulated an approach which located the events of the biblical narrative within the context of overall world history: Students should be "taught something of the great successive changes and events in the Jewish nation and world of mankind that connect the history of the Old and New Testaments."[31] Developing an overall outline of history by learning how the chronologies of scriptural and ecclesiastical events relate to each other, and to other world events, Edwards conceived as a major goal for students in his pedagogical program. Facilitating students in forming this perspective would help enable them to come to see Scripture as a meta-narrative in which is revealed the beginnings of "the greatest of all the works of God," the redemption of humanity as directed by God through the medium of history.[32] Instruction in this manner ideally would set the students on the path to viewing ongoing redemption history as the setting of the "divine drama" of God's interaction with humanity in which he calls them to participate.[33]

---

29. *LPW*, 409. Wheeler, "Edwards as Missionary," 203, 209, observes, "While Edwards was entirely conventional in his conviction that the Indians were in need of a 'civilized' education, his methods [of dialogic interaction and narrative-driven technique] proved innovative." This assists her in affirming, "Jonathan Edwards's work as a missionary reveals him to be a man of his times, with some notable differences."

30. See, e.g., Monaghan, *Learning to Read and Write in Colonial America*, 11; Smith, *American Reading Instruction*, 12; Spring, *American School, 1642–2000*, 13.

31. *LPW*, 410.

32. *HWR*, 512, 513. A crucial goal Edwards conceived was empowering students to come to see world history as being the history of God's work of redemption in which they could participate, as Edwards himself had done.

33. See Ashford, "Missions, the Global Church, and Christian Higher Education," 527, 527n6, for a basic perspective on Scripture: "One way to see the Bible's unity is to recognize the fact that its material organizes into the form of a *story*–a grand and overarching *narrative* that makes sense of God and the world. In other words, the Bible offers us the true story of the whole world" (emphasis added).

Bruner, *Divine Drama*, treats the theme of Scripture as an overarching storyline of "God's story," in which the individual participates and discovers meaning. Smith, *Divine Drama of History and Civilisation*, 1, considers history as "the progress of

Jonathan Edwards's Pedagogical Methodology

Although Edwards expected much from all his students, in practice, he accommodated his instructional technique to individual differences in capacities. If his pedagogical plan proved too ambitious for some and "if it be judged that it is needless to teach all the children all these things, some difference might be made in children of different genius."[34] As a natural corollary, "children of the best genius might be taught more things than others."[35]

Edwards realized, too, from his experiences as a father and from his observations at Northampton and at Stockbridge that children progress in developing mental capacities (but do so at different rates) as they mature. A "gross defect" of the instruction in reading when Edwards arrived at the mission was that students were acquiring nothing more than the "habit of making such and such sounds, on the sight of such and such letters," and not coming to connect the sounds with the appropriate words, and them with the ideas they represent.[36] Edwards was all too aware that this deficiency persisted after the children had developed the capacity to understand these connections, and to reflect speculatively on them, had they been led to be able to do so.

A significant aspect of Edwards's pedagogical concern for recognizing individual distinctions among students was his interest in rewarding excellent academic performance. Edwards was confident that measures could be devised that would "greatly ... encourage and animate [the students] in [learning], and excite a laudable ambition to excel." Proficiency in subjects taught at the school, such as "reading, writing, spelling,

---

human society," an archetypal providential story of interaction of divine direction and human participation. Vanhoozer, *Drama of Doctrine*, 37–38, 110, presents the gospel as a "theo-drama" of redemption in which God has communicated to human beings through Jesus Christ. Life is seen as "divine-human interactive theater," in which persons, through redemption, are called to perform truthful propositions (beliefs), experiences (feelings), and narratives (actions) to reflect God's comprehensive revelation in Christ. All of these works deal with the themes of a "divine drama" in which God, revealed in Scripture and acting in history, seeks to communicate with human beings. This communicating and interacting God is the One whom Edwards sought to have his students come to know through redemptive grace and the "new spiritual sense." See also Bartholomew and Goheen, *Drama of Scripture*.

34. *LPW*, 411. Potgeiter, "Education," 411, correctly notes, "Significantly, as Van Wyk (2016, 238–9) points out, Edwards differentiates [students] according to talent and not according to gender." Perhaps implicit, but not stated, is the fact that this differentiation is significant because Edwards specifically supported coeducation, a rarity at that time outside the home and a few "dame schools" of uneven quality.

35. *LPW*, 411.

36. *LPW*, 407.

arithmetic, knowledge in the principles of religion, [and] knowledge of church history," as demonstrated periodically at public examinations judged by school trustees, "and all in the town who are in any respect connected with Indian affairs," would be recognized with some form of "premium . . . that will very much please Indian children."[37] This would yield the beneficial results of encouraging the students to maintain their maximum efforts to meet the academic standards, and also of promoting community involvement and support of the school through display to those in and around the mission of the "best products" of the education there.[38]

Consistent with both his commitment regarding the spiritual goal of education and his social station in a British colonial setting, Edwards also championed the idea of rewards being given "to such [students] as, by the testimony of their teachers and governors, have excelled" in matters such as "virtue or diligence, in care to speak the truth, in strictly observing the sabbath, in good manners, [and] in respect to their superiors."[39] Development of the "total person" through acquisition of virtuous habits,

---

37. *LPW*, 412.

38. Edwards takes care to note that "the chiefs of the Indians be invited to attend" this ceremony; *LPW*, 412. Edwards "seems to understand that the effectiveness of education depends on a proper relationship between the school and the community." His proposal regarding holding an Awards Day-type event, attended by the children's families, tribal leaders, and local dignitaries, "was not, in itself, a new technique, but the idea that Indian families should be brought into the activity seems to have been a startling idea"; Dwight, *Life of President Edwards,* cxxxviii; Stelting, "Edwards as Educator," 180, 189n46.

39. *LPW*, 412. Although rejecting the "English system" of rote memorization alone as being an effective technique for learning, Edwards expected his Native American students to comply with typical English norms regarding behavior and mores. Edwards inherited by birth membership in a "ruling class" in which clergy figured prominently. An authority figure as an active minister who "had a very high regard for his clerical office" and whose status conferred on him membership in the "provincial gentry," Edwards expected from his students deference to his social standing, as well as to the stations of those considered equal to or above his social rank; Ball, *Approaching Jonathan Edwards*, 172; Sweeney, "River Gods and Related Minor Deities," 434; Minkema, "Writing and Preaching Sermons," 391. Thus we see that Edwards at Stockbridge exhibited both a forward-thinking mindset regarding teaching and learning processes and an outlook regarding deference to those in upper social status that was characteristic of his time. See Sweeney, "River Gods and Related Minor Deities," 1:341: "The ultimate source of authority was God, and the duty of men was to obey those whom God had set above them.... Ministers reiterated this hierarchic view of society in the eighteenth century and emphasized the need to obey those put in authority." The society in which Edwards participated (and, to an extent, dominated) was marked by "social hierarchies, mutual obligations, and obedience."

Jonathan Edwards's Pedagogical Methodology

customs, and mores is a vital aim of the learning process. Championing excellence in the areas named, therefore, is as important to the students' development as is academic achievement. Edwards's commitment to sharing the gospel with his Stockbridge Native students is undeniable, as was his respect of their ability to be taught on an equal basis as the Anglo-colonials. Nonetheless, his advocacy of the students' acquisition of refinements of "civilization" (i.e., "Anglicization") concerning "appropriate" demeanor and social deference reflected a desire for the Natives to comport themselves by standards sanctioned by the regnant socially stratified system.

Although the students maturing in areas of mind, heart, and soul is paramount to Edwards, important to him also is the children's social advancement. Observations and experience had led Edwards to conclude that "wise and skillful management" on the part of the teacher leading to "the habit of conversation on divine things" with those in his or her care would produce a dividend significant in the students' social interaction: "[G]radually [they would] be divested of that shyness and backwardness, usually discovered in children, to converse on such topics with their superiors."[40] Edwards thus demonstrated his awareness of education as a key agent in the development of social skills.

Noteworthy is the fact that Edwards viewed the village of Stockbridge as a matrix of social acculturation in which the school could serve as a medium. To this end, he planned a culturally diverse educational setting, in which "a number of English children might be put into the school with the Indian children."[41] He believed such an environment would not only assist in the Native American students to learn English, but help divest them of their "savage" and "barbarous" ways, as well. Moreover, in what he considers "the most effectual method of all" to aid the Indians in becoming "civilized," he advocates placing Native American children in carefully chosen colonial settlers' families to live for one to two years prior to their arrival at the school.[42]

---

40. *LPW*, 408.

41. *LPW*, 413. See also Claghorn in *LPW*, 22–23.

42. *LPW*, 413; Claghorn in *LPW*, 22–23. Blore, "Educational Philosophy of Jonathan Edwards," 78, praises this idea of Edwards as an innovation in "language immersion" centuries ahead of its time. On the other hand, Edwards seems to have considered neither the potential danger this could have posed to the host families nor the possibility that exposure to the host families of the Indians' "barbarous" way of life may have "lowered" them, rather than "elevating" the Native Americans to the hosts' cultural level. Noteworthy is the fact that "the Edwardses eventually took at least one Indian boy

Edwards's desire to place Native American children in colonial host families may seem today to indicate a condescending ethnocentrism present in his belief this was "absolutely necessary" in order to prepare them to learn at the school.[43] However, his plan to have the Native American and Anglo-colonial students integrated into a unified classroom setting reflected his assurance that students in both categories were equally capable of learning.[44]

Persons expecting "education in the hands of a repressive Puritan" from Edwards would be surprised by three facts regarding his pedagogical philosophy and methodology. Nowhere in his articles of faith on education does Edwards convey the impression that he considered learning to be a duty which students must bear and persevere through under any circumstances, at all costs. On the contrary, his intended outcome was to put an end to the "dull, wearisome task" which learning had become through rote memorization.[45] Edwards's conviction was that stimulation of the student's cognitive and reflective capabilities through teacher-student dialogue based on narrative-generated lessons would result in "the child's learning [being] rendered pleasant, entertaining and profitable."[46] Also of significance, the dialogic technique would transform the student from a passive recipient into an active participant in the learning process. This stimulation of the thought processes would enable the student to see how learning could be beneficial and something that could be explored more independently in due course.

Intriguing, too, is Edwards's desire to include singing in the curriculum at Stockbridge.[47] This plan indicates the complexity of Edwards's thinking as a philosopher, as a theologian, and as an educator. As discussed in chapter 3, Edwards held a theory of beauty in which music is an integral part of the natural, or secondary, beauty of the physical world.[48] From his theological viewpoint, Edwards believed the beauty of creation reflects the harmony of the Trinity and that it acted as a medium

---

into their home and perhaps others"; Marsden, *Jonathan Edwards: A Life*, 390, 580n27; *LPW*, 638; *LPW*, 666–67.

43. *LPW*, 413.

44. This cultural integration in a school setting was an "innovative step" at this time; Minkema, "Jonathan Edwards on Education," 34.

45. *LPW*, 408.

46. *LPW*, 408.

47. *LPW*, 411.

48. See Edwards, "The Mind. [1] Excellency," 335; *EW*, 96.

intended to enable students to understand how God seeks to communicate with them.[49]

Additionally, his view of music offers an instructive glimpse into Edwards's concept of human nature. Assured that "music, especially sacred music, has a powerful efficacy to soften the heart into tenderness, to harmonize the affections, and to give the mind a relish for objects of a superior character," Edwards was convinced of the transformative effects of teaching the Native Americans to sing.[50] The charms of music would enable them to "renounce the coarseness, and filth and degradation, of savage life," replacing these ills with "cleanliness, refinement and good morals."[51] So convinced was Edwards of the usefulness of the incorporation of singing into the school program that he wrote a letter to a singing teacher to meet "a very great need of somebody at Stockbridge to teach the Indians to sing."[52] His belief in the value of music is revealing of Edwards the worshiper as well as Edwards the thinker, as singing was a vital part of his personal, family, and corporate devotions.[53]

Yet another significant innovation Edwards conceived for the mission, one with far-reaching results, was coeducation. His plan for the school included an expressed commitment to teaching "*girls* as well as *boys.*"[54] Distinctions he made in his teaching methodology were to accommodate intellectual variations, not gender-based differences, among

---

49. See Delattre, *Beauty and Sensibility in the Thought of Jonathan Edwards,* 17; Edwards, "Chapter III," 561; *TV,* 27; Edwards, "Miscellany 332," 410 (emphasis added). See also Edwards, "Dissertation I," 434, 435; Mitchell, *Jonathan Edwards on the Experience of Beauty,* 4; Pauw, *Supreme Harmony of All;* Minkema, "Jonathan Edwards on Education," 34, 263n11; Marsden, *Infinite Fountain of Light,* 51–52; Erdt, "Art," 38–40. "Edwards appears to have commented more on the graciously efficacious power of music than on any other art form, perhaps because singing was a staple of Puritan worship"; Erdt, "Art," 39.

50. *LPW,* 411. See also Marsden, *Jonathan Edwards: A Life,* 79, 390; Jenson, "End is Music," 169. See Edwards, "Miscellany 188," 331: "The best, most beautiful, and most perfect way that we have of expressing a sweet concord of mind to each other, is by music."

51. *LPW,* 411.

52. *LPW,* 597.

53. Edwards, "Personal Narrative," 794; Hopkins, *Life of Edwards,* 44; Claghorn in *LPW,* 596; Minkema, "Jonathan Edwards on Education," 34, 263n11.

54. *LPW,* 411 (emphasis in original). Edwards recommends that prizes be given at the Stockbridge school to those who have attained "the greatest proficiency in learning to sew, to spin, to knit, etc."; *LPW,* 412. Presumably this was done with female students in mind. Significantly, however, Edwards does not suggest that the girls at the school should *not* be taught the same subjects as boys.

those he taught. This was contrary to the custom of mid-eighteenth-century colonial America, in which females were minimally educated outside the home. Commonly, the only settings for educating females beyond the home environment were the so-called "dame schools." These were typically operated by older women (including widows), who themselves may have been minimally educated, in their homes while going about household duties. In these, both boys and girls were taught rudimentary reading, writing, and arithmetic ("the three r's"), and girls were taught domestic skills, such as cooking, sewing, knitting, and embroidery.[55] Both genders received training in the Puritan religious precepts.

55. Minkema, "Jonathan Edwards on Education," 33; Cremin, *American Education*, 129, 129n19, 173–75, 187; Cubberley, *History of Education*, 447–48.
 Owing partially to individual abilities and drive and partially to their gentry status in society, Edwards's mother and sisters were exceptions to the general rule of their day regarding education outside the home being unavailable to females. During the colonial era, "there existed no real question as to the intelligence of women, it being generally accepted that they were inferior"; Woody, *History of Women's Education in the United States*, 1:92. In addition, the sphere for which they were fitted was that of hearth and home as wives and mothers, preparation for which was to be acquired in the home; Woody, *History of Women's Education in the United States*, 1:93. See also Rudolph, *American College and University*, 307–8. Therefore, since education beyond the home environment would not benefit them, plainly stated, "Colonial formal education for females hardly existed"; Reed, *History of Christian Education*, 322; "[W]omen in the seventeenth and eighteenth centuries [in colonial America] were, essentially, socially barred from higher education by virtue of their sex"; "Prior to the American Revolution, few avenues of formal education were open to girls and young women. Throughout the colonial period, young boys and girls typically learned to read at 'dame schools' run by women in their homes. Beyond this rudimentary level of instruction, educational options for young women were limited . . . . On the whole, little formal attention was paid to the education of women in the mid-eighteenth century"; Jannenga, "Making College Colonial," 1n2; McMahon, *Education of Girls and Women*; Kerber, *Women of the Republic: Ideology and Intellect in Revolutionary America*; Schwager, "Educating Women in America," 333–72 (see Schwager's extensive notes throughout); E. Dexter, *A History of Education in the United States*, 424: "We have little evidence that our forefathers of early colonial days felt the importance of educating their daughters"; Woody, *History of Women's Education in the United States*, 1:117, 117n14: "Even though a woman gave the first ground on which a free school was erected in [Massachusetts], her sex was zealously excluded from the benefits of schooling, and many of the New England towns appear, at first, to have considered the admission of girls to their schools as 'inconsistent with the design' thereof; "For most of the the colonial era, education [as a general rule] was not available to girls . . . . Boys were required to learn reading, writing, and arithmetic, but girls where limited to needlework and reading"; In the majority of colonial American schools that existed prior to the American Revolution, "no such opportunity was afforded girls to make the most of themselves [through education], as had been forced upon most boys for a half-dozen generations"; Boone, *Education in the United States*, 69; *Colonial Women: Literacy and Education*, www.encyclopedia.com/history/encyclopedia-almanacs-transcripts-and-maps/colonial-women; "[In] the

Jonathan Edwards's Pedagogical Methodology

The "dame schools" extended through the eighth grade, after which, the girls' formal education typically ended. Boys proceeded to grammar schools; there, a male teacher taught students more advanced math, Latin, and Greek, preparing those so inclined for admission to Harvard.[56] As examined previously, Edwards's support of coeducation was largely the result of Edwards's upbringing in an environment in which he and his sisters alike received educations of identical quality, as well as the influences of Comenius and Francke.

In summary, Edwards's mindset and worldview were partially rooted in his eighteenth-century milieu in three ways: as a Puritan, with his emphasis on the centrality of Scripture to instruction; as an appropriator and modifier of "Enlightenment(s)" ideas, with his epistemology evident in his teaching; and as a "typical" Anglo-colonial American of the time, with his attitude toward Native American culture at the beginning of his missionary service. On the other hand, Edwards was progressive-thinking insofar as his dialogic methodology, cultural integration, and coeducation in the classroom environment were all innovations for his

---

opinion of colonial America learning did not properly belong to women. Reading was demanded, writing desired, a little arithmetic might be studied. Beyond this [females] seldom went . . . . In New England . . . discrimination [against educating females] appears . . . in the schools of the period. The New Haven Hopkins Grammar School states the rule for the others of its kind: 'that all girls be excluded as Improper and inconsistent [with] such a Grammar School as ye law injoins, and is ye Design of this [settlement].' With regard to those lesser masters' schools which taught the three R's, the same rule held on the whole . . . . Of some two hundred towns whose records have been studied by Small [probably Walter Herbert Small, "The New England Grammar School, 1635–1700," in *School Review* X (Sept. 1902) 513–31; Small, *Early New England Schools*, 1914] and others, the present writer can find only eleven which admitted girls prior to 1770"; Monroe, *Cyclopedia of Education*, 2:123. The foregoing substantiates that, for the most part, schooling beyond the home (and possibly the "dame school") was routinely denied to those of the female gender during Edwards's lifetime in his New England setting. Therefore, his commitment to coeducation merits him acclaim as an education theorist and pedagogic practitioner.

A major justification for the Puritan assessment of the female intellect as inferior was Eve's falling prey to the serpent in Genesis 3 and her subsequent temptation of Adam, leading to the Fall and its resultant curse on their posterity; see, e.g., Abraham, *Eve*, 29–30; Hutchins, "Edwards and Eve," 675. Edwards held a more positive view of Eve than typically did his Puritan contemporaries and forebears; see Edwards, "Note 235," 187; Edwards, "Miscellany 674," 235n3; Edwards, "Miscellany 702," 288 [289]; Edwards, "Note 399," 397; Hutchins, "Edwards and Eve," 674: "When Calvin acknowledges Eve, he invariably criticizes her; Edwards, on the other hand, repeatedly finds opportunities to praise Eve and to call attention to her positive characteristics."

56. The calls of education reformers such as Comenius and Francke for universal coeducation went unheeded in colonial America (as demonstrated in the footnote above) until after Edwards's lifetime.

time and location. We shall now examine, to the extent evidence allows, Edwards's results as a teacher at Stockbridge.

EDWARDS'S RESULTS AS A TEACHER AT STOCKBRIDGE

Frustrating to the historian is the lack of direct evidence of Edwards's accomplishments as a teacher at Stockbridge. Although records exist of a few names of Native Americans who were prominent at the mission, they are not mentioned as having been students of Edwards. No records exist of anyone writing to or telling someone how his students there regarded his teaching.[57] This being the case, if one assesses the results of Edwards's teaching there, it must be on the basis of such indirect evidence as exists.

Not having learned the Indian languages, Edwards preached at Stockbridge through an interpreter. In his sermon on Ps 27:4, preached in October 1756, Edwards incorporated a writing exercise by one of his interpreters, Ebenezer Maunnauseet. This indicates that Maunnauseet was at least in the process of acquiring literacy skills.[58] Similarly, John Wauwaumpequumaut, another interpreter for Edwards, merits praise from Edwards as "an extraordinary man on some accounts; [one who] understands English well, [is] a good reader and writer and is an excellent interpreter."[59] Even more significantly, "[P]erhaps there was never an

---

57. Edwards, "Sermon 1175"; *Sermon Index (Canonical): Psalms 27*, www.edwards.yale.edu/research/sermon-index/canonical?chapter=27&book=19; Minkema, email to author, 02/25/2016; Minkema, "Maunnauseet, Ebenezer (dates unknown)," 367.

See Wheeler, *To Live Upon Hope*, 213: "There is no external evidence of Edwards's work as a teacher and no way of knowing to what extent he employed [his] theories of education during his time at Stockbridge." Nevertheless, she finds "echoes of his preaching style" in his pedagogical philosophy. In any case, it is known that Edwards taught those Native American students who remained at the mission on a weekly basis after the struggles involving control of the school were resolved and Reverend Isaac Hollis, "a member of the New England Company who independently supported specific educational projects in [Stockbridge]" and the chief English patron and benefactor of the mission, placed control in Edwards's hands in February 1754; Sweeney, "River Gods and Related Minor Deities," 459; Claghorn in *LPW*, 24; Marsden, *Jonathan Edwards: A Life*, 394; Smith, "God Has Made Us to Differ," 57.

58. *LPW*, 451–52. See also Wheeler, *To Live Upon Hope*, 220, 304n147.

59. *LPW*, 451–52. Interestingly, Rebecca Kellogg Ashley (1695–1757), younger sister of the Martin Kellogg whom Edwards held in contempt for his insufficiencies as a schoolteacher and his mistreatment of his Native charges, was also an interpreter for Edwards at Stockbridge. Fluent in the Iroquois tongue as a result of having been taken captive in the 1704 raid on Deerfield, Massachusetts, she was adopted by Mohawks and began to

Indian educated in America that exceeded him in knowledge, in divinity, [and] understanding of the Scriptures." Although Wauwaumpequumaut arrived at Stockbridge prior to Edwards's beginning as a missionary there, his education was completed under Edwards's care and mentorship.

Moreover, there is evidence of regeneration among the Native Americans at Stockbridge during Edwards's missionary service. In 1753, Edwards reported a change of conduct that seemed to indicate a positive response to the gospel: "Some of the Stockbridge Indians have of late been under considerable awakenings, especially two or three elderly men, that used to be vicious persons." Equally as notable, Edwards indicated that he had received professions of faith from some of the Natives, the longest of these from Cornelius and Mary Munneweaunummuck.[60] In addition, Edwards performed the rite of marriage for four Native American couples, celebrated communion with his Native American congregation on at least nine occasions at Stockbridge, and recognized some of the Native Americans there as full church members.[61]

Considering the seriousness during his Northampton pastorate with which he regarded admission to communion and church membership, and given that the professions of faith at Stockbridge follow the standards of the sample professions Edwards had composed for his Northampton congregants during the communion controversy, this evidence is especially noteworthy.[62] It is safe to conclude that a sub-

---

work as a translator for missions to indigenous peoples in the late 1740s. Edwards highly esteemed Ashley as someone "well acquainted with [the Mohawks's] language" and as one who had "a great interest in their affections." As a missionary to the Onohquaga on the Susquehanna River in the early 1750s, Gideon Hawley recorded in his journals that Ashley assisted him "with every aspect of the mission, from preaching to teaching to baptisms"; *LPW*, 496; Howard, "Ashley, Rebecca Kellogg (1695–1757)," 41–42. See also Howard, "Rebecca Kellogg Ashley."

60. *LPW*, 595; Edwards, "Profession of Faith, Two Drafts"; Wheeler, *To Live Upon Hope*, 221; Wheeler, *To Live Upon Hope*, 220, 304n150.

Although intoxication among the Natives seems to have been a recurring problem at the mission, Edwards found reason for hope because of improved behavior at one point toward the end of his ministry, possibly resulting from responsiveness to his sermons: "We have had less drunkenness of late among the Indians than for many years"; Edwards, "A222. Letter to Thomas Foxcroft, February 11, 1757."

61. Wheeler, *To Live Upon Hope*, 220, 304n149; Wheeler, "Lessons from Stockbridge," 136, 139n23; Edwards, *Diary and Memorandum Book, 1733–1757*; Marsden, *Jonathan Edwards: A Life*, 395, 581n42.

62. See Marsden, *Jonathan Edwards: A Life*, 394, 581n42. For an explanation of Edwards's view of the sacraments of baptism and communion, see Bezzant, "Ecclesiology and Sacraments," 267–80, especially 269–72.

stantive exchange had occurred between the candidates and Edwards regarding Christian faith and practice, which resulted in Edwards being convinced of the genuineness of conversion in these cases.[63] In instances of regeneration at the mission, the converts had come into "the way of grace" under Edwards's instruction in Scripture from the pulpit, his teaching at the school, or both.

Another piece of evidence supporting authentic engagement with Christianity by a Native American at the mission is provided by Hendrick Aupaumut, a sachem (i.e., a chief of a North American tribe) of the Stockbridge Indians, who was identified as a Christian and Mahican.[64] Aupaumut was born in Stockbridge in 1757 and, presumably, baptized by Edwards. As an adult, he sent a letter to Edwards's son Timothy, requesting, "I should be thankful if you would lend me a Book. The Author is your Father—Concerning [*Religious*] *Affections* or if you han't [*sic*] such—wish to have the other mention[ed]—the [*Freedom of the*] *Will*."[65] Moreover, a 1795 welcome from a tribal leader, likely Aupaumut, to missionaries from the Society of Friends (popularly known as Quakers), who had arrived at Stockbridge to undertake evangelism among Natives in the area, indicates that Edwards and the New Divinity ministers may have had some influence among the Natives: "Brothers, we heartily thank you for the many tokens of your *disinterested* love and friendship towards us poor Indians."[66]

While undergoing the trial by fire of his Stockbridge ordeal, Edwards demonstrated what are among the most important characteristics for an educator to have–the ability and the willingness to learn from one's students and to adapt as necessary to one's environment without altering

---

63. See Wheeler, *To Live Upon Hope*, 221. See also Wheeler, "Lessons from Stockbridge," 136; Wheeler, "Edwards as Missionary," 204.

64. See Wheeler, "Lessons from Stockbridge," 137.

65. "Hendrick A. to Hon'ble Timothy Edwards, Esq. Stockbridge or Wunnuqhqtoqhoke"; Wheeler, "Lessons from Stockbridge," 137, 140n29. See Wheeler, "Lessons from Stockbridge," 140n29: "The date on this letter was added later, and a more likely date is the early 1790s. I thank Lion Miles for pointing this out, personal communication, Aug. 31, 2004."

Hendrick acquired the volumes he sought from Timothy Edwards, and this exchange assisted in advancing Christianity among the Stockbridge Natives. See Hedberg, "Edwards, Timothy (son) (1738–1813)," 186–87, for this and other details of Timothy Edwards's life.

66. Sergeant, diary entry, dated May 18, 1795, Harvard Grants for Work among the Indians, *Journals of John Sergeant, 1790–1909*, Harvard University Archives; Wheeler, "Lessons from Stockbridge," 137n30 (emphasis added).

what is essential to convey. As noted previously in this study, Edwards accommodated his sermon style to his Native congregants without sacrificing the essence of the gospel in his presentation of Christ as being just in punishing sin but merciful to forgive sinners.

In addition to "doctrine and precept," Edwards communicated Christianity at Stockbridge by "instance and example."[67] In the course of his ministry to the indigenous people, he became accustomed to hearing their complaints against some of the Williamses and their allies. In order to determine the merits of their case, Edwards searched diligently through treaties signed between the Mohawks, Mahicans, and other area tribes, with the Massachusetts government. This investigation led Edwards to conclude that the Natives' resentment toward the Williamses regarding unjust land dealings was well-founded, as their exploitation was systematically violating official policy. On this and other matters, he uniformly demonstrated concern for the Indians' well-being through intervention on their behalf against those who opposed their interests by championing their cause to authorities against the Natives' exploiters. The exigencies of Stockbridge forged an Edwards who took shape as "a missionary deeply involved in the practical affairs" that pressed in on him, demanding his attention.[68]

Overall, in the midst of fending off attempts to dismiss him from the mission and of his assiduous study that produced his momentous writings during this period, Edwards "preached regularly to the Indians, catechized their children, visited the day school and the boarding school [and taught Indians and Anglo-colonials alike weekly at one point in his mission service], sorted out problems and complaints, fought for the rights of Indians against avaricious whites who, contrary to the declared policy of the government, were depriving them of their land, wrote to the Boston Commissioners and to sponsors in England to get more support for the Indian work, and planned and worked out strategies for further missionary thrusts in other places!"[69] The magnitude of his labors with

---

67. Quotations are in Edwards, "Author's Preface," 89. In writing this, "Edwards made clear that the Christian life is caught as well as taught, for we learn how to live as Christians not just from instruction but from example as well"; Bezzant, *Edwards the Mentor*, 93.

68. Marsden, *Jonathan Edwards: A Life*, 388. See, e.g., *LPW*, 437.

69. Davies, "Jonathan Edwards," 65. See also Grigg, "Missions," 421: "Wheeler [*To Live Upon Hope,*] (2008)] persuasively argues that the work of Edwards . . . played a role in enabling the Stockbridge Mahicans to remain on their land for several decades longer than might have been expected."

the aim of securing equitable treatment of the Natives in the face of abuse and exploitation "demonstrate that Edwards diligently defended Indian rights."[70]

A prime example is his determined (and ultimately successful) effort to have Captain Martin Kellogg ousted as schoolmaster. Kellogg had proved to be not only inadequate as a teacher but inimical to the purpose of the mission, as well.[71] Similarly, Edwards resisted the planned appointment of Abigail Sergeant Dwight (whom he considered ill-suited), regarding teaching a proposed girls' school.[72] Significantly, during a period of great tension and unrest at the mission, rooted in the disorder Kellogg had created at the school, Edwards facilitated the transition from Kellogg to the well-qualified Gideon Hawley (whom he had sought) as school teacher, to the Natives' tremendous satisfaction. Of equal significance, Edwards admonished the Natives that the English and Dutch who provided them rum did not have their customers' best interests in mind, and his Indian listeners aided their own exploitation and mistreatment by succumbing to intoxication. "Despite recurrent stress and public vilification," Edwards also brought information regarding mistreatment of the Indian children and news of their material needs, such as clothing, to the attention of authorities.[73]

70. Gibson, "Jonathan Edwards: A Missionary?"

71. See Claghorn in *LPW*, 23: "Edwards had been frustrated since his coming [to Stockbridge] by the ineptitude of Capt. Martin Kellogg, the man hired in 1748 to run the boys' boarding school"; Marsden, *Jonathan Edwards: A Life*, 388; Wheeler, "Edwards as Missionary," 201; Gibson, "Jonathan Edwards: A Missionary?" Gibson lists Edwards's letters to Isaac Hollis, Andrew Oliver, Joseph Paice, Thomas Foxcroft, and Thomas Hubbard, and concludes that the total is "too many to recount in detail here." See *LPW*, 61–70; *LPW*, 471–77; *LPW*, 494–509.

72. See Claghorn in *LPW*, 23. Compounding Edwards's exasperation with Kellogg, "When he learned that the [proposed] girls' school was to be run by another ill-trained local [Abigail Dwight], his disappointment with the mission could no longer be contained. See *LPW*, 424; Wheeler, "Edwards as Missionary," 200, 200n22. Firing off letter after letter to members of the New England Company [the Society for the Propagation of the Gospel in New England; renamed New England Company following the British Restoration], the general assembly, and British sponsors [such as Rev. Isaac Hollis], Edwards fought hard for complete control of both the mission and its schools." See *LPW*, 422–30; *LPW*, 431–34; *LPW*, 586–92. A proposed girls' school at Stockbridge proved unsuccessful, but Edwards taught boys and girls together during his duration as teacher there.

73. Quotation is in McDermott, "Jonathan Edwards and American Indians," 555; see *LPW*, 394–405; *LPW*, 400; *LPW*, 437; *LPW*, 583; *LPW*, 664; Martin, "Native Americans," 390–91. See also Minkema, "The Edwardses: A Ministerial Family in Eighteenth-Century New England," 376: "Drunkenness was a perennial problem

Jonathan Edwards's Pedagogical Methodology

During his missionary service at Stockbridge, Edwards and at least some of the Native Americans there became friends and he came to see them as "my people."[74] At one point while at the mission, despite its challenges, Edwards reflected on the contrast between the environment there and his contentions with many supposedly "civilized saints" of Northampton: "Here, at present, we live at peace; which has of long time been an unusual thing with us."[75]

Having been dismissed by his Northampton congregation, Edwards had arrived at Stockbridge as someone who was considered "not apt to teach" and as one who, in fact, disdained Native American ways.[76] Nevertheless, during his missionary service, he earned considerable respect from his Indian congregation through his ministry to them and his even-handed judgment of all people, regardless of ethnicity, by the same scriptural standards. In addition to his teaching once a week at the Stockbridge school and preaching regularly, Edwards and his family also lived

---

among the Indians [at Stockbridge], who would acquire liquor from the Williams trading post in town or from French traders to the west. Edwards found it necessary to address the vice specifically in several sermons." (However, see 215n60 para. 2, above.)

74. *LPW*, 610. See also Marsden, *Jonathan Edwards: A Life*, 394, 395; Wheeler, *To Live Upon Hope*, 220; McDermott, *Jonathan Edwards Confronts the Gods*, 203; Minkema, "Mahican (Stockbridge) Indians," 359: Edwards's experiences at Stockbridge convinced him "to regard some Indians as better Christians than many English." Apparently, Edwards's affection toward at least some of the Stockbridge Natives was evident to others and was known by members of his family. His daughter Sarah wrote in a letter to her sister Esther how their father had taken leave of "all his people and [family]" affectionately in his "Farewell Sermon to the Indians," 717n1.

See Ball, *Approaching Jonathan Edwards*, 171, 171n82, 171n84: A bond was formed between Edwards and the Stockbridge Indians because of the ill treatment by some of the Williamses toward both him and them. The fact that this family, which had increased its strength through intermarriage with a number of local power brokers, was instrumental in his dismissal from Northampton, also exploited them through manipulative and illegal land dealings, led to Edwards's commitment to protect the Indians' interests against a common foe. In sum, despite considerable opposition, such as some of the Williamses mounted, Edwards enjoyed substantial support for his undertakings among the Stockbridge Native residents, as well as among the Boston Commission of Indian Affairs and from colonial leaders such as Governor Jonathan Belcher; Claghorn in *LPW*, 24.

75. *LPW*, 420. In his letter to Gillespie cited in the note above, Edwards bemoaned, "I am still meeting with trouble, and expect no other as long as I live in this world"; 610. At another point, Edwards's disputes with his Northampton congregation provoked his lament, "It seems I am born to be a man of strife," yet he found a measure of peace amidst those he once scorned as "savage" and "barbarous" in his ordeal at Stockbridge; Marsden, *Jonathan Edwards: A Life*, 349, 349n16.

76. Quotation is in Williams, "Letter from Ephraim Williams, Jr. to Jonathan Ashley, May 2, 1751," 61.

among the Native population, rather than apart from them among the white settlers, as his predecessor John Sergeant and Abigail Williams had done after their marriage. Jonathan Jr., six years of age at the beginning of his father's missionary service, noted that Natives were his family's nearest neighbors; he daily interacted with boys of the Indian families at school and at play, commenting that "even all [his] thoughts ran in Indian" during this time period.[77]

Furthermore, daily interaction allowed, for example, Sarah and the Edwardses' daughters to share everyday concerns with indigenous families through experiences common to each, such as births, sicknesses, deaths, marriages, and care of children. This type of basic human contact, coupled with Edwards's pulpit proclamations, his teaching, and the concern he showed for his charges' material and spiritual needs, earned the friendship and respect of at least some of those to whom he so painstakingly ministered.[78] His exertions in the arena of Stockbridge left Edwards's energies considerably spent but himself confident in the knowledge that he had done his utmost to secure the Natives' fair treatment on earth and to promote, both behind the pulpit and at the teacher's desk, their salvation for the world hereafter.

---

77. Quotation is in Edwards, *Observations on the Language of the Muhhekaneew [Mohegan] Indians*, 3. See Wheeler, *To Live Upon Hope*, 220; Marsden, *Jonathan Edwards: A Life*, 394, 395; Smith, "God Has Made Us to Differ," 59; Baines, "Thy Kingdom Come," 100. See Holbrook, "Editor's Introduction," 21: At Stockbridge, in the end, notwithstanding the challenges Edwards faced regarding the mission environment and the Indians themselves, "Edwards won his way by just dealings and personal integrity." In doing so, he also won the admiration of some of those to whom he ministered and won souls to Christ. Lion Miles's claim that, as one of those who had tried to protect the Stockbridge Natives against the intimidating Ephraim Williams and his supporters, Edwards was "all but powerless," therefore, is not completely accurate.

78. See Marsden, *Jonathan Edwards: A Life*, 394. By the time of the death of John Sergeant, the original missionary to Stockbridge, in 1749, there were 218 Native Americans living at the mission, of whom 129 had been baptized and forty-two had become communicants at the Stockbridge church; Claghorn in *LPW*, 19. Parsons, *Life of Sir William Pepperrell, Bart*, 254, indicates that these individuals made up fifty-three families.

Although Wheeler, "Edwards as Missionary," 203, 209, 209n72, comments, "It is nearly impossible to assess the impact of Edwards's methods on the mission residents," she observes, "Like Edwards, Stockbridge Indian leaders over the years have consistently emphasized the importance of education and the imperatives of justice." This indicates the possibility of a positive influence of Edwards's pedagogy and his overall mission work on those to whom he ministered at Stockbridge and on their succeeding generations.

Jonathan Edwards's Pedagogical Methodology

Having examined Edwards's pedagogical philosophy and praxis at Stockbridge, we shall now move back in time but move on to two older age groups, in order to discuss him as a teacher of Bible students and ministerial candidates at Northampton.

EDWARDS AT NORTHAMPTON: TEACHING BIBLE STUDENTS

Examining Edwards as an instructor at Northampton in connection with his teaching at Stockbridge reveals both similarities and differences. At each location, Edwards used an identical technique of teacher-student dialogue involving questions, but, as one would expect, his expectations of the students were higher at Northampton. The catechists are those he considered "young people," in the fifteen-to-twenty-five year old age range.[79] The ministerial candidates are college graduates who, according to the custom of the day, sought individual study with an established minister.[80] We shall examine Edwards in each of these capacities in turn.

Edwards's firmly-held belief that the teaching function of the pastoral office necessitated both instruction in Scripture and mentoring of congregants led him to compose an "intricate, even daunting" set of "Questions for Young People" as a pedagogical aid.[81] Consistent with his early home environment, in which his sisters each received education equal to his, his instruction of his own children, and his later commitment to coeducation at Stockbridge, Edwards distributed these questions to young women and men alike. Sessions following up their distribution consisted of his questioning male and female students separately and eliciting their questions of him.

Drawn from Scriptures, the questions test both the students' knowledge of the history of Scripture events and their cognitive abilities: The correct answers require the abilities to relate passages to each other and

---

79. For Edwards's definition of "young person," see Minkema, "Jonathan Edwards on Education," 34, 263n2: "'Young people' Edwards defined as individuals from fifteen to twenty-five years old"; Minkema, "Old Age and Religion," 675; *LPW*, 116–17; Brekus, "Children of Wrath, Children of Grace," 302.

80. Minkema, "Jonathan Edwards on Education," 40.

81. Edwards, "Questions for Young People." See also Minkema, "Writing and Preaching Sermons," 391. One hundred fifteen of these questions are included as "Bible Questions for the Children of Northampton," in Edwards, *To the Rising Generation*, 162–77.

to draw conclusions from doing so.⁸² These examples illustrate the typical structure (question, Scripture where answer found, student to whom directed):

> 4. Where was the place where the tabernacle that Moses made in the wilderness was kept after the children of Israel were come up out [of]Egypt and settled in Canaan? Josh. 18:1. (Simeon Root)
>
> 15. How many kings reigned in Judah after the captivity of the Ten Tribes? Eight Kings. (Amos Negro)
>
> 19. Why was the city where the kings of Israel were wont to reside called Samaria, or whence was that name derived? I Kgs. 16:24. (Daniel Clark)
>
> 34. Who was the youngest King of whose age we have any account in SS [Scriptures] [?] Joash the son of Ahaziah 2. Chron. 24. 1. Elisha Strong
>
> 36. How many have we account of in SS. that fasted fourty [sic] days & forty nights [M]oses [and] Elijah 1 Kings 19. 8. & X [Christ]. Ebenezer Bartlet[t]
>
> 48. How often did the children of Israel come to the Red Sea after they departed from Mt. Sinai before they came to Canaan? Num. 6:33, 35;Num. 6:14, 25; Deut. 2:1, I Kgs. 9:26. (Joseph Parsons)⁸³

The list is revealing about Edwards's Northampton pastorate. Analysis of the handwriting and ink indicates a date of composition in the early- to mid-1730s, soon after Edwards became sole pastor upon the death of Solomon Stoddard in February 1729.⁸⁴ This timing may indicate that Edwards believed that instruction specifically of young persons in

---

82. See Minkema, "Jonathan Edwards on Education," 35.

83. Edwards, "Questions for Young People"; Minkema, "Jonathan Edwards on Education," 35. The sources of information on these questions are *Church and Pastoral Documents, WJEO*, vol. 39, and Minkema, "Jonathan Edwards on Education," 34–36.

84. Edwards, "Questions for Young People." Biographical data have been located on sixty-one of the sixty-six persons whose names are appended to questions. Of these, "at least two young men, Elisha Clark and Amos Negro, joined [Northampton church], respectively, when Stoddard was still keeping records and in the first year of Edwards's pastorate, and at least one boy, Simeon Root, never joined the Northampton church," indicating that Edwards's students may have included persons from the larger community; Edwards, "Questions for Young People."

Jonathan Edwards's Pedagogical Methodology

Scripture was significant enough to undertake as soon as possible after assuming sole pastoral authority.

The names of sixty-six males are assigned to questions, the total of which is roughly 150.[85] At least some of the names appear to be later additions, indicating that possibly Edwards formulated the questions earlier in his ministry and assigned the names later. Nearly all of the names are of persons born between 1716 and 1721, who became communicants at Northampton during the Connecticut Valley revival of 1734–1735. The questions are likely assigned to the particular students Edwards believed would most benefit from the correct answers, from the process of arriving at the correct answers, or both. The students probably met with Edwards *en masse* at his home for Bible study and catechetical instruction, during or shortly after the revival of 1734–1735.

Overall, the program Edwards designed indicated his interest in formulating questions on a general theme, such as, "Questions that must be answered by the knowledge of the harmony of the evangelists" and "Questions concerning the circumstances of Christ's last sufferings, out of my discourse [on] the sufferings of Christ."[86] The latter category likely indicates a ministerial concern with assuring catechists' attention to his sermons.

In addition, Edwards recorded a note to himself pertaining to the pedagogical technique to be employed: "[138. A]T ANOTHER TIME, put the [y]oung people upon giving [rea]sons of this or that, and proving such [and s]uch things by argument. [Also,] what arguments can you bring [for them], or how do you prove [them; wh]at can you mention that proves [them; what can] you give for this or that?"[87] This demonstrates that, outside his home, he had begun using the dialogic methodology centered around questions that he would continue to use at Northampton with aspiring clerics, with students at Stockbridge, and with the seniors at the College of New Jersey.

Also, his expectation of the knowledge of Scripture that the students would bring to study with him is higher than at Stockbridge, with respect to both the Native American and colonial students at the mission. The

---

85. The questions are written on two folio sheets. The ones on the first sheet are numbered 1–57; the ones on the second, 101–139; Edwards, "Questions for Young People."

86. Edwards, "Questions for Young People." Edwards, "Free and Voluntary Suffering and Death of Christ," 19:495–515, may be his reference here.

87. Edwards, "Questions for Young People."

young people who formed Edwards's Bible study and catechism classes at Northampton would have been receiving instruction in Scripture in their homes and at school contemporaneously with coming under his tutelage. In the cases of regenerate students, Edwards's purposes would have been to help move them further along on the Christian walk and perhaps to help some discern a possible call to pastoral ministry or to a mission field. We shall now move on to examine Edwards as a teacher of ministerial candidates.

EDWARDS AT NORTHAMPTON: TEACHING MINISTERIAL ASPIRANTS

During the time preceding the existence of seminaries in the United States, an aspirant to pastoral ministry who had graduated from college often entered into a form of "apprenticeship without contract" with an established minister to live in his home for a time, in order to "observe his practice in pastoral duties and to receive from him a closer supervision of preparation for the pulpit."[88] Originating in England from "the relatively common practice amongst disenfranchised English Puritans of building a local community of like-minded believers for training in preaching and godly living," by 1750 this practice had become formalized to the point of a clergyman's receiving several ministerial candidates at once and "conducting their training according to a general plan."[89] The widespread institutionalization of this means of education became known as the "Schools of the Prophets."[90]

---

88. Gambrell, "Ministerial Training in Eighteenth-Century New England," 101; Guelzo, *Edwards on the Will*, 91; Rogers, "Edward Dorr Griffin and the Edwardsian Second Great Awakening," 29. This action by ministerial candidates seems to have been necessitated by the fact that "when the schools ['of the prophets'] came into prominence, colleges were already beginning to pass over from theological to secular interests, [even] though there were as yet no established foundations for professional training in theology" (Gambrell, 103).

89. Bezzant, "'Singularly, Particularly, Closely,'" 232; Gambrell, "Ministerial Training in Eighteenth-Century New England," 101. See Haller, *Rise of Puritanism*, 26–30; Bezzant, "'Singularly, Particularly, Closely,'" 232: "These 'schools of the prophets,' drawing their inspiration from communities of prophesying leaders in 1 Samuel 19, or 2 Kings 2, where disciples were trained to handle the law, became a common and effective strategy for faith transmission in the seventeenth century. Not bound by church regulations or episcopal rule, these colleges of learning were united more radically by 'bonds of affection,' and generated great loyalty and common vision."

90. Gambrell, "Ministerial Training in Eighteenth-Century New England," 101;

Jonathan Edwards's Pedagogical Methodology

During and following the Great Awakening and the excitement the revivals comprising it created, "there seemed to arise among those aspiring to the ministry an eagerness to sit at the feet of the great revival preachers and to learn the secrets of their stirring success."[91] Some clerical aspirants were attracted to particular ministers by hearing their sermons; others, by reading their pulpit proclamations; still others, by reports circulated of eminent divines' successes.

Edwards's renown as a revivalist made him a popular choice for such instruction.[92] He welcomed a number of recent college graduates who aspired to the ministry into his home during his Northampton pastorate to instill in them an intellectual foundation in theology and to impart practical advice on ministerial practice. The exact number is unknown, but among them were John Searl(e), a "Northampton native and pastor successively of Sharon, Connecticut, Stoneham, Massachusetts, and Royalton, Vermont"; Samuel Buell, who, as a young evangelist,

---

Bezzant, "American Theological Education at the Beginning of the Nineteenth Century," 77, 77n7; Bezzant, *Edwards the Mentor*, 23–24. Clerical aspirants who had graduated from college and who were attracted to the revival preaching then occurring "refused to return to the village or town where they had grown up, if this meant being apprenticed to an unregenerate pastor," thus motivating relocation and searches for "prominent pro-revival clerics who turned their parsonages into 'schools of the prophets'"; Bezzant, "'Singularly, Particularly, Closely,'" 234; Conforti, *Samuel Hopkins and the New Divinity Movement,* 24. "The term, 'school of the prophets,' seems to have long been used in New England, and perhaps in old England as well, to denote an institution whose prime function was the education of the clergy." In Gambrell's usage, "schools of the prophets' will be used to mean only those private institutions where . . . an active pastor received into his home and his study considerable numbers of young men preparing for the ministry";Gambrell, "Ministerial Training in Eighteenth-Century New England," 102. See also Endy, "Theology and Learning in Early America," 125–51; and Minkema, "Informing of the Child's Understanding," 178–80.

91. Gambrell, "Ministerial Training in Eighteenth-Century New England," 103.

92. See Bezzant, "'Singularly, Particularly, Closely,'" 235; Foster, "Joseph Bellamy," 107, 107n1: "The impetus given by Edwards to New England theology began to exhibit itself before he himself passed off the scene. A figure [as] unique as his, and one of so great eminence as a practical worker, could not fail to attract attention and, in the paucity of teachers in New England, draw pupils for . . . instruction in the ministerial calling. It was in this way that he gained for the new principles that he was presenting two adherents who were to prove during his lifetime efficient collaborators with him in his practical efforts, and after his death successors and leaders in his school. These were Bellamy and Hopkins."

Edwards's success in the pulpit was not the only factor attracting clerical candidates to him. Significant, too, was his persuasion that "Learning was not something just for the classroom: the 'social acquisition of knowledge' was a deeply held conviction, energizing Edwards's approach to mentoring and fueling requests for residential internships;" Bezzant, *Edwards the Mentor*, 43, 43n14.

had brought a Northampton revival awakening to its height and who remained "a force in East Hampton for fifty-two years"; Job Strong, "another son of Northampton and pastor of Portsmouth, New Hampshire"; Elihu Spencer, "who with Strong spent the summer of 1749 at the Edwards parsonage, served as a missionary to the Oneidas, married Edwards's daughter Sarah, and served a variety of churches in New York, New Jersey, and Delaware"; Eleazar Wheelock, founder of Moor's Charity Indian School (forerunner of Dartmouth College) in 1754, founder of Dartmouth College in 1769; Benjamin Pomeroy, a trustee of Moor's Indian Charity School; trustee of Dartmouth College; member of Society in Scotland for Propagating Christian Knowledge); Daniel Brinsmade, "pastor of Washington, Connecticut, for much of the latter half of the eighteenth century"; and Gideon Hawley, "who after serving as teacher at Stockbridge under Edwards during the early 1750s, was the missionary to the Mashpee Indians on Cape Cod for nearly half a century."[93]

93. Minkema, "Informing of the Child's Understanding," 178; Minkema, "Jonathan Edwards on Education," 39; Cooley, 46–47; Bezzant, *Edwards the Mentor*, 43n11; Marsden, *Jonathan Edwards: A Life*, 317. See Gambrell, "Ministerial Training in Eighteenth-Century New England," 103: "The most prominent teachers [of the 'schools of the prophets'] were all of the New Divinity"; Sweeney, *American Evangelical Story*, 60: "Ministering as they did before the rise of modern seminaries, [New Divinity theologians] founded 'schools of the prophets' (*schola prophetarum*) in which to train the future clergy"; Conforti, *Samuel Hopkins and the New Divinity Movement*, 24–25: "Many of these schools [of the prophets] were run by New Divinity men who won over to their movement a significant portion of the next two generations of ministers in New England. The 'schools of the prophets,' moreover, stamped their graduates with the clerical values and style that marked the pattern of the New Divinity ministry"; Kling, "New Divinity Schools of the Prophets," 130–31: "[T]he informal 'schools of the prophets' provided the infrastructure for the growth and longevity of [the New Divinity] movement. For three generations, these schools transmitted New Divinity theological precepts and ministerial models.... Between 1750 and 1825, over five hundred clerical aspirants studied in New Divinity schools of the prophets." See Gambrell, "Ministerial Training in Eighteenth-Century New England," 123–26; Endy, "Theology and Learning in Early America," 127; and Kling, "New Divinity Schools of the Prophets," 137, for the names of some of the ministers, in addition to Bellamy and Hopkins, who trained prospective clergy at these "schools." Foremost examinations of the "New Divinity" ("the theological movement based on Edwards's ministry"; Sweeney, *American Evangelical Story,* 58; and "the first and perhaps the most enduring of indigenous theologies in America"; Kling, "New Divinity Schools of the Prophets," 131; see also Crisp and Sweeney, "Introduction," 4) include Sweeney, *American Evangelical Story,* 55–67; Kling, *Field of Divine Wonders*; and Kling, "New Divinity Schools of the Prophets," 129–47. See also Kling, "New Divinity Schools of the Prophets," 129–30n2, for an extensive list of other works dealing totally or substantially with the New Divinity.

Major works on Joseph Bellamy include Foster, "Joseph Bellamy," 107–28; Anderson, "Joseph Bellamy, 1719–1790"; Anderson, "Pope of Litchfield County"; Conforti,

Jonathan Edwards's Pedagogical Methodology

Those who studied with Edwards and those who followed in his tradition made a primary contribution to later developments in American theological, intellectual, and cultural history. This they did by providing a Calvinistic system that nineteenth-century theologians would modify for the American environment and for the global scene of their day, in the process forging "a school of thought that was a force to be reckoned with for a century after [Edwards the progenitor's] demise."[94] This theological and cultural *tour de force*, known as the "New Divinity," we will examine later in this chapter. We shall now examine the role education via dialogue based on theological questions played in the transmission of this tradition. Joseph Bellamy and Samuel Hopkins were the first and best-known aspiring ministers who came under Edwards's tutelage. Each shall be discussed in turn.

Joseph Bellamy (1719–1790) graduated from Yale in 1736 and shortly thereafter experienced conversion and began his study for the ministry.[95] A product of a rustic background in Cheshire, Connecticut, Bellamy became the first of Edwards's protégés for the ministry when he made a pilgrimage to Northampton shortly after graduation.[96] Bellamy's study with Edwards was short but productive: Lasting a little more than a year, it became the foundation of his later preaching and teaching in the Edwardsian tradition. "Bellamy came of age in the shadow of Edwards and under the force of the spiritual and social tumult known as the Great Awakening. These events shaped his private and public life for the first decade of his career."[97]

In his study with Edwards, Bellamy made notes in a notebook he kept in a folio ledger of approximately twenty pages (that survive) on readings which Edwards assigned him. Intriguingly, a number of entries coincide in subject matter with Edwards's "Miscellanies" during this time period. For example, Bellamy's entries on the unpardonable sin–the sin

---

"Joseph Bellamy," 126–38; Valeri, "Joseph Bellamy" ; Valeri, *Law and Providence*; Crisp, "Moral Government of God," 78–90. See also Hermes, "Joseph Bellamy," 108–9; Plato, "Bellamy, Joseph (1719–1790)," 67–68.

94. Quotation is in Crisp, "Preface," xiv; Woodbridge et al., *Gospel in America*, 3; Sweeney, "Foreword," 4.

95. See Minkema, "Jonathan Edwards on Education," 40; Conforti, *Jonathan Edwards, Religious Tradition, and American Culture*, 15; Plato, "Bellamy, Joseph (1719–1790)," 67–68; Karlsen and Crumpacker, *Journal of Esther Edwards Burr*, 63–65n30.

96. Conforti, *Jonathan Edwards, Religious Tradition, and American Culture*, 15; Minkema, "Edwardses," 412; Cooley, "New England Theology and the Atonement," 42.

97. Valeri, *Law and Providence*, 9; Bezzant, *Edwards the Mentor*, 42.

against the Holy Ghost—and baptism parallel themes Edwards explores in "Miscellanies" 694, 703, and 704.[98] Additionally, Mark Valeri has noted a similarity in tone of some of Bellamy's reading notes to Edwards's developing vision of the history of the work of redemption.[99]

Furthermore, Bellamy's citations of or quotations from several books in his notes are from works either Edwards recommended or Bellamy saw in Edwards's library that interested him—or possibly a combination of both. The primary text was *Theologia Reformata* by John Edwards (1637–1716), a Cambridge graduate and English Calvinist theologian, which was published in 1713, as "a synopsis of the main points of Reformed religion but also a polemic against contrary views."[100] Around this core text, the other works from which Edwards supervised Bellamy's study undergirded a substantial, erudite, and systematic program of research and reflection. Among the works which Bellamy cites that Edwards owned in his library or cites in his writings are *The Historie of the World* by Sir Walter Raleigh (1614), *The Reasonable and Certainty of the Christian Religion* by Robert Jenkins (2 vols., 1698), *A Discourse Concerning the Resurrection of Jesus Christ* by Humphrey Ditton (1712), and *A Defence of the Church-Government, Faith, Worship & Spirit of the Presbyterians* by John Anderson (1714).[101]

Bellamy's notebook demonstrates the progress of Edwards's first ministerial student through the course of study Edwards provided. The initial entries are "brief statements of major doctrinal loci or theological topics, indexed to the discussion of them in *Theologia Reformata*."[102]

---

98. Minkema, "Informing of the Child's Understanding," 180; Bezzant, *Edwards the Mentor*, 43, 43n15. This notebook is located at Joseph Bellamy, *Student Notebook* (Joseph Bellamy Papers, Miscellaneous Personal Papers, Ms Group 30, Box 179, Yale Divinity School Library, New Haven, CT, 1736); Bezzant, *Edwards the Mentor*, 44n17. It is from these "scrawled pages of excerpts, summaries, outlines, and lists that we can glean something of the shape of the mentoring relationship Edwards and Bellamy enjoyed"; Bezzant, *Edwards the Mentor*, 44.

99. Minkema, "Informing of the Child's Understanding," 180. See Minkema's note: "MS, 'Joseph Bellamy H[ome-] B[ased] 1736,' Yale Divinity School, Special Collections, pp. 3–4. I have made use of a transcript kindly provided by Mark Valeri [then] of Union Theological Seminary in Virginia."

100. Minkema, "Informing of the Child's Understanding," 180; Bellamy, "Joseph Bellamy H[ome-]B[ased] 1736," 13.

101. Minkema, "Informing of the Child's Understanding," 181. Minkema notes that Edwards used the third edition (1722) of Ditton's work.

102. Minkema, "Jonathan Edwards on Education," 41; Bezzant, *Edwards the Mentor*, 43–44, 44n16.

Jonathan Edwards's Pedagogical Methodology

Through dialogic interaction centered on Bellamy's readings, the entries grew to longer quotations to provide material for their discussions, and even essays. What began as a somewhat ordinary student notebook became a scaled-down version of Edwards's *Miscellanies* that evidences collaboration between teacher and student.[103]

Edwards's questions for Bellamy would have been drawn at least partially from one or both of two sets. One is "Questions on Theological Subjects," a list of fifty-three "problems in doctrine and theology, set down in a notebook constructed no earlier than September 1746," but which Edwards may have begun composing earlier.[104] A large portion of these relate to the atonement and Trinitarian theology. For example:

> Upon what accounts was it necessary that Christ should satisfy for the sins of men?
>
> How does Christ's death fulfill that threatening of that law, "the day that thou eatest [thou shalt surely die?" (Gen. 2:17)]. ["Miscellanies," nos.] 281, 357, 506
>
> How is it said that Christ redeems us to God by his blood?

Among the questions under the heading, "Questions concerning the part that the three persons of the Trinity sustain in the work of redemption," are:

> In what sense will Christ deliver up the kingdom to the Father? How far the unity of the Godhead may be argued from the manner of the creation?
>
> Whether the unity of the Godhead can be demonstrated *a priori*?[105]

At least four of the questions on this list are drawn from Edwards's *Miscellanies*, an indication that he was using these musings as pedagogical tools in instructing his students.

The second set of questions is under the heading, "The Theological Questions of President Edwards, Senior, and Dr. Edwards, His Son" and is contained in a pamphlet printed in 1822, along with a longer set by his

---

103. See Minkema, "Jonathan Edwards on Education," 41. See also Schuman, "Training Ministers of 'Light and Heat,'" 261–75; Potgieter, "Education," 410.

104. Edwards, "Questions on Theological Subjects."

105. Edwards, "Questions on Theological Subjects."

son, Jonathan Jr.[106] These *quaero* were published in *Bibliotheca Sacra* in 1882, which identifies them as intended for "their pupils in theology."[107] Unlike the "Questions on Theological Subjects," these are arranged systematically by subjects, beginning with the nature of God and ending with the nature of the Church. This may indicate an emerging effort on the part of Edwards to systematize his method of instruction to fit those studying with him. Among the senior Edwards's interrogatives for students in this category are:

> How do you prove the natural perfections of God, viz. his intelligence, infinite power, foreknowledge and immutability?
>
> How do you prove that the persons in the Trinity are one God?
>
> What is the true idea of God's decrees?
>
> Are [human beings] moral and free agents?
>
> How is absolute moral necessity, or inability, consistent with the free agency of man? In what manner did Christ atone for sin?
>
> Did Christ redeem all men, alike, elect and non elect?[108]

106. Edwards, "Theological Questions of President Edwards, Senior, and Dr. Edwards, His Son"; Minkema, "Informing of the Child's Understanding," 176–77; Minkema, "Jonathan Edwards on Education," 38–39. "The origin of this pamphlet is something of a mystery, but we can speculate that Sereno Dwight, Edwards' great-grandson, had a hand in it, since at this time he was preparing the ten-volume edition of Edwards' *Works* published in New York, 1829"; Minkema, "Informing of the Child's Understanding," 264n23. The elder Edwards's contribution consists of ninety queries; the Younger's total is 313, "incorporating many questions from his father's list but adding others that pertained to late eighteenth-century controversies and issues dear to the New Divinity." "Although some questions by father and son deal with the same general topic (e.g., the nature of the Sabbath), none of them correlate exactly"; Edwards, "Theological Questions of President Edwards, Senior, and Dr. Edwards, His Son"; Minkema, "Informing of the Child's Understanding," 177; Kling, "New Divinity Schools of the Prophets," 140. See Rogers, "Edward Dorr Griffin and the Edwardsian Second Great Awakening," 34: Jonathan Edwards Jr., "faced with the rising tide of Socinian and Unitarian criticism [in his day], listed ten questions on Christ's deity and eight on the Trinity." The distinctive New Divinity doctrines of "the distinction between natural and moral ability, the sinfulness of unregenerate doings, and the need for immediate repentance . . . are prominent in his 313 questions, and explained in a concise way in a piece he wrote describing ten 'improvements in theology' made by Edwards, Sr. and his followers"; see Rogers, "Edward Dorr Griffin and the Edwardsian Second Great Awakening," 34n45.

107. Tarbox, "Article VII," 367–81.

108. Edwards, "Theological Questions of President Edwards, Senior, and Dr. Edwards, His Son."

As one would expect, the topics which Edwards handles here are those which form his ongoing concerns: God's nature and sovereignty, divine foreknowledge, and human free will prominent among them.

Bellamy was called to preach at a church in Bethlehem, Connecticut and installed as pastor there in 1740, maintaining its pulpit for half a century. Perhaps exceeding expectations given his modest background, he became "recognized well beyond western Connecticut as Jonathan Edwards' foremost student and one of the ablest defenders of experimental piety."[109]

Singled out for praise as "one of the more effective stump preachers of the Great Awakening," Bellamy visited "over 250 congregations and [preached] twice that many times in less than eighteen months."[110] Edwards's first pastoral protégé achieved recognition as one of the outstanding pulpit proclaimers of mid-eighteenth-century New England, with an oratorical style that surpassed that of his mentor.[111] Upon hearing Bellamy preach in 1755, Samuel Hopkins declared, "[T]here is not a better Preacher in America—on all accounts."[112] Virtually all contemporary accounts of his pulpit performances agree that he was "to be reckoned among the sons of thunder," to the point of being considered the equal

---

109. Anderson, "Pope of Litchfield County," 162. Bellamy apparently had a somewhat contentious personality, even being described as "combative, pugnacious, and censorious"; Cooley, "New England Theology and the Atonement," 42. In spite of this, he and Edwards bonded to the point of Edwards considering him "one of the most intimate friends [he had] in the world, and that [he had] much acquaintance with"; *LPW*, 348.

110. Anderson, "Pope of Litchfield County," iii; Plato, "Bellamy, Joseph (1719–1790)," 67–68.

111. Conforti, *Jonathan Edwards, Religious Tradition, and American Culture*, 15.

112. Hopkins, "Diary. August 28, 1755"; Valeri, *Law and Providence*, 56. So highly regarded was Bellamy's preaching skill that in 1753, a Presbyterian church in New York City (unsuccessfully) offered him the highest salary of any minister in the colonies at that time to leave his Bethlehem, Connecticut pastorate; Cooley, "New England Theology and the Atonement," 43. Bellamy sought the counsel of Edwards and some other ministers regarding accepting this offer; he was advised to remain at his Bethlehem pastorate. Edwards considered the New York City congregation "too hasty" in extending its offer, but made clear that he considered Bellamy commensurate with the proposal. Although conceding Bellamy was "in some respects a little unpolished," Edwards extolled his "gifts and grace . . . activity, resolution, attended with sagacity and prudence," his outstanding management abilities, his "very good natural abilities, benevolent, agreeable," as well as (surprisingly) "sprightly and sociable." Most importantly, Edwards found impressive Bellamy's "extraordinary gifts for the pulpit," which included "the greatest ability to command the attention of an auditory, and reach the hearts of his hearers, of any man [Edwards knew] of"; *LPW*, 619.

of "the divine dramatist" himself, George Whitefield.[113] As described by an admiring listener, "When the law was [Bellamy's] theme, Mount-Sinai was all in smoke; the thunder and lightning issued from his lips.... [But] in what lovely pictures, [he] lay open the glories of heaven, and paint the joys of the paradise of God!"[114]

Having absorbed Edwards's lessons, Bellamy established his own "School of the Prophets" in 1750 in Bethlehem, Connecticut. Reputedly the earliest one actually to be known as such, it enabled its proprietor to become "the first great teacher and the pedagogical progenitor of a succession of others who followed him" as pastor-teacher/mentors.[115] For over three decades, Bellamy welcomed aspiring clergymen into his home and prepared them to proclaim the word of God and to shepherd the flock of Christ.[116] In doing so, he experienced extraordinary success with those who sought his tutelage, becoming probably the most influential of all the theological mentors of those who formed the New Divinity.[117] The course of study through which he guided students reflected both the systematic approach and dialogic methodology of his mentor, Edwards. As Bellamy described in his memoir, the curriculum began with natural religion, proceeded to revealed religion, and finished with ecclesiology.[118]

Bellamy made his library available for his students to use to compose answers to his questions, which he then critiqued, initiating a dialogue. The literary selections Bellamy offered may be considered

---

113. Valeri, *Law and Providence*, 200n12; Sprague, *Annals of the American Pulpit*, 1:410.

114. Benedict, *Sermon Delivered at the Funeral of Rev. Joseph Bellamy, D. D.*, 20. See also Trumbull, *Complete History of Connecticut*, 2:159; Gambrell, "Ministerial Training in Eighteenth-Century New England," 112; Minkema, "Jonathan Edwards on Education," 43.

115. Gambrell, "Ministerial Training in Eighteenth-Century New England," 105, 130; Kling, "New Divinity Schools of the Prophets," 136–37; Bezzant, "'Singly, Particularly and Closely,'" 212; Minkema, "Jonathan Edwards on Education," 42.

116. Sweeney and Guelzo, *New England Theology*, 71; Gambrell, "Ministerial Training in Eighteenth-Century New England," 105; Endy, "Theology and Learning in Early America," 127; Valeri, *Law and Providence*, 4; Bezzant, "'Singly, Particularly and Closely,'" 212.

117. See Bezzant, "'Singly, Particularly and Closely,'" 212; Kling, "New Divinity Schools of the Prophets," 137; Conforti, *Jonathan Edwards, Religious Tradition, and American Culture*, 15; Valeri, *Law and Providence*, 56; Minkema, "Jonathan Edwards on Education," 42.

118. Bellamy, *Works of Joseph Bellamy*, 1:lvii, 34; Minkema, "Jonathan Edwards on Education," 43. See also Gambrell, "Ministerial Training in Eighteenth-Century New England," 130, who goes into detail regarding the subject matter Bellamy taught; Valeri, *Law and Providence*, 56–57; Anderson, "Joseph Bellamy (1719–1790)," 651–57.

somewhat modest in sheer numbers, consisting of some one hundred volumes and "350 unnamed pamphlets."[119] Nevertheless, those eager to learn theology were provided with substantial fare, including works by John Calvin, Francis Turretin, and Edwards's favorite theologian, Peter van Mastricht.[120] To be well-acquainted with those on the opposing side, students were also required to read Lord Shaftesbury, Francis Hutcheson, and David Hume.[121]

Bellamy's students finished this program by writing and delivering sermons under his direction, both at the church Bellamy pastored and in those in the surrounding area. Those learning effective preaching would have had an impressive model in this "son of thunder."

Bellamy is regarded as the foremost teacher of clerical aspirants in New England in the second half of the eighteenth century, training over sixty ministers; these fanned out over New England and the middle colonies/states.[122] He not only emulated Edwards's example to him and welcomed would-be pastors in order to teach them, he "even erected a two-room 'Log College,' which provided classroom space, while the third floor of his parsonage served as a dormitory."[123] Following even further

---

119. Minkema, "Edwardses," 410; Minkema, "Jonathan Edwards on Education," 43; Gambrell, "Ministerial Training in Eighteenth-Century New England," 108. Gambrell here notes that Bellamy's library holdings also include "an Arian treatise on the doctrine of the Trinity by James Purves (1734–95)," tracts by Deist Thomas Chubb, and *The True Intellectual System of the Universe* (1678) by Ralph Cudworth, noteworthy Cambridge Platonist; Gambrell, "Ministerial Training in Eighteenth-Century New England," 108–9.

120. See *LPW*, 217. Edwards advises, "[Turretin and Van Mastricht] are both excellent. Turretin is on polemical divinity; on the Five Points [of Calvinism], and all other controversial points; and is much larger in these than Mastricht; and is better for one that desires only to be thoroughly versed in controversies. But take Mastricht for divinity in general, doctrine, practice, and controversy; or as an universal system of divinity and it is much better than Turretin or any other book in the world, excepting the Bible, in my opinion."

121. Minkema, "Jonathan Edwards on Education," 43.

122. Gambrell, "Ministerial Training in Eighteenth-Century New England," 130; Conforti, *Jonathan Edwards, Religious Tradition, and American Culture*, 15; Valeri, *Law and Providence*, 4, 56; Kling, "New Divinity Schools of the Prophets," 139; Plato, "Bellamy, Joseph (1719–1790)," 68; Cooley, "New England Theology and the Atonement," 42; Chisholm, *Encyclopaedia Britannica*, 3:694. Naylor, "Raising a Learned Ministry: American Education Society, 1815–1860," 170, puts the number of Bellamy's students at ninety. Bellamy's students included Jonathan Edwards Jr. and John Smalley, teacher of Nathanael Emmons; Minkema, "Edwardses," 410; Cooley, "New England Theology and the Atonement," 43.

123. Conforti, *Jonathan Edwards, Religious Tradition, and American Culture*, 15.

his mentor's pattern, Bellamy welcomed a contingent of Native American boys into his home for instruction. In this venture, he sought, and received, Edwards's counsel; the result was the type of dialogic program from which Bellamy had benefited and which he provided his pastoral students. A vital component of Bellamy's tutelage was mentoring students, counseling each one about the student's personal experience as a Christian.[124] Many graduates of Bellamy's school established "Schools of the Prophets" of their own modeled on that of their teacher.[125] The significance of such schools for the development of the New Divinity will be examined later in this chapter.

In addition to Bellamy's significance as a minister and a teacher, he wrote over twenty works, foremost of which is *True Religion Delineated*. This work established its author as a theologian of the first rank and became "one of the steady sellers of early America," being frequently reprinted both in the United States and England.[126] True religion, Bellamy expounds, "consists in a Conformity to the *Law* of God, and in a

---

124. Bellamy, "B115"; *LPW*, 688–89; Edwards, "Memoir of His Life and Character," 1:lix; Endy, "Theology and Learning in Early America," 128.

125. Conforti, *Jonathan Edwards, Religious Tradition, and American Culture*, 15; Chisholm, *Encyclopedia Britannica*, 3:694. See Cooley, "New England Theology and the Atonement," 27; Gambrell, "Ministerial Training in Eighteenth-Century New England," 113n29: "Bellamy taught Levi Hart, who taught Charles Backus, who taught Alvan Hyde; Bellamy also taught John Smalley, who was the teacher of Nathanael Emmons. All these continually instructed groups of theological students." Two lines of transmission of teacher-mentor to student that were typical of the New Divinity formation process that proved fruitful for the American theological and cultural scenes was Jonathan Edwards to Joseph Bellamy (and Samuel Hopkins) to Jonathan Edwards Jr. to Edward Dorr Griffin, and Jonathan Edwards to Joseph Bellamy to John Smalley to Nathanael Emmons. See also Breitenbach, "Consistent Calvinism," 241–64. Breitenbach, "Consistent Calvinism," 243, identifies "educational bloodlines running through Edwards himself through Samuel Hopkins and Joseph Bellamy, and then through Jonathan Edwards Jr., John Smalley, Levi Hart, Stephen West, Samuel Spring, Charles Backus, Timothy Dwight, Asahel Hooker, Nathanael Emmons, and so on." In addition, many "New Divinity ministers were interlinked by ties of blood and marriage. Timothy Dwight was the nephew of Jonathan Edwards Jr. and the grandson of Jonathan Edwards. Samuel Hopkins's brother Daniel was a New Divinity minister, as was his brother-in-law David Sanford. Levi Hart married the daughter of Joseph Bellamy. Nathanael Emmons had four brothers-in-law who were New Divinity ministers, including Samuel Spring and Leonard Worcester" (243–44). Thus, the "Founding Fathers" of the New Divinity were linked by loyalties both personal and theological.

126. "Bellamy, Joseph (1719–1790). American Eras," https://www.encyclopedia.com/people/philosophy-and-religion/protestant-christianity-biographies/joseph-bellamy; Chisholm, *Encyclopedia Britannica*, 3:694.

Compliance with the *Gospel* of Christ."[127] The first part of this treatise discusses the Law, "which it finds perfectly fulfilled in the one exercise of love." Its examination of the gospel leads to "the successive topics of the ruin of man, the atonement, and the application of that atonement through faith, together with the reward of everlasting life promised to the believer."[128] Its animating theme is that of affirmation of the Edwardsian theory of virtue.[129]

Overall, as a pulpit orator, as a teacher-mentor, and as a theologian, Bellamy made his mark on his own and on later times.[130] As a developer of Edwardsean theology, the "paradox of Bellamy's rhetoric—'the more unable to love God we are, the more we are to blame [because of moral, not natural, inability]'—became characteristic of the [New Divinity] school."[131] In summary, Bellamy's influence dominated the religious landscape of late eighteenth- and early nineteenth-century America. Bellamy's achievements in the didactic and ecclesiastical leadership spheres were recognized with an honorary Doctor of Divinity degree by the University of Aberdeen in 1768.[132] We shall now move on to an examination of Bellamy's twin in terms of being a product of Edwards's influence on him and of his influence on the New Divinity, Samuel Hopkins.

Samuel Hopkins (1721–1803) is known as Edwards's "most devoted New Divinity disciple," the first biographer of his teacher and mentor (author of a work that served for more than a generation as the authoritative

---

127. Bellamy, *True Religion Delineated*, 1. In his Preface to this work, Edwards expressed confidence that "the Matter and Substance that is to be found in this Discourse . . . will be very entertaining and profitable to every serious and impartial Reader, whether learned or unlearned"; Edwards, "Preface," viii. See Phillips, "Last Edwardsean," 15; Crisp, "Moral Government of God," 88–89; see Cooley, "New England Theology and the Atonement," 108–9, for an explanation of why Edwards endorsed this work despite possibly holding a different view of the atonement from that of Bellamy.

128. Foster, "Joseph Bellamy," 108.

129. Foster, "Joseph Bellamy," 108. See also Cooley, "New England Theology and the Atonement," 101–8, for an examination of *True Religion Delineated* regarding Bellamy's view of the atonement. *N.B.* Cooley, "New England Theology and the Atonement," 102: "Both Bellamy and Edwards wrote in defense of Reformed theology, responding to many of the same threats; however, each approached his work in his own way."

130. Crisp and Sweeney, "Introduction," 2.

131. Foster, "Joseph Bellamy," 111. See Crisp and Sweeney, "Introduction," 2, for a concise explanation of this distinction.

132. Sprague, *Annals of the American Pulpit*, 1:406; Chisholm, *Encyclopedia Britannica*, 694; Gambrell, "Ministerial Training in Eighteenth-Century New England," 107.

"life" of his mentor, Edwards), and the progenitor of New Divinity social reform.[133]

Hopkins was born into a pious home of "Puritan stock" at Waterbury, Connecticut, and graduated from Yale in 1741.[134] There, the "serious-minded, reserved, and taciturn" youth befriended David Brainerd, later to become the missionary paragon of Christian lore, who was then a Yale sophomore.[135] Brainerd, as a leader of student evangelism, discussed Hopkins's spiritual condition with him, thereby "'[striking] conviction' through him."[136] While still a Yale student, Hopkins's "eager spirit was kindled" upon hearing Gilbert Tennent, one of the foremost revival preachers of the Great Awakening, deliver one of his pulpit orations in New Haven.[137] This experience so captured Hopkins that he determined that Tennent would be his instructor.[138]

Hearing Edwards preach shortly thereafter, however, caused a change of mind: Hopkins developed such an admiration of Edwards as a person and of his preaching that he determined instead to learn from Edwards by traveling to live with him at his earliest opportunity. Putting his resolve into action, Hopkins arrived at the Edwards home in December 1741 while Edwards himself was away on a revival tour. Arriving in a "wretched and depressed" condition, he was nevertheless welcomed into the Edwards home, and studied with Edwards for a total of a little more than eight months.[139]

---

133. Conforti, *Jonathan Edwards, Religious Tradition, and American Culture*, 37, 38. See also Crisp and Sweeney, *After Jonathan Edwards*, 17; Jauhiainen, "Samuel Hopkins and Hopkinsianism," 107. Major works on Samuel Hopkins include Park, *Memoir of the Life and Character of Samuel Hopkins*, in *The Works of Samuel Hopkins. D. D.*, 3 vols.; Walker, "Samuel Hopkins," 313–57; Foster, *Genetic History of the New England Theology*, 129–61; Elsbree, "Samuel Hopkins and His Doctrine of Benevolence," 534–50; Lovejoy, "Samuel Hopkins," 227–43; Schultz, "Making of a Reformer," 350–65; Conforti, "Samuel Hopkins and the New Divinity," 572–89; Conforti, *Samuel Hopkins and the New Divinity Movement*. See also Brenneman, "Hopkins, Samuel," 551–55; Plato, "Hopkins, Samuel (1721–1803)," 304–6.

134. "Samuel Hopkins," http://www.bartleby.com/226/1303.html.

135. Quotation is in Walker, "Samuel Hopkins," 317.

136. Hopkins, *Sketches*, 33–37; Walker, "Samuel Hopkins," 319; Sweeney and Guelzo, *New England Theology*, 86.

137. Gambrell, "Ministerial Training in Eighteenth-Century New England," 104; Walker, "Samuel Hopkins," 319.

138. Gambrell, "Ministerial Training in Eighteenth-Century New England," 104. On Gilbert Tennent, see Coalter, *Gilbert Tennent, Son of Thunder*; Holloway, "Homiletical Theology of Jonathan Edwards," 55–59.

139. Park, *Memoir of the Life and Character of Samuel Hopkins, D. D.*, 23–24;

Jonathan Edwards's Pedagogical Methodology

Hopkins apparently sought spiritual counseling from Edwards at least as much as ministerial study. His misery when he encountered Edwards resulted from what he took to be his unregenerate condition. As he confided to Sarah Edwards, "I was in a Christless, graceless state," which had caused him anxiety for some months.[140] In a conversation which Hopkins records, Edwards asked why he had not expressed this feeling to him previously. Though Edwards "gave not his opinion expressly" at this time, Hopkins goes on immediately to observe, "From this time I turned my thoughts upon preaching the gospel," and set about becoming licensed to preach.[141]

This interaction is significant because the context is the First Great Awakening. During this period, the New Birth (regeneration) was the most vital theme and an unconverted ministry the foremost danger. Therefore, proclamation of the gospel was something Hopkins considered an unregenerate person unqualified to do.[142] Hopkins received assurance of his own salvation from Edwards before proceeding into the ministry.[143] Counseling Hopkins in this situation before Hopkins

---

Gambrell, "Ministerial Training in Eighteenth-Century New England," 128, 137; Marsden, *Jonathan Edwards: A Life*, 249–50; Cooley, "New England Theology and the Atonement," 44.

140. Hopkins, *Sketches*, 41. Sarah comforted Hopkins as "a member of the [Edwards] family for a season," and the two "entered into a free conversation" in which she assured him that he would "receive light and comfort" to relieve his anxiety, and that she "doubted not that God intended yet to do great things by [him]"; Hopkins, quoted in Dodds, *Marriage to a Difficult Man*, 59. Dodds notes, "Sarah then had seven small children clamoring for her attention and her husband was away, but she took time to note the need of a gloomy young stranger. He never forgot this."

141. Hopkins, *Sketches*, 43.

142. See Tennent, *The Danger of an Unconverted Ministry, Considered in a Sermon on Mark VI.34*; Minkema, "Informing of the Child's Understanding," 182–83; Conforti, *Samuel Hopkins and the New Divinity Movement*, 29: "Both in his earlier decision to live with Tennent and in his later selection of Edwards, Hopkins's intention was to seek guidance while praying for an outpouring of God's grace." Spiritual counseling was constantly a vital element of Edwards's ministry. Conforti notes, "in his *Life of Edwards*, Hopkins described the theologian's Northampton parsonage" during the height of the Great Awakening "as constantly 'thronged with persons to lay open their spiritual concerns to him, and seek his advice and direction.' Troubled souls from all over New England made their way to Edwards's doorstep, and he 'received and conversed with [them], with great freedom and pleasure, and had the best opportunity to deal in the most particular manner with each one'"; Conforti, *Samuel Hopkins and the New Divinity Movement*, 29; Hopkins, *Life of Edwards*, 55. Encouraging parishioners to visit him, rather than he call on them, was the norm for Edwards throughout his pastoral ministry; Stout, "Parish Ministry," 25; Marsden, *Jonathan Edwards: A Life*, 134–35.

143. Hopkins, *Sketches*, 38; Walker, "Samuel Hopkins," 320; Gambrell, "Ministerial

undertook his efforts to be recognized as a minister was consistent with the mentoring of students which Edwards made a crucial aspect of his teaching.[144]

In his study with Edwards, Hopkins availed himself extensively of Edwards's library, "which included works ranging from the classics of Reformed theology to the books of famous heretics."[145] Taking in as much as he could of the offerings there, he discussed his impressions as teacher and student dialogued. The questions Edwards asked likely came from one or both of the sets previously discussed. Given the interests which formed Hopkins's later writings, likely these are among the ones on which he pondered and wrote, and which he and Edwards discussed:

> Cannot God's decrees be demonstrated by his foreknowledge?
>
> Why did God decree sin?
>
> To whom are the promises of the gospel made, to the regenerate or unregenerate?
>
> What is true love to God?
>
> What is true benevolence to man?[146]

A later modification ("improvement") Hopkins and other early Edwardsians made to the lessons they were taught is demonstrated in these examples: "What is the essence of true virtue, or holiness?" and

---

Training in Eighteenth-Century New England," 104; Bezzant, *Edwards the Mentor*, 81. Minkema, "Edwardses," 256: "In 1741, Edwards gave the Yale commencement address, a critique of awakening phenomena that was published as *The Distinguishing Marks of a Work of the Spirit of God* (1741). Sitting in the audience was a young and searching Samuel Hopkins, who upon hearing the sermon decided to study with the great revivalist [Edwards]."

144. See Walker, "Samuel Hopkins," 322; Minkema, "Jonathan Edwards on Education," 44; Bezzant, *Edwards the Mentor*, 82: "Edwards deliberately intervened in the ministerial development of his mentee [Hopkins] at significant junctures, and this mentoring relationship nurtured Hopkins in his sense of ministerial agency." In this connection, "The authority of Edwards enabled [Hopkins to have] greater confidence, self-mastery, and emotional resilience"; Conforti, *Samuel Hopkins and the New Divinity Movement*, 29: "Once Hopkins revealed his soul to Edwards" and his mentor counseled and assured him, Hopkins "was ready to battle the unconverted ministers of New England"—and to win unconverted souls.

145. Conforti, *Samuel Hopkins and the New Divinity Movement*, 31.

146. Edwards, "Questions on Theological Subjects" and Edwards, "Theological Questions of President Edwards, Senior, and Dr. Edwards, His Son."

"Is not self-love the root of all virtue?"[147] In addition, Edwards's ongoing battle with Arminianism is reflected in questions such as, "Whether God's certain foreknowledge of future events is not as inconsistent with the Arminian notion of liberty as God's absolute decrees?" and "Are there not many inconsistencies in the Arminian notion of freedom of will?"[148]

After concluding study with Edwards, Hopkins pastored two churches; from 1743 to 1769, he served a church in what is now the Great Barrington parish at Housatonic, Massachusetts, and from 1770 until his death, he preached at First Congregational Church of Newport, Rhode Island. During the British occupation of Newport from 1776 to 1780, Hopkins preached at Newburyport, Massachusetts and at Canterbury and Stamford, Connecticut.

By common agreement, however, the gifts of this student of Edwards's lay more in the areas of systematician and disseminator of theology and of biographer than in that of pulpit orator.[149] In fact, it was mainly in Hopkins's hands that what became known as New Divinity was given its form. The identity of the New Divinity as a distinct movement can be dated to the publication in 1765 of Hopkins's work, *Enquiry Concerning the Promises of the Gospel*.[150]

The voice of Edwards countering the claims of proponents of innate morality and universal benevolence in human nature with Scripture's teaching regarding original sin and total depravity is given new expression

---

147. Edwards, "Theological Questions of President Edwards, Senior, and Dr. Edwards, His Son."

148. Edwards, "Questions on Theological Subjects."

149. See Gambrell, "Ministerial Training in Eighteenth-Century New England," 123n68; Walker, "Samuel Hopkins," 325; Sweeney and Guelzo, *New England Theology*, 86; Cooley, "New England Theology and the Atonement," 45; Elsbree, "Samuel Hopkins and His Doctrine of Benevolence," 537; Lovejoy, "Samuel Hopkins," 230. The Unitarian minister William Ellery Channing's assessment that Hopkins was "the very ideal of bad delivery" and that "such tones never came from any human voice within my hearing," may be hyperbole partially explicable because of antagonism over doctrinal issues; Channing, *Works of William Ellery Channing*, 4:348; Walker, "Samuel Hopkins," 325, 325n4. Apparently, however, Channing believed Hopkins's preaching conveyed a positive message; see Channing, *Works of William Ellery Channing*, 4:347-54, quoted in Schultz, "Making of a Reformer," 365n76: "In his youth in Newport, Channing had listened to Hopkins preach. He admitted his gratitude to the minister for 'turning my thoughts and heart to the claims and majesty of impartial, universal benevolence.'" See also Elsbree, "Samuel Hopkins and His Doctrine of Benevolence," 538, 538n6.

150. Sweeney and Guelzo, *New England Theology*, 86. Hopkins's *Enquiry Concerning the Promises of the Gospel*; also in Hopkins, *Works*, was a response to Jonathan Mayhew's *Striving to Enter in at the Strait Gate* . . . (1761).

in this polemic. Conversion is no mere "genteel embrace of polite morals"; rather, it occurs as a gift of grace only "when God gives a new heart in regeneration."[151] Only then is "a foundation . . . laid in the mind of a discerning of the truths of the gospel in their real beauty and excellency (to which the unregenerate heart . . . is wholly blind)."[152] Only this foundation enables "those right exercises, in which faith or Christian holiness consists."[153] The echoes of Edwards's expositions of the "new spiritual sense" being a "a new foundation laid in the nature of the soul" that allows regenerate persons ("saints") to experience "a real sense of the excellency of God, and [of] Jesus Christ, and of the work of redemption, and of the ways and works of God revealed in the gospel," could not be clearer.[154]

Even more revolutionary was Hopkins's *An Inquiry into the Nature of True Holiness* (1773). In this, another polemical work, Hopkins extends Edwards's contention that "true virtue" is "not duty but beauty," which is actually exercised by "benevolence to being in general."[155] Having taken, as Edwards had done, a key precept of the "Enlightenment(s)"—universal benevolence—for his own use, Hopkins went on to make it "the centerpiece of his theology."[156] As Hopkins explicates, benevolence must first be directed to "Being in general," that is, God, but it cannot stop there. It must be all-inclusive, encompassing "all beings which exist, capable of good, or that can be, in any sense or degree, objects of good will."[157] This precept encompassed "all sentient life, but particularly it embraced the poor, the illiterate, the slaves, the downtrodden everywhere."[158]

Daunting task is this! Yet it must be so to be genuine: "Any kind of good will, or anything which has the [mere] appearance of benevolence,

---

151. Hopkins, *Enquiry Concerning the Promises of the Gospel,* 28, 29, 77.

152. Hopkins, *Enquiry Concerning the Promises of the Gospel,* 77.

153. RA, 206.

154. Sweeney and Guelzo, *New England Theology,* 91; *TV,* 3; Schultz, "Making of a Reformer," 353–54. *The Nature of True Virtue* is included as "Dissertation II," in *EW,* 539–627 (The above quotation is on p. 540).

155. Jauhiainen, "Samuel Hopkins and Hopkinsianism," 107.

156. Jauhiainen, "Samuel Hopkins and Hopkinsianism," 107. See Hopkins, *Inquiry into the Nature of True Holiness,* 42–46.

157. Elsbree, "Samuel Hopkins and His Doctrine of Benevolence," 541; Hopkins, *Inquiry into the Nature of True Holiness,* 36–37.

158. Elsbree, "Samuel Hopkins and His Doctrine of Benevolence," 541, 548: One must not seek only the salvation of souls; one must also "strive for the alleviation of human suffering if he would prove the kinship of his regenerated being to that of divine love," 548; Hopkins, *Inquiry into the Nature of True Holiness,* 36, 88–89.

which is limited to particular objects, and will not extend to all towards which good will can be exercised... is essentially different from [universal benevolence], and quite of another nature."[159] Genuine benevolence is "not only all-embracing but also self-denying"; it "comprehends all the love to God, our neighbor, and ourselves, required in the law of God."[160] To summarize, "universal benevolence" is "the holy love which God requires, and is the whole of holiness." In perhaps the formulation of doctrine for which he is best-known, Hopkins contends that benevolence must be "disinterested"; it "seeketh not [its] own [demands or interests]" (1 Cor 13:5)." Hopkins waxes eloquently, "Holy love has no regard to self, as self, but is a regard to the greatest general good and interest, the glory of God in the highest glory of his kingdom, and the greatest good of the creation."[161]

In a radical application of this test of virtue, Hopkins establishes a person's willingness to be damned for the glory of God as the standard of true "benevolence to Being in general": No person can know that he or she truly loves God until "he seeks [God's] glory above all things, and is disposed to say, 'Let God be glorified, whatever may be necessary in order to [do] it,' without making any exception; and this [is] *to be willing to be damned*, if this be necessary for the glory of God."[162]

On a more positive note, the concept of "disinterested benevolence" provided the theological foundation for the "Benevolent Empire": the interconnection of home and foreign missions efforts and social reforms in the United States of the nineteenth century. Notable among the expressions of the "disinterested benevolent" impact on the American landscape are the early abolition efforts of Hopkins and Jonathan Edwards Jr.; the formation of the Pennsylvania Abolition Society (founded by anti-slavery Quakers in 1775; revived in 1784 with Benjamin Franklin as president and made open to members of various religious denominations); New York Manumission Society (founded by John Jay and later

---

159. Hopkins, *Inquiry into the Nature of True Holiness*, 37. See Elsbree, "Samuel Hopkins and His Doctrine of Benevolence," 541.

160. Sweeney and Guelzo, *New England Theology*, 91; Hopkins, *Inquiry into the Nature of True Holiness*, 77.

161. Sweeney and Guelzo, *New England Theology*, 91; Hopkins, *Works*, 3:74; Hopkins, *Inquiry into the Nature of True Holiness*, 86.

162. Hopkins, *Sketches*, 3:150 (emphasis added). See also Elsbree, "Samuel Hopkins and His Doctrine of Benevolence," 538, 538n8; Plato, "Hopkins, Samuel (1721–1803)," 304–6; Brenneman, "Hopkins, Samuel," 551–55.

claiming Alexander Hamilton as a member) in 1785; Connecticut Missionary Society (1797–98) and the Massachusetts Missionary Society (1799), culminating in the American Home Missionary Society (1826), which promoted preaching, church planting, and the distribution of Christian literature among the Native Americans and settlers of the West; the Society of the Brethren (1808), the first foreign missions institution indigenous to the United States; the American Board of Commissioners for Foreign Missions (1812), the first "sending agency" for international missions founded on American soil; the American Bible Society (1816); the American Education Society (formed in 1815; given current name in 1820), founded to educate for the ministry "young men of suitable character who have not the means of educating themselves"; American Temperance Society (1836) and the Women's Christian Temperance Union (1873), to battle the evils of alcohol.[163]

163. Regarding the era when the American republic was coming into its own, "This was the age, often called the Benevolent Empire, in which commitment to causes of reform, local evangelism, and global mission merged to reflect America's tumultuous beginnings and almost unlimited prospects;" Bezzant, *Edwards the Mentor*, 126. The New Divinity was instrumental in these projects, as its leaders formed "a tight-knit network agitating for theological and moral reform" (118). See also Bezzant, "American Theological Education," 79–80. Reflecting this activist spirit, "By the 1830s [the New Divinity-led] voluntary organizations for missions, evangelism, and reform had combined budgets larger than that of the federal government"; Marsden, *Jonathan Edwards: A Life*, 8. Regarding Jonathan Edwards Jr., see Hall, "Abolitionism of Samuel Hopkins," 311; "Jonathan Edwards Jr.," www.slavery.princeton.edu/stories/jonathan-edwards-jr: Abhorring slavery as a "cardinal sin against God," the younger Edwards distinguished himself as "a leading antislavery activist of the eighteenth century and one of the few abolitionists Princeton ever produced"; Minkema, "Edwardses," 454: "Even before the [American] Revolution began, New Divinity theologians were at the forefront of social reform as they attempted to implement the 'mentor's' views on true virtue, the social covenant, and the moral accountability of man to God. Influenced in part by the spirit of humanitarianism being fostered in Europe as well as millennialistic fervor, Edwards Jr. and his colleagues were especially active in two causes, the Christianization of the West and the abolition of slavery." The younger Edwards also figured prominently as a missions advocate as a founder of the Connecticut Missionary Society in 1798; Minkema, "Edwardses," 415; Sweeney, *American Evangelical Story*, 88–91, 114; American Education Society, *Brief View of the American Education Society*, 3; Elsbree, "Samuel Hopkins and His Doctrine of Benevolence," 541, 545: Hopkins's development and popularization of "disinterested benevolence" inspired the formation of organizations to support missions, temperance, pacificism, and abolitionism, Bible distribution, education, Sunday Schools, orphanages, "and in every possible way [to] promote humanitarianism"; Schultz, "Making of a Reformer," 350: "Hopkins revived, reinvigorated, and rechanneled a Protestant orthodoxy that informed many later nineteenth-century efforts for social reform"; Conforti, *Samuel Hopkins and the New Divinity Movement*, 175, 189: Sermons by New Divinity pastors in New England in the 1780s were a major factor in producing the revivals that began what is known as the Second Great Awakening (to be discussed

later in this chapter). The reform agencies generated by this religious outpouring "comprised a 'benevolent empire' whose function it was to make the new republic a truly Christian nation and to prepare the way for the coming kingdom of God.... The involvement of the New Divinity men in the benevolent empire was not restricted to the American Education Society and the [ABCFM]; it extended to other reform organizations that were an outgrowth of the Second Great Awakening"; 189n54; "The Benevolent Empire," www.courses.lumenlearning.com/suny-ushistory1ay/chapter/the-benevolent-empire; FitzGerald, *The Evangelicals: The Struggle to Shape America*, 34, 45; Kilsdonk, "Religious Groups, Benevolent Organizations, and American Pluralism," web.archive.org/web/20190906144650/http://are.as.wvu.edu/kilsdonk.htm; Young, "Confessional Protest," 660–88.

Regarding social reform efforts generally, see Conforti, *Samuel Hopkins and the New Divinity Movement*, 116–17: "[Hopkins'] radical call for self-denial, in conjunction with his efforts to amend what he saw as the abstract and aesthetic qualities of Edwards's interpretation of true virtue, broadened the theological base for social reform within the New Divinity movement"; Lovejoy, "Samuel Hopkins," 229: Hopkins, "probably more than any other member of his generation," successfully merged the religious argument against slavery with the egalitarian philosophy of the American Revolution in a way which extended "the scope of the Revolution beyond government and politics to society at large"; regarding abolitionism specifically, see Lovejoy, "Samuel Hopkins," 231: "[T]he essence of Hopkins' opposition to slavery he derived from his theology, his New Light Calvinism, much of which he learned from his master, Jonathan Edwards"; Conforti, *Samuel Hopkins and the New Divinity Movement*, 136: "From 1784 [following the official end of the American Revolution] until the ratification of the Federal Constitution ... few Americans ... exceeded Hopkins in the amount of time and energy devoted to the antislavery cause.... By the close of the decade, Hopkins's contributions to [the] antislavery movement had won him recognition as a reformer comparable to the repute he had already achieved as a theologian"; Saillant, "African American Engagements with Edwards in the Era of the Slave Trade," 145: "Edwards provided the linchpin of abolitionism as it developed in the second half of the eighteenth century–his notion of disinterested benevolence.... [T]he Edwardsean understanding of virtue was elemental in early abolitionism, both black and white." Second- and third-generation Edwardseans, such as Samuel Hopkins and Levi Hart, were instrumental in developing organized opposition to slavery; Hall, "Abolitionism of Samuel Hopkins," 311: Edwards was a "distant inspiration for the Abolitionist movement in ante-bellum America." More broadly, "It was the larger tradition of Puritanism, of which [Edwards], Hopkins, and [John] Brown were quintessentially representative, that was foundational to American Abolitionism"; Minkema, "Jonathan Edwards's Defense of Slavery," 23–59; Minkema and Stout, "Edwardsean Tradition and the Anti-Slavery Debate, 1740–1865," 47–74; Conforti, *Samuel Hopkins and the New Divinity Movement*, 125–41. Hopkins in particular distinguished himself "during the revolutionary era by calling for the immediate abolition of slavery," 47; Lowe, "Destruction and Benevolence," 108: "Applying his new, expanded definition of benevolence, Hopkins's abolitionism became the practical implication he found rooted in Edwards's teaching. Hopkins read Edwards's 'Being in general' as 'God and our neighbors,' and thus [taking] a humanitarian perspective on the doctrine." In Lowe's analysis, "Edwards would have approved how Hopkins built upon his doctrine" of Being-in-general to formulate "disinterested benevolence" for post-Revolutionary America, for "Hopkins agreed with Edwards that 'universal benevolence' should be oriented toward God, the 'highest happiness,' 'the true good,' and 'highest good of the whole,' as the pinnacle object." "In the end, both Edwards and

Hopkins . . . stressed the importance of benevolence toward God; Edwards directly to God, and Hopkins to God by serving others"; 107, 110. See also Minkema, "Edwardses," 372: "Love was the essence [of true virtue to Edwards]: love of God and your fellow creatures."

Regarding Hopkins and missions efforts specifically, see Chaney, "God's Glorious Work," 121, 129, 130: "Samuel Hopkins spanned the era of the Revolution. His system became a sort of theological conductor from colony to nation. But it is as he stood in the lineage of Edwards that his theology is most important for laying the ground work of mission[s]." The concept of disinterested benevolence "was so significant that it became one of the slogans for the great missionary advance of the Nineteenth Century . . . . [Hopkins'] greatest contribution to the development of missionary theology in America was his concept of disinterested benevolence . . . . Disinterested benevolence reached back to Edwards . . . . [Hopkins] denied that he had departed from Edwards. His was the 'same amount of holiness for substance, though under a different name'. . . . [It] was Hopkins' 'disinterested benevolence' and not Edwards' 'benevolence to being in general' that became the slogan of America's missionary movement in the early Nineteenth Century." See also Marsden, *Jonathan Edwards: A Life*, 499.

See Naylor, "Raising a Learned Ministry," 15n15, regarding a secular perspective on the institutionalized reform movements. Naylor, "Raising a Learned Ministry," 9–20, sets the voluntaristic reform societies within the context of the nineteenth-century Protestant response to domestic challenges to churches, including a population expanding westward into an irreligious environment. Foreign missions efforts assumed the major thrust of the nation's evangelistic impulse, becoming institutionalized in the formation of the American Board of Commissioners for Foreign Missions by interdenominational effort in 1810. Evangelistic and social reform activities resulted in the formation of no fewer than 160 voluntary societies, through which "a mingling in varying degrees of religious, patriotic, humanitarian, and social concerns" were given expression, as "virtually every conceivable cause soon had its own organization, as voluntary societies continued to proliferate throughout the country in the nineteenth century"; Naylor, "Raising a Learned Ministry," 15, 15n15, 14. "The voluntary societies played an important role in the Protestant quest for a Christian culture in America; indeed, an 1833 book [written by William Cogswell] describing the benevolent societies was entitled, *The Harbinger of the Millennium* [Boston: Peirce and Parker, 1833]. It noted that the societies 'have an interest in each other, depend upon each other, and assist each other'" (17–18). Naylor, "Raising a Learned Ministry," 18, contends that the designation, "benevolent empire" is a misnomer, as it exaggerates the network's power and degree of independence from ecclesiastical control. She contends the description "the united front," used by Charles Foster, is more accurate, recognizing the nature of an "informal alliance" in which the "leaders of the various societies shared a common outlook and supported the activities of the other societies," in a less grandiose fashion. (See Naylor, "Raising a Learned Ministry," 18n19.)

Naylor, "Raising a Learned Ministry," 33, notes that Jedediah Morse (1761–1826; Yale, MA, 1786; University of Edinburgh, DD, 1795, and significant in the founding of Andover Theological Seminary in 1807) and Heman Humphrey (1779–1861; Yale, MA, 1805; influential in the temperance movement; president of Amherst College, 1823–1845), were among those who "directly influenced or participated in the founding of the American [Education] Society" in 1815, one of the major social reform organizations of the nineteenth century, one which "campaigned in the pulpit and press for a thoroughly educated ministry and effectively furthered this goal by its financial assistance policies"; Naylor, "Raising a Learned Ministry," 326 ; Bezzant, "American

Jonathan Edwards's Pedagogical Methodology

Hopkins's monumental, eleven-hundred page work in two volumes, *System of Doctrines* (1793), codified New Divinity teachings in the first comprehensive work of systematic theology published in New England in nearly three-quarters of a century.[164] In his *magnum opus,* the product of ten years of intense labor, Hopkins staunchly defended "consistent Calvinism" and stood in opposition to its main rivals: Arminianism, antinomianism, and universalism. Through this momentous work, Hopkins created a genuinely indigenous American Calvinist theology that

---

Theological Education," 75. The AES was "one of the first of the national voluntary associations," and during its course, it "helped educate nearly five thousand young men ... including several thousand ministers." Overall, the AES "recruited candidates for the ministry, provided students for the seminaries by giving scholarship loans and grants, upheld the ideal of a learned ministry, helped raise and maintain standards of ministerial education, and shaped the pattern of theological education in a specialized, three-year, graduate-level institution"; Naylor, "Raising a Learned Ministry," 383–84. See also Naylor, "Raising a Learned Ministry," 378, where she notes that Moses Stuart (1780–1852; professor of Sacred Literature, Andover, 1810–1848; "Father of Biblical Science in America") "taught seventy men who became college presidents and professors"; see also Giltner, *Moses Stuart: The Father of Biblical Science in America*; Hansen, "Forgotten 'Father of Biblical Science.'" The AES was "brought to the forefront of the national benevolent societies" substantially through the work of Elias Cornelius (1794–1832), its first executive secretary; Naylor, "Raising a Learned Ministry," 390.

See Draper for an interpretation of the millennium being the impetus for Albert Barnes (1798–1870), American theologian, minister, abolitionist, social reform advocate, and author of well-known commentaries on Scripture, to promote social reforms. Draper, "Millennium as a Motivation," 286, argues that Barnes "was influenced by the postmillennialism of the Puritans and Jonathan Edwards specifically, which included ideas such as the papacy being the Antichrist, which stood in the way of the progress of Christ's kingdom." Barnes was a prominent figure in the development of the "Benevolent Empire," through his efforts to promote abolition of slavery, the temperance movement, and missions efforts in the United States and abroad. See Draper, "Millennium as a Motivation," 99: "Like Edwards, Hopkins, Bellamy, and [Timothy] Dwight (1752–1817; president of Yale, 1795–1817) Barnes adopted the afflictive view of millennialism."

164. Hopkins, *System of Doctrines*; Jauhiainen, "Samuel Hopkins and Hopkinsianism," 107; American Education Society, *Brief View of the American Education Society*, 3. Willard, *Compleat Body of Divinity,* was *System of Doctrines*' nearest chronological predecessor. See Hambrick-Stowe, "New England Theology in New England Congregationalism," 169–70: Cooley, "New England Theology and the Atonement," 54: A total of 1200 persons, from several states and even across the Atlantic, including laity, subscribed to this work, helping to offset publication costs. See Gambrell, "Ministerial Training in Eighteenth-Century New England," 22–28; Anderson and Fisch, *Philosophy in America From the Puritans to James,* 81: Edwards's "influence in his own century may be roughly gauged by comparing Hopkins's *System of Doctrines* (1793) with the first folio of theology published in America, Samuel Willard's *Compleat Body of Divinity* (1726), delivered between 1688 and 1707 as a course of two hundred and fifty expository lectures on the Westminster Shorter Catechism."

laid the foundation for the theological instruction of future Edwardsean ministers.[165] So far-reaching was this pastor-reformer's development of the doctrines of divinity he imbibed from his mentor Edwards that Hopkins became "the most controversial and the most influential theologian of the American Revolutionary period"; so deep was the impression made by his efforts that the New Divinity later came to be frequently known as "Hopkinsianism" or "Hopkintonianism."[166]

165. Cooley, "New England Theology and the Atonement," 45; Elsbree, "Samuel Hopkins and His Doctrine of Benevolence," 545; Plato, "Hopkins, Samuel (1721–1803)," 304–6; Jauhiainen, "Samuel Hopkins and Hopkinsianism," 107. When New Divinity tutor at Yale Ebenezer Fitch became president of Williams College in 1793, he promptly made Hopkins's *System of Doctrines* a required text; Kling, "New Divinity and Williams College, 1793–1836," 202–4, 210; Rogers, "Edward Dorr Griffin and the Edwardsian Second Great Awakening," 27. However, see Cooley, "New England Theology and the Atonement," 110n31. Overall, it became the standard theology textbook at the New Divinity-inspired schools such as Andover Theological Seminary and Yale College, and had no rival in systematizing New Divinity doctrines, standing uncontested as "the most complete statement of *the* New England theology"; Cooley, "New England Theology and the Atonement," 110; Conforti, *Samuel Hopkins and the New Divinity Movement*, 192 (emphasis in original).

166. Schultz, "Making of a Reformer," 350; Phillips, "Last Edwardsean," 15; Bezzant, *Edwards the Mentor*, 117; Kling, "Edwards in the Context of International Missions and Revivals," 65: "Whereas Edwards saw true virtue as culminating in holy *consciousness*"; Hopkins took this concept the next step and applied it as "culminating in holy *action* (emphasis added)"; Conforti, *Samuel Hopkins and the New Divinity Movement*, 123: For zealous religious reformers of the nineteenth century, "Hopkins furnished not only a dynamic theological doctrine but a role model as well. The American Revolution, the Newport slave trade, and the slave system itself presented Hopkins with opportunities to demonstrate his disinterested love of Being in general and to call for the reform of American society"; Crisp and Sweeney, "Introduction," 2. These designations marking the movement with his name were, however, given without Hopkins's consent; see letter from Samuel Hopkins to Samuel Miller, January 23, 1801, Folder 79, Box 7, *Samuel Miller Papers*, Princeton University Library, Princeton, New Jersey; Sweeney, "Nathaniel William Taylor and the Edwardsian Tradition," 87, 87n23. "Consistent Calvinists" was the preferred self-reference among New Divinity's adherents. See also Conforti, *Samuel Hopkins and the New Divinity Movement*, 3, 61; Endy, "Theology and Learning in Early America," 125.

Regarding the New Divinity movement overall, "historians distinguish at least two subtraditions": "one stemming from the sharp-edged polemics of Hopkinsians, the other emanating from the more pastoral and ecumenical strains of Joseph Bellamy (Edwards's student) and Timothy Dwight (Edwards's grandson)." Within the diversity were shared "a few core concerns," which, most importantly, constituted "two evangelistic foci from which all other doctrines . . . radiated: (1) a distinction between the natural and moral ability to convert and live a life that pleases God, and (2) a thoroughgoing insistence on immediate repentance (based on natural ability)"; D. Sweeney, "New Divinity," 400.

Regarding the degree of continuity/discontinuity between Edwards's theology and the New Divinity, "Scholars over the last century and a half have 'generally characterized

Jonathan Edwards's Pedagogical Methodology

Quaker poet and abolitionist John Greenleaf Whittier summarized the New England Theology as continuous' and 'any changes being consistent with Edwards's own intentions,' but 'critics have tended to discover discontinuity' with 'each development within the tradition viewed as a departure from Edwards's Calvinism;'"; Lowe, "Destruction and Benevolence," 87; Sweeney, "Edwards and His Mantle," 100. (An example focusing on the discontinuity is Post, "Disinterested Benevolence," 356–68.) Lowe's own analysis is the New Divinity figures had interacted with Edwards himself and/or had read his works, "and in their minds were taking the next step toward a 'consistent Calvinism' by promoting a new breed of socio-religious ethics that were distinctly Edwardsean–and at the same time not Edwardsean at all." Ultimately, after examining how Edwards and Hopkins each understood "the biblical view of 'neighbor,' Edwards would have approved how Hopkins built upon his doctrine" (93, 110). Cf. Conforti, "Samuel Hopkins and the New Divinity," 581, 583: "Edwards would not have recognized his concept of Being in general or the God of his Calvinism in Hopkins's [*An*] *Inquiry* [*into the Nature of True Holiness*]. On these two points Hopkins had greatly altered Edwards's thought . . . . Taken together, Hopkins's innovations represented an important shift away from the equivocal theological legacy of Edwards on the issue of worldly action toward an emphatic endorsement of social reform. Where Edwards saw true virtue as essentially a matter of right *affections*, Hopkins viewed it as right *actions*" (emphasis added); Hall, "Abolitionism of Samuel Hopkins," 299: "Hopkins made explicit the humanitarian implications of Edwards's theory of virtue, which he fully accepted and actually applied through his abolitionist efforts"; Loveland, "Evangelicalism and 'Immediate Emancipation' in American Anti-Slavery Thought," 172–88; "Action was the infallible test of true benevolence and charity"; Loveland, "Evangelicalism and 'Immediate Emancipation,'" 180.

Cf. Cooley, "New England Theology and the Atonement," 8: "Edwards did not advocate the concept of disinterested benevolence in the way that the New Divinity theologians [such as Hopkins] did." Cooley's study focuses on Edwards's view of the atonement and the extent to which it was transmitted through the line of pastor/theologians he taught, and, in turn, who taught others, to form the New Divinity movement. After examining the theories of the nature and extent of the atonement of Edwards and those of Bellamy, Hopkins, John Smalley, Jonathan Edwards Jr., and others, up to E. A. Park, Cooley, "New England Theology and the Atonement," 215, 217, concludes that, in the New Divinity, Edwards's successors forged a "living vibrant theology" by "creatively crafting their theology [drawn from Edwards's thought] in ways they believed improved upon John Calvin and Jonathan Edwards" to meet the new challenges of changing times. "[An] evangelical theology that might broadly be described as *Edwardsean* was necessarily revivalistic and practical, in that it required the genuine conversion of the sinner, and *Calvinistic*, in that it affirmed the traditional tenets of the Reformed faith such as human depravity and divine election. These fundamental attributes would remain identifiable characteristics of Edwardseanism in the nineteenth century throughout Edwards Park's lifetime"; Phillips, "Last Edwardsean," 11–12 (emphasis in original).

See also Davies, "Jonathan Edwards," 60–68; Mailer, "Freedom From Spiritual Slavery, But From Civil Too," 86. Edwards's worldview "heralded an anti-slavery legacy in the New Divinity movement," partially by influencing "subsequent generations who proposed the mutual necessity of religious revival across the color line," among slaveholders and enslaved persons alike. The New Divinity proponents actuated abolitionism for different reasons, to different degrees, and by different measures. Some opposed slavery "to remove a societal sin as a precursor to a new millennium" [see Draper,

Hopkins's imprint on the growing republic and on the world by memorializing him as "the friend of all mankind–the generous defender of the poor and the oppressed."[167] Some may consider such an accolade hyperbole, but undeniably this New Divinity co-progenitor and protagonist "bequeathed a religious legacy to subsequent nineteenth-century activists who crusaded against slavery and other social sins in America." The scope of Hopkins's New Divinity's compassion fully included "all sentient beings," particularly "the more unfortunate members of the human race."[168]

In addition to the influence he exerted on the American scene and the global landscape, Hopkins (along with Bellamy) became a close friend of Edwards.[169] Bellamy's and Hopkins's friendship circles had frequently intersected since they became acquainted in the 1740s. Despite having markedly different personalities, a desire to learn from Edwards had drawn these two together. While Edwards served as a missionary in Stockbridge, Hopkins lived in nearby Housatonic and was a frequent visitor; upon Edwards's passing, Hopkins became executor of his mentor's papers. It does not strain credulity to envision these three mighty

---

"Millennium as a Motivation for the Social Reform Activity of Albert Barnes," 286]; others emphasized the moral sense innate in humans to redeem society by opposing the institution of slavery; still others advocated a gradualist approach to abolitionism." Bezzant, *Edwards the Mentor*, 117, offers perhaps the most cogent analysis of the connection between Edwards and his theological successors: At the end of the eighteenth century, "the priorities of Edwards Senior were recalibrated, making his legacy not necessarily doctrinally homogenous but certainly denominationally *settled*, evangelistically *effective*, and socially *engaged* (emphasis in original)."

167. Whittier, *Works of Whittier*, 6:144.

168. Sprague, *Annals of the American Pulpit*, 1:432; Elsbree, "Samuel Hopkins and His Doctrine of Benevolence," 550; Hall, "Abolitionism of Samuel Hopkins," 296–313. See Schultz, "Making of a Reformer," 350–51: "Few individuals of the Revolutionary generation had as profound an impact upon religious thought or social practice" as did Hopkins.

169. "It is significant that the young men [i.e., Bellamy and Hopkins] who lived with [Jonathan and Sarah Edwards] most intimately became their stoutest friends"; Dodds, *Marriage to a Difficult Man*, 55. The friendship between Edwards and Bellamy may seem unusual: "Bellamy was everything that Edwards was not: loud, large, and louche. Known as a pugnacious preacher, from a different social background, and not averse to a kind of vulgarity, he nonetheless became Edwards's most intimate friend;" Bezzant, *Edwards the Mentor*, 43, 43n4, 43n5, 43n6, 43n7; *LPW*, 348. The two exchanged letters on topics ranging from the breeding and sale of sheep (*LPW*, 210–11 ("the first in a sequence on the subject that lasts seven years"; *LPW*, 210) to advice on the optimal curriculum for teaching Native American children (Bellamy, "B115"; *LPW*, 688–89) to Edwards's disclosure of his innermost feelings immediately preceding his dismissal from the Northampton church ("a time of great trial" for Edwards) ("Letter 106," 307–10).

Jonathan Edwards's Pedagogical Methodology

minds and kindred souls refining through discussion the works Edwards authored while laboring at the mission, and Edwards's original New Divinity disciples-*cum*-confidantes oversaw editing of their mentor's *Two Dissertations* (*A Dissertation Concerning the End For Which God Created the World* and *A Dissertation Concerning the Nature of True Virtue*). In recognition of the impression he made on the American theological and cultural scenes, Hopkins was awarded an honorary Doctor of Divinity degree in 1790 by Brown University.[170]

The surviving correspondence of Bellamy and Hopkins indicates that Edwards's instruction had made an indelible impression on them, Edwards's two earliest protégés and the co-progenitors of the New Divinity movement. A letter from Hopkins to Bellamy twice refers to Edwards as their "mentor," in one of the earliest appearances in English of this term.[171] Edwards's vision of the necessity of "training up leaders for the future of the revivalist cause in New England [and beyond], nurturing others' talents ... giving feedback on their competencies, encouraging biblical and theological discussions, [and] even permitting disagreements," which he began with them, had taken hold. Their mentor's influence on the two is evident in the serious thought they gave to how best to instruct the ministerial aspirants who were seeking out the New Divinity pastors. In 1756, Bellamy wrote to Hopkins urging him to join Bellamy in developing and distributing their own list of theological questions for instruction, as Edwards had done with them, for use in the instruction of young divinity students.[172] These "Philosophems," as Bellamy called

170. Bezzant, *Edwards the Mentor*, 1; Chaney, "God's Glorious Work," 129; Conforti, *Samuel Hopkins and the New Divinity Movement*, 193; Conforti, "Samuel Hopkins and the New Divinity," 572; email to me from Kenneth Minkema, 01/04/2024.

171. Hopkins, "C141a." See also Bezzant, *Edwards the Mentor*, 1; Bezzant, "'Singly, Particularly and Closely,'" 208: The word *mentor* "was first used in modern literature by [Archbishop Francois] Fénelon [1651–1715] at the end of the seventeenth century in the book *Les adventures de Télémaque*, and its first known appearance in English occurs in 1750 in the writings of [Philip Stanhope, (1694–1773),] Lord Chesterfield."

172. Bezzant, *Edwards the Mentor*, 2; Letter from Joseph Bellamy to Samuel Hopkins, January 30, 1756, Gratz MSS, Historical Society of Pennsylvania, Philadelphia, Pennsylvania. See Conforti, *Samuel Hopkins and the New Divinity Movement*, 37, 201n50; Kling, "New Divinity Schools of the Prophets," 139; Minkema, "Informing of the Child's Understanding," 181, 181n27: "See Bellamy, 'Questions in Theology,' appended to Stephen West's 1774 list of questions for theological students, American Antiquarian Society, as cited in Valeri [*Law and Providence in Joseph Bellamy's New England* (New York: Oxford University Press),] 1994:74n39." This note appears on p. 73 of the current edition of Valeri, *Law and Providence*, and also includes this: "For Hopkins's and Bellamy's correspondence concerning these 'Philosophems,' see [Glenn Paul] Anderson, ["Joseph Bellamy (1719–1790): The Man and his Work"], 651."

them, apparently never came to fruition, but the practice of passing along, and adding to, these syllabi was perpetuated among those who continued the New Divinity tradition. They signify an aspect of instruction that came to be distinctively Edwarsdean.[173] The course of study undertaken by and requirements exacted from students varied from teacher to teacher. Nevertheless, analyzing available evidence yields "a remarkably consistent pattern of training practices for three-quarters of a century."[174] Edwards's techniques of interrogative-based dialogue and mentoring of students individually lived on in succeeding generations.[175]

This legacy attained its functioning form as each teacher in the "schools of the prophets" interacted with his students, partially from an extensive list of questions covering a complete system of theology; the topics ranged from ontology to soteriology to eschatology.[176] Serving both theological and practical functions, these "supplied the outline of a complete course of study and anticipated doctrinal problems that would be raised at licensure."[177] Primarily from independent study of directed readings, the students wrote extensive answers called "dissertations," which formed the bases of teacher-student dialogue.[178]

---

173. Minkema, "Informing of the Child's Understanding," 181.

174. Kling, "New Divinity Schools of the Prophets," 139. See also Endy, "Theology and Learning in Early America," 138.

175. See, e.g., Bezzant, "American Theological Education," 77, 77n6: "Edwards mentored the next generation of leadership by asking questions, stimulating debate and conversation, offering a model, and empowering [mentees] through a relationship of trust"; Gambrell, "Ministerial Training in Eighteenth-Century New England," 131: The procedure of "grounding students in systematic or didactic divinity, through a series of questions and answers, prevailed to a greater or less[er] degree among all the theological teachers [in the New Divinity], being doubtless in most instances a matter of inheritance from teacher to pupil-teacher." For example, Nathanael Emmons adopted a plan of instruction similar to that of his own teacher, John Smalley, who likely had adopted his from that of his own teacher, Bellamy; Park, "Memoir of Nathanael Emmons," 1:217; Gambrell, "Ministerial Training in Eighteenth-Century New England" 131; Cooley, "New England Theology and the Atonement," 27.

176. Conforti, *Samuel Hopkins and the New Divinity Movement*, 37.

177. Conforti, *Samuel Hopkins and the New Divinity Movement*, 35.

178. "The New Divinity was incubated among Reformed clergy and churches in New England who traced their ecclesiastical heritage back to Jonathan Edwards and the first Great Awakening"; Bezzant, *Edwards the Mentor*, 117–18. See Sweeney, "New Divinity," 400; Bezzant, *Edwards the Mentor*, 119, 117–18; see especially Bezzant, *Edwards the Mentor*, 117n10, 118n11.

Jonathan Edwards's Pedagogical Methodology

In summary, "[For] about half a century from 1800 to 1850, Edwards was the polestar of the most formidable and influential American theology."[179] Together, Edwards, Bellamy, and Hopkins formed the preeminent "Trinity of the New Divinity," each enabling Reformed orthodoxy to meet the challenges of shifting theological and cultural landscapes in the journey from colonies to nationhood by relating Christian truths to the world in which each lived. Vital to their efforts in forming "the first indigenous school of American Christian thought" was teaching via the dialogic method and mentoring students, as the pastor-teachers strove to transmit the lessons of Scripture and the essence of the Christian life to those who followed them.[180]

Among those whom they taught, and who in turn taught others, were Nathanael Emmons, who instructed at least ninety aspirants to the ministry; Charles Backus, with approximately sixty graduates; Benjamin Trumbull, John Smalley, Levi Hart, Jonathan Edwards Jr., Nathan Perkins, and Ebenezer Porter educated an approximate total of ninety, ranging between ten and twenty each; Stephen West, Ephraim Judson, Jacob Catlin, Theophilus Packard, Alvan Hyde and Edward Dorr Griffin instructed a total of upwards of seventy-five students.[181]

---

179. Marsden, *Jonathan Edwards: A Life*, 499, 499n26. See also Byrd, "North America," 468; Conforti, *Jonathan Edwards, Religious Tradition, and American Culture*, 4.

180. Quotation is in Sweeney, "New Divinity," 400; see also Sweeney, "Evangelical Tradition in America," 225, 225n28; Bezzant, "American Theological Education," 76. See Park, *Memoir of Nathaniel Emmons*; also "Memoir of Nathanael Emmons," in *The Works of Nathanael Emmons, D. D.*, 1:221–63; Dahlquist, "Nathanael Emmons," 203–4; Cooley, "New England Theology and the Atonement," 27, 47; "Somers [Connecticut] School of the Prophets"; Plato, "Emmons, Nathaniel (1745–1840)," 194–95: "On the model of Edwards and Bellamy, Emmons ran a 'School of the Prophets' out of his home. At least ninety-two students, including Edwards Amasa Park, were instructed under him for the ministry"; Conforti, *Samuel Hopkins and the New Divinity Movement*, 35, 201n44; Kling, "New Divinity and Williams College"; Sweeney, "New Divinity," 403: During the period of Schools of the Prophets, which provided pastoral instruction through apprenticeship before the rise of seminaries, "New Divinity theologians such as Joseph Bellamy, Charles Backus, and Nathanael Emmons trained the lion's share of New England's future pastors."

Bezzant, *Edwards the Mentor*, 120, observes that, as influential as they would become, during Edwards's lifetime, his writings often had not yet been published or were accessible only limitedly. "It was rather [Edwards's] network of friends, ministry colleagues, and indeed mentees who in the first instance faithfully carried forward his influence through their own teaching, mentoring, and writing."

181. Kling, "New Divinity Schools of the Prophets," 139. See also Naylor, "Raising a Learned Ministry," 166, 166–7n10, 170.

To Understand *Things* as Well as *Words*

Along with instruction in the doctrines of theology, the teachers at these New Divinity schools conveyed a distinctive approach to the Christian life and set of professional values, which became characteristic of the ones who came to be known as "New Divinity men."[182] The New Divinity influence became institutionalized as these graduates attained professorships and presidencies at major colleges and seminaries: Jonathan Edwards Jr. at Union College (1799–1801), Timothy Dwight (1795–1817) and Nathaniel William Taylor (Dwight Professor of Didactic Theology, 1822–1858) at Yale, Edward Dorr Griffin at Williams College (1821–1836), and Edwards Amasa Park at Andover Seminary (Bartlett Professor of Sacred Rhetoric, 1836–1847; Abbot Professor of Christian Theology, 1847–1881), are among the most noteworthy.[183]

---

182. Conforti, *Samuel Hopkins and the New Divinity Movement*, 35.

183. "Much of the antebellum collegiate education [in the United States] was shaped by New Englanders with an Edwardsean heritage, [who] controlled most of the nation's leading colleges, including the state 'universities'"; Marsden, *Jonathan Edwards: A Life*, 8–9, 499; Stratton, "Jonathan Edwards' (1703–1758)," 3. "[The] Edwardsean project to integrate spiritual awakening and higher education became the foundation for much of the spiritual vitality of Christian colleges through the Civil War" (3). See Minkema, "Jonathan Edwards on Education," 49; Kling, "New Divinity Schools of the Prophets," 131n6: "The following Yale alumni who became college presidents received theological instruction in the schools of the prophets: Azel Backus (Hamilton, [1812–1816]), Henry Davis (Middlebury, [1809–1817]; Hamilton, [1817–1833]), Edward Dorr Griffin (Williams, [1821–1836]), Heman Humphrey (Amherst, [1823–1845]). Other New Divinity trained ministers who became college presidents included Jonathan Edwards Jr. (Union, [1799–1801]), Zephaniah Swift Moore (Williams, [1815–1821]); Amherst, [1821–1823], and Stephen Chapin (Columbian, [1828–1841])." "The foundation of Andover Theological Seminary in Massachusetts in [1807/]1808 (later named Andover Newton Theological Seminary), the first ever graduate school for ministry and missionary aspirants, was the result" of Edwards's commitment to provide education for those who desired to multiply the fruits of the Great Awakening; Bezzant, *Edwards the Mentor*, 127–28, 128n75, 1238n76; Bezzant, "American Theological Education," 75. On Griffin, see Kling, "Edwards in the Second Great Awakening," 130–41; Cooley, "New England Theology and the Atonement," 153–62; Rogers, "Edward Dorr Griffin and the Edwardsian Second Great Awakening." Griffin was instrumental in the founding of the American Bible Society and the United Foreign Missions Society. Azel Backus studied theology with his uncle, Charles Backus; Jonathan Edwards Jr. studied with Samuel Hopkins for one year and Joseph Bellamy for six months. "Though not the fountainhead, Edwards Junior was a tributary of the ministry tradition that came to be known as the New Divinity." The younger Edwards's life "spanned the period between the First and Second Awakenings, contributing a patina of Edwardsean color to theological and ethical debates of the period." He affected this era in practical terms by teaching in his home Jedidiah Morse (a founder of Andover Theological Seminary) and eventual college presidents Edward Dorr Griffin (Williams College), Samuel Austin (University of Vermont, 1815–1821), and Timothy Dwight (Yale, 1795–1817). Edwards Jr. taught via the question-based dialogic technique his father, Bellamy, and Hopkins had used, but

Jonathan Edwards's Pedagogical Methodology

This transmission from pastor-scholar to pastor-scholar gave birth to a "uniquely Edwardsean theological culture" which took shape as the instruction they provided forged a crucial link in the system of theological education in America. These schools exerted a profound and widespread influence on the eighteenth and early nineteenth-century American theological and social scenes, which "not only enabled the New Divinity movement to prosper, but distinguished these schools as America's single most important source of ministerial training from the mid-eighteenth century to the establishment of seminaries in the early nineteenth century."[184] By the end of the eighteenth century, New

---

expanded his father's set of questions from ninety to three hundred thirteen. He assigned these selectively to his students, however, rather than the entire sum to any one student. Samuel Nott Sr., a student of the younger Edwards who pastored Christ Church in Franklin, Connecticut for seventy years and who co-founded Dartmouth College, recorded that his "regular study of divinity under Dr. Edwards" was "of very special service to [him]"; Ewert, "Jonathan Edwards the Younger," 1:71; Edwards, "Theological Questions of President Edwards, Senior, and Dr. Edwards, His Son"; Bezzant, *Edwards the Mentor*, 114, 117; Minkema, "Edwardses," 428, 428n79, 428,80, 429, 429n81. See also Banks, "By the Same Spirit," 43: "In spite of an unfortunately short tenure [as Union College president], Edwards did much for the school's morale in settling student unrest, securing state funds, and assisting interdenominational cooperation." Yet, "Edwards Jr's. greatest contribution at the college came in the broader Presbyterian movement in which partnership with Congregationalists occurred in the Plan of Union (1801)," which "facilitated a mission partnership as the nation expanded westward."

Edwards Amasa Park exemplified the transmission of the New Divinity essence through generations of teachers and students: "My father [Calvin Park, 1774-1847] studied theology with Dr. [Nathaniel] Emmons. His father [Nathan Park(e), 1738-1806)] studied with Dr. [John] Smalley, and his father [Nathan Park(e), ca. 1705-1753)] with President [Jonathan] Edwards. I therefore can claim a right to the Edwardean theology by what scientists would call the law of heredity"; Park, "Address at the Alumni Dinner, 1881," quoted in Phillips, "Last Edwardsean," 6; Chisholm, *Encyclopaedia Britannica*, 20:825-26.

184. Sweeney, "New Divinity," 403; Kling, "New Divinity Schools of the Prophets," 131. See also Kling, "Edwards and the Edwardseans." Regarding the New Divinity's influence in ways not specifically theological, see Bezzant, *Edwards the Mentor*, 119, 119n19. Kling, "New Divinity Schools of the Prophets," 144, notes that the "schools of the prophets" did not close after the founding of Andover Seminary in 1808. "Even with the founding of additional seminaries (Princeton in 1812, Harvard in 1815, Bangor [Maine] in 1816, Auburn [New York] in 1818, General in 1819, and Yale in 1822), the schools of the prophets, albeit in considerably reduced numbers, persisted. We may view the years from 1808 to the mid-1820s as a transitional phase during which several options lay before clerical aspirants. Some continued to receive all of their post-graduate theological training with a New Divinity 'prophet'; others studied with a pastor and at a seminary; still others made the transition complete by preparing exclusively at one of the newly established divinity schools." Cf. Gambrell, "Ministerial Training in Eighteenth-Century New England," 142-47.

To Understand *Things* as Well as *Words*

England bore a distinctive Edwardsean imprint; the vast majority of its pulpits were filled by pastors who had graduated from the New Divinity-influenced schools.[185] Thus ensconced, Edwards's heirs stood poised to lead the major religious and cultural phenomenon known as the Second Great Awakening.[186]

Having examined Edwards's view of human nature insofar as it applies to children and Native Americans (two sets of students whom he taught), his pedagogical philosophy and methodology, and Edwards as a teacher from the time he instructed his children at home through his service as an educator at Stockbridge, we now arrive at the final stop on

---

185. Sweeney, *American Evangelical Story*, 60; Sweeney, *Nathanael Taylor, New Haven Theology, and the Legacy of Jonathan Edwards*, 34–35; Sweeney, "New Divinity," 403: "Edwardseans constituted the fastest-growing religious movement in [New England] by 1800"; Cooley, "New England Theology and the Atonement," 27–28; Rogers, "Edward Dorr Griffin and the Edwardsian Second Great Awakening," 21–22; Bezzant, "American Theological Education," 77–78; Zakai, "Jonathan Edwards, the Enlightenment, and the Formation of Protestant Tradition in America," 197.

186. Sweeney, *American Evangelical Story*, 60; Hopkins, *Works*, 1:237–38; Rogers, "Edward Dorr Griffin and the Edwardsian Second Great Awakening," 22; Byrd, "North America," 464. See Kling, "New Divinity Schools of the Prophets," 131n5: "These schools transmitted the piety, theology, and legacy of the First Great Awakening through several generations, and profoundly contributed to a 'Second' Great Awakening." "Edward Dorr Griffin was the most prominent and most successful" among the "New Divinity men" in preaching the revivals that constituted the "Second Great Awakening"; Rogers, "Edward Dorr Griffin and the Edwardsian Second Great Awakening," 22. See also Todd, "Populist Puritan," 137–52, for a more direct link between Edwards and the Second Great Awakening. Todd argues that because Edwards adopted and modified Enlightenment thought in defense of Reformed orthodoxy, he "reshaped and refashioned" a Puritan worldview in a way that, as a result, in the Second Great Awakening, "the religious populism of the new American nation took on many of the characteristics of its revivalist forebear Jonathan Edwards" (152; 152n73); Smith et al., "Editor's Introduction," vii. See Sweeney, *American Evangelical Story*, 76–78, for major works on the Second Great Awakening.

Cf. White, "Reformation Roots and Edwardsean Fruits," 72–73. White continues, "It is my conviction that the distinctive in Edwards [Sr.] which is lacking in the three representatives of the school which bore his name is that of a truly gracious affection for God.... While in relation to the work of missions, Edwards Sr. appears as one beggar telling another beggar where to find a feast, his son Jonathan, Hopkins and Bellamy all demonstrate some degree of studied abstraction from the task. Though many of the words are the same, there does not appear to be the same depth of conviction regarding the great doctrines of the faith referred to in the previous discussion" (100–101).

See also Chaney, 215–16, regarding involvement of some of the New Divinity men in missions efforts: "The General Association in Connecticut met in Durham in June, 1786. Joseph Bellamy was moderator." Jonathan Edwards Jr. and Timothy Dwight served on a committee "to discover what suitable measures should be taken to 'send suitable missionaries to preach the Gospel, gather churches, and administer Gospel ordinances' in [the] new communities in the wilderness"; see Chaney 216n1.

Jonathan Edwards's Pedagogical Methodology

Edwards's instructional journey: the College of New Jersey (currently Princeton).

EDWARDS TEACHING AT THE COLLEGE OF NEW JERSEY

Edwards's time at the College of New Jersey was brief, cut short by his unexpected passing during a smallpox epidemic despite an inoculation (or perhaps because of a too-virulent one). Notwithstanding the fact that this "chapter [in Edwards's life] is quickly told," it is not merely a postscript that should be glossed over.[187] Edwards had ties connecting him to the school that is now Princeton before he assumed its presidency. His friend and protégé David Brainerd became "arguably Princeton's first student" after his expulsion from Yale.[188] Furthermore, during his

---

187. Winslow, *Jonathan Edwards (1703-1758)*, 313; Crocco, "Jonathan Edwards and Princeton," 223. This chapter also appears as "Jonathan Edwards and Princeton," in *Princeton Seminary Bulletin*. Although, as noted above, the story of Edwards as President of the College of New Jersey is one that can be quickly told, it should be told completely. This, Baines, "Thy Kingdom Come," 81, does not do, Referring to Edwards's settlement at Stockbridge on February 22, 1751, Baines writes, "Except for a matter of a few weeks in Princeton, New Jersey, most of which [were] spent dealing with illness, this was to be his home for the remainder of his life." Although Baines's focus is on Edwards as a missionary, Edwards continuing his dialogic teaching technique with the seniors for his brief tenure at the college, as Hopkins, *Life of Edwards*, 24–25, records, to their delight, and his preaching there (however briefly), deserve to be mentioned.

Prior to his involvement with the College of New Jersey, Edwards gave some indication of his vision regarding the ideals it should exemplify had he lived long enough to implement them. In penning his thoughts on the Great Awakening, Edwards took "the liberty of an Englishman" and "the liberty of a minister of Christ" to implore that care be taken to ensure that colleges be "nurseries of piety," that students and administrators alike constantly bear in mind that they are "societies whose main design is to train up youth in Christian knowledge and eminent piety," that colleges should in fact be "holy societies" in which "extraordinary means should be used . . . for training up the students in vital religion and experimental and practical godliness" where "a great deal of pains [are] taken to bring those [who] are there educated, to the knowledge of Christ." An essential means of achieving this goal is "for the governors and instructors of the colleges particularly, singly and frequently to converse with the students about the state of their souls"; GA, 510–12. I am grateful to Potgieter, "Education," 407, for pointing this out.

188. Quotation is in Crocco, "Jonathan Edwards and Princeton," 223. See also Pilcher, "Preacher of the New Light," 17n37: "[David Brainerd's] expulsion from Yale in 1743 had actually triggered the founding of the College of New Jersey." See also Wertenbaker, *Princeton 1746-1896*, 18. See Harrod, *Theology and Spirituality in the Works of Samuel Davies*, 24n26, for criticisms of Pilcher's inaccuracies regarding confusing David Brainerd with his brother John (d. 1781) in the diary entry he cites. The connection between David Brainerd and the founding of the College of New Jersey is expounded by Crocco, "Jonathan Edwards and Princeton," 223.

Northampton pastorate, Edwards formed close ties with certain Presbyterian "New Light" (pro-revival) ministers. Among these were Jonathan Dickinson, Aaron Burr Sr., Samuel Blair, and Gilbert Tennent. The first two members of this illustrious group became presidents of the College of New Jersey, and the second two were elected trustees.[189] Significantly, Edwards expressed hearty approval of the college's purpose at its inception. In a letter to a Scottish correspondent (likely Rev. John MacLaurin), Edwards endorsed the "design of erecting a college" in New Jersey as being "very glorious, and very worthy to be encouraged, and promoted by all the friends of Zion."[190] With the completion of Nassau Hall in 1756,

---

189. See Jannenga, "Making College Colonial," 48, 49n33: The religious fervor that manifested itself in the (First) Great Awakening divided a number of churches into "New Light" (pro-revival) and "Old Light" (anti-revival) camps. "[T]he Awakening became, as Patricia Bonomi has argued, a significant disruptor of colonial institutions." The controversy extended even into proper ministerial qualifications, splitting some newly-formed congregations. The leaders of Harvard and Yale opposed the revivals of the Awakening. "One of the results of the disruptions brought about by the Great Awakening was the establishment of the College of New Jersey. Founded by New Light Presbyterians, the college was a vehicle for ensuring that their churches would live on after the passing of their founding congregants"; see also Bonomi, *Under the Cope of Heaven*, 8–10.

Rev. Jonathan Dickinson (1688–1747) was one of the founders of and the first president of the College of New Jersey, April-October 1747, and Rev. Aaron Burr Sr. was president, 1748–1757. Rev. Samuel Blair (1712–1751) was elected a trustee in 1747, but did not serve as president. His brother, Rev. John Blair (1720–1771), was a trustee of this college, 1766–1767, and vice president and acting president, 1767–1768. Rev. Gilbert Tennent (1703–1764) was elected a trustee in 1746. Rev. Richard Treat, D. D. (1708–1778), a prominent New Side Presbyterian who pastored Abington Presbyterian Church in Abington, Pennsylvania for forty-seven years, was also an original trustee; Stanton, "College of New Jersey," 99; Log College Press. www.logcollegepress-annex.com/richard-treat-17081778; Wertenbaker, *Princeton 1746–1896*, 24; Weis, *Colonial Clergy of the Middle Colonies, New York, New Jersey, and Pennsylvania, 1628–1776*, 181. Cf. Crocco, "Jonathan Edwards and Princeton," 223. See also Pilcher, *Samuel Davies*, 171–87; Roberts, *Samuel Davies*, 361–95.

See also Chaney, 165, for a missionary connection between Edwards and two of his College of New Jersey cohorts: "Samuel Davies and Gilbert Tennent toured Scotland and England on behalf of [raising funds for] the College of New Jersey in 1753–55. In Edinburgh, on May 30, 1754, Davies met with the SSPCK [Society in Scotland for Propagating Christian Knowledge] and gave them his 'best advice about the best method of conducting the mission among the Indians.' As soon as he had returned to Virginia he engrossed himself in securing missionaries for the Indians. A 'Society in Virginia for managing the Indian mission' was set up"; Chaney, "God's Glorious Work," 165n2, 165n3. See also Jannenga, "Making College Colonial," 56–58.

190. *LPW*, 184–85. Claghorn writes, "The recipient was probably Rev. John MacLaurin of Glasgow" (*LPW*, 180); Crocco, "Jonathan Edwards and Princeton," 235n6, is more definite in attributing MacLaurin as the recipient.

the College of New Jersey relocated from Newark to Princeton, and vigorous efforts and fervent prayers came to fruition as the school was settled on its present site. Lastly, Edwards's daughter Esther married Rev. Aaron Burr Sr. (destined to be the college's second president) in late June 1752 and his son Timothy enrolled as a student there the same year.[191] Thus, Edwards was connected to the school by loyalties to friendship, theological conviction, and family.

During the last months of Edwards's life, he accepted a call from the trustees of the college to fill the vacancy left by the death in September 1757 of his son-in-law, Aaron Burr Sr., as president. Edwards initially expressed reluctance, citing health concerns (in a remarkably candid and colorful description), difficulties involved in relocating his "numerous family" from Stockbridge, deficiencies in certain areas of learning, and his desire to finish the writing projects then engaging his attention.[192] Under pressure from the trustees to accept, and released from his duties at Stockbridge, Edwards acceded. However, he assumed a lighter load than had been borne by Burr, agreeing to preach and to undertake a reduced workload teaching.[193]

Edwards's ascension to the presidency was warmly greeted by trustees and students alike. Indeed, "No choice could have been more acceptable, for, as Gilbert Tennent declared, he was universally acclaimed 'in all the churches,' for his 'acumen, orthodoxy, learning, piety, and courage.'"[194] Samuel Hopkins, Edwards's earliest biographer, records that, during his former teacher's brief tenure, he "preached in the college hall Sabbath after Sabbath, to the great acceptance of his hearers."[195] Stephen Crocco has noted that, if Edwards was inoculated against smallpox on or around February 23, there would have been approximately two weeks before the onset of symptoms. "Assuming that Edwards was unable to

---

191. Crocco, "Jonathan Edwards and Princeton," *PSB*, 330.

192. *LPW*, 725–30. See also Minkema, "Edwardses," 384–85; Wertenbaker, *Princeton 1746–1896*, 43.

193. Wertenbaker, *Princeton 1746–1896*, 43. Edwards apparently believed that Burr's hectic work schedule had caused or significantly contributed to his death, and he himself was considerably exhausted by his experience at Stockbridge; see Minkema, "Jonathan Edwards on Education," 37. Regarding Aaron Burr Sr., see Wertenbaker, *Princeton 1746–1896*, 41, 41n116: "Princeton Library MSS, AM 8569."

194. Wertenbaker, *Princeton 1746–1896*, 42; Stanton, "College of New Jersey," 99–100. Obviously, this praise was somewhat hyperbolic concerning his acclaim in churches, considering his dismissal from Northampton.

195. Hopkins, *Life of Edwards*, 84.

preach after the smallpox blisters appeared, he could have preached for six or seven Sundays."[196]

Minkema has identified two sermons that Edwards preached at Princeton, both in February 1758.[197] In the first of these, Edwards expounded on the doctrine, "Divine revelation is like a light that shines in a dark place."[198] After engaging in a "grand survey of world religions, from Deism to Catholicism to Islam," Edwards concluded that Scripture is "the greatest and most important and most divine truth."[199] In the second of these messages, Edwards grandly reviewed the wonders of the Day of Judgment.[200]

Regarding instruction at Nassau Hall, Edwards continued the dialogic technique that he had firmly established, and which he had indicated to the college trustees would be his plan, by conducting the eighteenth-century equivalent of a seminar: He distributed "some questions in divinity to the senior class, to be answered before him; each one having opportunity to study and write what he thought proper upon them."[201] Thus, Edwards ended his pedagogic trek as he began, employing the method which, in his experience, was "the most entertaining and profitable, best tending to lead the mind to a view of the true spirit, design, life and soul of the Scriptures, as well as to their proper use and improvement;" viz., that of "in public and private lectures, proposing questions to be answered, and some to be discussed in writing and free conversation."[202] Among the questions from which the ones disbursed to the scholars of Nassau Hall came are:

> How do you prove the natural perfections of God, viz. his intelligence, omnipotence, omniscience, immutability, omnipresence and unity?

---

196. Crocco, "Jonathan Edwards and Princeton," 230.

197. Minkema, "Jonathan Edwards on Education," 37.

198. Edwards, "Light in a Dark World, a Dark Heart," 19:710. This sermon was originally preached at Northampton August 1737 and repreached at Princeton February 1758; see Minkema, "Jonathan Edwards on Education," 264n19.

199. Minkema, "Jonathan Edwards on Education," 37; Edwards, "Light in a Dark World, a Dark Heart," 19:721.

200. Edwards, "Sermon 742."

201. www.pr.princeton.edu/pub/presidents/edwards/index.html; Hopkins, *Life of Edwards*, 24–25.

202. *LPW*, 729.

Jonathan Edwards's Pedagogical Methodology

How do you prove the moral perfections of God, that he is a friend to virtue; absolutely holy, just, good and true?

Why are not mankind in all ages (their internal faculties and external advantages being sufficient) united in right sentiments of the one true God?

Whether a person's being absolutely assured of their salvation be inconsistent with a being yet continued in a state of probation?

What is the most proper course to be taken in order to [attain] growth in grace?

How do you prove absolute and particular election?

What is the nature of a Christian Church?[203]

The result was that, when the students assembled to answer them and to interact with Edwards, "they found so much ... profit by it, especially by the light and instruction Mr. Edwards communicated [in engaging with them], that they spoke of it with the greatest satisfaction and wonder."[204]

In summary, this chapter has discussed Edwards's perspective on the role of a teacher as being twofold: At its introductory level, an educator imparts information to students about the subject at hand and encourages individual formation and development of talents, values, wholesome habits, and life goals. In addition, a truly complete education experience entails placing students on the way to receive regenerating grace, and to assist those who have done so in moving further in the Christian walk. An essential component of this process is counseling with individual students "singly, particularly and closely" about each one's spiritual condition and concerns, addressing the needs of the "total person."[205]

---

203. Edwards, "Theological Questions of President Edwards, Senior, and Dr. Edwards, His Son"; Edwards, "Questions on Theological Subjects."

204. Hopkins, *Life of Edwards*, 24–25. See also Potgieter, "Education," 407.

205. Quotation is in *LPW*, 412. Kang, "Faith, Learning, and Catechesis," 367, 367n3, 367n4, 367n5, observes that the term *catechesis* encompasses much more than, as it may sometimes be understood, simply instructing by means of a formal catechism. It originates from a Greek compound word meaning "'resound exactly,' 'learn by nuanced repetition,' 'teach in a systematic detailed manner,' or 'share a communication that one receives,'" and goes on to explain, "It is one among a broad range of words that are used in the Bible to describe the holistic and comprehensive nature of the Christian formation process." Edwards's use of the *Westminster Shorter Catechism* and the *Westminster*

To Understand *Things* as Well as *Words*

We have also seen that a dialogic pedagogy was Edwards's *modus operandi* in teaching his own children, in instructing Bible students and ministerial candidates at his Northampton pastorate, in educating students at the Stockbridge mission, and in teaching senior-class students at the College of New Jersey. The dialogic method, *contra* rote memorization, revolutionized the role of student by making him or her an active participant in the learning process.

We now move a review of chapters 1 through 6 and will discuss the dimension of Edwards as a teacher as a key element of his commitment to Christian evangelism. Doing so will locate Edwards as a teacher within the discussion, "Is there an essential Edwards?" Also discussed will be the need for holistic dialogic education and for mentoring students today.

Confession of Faith was only one component of his praxis in facilitating the "Christian formation process."

7

Edwards as Educator
Review and Educating the "Total Person"

NOTED AT THE OUTSET of this study was Jonathan Edwards's resistance to precise categorization and the consequent widespread attention he has attracted from a number of perspectives. This attention has been spectacularly manifested in the "Edwards Renaissance" that exploded in the middle of the previous century, and continues to flourish today. As a result, this eighteenth-century polymath currently ranks as "one of the most studied figures in the history of Christian thought."[1] A major result of this plethora of dissections is that today, "Edwards is read by both scholars and laypersons with equal fascination," making him perhaps the most widely-read Christian theologian at this time.[2] Intriguingly, "His appeal encompasses Pentecostal pastors in the majority world as well as Harvard historians. Few theologians of any stripe can [accurately] claim

---

1. Minkema and Stout, "Jonathan Edwards Studies: The State of the Field," 251. See Stout et al., "Introduction," vi: Lesser's first two reference guides on Edwards, published in 1981 and 1994, "list an astounding total of over 3,000 books, articles, dissertations, theses, and other publications on Edwards, making him one of the most studied figures in American history and *the* most studied figure in the colonial period" (emphasis in original). Regarding the "Edwards Renaissance," see Sweeney, "Evangelical Tradition in America," 229–31, 229n42; Stout et al., "Introduction," vi; Sweeney and Stievermann, "Introduction," xv; Yeager, "Britain and Europe," 492; Lowe and Gullotta, "Introduction," 13.

2. Crisp, "Preface," xiv; McClymond and McDermott, *Theology of Jonathan Edwards*, 727; Strachan and Sweeney, *Essential Jonathan Edwards*, 9.

that."[3] A result of the wide-ranging attention accorded him is that Edwards is one of the most-studied of any figures of the past, and in fact he "has been studied and put to use among a wide—indeed, surprising and ironic—array of people, in nearly every part of the world."[4]

Questions which this study (and numerous other works) have sought to answer are, " Is Jonathan Edwards worth studying today, and, if so, why?" Pondering these questions leads to related queries: Hasn't quite a lot already been written about him? Is this figure from a long bygone era relevant today? In roughly two and one-quarter centuries, haven't all the questions that can be asked about him already been posed? One may be tempted to conclude, "Edwards has been analyzed by so many different historians using so many different angles that perhaps everything to say about him has been said already."[5]

It is truly difficult to believe that there could remain any lacunae in Edwards studies, given the copious and ever-increasing amount of attention devoted to this complex figure's life and works. Yet, perhaps, therein lies the key: The very complexity that this minister, theologian, philosopher, and educator presents to those who seek to delve into "Edwardseana" may ensure that the depths still have not been (and perhaps can never be) completely plumbed; that, while there yet remain treasures that may be mined from the Edwards field, some lodes remain (and perhaps will remain) untapped, some gems uncovered. For innumerable reasons, Edwards continues to fascinate; he continues to attract those who believe that not all questions that can be asked about him have as yet been asked and answered.

Asking the question, "Why study Edwards today?" leads to reasons that (unbelievable as it may seem) have not yet been fully explored. One such area is that of Edwards as an educator. Edwards's teaching endeavors throughout his adult life, the influences on his pedagogy, his pedagogical philosophy and his goals as an educator, the innovative nature of his dialogic methodology, cultural integration, and coeducational praxis

---

3. Crisp, "Preface," xiv. This complexity will be examined more fully in the following chapter.

4. Sweeney, *Jonathan Edwards and the Ministry of the Word*, 17; Crisp and Sweeney, "Postscript," 257. It is no exaggeration to say that, for many, Edwards holds a "seemingly boundless international appeal"; Sweeney, "Edwards Studies Today," 579.

5. Marsden, *Jonathan Edwards: A Life*, xvii; Gray, "Birthing the New Birth," 5. See also MacLeod, "Jonathan Edwards (1703–58)," *Witness*, 2011, www.christianstudylibrary.org/article/jonathan-edwards-1703-58: "Why should we study the life of Jonathan Edwards? What was special about him?"

employed with his students at Stockbridge, his consistent reliance on a dialogic pedagogy with each group of his students, the impact of the continuation of his question-based dialogic technique by his ministerial students Joseph Bellamy and Samuel Hopkins on the New Divinity movement, and the possibility and desirability of recovering this multidimensional eighteenth-century figure as a practitioner and proponent of a dialogical holistic educational model in our postmodern age, remain largely unexamined in a systematic, comprehensive manner. This is especially puzzling, considering the availability of ample evidence to sustain such studies.

This work seeks to fill this niche and, in doing so, to help bring deserved attention both to Edwards as an education theorist and as an educator, and to *educator* as being a key dimension of Edwards as a Christian evangelist. Doing this will situate Edwards within the discussion, "Is there an essential Edwards?" and will assist in advancing the current state of Edwards studies.[6] Moreover, a thorough analysis of Edwards's pedagogical philosophy and technique yields valuable results both for Edwards scholarship and also for the formulation of theory and praxis of education in the postmodern era.

At the outset of this study appeared a very few of the innumerable laudations heaped upon Edwards by some who have explored his life and works. One more will provide a basis for analysis as this study draws to a close. The eminent man of God Martyn Lloyd-Jones observed, "I am tempted . . . to compare the Puritans to the Alps, Luther and Calvin to the Himalayas, and Jonathan Edwards to Mount Everest! He has always seemed to me to be the man most like the Apostle Paul . . . . [Edwards] stands out, it seems to me, quite on his own amongst men."[7]

What merits such praise? From the moment of his conversion, Edwards felt the press of eternity inexorably on his life. Edwards lived acutely aware that, at each moment, he was a heartbeat away from eternity and the presence of the God he loved and served. "Edwards' eternal perspective . . . breathe[d] through his life."[8] This reality motivated him to be keenly conscious of his failings and shortcomings and of the fact

---

6. The issue of an "essential Edwards" will be examined in the following chapter, specifically regarding whether so complex a person can have an identifiable "essence."

7. Lloyd-Jones, "Jonathan Edwards and the Crucial Importance of Revival," 355. Lloyd-Jones "in many ways was the most influential Reformed theologian of the [twentieth] century"; MacLeod, "Jonathan Edwards (1703–58)."

8. Moody, *God-Centered Life*, 174.

that he could not overcome them alone. Regeneration enabled Jonathan Edwards to view the temporal and the transitory from the perspective of the enduring and the eternal. Simply put, "Edwards spent his whole life preparing to die."[9]

As part of that preparation, while an eighteen-year-old college student and as someone embarking on a New York pastorate (his first), he began writing "instructions for life, maxims to be followed in all respects" by which to chart his course, which he named his "Resolutions."[10] Written in a straightforward style and intended for his private use to measure his spiritual progress toward becoming "a soul fit for eternity with God," these have become "classics of American literature."[11] These seventy statements do not consist of idle hopes or empty dreams; rather, they indicate Edwards's determination to seek the Lord's help to follow the "paths of righteousness" (Ps 23:3b). These "Resolutions" make clear that Edwards's "sole ambition was to realize his greatest potential and maximum usefulness for the glory of God."[12]

In his preamble to these, Edwards acknowledges his dependence on divine aid: "Being sensible that I am unable to do anything without God's help, I do humbly entreat him by his grace to enable me to keep these Resolutions, so far as they are agreeable to his will, for Christ's sake." At the outset, what claims his devotion first of all is, "1. Resolved, that I will do whatsoever I think to be most to God's glory ... [for] the whole of my duration." He continues, "Resolved to do whatever I think to be my duty, and most for the good and advantage of mankind in general. Resolved to do this, whatever difficulties I meet with, how many and how great soever." they may be. Another of these convictions Edwards states early is, "4. Resolved, never to do any manner of thing ... but what tends to the glory of God." Signifying his consciousness of the eternal from the vantage point of the temporal is "7. Resolved, never to do anything, which I should be afraid to do, if it were the last hour of my life."[13]

Living out these maxims activated and endowed with purpose Edwards's adult thoughts and actions, which he executed through Christian evangelization. Communicating the gospel through his words and through his actions undergirded and animated Edwards's preaching,

---

9. Marsden, *Jonathan Edwards: A Life*, 490.
10. Claghorn, "Introduction," 16:753–59.
11. Claghorn, "Introduction," 741, 743.
12. Claghorn, "Introduction," 743.
13. Edwards, "Resolutions," 753.

pastoring, writing, teaching, and mentoring. Serving his Lord with total dedication in each of these capacities directed his awe-inspiring intellect and focused his tremendous zeal.[14]

Major themes of this study have been Edwards's complexity as an individual and his significance in bridging the two main intellectual and cultural eras of his lifetime. Undeniably an original thinker, Edwards nonetheless drew on ideas both of his Reformation and Puritan forebears and on thoughts in the philosophical and scientific worlds of the eighteenth century, and modified them to suit his own purposes. The major components of these currents of thought which influenced Edwards's pedagogy were examined in chapters 2 and 3, respectively. As a "scion of the Puritans," Edwards's upbringing was rooted in the centrality of Scripture to instruction and as the foundation for the living of this life and for preparation for the next; as "the ultimate source of all that is important to comprehend for salvation, well-being, and beneficence to others."[15] The Bible and the devotional aids that were the spiritual staples in Edwards's milieu and in his home when he came of age formed the basis of his pedagogical content in engaging with his students. Foundational, too, to his belief in coeducation was his home environment, in which his sisters received educations identical in quality to his. In addition, as discussed in chapter 3, Edwards adopted and modified John Locke's epistemology regarding ideas of the natural world originating from sensory impressions and the ideas formed by these impressions being either *simple* or *complex* in his conception of regeneration as a "new simple idea" imparted by God and originating from the "new spiritual sense."[16] Moreover, Edwards appropriated certain theories of Isaac Newton and Nicolas Malebranche in the formation of his own vision of all reality consisting in God, which is central to his theology of the God who seeks to communicate to human beings through acting in redemption history and through the revelations of creation and Scripture.

As discussed in chapter 4, likely influences on the formulation of Edwards's pedagogical philosophy and praxis were, as noted above, his early home environment, in which piety and erudition reigned, as well

14. *LPW*, 784; *LPW*, 518. See also *LPW*, 797, 800; *LPW*, 197.

15. Sweeney, "Edwards, Jonathan (1703–1758)," 397; Sweeney, *Edwards the Exegete*, 189.

16. See Edwards, "Farewell Sermon Preached at the First Precinct at Northampton," 484; Edwards, "Sermon 998," 739; Edwards, "Children Ought to Love," 167–80; *LPW*, 411; Wheeler, *To Live Upon Hope*, 213–14.

as the educators and reformers Jan (John) Amos Comenius and August Hermann Francke, through their theories of Scripture-based education being open to all, regardless of gender or economic class, and the philosopher Andrew Baxter, through his advocacy of dialogic-based instruction.

Examined in chapter 5 was the fact that Edwards held a view of human nature as being a paradox: Human beings are fallen and unregenerate in the natural state, yet rational and redeemable; children of the wrath of God because of sin arising from the fallen nature, yet children of the grace of God who are capable of receiving regeneration if instruction in Scripture is presented to their understanding. This means that, as a teacher, Edwards believed that natural, unregenerate reason was insufficient to understand "spiritual and divine things" unassisted, even though this was the chief purpose of this faculty. Learning, therefore, was "a chief of the means of grace" to effect regeneration and to place the regenerate in communion with God.[17]

During Edwards's span as an educator, he instructed both males and females ranging in age from pre-teens to college graduates up to their twenties (and perhaps older), and including Native Americans (persons generally disdained in colonial society of that time) and Anglo-colonials. Edwards consistently employed a question-based dialogic methodology with the students he taught. His pedagogic journey began with his own children, continued through Bible students and ministerial aspirants at Northampton, Native American and Anglo-colonial students at Stockbridge, and concluded with senior-class students at the College of New Jersey. This holistic dialogic methodology was a departure from the ineffective method of rote memorization in place at Stockbridge previous to his arrival, the typical instructional technique used in eighteenth-century colonial America with pre-college age students. Likewise revolutionary were the coeducation schema and cultural integration (Native Americans and Anglo-colonials together) Edwards practiced at the Stockbridge school.

Edwards's philosophy of the purpose of education was twofold. His introductory aim was to facilitate his students' understanding of the subject(s) being taught via teacher-student dialogic interaction. Posing questions taken from one or more of the sets that he composed, Edwards in turn encouraged students to ask him questions, thus initiating discussion via dialogue. In the case of the children at Stockbridge,

---

17. Edwards, "Importance and Advantage," 29, 35.

this methodology enabled the students to associate words with the ideas which the words signified and to reflect on these associations. This technique also stimulated an appetite for ongoing learning and encouraged students to read on their own once having acquired this skill. Thus, the formation of the student as a lifelong learner was stimulated.

This form of interaction also revolutionized the role of student, transforming the learner from a passive recipient of information into an active participant in the learning process, with a defined responsibility reciprocal with that of the teacher. Edwards's ultimate goal as a teacher was to enable students to understand "spiritual and divine things," which required the "new spiritual sense." With all his students, Edwards strove to engage the total personality of the learner by "informing [his or her] understanding, influencing his heart, and directing its practice."[18]

Edwards also employed the interrogative-based dialogic methodology with Bible students and clerical candidates at Northampton and with the students at the College of New Jersey during his brief service there. As discussed in chapter 6, sets of questions survive around which teacher-student dialogue was centered in each of these cases. Of equal significance as the dialogic methodology, mentoring was a key element of education for Edwards consistently with the students he taught. With students not yet "savingly wrought upon" and with regenerate students alike, Edwards set as his goal counseling each "singly, particularly and closely, about the state and concerns of his soul."[19]

This work's examination of Edwards as an educator has revealed him to have been both a person of his eighteenth-century environment and a person who transcended his milieu. His conviction that Scripture should be the foundation both for the living of this life and for preparation for the next, and, as such, should be central to instruction, arose

---

18. Quotations are in *RA*, 206, 260; Edwards, "Sermon 66. Jas. 1:17"; *LPW*, 409. See also Edwards, "Farewell Sermon Preached at the First Precinct at Northampton," 484; *RA*, 121. See Ward, "Teaching-Learning Process," 117–24.

N.B.: "The principles of teaching and learning are essentially the same regardless of the educational setting . . . . Learning involves a series of interrelated complex processes"; Ward, "Teaching-Learning Process," 117, 118. Ward here describes *Perceiving, Remembering, Applying,* and *Valuing* as components of the processes. This same engagement of a student's total faculties is involved in the processes which Edwards initiated and within which he interacted.

19. Quotations are in Edwards, e.g., *RA*, 136, *LPW*, 56, *LPW*, 118; *LPW*, 412. See Cremin, *American Education,* 404, 500–501; Blore, "Educational Philosophy of Jonathan Edwards," 78: "Edwards was one of the most innovative thinkers of his day, not just in theology, but in pedagogy as well."

from the Puritanism of his upbringing. His disdain for Native American culture as "savage" and "barbarous" at the beginning of his service at Stockbridge was common among British colonials of that era. On the other hand, Edwards demonstrated forward thinking in adopting and modifying "Enlightenment(s)" ideas for his own use in the service of Christ. Furthermore, the dialogic methodology in which he engaged with all of the student groups studied, and the cultural integration and coeducation involved in his pedagogical praxis at Stockbridge, signify Edwards as progressive-thinking.

The significance of Edwards as an educator lived on after his death through the continuation of his question-based dialogic technique by Bellamy, Hopkins, and students whom they taught, among those who comprised the New Divinity movement. The theological precepts forged and refined as they were learned and passed on in this way (notably the doctrine of "disinterested benevolence," for example) exerted a momentous impact on the eighteenth and nineteenth-century American theological, intellectual, and cultural scenes. This force was felt chiefly through the social reforms and missions movements constituting the "Benevolent Empire," the revivals comprising the Second Great Awakening, and the theological direction of such schools as Yale College and Andover Seminary.[20]

---

20. Kling, "New Divinity Schools of the Prophets," 131n5, 131n6; Conforti, *Samuel Hopkins and the New Divinity Movement*, 35; Sweeney, *American Evangelical Story*, 60; Crocco, "Edwards's Intellectual Legacy," 302, 302n8. Regarding Andover Seminary, see Bezzant, "American Theological Education," 74–87, and Bezzant, *Edwards the Mentor*, 127–30. "As Conforti boldly says, 'the Great Awakening became institutionalized at Andover Seminary,' with leaders of the New Divinity as its driving spirit . . . ." "In line with the professionalization of academic disciplines in the period, Andover Theological Seminary was to be a graduate school where only those with a previous degree could matriculate, and where three years of study were to be undertaken with emphasis on systematics and homiletics . . . . Andover was established to provide a new kind of theological education for a new kind of spiritual and political context . . . . In institutional guise, it was an expression of the voluntaristic impulse of the new nation and the revivalist spirit of the outgoing century, and espoused a longevity intended to sustain the movement of New Divinity through educational means"; Bezzant, *Edwards the Mentor*, 128–30; 128n75; Bezzant, "American Theological Education," 84; Conforti, *Jonathan Edwards, Religious Tradition, and American Culture*, 20. Naylor, "Raising a Learned Ministry," 173n15, provides an extensive list of sources regarding the founding and the history of Andover Seminary.

HOLISTIC DIALOGIC EDUCATION TODAY

In fact, the holistic dialogic methodology Edwards utilized consistently has continued to the present day. This method recognizes that, in order for education (the process(es) of transmission of knowledge and the formation and development of skills, values, goals, and character traits) to be effective, it must engage a person's intellect, will, and behavior to encompass the "total person." This is possible because a person's possessing cognitive, affective, and psychomotor functions is a result of creation in the *imago Dei*, in which a person is created to be *relational vertically* (to God) and *relational horizontally* (to other individuals and to human communities; to be discussed below).

Edwards grasped the necessity of "informing the [student's] understanding, influencing his [or her] heart, and directing its practice" for the education process to be truly complete. As discussed previously, this teaching technique embraces the role of the learner as being one of a functioning participant in the process through active dialogue. The reader will recall the insufficiencies of the "grossly defective" pedagogic system in place upon Edwards's arrival at Stockbridge: Mere rote memorization was producing students who could do no better than reproduce sounds at the sight of certain words, but who did not know the meanings of the words.[21] This was, to a large extent, the result of a tradition-bound, hierarchical-centered mindset in which teachers were viewed predominantly as authority figures in relation to students, rather than as facilitators of a process in which both teachers and students have reciprocal roles and responsibilities.

As Parker Palmer notes, "[W]hat scholars now say–and what good teachers have always known–is that real learning does not happen until students are brought into relationship with the teacher, with each other, and with the subject [being taught and learned]. We cannot learn deeply and well until a community of learning is created in the classroom."[22] Researchers in education have discovered that people, once within a community of learning, "learn more effectively through dialogue and analysis of previous experiences" than through traditional monologic means.[23] As learners, children benefit from a dialogic pedagogy which

---

21. *LPW*, 409.

22. Palmer, *To Know As We Are Known*, xvi.

23. Daley, "Case for Learner-Centered Teaching and Learning," 23; Colwill, "Dialogical Learning and a Renewed Epistemology," 2.

engages them as whole human beings (mind, will, and behavior) through which learning is measured not simply in acquisition of facts; knowledge is internalized and expressed in actions, as well. Of equal importance, they are set on the path of acquiring an appetite for learning at an early age and thus becoming lifelong learners. On the young adult and older adult levels, "Dialogical education affords both teacher and student the opportunity to collectively inquire into the connections of subject matter and real-life experience. Each person comes away with different areas of growth (in addition to what is learned about the particular field under study)."[24]

Furthermore, in effective dialogue between educator and student in which each is made in the *imago Dei*, meaning is found in the exchange between them. Such an interaction produces benefits for others in a *group* in addition to those particular *individuals* invested in the exchange: "The net result is that skilled dialogue has a synergistic effect on the group process, opening up new vistas of relationship, thought and action." This is the case partially because "Dialogue encourages people of diverse perspectives to collectively think and inquire together toward generative possibilities and creative solutions," and thus, to experience learning as a "pleasant, entertaining and profitable" exercise.[25]

This pedagogical methodology is learner-centered and premised on the reality that teacher and student alike are made in God's image and thereby derive their worth from being *persons*, rather than from external (e.g., social and economic) factors. Above all, before human beings are teachers or learners, a fundamental theological truth is that dignity and worth as human beings are rooted in their having been created in the *imago Dei*, because this is "the theological platform on which such concepts as human value, worth, and self-esteem can be founded."[26] Two key

---

24. Colwill, "Dialogical Learning and a Renewed Epistemology," 3. See also Coe, *What Is Christian Education?*, 24, 25, 54, 140–41, 168–69, 175; Wyckoff, "Jonathan Edwards' Contributions to Religious Education," 91. "Teaching is a creative profession, not a delivery system. Great teachers do pass on information, but what great teachers also do is *mentor, stimulate, provoke* [thinking in students], and *engage*"; Sir Ken Robinson, quoted on "Professor Claire E Ball-Smith," www.york.ac.uk/education/our-staff/academic/claire-ball-smith (emphasis added). See also "Why Christian Education Matters," www.educateforlife.org. Edwards typified each of these aspects of stellar teaching.

25. Buber, *Knowledge of Man*, 26; Colwill, "Dialogical Learning and a Renewed Epistemology," 33, iv; *LPW*, 408.

26. Szczerba, "Concept of *Imago Dei* as a Symbol of Religious Inclusion and Human Dignity," 32; Lidums, "Doctrine of *Imago Dei*," 44. See also Lidums, "Doctrine of *Imago Dei*," 11 (Counselor's view): "[S]ince humans have been created in the image of God,

aspects of this reality are: (1) that "being in God's image has to do with people as *entire beings* (whether humanity as a whole or its component members are in view)." One significant dimension of this truth is that a person in his or her *entirety* (intellect, will, and actions) is completely in the *imago Dei*, because persons in the post-Fall and postmodern world are still made in (according to) the *imago Dei*.[27]

Also importantly, (2) Although *persons* have been damaged and diminished by the Fall, the *imago Dei per se* has not. "Humanity's creation ... in God's 'likeness-image' (or simply 'image' or simply 'likeness') means the following: all people are created according to 'God's image,' which the New Testament identifies as Jesus Christ. From before the beginning of creation, God intended that humanity should conform to the divine image–to *Christ* .... After the Fall, however, people were marred in many ways and lost most of their ability to reflect God. They nevertheless continue to be in God's image, unique among creation as those whom God intends and will enable to become conformed to the divine image," which is Christ, who is undamaged by the Fall.[28]

Therefore, "Even 'being in' God's image has not been damaged, for to be in God's image is to be created according to that image, accountable to that standard .... Even with their many limitations, all people have a special connection with God and are intended to be a reflection of God."[29] To be truly effective, education must occur within contexts which

---

we have the capacity for relationships with God, others and the world .... *Imago Dei* is not lost in humans. It is marred and distorted, and needs to be restored in and through Jesus Christ, who is 'the only complete and valid revelation of what the image of God looks like.' [Cf. Kilner, "Made in the Image of God," 107: "No image [i.e., the image of God] has been damaged, for God's image is Christ–it is the standard of what God has always intended humanity to become." Humankind has been damaged by the Fall, but Christ, the *imago Dei*, has not been.] The distorted image is restored through being in Christ, in the Church, in meaningful relationships, and [in] receiving a continuous impact that helps in the process of restoration through these relationships"; Collins, *Biblical Basis of Christian Counseling for People Helpers*, 89; Lidums, "Doctrine of *Imago Dei*," 27: "God has created us in His own image, endowing us with personhood, so as to have an I-Thou relationship with us. God wants us to know Him, and He wants to be known by us." Lidums analyzes nine views, or "thematic positions and/or themes," of the *imago Dei* (9–41).

27. Kilner, "Made in the Image of God," 106. See also Kilner, "Special Connection and Intended Reflection," 135–60; Kilner, *Dignity and Destiny*.

28. Kilner, "Made in the Image of God," 107 (emphasis added). See also Fant, "Teaching and Learning in the Humanities," 216: A complete education, at its core, is spiritual. "It reflects a full-orbed view of human nature and our relationship with God .... To ignore it is to dehumanize the *imago Dei* that we all possess."

29. Kilner, "Made in the Image of God," 107.

acknowledge (indeed, embrace) these realities, ones which admit (and celebrate) that "Christians are not self-creations but creatures bound to God and one another; their behaviors, attitudes, and strivings take shape within those boundaries."[30]

In summary, teaching which engages all aspects of the "total person" is *possible* because these aspects of selfhood are present as a result of creation in the *imago Dei*, and teaching which does this is *most desirable* because education that engages all aspects of a person's selfhood best accomplishes the goals of truly complete pedagogical processes; viz., assisting most fully both in students' achieving their greatest individual potential and in being placed on the way of receiving regenerating grace or (in the case of Christian students) moving further along in their Christian lives. It bears repeating that education is not merely *informative*; in its truest sense, it is also *formative* and *transformative*. In a life in which education does its best work, learning and faith become fully integrated. Moreover, in an optimal teaching/learning process, both teacher and student grow as each one proceeds on life's journey: "Teaching must flow from a posture of personal growth in knowledge and skills.... [If] the teacher stops learning–stops growing, stops honing skills and being interested in the world of ideas–real teaching eventually dies."[31]

---

30. Charry, "Moral Function of Doctrine"; Huffman, "'Train Up a Child in the Way He Should Go,'" 16.

31. Regarding integrating faith and learning, see Kuyper, *Wisdom and Wonder*, 93; see also Backfish, "Biblical Wisdom as a Model for Christian Liberal Arts Education," 389; quotation is in Guthrie, "Study of Holy Scripture and the Work of Christian Higher Education," 82. Although Guthrie specifically discusses Bible study in higher education, this point applies to educators at all levels. See also Colwill, "Dialogical Learning and a New Epistemology," 159: "Transformative learning will affect the learner's spiritual development, cognitive structures, attitudes, values, perceptions, and behavior," i.e, will have a *holistic* effect; it will affect the whole person.

Backfish, "Biblical Wisdom as a Model for Christian Liberal Arts Education," 382–96, lists "six key traits that characterize biblical wisdom [which] should also characterize Christian liberal education." Such an education should be "foundationally theological, integrated, accessible, practical, transformative, and [should] foster lifelong learning." Drawing on Prov 1:2–7, Backfish demonstrates that this passage illustrates each of these aspects of a full-orbed model of biblical wisdom, and also argues convincingly that this should be the paradigm for Christian education today. Edwards's pedagogy evidenced each of these dimensions, indicating that study of him as an educator would be worthy of attention among scholars in the field of education today.

EDWARDS AS MENTOR

Edwards the mentor comes to the fore again in this study as being an essential aspect of his identity. His conviction that "the Christian life is *caught* as well as *taught*, for we learn how to live as Christians not just from *instruction* but from *example* as well," drove him to be a determined "advocate for pedagogical practices that were broader than pulpit ministry, including a vision for mentoring." To be sure, his dedication to the deep personal investment of himself in persons which mentoring requires was not undertaken lightheartedly or sporadically, but rather, "represented a deep appreciation of the value of personalized learning, conducted 'earnestly, affectionately and thoroughly.'"[32]

"Edwards's life of mentoring, the ways he built the practices of mentoring into his quotidian round of pastoral responsibilities, was of far-reaching consequence."[33] Edwards invested himself in mentoring others throughout his adult life, perhaps most famously with Bellamy and Hopkins, but also with his children, the teenage Deborah Hatheway, seeking counsel about the state of her soul (who, though she was an "isolated correspondent," received a response of which it can be said, "the relational dynamic expressed . . . was genuine and representative"), his parishioners, and others with whom his life intersected.[34] Those who prepared for the ministry under his tutelage were afforded a nurturing and erudite environment in which dialogue was the normal instructional technique. Among the many who took up temporary abode in the Edwards manse to study over the years, the experience of Hopkins is typical. From Edwards (and Sarah), Hopkins benefitted from "parent-like care." This made a deep and life-long impression on Edwards's earnest mentee: "I

---

32. Bezzant, *Edwards the Mentor*, 93, 65n147, 65n148; *LPW*, 94, emphasis added.

33. Bezzant, *Edwards the Mentor*, 45.

34. Bezzant, "'Singly, Particularly, Closely,'" 230; Bezzant, *Edwards the Mentor*, 66. *LPW*, 94; Bezzant, *Edwards the Mentor*, 65, 65n148. Hatheway, "an eighteen-year-old who was without a pastor," turned to Edwards, "a known, trusted adviser for counsel. Responding to her inquiry, Edwards wrote this guide for a young Christian, with emphasis upon attitude and behavior." A "serene tone" permeates this pastoral communication, echoing "the Shema, Psalms, and New Testament." This letter, "often reprinted, has become a classic of Christian devotion. Publication began in 1807 under the title *Advice to Young Converts*; beginning in 1827, the letter was widely distributed by the American Tract Society. By 1875, at least 328,000 copies had been issued. See Thomas H. Johnson, *The Printed Writings of Jonathan Edwards, 1703-1758, a Bibliography* [Princeton, 1940], pp. 99–101"; Claghorn in *LPW*, 90. This letter also appears as Edwards, "Letter to a Young Convert," 157–61.

hope I shall never forget the kindness I have received from Mr. Edwards, & Madam [i.e., Sarah]. I could not have expected more from my own father and mother (July 5, 1742)."[35] Integral to the sense of hospitality Edwards conveyed was the counsel he provided Hopkins and the mutually enriching dialogue it enabled.

Despite the innumerable seismic changes the world has undergone since Edwards's day, it remains fallen, and human nature has changed none at all since his time. Consequently, "Life is pressured" as we experience an increasingly fragmented and disconcerting world. "The challenges [Edwards] faced are ours in abundance." These realities make crucial the fact that mentoring, which can be defined as, "that intentional activity between two people which seeks to empower [each] for spiritual development, often with the result of enhancing skills and attitudes for leadership," is as necessary today as ever.[36] "Mentors can offer the benefits that only experience can yield: wisdom, insight, and discernment . . . . Mentors can polish rough edges, identify personal weaknesses, and point out latent potential."[37] Additionally, mentors themselves can also grow during the mentoring process. "To teach is to learn twice," and to counsel someone as Edwards and his New Divinity successors did, to help someone down a road the mentor has already walked (or may be walking with the mentee) is to develop new skills as a person, to enlarge one's sphere of usefulness, and (ideally) to affect eternity positively for someone who needs help.[38]

---

35. Bezzant, *Edwards the Mentor*, 66, 66n152; *Samuel Hopkins Journal*, 46.

36. Bezzant, *Edwards the Mentor*, 6; Bezzant, "'Singly, Particularly, Closely," 230. Bezzant continues, "It most often occurs through face-to-face encounters, and is supported through other strategies, like letter-writing, discussion of decision-making, and sharing resources"; Bezzant, "'Singly, Particularly, Closely," 230. Regarding Edwards's "vision of reality" and fruitful ways of applying it to the current world, see McDermott, *Everyday Reality*; Marsden, *Infinite Fountain of Light*. See also Coome, "Putting Edwards to Work," 122–29.

37. Fant, "Teaching and Learning in the Humanities," 217. N.B.: "A mentor who does not include a *spiritual* component is not educating the *whole person*; only a mentor who includes spiritual advice to mentees is performing discipleship. This means that an educator who prays with and for a student, who assigns readings that aim at spiritual transformation, and who exalts a spiritual understanding of vocation is doing the work of a more holistic teacher" (217, emphasis added).

38. The "to teach is to learn twice" quotation is attributed to Joseph Joubert (1754–1824), a French essayist.

AN APPLICATION OF EDWARDS'S PEDAGOGY TO EDUCATION TODAY

Robert Gordon Lee has proposed a teaching schema in the Edwardsean mold which he has designated with the acronym "ETHIC," for learning that centers around the *end*, or goal, of education (addressing the "basic values, principles, and ends which constitute the goal of education"); the nature of *truth* ("What theological, philosophical, and epistemological presuppositions guide [Edwards's] approach to reality?); the nature of *humanity* ("What does it mean to be human, and what dispositional norms ought to be cultivated to produce virtuous students?"); *instruction* methods ("What techniques did [Edwards] employ, and are they consistent with his aims, understanding of humanity, and understanding of truth?"); *curriculum* design ("How does current research confirm his practices in curriculum design and classroom instruction?")[39] In this model, the goal of education for Edwards "was always to communicate God's goodness to and through his creation." In this schema, "A desire for God's goodness, an appreciation of the harmony of his redemptive purpose, and an affectional longing for his presence are all intended outcomes."[40]

From Edwards's perspective, "not only should students come to know [God], but also they should learn to desire, admire, and experience his goodness."[41] According to Lee, "Research from twenty-one different studies by [Robert J.] Marzano, [Debra J.] Pickering, and [Jane L.] Pollack [*Classroom Instruction That Works* (Alexandria, VA: Association

---

39. Lee, "Edwards on Education," 8–9. These elements are illustrated in a chart on 114; he summarizes these on 131–3.

Lee does not accurately summarize my original dissertation in his "Literature Review" section, stating that it "traces the philosophical influences on Edwards's thought and examines how those influences affected his practice as a Christian evangelist and teacher at the Stockbridge school," but ignoring that the bulk of the dissertation examines in detail how Edwards applied a dialogic methodology to each group of students he taught, and it contends that Edwards should be recognized as much as an educator as a minister and theologian. In addition, Lee notes that I did not engage with Edwards's last (and therefore, most mature) works. He, nevertheless, reached substantially the same conclusions as I did regarding Edwards's pedagogy at Stockbridge as to its nature and purpose. Lastly, Lee does not indicate that Edwards's techniques at Stockbridge were consistent with those he used with other groups of students he taught. Nevertheless, I appreciate both Lee's ETHIC model of education and his application of it to the education landscape of today.

40. Lee, "Edwards on Education," 114, 131–33.
41. Lee, "Edwards on Education," 114, 131–33.

for Supervision and Curriculum Development, 2001)] all support many of Edwards' practices such as questions, stories and reciprocal learning employed in the arrangement of *HWR*." (Edwards's use of stories will be examined more fully below.) Furthermore, "of the nine strategies listed for effective instruction, Edwards has exhibited seven of them."[42] This type of pedagogical methodology, holistic and learner-centered that focuses on preparing students for this life and the life to come, is needed now as much as in Edwards's time.

The final aspect of Edwards's pedagogy that will be examined in this section is his use of stories to instruct his students at Stockbridge. As an educator drawing on parental, pastoral, and pedagogic experiences, Edwards understood the importance of communicating the meta-narrative of redemptive history through "the particular stories of the Scriptures, sometimes with one story, and then with another, before [the students] can obtain the knowledge of [the Scriptures] themselves, by reading."[43] Edwards knew what researchers up to the present day have confirmed: "The use of stories in [facilitating] moral development is critical."[44] This is true because of the holistic impact of narrative-centered communication as a key component of the pedagogic process: "Stories have been consistently proven to produce lasting change in the cognitive, affective, volitional, and behavioral aspects of the learner." As a result, "Stories have always been an important way of transmitting values and wisdom. They become all the more important in a society that, like ours [postmodern United States], has experienced so much disruption in the family and the community. The lessons contained in good stories are lessons the child might not get otherwise in a world of harried adults and fractured social institutions."[45] This is particularly important because "stories illustrate truths that are difficult to grasp in any other form. This is especially true for children who are not yet ready for abstract thinking."[46] Mary Lyn Huffman offers a perceptive observation about the utility of narratives to illustrate essential truths:

42. Marzano et al., *Classroom Instruction That Works*, 43, 7; Lee, "Edwards on Education," 132–33.

43. *LPW*, 409.

44. Newton, *Heart Deep Teaching*; Coley, *Teaching for Change*, 88; Huffman, "'Train Up a Child in the Way He Should Go,'" 70.

45. Lee, "Edwards on Education," 121; Kilpatrick, *Why Johnny Can't Tell Right from Wrong*, 28; Huffman, "Train Up a Child in the Way He Should Go," 70.

46. Clouse, *Teaching for Moral Growth*, 16; Huffman, "Train Up a Child in the Way He Should Go," 70.

> Being instructed about friendship is very different [from] hearing the story of David and Jonathan, Ruth and Naomi, or Helen Keller and Anne Sullivan. Being told to tell the truth is very different [from] hearing the story of Pinnochio, the emperor's new clothes, or the boy who cried wolf. Being told to work hard is different [from] hearing a work ethic illustrated through the ant and the grasshopper, the little red hen, or Tom Sawyer. Children are drawn into stories, and through relating to the characters connect with the story and the moral message.[47]

To state the obvious, narrative-driven communication must be done in a "developmentally sensitive manner," at the learner's development level (or one level above) to allow maximum ability to interact with the moral message.[48] Equally important as his work with children, Edwards illustrates the usefulness of narrative-driven communication with young adults and with older adults in his sermons at the Stockbridge mission.

Having briefly reviewed the findings of chapters 1 through 6, and having briefly discussed the value of holistic dialogic pedagogy today, in the final chapter we shall examine the aspect of *educator* as essential to his identity as a Christian evangelist. This is done in order to situate this complex figure within the discussion, "Is there an essential Edwards?"

---

47. Huffman, "Train Up a Child in the Way He Should Go," 70–71.

48. Huffman, "Train Up a Child in the Way He Should Go," 71. See also Huffman, "Train Up a Child in the Way He Should Go," 90, 95–96.

Similar to Edwards's narrative-driven dialogic pedagogy, Huffman utilizes series of age/stage-appropriate questions for parents/teachers to ask to enable children/students to identify moral messages in the narratives; see Huffman, "Train Up a Child in the Way He Should Go," 136–54.

8

Conclusion
Edwards as Multidimensional (and Multiple?)

EDWARDS SCHOLARS HAVE COMMENTED virtually unendingly on the many-sided nature both of his work and of the legacy he has left to successive generations. Possessing an "amazing subtlety and comprehensiveness of... mind," Edwards "remains of permanent interest to theological inquiry."[1] Theology is only one aspect of Edwards's thought which has generated interest. Chris Chun has observed, "The diversity of opinions [regarding how to interpret Edwards] arises precisely because there are diverse aspects within his corpus."[2] In his assessment, "Edwards is perceived as philosopher, theologian, scientist, apologist, revivalist, and a leader of a contemporary charismatic movement."[3]

In this regard, David Kling and Douglas Sweeney provide this insight: "Edwards continues to appeal to so many in part because his life and work are so challenging, his thought so creative and elusive.... His corpus is large, complicated, wide-ranging, and multi-faceted, attracting the attention of a broad range of interpreters—historians, theologians, philosophers, and biblical and literary scholars."[4] Among historians

---

1. Williamson, "Excellency of Christ," 4.

2. Chun, *Legacy of Jonathan Edwards in the Theology of Andrew Fuller*, 5.

3. Chun, *Legacy of Jonathan Edwards in the Theology of Andrew Fuller* 3–4; see Chun, *Legacy of Jonathan Edwards in the Theology of Andrew Fuller*, 3n8–4n13.

4. Kling and Sweeney, "Introduction," xii.

Conclusion

alone, as Sean Michael Lucas has observed, Edwards's many aspects have led to his being viewed from "a dizzying array of perspectives":

> For George Marsden, Edwards is the 'American Augustine' in opposition to the American Foucault that Stephen Daniel appreciates. Leon Chai believes that the Enlightenment compromised Edwards, while Alvin Plantinga and Stephen Nichols contend that Edwards' theological emphasis of Word and Spirit made him a critic of the Enlightenment. Anri Morimoto praises Edwards' 'Catholic' vision of salvation; Gerald McDermott looks to Jonathan's (sometimes) charitable dealings with non-Christian religions; Kenneth Minkema examines Edwards on slavery and the slave trade; and Amy Plantinga Pauw finds in Edwards a theology conducive to social action. Meanwhile, feminist scholars have focused attention on Edwards' view of women and children.[5]

Similarly, Josh Moody comments on Edwards, "He has been analysed as a philosopher, a theologian, a preacher, a pastor, a social theorist, and any number of interdisciplinary minglings. He has been known in [his] work both as a Hell-fire preacher and an artist, in [his] thinking both as a Lockean philosopher and a medieval traditionalist, in [his] character both as a family man and a withdrawn intellectual."[6] Peter J. Theusen has pointed out a consequence of the wide array of options Edwards studies affords: "Appraisals of Edwards remain widely diverse—and often openly contradictory . . . . [It] is only a slight exaggeration to say that there is an Edwards for everyone."[7]

Multiplicity of approaches to and viewpoints regarding the Edwards *persona* (perhaps *personae*) is not of recent origin. M. X. Lesser has observed of Edwards studies, "A troublesome, and largely unresolved, duality [has] haunted Edwards from the start—mystic and rationalist, philosopher and theologian, poet of the divine and scourger of the wicked— and hangs on even now."[8] Alfred Owen Aldridge and Joseph Haroutunian have commented in a similar vein: A "rational-supernatural dichotomy persists among Edwards' followers. Joseph Haroutunian has acutely remarked that those critics impressed by Edwards' spirituality 'have done no justice to his intelligence, and those impressed by his intelligence have

---

5. Lucas, "Jonathan Edwards," 236. See also 236n38–n41.
6. Moody, *Jonathan Edwards and the Enlightenment*, 3.
7. Theusen, "Jonathan Edwards as Great Mirror," 39–60. Quotations are on 41, 44.
8. Lesser, *Reading Jonathan Edwards*, 3–4.

been impervious to his 'sense of divine things.'"[9] Iain Murray has noted, "Edwards divided men in his lifetime and to no less degree he continues to divide his biographers.... The nature of his greatness, the significance of his life and thought, an assessment of his character and writings—on all these, and much else, judgments are divided."[10]

Perhaps this is to be expected. As the subject of varying analyses over many decades, Edwards has been evaluated by the touchstones of shifting intellectual and cultural milieux. This has resulted in multiple reincarnations of the "Edwards essence." From having been labeled an "anachronism" to a "contemporary," from a "fiery Puritan" to "a poet, mystic and philosopher of the feelings"; from "the last medieval American—at least among intellectuals" to "the first modern American" (alas, in any event, "an American tragedy"); moreover, "intellectually the most modern man of his [era]," "among the last of the Puritans' but "among the first Americans to embrace the Enlightenment"; from "first and last a Calvinist theologian" to a polymath who was "infinitely more than a theologian"; indeed, an "artist" who was "so much ahead of his time that our own can hardly be said to have caught up with him," Edwards's life's work and legacy have undergone periods of favor and disfavor as they have been sifted by interpreters intent on finding (or fashioning) one or more Edwardses "reshape[d] ... to fit current needs."[11] In summary, "Edwards's star has waxed and waned with the times," and during the times when it has waxed, its light has been refracted through a wide array of lenses.[12]

9. Aldridge, *Jonathan Edwards*, 150.

10. Murray, *Jonathan Edwards*, xix. See also Stein, "Introduction," 9: "Frankly, it is impossible to read about Edwards and to engage the scholarship that he has elicited without coming to some conflicted judgments regarding him and his place in American history."

11. Parrington, "Anachronism of Jonathan Edwards," 1:148–63; Schweitzer, *Jonathan Edwards as Contemporary*; Parkes, *Jonathan Edwards*; Riley, "Real Jonathan Edwards," 705–15; Gay, *Loss of Mastery*, 116; Lowe and Gullotta, "Introduction," 18; Miller, "Jonathan Edwards—The First Modern American," 22–36; Miller, *Jonathan Edwards*, 305; Cherry, *Theology of Jonathan Edwards*, xxiii; Miller, *Jonathan Edwards*, xii, xiii; Crocco, "Edwards's Intellectual Legacy," 301. See also Werkmeister, *History of Philosophical Ideas in America*, 32

12. Quotation is in Minkema, "Jonathan Edwards's Life and Career," 24. Cf. Crocco, "Edwards's Intellectual Legacy," 300–324. In addition to the widely varying categorizations noted above, Edwards has also been considered "the most influential religious thinker in American history" and as someone for whom it is "impossible to exaggerate the influence [he has] exerted on American theological and religious discussions and on American religious life," but also one who has had "no great impact on American

Conclusion

One scholar has sounded this note of caution: "All attempts to categorize [Edwards's] thought involve an interpretive risk."[13] Others in Edwards studies have shared this assessment. Among them, Stephen H. Daniel offers this insight: "Of the well-known philosophic minds of the seventeenth and eighteenth centuries, Jonathan Edwards (1703–1758) is perhaps one of the most successful in escaping the historiographic impulse to categorization."[14] Henry May concurs: "Like most profound thinkers, [Edwards] cannot be fitted into any [one] category"; "He seems both inexhaustible and impossible to pin down."[15] This has led still others to posit that continuous reinterpretation may be inevitable: "One concludes, unsurprisingly, that Edwards has been seen as his readers needed to see him."[16] May comments, "Much as I admire the Edwards scholarship of today, I do not want to imply that in the past people saw Edwards through a mist of prejudice, and now we look at him in the clear light of objectivity. I assume that we all look at Edwards from where we are, and that this will always be so."[17] Likewise Thuesen: "It should by now be clear that every observer sees Edwards with different eyes."[18] Lastly, Jennifer L. Leader summarizes the "dissensus" in Edwards studies:

> [T]here are many Jonathan Edwardses. The enormous scope of this eighteenth-century divine's erudition, public and personal

---

religious practice or thought"[!]; Sweeney, "Jonathan Edwards: Legacy"; DeWitt, "Jonathan Edwards," 105; Wills, *Head and Heart*, 114.

13. Williamson, "Excellency of Christ," 4.
14. Daniel, "Introduction," 1.
15. May, *Enlightenment in America*, 49; May, "Jonathan Edwards and America," 30. See also Smith, "Perennial Jonathan Edwards," 1–11; Spencer, "Jonathan Edwards and the Historiography of the American Enlightenment," 24, 24n11. Sweeney, *Edwards the Exegete*, 20, 219, astutely captures at least some of the reasons this figure, sometimes considered an "enigma," has remained elusive to so many: "[Edwards] was a 'both-and' thinker: traditional and modern, partisan and ecumenical, critical and edifying, catholic and anti-Catholic. He undermines–by straddling, combining, even melding–standard categories used to periodize Western thought." His thought world was shaped by forces sometimes in conflict with each other. This is evident in his work as an exegete, for example:"His biblical scholarship was shaped by both ancient and modern values, by Renaissance humanism and Reformation dogma, by scholastic orthodoxy and religions of the heart (Puritanism, Pietism, *Nadere Reformatie*), by Old Dissent in its diversity and nascent evangelicalism"; "[Edwards] was a 'both-and' exegete: traditional; and avant-garde, edifying and critical, profoundly theological and thoroughly historical." See also Moody, *Jonathan Edwards and the Enlightenment*, 3, 11n18.
16. Shea, "Jonathan Edwards," 185.
17. May, "Jonathan Edwards and America," 21; also, May, *Divided Heart*, 128.
18. Thuesen, "Jonathan Edwards as Great Mirror," 41.

writings, and historical influence makes him a crucial and controversial figure to students of American history, philosophy, theology, and literature alike. Laid claim to so stridently by so many . . . Edwards's identity as cultural icon and architect of the American mind is still up for grabs; the internecine debates initiated by Perry Miller in the middle of the last century continue unabated about whether Edwards the thinker was primarily indebted to the Enlightenment or to Calvinism and the Bible; whether he was a synthesizer or inventor; whether he was the last Puritan or the first modernist, postmodernist or a medievalist.[19]

Taking this assessment to its conclusion, Roland Delattre suggests that the challenge posed by Edwards's complexities allows only one, possibly not entirely satisfying, solution: "Perhaps it is best to acknowledge that we will never lay hold of 'the essential Edwards,' that like any truly powerful thinker, he is a complex figure, more like a set of overlapping selves whose integrity we seek but in whom we never find a simple unity."[20] "Fascinating and intriguing, as well as infuriating and frustrating," "elusive" and, fundamentally, an "enigma": Is there any hope of truly understanding this potent and intricate force on the American scene and on the world stage?[21]

Daunting a task though it may be, this study argues in part that, in the case of Edwards, complexity does not necessitate non-integration. Surrendering the possibility of discovering an "essential Edwards," resignation to recognizing only "overlapping selves" and multiple Edwardses that permit no cohesion into a unity, is in fact a counsel of despair that disregards compelling evidence from his own life.

---

19. Leader, "In Love With Image," 153, 153n1; Leader, *Knowing, Seeing, Being*, 15–16. See also Louie, "Theological Aesthetics of Jonathan Edwards," 2.

20. Delattre, "Recent Scholarship on Jonathan Edwards," 370. See also Minkema, "Jonathan Edwards's Life and Career: Society and Self," 22, 27n14. Spencer, "Jonathan Edwards and the Historiography of the American Enlightenment," 21–39, provides an insightful analysis of the many attempts scholars have made to classify Edwards, and concludes, "Still, one suspects Henry F. May's circumspect conclusion about the problem of categorizing Edwards will remain no less relevant, and no less enlightened," 39.

Crocco, "Edwards's Intellectual Legacy," 314, considers P. Miller's understanding of Edwards as expressed in his biography to be "a variation of the 'essence of Edwards' approach favored by enlightened interpreters who looked behind Edwards the theologian for the *real* Edwards (emphasis in original)." See note 25 below.

21. Crisp, "Preface," xiii; Ball, *Approaching Jonathan Edwards*, 1; Moody, "Introduction," 3.

Conclusion

Undeniably, this multifaceted presence on the American scene and on the world stage was an intriguingly intricate figure whose many dimensions have exerted a "multivalent influence" in the United States and around the world.[22] Yet, how precisely has this figure, who has been described as, "*somehow* a great man," made his presence felt?[23] As we have discovered, attempts to address this issue vary considerably. A recent observer has noted that the diversity evident in Edwards studies has resulted in "many attempts ... to elucidate an overarching motif or metathematic center for the theology of Jonathan Edwards."[24] Among those that have been advocated are "Divine sovereignty, grace, metaphysical ontology, typology, piety, the covenant history of redemption, divine glory or beauty, ethics, [and] Reformed apologetics through appropriation of Enlightenment philosophy."[25] One analyst of Edwardseana, in seeking resolution, has concluded, "[M]odern or medieval, advanced or retarded, for good or ill, Edwards was a 'Christian Philosopher.'"[26]

Although this attempt to bring order to the recent chaos in the field of Edwards studies is more astute than many previous judgments, the truth is even more basic. At his core, Edwards was a *Christian evangelist* and *apologist*. Christian evangelization, communicating the gospel through his words and through his actions, and defending the truth of Scripture and of the orthodox Christian faith, formed the foundation upon which Edwards erected the edifice consisting of preaching, writing, teaching, and mentoring. With an all-consuming determination, "glorifying God in the world" by working to achieve "the advancement and enlargement of Christ's kingdom on earth" were the great aims toward which he directed his considerable talents and energies.[27] In all of his capacities, the diverse

---

22. Noll, "Edwards' Theology after Edwards," 292.

23. Quotation is in May, "Jonathan Edwards and America," 30 (emphasis added).

24. Hastings, *Jonathan Edwards and the Life of God*, 1.

25. Hastings, *Jonathan Edwards and the Life of God*, 1. See also Leader, "'In Love with the Image,'" 175n11. The discussion Leader describes here illustrates the intricacy of Edwards's thinking and the complexity of his legacy. Undeniably, each of the elements she indicates occupied a significant place in Edwards's thought world. Which of these was *most central* to his life's work is beyond the scope of the present study. This study *does* contend that, complex though Edwards was, Christian evangelist/apologist was his central identity and that educator should be considered a key component of it.

26. Colacurcio, "Example of Edwards," 55.

27. Quotations are in Edwards, "Diary, February 5, 1723/24," 784; *LPW*, 518. See also *RA*, 85; *LPW*, 435. See also Sweeney, *Edwards the Exegete*, 218: "Though a literary artist, metaphysical theologian, moral prophet, college teacher, nature lover, and civic leader, [Edwards] was primarily a minister of the Word."

aspects of this divine and thinker's character and personality emanated from a foundational commitment to these life-defining objectives.

In the multitude of discussions of Edwards that have occurred during and since his lifetime, perhaps this reality has been too obvious to have captured attention. On the other hand, perhaps it may seem to be nothing short of undiluted audacity for someone to claim, "Aha! I have identified the essence of someone whom a multitude of scholars have maintained resisted simple categorization." Yet the evidence from his life unquestionably points toward this conclusion. Nearly four decades' worth of his devoted service was given to proclaiming Holy Writ as the Word of God that is able to "make [one] wise unto salvation through faith which is in Christ Jesus (2 Tim 3:15)" and to guide and comfort the people of God.[28]

Edwards held the conviction that "Ministers are set [in place] as . . . teachers" in order "to instruct and enlighten" their congregations.[29] In doing so, proclaimers and expositors of Scripture are divinely commissioned "to be lights to the souls of men . . . as they are to be the means of imparting divine truth to them."[30] Edwards approached this task with a hermeneutic which regarded Scripture as "God's own teaching and instructions," given so that his listeners would "know the Word of God, that [they] might be instructed by it."[31]

Instruction and evangelism were Edwards's driving forces in the schoolhouse and at the meetinghouse alike. He devoted nearly as much of his life to teaching and mentoring students as he did to pastoring congregants. Edwards's recognition of the inadequacy of rote memorization alone as an effective learning technique and his consistent reliance on a holistic technique and a dialogic instructional methodology instead earn him recognition as a preeminent education theorist and pedagogic practitioner. As this study has made clear, Edwards was dedicated to the goals of developing and stimulating students' intellects and, especially in the cases of children, encouraging and empowering them to become lifelong

---

28. See, e.g., Marsden, "Chronology of Edwards' Life and Times," xiii–xv. Edwards began his pastoral ministry at a church in New York City in 1722 and preached until shortly before his death in 1758.

29. Edwards, "A Farewell Sermon Preached at the First Precinct in Northampton," 466.

30. Edwards, "True Excellency of a Minister of the Gospel," 90.

31. Sweeney, "Edwards and the Bible," 67; Edwards, "Profitable Hearers of the Word," 265.

Conclusion

learners. With all students, Edwards sought to impart knowledge of the subject matter (Scripture to all; reading, spelling, arithmetic, history, and singing with the Stockbridge students; with the ministerial aspirants and college students, theology and pastoral advice), and also sought to enable them to reflect on the material in ways that best internalized it for the individual student.

He was not content to stop there, however. Edwards strove to enable those under his tutelage to understand "things divine and spiritual" in order to prepare the way for them to receive the "new spiritual sense," and thereby enter into communion with the God who sought to communicate his love to them.[32] Communion with God would result in the student's participation in a "God-given, God-centered, God-intoxicated, God-entranced vision of all things," and thereby enable consciously "join[ing] God in the purpose for which he created the universe."[33]

In sum, Edwards understood in his time a truth that still stands today: "Education is a matter of profound spiritual, moral, and intellectual consequence."[34] He exemplified the teacher who does the utmost,

---

32. Quotations are in Edwards, "Miscellany 962," 245; RA, 206, 260.

33. Piper, "God-Entranced Vision of All Things," 14, 24.

34. Ashford, "Missions, the Global Church, and Christian Higher Education," 525. Ashford continues, "In fact, in our twenty-first-century global context, higher education should be treated as a significant part of the Christian mission and a strategic component of Christian cross-cultural missions." The mission of God Ashford defines as, "[T]o glorify himself by redeeming humanity and bringing all things under his good rule. Subsequently, the Christian mission is to participate in God's mission, through words and deeds, in every sector of society and every sphere of culture, including higher education"; Ashford, "Missions, the Global Church, and Christian Higher Education," 525–26. A case can be made that this description should apply to all levels of education.

A major emphasis of this study is that Edwards considered education (both as a minister instructing parishioners and as a teacher instructing students) an essential element of his Christian calling to glorify God in the world by striving toward "the advancement and enlargement of Christ's kingdom on earth." This study also seeks to highlight Edwards as both a person who was subject to the limitations of his eighteenth-century Anglo-colonial setting, and yet as one who transcended his setting in significant ways. A key manifestation of this duality is Edwards's exercise of cross-cultural missions with the Native Americans at Stockbridge, which was complex. Nonetheless, two facts are incontrovertible: (1) Edwards displayed ethnocentrism toward the Natives in his conviction that their "Anglicization" was necessary for their evangelization; e.g., to learn English, to live with English settlers, and to adopt English customs and mores; (2): Edwards displayed an interest in the Natives' spiritual and material well-being sincere enough to convince at least some of those to whom he ministered to become friends and allies of his in the struggles at the mission against those who opposed the Natives' interests, and also against those who opposed his presence and his initiatives there.

through his or her teaching, to empower the "total person" of the student as someone made in the *imago Dei,* and who strives to enable the student to see, as Edwards himself did, the eternal from the perspective of the temporal. Therefore, this examination seeks to gain approbation for Edwards as an educator and as a pedagogical theorist. In so doing, it contends for *educator* as being as essential a dimension of his Christian evangelism as were *minister, theologian,* and *philosopher.*

CONCLUSION: EDWARDS EXPERIENCED "THE CRY OF THE TEACHER'S SOUL"

Toward this goal, we shall consider Edwards in relation to the image of *teacher* that emerges in Laurie Matthias's book, *The Cry of the Teacher's Soul.*[35] In this work, Matthias affirms, "While we [Christians generally and especially Christian teachers] should unapologetically hold to orthodox Christian doctrine, we must also realize that much of the Christian faith—and much of the teaching vocation—contain deep paradoxes that we are meant to embrace, as difficult as that can be."[36] Embracing this reality necessitates realizing that "Human knowing, rightly understood, has paradoxical roots–mind and heart, hard data and soft intuition, individual insight and communal sifting and winnowing."[37] Yet again, an insight of Parker Palmer proves valuable for this study, as he has pointed out the importance of avoiding fragmenting reality "into an endless series of *either-ors*" by embracing and living out the "both/ands" of paradox: Failure to do so results in "a fragmented sense of reality that destroys the wholeness and wonder of life."[38] In contrast, "By living the

---

35. Matthias, *Cry of the Teacher's Soul*. In this work, Matthias "weaves scholarly insights from theology, psychology, and education together with powerful, personal stories to provide a spiritually and pedagogically-sound resource"; Freytag, Review of *The Cry of the Teacher's Soul*, 1. See also Matthias, "Faith and Learning," 169–86. "At the heart of Christian higher education is the attempt to integrate faith and learning. This attempt draws from theological understandings of students as holistic human beings–with minds, souls, hearts, and bodies–each created uniquely in the image of God and meant to flourish as an integrated whole"; see Matthias, "Faith and Learning," 169n1; see also Dockery, "Christian Higher Education," 35: "While [the Christian] approach to higher education values and prioritizes the life of the mind, it is also a holistic call for the engagement of head, heart, and hands."

36. Matthias, *Cry of the Teacher's Soul*, xv. See also Palmer, *To Know As We Are Known*, 112, 112n9.

37. Palmer et al., *Heart of Higher Education*, 22.

38. Palmer, *Courage to Teach*, 62. See also Matthias, "Faith and Learning," 173:

contradictions, we will come to hope, and in hope we will be empowered to live life's contradictions," such as the contradiction of being "children of wrath" and yet "children of grace."[39]

In her discussion, Matthias observes that Scripture places a general call on all to follow Christ, but also speaks of God having created each person uniquely with special gifts to be used in his service.[40] "[W]hen God speaks of what he expects of us, he is after our hearts, calling us to the things that matter to him such as holiness, mercy, justice, and humility."[41] Following this call necessitates the living out of a paradox: One must die to self in order truly to live.[42] Living the eternal life in Christ that is the gift of divine grace requires (on earth) dying to self and "taking up [one's] cross daily" to follow Christ (Matt 16:24). Thus, Christians must live out a paradox: "We die in order to live. We lose our lives in order to save them (See Mark 8:34–36)."[43] This paradox is at the heart of the way of the cross, which "reminds us that despair and disillusionment are not dead ends but signs of impending resurrection," in which the Christian participates.[44]

Edwards experienced the general call to follow Christ and, as his life indicates, the specific call to him to evangelize as a *minister*, one who is "set [in place] . . . as [a teacher] . . . in order to instruct and enlighten" his congregation, and as a *teacher*, in order to present "spiritual and divine things," "a true sense of the divine excellency of the things revealed in the Word of God, and a conviction of the truth and reality of them, thence arising," to the understanding of students.[45] Anyone accepting the chal-

---

Christian institutions "insist that the integration enterprise [of combining an emphasis on faith with practical professional courses] remain central to the mission of their institutions since training students to think Christianly prepares them to live *holistically*, not just pragmatically. Once again, Christian education is a both/and enterprise rather than an either/or one" (emphasis added); Glanzer et al., *Restoring the Soul of the University*, especially 244–324.

39. Quotations are in Palmer, *Courage to Teach*, 62; Brekus, "Children of Wrath, Children of Grace," 300–328.

40. Matthias, *Cry of the Teacher's Soul*, 35.

41. Matthias, *Cry of the Teacher's Soul*, 36, 36n9.

42. Matthias, *Cry of the Teacher's Soul*, 37. Matthias here cites 1 Pet 2:24.

43. Matthias, *Cry of the Teacher's Soul*, 39.

44. Quotation is in Palmer, *Promise of Paradox*, 32; Matthias, *Cry of the Teacher's Soul*, 40.

45. Quotations are in Edwards, "Farewell Sermon," 466; Edwards, "Divine and Supernatural Light," 126. See Edwards, "Divine and Supernatural Light," 137: "'Tis by reason, that we become possessed of a notion of those doctrines that are the subject

lenge to teach should constantly treat as paramount (as Edwards did), not only the subject matter one teaches, but also the power of example of a life transformed by the combination of faith and learning that draws one irresistibly: "An educator who internalizes an insatiable curiosity, a passion for learning, and intellectual honesty will always inspire one's students. Never settle for stagnation or intellectual short-cuts and always remember that an educator's life example speaks very loudly in the ears of one's students."[46]

The significance of the holistic, dialogic praxis which Edwards consistently applied to teaching did not end with its use among those who comprised the New Divinity movement. In reality, its impact is still being felt. Anyone who has learned by having been made an active participant in the learning process, who has had his or her understanding expanded and a desire to learn stimulated through dialogue with a teacher, owes a debt to Jonathan Edwards. Anyone who has experienced learning as being "pleasant, entertaining and profitable" to his or her mind, heart, and behavior, rather than a "dull, wearisome task" to be endured, owes gratitude to Jonathan Edwards as both a pedagogical theorist and as a teacher.[47] Anyone who has come to see learning not simply as acquiring information, but rather as something that should affect one's entire life, should be thankful for Jonathan Edwards.

Just as significantly, anyone who teaches and sees him or herself, as well as students, as fallen by nature, yet made in God's image and loved by the God who seeks to communicate that love through creation and his Word, has Jonathan Edwards as a forebear.[48] Anyone who teaches today,

---

matter of this divine light; and reason may [in] many ways be indirectly, and remotely an advantage to it. And reason has also to do in the acts that are immediately consequent on this discovery: a seeing the truth of religion from hence, is by reason . . . . So reason has to do in that accepting of, and trusting in Christ, that is consequent on it."

46. Colwill, "Dialogical Learning and a New Epistemology," 159. See also Foord, "Elements of a Theology of Theological Education," 41: "Christian education is not simply imparting information but also illustrating it with one's life." This truth applies equally to education that is not done in specifically Christian contexts.

The power of teaching not only by "doctrine and precept" but by "instance and example" as well can affect lives in a positive, lasting way. Kang recognizes the "need to have teachers who are allowing themselves to be mastered by the Word and who can then pass this attitude on to students . . . . 'It is the personality of the teacher which is the text the pupils read; the text they will never forget'"; Edwards, "Author's Preface," 89; Kang, "Faith, Learning, and Catechesis," 380: Herschel, "Spirit of Jewish Education," 19, as quoted in Wilson, *Our Father Abraham*, 280.

47. Quotations are in *LPW*, 408.

48. See Matthias, *Cry of the Teacher's Soul*, 76: Human beings "are born with shalom

Conclusion

or who will teach in the future, whose heart's desire is to "teach transgressors [the LORD's] ways" (Ps 51:13) and who seeks to further a student's walk with Christ, to help a student find his or her place in the Kingdom of God, follows in the tradition of Jonathan Edwards, who experienced this same "cry of the teacher's soul, 'I am called to teach!'"[49]

An unrivaled intellect and devoted Christian evangelist, Edwards also exhibited "a compassion for others, a strong and feisty presence, and a persevering spirit" as a teacher.[50] Edwards knew and embraced the paradox of human nature, with its "shattered shalom," the *imago Dei* present in fallen but redeemable humanity. He grasped and practiced that teaching the "whole person" meant making the student aware (or more fully aware) that the God of creation seeks to draw him or her into "the dynamic beauty of God," to experience seeing "the beauty of the redemptive love of Christ as the true center of reality."[51] That is, Edwards strove to teach in a way that integrated and enlivened all of the capacities of the student, equipping him or her to participate most fully in the world. This is "integrative education," which "aims to 'think the world together' rather than 'think it apart,' to know the world in a way that empowers educated people to act on behalf of wholeness rather than fragmentation."[52] Edwards taught in such a way that indicated he knew the following truth:

> Doing integrative education well depends on our capacity to hold a paradox: we must open free space for the unpredictable *and* enforce an educative order. In contrast to a top-down

---

["holiness" and "wholeness"] shattered inherently within each one of us . . . . Some theologians have labeled us as 'totally depraved' in order to emphasize how this part of who we are permeates every aspect of our identity . . . . No matter how unpopular this view of humankind may be in today's society, it is an undeniable truth," a truth that, as Matthias notes, applies alike to students and to teachers.

49. Matthias, *Cry of the Teacher's Soul*, 29.

50. Matthias, *Cry of the Teacher's Soul*, 29. MacLeod aptly summarizes the total Edwards thus: "In Edwards were combined the deep thinker, the accomplished scholar, the evangelistic preacher, and the earnest, holy man of God"; MacLeod, "Jonathan Edwards (1703–58)." Not meaning to belabor this point, but this study contends that Edwards combined each of these elements to form an exemplary educator who deserves recognition and study as such today.

51. Marsden, *Infinite Fountain of Light*, 40; Marsden, *Jonathan Edwards: A Life*, 505.

52. Palmer et al., *Heart of Higher Education*, 22. See Glanzer et al., *Restoring the Soul of the University*, especially 113–220 and 244–324. See also Bezzant, *Edwards the Mentor*, 3: "[O]ur fragmenting world needs ministries that are integrative, helping people put the pieces back together again–no Humpty Dumpties here."

delivery of information that leaves the teacher in control, integrative pedagogies involve a communal exchange that is fluid, complex, and confusing. Teachers who use these methods must be able to think on their feet in order to help students learn to do the same.[53]

Just as true learning is not done in isolation but rather in a learning community, so too, is one who learns meant to interact with those outside him or herself. "In truthful knowing the knower becomes co-participant in a community of faithful relationships with other persons and creatures and things, with whatever our knowledge makes known."[54] A major emphasis of the present study is that Edwards strove through his teaching to put his students in communion with the God who communicates through creation, through Scripture, and through the Living Word of Christ to bring human beings into relationship with Him. This communion also brings them into faithful relationship (community) with each other.

Matthias observes that a divine calling is one in which Christians "are called primarily to *be*, not to *do*."[55] Edwards's life makes clear that this was true of him. The role of educator was so much a part of Edwards, so vital a component of his total ministry of evangelism, that, more than something he *did*, it was an element of who he *was*.

Lastly, we return to Stelting, who asks, "What, for Edwards, would have the whole purpose of education? What was his expectation for the educational enterprise?"[56] At its introductory level, education has utilitarian value for the individual and for the larger community of which he or she is a part: "By instruction, persons would be brought into behavior beneficial to the whole community . . . . [I]nstruction is necessary to overcome the evil which would engulf us all if left only to uninstructed human nature."[57] Yet, ultimately, education is intended to do much more than simply improve individuals and the world in which they live:

---

53. Palmer et al., *Heart of Higher Education*, 39. See also Palmer, *To Know As We Are Known*, xix; Backfish, "Biblical Wisdom as a Model for Christian Liberal Arts Education," 392. I am grateful to Backfish for her insights in this article.

54. Palmer, *To Know As We Are Known*, 32. See also Foord, "Elements of a Theology of Theological Education," 42: "Growing in a knowledge of God is a collective activity . . . . Friends teach, encourage, and rebuke each other . . . they pray with each other for growth in grace."

55. Matthias, *Cry of the Teacher's Soul*, 36

56. Stelting, "Edwards as Educator," 216.

57. Stelting, "Edwards as Educator," 217.

Conclusion

When Edwards mounted the pulpit, or approached the lectern, or sat beneath the tree in the churchyard on Sunday afternoons surrounded by children, it was for one purpose. He intended to create a context within which people might truly, fully, and savingly see God; and that God might enter into them, giving them, by apprehension, a truth they could not otherwise know. *He wished to teach people to know God as he knew God.*[58]

This insight raises two critical questions. First, how did Edwards know God? He experienced God as the one in whom all reality consists. As the source of "excellency"; the one in whom "the redeemed have all their objective good"; indeed, "their highest good."[59] As the one in whose image human beings are made, allowing Scripture to be presented to their understanding as a means of grace to receive the "new spiritual sense." As the one who seeks to use creation and Scripture to communicate His love to human beings, in order to draw them into participation in the "divine drama." As the One who brings into "his marvelous light" and makes alive the "'hidden wholeness' on which all life depends."[60] As the one who, if allowed to do so, restores the "shattered shalom," and thereby empowers human beings to live out their calling as divine image-bearers to the world.[61]

Second, how did Edwards strive to get others to know God? He did so through instruction in Scripture and in the things of divinity as a minister to his congregants and as a teacher to his students. And through mentoring students "singly, particularly and closely" about the conditions of their souls, because education extends to much more than simply filling the head full of facts. *It affects how a person lives.* May those

---

58. Stelting, "Edwards as Educator," 217 (emphasis added).

59. *FW*, 166, 399, 406; Edwards, "God Glorified in Man's Dependence," 208.

60. 1 Peter 2:9; Palmer, *To Know as We Are Known*, xix. See also Merton and Griffin, *Hidden Wholeness*; Palmer et al., *Heart of Higher Education*, x. Restored communion with the communicative God enables viewing the natural world, notwithstanding all the challenges it presents, as "the outpouring crescendo of God's innermost activity and essentially loving essence"; Coome, "Putting Edwards to Work," 127. "El-Roi (God Who Sees) sees us and knows our every need. He knows that we are broken and need to be remade, refilled, and renewed, and this is what He desires to do for us.... He wants to nourish us and to remind us of our inherent worth as His beloved ones"; Freytag, Review of *Cry of the Teacher's Soul*, 2.

61. Education should perform a vital part in facilitating this transformation. See Fant, "Teaching and Learning in the Humanities," 220: "[A] full-orbed humanities education emphasizes the shared humanity that [human beings] all possess as a part of our unique place as image bearers in true relationship with God." This emphasis should be true of all holistic teaching/learning.

who continue to believe that education should do this, those who continue to experience "the cry of the teacher's soul: I feel called to teach," and those who feel "called to learn," indeed, all those who feel called to be co-participants in the learning, teaching, and knowing communities in a way that transforms one's whole being, be inspired by Jonathan Edwards. In the end, the only commemoration worthy of Edwards today is a fair evaluation of his life and work. Thorough analysis of his excellence in theory and praxis of education, and the emulation which such a review should engender, are honors he richly deserves.

Bibliography

Aaron, Richard I. *John Locke.* 2nd ed. Oxford: Clarendon, 1955.
Abraham, Joseph. *Eve: Accused or Acquitted?: An Analysis of Feminist Readings of the Creation Narrative Texts in Genesis 1–3.* Eugene, OR: Wipf & Stock, 2002.
Adams, Henry Brooks. *The Education of Henry Adams.* Boston: Houghton Mifflin, 1918.
Adams, William. *God's Eye on the Contrite.* Boston: Richard Pierce, 1685.
Adamson, John William. "The Great Didactic." In *Pioneers of Modern Education*, edited by John William Adamson, 58–79. Cambridge: Cambridge University Press, 1921.
Ahlstrom, Sydney E. "Jonathan Edwards, the Enlightenment, and the New Divinity." In *The Shaping of American Religion,* edited by James Ward Smith and A. Leland Jamison, 243–51. Princeton, NJ: Princeton University Press, 1961.
———. "The Puritan Impulse." In *The Shaping of American Religion*, edited by James Ward Smith and A. Leland Jamison, 236–43. Princeton, NJ: Princeton University Press, 1961.
———. "The Scottish Philosophy and American Theology." *Church History* 24 (1955) 257–72.
———. "Theology in America: A Historical Survey." In *The Shaping of American Religion*, edited by James Ward Smith and A. Leland Jamison, 232–35. Princeton, NJ: Princeton University Press, 1961.
———. *Theology in America: The Major Protestant Voices from Puritanism to Neo-Orthodoxy.* Indianapolis: Bobbs-Merrill, 1967.
Alden, John. "The Bible as Printed Word." In *The Bible and Bibles in America,* edited by Ernest S. Frerichs, 9–28. Atlanta: Scholars, 1988.
Aldridge, Alfred Owen. *Benjamin Franklin and Nature's God.* Durham, NC: Duke University Press, 1967.
———. "Edwards and Hutcheson." *Harvard Theological Review* 44 (1951) 35–53.
———. "Enlightenment and Awakening in Edwards and Franklin." In *Benjamin Franklin, Jonathan Edwards, and the Representation of American Culture,* edited by Barbara B. Oberg and Harry S. Stout, 27–41. New York: Oxford University Press, 1993.
———. *Jonathan Edwards.* New York: Washington Square, 1964.
Allen, Alexander Viets Griswold. *Life and Writings of Jonathan Edwards.* Edinburgh: T. & T. Clark, 1889.

Bibliography

———. "The Place of Edwards in History." In *Jonathan Edwards: A Retrospect*, edited by H. Norman Gardiner, 3–31. Boston: Houghton Mifflin, 1901.
Allen, Russell J. "Children as 'White Paper': Jonathan Edwards and Enlightenment Childhood." *Jonathan Edwards within the Enlightenment: Controversy, Experience, and Thought*, edited by John T. Lowe and Daniel N. Gullotta, 169–85. Göttingen: Vandenhoeck & Ruprecht, 2020.
———. "Holy Children are Happy Children: Jonathan Edwards and Puritan Childhood." MA thesis, Liberty University, 2016.
American Education Society. *A Brief View of the American Education Society*. Andover, MA: Flagg and Gould, 1826.
Ames, William. *Conscience with the Power and Cases Thereof*. Reprint, Norwood, NJ: Walter J. Johnson, 1975.
———. *The Marrow of Theology*. Translated by John Dykstra Eusden. Grand Rapids: Baker, 1968.
Amory, Hugh. "'A Bible and Other Books': Enumerating the Copies in Seventeenth-Century Essex County." In *Bibliography and the Book Trades: Studies in the Print Culture of Early New England*, edited by David D. Hall, 58–79. Philadelphia: University of Pennsylvania Press, 2005.
———. "A Boston Society Library: The Old South Church and Thomas Prince." In *Bibliography and the Book Trades: Studies in the Print Culture of Early New England*, edited by David D. Hall, 146–62. Philadelphia: University of Pennsylvania Press, 2005.
———. "The New England Book Trade, 1713–1790." In *The Colonial Book in the Atlantic World*, edited by Hugh Amory and David D. Hall, 314–46. Chapel Hill: University of North Carolina Press, 2007.
———. "Printing and Bookselling in New England, 1638–1713." In *The Colonial Book in the Atlantic World*, edited by Hugh Amory and David D. Hall, 83–116. Chapel Hill: University of North Carolina Press, 2007.
———. "Reinventing the Colonial Book." In *The Colonial Book in the Atlantic World*, edited by Hugh Amory and David D. Hall, 26–54. Chapel Hill: University of North Carolina Press, 2007.
Amory, Hugh, and David D. Hall. *The Colonial Book in the Atlantic World*. Chapel Hill: University of North Carolina Press, 2010.
Anchor, Robert. *The Enlightenment Tradition*. Berkeley: University of California Press, 1979.
Anderson, Glenn Paul. "Joseph Bellamy, 1719–1790: The Man and His Work." PhD diss., Boston University, 1971.
Anderson, Michael Patrick. "The Pope of Litchfield County: An Intellectual Biography of Joseph Bellamy, 1719–1790." PhD diss., Claremont Graduate School, 1980.
Anderson, Paul Russell, and Max Harold Fisch. *Philosophy in America From the Puritans to James*. Reprint, New York: Octagon, 1969.
Anderson, Virginia DeJohn. "Migrants and Motives: Religion and the Settlement of New England, 1630–1640." *New England Quarterly* 58 (1985) 339–83.
———. *New England's Generation: The Great Migration and the Formation of Society and Culture in the Seventeenth Century*. Cambridge: Cambridge University Press, 1991.
Anderson, Wallace E. "Biographical Background." In *Works of Jonathan Edwards Online*, edited by Wallace E. Anderson, 6:17–21. http://edwards.yale.edu.

Bibliography

———. "The Development of Edwards' Philosophical Thought." In *Works of Jonathan Edwards Online*, edited by Wallace E. Anderson, 6:52–136. http://edwards.yale.edu.

———. "Editor's Introduction." In *Works of Jonathan Edwards Online*, edited by Wallace E. Anderson, 6:7–27. http://edwards.yale.edu.

———. "Immaterialism in Jonathan Edwards' Early Philosophical Notes." *Journal of the History of Ideas* 25 (1964) 181–200.

———. "Mind and Nature in the Early Philosophical Writings of Jonathan Edwards." PhD diss., University of Minnesota, 1961.

———. "'Natural Philosophy' and Related Papers." In *Works of Jonathan Edwards Online*, edited by Wallace E. Anderson, 6:234. http://edwards.yale.edu.

———. "Note on 'Natural Philosophy.'" In *Works of Jonathan Edwards Online*, edited by Wallace E. Anderson, 6:173–91. http://edwards.yale.edu.

———. "The 'Spider Papers.'" In *Works of Jonathan Edwards Online*, edited by Wallace E. Anderson, 6:159. http://edwards.yale.edu.

"Andrew Baxter: Scottish Philosopher." www.britannica.com/topic/rationalism.

Andrews, Charles M. *The Colonial Period of American History: The Settlements*. Vol. 1 of *The Colonial Period of American History*. New Haven, CT: Yale University Press, 1934.

———. *The Fathers of New England: A Chronicle of the Puritan Commonwealths*. New York: United States Publishers Association, 1919.

Angoff, Charles. *A Literary History of the American People. Vol. 1: From 1607 to the Beginning of the Revolutionary Period*. New York: Tudor, 1935.

Anonymous. "Harvard College, 1636–1654." *American Journal of Education* 9 (1860) 135.

Antipas. "The Comparative Importance of Moral and Intellectual Culture." *The Spirit of the Pilgrims* 3 (1830) 572–75.

Armstrong, Chris R. *Patron Saints for Postmoderns: Ten From the Past Who Speak to Our Future*, 92–111. Downers Grove, IL: InterVarsity, 2009.

Ashford, Bruce Riley. "Missions, the Global Church, and Christian Higher Education." In *Christian Higher Education: Faith, Teaching, and Learning in the Evangelical Tradition*, edited by David S. Dockery and Christopher W. Morgan, 525–43. Wheaton, IL: Crossway, 2018.

Axtell, James. "The 'Education' in Context." In *The Educational Writings of John Locke*, 49–68. Cambridge: Cambridge University Press, 1968

———. *The European and the Indian: Essays in the Ethnohistory of Colonial North America*. New York: Oxford University Press, 1981.

———. *The Invasion Within: The Contest of Cultures in Colonial North America*. New York: Oxford University Press, 1985.

———. *The School Upon a Hill: Education and Society in Colonial New England*. New Haven, CT: Yale University Press, 1974.

Ayer, A. J. "Editorial Foreword." In D. J. O'Connor, *John Locke*, 11–22. New York: Dover, 1967.

Backfish, Elizabeth H. P. "Biblical Wisdom as a Model for Christian Liberal Arts Education." *Christian Higher Education* 18 (2019) 382–96.

———. "Transformative Learning Theory as a Hermeneutic for Understanding Tensions within Scripture." *Christian Scholar's Review* 50 (2021) 195–281.

Bibliography

Bailey, Richard A. "Driven by Passion: Jonathan Edwards and the Art of Preaching." In *The Legacy of Jonathan Edwards: American Religion and the Evangelical Tradition*, edited by D. G. Hart et al., 64–78. Grand Rapids: Baker, 2003.

Bailyn, Bernard. *Education in the Forming of American Society: Needs and Opportunities for Study*. New York: W. W. Norton & Co., 1960.

Baines, Ronald S. "Thy Kingdom Come: The Missionary Theology and Practice of Jonathan Edwards." MAR thesis, Reformed Theological Seminary, 2006.

Ball, Carol. *Approaching Jonathan Edwards: The Evolution of a Persona*. Burlington, VT: Ashgate, 2015.

Banks, John Sherwin. "By the Same Spirit: Edwardsean Pneumatology in the Younger Edwards." ThM thesis, Southern Baptist Theological Seminary, 2020.

Bardout, J.-C. *La vertu de la philosophie: Essai sur la morale de Malebranche*. Hildesheim: Georg Olms Verlag, 2000.

———. *Malebranche et la métaphysique*. Paris: Presses Universitaires de France, 1999.

Barker, William S. *Puritan Profiles*. Ross-shire, Scotland: Mentor, 1999.

Barnett, Das Kelly. "The Doctrine of Man in the Theology of Jonathan Edwards." PhD diss., Southern Baptist Theological Seminary, 1943.

Barnett, S. J. *The Enlightenment and Religion: The Myths of Modernity*. Manchester: University of Manchester Press, 2003.

Barshinger, David P. "Sin and Evil." In *The Oxford Handbook of Jonathan Edwards*, edited by Douglas A. Sweeney and Jan Stievermann, 235–49. New York: Oxford University Press, 2021.

Bartholomew, Craig G. and Goheen, Michael W. *The Drama of Scripture: Finding Our Place in the Biblical Story*. Grand Rapids: Baker Academic, 2014.

Baxter, Andrew. *An Enquiry Into the Nature of the Human Soul*. London: Printed for A. Millar, 1745.

———. *Matho: or, Cosmotheoria Puerilis, a Dialogue*. 2 vols. London: Printed for A. Millar, 1740.

Baxter, Richard. *The Autobiography of Richard Baxter*. Edited by N. H. Keeble. London: Dent, 1974.

———. *A Holy Commonwealth*. London: Printed for Thomas Underhill and Francis Tyson, 1659.

Baylin, Bernard. *Education in the Forming of American Society: Needs and Opportunities for Study*. New York: W. W. Norton & Co., 1960.

Bayly, Lewis. *The Practice of Piety*. London: Edward Brewster, 1695.

Beales, Ross W. "The Search for the Historical Child: Miniature Adulthood and Youth in Colonial New England" *American Quarterly* 27 (1975) 379–98.

Beales, Ross W., and E. Jennifer Monaghan. "Literacy and Schoolbooks." In *A History of the Book in America: The Colonial Book in the Atlantic World*, edited by Hugh Amory and David D. Hall, 1:380–87. Chapel Hill: University of North Carolina Press, 2007.

Beall, Otho T., Jr., and Richard H. Shryock. *Cotton Mather: First Significant Figure in American Medicine*. Baltimore: Johns Hopkins University Press, 1954.

Beard, Charles A. "On Puritans." In *Puritanism in Early America*, edited by George M. Waller, 1–4. Boston: D. C. Heath, 1950.

Beaver, R. Pierce. *Pioneers in Mission: The Early Missionary Ordination Sermons, Charges, and Instructions*. Grand Rapids: Eerdmans, 1966.

Bibliography

Beck, Lewis White. "Introduction." In *Eighteenth-Century Philosophy*, 1–11. New York: Free, 1966.

Benedict, Noah. *A Sermon Delivered at the Funeral of Rev. Joseph Bellamy, D. D.*, 20. New Haven, CT: Thomas and Samuel Green, 1790.

Behrens, Betty. Book Review of *The Enlightenment: An Interpretation*, by Peter Gay. *The Historical Journal* 11 (1968) 190–95.

Ball, Carol. *Approaching Jonathan Edwards: The Evolution of a Persona*. Burlington, VT: Ashgate, 2015.

Beattie, James. *An Essay on the Nature and Immutability of Truth in Opposition to Sophistry and Scepticism*. 6th ed. Edinburgh: Printed for Denham & Dick, 1805.

Bellamy, Joseph. "B115. Letter from Joseph Bellamy [to Jonathan Edwards], May 31, 1756." In *Works of Jonathan Edwards Online*, edited by Jonathan Edwards Center, 32:n.d. http://edwards.yale.edu.

———. "Letter to Samuel Hopkins, January 30, 1756." Gratz MSS, Historical Society of Pennsylvania, Philadelphia, Pennsylvania.

———. "MS, 'Joseph Bellamy H[ome-] B[ased] 1736." Yale Divinity School, Special Collections, 3–4.

———. *True Religion Delineated*. Boston: S Kneeland, 1750.

———. *The Works of Joseph Bellamy, D. D., First Pastor of the Church in Bethlam [sic], Conn., with a Memoir of His Life and Character*. Boston: Doctrinal Tract and Book Society, 1853.

Benz, Ernst. "Ecumenical Relations Between Boston Puritanism and German Pietism: Cotton Mather and August Hermann Francke." *Harvard Theological Review* 54 (1961) 159–93.

———. "Pietist and Puritan Sources of Early Protestant World Missions (Cotton Mather and A. H. Francke)." *Church History* 20 (1951) 28–55.

Bercovitch, Sacvan. "Cotton Mather." In *Major Writers of Early American Literature*, edited by Everett Emerson, 93–149. Madison: University of Wisconsin Press, 1972.

———. "New England Epic: Cotton Mather's *Magnalia Christi Americana*." *English Literary History* 33 (1966) 337–50.

———. "New England Epic: A Literary Study of Cotton Mather's *Magnalia Christi Americana*." PhD diss., Claremont Graduate School, 1965.

———. *The Puritan Origins of the American Self*. New Haven, CT: Yale University Press, 1975.

Best, John Hardin, and Robert T. Sidwell. *The American Legacy of Learning: Readings in the History of Education*. Philadelphia: J. B. Lippincott, 1967.

Bezzant, Rhys. "American Theological Education at the Beginning of the Nineteenth Century: The Edwardsean Legacy." In *Theological Education: Foundations, Practices, and Future Directions*, edited by Andrew M. Bain and Ian Hussey, 74–87. Eugene, OR: Wipf & Stock, 2018.

———. "Ecclesiology and Sacraments." In *The Oxford Handbook of Jonathan Edwards*, edited by Douglas A. Sweeney and Jan Stievermann, 267–80. New York: Oxford University Press, 2021.

———. *Edwards the Mentor*. New York: Oxford University Press, 2019.

———. "Introduction." In *Edwards, Germany, and Transatlantic Contexts*, edited by Rhys Bezzant, 7–10. Göttingen: Vandenhoeck & Ruprecht, 2022.

Bibliography

———. "Pepperrell, William (1696–1759)." In *The Jonathan Edwards Encyclopedia*, edited by Harry S. Stout et al., 436–37. Grand Rapids: Eerdmans, 2017.

———. "'Singly, Particularly, Closely': Edwards as Mentor." *Jonathan Edwards Studies* 4 (2014) 228–46.

———. "'Singly, Particularly, Closely': Edwards as Mentor." *Theologica Wratislaviensia* 7 (2012) 205–25.

Bezzant, Rhys, ed. *The Global Edwards: Papers from the Jonathan Edwards Congress held in Melbourne, August 2015*. Eugene, OR: Wipf & Stock, 2017.

Biehl, Craig. "*Original Sin* (1758)." In *The Jonathan Edwards Encyclopedia*, edited by Harry S. Stout et al., 427–30. Grand Rapids: Eerdmans, 2017.

Bierma, Lyle D. "The Role of Covenant Theology in Early Reformed Orthodoxy." *Sixteenth Century Journal* 21 (1990) 453–62.

Blore, Erick John. "The Educational Philosophy of Jonathan Edwards: An Analysis and Application of His Calvinistic Psychology." MAR thesis, Reformed Theological Seminary, 2007.

Blumenthal, Joseph. *The Printed Book in America*. Boston: David R. Godine, 1977.

Bogue, Carl W. *Jonathan Edwards and the Covenant of Grace*. Cherry Hill, NJ: Mack, 1975.

Bolton, Charles Knowles. *American Library History*. Chicago: American Library Association, 1911.

———. *Proprietary and Subscription Libraries*. Chicago: American Library Association, 1917.

Bombaro, John J. *Jonathan Edwards's Vision of Reality: The Relationship of God to the World, Redemption History, and the Reprobate*. Eugene, OR: Wipf & Stock, 2012

Bonomi, Patricia U. *Under the Cope of Heaven: Religion, Society, and Politics*. New York: Oxford University Press, 1986.

Boone, Richard G. *Education in the United States: Its History from the Earliest Settlements*. New York: D. Appleton and Co., 1907.

Boorstin, Daniel J. *The Americans: The Colonial Experience*. New York: Random House, 1958.

———. "The Myth of an American Enlightenment." In *America and the Image of Europe*, 65–78. New York: World, 1960.

Boss, Sarah B. "The Wheels of a Watch: Jonathan Edwards's Emblematic Philosophy of Time." In *Jonathan Edwards within the Enlightenment: Controversy, Experience, and Thought*, edited by John T. Lowe and Daniel N. Gullotta, 263–81. Göttingen: Vandenhoeck & Ruprecht, 2020.

Bossuiet, Jacques-Benigne. *Politics Drawn from the Very Words of Holy Scripture*. Translated and edited by Patrick Riley. Cambridge: Cambridge University Press, 1990.

Botein, Stephen. "The Anglo-American Book Trade before 1776: Personnel and Strategies." In *Printing and Society in Early America*, edited by William L. Joyce et al., 48–82. Worcester, MA: American Antiquarian Society, 1983.

Bowden, Henry Warner. *American Indians and Christian Missions: Studies in Cultural Conflict*. Chicago: University of Chicago Press, 1981.

Bracken, Harry M. "Andrew Baxter, Critic of Berkeley." *Journal of the History of Ideas* 18 (1957) 183–84.

Brauer, Jerald C. "Reflections on the Nature of English Puritanism." *Church History* 23 (1954) 99–108.

Bibliography

Breen, T. H. "Persistent Localism: English Social Change and the Shaping of New England Institutions." *William and Mary Quarterly* 3 (1975) 3–28.

Breen, T. H., and Stephen Foster. "Moving to the New World: The Character of Early Massachusetts Immigration." *William and Mary Quarterly* 3rd Series 30 (1973) 189–222.

Breitenbach, William K. "The Consistent Calvinism of the New Divinity Movement." *William and Mary Quarterly* 41 (1984) 241–64.

———. "The New Divinity and the Era of Moral Accountability." PhD diss., Yale University, 1978.

———. "Piety and Moralism: Edwards and the New Divinity." In *Jonathan Edwards and the American Experience*, edited by Nathan O. Hatch and Harry S. Stout, 177–204. New York: Oxford University Press, 1989.

———. "Religious Affections and Religious Affectations: Antinomianism and Hypocrisy in the Writings of Edwards and Franklin." In *Benjamin Franklin, Jonathan Edwards, and the Representation of American Culture*, edited by Barbara B. Oberg and Harry S. Stout, 13–26. New York: Oxford University Press, 1993.

Brekus, Catherine A. "Children of Wrath, Children of Grace: Jonathan Edwards and the Puritan Culture of Child Rearing." In *The Child in Christian Thought*, edited by Marcia J. Bunge, 300–328. Grand Rapids: Eerdmans, 2001.

———. "Remembering Jonathan Edwards's Ministry to Children." In *Jonathan Edwards at Home and Abroad: Historical Memories, Cultural Movements, Global Horizons*, edited by David W. Kling and Douglas A. Sweeney, 40–60. Columbia: University of South Carolina Press, 2003.

Bremer, Francis J. "Bible." In *Puritans and Puritanism in Europe and America*, edited by Francis J. Bremer and Tom Webster, 2:323–24. Oxford: ABC-CLIO, 2006.

———. "Introduction." In *Puritans and Puritanism in Europe and America: A Comprehensive Encyclopedia*, edited by Francis J. Bremer and Tom Webster, 1:xiii–xv. Oxford: ABC-CLIO, 2006.

———. "Puritan Childrearing." In *Puritans and Puritanism in Europe and America: A Comprehensive Encyclopedia*, edited by Francis J. Bremer and Tom Webster, 2:502–3. Oxford: ABC-CLIO, 2006.

———. "The Puritan Experiment in New England, 1630–1660." In *The Cambridge Companion to Puritanism*, edited by John Coffey and Paul C. H. Lim, 127–42. Cambridge: Cambridge University Press, 2008.

———. *The Puritan Experiment: New England Society from Bradford to Edwards*. New York: St Martin's, 1976.

———. *Puritanism: A Very Short Introduction*. Oxford: Oxford University Press, 2009.

———. *Shaping New Englands: Puritan Clergymen in Seventeenth-Century England and New England*. New York: Twayne, 1994.

Brenneman, Todd. "Hopkins, Samuel." In *Dictionary of Early American Philosophers*, edited by John R. Shook, 551–55. New York: Bloomsbury, 2012.

Brock, William R. *Scotus Americanus: A Survey of the Sources for Links Between Scotland and America in the Eighteenth Century*. Edinburgh: University of Edinburgh Press, 1982.

Brown, Matthew Pentland. "Orbits of Reading: The Presence of the Text in Early New England." PhD diss., University of Virginia, 1996.

———. *The Pilgrim and the Bee: Reading Rituals and Book Culture in Early New England*. Philadelphia: University of Pennsylvania Press, 2007.

Bibliography

Brown, Robert E. "The Bible." In *The Princeton Companion to Jonathan Edwards*, edited by Sang Hyun Lee, 87–102. Princeton, NJ: Princeton University Press, 2005.

———. "Biblical Exegesis." In *The Oxford Handbook of Jonathan Edwards*, edited by Douglas A. Sweeney and Jan Stievermann, 337–86. New York: Oxford University Press, 2021.

———. "Edwards, Locke, and the Bible." *Journal of Religion* 79 (1999) 361–84.

Bruner, Kurt. *The Divine Drama: Discovering Your Part in God's Story*. Wheaton, IL: Tyndale House, 2001.

Bryant, Louise May, and Mary Patterson. "The List of Books Sent by Jeremiah Dummer." In *Papers in Honor of Andrew Keogh*, edited by Mary C. Withington, 423–92. New Haven, CT: Privately printed, 1938.

Bryson, Gladys. *Man and Society: The Scottish Inquiry of the Eighteenth Century*. Princeton, NJ: Princeton University Press, 1945.

Buber, Martin. *The Knowledge of Man: Selected Essays*. New York: Harper & Row, 1965.

Bunge, Marcia J. "Education and the Child in Eighteenth-Century German Pietism: Perspectives from the Work of A. H. Francke." In *The Child in Christian Thought*, edited by Marcia J. Bunge, 247–78. Grand Rapids: Eerdmans, 2001.

Burr, Esther Edwards. *The Journal of Esther Edwards Burr. 1754–1757*, edited by Carol F. Karlsen and Laurie Crumpacker. New Haven, CT: Yale University Press, 2022.

Bush, Michael David. "Jesus Christ in the Theology of Jonathan Edwards." PhD diss., Princeton Theological Seminary, 2003.

Bushman, Richard L. "Jonathan Edwards and Puritan Consciousness." In *Puritan New England: Essays on Religion, Society, and Culture*, edited by Alden T. Vaughan and Francis J. Bremer, 346–62. New York: St. Martin's, 1977.

———. "Jonathan Edwards as Great Man: Identity, Conversion, and Leadership in the Great Awakening." *Soundings, an Interdisciplinary Journal* 52 (1969) 15–46.

Butts, Francis T. "The Myth of Perry Miller." *American Historical Review* 87 (1982) 665–94.

———. "Perry Miller and the Ordeal of American Freedom." PhD diss., Queen's University, 1980.

Byrd, James P. "North America." In *The Oxford Handbook of Jonathan Edwards*, edited by Douglas A. Sweeney and Jan Stievermann, 463–78. New York: Oxford University Press, 2021.

Byrne, Herbert W. *A Christian Approach to Education: Education Theory and Practice*. Grand Rapids: Baker, 1988.

Cadbury, Henry J. "Harvard College Library and the Libraries of the Mathers." *Proceedings of the American Antiquarian Society* 50 (1941) 20–48.

———. "Bishop Berkeley's Gifts to the Harvard Library." *Harvard Library Bulletin* 7 (1953) 73–87, 196–207.

———. "John Harvard's Library." *Publications of the Colonial Society of Massachusetts* 34 (1943) 353–77.

Cady, Edwin H. "The Artistry of Jonathan Edwards." *New England Quarterly* 22 (1949) 61–72.

Caldwell, Robert W., III. "Pneumatology." In *The Oxford Handbook of Edwards*, edited by Douglas A. Sweeney and Jan Stievermann, 151–64. New York: Oxford University Press, 2021.

Bibliography

Cambers, Andrew. "Defining Puritanism and Godly Culture." In *Godly Reading: Print, Manuscript and Puritanism in England, 1580-1720*, 10-16. Cambridge: Cambridge University Press, 2011.

———. *Godly Reading: Print, Manuscript and Puritanism in England, 1580-1720*. Cambridge: Cambridge University Press, 2011.

Campos, Heber Carlos de. "Latin America." In *The Oxford Handbook of Jonathan Edwards*, edited by Douglas A. Sweeney and Jan Stievermann, 555-67. New York: Oxford University Press, 2021.

———. "A Re-formed Understanding of Imputation in Jonathan Edwards's Original Sin." In *The Global Edwards: Papers from the Jonathan Edwards Congress held in Melbourne, August 2015*, 223-43. Eugene, OR: Wipf & Stock, 2017.

Capaldi, Nicholas. "Introduction." In *The Enlightenment: The Proper Study of Mankind*, edited by Nicholas Capaldi, 7-40. New York: Capricorn, 1967.

Capaldi, Nicholas, ed. *The Enlightenment: The Proper Study of Mankind*. New York: Capricorn, 1967.

Caradonna, Jeremy L. "Roundtable Discussion Conclusion." *Eighteenth-Century Studies* 49 (2015) 87-88.

———. "There Was No Counter-Enlightenment." *Eighteenth-Century Studies* 49 (2015) 51-69.

Carden, Allen. *Puritan Christianity in America: Religion and Life in Seventeenth-Century Massachusetts*. Grand Rapids: Baker, 1990.

Cappello, Mary. "The Authority of Self-Definition in Thomas Shepard's *Autobiography* and *Journal*." *Early American Literature* 24 (1989) 35-51.

Carden, Allen. *Puritan Christianity in America: Religion and Life in Seventeenth-Century Massachusetts*. Grand Rapids: Baker, 1990.

———. "The Word of God in Puritan New England: Seventeenth-Century Perspectives on the Nature and Authority of the Bible." *Andrews University Seminary Studies* 18 (1980) 1-16.

Carpenter, Frederic I. "The Radicalism of Jonathan Edwards." *New England Quarterly* 4 (1931) 629-44.

Carré, M. H. "The Earlier Conflict with Science." *Church Quarterly Review* 167 (1966) 347-54.

Carroll, Peter N. *Puritanism and the Wilderness: The Intellectual Significance of the New England Frontier, 1629-1700*. New York: Columbia University Press, 1969.

Cassara, Ernest. *The Enlightenment in America*. Boston: Twayne, 1975.

Cassirer, Ernst. *The Philosophy of the Enlightenment*. Translated by Fritz C. A. Koelln and James P. Pettegrove. Princeton, NJ: Princeton University Press, 1951.

Chai, Leon. *Jonathan Edwards and the Limits of Enlightenment Philosophy*. New York: Oxford University Press, 1998.

Chamberlain, Ava. "Editor's Introduction." In *Works of Jonathan Edwards Online*, edited by Ava Chamberlain, 18:1-47. http://edwards.yale.edu.

———. "Edwards and Social Issues." In *The Cambridge Companion to Jonathan Edwards*, edited by Stephen J. Stein, 325-44. New York: Cambridge University Press, 2007.

———. "Family Life." In *The Oxford Handbook of Jonathan Edwards*, edited by Douglas A. Sweeney and Jan Stievermann, 3-16. New York: Oxford University Press, 2021.

Chaney, Charles Leonard. "God's Glorious Work: The Theological Foundations of the Early Missionary Societies in America, 1787-1817." PhD diss., University of Chicago, 1973.

Bibliography

Channing, William Ellery. *The Works of William E. Channing.* Boston: James Munroe and Co., 1848.

Charry, Ellen T. "The Moral Function of Doctrine." *Theology Today* 49 (1992) 31–45.

Cherry, Conrad. "Imagery and Analysis: Jonathan Edwards on Revivals of Religion." In *Jonathan Edwards: His Life and Influence,* edited by Charles Angoff, 19–28. Rutherford, NJ: Farleigh Dickinson University Press, 1975.

———. *The Theology of Jonathan Edwards: A Reappraisal.* Reprint, Bloomington: Indiana University Press, 1990.

Chisholm, Hugh. *Encyclopaedia Britannica.* Cambridge: Cambridge University Press, 1911.

Chun, Chris. *The Legacy of Jonathan Edwards in the Theology of Andrew Fuller.* Leiden: Brill, 2012.

Claghorn, George S. "Introduction." In *Works of Jonathan Edwards Online,* edited by George S. Claghorn, 16:3–27. http://edwards.yale.edu.

Clap(p), Roger. *The Memoirs of Capt. Roger Clapp [of Dorchester], 1630.* Reprint, Boston: Printed by David Clapp Jr., 1844.

Clark, Gordon H. *A Christian Philosophy of Education.* Grand Rapids: Eerdmans, 1946.

Clement, Richard W. "Colonial Book Production, 1638–1783." In *The Book in America: A History of the Making and Selling of Books in the United States,* edited by Hellmut Lehmann-Haupt, 7–35. Golden, CO: Fulcrum, 1996.

Clifton-Soderstrom, Michelle A. *Angels, Worms, and Bogeys: The Christian Ethics of Pietism.* Eugene, OR: Wipf & Stock, 2010.

Clouse, Bonnidell. *Teaching for Moral Growth: A Guide for the Christian Community-Teachers, Parents, and Pastors.* Wheaton, IL: Victor, 1993.

Coalter, Milton J. *Gilbert Tennent, Son of Thunder: A Case Study of Continental Pietism's Impact on the First Great Awakening in the Middle Colonies.* New York: Greenwood, 1986.

Cochran, Elizabeth Agnew. "Ethics." In *The Oxford Handbook of Jonathan Edwards,* edited by Douglas A. Sweeney and Jan Stievermann, 281–95. New York: Oxford University Press, 2021.

Cochran, Joseph T. "Jonathan Edwards and His World of Harmony." *Jonathan Edwards Studies* 13 1–2 (2023) 23–44.

———. "Jonathan Edwards for the Next Generation." *Fides et Historia* 53 (2021) 1–9. New York: Oxford University Press, 2021.

———. Review of *Edwards the Mentor,* by Rhys S. Bezzant. www.pastortheologians.com/book-reviews-archive/2019/12/5/edwards-the-mentor-rhys-s-bezzant.

Coe, George Albert. *What Is Christian Education?* New York: C. Scribner's Sons, 1929.

Coffey, John. "Puritan Legacies." In *The Cambridge Companion to Puritanism,* edited by John Coffey and Paul C. H. Lim, 327–45. Cambridge: Cambridge University Press, 2008.

Coffey, John, and Paul C. H. Lim. "Introduction." In *The Cambridge Companion to Puritanism,* edited by John Coffey and Paul C. H. Lim, 1–15. Cambridge: Cambridge University Press, 2008.

Cohen, Charles L. "Conversion Among Puritans and Amerindians: A Theological and Cultural Perspective." In *Puritanism: Transatlantic Perspectives on a Seventeenth-Century Anglo-American Faith,* edited by Francis J. Bremer, 233–56. Boston: Massachusetts Historical Society, 1993.

Bibliography

Colacurcio, Michael J. "The Example of Edwards: Idealist Imagination and the Metaphysics of Sovereignty." In *Puritan Influences in American Literature*, edited by Eliot Emery, 55–106. Urbana: University of Illinois Press, 1979.

Coley, Kenneth S. *Teaching for Change: 8 Keys for Transformational Bible Studies with Teens*. Nashville: Randall House, 2017.

Coley, Kenneth S., et al. *Transformational Teaching: Instructional Designs for Christian Educators*. Brentwood, TN: B & H Academic, 2023.

Collins, Gary R. *Biblical Basis of Christian Counseling for People Helpers*. Colorado Springs, CO: NavPress, 1993.

Collinson, Patrick. *The Birthpangs of Protestant England: Religious and Cultural Change in the Sixteenth and Seventeenth Centuries*. London: Palgrave Macmillan, 1988.

———. *Elizabethans*. London: Cambridge University Press, 2003.

———. *The Puritan Character: Polemics and Polarities in Early Seventeenth-Century English Culture*. Los Angeles: University of California, 1989.

Colwell, S. "The Glory of God's Justice and the Glory of God's Grace: Contemporary Reflections on the Doctrine of Hell in the Teaching of Jonathan Edwards." *Evangelical Quarterly* 67 (1995) 291–308.

Colwill, Deborah A. "Dialogical Learning and a New Epistemology: Analysis of Cultural and Educational Shifts from Modernity toward Postmodernity." PhD diss., Trinity International University, 2005.

"Comenius." *New World Encyclopedia*. Updated January 8, 2024. https://www.newworldencyclopedia.org/p/index.php?title=Comenius&oldid=1132504.

Comenius, John Amos. *The Great Didactic*. Translated by M. W. Keatinge. London: Adam and Charles Black, 1907.

———. *On Education*. New York: Teachers College Press, Columbia University, 1967.

———. *Outline of a Pansophic School (Delineatio)*. In *Opera Didactia Omnia*, 35–60. Pragae: Bohemoslovenicae, 1957.

———. *The Orbis Pictus of John Amos Comenius*. Syracuse, NY: C. W. Bardeen, 1887.

———. *Pampaedia, or Universal Education*. Translated by A. M. Dobbie. Dover: Buckland, 1986.

———. *A Patterne of Universall Knowledge, in a Plaine and True Draught*. Translated by Jeremy Collier. Cambridge: T. H. and Jo Collins, 1651.

———. *Via Lucis*. Translated by E. T. Campagnac. Liverpool: University of Liverpool Press, 1938.

Commager, Henry Steele. *The Empire of Reason: How Europe Imagined and America Realized the Enlightenment*. Garden City, NY: Doubleday, 1977.

Conforti, Joseph A. "The Invention of the Great Awakening, 1795–1842." *Early American Literature* 26 (1991) 99.

———. *Jonathan Edwards, Religious Tradition, and American Culture*. Chapel Hill: University of North Carolina Press, 1995.

———. "Samuel Hopkins and the New Divinity: Theology, Ethics, and Social Reform in Eighteenth-Century New England." *William and Mary Quarterly* 34 (1977) 572–89.

———. *Samuel Hopkins and the New Divinity Movement*. Eugene, OR: Wipf & Stock, 1981.

Cooey, Paula M. *Jonathan Edwards on Nature and Destiny: A Systematic Analysis*. Lewiston, NY: Edwin Mellen, 1985.

Cooley, Daniel. "The New England Theology and the Atonement: Jonathan Edwards to Edwards Amasa Park." PhD diss., Trinity Evangelical Divinity School, 2014.

Bibliography

Coome, Christopher. "Putting Edwards to Work: Marsden, McDermott, and the Crisis of Modernity." Review Essay of George Marsden, *An Infinite Fountain of Light: Jonathan Edwards for the Twenty-First Century*, and Gerald R. McDermott, *Everyday Glory: The Revelation of God in All Reality. Jonathan Edwards Studies* 14 (2024) 122–29.

Cooper, Anthony Ashley. *An Inquiry Concerning Virtue, or Merit*. Manchester, UK: Manchester University Press, 1977.

Copan, Paul. "Jonathan Edwards' Philosophical Influences: Lockean or Malebranchean?" *Journal of the Evangelical Theological Society* 44 (2001) 107–24.

Cotton, John. *Spiritual Milk for Boston Babes, Drawn Out of the Breasts of Both Testaments*. Boston: Printed by S[amuel] G[reen] for Hezekiah Usher, 1656.

Crabtree, Arthur Bamford. *Jonathan Edwards' View of Man: A Study in Eighteenth-Century Calvinism*. Wallington, GB: Religious Education, 1948.

Cragg, Gerald R. *The Church and the Age of Reason (1648–1789)*. Baltimore, MD: Penguin, 1960.

———. *Reason and Authority in the Eighteenth Century*. Reprint, Cambridge: Cambridge University Press, 2013.

———. "Training in the Ministry—The Older Tradition." *Andover Newton Quarterly* 8 (1968) 226–29.

Cremin, Lawrence A. *American Education: The Colonial Experience, 1607–1783*. New York: Harper & Row, 1970.

Cressy, David. "Books as Totems in Seventeenth-Century England and New England." *Journal of Library History* 21 (1986) 92–106.

Crisp, Oliver D. "Jonathan Edwards's Ontology: A Critique of Sang Hyun Lee's Dispositional Account of Edwardsian Metaphysics" *Religious Studies* 46 (2010) 1–20.

———. "The Moral Government of God: Jonathan Edwards and Joseph Bellamy on the Atonement." In *After Jonathan Edwards: The Courses of the New England Theology*, edited by Oliver D. Crisp and Douglas A. Sweeney, 78–89. New York: Oxford University Press, 2012.

———. "On the Theological Pedigree of Jonathan Edwards' Doctrine of Imputation." *Scottish Journal of Theology* 56 (2003) 308–27.

———. "Preface." In *Jonathan Edwards Among the Theologians*, by Oliver D. Crisp, xiii–xx. Grand Rapids: Eerdmans, 2015.

Crisp, Oliver D., and Douglas A. Sweeney, eds. *After Jonathan Edwards: The Courses of the New England Theology*. New York: Oxford University Press, 2012.

———. "Introduction." In *After Jonathan Edwards: The Courses of New England Theology*, edited by Oliver D. Crisp and Douglas A. Sweeney, 1–14. New York: Oxford University Press, 2012.

———. "Postscript." In *After Jonathan Edwards: The Courses of New England Theology*, edited by Oliver D. Crisp and Douglas A. Sweeney, 254–57. New York: Oxford University Press, 2012.

Crocco, Stephen D. "Edwards's Intellectual Legacy." In *The Cambridge Companion to Jonathan Edwards*, edited by Stephen J. Stein, 300–24. New York: Cambridge University Press, 2007.

———. "Jonathan Edwards and Princeton." In *Jonathan Edwards as Contemporary: Essays in Honor of Sang Hyun Lee*, edited by Don Schweitzer, 240–55. New York: Peter Lang, 2010.

Bibliography

———. "Jonathan Edwards and Princeton." *Princeton Seminary Bulletin New Series* 24 (2003) 328–42.

Crockett, Bryan. "Geneva Bible." In *Puritans and Puritanism in Europe and America: A Comprehensive Encyclopedia*, edited by Francis J. Bremer and Tom Webster, 2:402–4. Santa Barbara, CA: ABC-CLIO, 2006.

Cubberley, Elwood P. *The History of Education: Educational Practice and Progress Considered as a Phase of the Development and Spread of Western Civilization.* New York: Houghton Mifflin Co., 1920.

———. *Readings in the History of Education.* New York: Houghton Mifflin Co., 1920.

———. *Public Education in the United States: A Study and Interpretation of American Educational History.* Rev. ed. New York: Houghton Mifflin, 1947.

Curti, Merle. *The Growth of American Thought.* 3rd ed. New York: Harper & Row, 1964.

Cuthbert, Christian. "'More Swiftly Propagating the Gospel': Jonathan Edwards, Col. John Stoddard, and the Invasion of Canada." In *Jonathan Edwards within the Enlightenment: Controversy, Experience, and Thought*, edited by John T. Lowe and Daniel Gullotta, 153–67. Göttingen: Vandenhoeck & Ruprecht, 2020.

Dahlquist, John Terrence. "Nathaniel Emmons: His Life and Work." PhD diss., Boston University, 1974.

Daley, Barbara. "A Case for Learner-Centered Teaching and Learning." *New Directions for Adult and Continuing Education* 98 (2003) 23–30.

Danaher, William J. "Beauty, Benevolence, and Virtue in Jonathan Edwards's *The Nature of True Virtue.*" *Journal of Religion* 87 (2007) 386–410.

Daniel, Stephen H. "Edwards as Philosopher." In *The Cambridge Companion to Jonathan Edwards*, edited by Stephen J. Stein, 162–80. New York: Cambridge University Press, 2007.

———. "Edwards' Occasionalism." In *Jonathan Edwards as Contemporary: Essays in Honor* of Sang Hyun Lee, edited by Don Schweitzer, 1–14. New York: Peter Lang, 2010.

———. "Introduction." In *The Philosophy of Jonathan Edwards: A Study in Divine Semiotics*, 1–10. Bloomington: Indiana University Press, 1994.

Daniels, Bruce Colin. *New England Nation: The Country the Puritans Built.* New York: Palgrave Macmillan, 2012.

———. *Puritans at Play: Leisure and Recreation in Colonial New England.* New York: St. Martin's, 1995.

Davenport, John. *God's Call to His People to Turn Unto Him.* Cambridge: Printed for S. G. and M. J. for John Usher of Boston, 1699

Davidson, Edward H. *Jonathan Edwards: The Narrative of a Puritan Mind.* Cambridge, MA: Harvard University Press, 1968.

———. "From Locke to Edwards." *Journal of the History of Ideas* 24 (1963) 355–72.

Davies, Ronald E. "Jonathan Edwards: Missionary Biographer, Theologian, Strategist, Administrator, Advocate–and Missionary" *International Bulletin of Mission Research* 21 (1997) 60–68.

———. "'Prepare Ye the Way of the Lord': The Missiological Thought and Practice of Jonathan Edwards (1703–1758)." PhD diss., Fuller Theological Seminary, 1989.

Davis, Donald G., and John Mark Tucker, *American Library History: A Comprehensive Guide to the Literature.* Santa Barbara, CA: ABC-CLIO, 1989.

Bibliography

De Castell, Suzanne, et al. "On Defining Literacy." In *Literacy, Society, and Schooling: A Reader*, edited by Suzanne de Castell et al., 3–14. Cambridge: Cambridge University Press, 1986.

Degler, Carl N. "Were the Puritans 'Puritanical'?" In *Out of Our Past: The Forces that Shaped Modern America*, 9–22. New York: Harper & Row, 1984.

Delattre, Roland A. *Beauty and Sensibility in the Thought of Jonathan Edwards*. Eugene, OR: Wipf & Stock, 2006.

———. "Recent Scholarship on Jonathan Edwards." *Religious Studies Review* 24 (1998) 369–75.

Delbanco, Andrew. "Cotton Mather (1663–1728)." In *The Puritans in America: A Narrative Anthology*, edited by Alan Heimert and Andrew Delbanco, 316–19. Cambridge, MA: Harvard University Press, 1985.

Delbanco, Andrew, ed. *Writing New England: An Anthology from the Puritans to the Present*. Cambridge, MA: Belknap Press of Harvard University Press, 2001.

Demos, John. *A Little Commonwealth: Family Life in Plymouth Colony*. New York: Oxford University Press, 1970.

DeWitt, John. "Jonathan Edwards: A Study: An Address Delivered at Stockbridge, Massachusetts October 5, 1903." *The Princeton Theological Review* (January 1904) 88–109.

Dexter, Edwin Grant. *A History of Education in the United States*. New York: Macmillan, 1904.

Dexter, Franklin Bowditch. *The Influence of the English Universities on the Development of New England*. Cambridge, MA: Harvard University Press, 1880.

Dockery, David S. "Christian Higher Education: An Introduction." In *Christian Higher Education: Faith, Teaching, and Learning in the Evangelical Tradition*, edited by David S. Dockery and Christopher W. Morgan, 17–37. Wheaton, IL: Crossway, 2018.

Dodds, Elisabeth D. *Marriage to a Difficult Man: The "Uncommon Union" of Jonathan and Sarah Edwards*. Philadelphia: Westminster, 1971.

Downing, L. "Occasionalism and Strict Mechanism: Malebranche, Berkeley, Fontenelle." *Early Modern Philosophy: Mind, Matter, and Metaphysics*, edited by C. Mercer and E. O'Neill, 206–30. Oxford: Oxford University Press, 2005.

Draper, Andrew Sloan. "Public School Pioneering in New York and Massachusetts." *Educational Review* 5 (1893) 345–62.

Draper, Mark. "The Millennium as a Motivation for the Social Reform Activity of Albert Barnes." PhD diss., Trinity International University, 2014.

Dreisbach, Daniel L. "The Bible and the Political Culture of the American Founding." In *Faith and the Founders of the American Republic*, edited by Daniel L. Dreisbach and Mark David Hall, 144–73. Oxford: Oxford University Press, 2014.

Dreisbach, Daniel L., and Mark David Hall. "Introduction." In *Faith and the Founders of the American Republic*, edited by Daniel L. Dreisbach and Mark David Hall, 1–10. Oxford: Oxford University Press, 2014.

Drucker, Peter F. *The New Realities*. New Brunswick, NJ: Transaction, 2003.

Dyrness, William, and Christi Wells. "Aesthetics." In *The Oxford Handbook of Jonathan Edwards*, edited by Douglas A. Sweeney and Jan Stievermann, 296–308. New York: Oxford University Press, 2021.

Bibliography

Dupré, Louis. "A Definition and a Provisional Justification." In *The Enlightenment and the Intellectual Foundations of Modern Culture*, 1–7. New Haven, CT: Yale University Press, 2008.

Dwight, Sereno Edwards. *Life of President Edwards*. New York: G. & C. & H. Carvill, 1830.

———. "Memoirs of Jonathan Edwards, A. M." In *The Works of Jonathan Edwards, A M . . . and a Memoir by Sereno E. Dwight*, edited by E. Hickman. London: Ball, Arnold, and Co., 1840.

Eames, Wilberforce. Review of *The New England Primer: A History of its Origin and Development*, edited Paul Leicester Ford. *American Historical Review* 3 (1898) 372–73.

Eavey, C. B. *History of Christian Education*. Chicago: Moody, 1964.

Eberling, Eric R. "Latin Grammar Schools." In *Historical Dictionary of American Education*, edited by Richard J. Altenbaugh, 210. Westport, CT: Greenwood, 1999.

———. "Massachusetts Education Laws of 1642, 1647, and 1648." In *Historical Dictionary of American Education*, edited by Richard J. Altenbaugh, 225–26. Westport, CT: Greenwood, 1999.

Edwards, Jonathan. "1003. No Text." In *Works of Jonathan Edwards Online*, edited by Jonathan Edwards Center, 69:n.d. http://edwards.yale.edu.

———. "1225. No text. Fragment: 'Tis the will of Christ that all nations should be taught'; on back of fragment of letter from Gideon Hawley, Dec. 28, 1756." In *Works of Jonathan Edwards Online*, 25:759–60, edited by Wilson H. Kimnach. http://edwards.yale.edu.

———. "A222. Letter to Thomas Foxcroft, February 11, 1757." In *Works of Jonathan Edwards Online*, edited by Jonathan Edwards Center, 32:n.d. http://edwards.yale.edu.

———. "Approaching the End of God's Grand Design." In *Works of Jonathan Edwards*, edited by Wilson H. Kimnach, 25:116, 117. New Haven, CT: Yale University Press, 2006.

———. "Author's Preface." In *Works of Jonathan Edwards Online*, edited by Norman Pettit, 7:89–98. http://edwards.yale.edu.

———. "Beauty of the World." In *Works of Jonathan Edwards*, edited by Wallace E. Anderson, 6:306–7. New Haven, CT: Yale University Press, 1980.

———. The "Blank Bible." In *Works of Jonathan Edwards Online*, edited by Stephen J. Stein, 24:458. http://edwards.yale.edu.

———. *Catalogues of Books*. In *Works of Jonathan Edwards Online*, edited by Peter J. Thuesen, 26:39, 75, 165, 182, 185, 197, 198. http://edwards.yale.edu.

———. "Chapter III. Concerning the Secondary and Inferior Kind of Beauty." In *Works of Jonathan Edwards*, edited by Paul Ramsey, 8:561. New Haven, CT: Yale University Press, 1989.

———. "Chapter IV." In *Works of Jonathan Edwards Online*, edited by Clyde. A. Holbrook, 3:424. http://edwards.yale.edu.

———. "Chapter IV: Literary Theory and Practice." In *Works of Jonathan Edwards Online*, edited by Wilson H. Kimnach, 10:195. http://edwards.yale.edu.

———. "Children Ought to Love the Lord Jesus Christ Above All." In *Works of Jonathan Edwards Online*, edited by Harry S. Stout, 22:167–80. http://edwards.yale.edu.

Bibliography

———. "CHRISTIAN KNOWLEDGE." *Sermons, Series II, 1739.* In *Works of Jonathan Edwards Online,* edited by Jonathan Edwards Center, 54:n.d. http://edwards.yale.edu.

———. "The Church's Marriage to Her Sons, and to Her God." In *Works of Jonathan Edwards,* edited by Wilson H. Kimnach, 25:169-87. New Haven, CT: Yale University Press, 20

———. "Conclusion." In *Works of Jonathan Edwards Online,* edited by Clyde A. Holbrook, 3:437. http://edwards.yale.edu.

———. "Controversies" Notebook. In *Works of Jonathan Edwards Online,* edited by Jonathan Edwards Center, 27:4-6, 10b, 11a, 15, 33, 51, 56, 59-60, 63, 65-6, 69, 73, 80, 87. http://edwards.yale.edu.

———. *Diary and Memorandum Book, 1733-1757.* Box 21, f. 1267, *Jonathan Edwards Collection,* Gen. MSS 151, Beinecke Library, Yale University. www.collections.library.yale.edu/catalog2026515.

———. "Diary: February 5, 1723/24." In *Works of Jonathan Edwards Online,* edited by George S. Claghorn, 16:784. http://edwards.yale.edu.

———. "Discourse on the Trinity." In *The Works of Jonathan Edwards Online,* edited by Sang Hyun Lee, 21:116, 141, 143. http://edwards.yale.edu.

———. "Dissertation I. Concerning the End for which God Created the World. Chapter Two, Section VII." In *The Works of Jonathan Edwards Online,* edited by Paul Ramsey, 8:531. http://edwards.yale.edu.

———. "Dissertation II. The Nature of True Virtue." In *Works of Jonathan Edwards Online,* edited by Paul Ramsey, 8:539-627. http://edwards.yale.edu.

———. "A Divine and Supernatural Light." In *The Sermons of Jonathan Edwards: A Reader,* edited by Wilson H. Kimnach et al., 121-40. New Haven, CT: Yale University Press, 1999.

———. "A Divine and Supernatural Light." In *Works of Jonathan Edwards Online,* edited by Mark Valeri, 17:408-27. http://edwards.yale.edu.

———. "Divine Love Alone Lasts Eternally." In *Works of Jonathan Edwards,* edited by Paul Ramsey, 8:363. New Haven, CT: Yale University Press, 1989.

———. "The Duty of Hearkening to God's Voice." In *Works of Jonathan Edwards,* edited by Wilson H. Kimnach, 10:440-41. New Haven, CT: Yale University Press, 1992.

———. "Early Piety Is Especially Acceptable to God." In *To the Rising Generation: Addresses Given to Children and Young Adults,* 1-7. Lake Mary, FL: Soli Deo Gloria, 2005.

———. *Ecclesiastical Writings.* In *Works of Jonathan Edwards Online,* edited by David D. Hall, 12: 73-77, 351-497. http://edwards.yale.edu.

———. "The End of the Wicked Contemplated by the Righteous." In *Works of Jonathan Edwards Online,* edited by Harry S. Stout, 13:56. http://edwards.yale.edu.

———. "The Excellency of Christ." In *Works of Jonathan Edwards Online,* edited by M. X. Lesser, 19:563-95. http://edwards.yale.edu.

———. *A Faithful Narrative of the Surprising Work of God.* London: John Oswald, 1737. Boston: S. Kneeland, 1738.

———. "A Farewell Sermon Preached At The First Precinct In Northampton . . . " In *Works of Jonathan Edwards Online,* edited by Wilson H. Kimnach, 25:466-84. http://edwards.yale.edu.

———. *The Great Awakening.* In *Works of Jonathan Edwards Online,* edited by C. C. Goen, 4:546-47. http://edwards.yale.edu.

Bibliography

———. "Freedom of the Will." In *Works of Jonathan Edwards*, edited by Paul Ramsey, 1:131. New Haven, CT: Yale University Press, 2009.

———. *The Great Christian Doctrine of Original Sin Defended*. In *Works of Jonathan Edwards Online*, edited by Clyde A. Holbrook, 3:102–437. http://edwards.yale.edu.

———. "God Glorified in Man's Dependence." In *Works of Jonathan Edwards Online*, edited by Mark Valeri, 17:208. http://edwards.yale.edu.

———. "God Is Infinitely Strong." In *Works of Jonathan Edwards Online*, edited by Wilson H. Kimnach, 25:641–46. http://edwards.yale.edu.

———. "God Is Very Angry at the Sins of Children." In *To the Rising Generation: Addresses Given to Children and Young Adults*, edited by Don Kistler, 57. Lake Mary, FL: Soli Deo Gloria, 2005.

———. "God's Use of Affliction." In *Works of Jonathan Edwards Online*, edited by Wilson H. Kimnach, 25:646–53. http://edwards.yale.edu.

———. "[7] Gravity [*Unnumbered Series*]." In *Works of Jonathan Edwards Online*, edited by Wallace E. Anderson, 6:265–66. http://edwards.yale.edu.

———. "The Great Awakening." In *Works of Jonathan Edwards Online*, edited by C. C. Goen, 4:199–205. http://edwards.yale.edu.

———. "Heeding the Word, and Losing It." In *Works of Jonathan Edwards Online*, edited by M. X. Lesser, 19:46. New Haven, CT: Yale University Press, 2001.

———. "Honey from the Rock." In *Works of Jonathan Edwards Online*, edited by Mark Valeri, 17:136. http://edwards.yale.edu.

———. "Images of Divine Things 7." In *Works of Jonathan Edwards Online*, edited by Wallace E. Anderson et al., 11:328. http://edwards.yale.edu.

———. *Images or Shadows of Divine Things*. Edited by Perry Miller. New Haven, CT: Yale University Press, 1948.

———. "The Importance and Advantage of a Thorough Knowledge of Divine Truth." In *The Sermons of Jonathan Edwards: A Reader*, edited by Wilson H. Kimnach et al., 26–48. New Haven, CT: Yale University Press, 1999.

———. "The Importance and Advantage of a Thorough Knowledge of Divine Truth." In *Works of Jonathan Edwards Online*, edited by Harry S. Stout, 22:83–102. http://edwards.yale.edu.

———. "A Letter to a Young Convert." In *To the Rising Generation: Addresses Given to Children and Young Adults*, edited by Don Kistler, 157–61. Lake Mary, FL: Soli Deo Gloria, 2005.

———. *Letters and Personal Writings*. In *Works of Jonathan Edwards Online Volume 16*, edited by George S. Claghorn. http://edwards.yale.edu.

———. "Light in a Dark World, a Dark Heart." In *Works of Jonathan Edwards Online*, edited by M. X. Lesser, 19:710. http://edwards.yale.edu.

———. "The Mind." In *Works of Jonathan Edwards Online*, edited by Wallace E. Anderson, 6:333–86. http://edwards.yale.edu.

———. "The Mind [1]. Excellency." In *Works of Jonathan Edwards Online*, edited by Wallace E. Anderson, 6:332–38. http://edwards.yale.edu.

———. "The Mind [10]." In *Works of Jonathan Edwards Online*, edited by Wallace E. Anderson, 6:342. http://edwards.yale.edu.

———. "The Mind [39]. CONSCIENCE." In *Works of Jonathan Edwards Online*, edited by Wallace E. Anderson, 6:356. http://edwards.yale.edu.

Bibliography

———. "The Mind [42]." In *Works of Jonathan Edwards Online*, edited by Wallace E. Anderson, 6:360–61. http://edwards.yale.edu.

———. "The Mind [45]. Excellence. 9." In *Works of Jonathan Edwards Online*, edited by Wallace E. Anderson, 6:364. http://edwards.yale.edu.

———. "The Mind [61]. SUBSTANCE." In *Works of Jonathan Edwards Online*, edited by Wallace E. Anderson, 6:376-80. http://edwards.yale.edu.

———. "The Mind [71]." In *Works of Jonathan Edwards Online*, edited by Wallace E. Anderson, 329. http://edwards.yale.edu.

———. "Miscellany 40. Ministers." In *Works of Jonathan Edwards Online*, edited by Thomas A. Schafer, 13:222. http://edwards.yale.edu.

———. "Miscellany 94. TRINITY." In *Works of Jonathan Edwards Online*, edited by Thomas S. Schafer, 13:262. New Haven, CT: Yale University Press, 1994. http://edwards.yale.edu.

———. "Miscellany 96. Trinity." In *Works of Jonathan Edwards Online*, edited by Harry S. Stout, 13:263–64. http://edwards.yale.edu.

———. "Miscellany 104. End of the Creation." In *Works of Jonathan Edwards Online*, edited by Harry S. Stout, 13:272. http://edwards.yale.edu.

———. "Miscellany 119. Types." In *Works of Jonathan Edwards Online*, edited by Harry S. Stout, 13:284. http://edwards.yale.edu.

———. "Miscellany 188. HEAVEN." In *Works of Jonathan Edwards Online*, edited by Harry S. Stout, 13:331. http://edwards.yale.edu.

———. "Miscellany 210. Spirit of God." In *Works of Jonathan Edwards Online*, edited by Harry S. Stout, 13:n.d. http://edwards.yale.edu.

———. "Miscellany 271. End of the Creation." In *Works of Jonathan Edwards Online*, edited by Harry S. Stout, 13:374. http://edwards.yale.edu.

———. "Miscellany 301. SIN AND ORIGINAL SIN." In *Works of Jonathan Edwards Online*, edited by Harry S. Stout, 13:387–89. http://edwards.yale.edu.

———. "Miscellany 302. Conversion." In *Works of Jonathan Edwards Online*, edited by Harry S. Stout, 13:389. http://edwards.yale.edu.

———. "Miscellany 332. End of the Creation." In *Works of Jonathan Edwards Online*, edited by Harry S. Stout, 13:410. http://edwards.yale.edu.

———. "Miscellany 362. Trinity." In *Works of Jonathan Edwards Online*, edited by Harry S. Stout, 13:434. http://edwards.yale.edu.

———. "Miscellany 370. Trinity." In *Works of Jonathan Edwards Online*, edited by Harry S. Stout, 13:442. http://edwards.yale.edu.

———. "Miscellany 405. Trinity." In *Works of Jonathan Edwards Online*, edited by Harry S. Stout, 13:468. http://edwards.yale.edu.

———. "Miscellany 410. FAITH." In *Works of Jonathan Edwards Online*, edited by Harry S. Stout, 13:470–71. http://edwards.yale.edu.

———. "Miscellany 448. End of the Creation." In *Works of Jonathan Edwards Online*, edited by Harry S. Stout, 13:495. http://edwards.yale.edu.

———. "Miscellany 539. Means of Grace." In *Works of Jonathan Edwards Online*, edited by Ava Chamberlain, 18:84, 88. http://edwards.yale.edu.

———. "Miscellany 553. End of the Creation." In *Works of Jonathan Edwards Online*, edited by Ava Chamberlain, 18:97. http://edwards.yale.edu.

———. "Miscellany 674. Conviction. Humiliation." In *Works of Jonathan Edwards Online*, edited by Ava Chamberlain, 18:235.

Bibliography

———. "Miscellany 702. Work of Creation. Providence. Redemption." In *Works of Jonathan Edwards Online*, edited by Ava Chamberlain, 18:284–309.

———. "Miscellany 706. Sin Against the Holy Ghost, Why Unpardonable." In *Works of Jonathan Edwards Online*, edited by Ava Chamberlain, 18:324. http://edwards.yale.edu.

———. "Miscellany 769." In *Works of Jonathan Edwards Online*, edited by Ava Chamberlain, 18:415–18. http://edwards.yale.edu.

———. "Miscellany 782. Ideas. Sense of the Heart. Spiritual Knowledge or Conviction. Faith." In *Works of Jonathan Edwards Online*, edited by Ava Chamberlain, 18:452–66. http://edwards.yale.edu.

———. "Miscellany 849." In *Works of Jonathan Edwards Online*, edited by Amy Plantinga Pauw, 20:76. http://edwards.yale.edu.

———. "Miscellany 880." In *Works of Jonathan Edwards Online*, edited by Amy Plantinga Pauw, 20:121–39. http://edwards.yale.edu.

———. "Miscellany 931. Hell Torments. Conflagration." In *Works of Jonathan Edwards Online*, edited by Amy Plantinga Pauw, 20:185. http://edwards.yale.edu.

———. "Miscellany 962. Traditions of the Heathen." In *Works of Jonathan Edwards Online*, edited by Amy Plantinga Pauw, 20:245. http://edwards.yale.edu.

———. "Miscellany 976. Being of God. Unity of the World. Unity of God." In *Works of Jonathan Edwards Online*, edited by Amy Plantinga Pauw, 20:280–86. http://edwards.yale.edu.

———. "Miscellany 984. Christian Religion. Evidences That the World of Mankind Cannot be Much Older Than is Represented in Scripture." In *Works of Jonathan Edwards Online*, edited by Amy Plantinga Pauw, 20:309. http://edwards.yale.edu.

———. "Miscellany 986. Revealed Religion." In *Works of Jonathan Edwards Online*, edited by Amy Plantinga Pauw, 20:310. http://edwards.yale.edu.

———. "Miscellany 1077. GOD'S HOLINESS." In *Works of Jonathan Edwards Online*, edited by Amy Plantinga Pauw, 20:460. http://edwards.yale.edu.

———. "Miscellany 1084. End of the Creation." In *Works of Jonathan Edwards Online*, edited by Amy Plantinga Pauw, 20:467. http://edwards.yale.edu.

———. "Miscellany 1094. End of the Creation. Glory of God." In *Works of Jonathan Edwards Online*, edited by Amy Plantinga Pauw, 20:483. http://edwards.yale.edu.

———. "Miscellany 1226." In *Works of Jonathan Edwards Online*, edited by Douglas A. Sweeney, 23:158. http://edwards.yale.edu.

———. "Miscellany 1253. Trinity." In *Works of Jonathan Edwards Online*, edited by Douglas A. Sweeney, 23:186–88. http://edwards.yale.edu.

———. "Miscellany 1263. God's Immediate and Arbitrary Operation." In *Works of Jonathan Edwards Online*, edited by Douglas A. Sweeney, 23:201–12. http://edwards.yale.edu.

———. "Miscellany n. Damnation of Infants." In *Works of Jonathan Edwards Online*, edited by Harry S. Stout, 13:169. http://edwards.yale.edu.

———. "Miscellany pp. God." In *Works of Jonathan Edwards Online*, edited by Harry S. Stout, 13:188. http://edwards.yale.edu.

———. "The Most Direct Way to Happiness." In *To the Rising Generation: Addresses Given to Children and Young Adults*, edited by Don Kistler, 53–55. Lake Mary, FL: Soli Deo Gloria, 2005.

———. "Miscellany qq. Ministers." In *Works of Jonathan Edwards Online*, edited by Harry S. Stout, 13:188. http://edwards.yale.edu.

Bibliography

———. "Much in Deeds of Charity." In *Sermons of Jonathan Edwards: A Reader*, edited by Wilson H. Kimnach et al., 197–211. New Haven, CT: Yale University Press, 1999.

———. "The Nature of True Virtue." In *Works of Jonathan Edwards Online*, edited by Paul Ramsey, 8:539–627. http://edwards.yale.edu.

———. "Note 235." In *Works of Jonathan Edwards Online*, edited by Stephen J. Stein, 15:185-87. http://edwards.yale.edu.

———. "Note 399. Genesis 3:20." In *Works of Jonathan Edwards Online*, edited by Stephen J. Stein, 15:396–99. http://edwards.yale.edu.

———. "Notes on Knowledge and Existence." In *Works of Jonathan Edwards Online*, edited by Wallace E. Anderson, 6:399. http://edwards.yale.edu.

———. "Of Atoms." In *Works of Jonathan Edwards Online*, edited by Wallace E. Anderson, 6:209–19. http://edwards.yale.edu.

———. Of Being." In *Works of Jonathan Edwards Online*, edited by Wallace E. Anderson, 6:203–8. http://edwards.yale.edu.

———. "Of the Rainbow." In *Works of Jonathan Edwards Online*, edited by Wallace E. Anderson, 6:298–302. http://edwards.yale.edu.

———. "Part III: First Sign." In *Works of Jonathan Edwards Online*, edited by Paul Ramsey, 2:208–39. http://edwards.yale.edu.

———. "Personal Narrative." In *Works of Jonathan Edwards Online*, edited by George S. Claghorn, 16:801–4. http://edwards.yale.edu.

———. "The Pleasantness of Religion." In *Works of Jonathan Edwards Online*, edited by Kenneth P. Minkema, 14:102. http://edwards.yale.edu.

———. "Profession of Faith, Two Drafts." N.d., 21/1245, *Jonathan Edwards Collection*, Gen. MSS 151, Beinecke Library, Yale University. www.collections.library.yale.edu/catalog2026514.

———. "Profitable Hearers of the Word." In *Works of Jonathan Edwards Online*, edited by Kenneth P. Minkema, 4:246–77. http://edwards.yale.edu.

———. "Ps 119:60a (n.d. [Summer 1724])." In *Works of Jonathan Edwards Online*, edited by Kenneth P. Minkema, 14:543. http://edwards.yale.edu.

———. "The Pure in Heart Blessed." In *Works of Jonathan Edwards Online*, edited by Mark Valeri, 17:61, 67. http://edwards.yale.edu.

———. "Questions for Young People." In *Works of Jonathan Edwards Online*, edited by Jonathan Edwards Center, 39:n.d. http://edwards.yale.edu.

———. "Questions on Theological Subjects." In *Works of Jonathan Edwards Online*, edited by Jonathan Edwards Center, 39:n.d. http://edwards.yale.edu.

———. "The Reality of Conversion." In *The Sermons of Jonathan Edwards: A Reader*, edited by Wilson H. Kimnach et al., 83–104. New Haven, CT: Yale University Press, 1999.

———. *Religious Affections*. In *Works of Jonathan Edwards Online*, edited by John E. Smith, 2:201, 205–39, 256. http://edwards.yale.edu.

———. "Resolutions." In *Works of Jonathan Edwards Online*, edited by George S. Claghorn, 16:753–59. http://edwards.yale.edu.

———. "Sermon 66. Jas. 1:17." In *Works of Jonathan Edwards Online*, edited by Jonathan Edwards Center, 43:n.d. http://edwards.yale.edu.

———. "Sermon 086. *Luke 14:16*." In *Works of Jonathan Edwards Online*, edited by Jonathan Edwards Center, 43:n.d. http://edwards.yale.edu.

Bibliography

———. "Sermon 105. Rev 3:15. Spring 1729." In *Works of Jonathan Edwards Online*, edited by Jonathan Edwards Center, 44:n.d. http://edwards.yale.edu.

———. "Sermon 110. On Job 31:3, 1729." In *Works of Jonathan Edwards Online*, edited by Wilson H. Kimnach, 10:195. http://edwards.yale.edu.

———. "Sermon 136. Job 1:5." In *Works of Jonathan Edwards Online*, edited by Kenneth P. Minkema, 14:549. http://edwards.yale.edu.

———. "Sermon 251. I Cor 8:13." In *Works of Jonathan Edwards Online*, edited by Jonathan Edwards Center, 47:n.d. http://edwards.yale.edu.

———. "Sermon 152. Mark 9:44." In *Works of Jonathan Edwards Online*, edited by Jonathan Edwards Center, 45:n.d. http://edwards.yale.edu.

———. "Sermon 274. Job 20:11, To the Young People at a Private [M]arch 1733 meeting." In *Works of Jonathan Edwards Online*, edited by Jonathan Edwards Center, 48:n.d. http://edwards.yale.edu.

———. "Sermon 297. Psalm 139:23-24. Sept. 1733." In *Works of Jonathan Edwards Online*, edited by Mark Valeri, 17:457. http://edwards.yale.edu.

———. "Sermon 307. Ecclesiastes 9:10(b). 'Persons ought to do what they can for their salvation.' Dec. 1733." In *Works of Jonathan Edwards Online*, edited by Jonathan Edwards Center, 48:nd. http://edwards.yale.edu.

———. "Sermon 323. Prov. 24:13-14(b)." In *Works of Jonathan Edwards Online*, edited by Jonathan Edwards Center, 49:n.d. http://edwards.yale.edu.

———. "Sermon 341. 2 Chronicles 34:2-3. 'Early piety is especially acceptable to God." Private meeting. Nov. 1734." In *Works of Jonathan Edwards Online*, edited by M. X. Lesser, 19:801. http://edwards.yale.edu.

———. "Sermon 345. John 3:8. Decem[ber] 1734." In *Works of Jonathan Edwards Online*, edited by Jonathan Edwards Center, 49:n.d. http://edwards.yale.edu.

———. "Sermon 373. Rom. 2:10. Decem[ber] 17, 1735." In *Works of Jonathan Edwards Online*, edited by Jonathan Edwards Center., 50:n.d. http://edwards.yale.edu.

———. "Sermon 525. Heb. 5:12. Christian Knowledge." In *Works of Jonathan Edwards Online*, edited by Jonathan Edwards Center, 54:n.d. http://edwards.yale.edu.

———. "Sermon 585. Is. 33:14(b)." In *Works of Jonathan Edwards Online*, edited by Jonathan Edwards Center, 56:n.d. http://edwards.yale.edu.

———. "Sermon 592. 'God is very angry at the sins of children.' Feb. 1741. To the children at a private meeting." In *Works of Jonathan Edwards Online*, edited by Harry S. Stout, 22:544. http://edwards.yale.edu.

———. "Sermon 795. Galatians 5:17. Sept. 1745." In *Works of Jonathan Edwards Online*, edited by Wilson H. Kimnach, 25:n.d. http://edwards.yale.edu.

———. "Sermon 742. Jude 6." In *Works of Jonathan Edwards Online*, edited by Jonathan Edwards Center, 62:n.d. http://edwards.yale.edu.

———. "Sermon 891. Eph. 6:4. Quarterly Lecture Feb. 1747/8." In *Works of Jonathan Edwards Online*, edited by Jonathan Edwards Center, 66:n.d. http://edwards.yale.edu.

———. "Sermon 973. Matt 7:13-14(b). Jan. 1751. Stockbridge Indians." In *Works of Jonathan Edwards Online*, edited by Wilson H. Kimnach, 25:739. http://edwards.yale.edu.

———. "Sermon 975. Mark 16:15-16. Jan. 1751. Stockbridge Indians. Repreached Feb. 1752 to Mohawks." Published as "He That Believeth Shall Be Saved." In *The Sermons of Jonathan Edwards: A Reader*, edited by Wilson H. Kimnach et al., 111-20. New Haven, CT: Yale University Press, 1999.

Bibliography

———. "Sermon 998, on Gen 1:27, preached August 1751 to Stockbridge Indians and Mohawks." In *Works of Jonathan Edwards Online*, edited by Wilson H. Kimnach, 25:739. http://edwards.yale.edu.

———. "Sermon 1007. Oct. 1751. Stockbridge." In *Works of Jonathan Edwards Online*, edited by Wilson H. Kimnach, 25:742. http://edwards.yale.edu.

———. "Sermon 1008. Luke 24:47. Oct. 1751. Stockbridge Indians and Mohawks." In *Works of Jonathan Edwards Online*, edited by Wilson H. Kimnach, 25:742. http://edwards.yale.edu.

———. "Sermon 1031. Ps. 27:4(b). 'Tis the heart of a truly good man to love God above all things.' Mar. 1752. Lecture before sacrament. Stockbridge Indians." In *Works of Jonathan Edwards Online*, edited by Wilson H. Kimnach, 25:743. http://edwards.yale.edu.

———. "Sermon 1082. Acts 14:26-27. Private Meeting on Occasion of Mssrs W——ge's & Hawley going into the Country of the Six Nations." In *Works of Jonathan Edwards Online*, edited by Jonathan Edwards Center, 71:n.d. http://edwards.yale.edu.

———. "Sermon 1152. Matt 1:21. Sept. 1755. Stockbridge Indians." In *Works of Jonathan Edwards Online*, 25:752-53. http://edwards.yale.edu.

———. "Sermon 1166. Proverbs 19:8(b)." In *Works of Jonathan Edwards Online*, edited by Wilson H. Kimnach, 25:754. http://edwards.yale.edu.

———. "Sermon 1171. Prov. 8:17(b)." In *Works of Jonathan Edwards Online*, edited by Jonathan Edwards Center, 73:n.d. http://edwards.yale.edu.

———. "Sermon 1175. Psalms 27:4(c). Oct. 1756. Stockbridge Indians." In *Works of Jonathan Edwards Online*, edited by Wilson H. Kimnach, 25:753. http://edwards.yale.edu.

———. "Sermon Three." In *Works of Jonathan Edwards Online*, edited by John F. Wilson, 9:155. http://edwards.yale.edu.

———. "Sermon Twenty-Four." In *Works of Jonathan Edwards Online*, edited by John F. Wilson, 9:433-34. http://edwards.yale.edu.

———. *Sermons and Discourses, 1739-1742*. In *Works of Jonathan Edwards Online*, edited by Harry S. Stout, 22:n.d. http://edwards.yale.edu.

———. *Sermons and Discourses, 1743-1758*. In *Works of Jonathan Edwards Online*, edited by Wilson H. Kimnach, 25:n.d. http://edwards.yale.edu.

———. "Sin and Wickedness Bring Calamity and Misery on a People." In *Works of Jonathan Edwards Online*, edited by Kenneth P. Minkema, 14:487-505. http://edwards.yale.edu.

———. "The Sins of Youth Go with Them to Eternity." In *To the Rising Generation: Addresses Given to Children and Young Adults*, edited by Don Kistler, 35. Lake Mary, FL: Soli Deo Gloria, 2005.

———. "Sinners in Zion." In *Works of Jonathan Edwards Online*, edited by Harry S. Stout, 22:283, 284. http://edwards.yale.edu.

———. "Some Thoughts Concerning the Revival: Part III." In *Works of Jonathan Edwards Online*, edited by C. C. Goen, 4:394. http://edwards.yale.edu.

———. "Some Thoughts Concerning the Revival: Part IV." In *Works of Jonathan Edwards Online*, edited by C. C. Goen, 4:528. http://edwards.yale.edu.

———. "Subjects to be Handled in the Treatise on the Mind." In *Works of Jonathan Edwards Online*, edited by Wallace E. Anderson, 6:390. http://edwards.yale.edu.

Bibliography

———. "The Theological Questions of President Edwards, Senior, and Dr. Edwards, His Son." In *Works of Jonathan Edwards Online*, 39:n.d. http://edwards.yale.edu.

———. "The Things That Belong To True Religion." In *Works of Jonathan Edwards Online*, edited by Wilson H. Kimnach, 25:570–74. http://edwards.yale.edu.

———. "Things to be Considered an(d) Written Fully About, [*Long Series*]." In *Works of Jonathan Edwards Online*, edited by Wallace E. Anderson, 6:231. http://edwards.yale.edu.

———. "The Time of Youth Is the Best Time to Be Improved for Religious Purposes." In *To the Rising Generation: Addresses Given to Children and Young Adults*, 12–25. Lake Mary, FL: Soli Deo Gloria, 2005.

———. "To the Mohawks at the Treaty, August 16, 1751." In *The Sermons of Jonathan Edwards: A Reader*, edited by Wilson H. Kimnach et al., 105–11. New Haven, CT: Yale University Press, 1999.

———. "To a Singing Teacher. Windsor. June 4, 1753." In *Works of Jonathan Edwards Online*, edited by George S. Claghorn, 16:597. http://edwards.yale.edu.

———. "A Treatise Concerning Religious Affections." In *A Jonathan Edwards Reader*, edited by John E. Smith et al., 137–71. New Haven, CT: Yale University Press, 1995.

———. "The True Excellency of a Minister of the Gospel (August 30, 1744)." In *Works of Jonathan Edwards Online*, edited by Wilson H. Kimnach, 25:85–103. http://edwards.yale.edu.

———. "Two Notable Converts." In *Works of Jonathan Edwards Online*, edited by C. C. Goen, 4:199–200. http://edwards.yale.edu.

———. "The Value of Salvation." In *Works of Jonathan Edwards Online*, edited by Wilson H. Kimnach, 10:309. http://edwards.yale.edu.

———. "A Warning to Professors [of Christianity]." In *The Works of President Edwards*, edited by Sereno Edwards Dwight, 4:531. New York: Leavitt & Allen 1856.

———. "Wicked Men's Slavery to Sin." In *Works of Jonathan Edwards Online*, edited by Wilson H. Kimnach, 10:347. http://edwards.yale.edu.

———. "Wisdom in the Contrivance of the World." In *Works of Jonathan Edwards Online*, edited by Wallace E. Anderson, 6:307–10. http://edwards.yale.edu.

Edwards, Jonathan, Jr. *Observations on the Language of the Muhhekaneew [Mohegan] Indians*. New Haven, CT: Printed by Josiah Meigs, 1788.

Edwards, Steve. "Affections." In *The Jonathan Edwards Encyclopedia*, edited by Harry S. Stout et al., 8–13. Grand Rapids: Eerdmans, 2017.

Edwards, Tryon. "A Memoir of His Life and Character." In *The Works of Joseph Bellamy, D. D., First Pastor of the Church in Bethlam [sic], Conn., with a Memoir of His Life and Character*, 1:lix. Boston: Doctrinal Tract and Book Society, 1853.

Elias, John L. *A History of Christian Education: Protestant, Catholic, and Orthodox Perspectives*. Malabar, FL: Krieger, 2002.

Eliot, John. *The Harmony of the Gospels*. Boston: Printed by John Foster, 1678.

———. *New Englands First Fruits*. Printed by R. O. and G. D. for Henry Overton, 1643.

Eliot, John, and Thomas Mayhew. *Tears of Repentance: Or, a further narrative of the Progress of the Gospel Amongst the Indians in New-England*. London: Peter Cole, 1653.

Eliot, Simon, and Beverly Stern. "Introduction." In *The Age of Enlightenment*, 1:1–5. London: Open University Press, 1979.

Bibliography

Elliott, Emory. *Power and the Pulpit in Puritan New England*. Princeton, NJ: Princeton University Press, 2015.

Elsbree, Oliver Wendell. "Samuel Hopkins and His Doctrine of Benevolence." *New England Quarterly* 8 (1935) 534–50.

Elwood, Douglas J. "Introduction: Edwards and the Third Way." In *The Philosophical Theology of Jonathan Edwards*, 1–11. New York: Columbia University Press, 1960.

Elwood, Douglas J. *The Philosophical Theology of Jonathan Edwards*. New York: Columbia University Press, 1960.

Emerson, Everett H. *English Puritanism from John Hooper to John Milton*. Durham, NC: Duke University Press, 1968.

———. *John Cotton*. New York: Twayne, 1965.

———. *Puritanism in America, 1620–1750*. Boston: G. K. Hall, 1977.

———. "Thomas Hooker: The Puritan as Theologian." *Anglican Theological Review* 49 (1967) 190–203.

Endy, Melvin B., Jr. "Theology and Learning in Early America." In *Schools of Thought in the Christian Tradition*, edited by Patrick Henry, 125–51. Philadelphia: Fortress, 1984.

Erdt, Terrence. "Art." In *The Jonathan Edwards Encyclopedia*, edited by Harry S. Stout et al., 38–40. Grand Rapids: Eerdmans, 2017.

———. *Jonathan Edwards: Art and the Sense of the Heart*. Amherst: University of Massachusetts Press, 1980.

Eusden, John Dykstra. "Introduction." In *The Marrow of Theology*, by William Ames, 1–66. Grand Rapids: Baker, 1968.

Everhard, Matthew. "Jonathan Edwards: An Intellect Precariously Astride Two Diverging Epochs." In *Jonathan Edwards within the Enlightenment: Controversy, Experience, and Thought*, edited by John T. Lowe and Daniel N. Gullotta, 317–34. Göttingen: Vandenhoeck & Ruprecht, 2020.

———. "Original Sin [Doctrine]." In *The Jonathan Edwards Encyclopedia*, edited by Harry S. Stout et al., 424–27. Grand Rapids: Eerdmans, 2017.

Ewert, Wesley Carl. "Jonathan Edwards the Younger: A Biographical Essay." ThD diss., Hartford Theological Seminary, 1953.

Ewing, George W. "Introduction." In *On the Reasonableness of Christianity As Delivered in the Scriptures*, by John Locke, vii–xix. Chicago: Regnery, n.d.

Fairbairn, Andrew Martin. "Jonathan Edwards." In *Prophets of the Christian Faith*, edited by F. W. Farrar et al., 151–71. London: James Clarke, 1897.

Fairchild, Byron. "Pepperrell, Sir William." *Dictionary of Canadian Biography*. Toronto: University of Toronto, 1974. www.biographi.ca/en/bio/pepperrell_william_3E.html.

Falbusch, Erwin, ed. "Francke, August Hermann." In *The Encyclopedia of Christianity*, 2:345. Leiden: Brill, 2001.

Fant, Gene C., Jr. "Teaching and Learning in the Humanities." In *Christian Higher Education: Faith, Teaching, and Learning in the Evangelical Tradition*, edited by David S. Dockery and Christopher W. Morgan, 205–23. Wheaton, IL: Crossway, 2018.

Farren, Donald. "Subscription: A Study of the Eighteenth-Century American Book Trade." DLS thesis, Columbia University, 1982.

Bibliography

Faust, Clarence H. "Introduction." In *Jonathan Edwards: Representative Selections*, edited by Clarence H. Faust and Thomas H. Johnson, xi–cxv. New York: American Book Co., 1935.

———. "Jonathan Edwards' View of Human Nature." PhD diss., University of Chicago, 1935.

Faust, Clarence H., and Thomas H. Johnson, eds. *Jonathan Edwards: Representative Selections*. New York: American Book Co. 1935.

Ferm, Robert L. *Jonathan Edwards the Younger, 1745–1801: A Colonial Pastor*. Grand Rapids: Eerdmans, 1976.

Fiering, Norman S. *Jonathan Edwards's Moral Thought and its British Context*. Chapel Hill: University of North Carolina Press, 1981.

———. *Moral Philosophy at Seventeenth-Century Harvard: A Discipline in Transition*. Chapel Hill: University of North Carolina Press, 1981.

———. "The Rationalist Foundations of Jonathan Edwards's Metaphysics." In *Jonathan Edwards and the American Experience*, edited by Nathan O. Hatch and Harry S. Stout, 73–101. New York: Oxford University Press, 1988.

———. "The Transatlantic Republic of Letters: A Note on the Circulation of Learned Periodicals to Early Eighteenth-Century America." *William and Mary Quarterly* 33 (1976) 642–60.

———. "Will and Intellect in the New England Mind." *William and Mary Quarterly* 3 (1972) 515–58.

Fink, Jerome Sanford. "The Purposes of the American Colonial Colleges." EdD diss, Stanford University, 1958.

FitzGerald, Frances. *The Evangelicals: The Struggle to Shape America*. New York: Simon & Schuster, 2017.

Fleming, Sandford. *Children and Puritanism: The Place of Children in the Life and Thought of the New England Churches, 1620–1847*. Reprint, New York: Arno, 1969.

Flower, Elizabeth, and Murray G. Murphey. "Early American Philosophy: The Puritans." In *A History of Philosophy in America*, edited by Elizabeth Flower and Murray G. Murphey, 1:3–58. New York: G. P. Putnam's Sons, 1977.

———. "The Impact of Science." In *A History of Philosophy in America*, edited by Elizabeth Flower and Murray G. Murphey, 1:61–134. New York: G. P. Putnam's Sons, 1977.

———. "Jonathan Edwards." In *A History of Philosophy in America*, edited by Elizabeth Flower and Murray G. Murphey, 1:137–99. New York: G. P. Putnam's Sons, 1977.

Flynt, Josiah. "Sermon" [1670s]. Harvard University MS, 274.

Foord, Martin. "The Elements of a Theology of Theological Education." In *Theological Education: Foundations, Practices, and Future Directions*, edited by Andrew M. Bain and Ian Hussey, 29–43. Eugene, OR: Wipf & Stock, 2018.

Foote, Henry Wilder. "An Account of the Bay Psalm Book." *Papers of the Hymn Society of America* 7 (1940) 3–18.

Ford, Paul Leicester, ed. *The New England Primer: A History of Its Origin and Development*. New York: Printed for Dodd, Mead, and Co., 1897.

Ford, Worthington Chauncey. *The Boston Book Market, 1679–1700*. New York: Burt Franklin, 1972.

Foster, Frank Hugh. *A Genetic History of the New England Theology*. Reprint, New York: Garland, 1987.

———. "Joseph Bellamy." In *A Genetic History of the New England Theology*, 107–28. New York: Garland, 1987.

Foster, Stephen. "Hooker, Thomas (1586–1647)." In *Puritans and Puritanism in Europe and America: A Comprehensive Encyclopedia*, edited by Francis J. Bremer and Tom Webster, 1:130–32. Santa Barbara, CA: ABC-CLIO, 2006.

———. *The Long Argument: English Puritanism and the Shaping of New England Culture, 1570–1700*. Chapel Hill: University of North Carolina Press, 1991.

Foxcroft, Thomas. *Cleansing our Way in Youth Press'd, As of the Highest Importance*. Boston: Printed by S. Kneeland, for S. Gerrish, 1719.

"Francke, August Hermann." In *Encyclopedia Americana*, 11:752. New York: Encyclopedia Americana Corp., 1920.

Francke, August Hermann. *Faith's Work Perfected: or, Francke's Orphan House at Halle*. Edited and Translated by William L. Gage. London: Sampson Low, Son, & Marston, 1867.

———. *Lectiones Paraeneticae 7 Teile*. Halle: im Waysen-Haus, 1736.

———. *Paedagogische Schriften*. Edited by Gustav Kramer. Langensalza: Hermann Beyer, 1876.

Frankena, William K. "Foreword." In *The Nature of True Virtue*, v–xiii. Ann Arbor: University of Michigan Press, 1960.

———. "A Model for Analyzing a Philosophy of Education." In *The High School Journal* 50 (1966) 8–13.

Franklin, Benjamin. "Letter to Ezra Stiles. March 9, 1790." In *The Writings of Benjamin Franklin*, edited by Albert Henry Smyth, 10:83–85. New York: Macmillan, 1907.

Franklin, Brian Russell. "Missions and Missiology." In *The Jonathan Edwards Encyclopedia*, edited by Harry S. Stout et al., 384–85. Grand Rapids: Eerdmans, 2017.

Fraser, Alexander Campbell, ed. *The Works of George Berkeley*. Reprint, Frankfurt: Anatiposi, 2023.

Fraser, James W., ed. *The School in the United States: A Documentary History*. 4th ed. London: Routledge, 2019.

Frazier, Patrick. *The Mohicans of Stockbridge*. Lincoln: University of Nebraska Press, 1992.

Freytag, Cathy E. Review of *The Cry of the Teacher's Soul*, by Laurie R. Matthias. *International Christian Community of Teacher Educators Journal* 11 (2016) 1–2.

Friedman, Rachelle E. "Puritan Historians." In *Puritans and Puritanism in Europe and America: A Comprehensive Encyclopedia*, edited by Francis J. Bremer and Tom Webster, 2:503–9. Oxford: ABC-CLIO, 2006.

Gambrell, Mary Latimer. "Ministerial Training in Eighteenth-Century New England." PhD diss., Columbia University, 1937.

Gardiner, H. Norman. "The Early Idealism of Edwards." In *Jonathan Edwards: A Retrospect*, edited by H. Norman Gardiner, 115–60. Boston: Houghton Mifflin, 1901.

———. "The Early Idealism of Jonathan Edwards." *Philosophical Review* 9 (1900) 573–96.

Garrard, Graeme. "Tilting at Counter-Enlightenment Windmills." *Eighteenth-Century Studies* 49 (2015) 77–81.

Bibliography

Gaustad, Edwin S. "The Nature of True—and Useful—Virtue: From Edwards to Franklin." In *Benjamin Franklin, Jonathan Edwards, and the Representation of American Culture*, 42–57. New York: Oxford University Press, 1993.
Gay, Peter. *The Enlightenment: The Rise of Modern Paganism*. New York: Knopf, 1966.
———. *An Interpretation: The Rise of Modern Paganism*. New York: Knopf, 1966.
———. "Jonathan Edwards: An American Tragedy." In *A Loss of Mastery: Puritan Historians in Colonial America*, 88–118. Berkeley: University of California Press, 1966.
———. *A Loss of Mastery: Puritan Historians in Colonial America*. Berkeley: University of California Press, 1966.
George, Charles, and Katherine George. *The Protestant Mind of the English Reformation, 1570–1640*. Princeton, NJ: Princeton University Press, 1961.
Gerstner, John H. "Jonathan Edwards's Place in the History of Christian Thought." In *Jonathan Edwards: A Mini-Theology*, edited by John H. Gerstner, 13–19. Wheaton, IL: Tyndale, 1987.
Gibson, Jonathan. "Jonathan Edwards: A Missionary?" *Themelios* 36 (2011) 380–402.
Gierer, Emily Dolan. "Hannah Edwards Wetmore and Her Joyful Death: The Deathbed Confessional During the Enlightenment." In *Jonathan Edwards within the Enlightenment: Controversy, Experience, and Thought*, edited by John T. Lowe and Daniel N. Gullotta, 189–206. Göttingen: Vandenhoeck & Ruprecht, 2020.
Gill, M. B. "Lord Shaftesbury [Anthony Ashley Cooper, 3rd Earl of Shaftesbury]." https://plato.stanford.edu/entries/shaftesbury/.
Gilman, Daniel Coit, et al., eds. "Comenius, Johann Amos." In *The New International Encyclopedia*, 5:198-200. New York: Dodd, Mead, and Co., 1905.
Giltner, John H. *Moses Stuart: The Father of Biblical Science in America*. Atlanta: Scholars, 1988.
Ginsberg, Morris. "Translator's Preface." In *Dialogues on Metaphysics and on Religion*, by Nicolas Malebranche, 16. New York: Macmillan, 1923.
Glanzer, Perry L., et al. *Restoring the Soul of the University: Unifying Christian Higher Education in a Fragmented Age*. Westmont, IL: InterVarsity Academic, 2017.
Goen, C. C. "[All Christians Should Honor God in Every Way]." In *Works of Jonathan Edwards Online*, edited by C. C. Goen, 4:528. http://edwards.yale.edu.
———. "Editor's Introduction." In *Works of Jonathan Edwards Online*, edited by C. C. Goen, 4:1–95. http://edwards.yale.edu.
Gordis, Lisa M. *Opening Scripture: Bible Reading and Interpretive Authority in Puritan New England*, 1–11. Chicago: University of Chicago Press, 2003.
Gordon, Edward E., and Elaine H. Gordon. *Literacy in America: Historic Journey and Contemporary Solutions*. Westport, CT: Praeger, 2003.
Gouge, William. *Of Domesticall Duties: Eight Treatises*. London: Printed by John Haviland for William Bladen, 1622.
Graff, Harvey J. *The Legacies of Literacy: Continuities and Contradictions in Western Culture and Society*. Bloomington: Indiana University Press, 1987.
Grant, Leonard. "Puritan Catechizing." *Journal of Presbyterian History* 46 (1968) 107–27.
Gray, Lauren Davis. "Birthing the New Birth: The Natural Philosophy of Childbirth in the Theology of Jonathan Edwards." MA thesis, Florida State University, 2009.
Greaves, Richard L. *The Puritan Revolution and Educational Thought: Background for Reform*. New Brunswick, NJ: Rutgers University Press, 1969.

Bibliography

Greene, Jack P. "The Development of Early American Culture." In *Interpreting Early America: Historiographical Essays*, edited by Jack P. Greene, 120–25. Charlottesville: University Press of Virginia, 1996.

Gribben, Crawford. "The Eschatology of the Puritan Confessions." *Scottish Bulletin of Evangelical Theology* 20 (2002) 51–78.

Grigg, John A. "Missions." In *The Oxford Handbook of Jonathan Edwards*, edited by Douglas A. Sweeney and Jan Stievermann, 416–30. New York: Oxford University Press, 2021.

Griswold, Jerry. "Children's Literature in the USA: A Historical Overview." In *International Companion Encyclopedia of Children's Literature*, edited by P. Hunt, 860–70. London: Routledge, 2004.

Guelzo, Allen C. "Edwards, Jonathan." In *Encyclopedia of the Enlightenment*, edited by Alan Charles Kors, 1:390–92. Oxford: Oxford University Press, 2003.

———. *Edwards on the Will: A Century of American Theological Debate*. Middletown, CT: Wesleyan University Press, 1989.

———. "Learning is the Handmaid of the Lord: Jonathan Edwards, Reason, and the Life of the Mind." *Midwest Studies in Philosophy* 28 (2004) 1–18.

Gundlach, Bradley J. "Foundations of Christian Higher Education: Learning from Church History." In *Christian Higher Education: Faith, Teaching, and Learning in the Evangelical Tradition*, edited by David S. Dockery and Christopher W. Morgan, 121–38. Wheaton, IL: Crossway, 2018.

Gura, Philip F. "Edwards and American Literature." In *The Cambridge Companion to Jonathan Edwards*, edited by Stephen J. Stein, 272–79. New York: Cambridge University Press, 2007.

Gustafson, Sandra M. "Edwards's Place in Anglo-American Literature." In *The Oxford Handbook of Jonathan Edwards*, edited by Douglas A. Sweeney and Jan Stievermann, 495–513. New York: Oxford University Press, 2021.

Guthrie, Donald C. "Faith and Teaching." In *Christian Higher Education: Faith, Teaching, and Learning in the Evangelical Tradition*, edited by David S. Dockery and Christopher W. Morgan, 149–67. Wheaton, IL: Crossway, 2018.

Guthrie, Goerge H. "The Study of Holy Scripture and the Work of Higher Education." In *Christian Higher Education: Faith, Teaching, and Learning in the Evangelical Tradition*, edited by David S. Dockery and Christopher W. Morgan, 81–100. Wheaton, IL: Crossway, 2018.

Gwyn, Julian. "Pepperrell, Sir William." In *The Canadian Encyclopedia*. www.thecanadianencyclopedia.ca/en/article/sir-william-pepperrell.

Hackel, Heidi Brayman, and Catherine E. Kelly. "Introduction." In *Reading Women: Literacy, Authorship, and Culture in the Atlantic World, 1500–1800*, edited by Heidi Brayman Hackel and Catherine E. Kelly, 1–10. Philadelphia: University of Pennsylvania Press, 2008.

Hale, Richard Walden, Jr. *Tercentenary History of the Roxbury Latin School, 1645–1945*. Cambridge, MA: Riverside, 1946.

Hall, Basil. "'Calvin Against the Calvinists.'" *Proceedings of the Huguenot Society of London* 20 (1962) 284–301.

———. "Puritanism: The Problem of Definition." In *Studies in Church History*, edited by G. J. Cuming, 2:283–96. Camden, NJ: Nelson, 1965.

Hall, David D. *The Faithful Shepherd: A History of the New England Ministry in the Seventeenth Century*. Chapel Hill: University of North Carolina Press, 1972.

Bibliography

———. "Introduction." In *Puritans in the New World: A Critical Anthology*, edited by David D. Hall, ix-xv. Princeton, NJ: Princeton University Press, 2004.

———. "Introduction—Part 1: Some Contexts and Questions." In *A History of the Book in America: The Colonial Book in the Atlantic World*, edited by Hugh Amory and David D. Hall, 1–12. Chapel Hill: University of North Carolina Press, 2007.

———. "Introduction—Part 2: The Europeans' Encounter with Native Americans." In *A History of the Book in America: The Colonial Book in the Atlantic World*, edited by Hugh Amory and David D. Hall, 13–25. Chapel Hill: University of North Carolina Press, 2007.

———. "Learned Culture in the Eighteenth Century." In *A History of the Book in America: The Colonial Book in the Atlantic World*, edited by Hugh Amory and David D. Hall, 411–33. Chapel Hill: University of North Carolina Press, 2007.

———. "Misrepresentations Corrected." In *Works of Jonathan Edwards Online*, edited by David D. Hall, 12:74–77. http://edwards.yale.edu.

———. "New England, 1660–1730." In *The Cambridge Companion to Puritanism*, edited by John Coffey and Paul C. H. Lim, 143–58. Cambridge: Cambridge University Press, 2008.

———. "The New England Background." In *The Cambridge Companion to Jonathan Edwards*, edited by Stephen J. Stein, 61–79. Cambridge: Cambridge University Press, 2006.

———. "Readers and Reading in America: Historical and Critical Perspectives." In *Cultures of Print: Essays in the History of the Book*, edited by David D. Hall, 172–73. Amherst: University of Massachusetts Press, 1996.

———. "Readers and Writers in Early New England." In *A History of the Book in America: The Colonial Book in the Atlantic World*, edited by Hugh Amory and David D. Hall, 145–79. Chapel Hill: University of North Carolina Press, 2007.

———. "Understanding the Puritans." In *The State of American History*, edited by Herbert J. Bass, 343–44. Chicago: Quadrangle, 1970.

———. "The Uses of Literacy in New England, 1600–1850." In *Printing and Society in Early America*, edited by William L. Joyce et al., 1–47. Worcester, MA: American Antiquarian Society, 1983.

———. *Worlds of Wonder, Days of Judgment: Popular Religious Belief in Early New England*. Cambridge, MA: Harvard University Press, 1990.

Hall, David D., ed. *Bibliography and the Book Trades: Studies in the Print Culture of Early New England*. Philadelphia: University of Pennsylvania Press, 2005

———. *Cultures of Print: Essays in the History of the Book*. Amherst: University of Massachusetts Press, 1996.

———. *Puritans in the New World: A Critical Anthology*. Princeton, NJ: Princeton University Press, 2004.

Hall, David D., and Elizabeth Carroll Reilly. "Practices of Reading: Introduction." In *A History of the Book in America: The Colonial Book in the Atlantic World*, edited by Hugh Amory and David D. Hall, 377–80. Chapel Hill: University of North Carolina Press, 2007.

Hall, Richard. "The Abolitionism of Samuel Hopkins: An Application of Edwards's Doctrine of True Virtue." In *The Global Edwards: Papers from the Jonathan Edwards Congress held in Melbourne, August 2015*, 296–313. Eugene, OR: Wipf & Stock, 2017.

Bibliography

———. "Enlightenment." In *The Jonathan Edwards Encyclopedia*, edited by Harry S. Stout et al., 198–200. Grand Rapids: Eerdmans, 2017.

Hall, Thomas Cuming. *The Religious Background of American Culture*. New York: Frederick Ungar, 1959.

Haller, William. *The Rise of Puritanism, or, The Way to the New Jerusalem as Set Forth in Pulpit and Press from Thomas Cartwright to John Lilburne and John Milton, 1570–1643*. New York: Columbia University Press, 1938.

Hambrick-Stowe, Charles. "All Things Were New and Astonishing: Edwardsian Piety, the New Divinity, and Race." In *Jonathan Edwards at Home and Abroad: Historical Memories, Cultural Movements, Global Horizons*, edited by David W. Kling and Douglas A. Sweeney, 121–36. Columbia: University of South Carolina Press, 2003.

———. "The 'Inward, Sweet Sense' of Christ in Jonathan Edwards." In *The Legacy of Jonathan Edwards: American Religion and the Evangelical Tradition*, edited by D. G. Hart et al., 79–95. Grand Rapids: Baker Academic, 2003.

———. "The New England Theology in New England Congregationalism." In *After Jonathan Edwards: The Courses of the New England Theology*, edited by Oliver D. Crisp and Douglas A. Sweeney, 165–77. New York: Oxford University Press, 2012.

———. "Practical Divinity and Spirituality." In *The Cambridge Companion to Puritanism*, edited by John Coffey and Paul C. H. Lim, 191–205. Cambridge: Cambridge University Press, 2008.

———. "Spirituality and Devotion." In *The Oxford Handbook of Jonathan Edwards*, edited by Douglas A. Sweeney and Jan Stievermann, 353–69. New York: Oxford University Press, 2021.

Hampson, Norman. *The Enlightenment*. Reprint, New York: Penguin, 1981.

Han, Dongsoo. "Asia." In *The Oxford Handbook of Jonathan Edwards*, edited by Douglas A. Sweeney and Jan Stievermann, 514–27. New York: Oxford University Press, 2021.

Hangartner, Carl Albert. "Movements to Change American College Teaching, 1700–1830." PhD diss., Yale University, 1955.

Hankins, Jean Fittz. "Bringing the Good News: Protestant Missionaries to the Indians of New England and New York, 1700–1775." PhD diss., University of Connecticut, 1993.

Hans, Nicholas A. *New Trends in Education in the Eighteenth Century*. London: Routledge & Kegan Paul Ltd., 1951.

Hansen, Collin. "Forgotten 'Father of Biblical Science': Moses Stuart Pioneered Modern Biblical Study in America." *Christianity Today*, December 8, 2009. www.christianitytoday.com/history/2009/december/forgotten-father-of-biblical-science.html.

———. "Young, Restless, and Reformed." *Christianity Today* 50 (2006) 33–38.

Harder, Michael. "True Excellency: The Missionary Preaching of Jonathan Edwards." PhD diss., Southeastern Baptist Theological Seminary, 2022.

Harris, Michael H., and Donald G. Davis, *American Library History: A Bibliography*. Austin: University of Texas Press, 1978.

Harrod, Joseph C. *Theology and Spirituality in the Works of Samuel Davies*. Göttingen: Vandenhoeck & Ruprecht, 2019.

Hart, D. G. "Before the Young, Restless, and Reformed: Edwards's Appeal to Post–World War II Evangelicals." In *After Jonathan Edwards: The Courses of the New England Theology*, edited by Oliver D. Crisp and Douglas A. Sweeney, 237–53. New York: Oxford University Press, 2012.

Bibliography

Hart, James D. *The Popular Book: A History of America's Literary Taste*. New York: Oxford University Press, 1950.

Harwood, Grace Sara. "Perhaps No One General Answer Will Do: Cotton Mather's Commentary on the Synoptic Gospels in 'Biblia Americana.'" PhD diss., Georgia State University, 2018.

Hastings, W. Ross. *Jonathan Edwards and the Life of God: Toward an Evangelical Theology of Participation*. Minneapolis: Fortress, 2015.

Hatch, Nathan O., and Harry S. Stout. "Introduction." In *The Bible in America: Essays in Cultural History*, edited by Nathan O. Hatch and Mark A. Noll, 3–18. New York: Oxford University Press, 1982.

Hazard, Paul. *The European Mind: The Critical Years, 1680–1715*. New Haven, CT: Yale University Press, 1953.

———. *European Thought in the Eighteenth Century: From Montesquieu to Lessing*. New Haven, CT: Yale University Press, 1954.

Hedberg, Allan G. "Child Rearing." In *The Jonathan Edwards Encyclopedia*, 87. Grand Rapids: Eerdmans, 2017.

———. "Edwards, Timothy (son) (1738–1813)." In *The Jonathan Edwards Encyclopedia*, 186–87. Grand Rapids: Eerdmans, 2017.

Heidegger, Martin. "The Age of World Picture." In *The Question Concerning Technology and Other Essays*, by Martin Heidegger, 115–54. Translated by William Lovitt. New York: Harper Torchbooks, 1977.

Heim, Karl. *Christian Faith and Natural Science*. London: SCM, 1953.

Heimert, Alan, and Andrew Delbanco. *The Puritans in America: A Narrative Anthology*. Cambridge, MA: Harvard University Press, 1985.

Helm, Paul. "A Different Kind of Calvinism? Edwardsianism Compared with Older Forms of Reformed Thought." In *After Jonathan Edwards: The Courses of the New England Theology*, edited by Oliver D. Crisp and Douglas A. Sweeney, 91–103. New York: Oxford University Press, 2012.

———. "Epistemology." In *The Oxford Handbook of Edwards*, edited by Douglas A. Sweeney and Jan Stievermann, 104–17. New York: Oxford University Press, 2021.

———. "A Forensic Dilemma: John Locke and Jonathan Edwards on Personal Identity." In *Jonathan Edwards: Philosophical Theologian*, edited by Paul Helm and Oliver D. Crisp, 45–59. Burlington, VT: Ashgate, 2003.

———. "The Human Self and the Divine Trinity." In *Jonathan Edwards as Contemporary: Essays in Honor of Sang Hyun Lee*, edited by Don Schweitzer, 93–106. New York: Peter Lang, 2010.

———. "John Locke and Jonathan Edwards: A Reconsideration." *Journal of the History of Philosophy* 7 (1969) 51–61.

———. "Jonathan Edwards on Original Sin." In *Faith and Understanding*, by Paul Helm, 152–76. Edinburgh: Edinburgh University Press, 1997.

Helm, Paul, and Oliver D. Crisp. "The Human Self and the Divine Trinity." In *Jonathan Edwards as Contemporary: Essays in Honor of Sang Hyun Lee*, edited by Don Schweitzer, 110–23. New York: Peter Lang, 2010.

———. "Introduction: The Rehabilitation of Jonathan Edwards." In *Jonathan Edwards: Philosophical Theologian*, edited by Paul Helm and Oliver D. Crisp, ix-xi. Burlington, VT: Ashgate, 2003.

Henderson, G. D. *The Burning Bush: Studies in Scottish Church History*. Edinburgh: St. Andrew, 1957.

Bibliography

———. "Puritanism in Eighteenth-Century Scotland." *Evangelical Quarterly* (July 1947) 211–21.

"Hendrick A. to Hon'ble Timothy Edwards, Esq. Stockbridge or Wunnuqhqtoqhoke." 1775. Stockbridge Library, Stockbridge, Massachusetts.

Henry, Caleb. "Locke, John (1632–1704)." In *The Jonathan Edwards Encyclopedia*, edited by Harry S. Stout et al., 353–54. Grand Rapids: Eerdmans, 2017.

Herbert, Arthur Sumner. *Historical Catalogue of Printed Editions of the English Bible, 1525–1961.* New York: American Bible Society, 1968.

Hermes, Katherine. "Joseph Bellamy." In *Dictionary of Early American Philosophers*, edited by John R. Shook, 108–9. London: Continuum, 2012.

Herrick, C. A. "The Early New Englanders: What Did They Read?" *The Library* 33 (1918) 1–17.

Herzog, Frederick. *European Pietism Reviewed.* Eugene, OR: Pickwick, 2003.

Hessinger, Rodney. "Classical Curriculum." In *Historical Dictionary of American Education*, edited by Richard J. Altenbaugh, 81–82. Westport, CT: Greenwood, 1999.

Hewes, Dorothy W. "Dame Schools." In *Historical Dictionary of American Education*, edited by Richard J. Altenbaugh, 106. Westport, CT: Greenwood, 1999.

Higginson, John. "An Attestation to this Church-History of New-England." In *Preface to Cotton Mather, Magnalia Christi Americana, Books I and II*, edited by Kenneth B. Murdock and Elizabeth W. Miller, 63–88. Cambridge, MA: Harvard University Press, 1977.

Hill, Alan G. "Wordsworth, Comenius, and the Meaning of Education." *Review of English Studies* 26 (1975) 301–12.

Hill, Christopher. "The Definition of a Puritan." In *Society and Puritanism in Pre-Revolutionary England*, 1–15. London: Seeker and Warburg, 1964.

———. *The English Bible and the Seventeenth-Century Revolution.* New York: Penguin, 1993.

Hill, Jonathan. *Faith in the Age of Reason: The Enlightenment from Galileo to Kant.* Oxford: Lion Hudson, 2004.

Hills, Margaret T. *The English Bible in America: A Bibliography of the Editions of the Bible and the New Testament Published in America, 1777–1957.* New York: American Bible Society, 1961.

Himmelfarb, Gertrude. *The Roads to Modernity: The British, French, and American Enlightenments.* New York: Vintage, 2004.

Hindson, Edward. "Introduction to the Puritans." In *Introduction to Puritan Theology*, edited by Edward Hindson, 17–27. Grand Rapids: Baker, 1976.

Hoeveler, David. *Creating the American Mind: Intellect and Politics in the Colonial Colleges.* Lanham, MD: Rowman & Littlefield, 2007.

Holbrook, Clyde A. "Editor's Introduction." In *Works of Jonathan Edwards Online*, edited by Clyde A. Holbrook, 3:23–25, 67–68. http://edwards.yale.edu.

———. *The Ethics of Jonathan Edwards: Morality and Aesthetics.* Ann Arbor: University of Michigan Press, 1973.

———. "Jonathan Edwards and His Detractors." *Theology Today* 10 (1953) 384–96.

———. "The Major Patterns." In *The Ethics of Jonathan Edwards: Morality and Aesthetics*, 1–2. Ann Arbor: University of Michigan Press, 1973.

Bibliography

Holifield, E. Brooks. "Edwards as Theologian." In *Cambridge Companion to Jonathan Edwards*, edited by Stephen J. Stein, 144–61. Cambridge: Cambridge University Press, 2007.

Hollister, Gideon Hiram. *The History of Connecticut From the First Settlement of the Colony to the Adoption of the Present Constitution*. Hartford, CT: L. Stebbins & Co., 1858.

Holloway, Charles Stewart. "The Homiletical Theology of Jonathan Edwards, Gilbert Tennent, and Samuel Davies." PhD diss., Southwestern Baptist Theological Seminary, 2008.

Holmes, Oliver Wendell Sr. *Elsie Venner: A Romance of Destiny*. Boston: Houghton, Mifflin, 1862.

Holmes, Stephen R. "Does Jonathan Edwards Use a Dispositional Ontology? A Response to Sang Hyun Lee." In *Jonathan Edwards: Philosophical Theologian*, edited by Paul Helm and Oliver D. Crisp, 99–114. Burlington, VT: Ashgate, 2003.

———. *God of Grace and God of Glory: An Account of the Theology of Jonathan Edwards*. Edinburgh: T. & T. Clark, 2000.

Holmes, Thomas James. "Preface." In *Cotton Mather: A Bibliography of His Works*. Cambridge, MA: Harvard University Press, 1940.

Hooker, Thomas. *The Application of Redemption by the Effectual Work of the Word, and Spirit of Christ*. Reprint, New York: Arno, 1972.

———. *The Soules Vocation, or Effectual Calling to Christ*. London: Printed by John Haviland, for Andrew Crooke, 1638.

———. *The Unbeleevers Preparing for Christ*. London: Printed by the Cotes for Andrew Crooke, 1638.

Hopkins, Samuel. "C141a. Samuel Hopkins to Joseph Bellamy, January 19, 1758." In *Works of Jonathan Edwards Online*, edited by Jonathan Edwards Center. http://edwards.yale.edu.

———. "Diary. August 28, 1755." *Samuel Hopkins Papers*. Trask Memorial Library, Andover-Newton Theological School, South Andover, Massachusetts.

———. *Enquiry Concerning the Promises of the Gospel*. Boston: W. M'Alpine and J. Fleming, 1765.

———. *An Inquiry into the Nature of True Holiness*. New York: Reprinted for M. Smith and C. Davis, by William Durell, 1791.

———. *Life and Character of the Late Reverend Mr. Jonathan Edwards*. Boston: S. Kneeland, 1765.

———. *Samuel Hopkins Journal, 1741-1751*. Historical Society of Pennsylvania, MS Sermons Formerly Box 6, now Box 322, vol. 18 (Gratz Collection 250B).

———. *Sketches of the Life of the Late Rev. Samuel Hopkins, D. D.* Edited by Stephen West. Hartford, CT: Hudson and Goodwin, 1805.

———. *System of Doctrines, Contained in Divine Revelation, Explained and Defended*. Boston: Printed by Isaiah Thomas and Ebenezer T, Andrews, 1793.

———. *The Works of Samuel Hopkins, D D*. Boston: Doctrinal Tract and Book Society, 1854.

Hornberger, Theodore. "The Date . . ." *American Literature* 6 (1935) 413–20.

———. "The Effect of the New Science upon the Thought of Jonathan Edwards." *American Literature* 9 (1937) 196–207.

———. *Scientific Thought in the American Colleges, 1638-1800*. Austin: University of Texas Press, 1946.

Bibliography

Horton, Douglas. "Let Us Not Forget the Mighty William Ames." *Religion in Life* 19 (1960) 434–35.

Hoselton, Ryan P. "Ames, William (1565–1633)." In *The Jonathan Edwards Encyclopedia*, edited by Harry S. Stout et al., 20–21. Grand Rapids: Eerdmans, 2017.

———. "The Bible in Early Pietist and Evangelical Missions." In *The Bible in Early Transatlantic Pietism and Evangelicalism*, edited by Ryan P. Hoselton et al., 109–28. University Park: Pennsylvania State University, 2022.

———. "Introduction." In *The Bible in Early Transatlantic Pietism and Evangelicalism*, edited by Ryan P. Hoselton et al., 1–14. University Park: Pennsylvania State University, 2022.

———. "Jonathan Edwards, Halle Pietism, and Benevolent Activism in Early Awakened Protestantism." In *Edwards, Germany, and Transatlantic Contexts*, edited by Rhys Bezzant, 51–68. Göttingen: Vandenhoeck & Ruprecht, 2021.

———. "Mather, Cotton (1663–1728)." In *The Jonathan Edwards Encyclopedia*, edited by Harry S. Stout et al., 366. Grand Rapids: Eerdmans, 2017.

Hourly History. *The Age of Enlightenment: A History from Beginning to End*. https://hourlyhistory.com/free-history-ebooks/age-of-enlightenment/?doing_wp_cron=1730742763.5126080513000488281250.

Howard, Leon. *"The Mind" of Jonathan Edwards: A Reconstructed Text*. Berkeley: University of California Press, 1963.

———. "The Puritans in Old and New England." In *Essays on Puritans and Puritanism*, edited by James Barbour and Thomas Quirk, 87–112. Albuquerque: University of New Mexico Press, 1986.

Howard, Joy A. J. "Ashley, Rebecca Kellog (1695–1757)." In *The Jonathan Edwards Encyclopedia*, edited by Harry S. Stout et al., 41–42. Grand Rapids: Eerdmans, 2017.

———. "Rebecca Kellogg Ashley: Negotiating Identity on the Early American Borderlands, 1704–1757." In *Women in Early America: Transnational Histories, Rethinking Master Narratives*, edited by Thomas A. Foster, 118–38. New York: New York University Press, 2015.

Huffman, Mary Lyn. "'Train Up a Child in the Way He Should Go': Parental Use of Biblical Stories in Teaching for Moral Growth." MA thesis, Reformed Theological Seminary, 2005.

Hussey, Phillip, and Michael McClymond. "Creation and Predestination." In *The Oxford Handbook of Edwards*, edited by Douglas A. Sweeney and Jan Stievermann, 199–214. New York: Oxford University Press, 2021.

Hutcheson, Francis. *An Inquiry into the Original of Our Ideas of Beauty and Virtue*. London: Printed for D. Midwinter, et al., 1738.

———. *A Short Introduction to Moral Philosophy, in Three Books*. Glasgow: Robert & Andrew Foulis, 1753.

Hutchins, Zachary. "Edwards and Eve: Finding Feminist Strains in the Great Awakening's Patriarch." *Early American Literature* 43 (2008) 671–86.

Ingraffia, Brian D. *Postmodern Theory and Biblical Theology: Vanquishing God's Shadow*, 126. Cambridge: Cambridge University Press, 1995.

James, Sydney V. "Introduction." In *The New England Puritans*, edited by Sydney V. James, 1–11. New York: Harper & Row, 1968.

Jannenga, Stephanie C. "Making College Colonial: The Transformation of English Culture in Higher Education in Pre-Revolutionary America" PhD diss., Kent State University, 2020.

Bibliography

Jarvis, F. Washington. *Schola Illustris: The Roxbury Latin School, 1645-1995*. Boston: David R. Godine, 1996.

Jauhiainen, Peter. "Samuel Hopkins and Hopkinsianism." In *After Jonathan Edwards: The Courses of the New England Theology*, edited by Oliver D. Crisp and Douglas A. Sweeney, 106-17. New York: Oxford University Press, 2012.

Jennings, Francis. *The Invasion of America: Indians, Colonialism, and the Cant of Conquest*. Chapel Hill: University of North Carolina Press, 1975.

Jenson, Robert W. *America's Theologian: A Recommendation of Jonathan Edwards*. New York: Oxford University Press, 1988.

———. "Christology." In *The Princeton Companion to Jonathan Edwards*, edited by Sang Hyun Lee, 72-86. Princeton, NJ: Princeton University Press, 2005.

———. "The End is Music." In *Edwards in Our Time: Jonathan Edwards and the Shaping of American Religion*, edited by Sang Hyun Lee and Allen C. Guelzo, 161-72. Grand Rapids: Eerdmans, 1999.

———. "How I Stole from Edwards." In *Jonathan Edwards as Contemporary: Essays in Honor of Sang Hyun Lee*, edited by Don Schweitzer, 276-80. New York: Peter Lang, 2010.

Jernegan, Marcus W. "The Beginnings of Public Education in New England." *School Review* 23 (1915) 319-30.

———. "Compulsory Education in the American Colonies." 735-36. www.journals.uchicago.edu/doi/pdfplus/10.1086/436982.

Jeske, Jeffrey. "Cotton Mather, Physico-Theologian." *Journal of the History of Ideas* 47 (1986) 583-94.

Johnson, Edward. *A History of New-England*. London: Printed for Nath: Brooke, 1654.

Johnson, Samuel. *Samuel Johnson, President of King's College: His Career and Writings*. Edited by Herbert Wallace Schneider. New York: Columbia University Press, 1929.

Johnson, Thomas H. "Jonathan Edwards' Background of Reading." *Publications of the Colonial Society of Massachusetts* 28 (1931) 193-222.

Jones, Phyllis M., and Nicholas R. Jones. "Introduction." In *Salvation in New England: Selections From the Sermons of the First Preachers*, edited by Phyllis M. Jones and Nicholas R. Jones, 3-5. Austin: University of Texas Press, 1977.

Kang, S. Steve. "Faith, Learning, and Catechism." In *Christian Higher Education: Faith, Teaching, and Learning in the Evangelical Tradition*, edited by David S. Dockery and Christopher W. Morgan, 365-83. Wheaton, IL: Crossway, 2018.

Karlsen, Carol F., and Laurie Crumpacker, eds. *The Journal of Esther Edwards Burr, 1754-1757*. New Haven, CT: Yale University Press, 1984.

Keating, Jerome Francis. "Personal Identity in Jonathan Edwards, Ralph Waldo Emerson, and Alfred North Whitehead." PhD diss., Syracuse University, 1972.

Keatinge, M. W. *The Great Didactic of John Amos Comenius*. London: Adam and Charles Black, 1907.

Keeble, N. H. "Puritanism and Literature." In *The Cambridge Companion to Puritanism*, edited by John Coffey and Paul C. H. Lim, 309-24. Cambridge: Cambridge University Press, 2008.

Keep, Austin Baxter. *History of the New York Society Library, with an Introductory Chapter on Libraries in Colonial New York, 1698-1776*. Boston: Gregg, 1972.

Kennedy, Rick. *The First American Evangelical: A Short Life of Cotton Mather*. Grand Rapids: Eerdmans, 2015.

Bibliography

Kerber, Linda K. *Women of the Republic: Ideology and Intellect in Revolutionary America.* Chapel Hill: University of North Carolina Press, 1980.

Kesler, Charles R. "The Different Enlightenments: Theory and Practice in the Enlightenment." In *The Ambiguous Legacy of the Enlightenment*, edited by William A. Rusher and Ken Masugi, 102–19. Lanham, MD: University Press of America, 1995.

Kidd, Thomas S. *The Protestant Interest: New England After Puritanism.* New Haven, CT: Yale University Press, 2004.

Kilgour, Frederick C. "The First Century of Scientific Books in the Harvard College Library." *Harvard Library Notes* 3 (1939) 217–19.

Kilner, John F. *Dignity and Destiny: Humanity in the Image of God.* Grand Rapids: Eerdmans, 2015.

———. "Made in the Image of God: *Implications for Teaching and Learning.*" In *Christian Higher Education: Faith, Teaching, and Learning in the Evangelical Tradition*, edited by David S. Dockery and Christopher W. Morgan, 101–19. Wheaton, IL: Crossway, 2018.

———. "Special Connection and Intended Reflection: Creation in God's Image and Human Significance." In *Why People Matter: A Christian Engagement with Rival Views of Human Significance*, edited by John F. Kilner, 135–60. Grand Rapids: Baker Academic, 2017.

Kilpatrick, William K. *Why Johnny Can't Tell Right from Wrong.* New York: Simon & Schuster, 1992.

Kim, Hyunkwan. "Jonathan Edwards's Reshaping of Lockean Terminology into a Calvinistic Aesthetic Epistemology in his *Religious Affections.*" *Puritan Reformed Journal* 6 (2014) 103–22.

Kimnach, Wilson H. "The Brazen Trumpet: Jonathan Edwards's Conception of the Sermon." In *Jonathan Edwards: His Life and Influence*, edited by Charles Angoff, 29–44. Rutherford, NJ: Farleigh Dickinson University Press, 1975.

———. "Early Experiences and Formal Education." In *Works of Jonathan Edwards Online*, edited by Wilson H. Kimnach, 10:4. http://edwards.yale.edu.

———. "The Sermons: Concept and Execution." In *The Princeton Companion to Jonathan Edwards*, edited by Sang Hyun Lee, 243–57. Princeton, NJ: Princeton University Press, 2005.

———. "The Stockbridge Mission." In *Works of Jonathan Edwards Online*, edited by Wilson H. Kimnach, 25:24–32. http://edwards.yale.edu.

Kimnach, Wilson H., et al. "Editors' Introduction." In *The Sermons of Jonathan Edwards: A Reader*, edited by Wilson H. Kimnach et al., ix-xlvii. New Haven, CT: Yale University Press, 1999.

———. *The Sermons of Jonathan Edwards: A Reader.* New Haven, CT: Yale University Press, 1999.

King, Henry Churchill. "Jonathan Edwards as Philosopher and Theologian." *Hartford Seminary Record* 14 (1903) 23–57.

Kistler, Don. "Preface." In *To the Rising Generation: Addresses Given to Children and Young Adults.* Lake Mary, FL: Soli Deo Gloria, 2005, v.

Kling, David W. "Edwards in the Context of International Revivals and Missions." In *The Oxford Handbook of Jonathan Edwards*, edited by Douglas A. Sweeney and Jan Stievermann, 51–68. New York: Oxford University Press, 2021.

Bibliography

———. "Edwards in the Second Great Awakening: The New Divinity Contributions of Edward Dorr Griffin and Asahel Nettleton." In *After Jonathan Edwards: The Courses of the New England Theology*, edited by Oliver D. Crisp and Douglas A. Sweeney, 130–41. New York: Oxford University Press, 2012.

———. *A Field of Divine Wonders: The New Divinity and Village Revivals in Northwestern Connecticut, 1792–1822*. University Park: Pennsylvania State University Press, 1993.

———. "The New Divinity and Williams College, 1793–1836." *Religion and American Culture* 6 (1996) 195–223.

———. "New Divinity Schools of the Prophets, 1750–1825: A Case Study in Ministerial Education." *History of Education Quarterly* 37 (1997) 185–206.

Kling, David W., and Douglas A. Sweeney. "Introduction." In *Jonathan Edwards at Home and Abroad: Historical Memories, Cultural Movements, Global Horizons*, edited by David W. Kling and Douglas A. Sweeney, xiii–xxiii. Columbia: University of South Carolina, 2003.

Kloppenberg, James T. "Knowledge and Belief in American Public Life." In *Knowledge and Belief in America: Enlightenment Traditions and Modern Religious Thought*, edited by William M. Shea and Peter A. Huff, 27–51. Washington, DC: Woodrow Wilson Center Press and Cambridge University Press, 1995.

Knappen, M. M. *Tudor Puritanism: A Chapter in the History of Idealism*. Chicago: University of Chicago Press, 1939.

Knight, George R. *Philosophy of Education: An Introduction in Christian Perspective*. Berrien Springs, MI: Andrews University Press, 1980.

Knight, Janice. *Orthodoxies in Massachusetts: Rereading American Puritanism*. Cambridge, MA: Harvard University Press, 1994.

———. "Typology." In *The Princeton Companion to Jonathan Edwards*, edited by Sang Hyun Lee, 190–209. Princeton, NJ: Princeton University Press, 2005.

Kuyper, Abraham. *Wisdom and Wonder: Common Grace in Science and Art*. Edited by Jordan J. Ballor and Stephen J. Grabill. Translated by Nelson Deyo Kloosterman. Grand Rapids: Christian Library's Press, 2011.

Lake, Peter. "Defining Puritanism—Again?" In *Puritanism: Transatlantic Perspectives on a Seventeenth-Century Anglo-American Faith*, edited by Francis J. Bremer, 3–29. Boston: Massachusetts Historical Society, 1993.

———. "Introduction: Laurence Chaderton and the Problem of Puritanism." In *Moderate Puritans and the Elizabethan Church*, 1–15. Cambridge: Cambridge University Press, 1982.

———. *Moderate Puritans and the Elizabethan Church*. Cambridge: Cambridge University Press, 1982.

Lakoff, George, and Mike Johnson. *Philosophy in the Flesh: The Embodied Mind and Its Challenge to Western Thought*. New York: Basic Books, 1999.

Lamberton, E. V. "Colonial Libraries of Pennsylvania." *Pennsylvania Magazine of History and Biography* 42 (1918) 193–234.

Lane, Belden C. "Jonathan Edwards on Beauty, Desire, and the Sensory World." *Theological Studies* 65 (2004) 44–72.

Laska, John A. *Schooling and Education: Basic Concepts and Problems*. New York: Van Nostrand, 1976.

Laurence, David. "Jonathan Edwards, John Locke, and the Canon of Experience." *Early American Literature* 15 (1980) 107–23.

Bibliography

Laurie, S. S. *John Amos Comenius, Bishop of the Moravians: His Life and Educational Works*. Cambridge: Cambridge University Press, 1887.

The Laws and Liberties of Massachusetts. Introduction by Max Farrand. Cambridge, MA: Harvard University Press, 1929.

Lawson, Deodat. *The Duty and Property of a Religious Householder*. Boston: Printed by Bartholomew Green, 1693.

Leader, Jennifer L. "'In Love with the Image': Transitive Being and Typological Desire in Jonathan Edwards." *Early American Literature* 41 (2006) 153–81.

———. *Knowing, Seeing, Being: Jonathan Edwards, Emily Dickinson, Marianne Moore, and the American Typological Tradition*. Boston: University of Massachusetts Press, 2016.

Ledwith, Daniel R. "Family." In *The Jonathan Edwards Encyclopedia*, edited by Harry S. Stout et al., 221–24. Grand Rapids: Eerdmans, 2017.

Lee, Robert Gordon. "Edwards on Education: A Content Analysis of the Philosophy of Education of Jonathan Edwards with Implications for Christian Educators." EdD diss., Southeastern Baptist Theological Seminary, 2023.

Lee, Sang Hyun. *The Concept of Habit in the Thought of Jonathan Edwards*. Cambridge, MA: Harvard University Press, 1972.

———. "Does History Matter to God?: Jonathan Edwards's Dynamic Re-conception of God's Relation to the World." In *Jonathan Edwards at 300: Essays on the Tercentenary of His Birth*, edited by Harry S. Stout et al., 3–13. New York: University Press of America, 2005.

———. "Edwards on God and Nature: Resources for Contemporary Theology." In *Edwards in Our Time: Jonathan Edwards and the Shaping of American Religion*, edited by Sang Hyun Lee and Allen C. Guelzo, 15–44. Grand Rapids: Eerdmans, 1999.

———. "God's Relation to the World." In *The Princeton Companion to Jonathan Edwards*, edited by Sang Hyun Lee, 292–308. Princeton, NJ: Princeton University Press, 2005.

———. *The Philosophical Theology of Jonathan Edwards*. Princeton: Princeton University Press, 2000.

Lee, Sukjae. "Occasionalism." In *Stanford Encyclopedia of Philosophy*. www.plato.stanford.edu/entries/occasionalism.

Lei, Xiao-Xiao (Sharon). "To 'Make a Travailer of Thee': A Study of John Bunyan's Pastoral Theology with Particular Focus on Assurance." PhD diss., Trinity Evangelical Divinity School, 2014.

Lennon, Thomas M., and Paul J. Olscamp. "Introduction." In *The Search After Truth and Elucidations of The Search After Truth*, by Nicolas Malebranche and edited by Thomas M. Lennon and Paul J. Olscamp, vii–xxiii. Cambridge: Cambridge University Press, 1997.

Lepore, Jill. "Literacy and Reading in Puritan New England." In *Perspectives on American Book History: Artifacts and Commentary*, edited by Scott E. Casper et al., 17–46. Amherst: University of Massachusetts Press, 2002.

Lesser, M. X. "Edwards in 'American Culture.'" In *The Cambridge Companion to Jonathan Edwards*, edited by Stephen J. Stein, 289–99. New York: Cambridge University Press, 2007.

Bibliography

———. "Introduction." In *Reading Jonathan Edwards: An Annotated Bibliography in Three Parts, 1729-2005*, edited by M. X. Lesser, 3-46. Grand Rapids: Eerdmans, 2008.

———. *Jonathan Edwards: An Annotated Bibliography, 1979-1993*. Westport, CT: Greenwood, 1994.

———. *Jonathan Edwards: A Reference Guide*. Boston: G. K. Hall, 1981.

Lesser, M. X., ed. *Reading Jonathan Edwards: An Annotated Bibliography in Three Parts, 1729-2005*. Grand Rapids: Eerdmans, 2008.

"Letter from William Smith to William Johnson, March 16, 1767." In *The Papers of Sir William Johnson*, edited by James Sullivan et al., 5:511. Albany, NY: University of the State of New York, 1931.

Levin, David, ed. *Jonathan Edwards: A Profile*. New York: Hill & Wang, 1969.

Lewin, James. *Die Lehre von den Ideen bei Malebranche*. Halle: E. Karras, 1912.

Lidums, Gatis. "The Doctrine of *Imago Dei* and its Relation to Self-Transcendence in the Context of Practical Theology." PhD diss., University of Helsinki, 2004.

Lindberg, Carter. "Introduction." In *The Pietist Theologians: An Introduction to Theology in the Seventeenth and Eighteenth Centuries*, edited by Carter Lindberg, 1-20. Malden, MA: Blackwell, 2005.

Lisa, Andrew. "History of the American Education System." Stacker (December 10, 2020). https://stacker.com/education/history-american-education-system.

Littlefield, George Emery. *Early Schools and School-Books of New England*. Boston: Club of Odd Volumes, 1904.

Litton, Edward Arthur. *Introduction to Dogmatic Theology on the Basis of the Thirty-Nine Articles*. Edited by Philip E. Hughes. Eugene, OR: Wipf & Stock, 2018.

Liturgische Konferenz. "Das Kirchenjahr: Evangelischer Sonn-und Feiertagskalender 2016/2017." www.eivelkirche.ekir.de/wp-content/uploads/2016/2017.

Lloyd-Jones, D. M. "Jonathan Edwards and the Crucial Importance of Revival." In *The Puritans: Their Origins and Successors*, edited by D. M. Lloyd-Jones, 348-71. Carlisle, PA: Banner of Truth Trust, 1987.

———. "Puritanism and Its Origins." In *The Puritans: Their Origins and Successors*, edited by D. M. Lloyd-Jones, 237-59. Carlisle, PA: Banner of Truth Trust, 1987.

Loch, Werner. "Historische Zusammenhänge und phänomenologische Unterschiede." In *Geschichte des Pietismus: Im Auftrag der Historischen Kommission zur Erforschung des Pietismus*, 4:264-68. Göttingen: Vandenhoeck & Ruprecht, 1966(?).

———. "Die Konzeption der Kindheit als Prinzip der Pädagogik." In *Geschichte des Pietismus: Im Auftrag der Historischen Kommission zur Erforschung des Pietismus*, 4:272. Göttingen: Vandenhoeck & Ruprecht, 1966(?).

———. "Weltverbesserung durch Erziehungseinrichtungen." In *Geschichte des Pietismus: Im Auftrag der Historischen Kommission zur Erforschung des Pietismus*, 4:279. Göttingen: Vandenhoeck & Ruprecht, 1966(?).

Locke, John. *An Essay Concerning Human Understanding*. London: Eliz. Holt, 1690.

———. "A Letter to the Reverend Mr. Richard King, August 25, 1703." In *The Works of John Locke*, by John Locke, 10:306. London: C. and J. Rivington, 1824.

———. "A Letter to the Right Reverend Edward, Lord Bishop of Worcester, Concerning Some Passages Relating to Mr. Locke's *Essay of Human Understanding*, January 7, 1697." In *The Works of John Locke*, by John Locke, 4:96. London: C. and J. Rivington, 1824.

Bibliography

———. *Of the Conduct of the Understanding*. Edited by Bolton Corney. London: Bell and Daldy, 1859.

———. *The Reasonableness of Christianity as Delivered in the Scriptures*. London: A. Bettesworth and C. Hitch, 1731.

———. *Some Thoughts Concerning Education*. Cambridge: Cambridge University Press, 1889.

———. *The Works of John Locke*. London: Printed for Thomas Tegg et al., 1823.

Lockridge, Kenneth A. "The History of a Puritan Church, 1637–1736." *New England Quarterly* 40 (1967) 399–424.

———. *Literacy in Colonial New England : An Enquiry into the Social Context of Literacy in the Early Modern West*. New York: Norton, 1974.

———. "Literacy in Early America, 1650–1800." In *Literacy and Social Development in the West*, edited by Harvey J. Graff, 183–200. Cambridge: Cambridge University Press, 1981.

Loeb, Louis E. *From Descartes to Hume: Continental Metaphysics and the Development of Modern Philosophy*. Ithaca, NY: Cornell University Press, 1981.

LoLordo, A. "Descartes and Malebranche on Thought, Sensation and the Nature of Mind." *Journal of the History of Philosophy* 43 (2005) 387–402.

Lough, John. "Reflections on Enlightenment and Lumières." *Journal for Eighteenth-Century Studies* 8 (1985) 1–15.

Louie, Kin Yip. "The Theological Aesthetics of Jonathan Edwards." PhD diss., University of Edinburgh, 2007.

Lovejoy, David S. "Samuel Hopkins: Religion, Slavery, and the Revolution." *New England Quarterly* 40 (1967) 227–43.

Lovelace, Richard F. *The American Pietism of Cotton Mather: Origins of American Evangelicalism*. Grand Rapids: Christian University Press, 1979.

Loveland, Anne C. "Evangelicalism and 'Immediate Emancipation' in American Anti-Slavery Thought." *Journal of Southern History* 32 (1966) 172–88.

Lowe, John T. "Destruction and Benevolence: The New Divinity and Origins of Abolitionism in Edwardsean Tradition." In *Jonathan Edwards within the Enlightenment: Controversy, Experience, and Thought*, edited by John T. Lowe and Daniel N. Gullotta, 87–110. Göttingen: Vandenhoeck & Ruprecht, 2020.

Lowe, John T., and Daniel N. Gullotta. "Introduction." In *Jonathan Edwards within the Enlightenment: Controversy, Experience, and Thought*, edited by John T. Lowe and Daniel N. Gullotta, 13–18. Göttingen: Vandenhoeck & Ruprecht, 2020.

Lowens, Irving. "*The Bay Psalm Book* in Seventeenth-Century New England." *Journal of the American Musicological Society* 8 (1955) 22–29.

Lucas, Sean Michael. "Jonathan Edwards: Between Church and Academy: A Bibliographic Essay." In *The Legacy of Jonathan Edwards: American Religion and the Evangelical Tradition*, edited by D. G. Hart et al., 228–47. Grand Rapids: Baker, 2003.

Lucci, Diego. *Scripture and Deism: The Biblical Criticism of the Eighteenth-Century British Deists*. New York: Peter Lang, 2008.

Lukasik, Christopher. "Feeling the Force of Certainty: The Divine Science, Newtonianism, and Jonathan Edwards' 'Sinners in the Hands of an Angry God.'" *New England Quarterly* 73 (2000) 222–45.

Lynch, Jack. "'Every Man Able to Read': Literacy in Early America." *Colonial Williamsburg Journal* 33 (2011) 24–29.

Bibliography

Lyon, Georges. *L'Idealisme en Angleterre au XVIIIe siècle*. Paris: Ancienne Librarie Germer Bailliére et cie, 1888.

Lyttle, David. "Jonathan Edwards on Personal Identity." In *Studies in Religion in Early American Literature*, by David Lyttle, 21–32. Lanham, MD: University Press of America, 1983.

———. "The Sixth Sense of Jonathan Edwards." *Church Quarterly Review* 167 (1966) 50–59.

———. "The Supernatural Light." In *Studies in Religion in Early American Literature*, by David Lyttle, 1–20. Lanham, MD: University Press of America, 1983.

MacCracken, John H. "The Sources of Jonathan Edwards' Idealism." *The Philosophical Review* 11 (1902) 26–42.

MacLean, Kenneth. *John Locke and English Literature of the Eighteenth Century*. New Haven, CT: Yale University Press, 1936.

Maclear, James F. "New England and the Fifth Monarchy: The Quest for the Millennium in Early American Puritanism." In *Puritan New England: Essays on Religion, Society, and Culture*, edited by Alden T. Vaughan and Francis J. Bremer, 66–91. New York: St. Martin's, 1977.

MacLeod, William. "Jonathan Edwards (1703–58)." *Witness*, 2009. https://www.christianstudylibrary.org/article/jonathan-edwards.

Mailer, Gideon. "Freedom from Spiritual Slavery, but from Civil Too." In *Jonathan Edwards within the Enlightenment: Controversy, Experience, and Thought*, edited by John T. Lowe and Daniel N. Gullotta, 61–86. Göttingen: Vandenhoeck & Ruprecht, 2020.

Maizlish, Rivka. "Perry Miller and the Puritans: An Introduction." *Society for US Intellectual History* (May 8, 2013). www.s-usih.org/2013/05/perry-miller-and-the-puritans-an-introduction/.

Malebranche, Nicolas. *Dialogues on Metaphysics*. Translated by Willis Doney. New York: Abaris, 1980.

———. *Dialogues on Metaphysics and on Religion*. Translated by Morris Ginsberg. New York: Macmillan, 1923.

———. *Oeuvres completes de Malebranche*. Edited by André Robinet. Paris: J. Vrin, 1958–84.

———. *The Search After Truth and Elucidations of The Search After Truth*. Edited by Thomas M. Lennon and Paul J. Olscamp. Cambridge: Cambridge University Press, 1997.

———. *Treatise on Nature and Grace*. Translated by Patrick Riley. Oxford: Clarendon, 1992.

Marini, Amelia. "Seeing Happiness: Jonathan Edwards and the Art of Perception." In *Jonathan Edwards within the Enlightenment: Controversy, Experience, and Thought*, edited by John T. Lowe and Daniel N. Gullotta, 239–59. Göttingen: Vandenhoeck & Ruprecht, 2020.

Marko, Jonathan S. "Deism." In *The Jonathan Edwards Encyclopedia*, edited by Harry S. Stout et al., 136–38. Grand Rapids: Eerdmans, 2017.

Marsden, George M. "Biography." In *The Cambridge Companion to Jonathan Edwards*, edited by Stephen J. Stein, 19–38. New York: Cambridge University Press, 2007.

———. "Challenging the Presumptions of the Age: The Two Dissertations." In *The Legacy of Jonathan Edwards: American Religion and the Evangelical Tradition*, edited by D. G. Hart et al., 99–113. Grand Rapids: Baker, 2003.

Bibliography

———. "Chronology of Edwards' Life and Times." In *Jonathan Edwards: A Life*, xiii–xv. New Haven, CT: Yale University Press, 2003.

———. "Foreword." In *The Jonathan Edwards Encyclopedia*, vi–viii. Grand Rapids: Eerdmans, 2017.

———. "Historical and Ecclesiastical Contexts." In *The Oxford Handbook of Edwards*, edited by Douglas A. Sweeney and Jan Stievermann, 33–50. New York: Oxford University Press, 2021.

———. *An Infinite Fountain of Light: Jonathan Edwards for the Twenty-First Century.* Downer's Grove, IL: InterVarsity, 2023.

———. *Jonathan Edwards: A Life.* New Haven, CT: Yale University Press, 2003.

———. "Jonathan Edwards in the Twenty-First Century." In *Jonathan Edwards at 300: Essays on the Tercentenary of His Birth*, edited by Harry S. Stout et al., 152–64. Lanham, MD: University Press of America, 2005.

———. "Perry Miller's Rehabilitation of the Puritans: A Critique." *Church History* 39 (1970) 91–105.

———. "The Quest for the Historical Edwards: The Challenge of Biography." In *Jonathan Edwards at Home and Abroad: Historical Memories, Cultural Movements, Global Horizons*, edited by David W. Kling and Douglas A. Sweeney, 3–15. Columbia: University of South Carolina Press, 2003.

Martin, George H. *The Evolution of the Massachusetts Public School System: A Historical Sketch.* New York: D. Appleton and Co., 1915.

Marzano, Robert J., et al. *Classroom Instruction That Works: Research-Based Strategies for Increasing Student Achievement.* Alexandria, VA: Association for Supervision and Curriculum Development, 2001.

Mather, Cotton. *Diary of Cotton Mather, 1681–1724. Collections of the Massachusetts Historical Society* 7th Series 7. N.d.: Boston, 1911.

———. *A Family Well-Ordered.* Reprint, Morgan, PA: Soli Deo Gloria, 2001.

———. *India Christiana.* Boston: Printed by B. Green, 1721.

———. "Introduction." In *The Christian Philosopher*, edited by Winton U. Solberg, xxii–xxiv. Urbana: University of Illinois Press, 1994.

———. *Man Eating the Food of Angels.* Boston: Printed for Benj[amin] Eliot, 1710.

———. *Manuductio ad Ministerium.* London: Printed for Charles Dilly, 1781.

———. *The Minister: a sermon, offer'd unto the anniversary convention of ministers, from several parts of New-England, met at Boston, 31 d. iii m.* Boston: n.d., 1722.

———. *Nuncia Bona e Terra Longinqua.* Boston: Printed by B. Green, for Samuel Gerrish, 1715.

———. "Preface." In *Utilia: Real and Vital Religion Served, in the Various and Glorious Intentions of It.* Boston: T. Fleet and T. Crump, 1716.

Mather, Increase. *David Serving His Generation.* Boston: B. Green and J. Allen, 1698.

———. *The Latter Sign Discoursed of In a Sermon Preached at the Lecture of Boston in New England; August 31, 1682. In A Discourse Concerning Comets*, by Increase Mather, Boston: S G. for S. S., 1683.

———. *Substance of Sermons Delivered by Several Ministers in Boston.* MS Collection, Huntington Library, San Marino, CA.

Mathews, Mitford M. *Teaching to Read Historically Considered.* Chicago: University of Chicago Press, 1966.

Matthews, Albert. "Comenius and Harvard College." *Publications of the Colonial Society of Massachusetts* 21 (1919) 146–90.

Bibliography

Matthias, Laurie R. *The Cry of the Teacher's Soul*. Eugene, OR: Wipf & Stock, 2015.

———. "Faith and Learning." In *Christian Higher Education: Faith, Teaching, and Learning in the Evangelical Tradition*, edited by David S. Dockery and Christopher W. Morgan, 169–86. Wheaton, IL: Crossway, 2018.

Matthias, Markus. "August Hermann Francke (1663–1727)." In *The Pietist Theologians: An Introduction to Theology in the Seventeenth and Eighteenth Centuries*, edited by Carter Lindberg, 100–114. Malden, MA: Blackwell, 2005.

Mattes, Mark Alan, ed. *Handwriting in Early America: A Media History*. Amherst: University of Massachusetts Press, 2023.

Maurer, Armand A. "Edwards, Jonathan." In *The Encyclopedia of Philosophy*, edited by Paul Edwards, 8:422. New York: Macmillan, 1972.

May, Henry F. *The Divided Heart: Essays on Protestantism and the Enlightenment in America*. New York: Oxford University Press, 1991.

———. *The Enlightenment in America*. New York: Oxford University Press, 1976.

———. "Jonathan Edwards and America." In *Jonathan Edwards and the American Experience*, edited by Nathan O. Hatch and Harry S. Stout, 19–33. New York: Oxford University Press, 1988.

Mayer, Frederick. *Road to Modern Education*. Lanham, MD: Rowman & Littlefield, 1966.

McClymond, Michael J. "Hearing the Symphony: A Critique of Some Critics of Sang Lee's and Amy Pauw's Accounts of Jonathan Edwards's View of God." In *Jonathan Edwards as Contemporary: Essays in Honor of Sang Hyun Lee*, edited by Don Schweitzer, 67–92. New York: Peter Lang, 2010.

———. "Spiritual Perception in Jonathan Edwards." *Journal of Religion* 77 (1997) 195–216.

McClymond, Michael J., and Gerald R. McDermott. *The Theology of Jonathan Edwards*. New York: Oxford University Press, 2012.

McCracken, Charles. *Malebranche and British Philosophy*. Oxford: Clarendon, 1983.

McDermott, Gerald R. "Conclusion: Edwards's Relevance Today." In *Understanding Jonathan Edwards: An Introduction to America's Theologian*, edited by Gerald R. McDermott, 210–17. New York: Oxford University Press, 2009.

———. "Edwards and the World Religions." In *Understanding Jonathan Edwards: An Introduction to America's Theologian*, edited by Gerald R. McDermott, 177–94. New York: Oxford University Press, 2009.

———. *Everyday Reality: The Revelation of God in All of Reality*. Grand Rapids: Baker Academic, 2018.

———. "Franklin, Jefferson, and Edwards on Religion and Religions." In *Jonathan Edwards at 300: Essays on the Tercentenary of his Birth*, edited by Harry S. Stout et al., 65–85. Lanham, MD: University Press of America, 2005.

———. "Introduction: How to Understand the American Theologian." In *Understanding Jonathan Edwards: An Introduction to America's Theologian*, edited by Gerald R. McDermott, 3–14. New York: Oxford University Press, 2009.

———. "Jonathan Edwards and American Indians: The Devil Sucks Their Blood." *New England Quarterly* 72 (1999) 539–57.

———. "Jonathan Edwards and the Future of Global Christianity." *Theologica Wratislaviensia* 7 (2012) 13–19.

———. *Jonathan Edwards Confronts the Gods: Christian Theology, Enlightenment Religion, and Non-Christian Faiths*. New York: Oxford University Press, 2000.

Bibliography

———. "Missions and Native Americans." In *The Princeton Companion to Jonathan Edwards*, edited by Sang Hyun Lee, 258–73. Princeton, NJ: Princeton University Press, 2005.

———. "Nathanael Emmons and the Decline of Edwardsian Theology." In *After Jonathan Edwards: The Courses of the New England Theology*, edited by Oliver D. Crisp and Douglas A. Sweeney, 118–29. New York: Oxford University Press, 2012.

———. *One Holy and Happy Society: The Public Theology of Jonathan Edwards.* University Park: Pennsylvania State University Press, 1992.

———. "Theology in the Hands of a Literary Artist: Jonathan Edwards as Preacher." *Theologica Wratislaviensia* 7 (2012) 115–27.

McGiffert, Arthur Cushman Jr. *Jonathan Edwards*. New York: Harper & Brothers, 1932.

McGiffert, Michael. "American Puritan Studies in the 1960's." *William and Mary Quarterly* 3 (1970) 36–67.

———. "Grace and Works: The Rise and Division of Covenant Divinity in Elizabethan Puritanism." *Harvard Theological Review* 75 (1982) 463–502.

———. "Shepard, Thomas (1605–1649)." In *Puritans and Puritanism in Europe and America: A Comprehensive Encyclopedia*, edited by Francis J. Bremer and Tom Webster, 1:231–33. New York: ABC-Clio, 2006.

McLachlan, H[erbert]. *The Religious Opinions of Milton, Locke, and Newton.* Manchester: Manchester University Press, 1941.

McLoughlin, William G. "Pietism and the American Character." *American Quarterly* 17 (1965) 163–86.

McMahon, Lucia. *Education of Girls and Women.* www.encyclopedia.com/history/encyclopedia-almanacs-transcripts-and-maps/education-girls-and-women.

McMullen, Michael David, ed. *The Blessing of God: Previously Unpublished Sermons of Jonathan Edwards.* Brentwood, TN: Broadman & Holman, 2003.

Melton, James Van Horn. "Pietism, Politics, and the Public Sphere in Germany." In *Religion and Politics in Enlightenment Europe*, edited by James E. Bradley and Dale K. Van Kley, 294–333. Notre Dame, IN: University of Notre Dame Press, 2001.

Mencken, H. L. *A Mencken Chrestomathy.* New York: Vintage, 1982.

Mencken, H. L., and George Jean Nathan. "Clinical Notes." *American Mercury* 4 (1925) 59.

Merriam, Sharan B., et al. *Learning in Adulthood: A Comprehensive Guide.* 3rd ed. San Francisco: Jossey-Bass, 2007.

Merton, Thomas, and John Howard Griffin. *A Hidden Wholeness: The Visual World of Thomas Merton.* Boston: Houghton Mifflin Co., 1979.

Meyer, Donald Harvey *The Democratic Enlightenment.* New York: Capricorn, 1976.

———. "The Uniqueness of the American Enlightenment." *American Quarterly* 28 (1976) 165–86.

Mezirow, Jack. "Perspective Transformation." *Adult Education* 28 (1978) 100–110.

———. "Transformative Learning: Theory to Practice." *New Directions for Adult and Continuing Education* 74 (1997) 5.

Middlekauff, Robert. *Ancients and Axioms: Secondary Education in Eighteenth-Century New England.* New Haven, CT: Yale University Press, 1963.

———. *The Mathers: Three Generations of Puritan Intellectuals, 1596–1728.* Berkeley: University of California Press, 1999.

———. "Perry Miller." In *Pastmasters: Some Essays on American Historians*, edited by Marcus Cunliffe and Robin Winks, 167–90. New York: Harper & Row, 1969.

Bibliography

———. "Piety and Intellect in Puritanism." *William and Mary Quarterly* 3 (1965) 457–70.

Middleton, Richard. *Colonial America: A History, 1565–1776*. 3rd ed. Malden, MA: Blackwell, 2002.

Miles, Lion. "The Red Man Dispossessed: The Williams Family and the Alienation of Indian Land in Stockbridge, Massachusetts, 1736–1818." *New England Quarterly* 67 (1994) 46–76.

Miller, Howard. "Evangelical Religion and Colonial Princeton." In *Schooling and Society: Studies in the History of Education*, edited by Lawrence Stone, 115–45. Baltimore: Johns Hopkins University Press, 1976.

Miller, Perry. "Declension in a Bible Commonwealth." In *Proceedings of the American Antiquarian Society* 51 (1941) 37–94.

———. "Edwards, Locke, and the Rhetoric of Sensation." In *Critical Essays on Jonathan Edwards*, edited by William J. Scheick, 120–35. Boston: G. K. Hall, 1980.

———. *Errand into the Wilderness*. Cambridge, MA: Harvard University Press, 1956.

———. "General Editor's Note." In *Works of Jonathan Edwards*, edited by Paul Ramsey, 1:vii–viii. New Haven, CT: Yale University Press, 1949.

———. *Jonathan Edwards*. Reprint, Lincoln: University of Nebraska Press, 2005.

———. "Jonathan Edwards—The First Modern American." In *Jonathan Edwards and the Enlightenment*, edited by John Opie, 22–36. Lexington, MA: D. C. Heath, 1969.

———. "Jonathan Edwards on the Sense of the Heart." *Harvard Theological Review* 41 (1948) 123–45.

———. "The Marrow of Puritan Divinity." In *Puritan New England: Essays on Religion, Society, and Culture*, edited by Alden T. Vaughan and Francis J. Bremer, 44–63. New York: St. Martin's, 1977.

———. *Nature's Nation*. Cambridge, MA: Harvard University Press, Belknap, 1967.

———. *The New England Mind: From Colony to Province*. Cambridge, MA: Harvard University Press, 1953.

———. *The New England Mind: The Seventeenth Century*. Cambridge, MA: Harvard University Press, 1953.

———. *Orthodoxy in Massachusetts, 1630–1650*. New York: Harper & Row, 1970.

———. "The Piety and the Federal Theology." In *Tensions in American Puritanism*, edited by Richard Reinitz, 17–37. New York: John Wiley & Sons, 1970.

———. "The Puritan Way of Life." In *Puritanism in Early America*, edited by George M. Waller, 4–22. Boston: D. C. Heath, 1950.

———. "Speculative Genius." Review of *Jonathan Edwards, 1703–1758: A Biography*, *Saturday Review of Literature* 31(1940) 6–7.

Miller, Perry, and Thomas H. Johnson. *The Puritans: A Sourcebook of Their Writings*. New York: American Book, 1938.

Miller, Samuel. *A Brief Retrospect of the Eighteenth Century*. 2 vols. New York: T. and J. Swords, 1803.

Miller, Thomas P. *The Evolution of College English: Literacy Studies from the Puritans to the Postmoderns*. Pittsburgh: University of Pittsburgh Press, 2014.

Milton, John. "The Milton Reading Room." www.dartmouth.edu/~milton/reading_room/of_education /text.shtml.

Minkema, Kenneth P. "Appendix A." In *Works of Jonathan Edwards Online*, edited by Peter J. Thuesen, 26:363. http://edwards.yale.edu.

Bibliography

———. "Cotton Mather, Jonathan Edwards, and the Relationship Between Historical and Spiritual Exegesis in Early Evangelicalism." In *The Bible in Early Transatlantic Pietism and Evangelicalism*, edited by Ryan P. Hoselton et al., 182–99. University Park: Pennsylvania State University, 2022.

———. "Cooper, Anthony A., Third Earl of Shaftesbury (1671–1713)." In *The Jonathan Edwards Encyclopedia*, edited by Harry S. Stout et al., 114. Grand Rapids: Eerdmans, 2017.

———. "A 'Dordtian Philosophe': Jonathan Edwards, Calvin, and Reformed Orthodoxy." *Church History and Religious Culture* 91 (2011) 241–53.

———. "The Edwardses: A Ministerial Family in Eighteenth-Century New England." PhD diss., University of Connecticut, 1988.

———. "Edwards, Esther Stoddard (1672–1771)." In *The Jonathan Edwards Encyclopedia*, edited by Harry S. Stout et al., 177–78. Grand Rapids: Eerdmans, 2017.

———. "Mary Edwards (1701–1776)." In *The Jonathan Edwards Encyclopedia*, edited by Harry S. Stout et al., 181. Grand Rapids: Eerdmans, 2017.

———. "Edwards, Timothy (father) (1669–1758)." In *The Jonathan Edwards Encyclopedia*, 185–86. Grand Rapids: Eerdmans, 2017.

———. "Foreword." In *The Global Edwards: Papers from the Jonathan Edwards Congress held in Melbourne, August 2015*, xiii–xiv. Eugene, OR: Wipf & Stock, 2017.

———. "Foreword." In *Jonathan Edwards within the Enlightenment: Controversy, Experience, and Thought*, edited by John T. Lowe and Daniel N. Gullotta, 11–12. Göttingen: Vandenhoeck & Ruprecht, 2020.

———. "Francke, August Hermann (1663–1727)." In *The Jonathan Edwards Encyclopedia*, edited by Harry S. Stout et al., 233. Grand Rapids: Eerdmans, 2017.

———. "Hannah and Her Sisters: Sisterhood, Courtship, and Marriage in the Edwards Family in the Early Eighteenth Century." *New England Historical and Genealogical Register* 146 (1992) 35–56

———. "Hutcheson, Francis (1694–1746)." In *The Jonathan Edwards Encyclopedia*, edited by Harry S. Stout et al., 312–13. Grand Rapids: Eerdmans, 2017.

———. "'Informing of the Child's Understanding, Influencing his Heart, and Directing its Practice': Jonathan Edwards on Education." *Acta Theologica* 31 (2011) 159–89.

———. "Jonathan Edwards: A Theological Life." In *The Princeton Companion to Jonathan Edwards*, edited by Sang Hyun Lee, 1–15. Princeton, NJ: Princeton University Press, 2005.

———. "Jonathan Edwards in the Twentieth Century." *Journal of the Evangelical Theological Society* 47 (2004) 659–87.

———. "Jonathan Edwards on Education and His Educational Legacy." In *After Jonathan Edwards: The Courses of the New England Theology*, edited by Oliver D. Crisp and Douglas A. Sweeney, 31–50. New York: Oxford University Press, 2012.

———. "Jonathan Edwards's Defense of Slavery." *Massachusetts Historical Review* 4 (2002) 23–59.

———. "Jonathan Edwards's Life and Career: Society and Self." In *Understanding Jonathan Edwards: An Introduction to America's Theologian*, edited by Gerald R. McDermott, 15–28. New York: Oxford University Press, 2009.

———. "Maunnauseet, Ebenezer (dates unknown)." In *The Jonathan Edwards Encyclopedia*, edited by Harry S. Stout et al., 367. Grand Rapids: Eerdmans, 2017.

———. "Mahican (Stockbridge) Indians." In *The Jonathan Edwards Encyclopedia*, edited by Harry S. Stout et al., 359–60. Grand Rapids: Eerdmans, 2017.

Bibliography

———. "Malebranche, Nicolas (1638-1715)." In *The Jonathan Edwards Encyclopedia*, edited by Harry S. Stout et al., 360. Grand Rapids: Eerdmans, 2017.

———. "Old Age and Religion in the Writings and Life of Jonathan Edwards." *Church History* 70 (2001) 674-704.

———. "The Private Writings of Hannah Edwards (Hannah Edwards Wetmore)." In *Works of Jonathan Edwards Online*, edited by Jonathan Edwards Center, 41:nd. http://edwards.yale.edu.

———. "Reforming Harvard: Cotton Mather on Education at Cambridge" *New England Quarterly* 87 (2014) 319-40.

———. "'Universal Education' in Early New Haven." Lecture given at New Haven Museum, April 2013.

———. "Writing and Preaching Sermons." In *The Oxford Handbook of Jonathan Edwards*, edited by Douglas A. Sweeney and Jan Stievermann, 387-403. New York: Oxford University Press, 2021.

Minkema, Kenneth P., and Harry S. Stout. "The Edwardsean Tradition and the Anti-Slavery Debate, 1740-1865." *Journal of American History* 92 (2005) 47-74.

———. "Jonathan Edwards Studies: The State of the Field." In *Jonathan Edwards as Contemporary: Essays in Honor of Sang Hyun Lee*, edited by Don Schweitzer, 239-58. New York: Peter Lang, 2010.

Mintz, Steven. *Huck's Raft: A History of American Childhood*. Cambridge, MA: Harvard University Press, 2004.

Mitchell, Louis J. *Jonathan Edwards on the Experience of Beauty*. Eugene, OR: Wipf & Stock, 2003.

Monaghan, E. Jennifer. *Learning to Read and Write in Colonial America*. Amherst: University of Massachusetts Press, 2005.

———. "Literacy Instruction and Gender in Colonial New England." *American Quarterly* 40 (1988) 18-41.

Monaghan, E. Jennifer, and Arlene L. Barry. *Writing the Past: Teaching Reading in Colonial America and the United States, 1640-1940*. An exhibition presented at the 44th Annual Convention of the International Reading Association, San Diego, California, May 2-7, 1999.

Monroe, Paul. *A Cyclopedia of Education*. 5 vols. New York: Macmillan, 1911-1918.

Monroe, Will S. *Comenius and the Beginnings of Educational Reform*. New York: Arno Press and The New York Times, 1971.

Moody, Josh. *The God-Centered Life: Insights from Jonathan Edwards for Today*. Vancouver, BC: Regent College Press, 2007.

———. *Jonathan Edwards and the Enlightenment: Knowing the Presence of God*. New York: University Press of America, 2005.

Moodey, Samuel. *The Vain Youth Summoned to Appear at Christ's Bar*. Boston: Printed by Timothy Green, 1707.

Morais, Herbert M. *Deism in Eighteenth Century America*. New York: Russell & Russell, 1960.

Moran, Gerald F., and Maris A. Vinovskis. "Literacy and Education in Eighteenth-Century North America." In *The World Turned Upside-Down: The State of Eighteenth-Century American Studies at the Beginning of the Twenty-First Century*, edited by Michael V. Kennedy and William G. Shade, 186-223. Bethlehem, PA: Lehigh University Press, 2001.

Bibliography

Morgan, Edmund S. "The Historians of Early New England." In *Reinterpretation of Early American History*, edited by Ray Allen Billington, 41–63. New York: Norton, 1968.

———. "New England Puritanism: Another Approach." *William and Mary Quarterly* 3rd Series 18 (1961) 236–42.

———. *The Puritan Family: Religion and Domestic Relations in Seventeenth-Century New England*. New York: Harper & Row, 1966.

———. *Visible Saints: The History of a Puritan Idea*. New York: New York University Press, 1963.

Morgan, John. *Godly Learning: Puritan Attitudes Toward Reason, Learning, and Education, 1560–1640*. New York: Cambridge University Press, 1986.

———. "The Problem of Definition." In *Godly Learning: Puritan Attitudes Toward Reason, Learning, and Education, 1560–1640*, 9–22. New York: Cambridge University Press, 1986.

Morison, Samuel Eliot. "Builders of the Bay Colony." In *Puritanism in Early America*, edited by George M. Waller, 62–68. Boston: D. C. Heath, 1950.

———. *The Founding of Harvard College*. Cambridge, MA: Harvard University Press, 1935.

———. *The Intellectual Life of Colonial New England*. New York: New York University Press, 1956.

———. "The Puritan Pronaos." In *Puritanism in Early America*, edited by George M. Waller, 68–79. Boston: D. C. Heath, 1950.

———. *Three Centuries of Harvard, 1636–1936*. Cambridge, MA: Harvard University Press, 1965.

Morris, Amy. "The Art of Purifying: *The Bay Psalm Book* and Colonial Puritanism." *Early American Literature* 42 (2007) 107–30.

Morris, William S. "The Genius of Jonathan Edwards." In *Reinterpretation in American Church History*, edited by Jerald C. Brauer, 29–65. Chicago: University of Chicago Press, 1968.

———. "The Reappraisal of Edwards." *New England Quarterly* 30 (1957) 515–25.

———. *The Young Jonathan Edwards: A Reconstruction*. New York: Carlson, 1991.

Müller-Bahlke, Thomas. "Naturwissenschaft und Technik im Gedankenhorizont des Halleschen Pietismus." In *Geschichte des Pietismus: Im Auftrag der Historischen Kommission zur Erforschung des Pietismus*, 4:363–64, Göttingen: Vandenhoeck & Ruprecht, 1966(?).

Muller, Richard A. "Jonathan Edwards and the Absence of Free Choice: A Parting of Ways in the Reformed Tradition." *Jonathan Edwards Studies* 1 (2011) 3–22.

Murdoch, Kenneth B. *The Day of Doom*. New York: Spiral, 1929.

Murdock, Kenneth B. *Literature and Theology in Colonial New England*. Westport, CT: Greenwood, 1949.

———. "The Puritan Legacy." In *Puritanism and the American Experience*, edited by Michael McGiffert, 260–74. Reading, MA: Addison-Wesley, 1969.

———. "The Puritan Literary Attitude." In *Puritanism in Early America*, edited by George M. Waller, 89–98. Boston: D. C. Heath, 1950.

———. "The Teaching of Latin and Greek at the Boston Latin School in 1712." *Publications of the Colonial Society of Massachusetts* 27 (Transactions, 1927–1930) 21–29.

Bibliography

Murphy, Daniel. *Comenius: A Critical Reassessment of His Life and Work*. Cambridge: Cambridge University Press, 1995.

Murray, Iain. *Jonathan Edwards: A New Biography*. Carlisle, PA: Banner of Truth Trust, 1987.

Nadler, Steven, ed. *The Cambridge Companion to Malebranche*. Cambridge: Cambridge University Press, 2000.

———. *Malebranche and Ideas*. Oxford: Oxford University Press, 1992.

Naylor, Natalie Ann. "Raising a Learned Ministry: American Education Society, 1815–1860." EdD diss., Columbia University, 1971.

Neal, Daniel. *The History of New-England, Containing an Impartial Account of the Civil and Ecclesiastical Affairs of the Country, to the Year of our Lord, 1700*. 2 vols. London: J. Clark, R. Ford, and R. Cruttenden, 1720.

Neele, Adriaan C. "Africa." In *The Oxford Handbook of Jonathan Edwards*, edited by Douglas A. Sweeney and Jan Stievermann, 542–54. New York: Oxford University Press, 2021.

New, John F. H. *Anglican and Puritan: The Basis of Their Opposition, 1558–1640*. Stanford, CA: Stanford University Press, 1964.

Newcomb, Harvey. *Memoir of Phebe Bartlett, of Nothampton, Massachusetts*. Northampton, MA(?): American Sunday School Union, 1831.

Newton, Gary. *Heart Deep Teaching: Engaging Students for Transformed Lives*. Nashville: B & H Academic, 2012.

Newton, Isaac. *The Chronology of the Ancient Kingdoms Amended*. London: Printed for J. Tonson, and J. Osborn and T. Longman, 1728.

———. *Four Letters from Sir Isaac Newton to Doctor Bentley Containing Some Arguments in Proof of a Deity*. London: Printed for R. and J. Dodsley, 1756.

———. *Opticks, or, A Treatise of the Reflexions, Refractions, Inflexions, and Colours of Light*. London: Sam[uel] Smith and Benj[amin] Walford, 1704.

———. *Philosophiae Naturalis Principia Mathematica*. 2nd ed. Cambridge, 1713.

Nichols, Stephen J. *An Absolute Sort of Certainty: The Holy Spirit and the Apologetics of Jonathan Edwards*. Phillipsburg, NJ: P & R, 2003.

———. *Jonathan Edwards: A Guided Tour of His Life and Thought*. Phillipsburg, NJ: P & R, 2001.

———. "Jonathan Edwards: His Life and Legacy." In *A God-Entranced Vision of all Things: The Legacy of Jonathan Edwards*, edited by John Piper and Justin Taylor, 35–54. Wheaton, IL: Crossway, 2004.

———. "Last of the Mohican Missionaries: Jonathan Edwards at Stockbridge." In *The Legacy of Jonathan Edwards: American Religion and the Evangelical Tradition*, edited by D. G. Hart et al., 47–63. Grand Rapids: Baker, 2003.

Nichols, Stephen R. C. "Revelation." In *The Oxford Handbook of Jonathan Edwards*, edited by Douglas A. Sweeney and Jan Stievermann, 163–82. New York: Oxford University Press, 2021.

Nicolson, Harold. *The Age of Reason (1700–1789)*. London: Constable, 1960.

Noddings, Nel. *Philosophy of Education*. London: Routledge, 2018.

Noll, Mark A. "American Christian Politics." Review of *Godly Republicanism*, by Michael P. Winship, *Christianity Today/Books and Culture*, www.booksandculture.com/articles/2012/novdec/american.

Bibliography

———. "Edwards' Theology after Edwards." In *The Princeton Companion to Jonathan Edwards*, edited by Sang Hyun Lee, 292–308. Princeton, NJ: Princeton University Press, 2005.

———. "Jonathan Edwards and Nineteenth-Century Theology." In *Jonathan Edwards and the American Experience*, edited by Nathan O. Hatch and Harry S. Stout, 260–87. New York: Oxford University Press, 1988.

———. *Protestants in America*. Oxford: Oxford University Press, 2000.

———. "The Rise and Long Life of the Protestant Enlightenment in America." In *Knowledge and Belief in America: Enlightenment Traditions and Modern Religious Thought*, edited by William M. Shea and Pater A. Huff, 88–124. Cambridge: Cambridge University Press, 1995.

Nord, David Paul. *Faith in Reading: Religious Publishing and the Birth of Mass Media in America*. New York: Oxford University Press, 2004.

Norton, Arthur O. "Harvard Text-Books and Reference Books of the Seventeenth Century." *Publications of the Colonial Society of Massachusetts* 28 (1935) 361–438.

Oakes, Urian. *The Unconquerable, All-Conquering, and More-Than-Conquering Souldier* [sic]. Cambridge, MA: Samuel Green, 1674.

Oberg, Barbara B., and Harry S. Stout. "Introduction." In *Benjamin Franklin, Jonathan Edwards, and the Representation of American Culture*, edited by Barbara B. Oberg and Harry S. Stout, 3–9. New York: Oxford University Press, 1993.

Oberholzer, Emil. "The Church in New England Society." In *Seventeenth-Century America: Essays in Colonial History*, edited by James Morton Smith, 143–65. Chapel Hill: University of North Carolina, 1959.

Obst, Helmut. *August Hermann Francke und Sein Werk*. Halle: Franckeschen Stiftungen zu Halle, 2013.

O'Connor, D. J. *John Locke*. Baltimore: Penguin, 1952.

Oliphint, K. Scott. "Jonathan Edwards on Apologetics: Reason and the Noetic Effects of Sin." In *The Legacy of Jonathan Edwards: American Religion and the Evangelical Tradition*, edited by D. G. Hart et al., 131–46. Grand Rapids: Baker Academic, 2003.

Olsen, Wesley A. "The Philosophy of Jonathan Edwards and its Significance for Educational Thinking." EdD diss., Rutgers University, 1973.

Olson, Roger E. "Pietism: Myths and Realities." In *The Pietist Impulse in Christianity*, edited by Christian T. Collins Winn et al., 8–26. Eugene, OR: Wipf & Stock, 2011.

Opie, John. "Introduction." In *Jonathan Edwards and the Enlightenment*, i–xiv. Lexington, MA: D. C. Heath, 1969.

Ormond, Alexander T. "Greeting from Princeton University." In *Jonathan Edwards: A Retrospect*, edited by H. Norman Gardiner, 80–86. Boston: Houghton Mifflin, 1901.

Outram, Dorinda. *The Enlightenment*. 3rd ed. Cambridge: Cambridge University Press, 2013.

———. "What Is Enlightenment?" In *The Enlightenment: New Approaches to European History*, 1–9. Cambridge: Cambridge University Press, 2019.

Oviatt, Edwin. *The Beginnings of Yale (1701–1726)*. New Haven, CT: Yale University Press, 1916.

Packer, James I. "Foreword." In *Introduction to Puritan Theology: A Reader*, edited by Edward Hindson, 9. Grand Rapids: Baker, 1976.

———. "Introductory Essay." In *The Death of Death in the Death of Christ*, by John Owen, 1. London: Banner of Truth, 1963.

Bibliography

———. *A Quest for Godliness: The Puritan Vision of the Christian Life*. Wheaton, IL: Crossway, 1990.

Pagden, Anthony. *The Enlightenment and Why It Still Matters*. New York: Random House, 2013.

Paine, Thomas. *The Doctrine of Original Sin Proved and Applyed*. Boston: Printed by B. Green for Danial Henchman, 1724.

———. *The Writings of Thomas Paine, vol. IV. 1794–1796*. www.gutenberg.org/files/3743/3743-h/3743- h.htm#link2HCH0001.

Palmer, Parker J. *Courage to Teach: Exploring the Inner Landscape of a Teacher's Life*. San Francisco: Jossey-Bass, 1998.

———. *The Promise of Paradox: A Celebration of Contradictions in the Christian Life*. San Francisco: Jossey-Bass, 2008.

———. *To Know As We Are Known: Education as a Spiritual Journey*. San Francisco: Harper Collins, 1993.

Palmer, Parker J., et al. *The Heart of Higher Education: A Call to Renewal*. San Francisco: Jossey-Bass, 2010.

Park, Edwards Amasa. *Memoir of the Life and Character of Samuel Hopkins, D. D.* Boston: Leonard W. Kimball, 1830.

———. "Memoir of Nathanael Emmons." In *The Works of Nathanael Emmons*, edited by Jacob Ide, 1:1–468. Boston: Congregational Board of Publication, 1861.

Park, Paul J. "Stoddard, Solomon (1643–1729)." In *The Jonathan Edwards Encyclopedia*, edited by Harry S. Stout et al., 553. Grand Rapids: Eerdmans, 2017.

Parker, Nathan. "Bartlett, Phebe (1731–1805)." In *The Jonathan Edwards Encyclopedia*, edited by Harry S. Stout et al., 59–60. Grand Rapids: Eerdmans, 2017.

Parkes, Henry Bamford. *Jonathan Edwards: The Fiery Puritan*. New York: Minton, Balch, 1930.

Parrington, Vernon Louis. "The Anachronism of Jonathan Edwards." In *Main Currents in American Thought*, 1:148–63. New York: Harcourt, Brace and Co., 1927.

Parsons, Usher. *The Life of Sir William Pepperrell, Bart*. Boston: Little, Brown and Co., 1856.

Pauw, Amy Plantinga. *The Supreme Harmony of All: The Trinitarian Theology of Jonathan Edwards*. Grand Rapids: Eerdmans, 2002.

Pederson, Randall J. "Orthodoxy." In *The Jonathan Edwards Encyclopedia*, edited by Harry S. Stout et al. 430–31. Grand Rapids: Eerdmans, 2017.

Perry, Lewis. *Intellectual Life in America: A History*. New York: Franklin Watts, 1984.

Perry, Ralph Barton. "The Moral Athlete." In *Puritanism in Early America: Problems in American Civilization*, edited by George M. Waller, 98–107. Boston: D. C. Heath, 1950.

———. *Puritanism and Democracy*. New York: Vanguard, 1944.

Phillips, Charles. "Edwards Amasa Park: The Last Edwardsian." In *After Jonathan Edwards: The Courses of the New England Theology*, edited by Oliver D. Crisp and Douglas A. Sweeney, 151–61. New York: Oxford University Press, 2012.

———. "The Last Edwardsean: Edwards Amasa Park and the Rhetoric of Improved Calvinism." PhD diss., University of Stirling, 2005.

Piggin, Stuart. "Australia." In *The Oxford Handbook of Jonathan Edwards*, edited by Douglas A. Sweeney and Jan Stievermann, 528–41. New York: Oxford University Press, 2021.

Bibliography

Pilcher, George William. "Preacher of the New Light, Samuel Davies, 1724 [sic]-1761." PhD diss., University of Illinois, 1963.

———. *Samuel Davies: Apostle of Dissent in Colonial Virginia.* Knoxville: University of Tennessee Press, 1971.

Piper, John. "A God-Entranced Vision of All Things: Why We Need Jonathan Edwards 300 Years Later." In *A God-Entranced Vision of all Things: The Legacy of Jonathan Edwards,* edited by John Piper and Justin Taylor, 21–34. Wheaton, IL: Crossway, 2004.

Piper, John, and Justin Taylor, eds. *A God-Entranced Vision of all Things: The Legacy of Jonathan Edwards.* Wheaton, IL: Crossway, 2004.

Piper, Noel. "Sarah Edwards: Jonathan's Home and Haven." In *A God-Entranced Vision of all Things: The Legacy of Jonathan Edwards,* edited by John Piper and Justin Taylor, 55–78. Wheaton, IL: Crossway, 2004.

Piirimäe, Eva. "Berlin, Herder, and the Counter-Enlightenment." *Eighteenth-Century Studies* 49 (2015) 71–76.

Platner, John Winthrop, et al. *The Religious History of New England.* Cambridge, MA: Harvard University Press, 1917.

Plato, Michael J. "Bellamy, Joseph (1719–1790)." In *The Jonathan Edwards Encyclopedia,* edited by Harry S. Stout et al., 67–68. Grand Rapids: Eerdmans, 2017.

———. "Emmons, Nathaniel (1745–1840)." In *The Jonathan Edwards Encyclopedia,* edited by Harry S. Stout et al., 194–95. Grand Rapids: Eerdmans, 2017.

———. "Hopkins, Samuel (1721–1803)." In *The Jonathan Edwards Encyclopedia,* edited by Harry S. Stout et al., 304–6. Grand Rapids: Eerdmans, 2017.

———. "Newton, Isaac (1642–1727)." In *The Jonathan Edwards Encyclopedia,* edited by Harry S. Stout et al., 407. Grand Rapids: Eerdmans, 2017.

Plunkett, Mrs. H. M. "Ten Co-educated Girls Two Hundred Years Ago." *Scribner's Magazine* 33 (1903) 450–56.

Pocock, J. G. A. *Barbarism and Religion.* Cambridge: Cambridge University Press, 1999.

———. "Post-Puritan England and the Problem of the Enlightenment." In *Culture and Politics from Puritanism to the Enlightenment: The Enlightenment in National Context,* edited by Perez Zagorin, 91–112. Los Angeles: University of California Press, 1980.

———. "The Re-Description of Enlightenment." *Proceedings of the British Academy* 125 (2004) 101–17.

Pope, Robert G. *The Half-Way Covenant: Church Membership in Puritan New England.* Princeton, NJ: Princeton University Press, 1969.

———. "New England Versus the New England Mind: The Myth of Declension." *Journal of Social History* 3 (1969/1970) 95–198.

Porterfield, Amanda. *The Protestant Experience in America.* Westport, CT: Greenwood, 2006.

Post, Stephen. "Disinterested Benevolence: An American Debate Over the Nature of Christian Love." *Journal of Religious Ethics* 14 (1986) 356–68.

Potgieter, Esmari. "Education." In *The Oxford Handbook of Jonathan Edwards,* edited by Douglas A. Sweeney and Jan Stievermann, 404–15. New York: Oxford University Press, 2021.

———. "Jonathan Edwards and a Reformational View of the Purpose of Education." In *Die Skriflig/In Luce Verbi* 50 (2016) 1–9.

Potter, Alfred Claghorn. "Catalogue of John Harvard's Library." *Publications of the Colonial Society of Massachusetts* 21 (1919) 190–230.

Bibliography

———. "The Harvard College Library, 1723–1735." *Publications of the Colonial Society of Massachusetts* 25 (1924) 1–13.

Powers, Cornelia. "Women in Colonial America Were More Powerful Than We Give Them Credit For." *TIME* (March 16, 2022). www.time.com/6157132/colonial-women-history-esther-aaron-burr.

Preston, John. *Life Eternall; or, A Treatise of the knowledge of the Divine Essence and Attributes, Delivered in XVIII Sermons.* London, 1631.

Price, Rebecca R. "Jonathan Edwards as a Christian Educator." PhD diss., New York University, 1938.

Pryde, George Smith. *The Scottish Universities and the Colleges of Colonial America.* Glasgow: Jackson, Son & Co., 1957.

Quincy, Josiah. *The History of Harvard University.* Boston: Crosby, Nichols, Lee, 1840.

Quinn, Philip L. "The Master Argument of The Nature of True Virtue." In *Jonathan Edwards: Philosophical Theologian*, edited by Paul Helm and Oliver D. Crisp, 79–97. Burlington, VT: Ashgate, 2003.

Radner, Daisie. *Malebranche: A Study of a Cartesian System.* Assen: Van Gorcum, 1978.

Ramsey, Paul. "Editor's Introduction." In *Works of Jonathan Edwards Online*, edited by Paul Ramsey, 8:1–12. http://edwards.yale.edu.

———. "Edwards and John Locke." In *Works of Jonathan Edwards Online*, edited by Paul Ramsey, 1:47–65. http://edwards.yale.edu.

———. "Edwards and His Antagonists: THOMAS CHUBB, DANIEL WHITBY, and ISAAC WATTS." In *Works of Jonathan Edwards Online*, edited by Paul Ramsey, 1:65–118. http://edwards.yale.edu.

Rand, Edward Kennard. "Liberal Education in Seventeenth-Century Harvard." *New England Quarterly* 6 (1933) 525–51.

Ranz, James. "The History of the Printed Book Catalogue in the United States." PhD thesis, University of Illinois, 1960.

Redwood, John. *Reason, Ridicule and Religion: The Age of Enlightenment in England, 1660–1750.* Cambridge, MA: Harvard University Press, 1976.

Reed, James E. *A History of Christian Education.* Nashville: Broadman & Holman, 1993.

Rehnman, Sebastian. *Edwards on God.* London: Routledge, 2021.

———. "Idealism and Aetiology." In *The Oxford Handbook of Jonathan Edwards*, edited by Douglas A. Sweeney and Jan Stievermann, 337–50. New York: Oxford University Press, 2021.

Reid, Thomas. *An Inquiry into the Human Mind on the Principles of Common Sense.* 5th ed. Edinburgh: Printed for Bell & Bradfute, et al., 1801.

Reinitz, Richard. "Introduction." In *Tensions in American Puritanism*, edited by Richard Reinitz, 2–3. New York: John Wiley & Sons, 1970.

———. "Perry Miller and Recent American Historiography." *Bulletin, British Association for American Studies* 8 (1964) 27–35.

———. *Tensions in American Puritanism: Problems in American History.* New York: John Willey & Sons, 1970.

Reklis, Kathryn. "Imagination and Hermeneutics." In *The Oxford Handbook of Jonathan Edwards*, edited by Douglas A. Sweeney and Jan Stievermann, 309–23. New York: Oxford University Press, 2021.

Riley, I. Woodbridge. "Jonathan Edwards." In *Critical Essays on Jonathan Edwards*, edited by William J. Scheick, 97–119. Boston: G. K. Hall, 1980.

———. "The Real Jonathan Edwards." *The Open Court* 22 (1908) 705–15.

Bibliography

Riley, Patrick. "Biographical Note." In *Treatise on Nature and Grace*, by Nicolas Malebranche, 11–13. Translated by Patrick Riley. Oxford: Clarendon, 1992.

——. "Introduction." In *Politics Drawn from the Very Words of Holy Scripture*, by Jacques-Benigne Bossuet, translated and edited by Patrick Riley, viii-lxviii. Cambridge: Cambridge University Press, 1990.

Ripley, George, and Charles A. Dana, eds. "Francke, August Hermann." In *The American Cyclopaedia*, 7:427. New York: D. Appleton & Co., 1879.

Roberts, Dewey. *Samuel Davies: Apostle to Virginia*. Destin, FL: Sola Fide, 2017.

Robinet, André. *Système et existence dans l'oeuvre de Malebranche*. Paris: J. Vrin, 1965.

Robson, David W. *Educating Republicans: The College in the Era of the American Revolution, 1750–1800*. Westport, CT: Greenwood, 1985.

Rodis-Lewis, Geneviève. *Nicolas Malebranche*. Paris: Presses Universitaires de France, 1963.

Rogers, Mark. "Edward Dorr Griffin and the Edwardsian Second Great Awakening." PhD diss., Trinity Evangelical Divinity School, 2012.

Rolde, Neil. *Sir William Pepperrell of Colonial New England*. Brunswick, ME: Harpswell, 1982.

Rome, Beatrice K. *The Philosophy of Malebranche*. Chicago: Regnery, 1963.

Rose, Walter H. "Alternative Viewpoint: Edwards and the Bible." In *Understanding Jonathan Edwards: An Introduction to America's Theologian*, edited by Gerald R. McDermott, 83–89. New York: Oxford University Press, 2009.

Roucek, Joseph S. "Czechoslovakia's Higher Education and Its Changing Fortunes." *Journal of Higher Education* 27 (1956) 21–24, 55–56.

Rowe, Karen E. "Introduction." In *The Puritan Character: Polemics and Polarities in Early Seventeenth-Century English Culture*, edited by Patrick Collinson, v-xvi. Los Angeles: Clark Memorial Library, UCLA, 1989.

Royster, Paul. *Milk for Babes. Drawn Out of the Breasts of Both Testaments. Chiefly, for the Spirituall Nourishment of Boston Babes in Either England: But May Be of Like Use for Any Children*. 1646. https://digitalcommons.unl.edu/cgi/viewcontent.cgi?article=1018&context=etas.

Rudolph, Frederick. *The American College and University: A History*. Athens: University of Georgia Press, 1990.

Ruland, Richard, and Malcolm Bradbury. *From Puritanism to Postmodernism: A History of American Literature*. New York: Viking, 1991.

Rupp, George. "The 'Idealism' of Jonathan Edwards." *Harvard Theological Review* 62 (1969) 209–26.

Rutman, Darrett B. *American Puritanism: Faith and Practice*. New York: Lippincott, 1970.

——. "The Mirror of Puritan Authority." In *Puritanism and the American Experience*, edited by Michael McGiffert, 67. Reading, MA: Addison-Wesley, 1969.

——. "What Is Puritanism? Several Definitions and an Approach." In *American Puritanism: Faith and Practice*, by Darrett D. Rutman, 4–10. New York: Lippincott, 1970.

Ryken, Leland. *Worldly Saints: The Puritans as They Really Were*. Grand Rapids: Academie, 1986.

Sabin, Joseph, ed. *Bibliotheca Americana: A Dictionary of Books Relating to America: From its Discovery to the Present Time*. 29 vols. New York: J. Sabin's Son, 1881.

Bibliography

Sadler, John Edward. *J. A. Comenius and the Concept of Universal Education*. London: George Allen & Unwin, 1966.

Saebø, Magne, et al., eds. "Francke, August Hermann." In *Hebrew Bible, Old Testament: The History of Its Interpretation*, 2:909. Göttingen: Vandenhoeck & Ruprecht, 1996.

Saillant, John. "African American Engagements with Edwards in the Era of the Slave Trade." In *Jonathan Edwards at 300: Essays on the Tercentenary of His Birth*, 141–51. Lanham, MD: University Press of America, 2005.

———. "Ministry to the Bound and Enslaved." In *The Oxford Handbook of Jonathan Edwards*, edited by Douglas A. Sweeney and Jan Stievermann, 431–45. New York: Oxford University Press, 2021.

Sattler, Gary R. *God's Glory, Neighbor's Good: A Brief Introduction to the Life and Writings of August Hermann Francke*. Chicago: Covenant, 1982.

———. *Nobler Than the Angels, Lower Than a Worm: The Pietist View of the Individual in the Writings of Heinrich Müller and August Hermann Francke*. Lanham, MD: University Press of America, 1989.

Savelle, Max. *The Colonial Origins of American Thought*. Princeton, NJ: Van Nostrand, 1964.

———. *Seeds of Liberty: The Genesis of the American Mind*. Seattle: University of Washington Press, 1965.

Schafer, Thomas Anton. "The Concept of Being in the Thought of Jonathan Edwards." PhD thesis, Duke University, 1951.

Scheiding, Oliver. "The World as Parish: Cotton Mather, August Hermann Francke, and Transatlantic Religious Networks." In *Cotton Mather and Biblia Americana, America's First Bible Commentary: Essays in Reappraisal*, 131–66. Grand Rapids: Baker Academic, 2010.

Schlaeger, Margaret Clare. "Jonathan Edwards' Theory of Perception." PhD diss., University of Illinois, 1964.

Schlatter, Richard. "Introductory Essay: The Puritan Strain." In *Puritanism and the American Experience*, edited by Michael McGiffert, 3–19. Reading, MA: Addison-Wesley, 1969.

Schmadel, Lutz. *Dictionary of Minor Planet Names*. 5th ed. Heidelberg: Springer, 2003.

Schmaltz, Tad. "Cartesian Causation: Body-Body Interaction, Motion, and Eternal Truths." *Studies in History and Philosophy of Science* 34 (2003) 362–73

———. *Malebranche's Theory of the Soul*. Oxford: Oxford University Press, 1996.

———. "Nicolas Malebranche." *Stanford Encyclopedia of Philosophy*. www.plato.stanford.edu/entries/malebranche.

———. "Occasionalism and Mechanism: Fontenelle's Objections to Malebranche." *British Journal for the History of Philosophy* 16 (2008) 293–313.

Schmid, Heinrich. *Die Geschichte des Pietismus*. Nördlingen: C. H. Buck'schen, 1863.

Schmidt, James. "The Counter-Enlightenment: Historical Notes on a Concept Historians Should Avoid." *Eighteenth-Century Studies* 49 (2015) 83–86.

Schmidt, Martin. *Wiedergeburt und Neuer Mensch: Gesammelte Studien zur Geschichte des Pietismus*. Witten: Luther, 1969.

Schneider, Herbert W. *A History of American Philosophy*. 2nd ed. New York: Columbia University Press, 1963.

———. *The Puritan Mind*. Ann Arbor: University of Michigan Press, 1958.

Bibliography

Schnittjer, Gary E. "The Ingredients of Effective Mentoring: The Log College as a Model for Mentorship." *Christian Education Journal* 15 (1994) 86–100.

Schultz, Stanley K. "The Making of a Reformer: The Reverend Samuel Hopkins as an Eighteenth-Century Abolitionist." *Proceedings of the American Philosophical Society* 115 (1971) 350–65.

Schuman, Andrew. "Training Ministers of 'Light and Heat': Jonathan Edwards's Home-Based Educational Approach and Its Legacy." In *The Global Edwards: Papers from the Jonathan Edwards Congress held in Melbourne, August 2015*, 261–76. Eugene, OR: Wipf & Stock, 2017.

Schwager, Sally. "Educating Women in America." *Signs* 12 (1987) 333–72.

Schweitzer, Don, ed. *Jonathan Edwards as Contemporary: Essays in Honor of Sang Hyun Lee*. New York: Peter Lang, 2010.

Schweitzer, William M. *God Is a Communicative Being: Divine Communicativeness and Harmony in the Theology of Jonathan Edwards*. New York: T. & T. Clark, 2012.

Scotchmer, Paul F. "The Aims of American Education: A Review from Colonial Times to the Present." *Christian Scholars Review* 13 (1984) 99–119.

Scott, Lee Osborne. "The Concept of Love as Universal Disinterested Benevolence in the Early Edwardeans." PhD diss., Yale University, 1952.

Sedgwick, Sarah Cabot, and Christina Marquand. *Stockbridge 1739-1974*. Stockbridge, MA: Berkshire Traveller, 1974.

Seigel, Jules Paul. "Puritan Light Reading." *New England Quarterly* 37 (1964) 185–99.

Senex. "On Christian Education." *The Spirit of the Pilgrims* 1 (1828) 561–72.

Sergeant, John. *A Valedictorian Oration by John Sergeant, Delivered at Yale College in the Year 1729*. New York: Henry W. Turner, 1882.

Shantz, Douglas H. "Bible Editions, Translations, and Commentaries in German Pietism." In *The Bible in Early Transatlantic Pietism and Evangelicalism*, edited by Ryan P. Hoselton et al., 17–35. University Park: Pennsylvania State University, 2022.

———. *An Introduction to German Pietism: Protestant Renewal at the Dawn of Modern Europe*. Baltimore: Johns Hopkins University Press, 2013.

Shea, Daniel B. "Jonathan Edwards: The First Two Hundred Years." *Journal of American Studies* 14 (1980) 181–97.

Shepard, Thomas. *The Clear Sun-Shine of the Gospel Breaking Forth upon the Indians in New-England*. London: Printed by R. Cotes for John Bellamy, 1648.

———. "Salvation by Covenant." In *The Gospel Covenant, or The Covenant of Grace Opened*, by Peter Bulkeley, vii-viii. 2nd ed. London: Matthew Simmons, 1653.

———. *A Short Catechism Familiarly Teaching the Knowledg[e] of God, and of our Selves*. Cambridge, MA: Samuel Green, 1654.

———. *The Sincere Convert: Discovering the Small Number of True Believers, and the Great Difficulty of Saving Conversion*. In *The Works of Thomas Shepard*, 9–17. Boston: Doctrinal Tract and Book Society, 1853.

———. *The Sound Beleever, or, A Treatise of Evangelicall Conversion, Discovering the Work of Christs Spirit, in Reconciling of a Sinner to God*. London: Printed for Andrew Crooke, 1653.

———. *Theses Sabbaticae*. Printed for T. R. and E. M., for John Rothwell, 1649.

———. *The Works of Thomas Shepard*. 3 vols. Boston: Doctrinal Tract and Book Society, 1853.

Bibliography

Shera, Jesse H. *Foundations of the Public Library: The Origins of the Public Library Movement in New England, 1629–1855*. Chicago: University of Chicago Press, 1949.

Sherman, D. *Sketches of New England Divines*. New York: Carlton & Porter, 1860.

Shewmaker, William O. "The Training of the Protestant Ministry in the United States of America, before the Establishment of Theological Seminaries." *Papers of the American Society of Church History* 2 (1921) 71–101.

Shields, David S. "Eighteenth-Century Literary Culture." In *A History of the Book in America: The Colonial Book in the Atlantic World*, edited by Hugh Amory and David D. Hall, 434–76. Chapel Hill: University of North Carolina Press, 2007.

Shipton, Clifford K. "A Plea for Puritanism." In *American Historical Review* 40 (1935) 460–67.

———. "Secondary Education in the Puritan Colonies." *New England Quarterly* 7 (1934) 646–61.

Shores, Louis. *Origins of the American College Library, 1638–1800*. New York: Barnes & Noble, 1935.

Shuffelton, Frank. "Introduction." In *The American Enlightenment*, edited by Frank Shuffelton, ix–xxiii. Rochester, NY: University of Rochester Press, 1993.

Sibley, John Langdon. *Sibley's Harvard Graduates, the Classes of 1746–1750*. Edited by Clifford K. Shipton. Massachusetts Historical Society, 1962.

Silverman, Kenneth. *The Life and Times of Cotton Mather*. New York: Harper & Row, 1984.

Simmons, Richard C. "Godliness, Property, and the Franchise in Puritan Massachusetts: An Interpretation." *Journal of American History* 55 (1968) 495–511.

Simonson, Harold P. *Jonathan Edwards: Theologian of the Heart*. Grand Rapids: Eerdmans, 1964.

Simpson, Alan. *Puritanism in Old and New England*. Chicago: University of Chicago Press, 1955.

———. "The Puritan Thrust." In *Puritanism in Old and New England*, 1–18. Chicago: University of Chicago Press, 1955.

———. "The Puritan Tradition." In *The New England Puritans*, edited by Sydney V. James, 159–66. New York: Harper & Row, 1968.

Simpson, Samuel. "Early Ministerial Training in America." *Papers of the American Society of Church History* 2nd Series 2 (1910) 117–29.

———. "Jonathan Edwards—A Historical Review." *Hartford Seminary Record* 14 (1903) 3–22.

Slater, Peter Gregg. *Children in the New England Mind in Death and in Life*. Hamden, CT: Archon, 1977.

Sleeper, Stephanie. "Puritan Best-Sellers." In *Puritans and Puritanism in Europe and America: A Comprehensive Encyclopedia*, edited by Francis J. Bremer and Tom Webster, 2:501–2. Oxford: ABC-CLIO, 2006.

———. "Puritan Prayer Books." In *Puritans and Puritanism in Europe and America: A Comprehensive Encyclopedia*, edited by Francis J. Bremer and Tom Webster, 2:510. Oxford: ABC-CLIO, 2006.

Sliwoski, Richard S. "Doctoral Dissertations on Jonathan Edwards." *Early American Literature* 14 (1979/1980) 318–27.

Sloan, Douglas. *The Great Awakening and American Education: A Documentary History*. New York: Columbia University Press, 1973.

Bibliography

———. *The Scottish Enlightenment and the American College Ideal.* New York: Columbia University Press, 1971.
Small, Walter Herbert. *Early New England Schools.* Boston: Ginn, 1914.
Smith, Claude A. "Jonathan Edwards and 'the Way of Ideas.'" *Harvard Theological Review* 59 (1966) 153–73.
Smith, E. "The Descendants of William Edwards." *The New York Genealogical and Biographical Record* 71 (1940) 217–24, 323–32.
———. "The Descendants of William Edwards." *The New York Genealogical and Biographical Record* 72 (1941) 124–25.
Smith, James. *The Divine Drama of History and Civilisation.* London: Chapman and Hall, 1854.
Smith, James K. A. *You Are What You Love: The Spiritual Power of Habit.* Grand Rapids: Brazos, 2016.
Smith, John E. "Jonathan Edwards as Philosophical Theologian." *The Review of Metaphysics* 30 (1976) 306–24.
———. "Jonathan Edwards: Piety and Practice in the American Character." *Journal of Religion* 54 (1974) 166–80.
———. *Jonathan Edwards: Puritan, Preacher, Philosopher.* South Bend, IN: University of Notre Dame Press, 1992.
———. "The Perennial Jonathan Edwards." In *Edwards in Our Time: Jonathan Edwards and the Shaping of American Religion,* edited by Sang Hyun Lee and Allen C. Guelzo, 1–11. Grand Rapids: Eerdmans, 1999.
———. "Puritanism and Enlightenment: Edwards and Franklin." In *Knowledge and Belief in America: Enlightenment Traditions and Modern Religious Thought,* edited by William M. Shea and Peter A. Huff, 195–226. Washington, DC: Woodrow Wilson Center Press and Cambridge University Press, 1995.
———. "Religious Affections and the 'Sense of the Heart.'" In *The Princeton Companion to Jonathan Edwards,* edited by Sang Hyun Lee, 103–14. Princeton, NJ: Princeton University Press, 2005.
Smith, John E., et al. "Editors' Introduction." In *A Jonathan Edwards Reader,* edited by John E. Smith et al., vii–xl. New Haven, CT: Yale University Press, 2003.
———. *A Jonathan Edwards Reader.* New Haven, CT: Yale University Press, 2003.
Smith, John Howard. "God Has Made Us to Differ: Jonathan Edwards, the Enlightenment, and the American Indian." In *Jonathan Edwards within the Enlightenment: Controversy, Experience, and Thought,* edited by John T. Lowe and Daniel N. Gullotta, 43–59. Göttingen: Vandenhoeck & Ruprecht, 2020.
Smith, Nila Banton. *American Reading Instruction: Its Development and its Significance in Gaining a Perspective on Current Practices in Reading.* Newark, DE: International Reading Association, 1965.
Smith, Samuel James. "The New-England Primer." *Britannica.* www.britannica.com/topic/The-New-England-Primer.
Smolinski, Reiner. "How to Go to Heaven, or How Heaven Goes?: Natural Science and Interpretation in Cotton Mather's *Biblica Americana* (1693–1728)." *New England Quarterly* 81 (2008) 278–329.
Snoddy, Richard. "Preaching." In *The Jonathan Edwards Encyclopedia,* edited by Harry S. Stout et al., 457–59. Grand Rapids: Eerdmans, 2017.
Snow, Louis Franklin. *The College Curriculum in the United States.* New York: Columbia University Teachers College Press, 1907.

Bibliography

"Somers School of the Prophets." Connecticut History, November 30, 2022. www.connecticuthistory.org/somers-school-of-the-prophets/

Sommerville, C. John. *The Rise and Fall of Childhood*. rev. ed. New York: Vintage, 1990.

Sparn, Walter. "Der Philosophiebegriff in Halle." In *Geschichte des Pietismus: Im Auftrag der Historischen Kommission zur Erforschung des Pietismus*, 4:233–40. Göttingen: Vandenhoeck & Ruprecht, 1966(?).

Spencer, Mark G. "Jonathan Edwards and the Historiography of the American Enlightenment." In *Jonathan Edwards within the Enlightenment: Controversy, Experience, and Thought*, edited by John T. Lowe and Daniel N. Gullotta, 21–39. Göttingen: Vandenhoeck & Ruprecht, 2020.

Spinka, Matthew. *John Amos Comenius: That Incomparable Moravian*. New York: Russell & Russell, 1967.

Splitter, Wolfgang. "The Fact and Fiction of Cotton Mather's Correspondence with German Pietist August Hermann Francke" *New England Quarterly* 83 (2010) 102–22.

Spohn, William C. "Sovereign Beauty: Jonathan Edwards and the *Nature of True Virtue*." *Theological Studies* 42 (1981) 394–421.

Sprague, William Buell. *Annals of the American Pulpit*. New York: Robert Carter & Brothers, 1859.

Spring, Joel. *American School, 1642-2000*. 5th ed. New York: McGraw-Hill, 2001.

———. *American School From the Puritans to No Child Left Behind*. New York: McGraw-Hill, 2007.

Sprunger, Keith L. "Ames, Ramus, and the Method of Puritan Theology." *Harvard Theological Review* 59 (1966) 133–51.

———. *The Learned Doctor William Ames: Dutch Backgrounds of English and American Puritanism*. Urbana: University of Illinois Press, 1972.

———. "William Ames and the Settlement of Massachusetts Bay." *New England Quarterly* 39 (1966) 66–79.

Staloff, Darren. *The Making of an American Thinking Class: Intellectuals and Intelligentsia in Puritan Massachusetts*. New York: Oxford University Press, 1998.

Stanton, Allen. "College of New Jersey." In *The Jonathan Edwards Encyclopedia*, edited by Harry S. Stout et al., 99–100. Grand Rapids: Eerdmans, 2017.

Stearns, Raymond P. "Assessing the New England Mind." *Church History* 10 (1941) 246–62.

Stein, Stephen J. "Introduction." In *The Cambridge Companion to Jonathan Edwards*, edited by Stephen J. Stein, 1–15. New York: Cambridge University Press, 2007.

Stelting, Donald Edd. "Edwards as Educator: His Legacy of Educational Thought and Practice." PhD diss., University of Kansas, 1998.

Stencil, E. "Malebranche and the General Will of God." *British Journal for the History of Philosophy* 19 (2011) 1107–29.

Stephen, Leslie. "Baxter, Andrew (1686-1750)." In *Dictionary of National Biography*, edited by Leslie Stephen, 3:425. New York: Macmillan, 1885.

———. *History of English Thought in the Eighteenth Century*. 2nd ed. London: Smith, Elder, & Co., 1881.

Stephenson, George M. *The Puritan Heritage*. New York: Macmillan, 1952.

Stevens, Edward W., Jr., "Literacy." In *Historical Dictionary of American Education*, edited by Richard J. Altenbaugh, 216–18. Westport, CT: Greenwood, 1999.

Bibliography

Stewart, Dugald. *The Collected Works of Dugald Stewart.* Edited by Sir William Hamilton. Edinburgh: Thomas Constable and Co., 1854.

Stievermann, Jan. "General Introduction." In *Cotton Mather and Biblia Americana—America's First Bible Commentary: Essays in Reappraisal,* edited by Reiner Smolinski and Jan Stievermann, 1–60. Tübingen: Mohr Siebeck, 2010.

———. "German Pietism." In *The Jonathan Edwards Encyclopedia,* edited by Harry S. Stout et al., 247–51. Grand Rapids: Eerdmans, 2017.

———. "History, Providence, and Eschatology." In *The Oxford Handbook of Jonathan Edwards,* edited by Douglas A. Sweeney and Jan Stievermann, 215–34. New York: Oxford University Press, 2021.

———. "Studying the History of American Protestantism through Jonathan Edwards: Versions of 'America's Theologian' at Mid-Century." *Theologica Wratislaviensia* 7 (2012) 69–91.

Stievermann, Jan, and Ryan P. Hoselton. "Spiritual Meaning and Experimental Piety in the Exegesis of Cotton Mather and Jonathan Edwards." In *Jonathan Edwards and Scripture: Biblical Exegesis in British North America,* edited by David P. Barshinger and Douglas A. Sweeney, 144–62. New York: Oxford University Press, 2018.

Stoddard, Solomon. "Letter to [Massachusetts Bay] Gov. [Joseph] Dudley, Oct. 22, 1703." *Collections of the Massachusetts Historical Society* 4th ser., 2:235-37. Boston: Crosby, Nichols, and Co., 1854.

———. *Question: Whether God is Not Angry with the Country for Doing So Little Towards the Conversion of the Indians?* Boston: Printed by B. Green, 1723.

Stoeffler, F. Ernest. *Continental Pietism and Early American Christianity.* Grand Rapids: Eerdmans, 1976.

———. *German Pietism During the Eighteenth Century.* Leiden: Brill, 1973.

Stokes, Anson Phelps. *Memorials of Eminent Yale Men.* New Haven, CT: Yale University Press, 1914.

Storms, C. Samuel. *Tragedy in Eden: Original Sin in the Theology of Jonathan Edwards.* Lanham, MD: University Press of America, 1985.

Stoughton, John A. *"Windsor Farmes": A Glimpse of an Old Parish.* Hartford, CT: Clark and Smith, 1853.

Stout, Harry S. "Edwards as Revivalist." In *The Cambridge Companion to Jonathan Edwards,* edited by Stephen J. Stein, 125–43. New York: Cambridge University Press, 2007.

———. "Introduction." In *Edwards in Our Time: Jonathan Edwards and the Shaping of American Religion,* edited by Sang Hyun Lee and Allen C. Guelzo, ix-xvi. Grand Rapids: Eerdmans, 1999.

———. "Jonathan Edwards' Tri-World Vision." In *The Legacy of Jonathan Edwards: American Religion and the Evangelical Tradition,* edited by D. G. Hart et al., 27–46. Grand Rapids: Baker, 2003.

———. *The New England Soul: Preaching and Religious Culture in Colonial New England.* New York: Oxford University Press, 1986.

———. "Parish Ministry." In *The Oxford Handbook of Jonathan Edwards,* edited by Douglas A. Sweeney and Jan Stievermann, 17–32. New York: Oxford University Press, 2021.

———. "Preface." In *Cotton Mather and Biblia Americana, America's First Bible Commentary: Essays in Reappraisal,* edited by Reiner Smolinski and Jan Stievermann, ix-x. Grand Rapids: Baker Academic, 2010.

Bibliography

———. "Preface to the Period." In *Works of Jonathan Edwards Online*, edited by Harry S. Stout, 22:9–23. http://edwards.yale.edu.

———. "Puritanism." In *The Jonathan Edwards Encyclopedia*, edited by Harry S. Stout et al., 479–81. Grand Rapids: Eerdmans, 2017.

———. "The Puritans and Edwards." In *The Princeton Companion to Jonathan Edwards*, edited by Sang Hyun Lee, 274–91. Princeton, NJ: Princeton University Press, 2005.

———. "Revivals as Millennial Harbingers." In *Works of Jonathan Edwards Online*, edited by Harry S. Stout, 22:24. http://edwards.yale.edu.

———. "Word and Order in Colonial New England." In *The Bible in America: Essays in Cultural History*, edited by Nathan O. Hatch and Mark A. Noll, 19–38. New York: Oxford University Press, 1982.

Stout, Harry S., et al. "Introduction." In *The Jonathan Edwards Encyclopedia*, edited by Harry S. Stout et al., ix-xi. Grand Rapids: Eerdmans, 2017.

Stoute, Douglas Andrew. "The Origins and Early Development of the Reformed Idea of the Covenant." DPhil thesis, King's College, Cambridge University, 1979.

Strachan, Owen, and Douglas A. Sweeney. *The Essential Jonathan Edwards: An Introduction to the Life and Teaching of America's Greatest Theologian*. Chicago: Moody, 2018.

Stratton, Gary David. "Jonathan Edwards' (1703-1758) Theology of Spiritual Awakening and Spiritual Formation Leadership in Higher Education." PhD diss., Biola University, 2009.

Strobel, Kyle. "Being Seen and Being Known: Jonathan Edwards's Theological Anthropology." In *The Global Edwards: Papers from the Jonathan Edwards Congress held in Melbourne, August 2015*, edited by Rhys S. Bezzant, 158–78. Eugene, OR: Wipf & Stock, 2017.

———. *Jonathan Edwards's Theology: A Reinterpretation*. New York: Bloomsbury, 2013.

———. "The Nature of God and the Trinity." In *The Oxford Handbook of Edwards*, edited by Douglas A. Sweeney and Jan Stievermann, 118–34. New York: Oxford University Press, 2021.

Studebaker, Steven M. *Jonathan Edwards' Social Augustinian Trinitarianism in Historical and Contemporary Perspectives*. Piscataway, NJ: Gorgias, 2013.

Suter, Rufus O. "The Concept of Morality in the Philosophy of Jonathan Edwards." *Journal of Religion* 14 (1934) 265–72.

———. "The Philosophy of Jonathan Edwards." PhD diss., Harvard University, 1932.

Swazo, Norman K. *Crisis Theory and World Order: Heideggerian Reflections*, 97–99. Albany, NY: State University of New York Press, 2002.

Sweeney, Douglas A. *The American Evangelical Story: A History of the Movement*. Grand Rapids: Baker, 2005.

———. "Edwards and His Mantle: The Historiography of the New England Theology." in *New England Quarterly* 71 (1998) 97–119.

———. "Edwards and the Bible." In *Understanding Jonathan Edwards: An Introduction to America's Theologian*, edited by Gerald R. McDermott, 63–82. New York: Oxford University Press, 2009.

———. "Edwards, Jonathan (1703–1758)." In *Dictionary of Major Biblical Interpreters*, edited by Donald K. McKim, 397–400. Downers Grove, IL: IVP Academic, 2007.

Bibliography

———. "Edwards Studies Today." In *The Oxford Handbook of Edwards*, edited by Douglas A. Sweeney and Jan Stievermann, 658-81. New York: Oxford University Press, 2021.

———. *Edwards the Exegete: Biblical Interpretation and Anglo-Protestant Culture on the Edge of the Enlightenment*. Oxford: Oxford University Press, 2016.

———. "Evangelical Tradition in America." In *The Cambridge Companion to Jonathan Edwards*, edited by Stephen J. Stein, 217-38. New York: Cambridge University Press, 2007.

———. "Foreword." In *Samuel Hopkins and the New Divinity Movement*, by Joseph Conforti, 1-7. Eugene, OR: Wipf & Stock, 1981.

———. *Jonathan Edwards and the Ministry of the Word*. Downers Grove, IL: IVP Academic, 2009.

———. "Jonathan Edwards: Legacy." www.edwards.yale.edu/research/about-edwards/legacy.

———. "Nathaniel William Taylor and the Edwardsian Tradition: Evolution and Continuity in the Culture of the New England Theology." PhD diss., Vanderbilt University, 1995.

———. "New Divinity." In *The Jonathan Edwards Encyclopedia*, edited by Harry S. Stout et al., 400-404. Grand Rapids, Eerdmans, 2017.

———. "Taylorites and Tylerites." In *After Jonathan Edwards: The Courses of the New England Theology*, edited by Oliver D. Crisp and Douglas A. Sweeney, 142-50. New York: Oxford University Press, 2012.

Sweeney, Douglas A., and Allen C. Guelzo. *The New England Theology: From Jonathan Edwards to Edwards Amasa Park*. Grand Rapids: Baker, 2006.

Sweeney, Douglas A., and Jan Stievermann. "Introduction." In *The Oxford Handbook of Jonathan Edwards*, edited by Douglas A. Sweeney and Jan Stievermann, xv-xix. Oxford: Oxford University Press, 2021.

Sweeney, Kevin Michael. "River Gods and Related Minor Deities: The Williams Family and the Connecticut River Valley, 1637-1790." PhD diss. Yale University, 1986.

Sweet, William Warren. *Religion in the Development of American Culture, 1765-1840*. New York: Scribner, 1952.

Szczerba, Wojciech. "The Concept of *Imago Dei* as a Symbol of Religious Inclusion and Human Dignity." *Forum Philosophicum* 25 (2020) 13-36.

Tan, Seng-Kong. "Anthropology, Affections, and Free Will." In *The Oxford Handbook of Jonathan Edwards*, edited by Douglas A. Sweeney and Jan Stievermann, 250-266. New York: Oxford University Press, 2021.

———. *Fullness Received and Returned: Trinity and Participation in Jonathan Edwards*. Minneapolis: Fortress, 2014.

———. "Learning from Jonathan Edwards: Toward a Trinitarian Theology of Contemplation and Action." In *The Global Edwards: Papers from the Jonathan Edwards Congress held in Melbourne, August 2015*, edited by Rhys S. Bezzant, 179-202. Eugene, OR: Wipf & Stock, 2017.

Tappert, Theodore. "The Influence of Pietism in Colonial American Lutheranism." In *Continental Pietism and Early American Christianity*, edited by F. Ernest Stoeffler, 13-33. Grand Rapids: Eerdmans, 1976.

Tarbox, I. N. "Article VII. Theological Education. No. IX–Questions of the Two Edwardses for their Pupils in Theology." In *Bibliotheca Sacra* 39 (1882) 367-81.

Bibliography

Taylor, Charles. *Sources of the Self: The Making of the Modern Identity.* Cambridge: Cambridge University Press, 1989.

Taylor, Justin. "Introduction." In *A God-Entranced Vision of all Things: The Legacy of Jonathan Edwards*, edited by John Piper and Justin Taylor, 13-18. Wheaton, IL: Crossway, 2004.

Tewksbury, Donald George. *Founding of American Colleges and Universities Before the Civil War.* PhD diss,, Columbia University Teachers College, 1932.

Thomas, Isaiah. *The History of Printing in America.* 2 vols. Albany, NY: Joel Munsell, 1874.

Thomas, Keith. "The Great Fight Over the Enlightenment." Review of *The Enlightenment: And Why It Still Matters*, by Anthony Pagden, and *Solomon's Secret Arts: The Occult in the Age of Enlightenment*, by Paul Kleber Monod, *The New York Review of Books*, April 3, 2014, 68-72.

Thuesen, Peter J. "Editor's Introduction." In *Works of Jonathan Edwards Online*, edited by Peter J. Thuesen, 26:1-116. http://edwards.yale.edu.

———. "Edwards' Intellectual Background." In *The Princeton Companion to Jonathan Edwards*, edited by Sang Hyun Lee, 16-33. Princeton, NJ: Princeton University Press, 2005.

———. "Jonathan Edwards as Great Mirror." *Scottish Journal of Theology* 50 (1997) 39-60.

———. "Sources of Edwards's Thought." In *The Oxford Handbook of Jonathan Edwards*, edited by Douglas A. Sweeney and Jan Stievermann, 69-88. New York: Oxford University Press, 2021.

Thwing, Charles Franklin. *A History of Higher Education in America.* New York: D. Appleton, 1906.

Tindall, William York. *John Bunyan, Mechanick Preacher.* New York: Columbia University Press, 1934.

Todd, Margo. "Puritan Self-Fashioning." In *Puritanism: Transatlantic Perspectives on a Seventeenth-Century Anglo-American Faith*, edited by Francis J. Bremer, 57-87. Boston: Massachusetts Historical Society, 1993.

Todd, Obbie Tyler. "The Populist Puritan: Jonathan Edwards and the Rise of American Populism." In *Jonathan Edwards within the Enlightenment: Controversy, Experience, and Thought*, edited by John T. Lowe and Daniel N. Gullotta, 137-52. Göttingen: Vandenhoeck & Ruprecht, 2020.

Tomas, Vincent. "The Modernity of Jonathan Edwards." *New England Quarterly* 25 (1952) 60-84.

Townsend, Harvey G. "Introduction." In *The Philosophy of Jonathan Edwards from His Private Notebooks*, edited by Harvey G. Townsend, v-xxii. Eugene, OR: University of Oregon Press, 1955.

Trent, William P., and Benjamin W. Wells. *Colonial Prose and Poetry: The Beginnings of Americanism, 1650-1710.* New York: Thomas Y. Crowell, 1903.

Trinterud, Leonard J. "The Origins of Puritanism." *Church History* 20 (1951) 37-57.

Trumbull, Benjamin. *Complete History of Connecticut, Civil and Ecclesiastical.* New London, CT: H. D. Utley, 1898.

Trueman, Carl R. "Heaven and Hell: 12 in Puritan Theology" *Epworth Review* 22 (1995) 75-85.

Turnbull, G. H. *Hartlib, Dury and Comenius: Gleanings from Hartlib's Papers.* London: University Press of Liverpool, 1947.

Turner, Jack. "John Locke, Christian Mission, and Colonial America." *Modern Intellectual History* 8 (2011) 267-97.

Bibliography

Tuttle, Julius Herbert. "The Libraries of the Mathers." *Proceedings of the American Antiquarian Society* 20 (1911) 296–356.

Tyack, David B. "A City upon a Hill: Education in the Massachusetts Bay Colony." In *Turning Points in American Educational History*, 1–27. Waltham, MA: Blaisdell, 1967.

Urban, Wayne J., and Jennings L. Wagoner, Jr. *American Education: A History*. New York: McGraw-Hill, 2004.

Unger, Harlow G. "Massachusetts Laws of 1642 and 1647." In *Encyclopedia of American Education*, 645–46. New York: Facts on File, 2001.

Valeri, Mark. "Joseph Bellamy: Conversion, Social Ethics, and Politics in the Thought of an Eighteenth Century Calvinist." PhD diss., Princeton University, 1985.

———. *Law and Providence in Joseph Bellamy's New England: The Origins of the New Divinity in Revolutionary America*. New York: Oxford University Press, 1994.

———. "Politics and Economics." In *The Oxford Handbook of Jonathan Edwards*, edited by Douglas A. Sweeney and Jan Stievermann, 446–60. New York: Oxford University Press, 2021.

Vander Molen, Ronald J. "Anglican Against Puritan: Ideological Origins During the Marian Exile." In *Puritan New England: Essays on Religion, Society, and Culture*, edited by Alden T. Vaughan and Francis J. Bremer, 2–18. New York: St. Martin's, 1977.

Van Dixhoorn, Chad B. "The New Taxonomies of the Westminster Assembly (1643–52): The Creedal Controversy." *Reformation and Renaissance Review* 6 (2004) 82–106.

Vanhoozer, Kevin J. *The Drama of Doctrine: A Canonical-Linguistic Approach to Christian Theology*. Louisville, KY: Westminster John Knox, 2005.

Van Vlastuin, Willem. "Federalism and Reformed Scholasticism." In *The Oxford Handbook of Edwards*, edited by Douglas A. Sweeney and Jan Stievermann, 183–98. New York: Oxford University Press, 2021.

Vartanian, Pershing. "Cotton Mather and the Puritan Transition into the Enlightenment." *Early American Literature* 7 (1973) 213–24.

Vaughan, Alden T. "Introduction." In *The Puritan Tradition in America, 1620–1730*, edited by Alden T. Vaughan, xi–xxxiv. Hanover, NH: University Press of New England, 1972.

———. *New England Frontier: Puritans and Indians, 1620–1675*. Boston: Little, Brown, 1965.

Vaughan, Alden T., ed. *The Puritan Tradition in America, 1620–1730*. Hanover, NH: University Press of New England, 1972.

Vaughan, Alden T., and Francis J. Bremer. "The English Background of Puritan New England." In *Puritan New England: Essays on Religion, Society, and Culture*, edited by Alden T. Vaughan and Francis J. Bremer, 1. New York: St. Martin's, 1977.

———. "The Puritan Legacy." In *Puritan New England: Essays on Religion, Society, and Culture*, edited by Alden T. Vaughan and Francis J. Bremer, 363. New York: St. Martin's, 1977.

Vella, Jane. "A Spirited Epistemology: Honoring the Adult Learner as Subject." *New Directions for Adult and Continuing Education* 85 (2000) 7–16.

Vetö, Miklos. "Edwards and Philosophy." In *Understanding Jonathan Edwards: An Introduction to America's Theologian*, edited by Gerald R. McDermott, 151–70. New York: Oxford University Press, 2009.

Bibliography

Von Rohr, John. "Covenant and Assurance in Early English Puritanism." *Church History* 34 (1965) 195–203.

Wainwright, William J. "Ontology." In *The Oxford Handbook of Jonathan Edwards*, edited by Douglas A. Sweeney and Jan Stievermann, 91–103. New York: Oxford University Press, 2021.

Walker, Williston. *Creeds and Platforms of Congregationalism*. New York: Charles Scribner's Sons, 1893.

———. "Jonathan Edwards." In *Ten New England Leaders*, 217–63. Reprint, New York: Arno, 1969.

———. "Samuel Hopkins." In *Ten New England Leaders*, 313–57. Reprint, New York: Arno, 1969.

Waller, George M. "Introduction." In *Puritanism in Early America*, edited by George M. Waller, v–x. Boston: D. C. Heath, 1950.

Wallmann, Johannes. *Der Pietismus*. Göttingen: Vandenhoeck & Ruprecht, 2005.

Walsh, Frances. "New England Primer." In *Historical Dictionary of American Education*, edited by Richard J. Altenbaugh, 257–58. Westport, CT: Greenwood, 1999.

Walsham, Alexandra. "The Godly and Popular Culture." In *The Cambridge Companion to Puritanism*, edited by John Coffey and Paul C. H. Lim, 277–93. Cambridge: Cambridge University Press, 2008.

———. *Providence in Early Modern England*. Oxford: Oxford University Press, 1999.

Walter, Scott, and William J. Reese. "Boston Latin Grammar School." In *Historical Dictionary of American Education*, edited by Richard J. Altenbaugh, 53. Westport, CT: Greenwood, 1999

Walton, Brad. *Jonathan Edwards, Religious Affections, and the Puritan Analysis of True Piety, Spiritual Sensation, and Heart Religion*. Lewiston, ME: Edwin Mellen, 2002.

Warburton, William. "Letter CXXVII to Richard Hurd, March 3, 1759." In *William Warburton, Letters from a Late Eminent Prelate to One of His Friends*. 2nd ed. London: Printed for T. Cadell and W. Davies, 1809.

Warch, Richard. *School of the Prophets: Yale College, 1701–1740*. New Haven, CT: Yale University Press, 1973.

Ward, Mark L., Jr. "Love." In *The Jonathan Edwards Encyclopedia*, edited by Harry S. Stout et al., 355–57. Grand Rapids: Eerdmans, 2017.

Ward, Ted. "The Teaching-Learning Process." In *Introducing Christian Education: Foundations for the 21st Century*, edited by Michael Anthony, 117–24. Grand Rapids: Baker Academic, 2001.

Ward, W. R. *The Protestant Evangelical Awakening*. Cambridge: Cambridge University Press, 1992.

Weaver, G. Stephen Jr. "Burr, Esther Edwards (1732–1758)." In *The Jonathan Edwards Encyclopedia*, edited by Harry S. Stout et al., 78–79. Grand Rapids: Eerdmans, 2017.

Weber, Donald Louis. "The Image of Jonathan Edwards in American Culture." PhD diss., Columbia University, 1978.

———. "The Recovery of Jonathan Edwards." In *Jonathan Edwards and the American Experience*, edited by Nathan O. Hatch and Harry S. Stout, 50–67. New York: Oxford University Press, 1988.

Weis, Frederick Lewis. *Colonial Clergy of the Middle Colonies, New York, New Jersey, and Pennsylvania, 1628–1776*. Worcester, MA: American Antiquarian Society, 1957.

Bibliography

Wendell, Barrett. *Cotton Mather: The Puritan Priest.* New York: Dodd, Mead, and Co., 1891.

———. *A Literary History of America.* New York: Charles Scribner's Son, 1901.

Werkmeister, W. H. *A History of Philosophical Ideas in America.* New York: Ronald, 1949.

Wertenbaker, Thomas Jefferson. *The First Americans, 1607–1690.* Edited by Arthur M. Schlesinger and Dixon Ryan Fox. New York: Macmillan, 1927.

———. *The Golden Age of Colonial Culture.* Ithaca, NY: Cornell University Press, 1949.

———. *Princeton, 1746–1896.* Princeton, NJ: Princeton University Press, 1946.

———. "The Puritan Oligarchy." In *Puritanism in Early America*, edited by George M. Waller, 108–12. Boston: D. C. Heath, 1950.

The Westminster Confession of Faith. https://westminsterstandards.org/westminster-confession-of-faith/.

Westra, Helen Petter. "Jonathan Edwards and 'What Reason Teaches.'" *Journal of the Evangelical Theological Society* 34 (1991) 495–503.

———. *The Minister's Task and Calling in the Sermons of Jonathan Edwards.* Lewiston, NY: Edwin Mellen, 1986.

Wetmore, James Carnahan. *The Wetmore Family of America and Its Collateral Branches.* Albany: Munsell & Rowland, 1861.

Wheeler, Nathan G. "History." In *The Jonathan Edwards Encyclopedia*, edited by Harry S. Stout et al., 291–92. Grand Rapids: Eerdmans, 2017.

Wheeler, Rachel. "Edwards as Missionary." In *The Cambridge Companion to Jonathan Edwards*, edited by Stephen J. Stein, 196–214. Cambridge: Cambridge University Press, 2007.

———. "'Friends to Your Souls': Jonathan Edwards' Indian Pastorate and the Doctrine of Original Sin." *Church History* 72 (2003) 736–65.

———. "Jonathan Edwards: Missionary." www.edwards.yale.edu/research/about-edwards/missionary.

———. "Lessons from Stockbridge: Jonathan Edwards and the Stockbridge Indians." In *Jonathan Edwards at 300: Essays on the Tercentenary of His Birth*, edited by Harry S. Stout et al., 131–40. Lanham, MD: University Press of America, 2005.

———. *To Live Upon Hope: Mohicans and Missionaries in the Eighteenth-Century Northeast.* Ithaca, NY: Cornell University Press, 2008.

White, Francis David. "The Reformation Roots and Edwardsean Fruits of the Missiology of Jonathan Edwards' Interleaved Bible." ThM thesis, Westminster Theological Seminary, 1991.

White, Hayden V. "Editor's Introduction." In *The Enlightenment Tradition*, by Robert Anchor, ix–xix. Berkeley: University of California Press, 1967.

White, Morton. *Science and Sentiment in America: Philosophical Thought from Jonathan Edwards to John Dewey.* Oxford: Oxford University Press, 1973.

Whittier, John Greenleaf. *The Works of John Greenleaf Whittier, Vol. VI.* https://www.gutenberg.org/files/9594/9594-h/9594-h.htm

Wigglesworth, Michael. *The Day of Doom; or, A Poetical Description of the Great and Last Judgment.* Reprint, New York: American News, 1867.

Willard, Samuel. *A Compleat Body of Divinity . . .* Boston: Printed by B. Green and S. Kneeland, for B. Eliot and D. Henchman, 1726.

———. *The Mourners Cordial Against Excessive Sorrow.* Boston: Printed by Benjamin Harris, and John Allen, 1691.

Bibliography

Williams, Ephraim, Jr. "Letter from Ephraim Williams Jr. to Jonathan Ashley, May 2, 1751." In *Colonel Ephraim Williams: A Documentary Life*, 61. Berkshire County, MA: Berkshire County Historical Society, 1970.

Williamson, Joseph Crawford. "The Excellency of Christ: A Study in the Christology of Jonathan Edwards." PhD diss., Harvard University, 1968.

Wills, Garry. *Head and Heart: A History of Christianity in America*. Westminster, GB: Penguin, 2007.

Wilson, John F. "History." In *The Princeton Companion to Jonathan Edwards*, edited by Sang Hyun Lee, 210–25. Princeton, NJ: Princeton University Press, 2005.

Wilson, Marvin R. *Our Father Abraham: Jewish Roots of the Christian Faith*. Grand Rapids: Eerdmans, 1989.

Wilson, James Grant, and John Fiske, eds. *Appleton's Cyclopaedia of American Biography*. New York: D. Appleton and Co., 1888.

Willey, Basil. *The Eighteenth-Century Background: Studies on* the *Idea of Nature in the Thought of the Period*. London: Chatto & Windus, 1950.

Winiarski, Douglas L. "Native American Popular Religion in New England's Old Colony, 1670–1770." *Religion and American Culture* 15 (2005) 147–86.

Winship, Michael P. *Godly Republicanism: Puritans, Pilgrims, and a City on a Hill*. Cambridge, MA: Harvard University Press, 2012.

———. "Mather, Cotton." In *Puritans and Puritanism in Europe and America: A Comprehensive Encyclopedia*, edited by Francis J. Bremer and Tom Webster, 1:166–67. Santa Barbara, CA: ABC-CLIO, 2006.

———. "'The Most Glorious Church in the World': The Unity of the Godly in Boston, Massachusetts, in the 1630s." *Journal of British Studies* 39 (2000) 71–98.

Winslow, Ola Elizabeth. *Jonathan Edwards (1703–1758): A Biography*. New York: Macmillan, 1940.

Winthrop, John. "A Modell of Christian Charity." In *Massachusetts Historical Society* 3rd Series 7:31–48. Boston: n.d., 1838.

Woodbridge, John D. "The Authority of Holy Scripture: Commitments for Christian Higher Education in the Evangelical Tradition." In *Christian Higher Education: Faith, Teaching, and Learning in the Evangelical Tradition*, edited by David S. Dockery and Christopher W. Morgan, 59–79. Wheaton, IL: Crossway, 2018.

Woodbridge, John D., and Frank A. James III. *From Pre-Reformation to the Present Day: The Rise and Growth of the Church in Its Cultural, Intellectual, and Political Context*. Grand Rapids: Zondervan, 2013.

Woodbridge, John D., et al. *The Gospel in America: Themes in the Story of America's Evangelicals*. Grand Rapids: Zondervan, 1979.

Woodhouse, A. S. P. *Puritanism and Liberty*. Chicago: University of Chicago Press, 1951.

Woody, Thomas. *A History of Women's Education in the United States*. Reprint, New York: Octagon, 1966.

Wotton, William. *Reflections upon Ancient and Modern Learning*. London: J. Leake, 1697.

Woznicki, Christopher. "To Hell with the Enlightenment: Jonathan Edwards and the Doctrine of Hell." In *Jonathan Edwards within the Enlightenment: Controversy, Experience, and Thought*, edited by John T. Lowe and Daniel N. Gullotta, 299–315. Göttingen: Vandenhoeck & Ruprecht, 2020.

Bibliography

Wright, Louis B. *The Cultural Life of the American Colonies, 1607–1763*. New York: Harper & Row, 1957.

Wright, Thomas Goddard. *Literary Culture in Early New England, 1620–1730*. New York: Russell & Russell, 1966.

Wright, Wyllis Eaton. *Colonel Ephraim Williams: A Documentary Life*. Pittsfield, MA: Berkshire County Historical Society, 1970.

Wroth, Lawrence C. *The Colonial Printer*. Portland, ME: Southworth-Anthoensen, 1938.

———. "Printing in the Colonial Period, 1638–1783: The Establishment of the Presses in New England." In *The Book in America: A History of the Making and Selling of Books in the United States*, edited by Hellmut Lehmann-Haupt, 7–11. New York: R. R. Bowker, 1952.

Wyckoff, D. Campbell. *The Gospel and Christian Education: A Theory of Christian Education for Our Times*. Philadelphia: Westminster, 1959.

———. "Jonathan Edwards' Contributions to Religious Education." PhD diss., New York University, 1948.

———. *The Task of Christian Education*. Philadelphia: Westminster, 1955.

———. *Theory and Design of Christian Education Curriculum*. Philadelphia: Westminster, 1961.

Wyss, Hilary E. *English Letters and Indian Literacies: Reading, Writing, and New England Missionary Schools, 1750–1830*. Philadelphia: University of Pennsylvania Press, 2012.

———. *Writing Indians: Literacy, Christianity, and Native Community in Early America*. Amherst: University of Massachusetts Press, 2000.

Yeager, Jonathan. "Britain and Europe." In *The Oxford Handbook of Jonathan Edwards*, edited by Douglas A. Sweeney and Jan Stievermann, 479–94. New York: Oxford University Press, 2021.

Yeide, Harry, Jr. *Studies in Classical Pietism: The Flowering of the Ecclesiola*. New York: Peter Lang, 1997.

Yoder, Peter James. *Pietism and the Sacraments: The Life and Theology of August Hermann Francke*. University Park: Pennsylvania State University Press, 2021.

Yolton, John W. "Introduction." In *The Locke Reader: Selections from the Works of John Locke with a General Introduction and Commentary*, edited by John W. Yolton, 1–9. New York: Cambridge University Press, 1977.

———. *John Locke and Education*. New York: Random House, 1971.

———. *Locke: An Introduction*. New York: Basil Blackwell, 1985.

———. "Preface." In *John Locke and the Way of Ideas*, ix. Oxford: Clarendon, 1956.

Yolton, John W., and Jean S. Yolton. "Introduction." In *Some Thoughts Concerning Education*, by John Locke, 18. Oxford: Clarendon, 1989.

Young, Michael P. "Confessional Protest: The Religious Birth of U. S. National Social Movements." *American Sociological Review* 67 (2002) 660–88.

Zahl, Paul F. M. *The Protestant Face of Anglicanism*. Grand Rapids: Eerdmans, 1998.

Zakai, Avihu. "The Age of Enlightenment." In *The Cambridge Companion to Jonathan Edwards*, edited by Stephen J. Stein, 80–99. New York: Cambridge University Press, 2007.

———. "Jonathan Edwards, the Enlightenment, and the Formation of Protestant Tradition in America." In *The Creation of the British Atlantic World*, edited by Elizabeth Mancke and Carole Shammas, 182–208. Baltimore: Johns Hopkins University Press, 2005.

Bibliography

———. *Jonathan Edwards's Philosophy of History: The Reenchantment of the World in the Age of Enlightenment*. Princeton, NJ: Princeton University Press, 2003.

———. *Jonathan Edwards's Philosophy of Nature: The Re-enchantment of the World in the Age of Scientific Reasoning*. New York: T. & T. Clark, 2010.

———. "The Medieval and Scholastic Dimensions of Edwards' Philosophy of Nature." In *Jonathan Edwards as Contemporary*, edited by Don Schweitzer, 15–31. New York: Peter Lang, 2010.

———. "The Natural Sciences and Philosophy of Nature." In *The Oxford Handbook of Jonathan Edwards*, edited by Douglas A. Sweeney and Jan Stievermann, 324–36. New York: Oxford University Press, 2021.

Zenos, A. C. Review of *The Church of Christ*, by E. A. Litton. *American Journal of Theology* 3 (1899) 406–7.

Zhu, Victor. "Jonathan Edwards Chinese Millennial Movements." In *The Global Edwards: Papers from the Jonathan Edwards Congress held in Melbourne, August 2015*, edited by Rhys S. Bezzant, 43–58. Eugene, OR: Wipf & Stock, 2017.

Ziff, Larzer. *Puritanism in America*. New York: Viking, 1973.

www.ingramcontent.com/pod-product-compliance
Lightning Source LLC
Chambersburg PA
CBHW071144300426
44113CB00009B/1081